Foot[illegible]
Highlands & Islands

Alan Murphy
Colin Hutchison
3rd edition

*"From the lone shielding on the misty island
Mountains divide us, and the waste of seas
But still the blood is strong, the heart is Highland,
And we in dreams behold the Hebrides"*

Canadian Boat Song, Unattributed

❶ Sandwood Bay
Sit on the beach and watch the sun set with a loved one and a bottle of your favourite single malt

❷ St Kilda
Voyage across perilous seas to these mysterious, haunted islands for the ultimate adventure

❸ Calanais
5000-year-old standing stones in a beautiful setting

❹ Inverewe
Enjoy someone else's garden; over 50 acres of horticultural heaven

❺ Applecross
Climb over Scotland's highest driveable pass to a great seafront pub serving super-fresh seafood

❻ Loch Coruisk
Sail into the gaping maw of this loch for a close up view of the mighty Cuillins

❼ Barra
Fly to Barra and land on the world's only beach runway

❽ West Highland railway
Climb aboard for one of the world's great train rides

❾ Glen Coe
The glen that's got it all: amazing scenery, a tragic past, a great pub, a classic ridge walk, and even a ski centre

Scotland Highlands & Islands Highlights

See colour maps at back of book

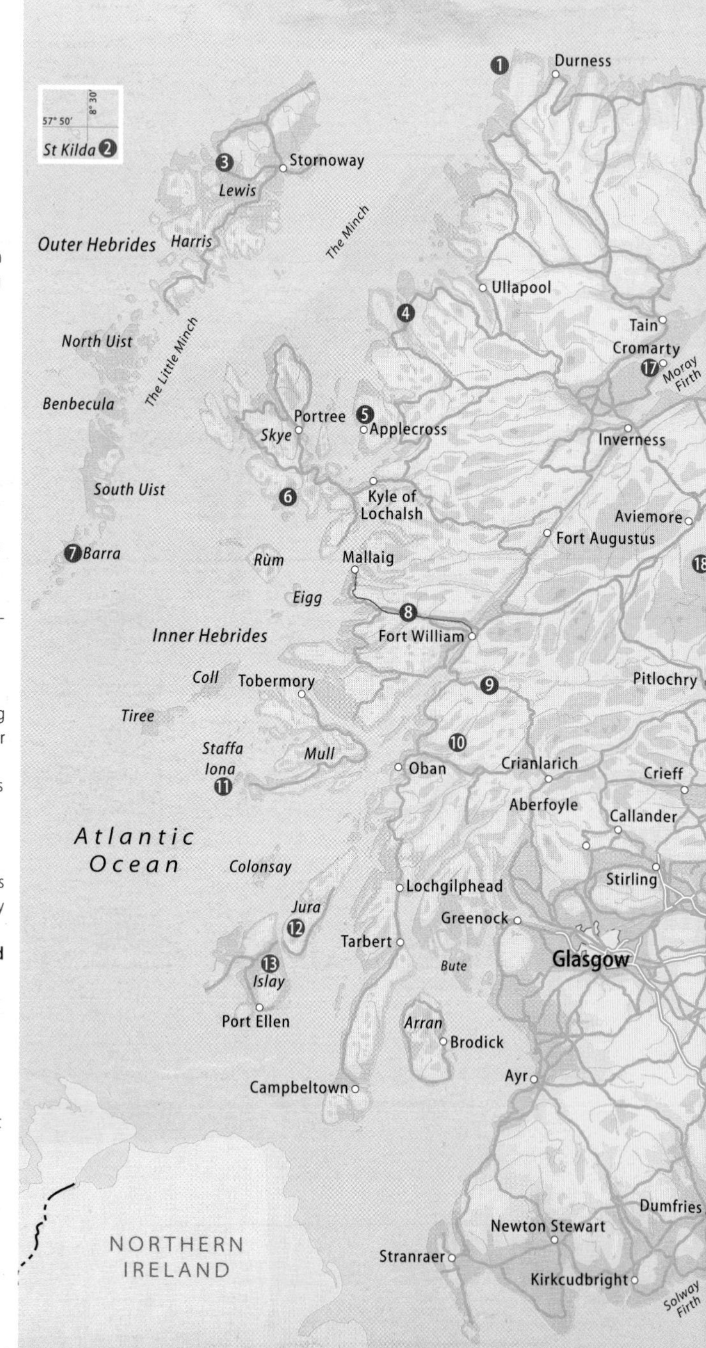

⑩ Loch Etive
Take a cruise on this hidden watery jewel

⑪ Iona
Hire a bike and explore this divine little island

⑫ Jura
Take a ferry to Jura, where George Orwell wrote *1984*, and trek to the legendary Corryvreckan, the second largest whirlpool in the world

⑬ Islay distillery
Savour the delights of an Islay malt on a tour of one of the island's distilleries

⑭ Hermaness National Nature Reserve
Explore the dramatic coastal scenery of this bird sanctuary at the top of the world

⑮ Shetland Folk Festival
The best of traditional Celtic music, crammed into three glorious days and nights

⑯ Skara Brae
Be blown away at Europe's best-preserved Stone Age village

⑰ Cromarty
Timeless village where you can see the resident dolphins at play from the shore

⑱ Lairig Ghru
Explore the heart of the mighty Cairngorm mountains on this classic hike

Contents

The Burg, on the island of Mull, is aptly known as 'The Wilderness'.

Unst, in Shetland, is the most northerly inhabited island in Britain and a haven for wildlife.

Goatfell is Arran's highest peak, at 2866 ft, and the views from the top are breathtaking.

Skye & the Small Isles

Outer Hebrides

Orkney & Shetland

Background

Footnotes

Inside front cover

Sleeping and eating price codes

Inside back cover

Author biography

A distinctive feature of the Shetland landscape are the famously small native ponies.

A foot in the door

Every self-respecting Scot comes over all proprietorial when introducing the glories of their country to a friend or loved one for the first time. So much so, you'd think they'd designed the whole place themselves. As if the jaw-dropping scenery of Wester Ross or the Trossachs was some kind of DIY makeover: "oh, yes, we got rid of all that woodchip and planted the hillsides in Caledonian pine forest. The native woodland look is in this year."

The Scots have every right to be proud, for when the rain stops falling and the mist clears, there is, quite simply, no more beautiful place on Earth. If there is a heaven, it must surely look like the Highlands and Islands, but let's hope the petrol's cheaper.

Scotland is one of the least densely populated countries in Europe. Not much smaller than its southern neighbour, England, it has only a tenth of its population – and most of those are crammed into the narrow central belt, leaving two-thirds of the country virtually empty. This is Europe's last great wilderness; one of the few places in this increasingly cluttered continent where you can really get away from it all.

About the only thing the Highlands doesn't have going for it is a dependable climate. Let's face it; if you want to lie on a beach all day soaking up rays, then you really ought to try somewhere else. Ironically, though, this makes the Scottish Highlands and Islands the perfect destination for a romantic break. Think about it: if the weather's rubbish then you'll have more time to stay in bed. It could give a whole new meaning to the term Highland fling.

An' ye had been whaur I hae been
Killiecrankie, near Pitlochry, was the site of a famous battle, in 1689, during the first Jacobite rebellion.

10 Gaelic symbol

Like many beautiful parts of the world, the landscape has a tragic and painful story to tell. The Highlands and Islands of Scotland are still haunted by the Clearances of the 19th century; those years of state-sponsored genocide that followed in the wake of two successive failed Jacobite rebellions in the 18th century and which sealed the fate of the traditional Highland way of life. However, after two centuries of decline, Gaelic, the ancient language of the Highlands and Islands, has been making a comeback, thanks to financial help from government agencies and the European Union. There has also been a resurgence of confidence in Gaelic culture, spurred on by the commercial success of Gaelic-language bands such as Runrig and Capercaillie. The Free Church of Scotland has played a crucial role too; a bastion of tradition in the Outer Herbides, where religion still plays a vitally important role in the islanders' lives.

For these are my mountains
The mighty Cuillins, the greatest concentration of peaks in the UK, are the dominant feature on the Isle of Skye, both geographically and culturally.

Highland coup

Life in the Highlands and Islands has changed dramatically for many people following the new Scottish Parliament's most radical and far-reaching legislation, the Land Reform (Scotland) Act of 2003. Among other things, the act gives crofters – small tenant farmers – the right to collectively purchase the land on which they live and work, whether or not the landowner wants to sell. It also grants them fishing and mineral rights on and contiguous with the land. The act has not gone down too well with Scotland's big estate owners, many of whom are apoplectic with rage, describing it as a brand of Marxism and comparing the move to the seizure of white-owned land by Zimbabwe's President, Robert Mugabe. Many will find such a response risible. Few tears will be shed for Scotland's 343 landowners who, between them, own half of all private land in the country. Those with longer memories may see this simply as a payback for the iniquities of the Highland Clearances.

Stoned love

The 5000-year-old standing stones at Calanais on Lewis attract tourists and New Age travellers in their droves to marvel at their beauty and spiritual power.

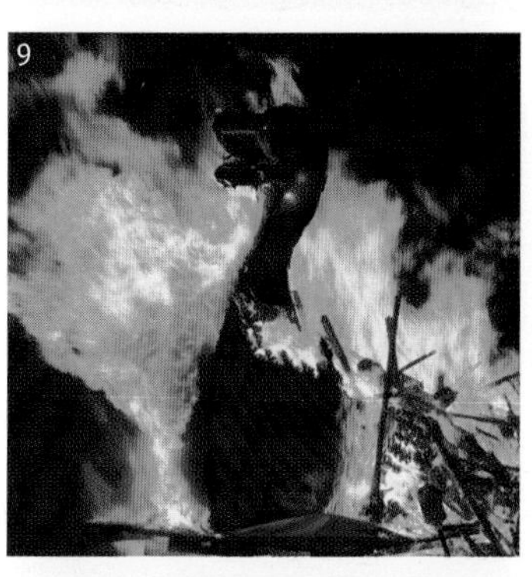

1 *The Old Man of Hoy, one of Orkney's most famous landmarks, can be reached by a spectacular clifftop walk.* ▸▸ *See page 353.*

2 *The bicycle was invented in Scotland, so it seems entirely appropriate that the country is now regarded as one of the top mountain biking destinations in the world.* ▸▸ *See page 52.*

3 *The ptarmigan is a master of camouflage. It goes through an incredible phase of moult from dark brown in summer to pure white in winter.* ▸▸ *See page 416.*

4 *There is surely no prettier port in the west of Scotland than Tobermory, Mull's main village.* ▸▸ *See page 147.*

5 *The sound of the sea crashing against the black crystalline columns of Fingal's Cave inspired Mendelssohn to compose his* Hebrides Overture ▸▸ *See page 149.*

6 *Hill House in Helensburgh is one of the best examples of the work of renowned architect, Charles Rennie Mackintosh.* ▸▸ *See page 133.*

7 *The tiny island of Iona, once the most sacred religious site in Europe, still draws pilgrims in their thousands to visit its beautiful 13th-century abbey.* ▸▸ *See page 151.*

8 *The north coast of Scotland attracts some of the world's greatest surfers.* ▸▸ *See page 58.*

9 *Every year on Shetland, locals celebrate Up-Helly-Aa, a spectacular Viking fire festival.* ▸▸ *See page 381.*

10 *Impromptu folk jamming sessions are an integral part of Orkney life.* ▸▸ *See page 362.*

11 *Among the many beautiful castles in the northeast is Drum, near Aberdeen.* ▸▸ *See page 90.*

12 *Skara Brae on Orkney is the best-preserved Stone Age village in northern Europe.* ▸▸ *See page 347.*

14 Northern exposure

The Scottish mainland is surrounded by hundreds of islands, each one with its own distinct history and culture. Crossing to these islands doesn't just feel like entering a different country, but stepping into another time zone. Where else could you find a police station using gerbils as paper shredders, people living by the the old Julian calendar, or the swings in children's playgrounds being padlocked to ensure strict observance of the Sabbath?

Lying off the west coast are the Hebrides, home of the Gaelic culture, where the road signs include English spellings almost as an afterthought and local people speak Gaelic as their native tongue. Off the northern tip of the mainland is Orkney, an archipelago of 70 islands, which has spawned some of Scotland's greatest writers; not surprising, perhaps, given that Orkney has such a fascinating and eventful history. The islands were ruled by the Vikings for 650 years, until the 15th century and, despite their remote location, played a dramatic role at the end of the First World War when the German fleet was scuttled in Scapa Flow. But if you think Orkney seems remote, you ain't seen nothing yet. The Shetland Isles are so far north they can only be included on maps as an inset and the nearest mainland town is Bergen, in Norway. Unbelievable as it may seem, even Shetland is made to look like the hub of civilization by St Kilda, the most remote community in Europe until evacuation of its entire population in 1930. The white-knuckle boat trip across perilous Atlantic seas must surely rank as one of the great adventures.

There isn't a legal limit to cuteness, but if there were, the village of Plockton, on the northwest coast, would be way, way over it.

Glen Coe stirs the emotions like no other place on the Scottish mainland. It can be stunning, it can be challenging and, on a dark winter's night, it can be downright spooky.

Going to extremes

Scotland has never been a place for softies. Its challenging weather and dramatic scenery really do convey a sense of being in the great outdoors. There are mountains galore to climb, lochs to fish and wildlife to watch; or you can just sit back and take in all that stunning scenery. There are countless opportunities to leave civilization a long way behind. You could explore Scotland's long-distance footpaths, such as the West Highland Way, which snake through some of the country's finest scenery. The more adventurous can try their hand (or feet) at 'Munro bagging', which is not some dubious public school practice but the name given to the popular pursuit of climbing Scotland's 284 mountains higher than 3000 feet. This offers the chance to explore wild areas of unparalleled beauty such as Glen Coe, Torridon, Kintail or the Cairngorms. If even that is too tame for you, then don't worry, Scotland is fast becoming the extreme sports capital of the Northern Hemisphere, with some of the best diving, surfing and mountain biking in the world, as well as new pursuits like canyoning, fun-yakking and the positively terrifying Tyrolean Traverse.

Scotland's wide, open spaces are also home to a rich and diverse wildlife. On land, you can see pine martens, red squirrels, wildcats, even reindeer, while golden eagles, ospreys and rare sea eagles rule the skies. In the lochs and seas that punctuate much of the northwest Highlands live otters, dolphins, porpoises, whales and, according to some, even the occasional prehistoric monster.

A breed apart

The remote islands of St Kilda, more than 40 miles west of Lewis, are the most important seabird breeding station in northwest Europe, as well as being home to the highest sea cliffs in Britain (430 m), at Conachair.

Essentials

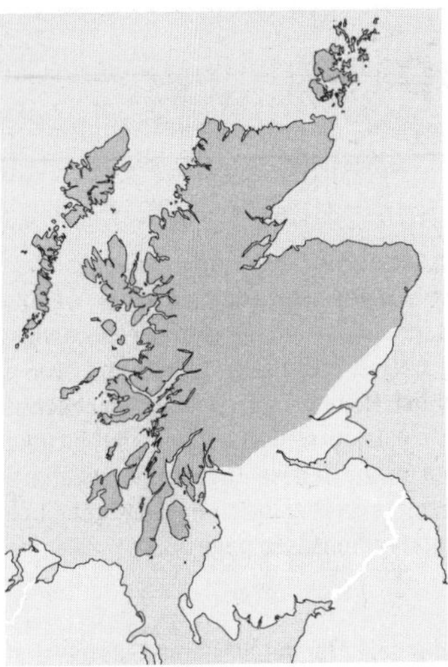

Footprint features

Planning your trip

Where to go

Scotland is a small country but there's a lot to see and trying to cram everything into a first visit can be very frustrating. There are many, many places of great natural beauty and the country's long, turbulent history has left a rich heritage of medieval castles, cathedrals, palaces, abbeys, neolithic stone circles, Bronze Age brochs and even a 5000-year-old village. Which parts of the Scottish Highlands and Islands you choose will be determined by your own particular interests, as well as by the length of your stay and the size of your wallet. It goes without saying (but we'll say it anyway), that a longer trip will allow you to visit the wild and remote parts of the country and get much more out of your visit. For details of all transport options, see page 36.

One week

If you only have a week or two, you can head straight for the hills from Glasgow and Edinburgh. A short distance north of Glasgow is Loch Lomond, gateway to the Western Highlands and a beautiful introduction to the spectacular sights which lie in wait further north. From Loch Lomond you should head north through Glen Coe – one of the main highlights of a visit to Scotland – to Fort William, the main tourist centre for the Western Highlands. From Fort William there are two routes to another of Scotland's most popular attractions, the Isle of Skye. The quickest route is by road and bridge, via Kyle of Lochalsh, but by far the most romantic and scenic route is by train from Fort William to Mallaig, and by ferry from there to Armadale. You should then leave at least three days to explore the island, or more if you plan to do any walking.

Alternatively, it's only a short drive north from Edinburgh to Perthshire. Though not as dramatic as the northwest, the mountains, rivers, lochs and glens of the Perthshire Highlands are very beautiful and easily accessed from the town of Perth. Perthshire leads seamlessly into the visual delights of the Trossachs, a thick wedge of lochs, forests and mountains forever associated with Sir Walter Scott, tucked in between Stirling and Loch Lomond.

Two weeks

An alternative to Fort William and Skye, or in addition if you have more time, would be to head to Oban, the main ferry port of the west coast, and make the short trip to the beguiling Isle of Mull, which tends to attract fewer visitors than Skye in the summer months, and from where you can pop across to its divine neighbour, Iona, or explore the inspirational Fingal's Cave on Staffa. Alternatively, you could head south from Oban, through Argyll, with its many prehistoric sites, and take a ferry to the little-visited islands of Islay, famous for its malt whiskies, and Jura. Both are great places for walking holidays. Also within reach of Argyll, or Ayrshire, is the island of Arran, described as 'Scotland in miniature' and ideal for walking or cycling.

Three to four weeks

If you have three or four weeks at your disposal then you can follow the long and winding road north from Kyle of Lochalsh, as it twists and turns along the coast to Ullapool. Most visitors don't make it north of Ullapool but those who do are rewarded with the starkly beautiful, almost primeval landscapes of the far northwest. You can sail from Ullapool across to the Outer Hebrides, a long, narrow archipelago stretching from Lewis and Harris in the north to Barra in the south. Alternatively, you could include a trip to the Orkney Islands, littered with important Stone Age ruins and also one of the world's best cold water dive sites. If time and money really are no object, then head for the culturally distinct Shetland Isles, home to Viking festivals and millions of seabirds, so far north of the mainland that they can only be included on maps as an inset.

When to go

The high season is from May to September, and this is when Scotland receives the vast majority of visitors. Though the weather tends to be better during the summer months, prices for accommodation are higher and hotels and guesthouses in the most popular places need to be booked in advance. It's also a good idea to make reservations at this time on ferries to the islands, especially to Skye and Mull. A major advantage to visiting in the summer months is the long hours of daylight, especially in the far north, where the sun doesn't set till around 2300 or later in June and July.

From October to Easter, many tourist sights are closed, and travelling around the Highlands and Islands can be difficult as public transport services are limited. Many of the smaller tourist offices are also closed during the low season. Although some hotels and guesthouses close too, the majority are now open all year round, as are most restaurants. Taking everything into consideration, May and September are probably the best months to visit the Scottish Highlands and Islands.

Climate

The Scottish climate is notoriously unpredictable, especially on the west coast, where a bright, sunny morning can turn into a downpour in the time it takes to butter your toast. Predicting the weather is not an exact science and tables of statistics are most likely a waste of time. There's an old saying in Scotland that if you don't like the weather, then wait 20 minutes, and this just about sums it up. The west coast receives far more rain than the rest of the country and the east coast gets more sunshine. The west coast is also milder in the winter due to the relatively warm waters of the Gulf Stream. Winters in the north can be very harsh, especially in the mountains and glens, making hiking conditions treacherous. Winter storms also make it difficult to travel around the islands as ferry services are often cancelled. Generally speaking, May to September are the warmest months, with an average summer high of around 18-19°C and, though they are often the driest months, you can expect rain at any time of the year, even in high summer. So, you'll need to come prepared, and remember the old hikers' adage that there's no such thing as bad weather, only inadequate clothing.

The MET office Weather Call service provides weather forecasts. Call T09014 722 plus the following three digits: Central Scotland 071; Borders 072; East Highlands 074; West Highlands and Islands 075; Orkney and Shetland 076. (60p per minute).

Tour operators

There are many companies offering general interest or special interest tours of Scotland. Travel agents will have details, or you can check the small advertisements in the travel sections of newspapers, or contact the British Tourist Authority or Scottish Tourist Board for a list of operators.

In the UK

Assynt Guided Holidays, Birchbank, Knockan, Elphin, Sutherland, T/F01854-666215. Specialize in walking tours of this rugged corner of the northwest.

Avalon Trekking Scotland, Bowerswell Lane, Kinnoull, Perth, PH2 TDL, T/F01738-624194. Good all-round hillwalking tours.

Bespoke Highland Tours, T/F0141-342 4576, www.highland-tours.co.uk. Personalized walking, cycling and long-distance trekking.

On the buses

A great cheap way to get around Scotland is on one of the jump-on-jump-off backpacker bus tours. These leave from Edinburgh Monday to Saturday, and stop off at independent hostels in Perth, Pitlochry, Inverness, Loch Ness, the Isle of Skye, Fort William, Glen Coe, Oban and Glasgow. You can hop on and off whenever you please, and you don't need to stay at any of the hostels. Prices start at around £59. The same companies also run excellent-value Highland tours, leaving from Edinburgh. Prices start at around £79 for three days, up to £200 and more for 6-7 days. Prices do not include accommodation or food. See Tour operators, below, for details of companies offering these tours.

Classique Tours, Glasgow, T0141-8894050, www.classiquetours.co.uk. For those who prefer something a wee bit different, tartan-free tours of the 'real Scotland' in a vintage bus. 5-day tours start at £275 and their 7-day Grand Hebridean Tour is £485.
Cndo Scotland, 32 Stirling Enterprise Park, Stirling, T01786-445703, www.cndo scotland.co.uk. Walking holidays in NW and islands, from £420 per week including accommodation and ferries.
Escape 2 Scotland, 27/10 Maxwell St, Edinburgh, EH10 5HT, T/F0131-4472570, www.escape2scotland.co.uk. Organizes tailor-made trips for groups and individuals.
Explore NW Scotland, 65 Cradlehall Park, Westhill, Inverness, T077489-75638 (mob), www.explorenwscotland.co.uk. Highly recommended walking and sailing holiday company run by Richard Knotts. Offers a variety of 6-day packages for groups of up to 5, with accommodation in tents, bothies, bunkhouses or guesthouses. Prices range from £395 up to £535 for single travellers, less for 2 or more.
Gael Connexions, T01855-841219, T0776-99 22463 (mob), www.gaelconnexions.co.uk. Fort William-based company organizing genealogy tours for foreigners wishing to trace their ancestors. Their guide and researcher will point you in the right direction or plan your entire journey. Free consultation offered.
Go Blue Banana, Edinburgh, T0131-5562000, www.gobluebanana.com. Backpacker bus tour operators, see box, above.
Haggis Backpackers, 11 Blackfriars St, Edinburgh, EH1 1NB, T0131-5579393, www.haggisadventures.com. Backpacker bus tour operators, see box, above.
Heart of Scotland Tours, T0131-558 8855, www.heartofscotlandtours.co.uk. Run 1- and 2-day coach tours, £27-57, departing from Edinburgh Backpackers Hostel.
Lomond Walking Holidays, 34c James St, Riverside, Stirling, FK8 1UG, T/F01786-447752, www.biggar-net.co.uk/lomond. Offer a variety of walking packages.
Macbackpackers, Edinburgh, T0131-5589900, www.macbackpackers.com. Backpacker bus tour operators, see box, above.
North-West Frontiers, 18A Braes, Ullapool, IV26 28Z, T/F01854-612628, www.nwfront iers.com. Walking tours for small groups. A bit more hardcore than the rest.
Ossian Guides, Sanna, Newtonmore, Inverness, PH20 1DG, T/F01540-673402. Reliable walking guide company.
Timberbush Tours, 555 Castlehill, Edinburgh, T0131-226 6066, www.timber bush-tours.co.uk. Run a variety of 1- to 3-day guided coach tours around the country, £22-90.
Walkabout Scotland, 2 Rossie Place, Edinburgh, T0131-661 7168, www.walk aboutscotland.com. Walking tours around Edinburgh and the Highlands.
Wild in Scotland, 9 South St Andrew St, Edinburgh, T0131-478 6500, www.wild -in-scotland.com. Runs various coach tours from 3 days (£65) to 6 days (£119).
Wilderness Scotland,T0131-6256635, www.wildernessscotland.com. Specialist Edinburgh based adventure tour operator offering walking, climbing, kayaking, hiking and photographic trips into Scotland's wild places, plus tailor-made trips.

In North America

Abercrombie & Kent, T1-800-3237308, www.abercrombiekent.com. General sightseeing tours.
Above the Clouds Trekking, T800-2334499, www.gorp.com/abvclds.htm. Walking tours.
British Coastal Trails, T800-4731210, www.bctwalk.com. Walking tours.
Cross-Culture, 52 High Point Dr, Amherst MA01002-1224, T800-4911148, www.cross cultureinc.com. General sightseeing tours.
Golf International Inc, T1-800-8331389. Golfing tours from the USA offered.
Jerry Quinlan's Celtic Golf, T1-800-5356148, www.jqceltiicgolf.com. Organizes golfing packages from the USA.
Prestige Tours, T1-800-8907375. General sightseeing tours.
Saga, 222 Berkeley St, Boston, MA 02116, USA. General sightseeing tours.
Sterling Tours, T1-800-7274359, www.sterlingtours.com. General sightseeing tours.

In Australia and New Zealand

Adventure Specialists, 69 Liverpool St, Sydney, T02-92612927. Adventure tours.
Adventure Travel Company, 164 Parnell Rd, Parnell, East Auckland, T09-3799755. New Zealand agents for **Peregrine Adventures**. Offers a range of activity tours.
Peregrine Adventures, 258 Lonsdale St, Melbourne, T03-96638611, www.peregrine.net.au; also branches in Brisbane, Sydney, Adelaide and Perth. Offers a wide range of activity tours throughout Scotland.
Saga, Level 1, 10-14 Paul St, Milsons Point, Sydney 2061. General sightseeing tours.

Finding out more

The best way of finding out more information for your trip to Scotland is to contact **Visit Britain** ⓘ *www.visitbritain.com*, the overseas representative for **Visit Scotland** ⓘ *www.visitscotland.com*. Their website is very useful as a first-stop directory for accommodation. Alternatively, you can email Visit Scotland. Both organizations can provide a wealth of free literature and information such as maps, city guides, events calendars and accommodation brochures. If you want more detailed information on a particular area, contact the area tourist boards.

Scottish Tourist Boards

VisitScotland, 23 Ravelston Terr, Edinburgh, EH4 3EU, T0131-3322433, www.visitscotland.com; and 19 Cockspur St, London SW1 5BL, T020-7930 2812.
Aberdeen & Grampian Tourist Board, 27 Albyn Pl, Aberdeen, AB10 1YL, T01224-632727, www.aberdeen-grampian.com.
Argyll, the Isles, Loch Lomond, Stirling & Trossachs Tourist Board, 7 Alexandra Par, Dunoon, Argyll, PA23 8AB, T01369-701000, www.visitscottish heartlands.com.
Ayrshire & Arran Tourist Board, Burns House, Burns Statue Sq, Ayr, KA7 1UP, T01292-288688, www.ayrshire-arran.com.
The Highlands of Scotland Tourist Board, Peffery House, Strathpeffer, IV14 9HA, T01479-810363, UK T0870-5143070, www.visithighlands.com.
Orkney Tourist Board, 6 Broad St, Kirkwall, Orkney, KW15 1NX, T01856-872856, www.visitorkney.com.
Perthshire Tourist Board, Lower City Mills, West Mill St, Perth, PH1 5QP, T01738-627958, www.perthshire.co.uk.
Shetland Islands Tourism, Market Cross, Lerwick, Shetland, ZE1 0LU, T01595-693434, www.visitshetland.com.
Western Isles Tourist Board, 26 Cromwell St, Stornoway, Isle of Lewis, HS1 2DD, T01851-703088, www.visithebrides.com.

Useful websites

The VisitScotland site and the various area tourist board sites have information on accommodation, transport and tourist sights as well as outdoor activities such as walking, skiing, fishing, etc. See also page 59.

Travel and leisure

www.aboutscotland.co.uk Useful for information on accommodation.
www.bbc.co.uk The UK's most popular site with an excellent what's on guide.
www.britannia.com A huge UK travel site. Click on 'Scotland guide' for a massive selection of subjects plus links to various sites including newspapers.
www.hebrides.com Comprehensive site.
www.scotland-info.co.uk Good for local information on hotels, shops and restaurants.
www.scotland.net Scotland online with good information on golf, walking and climbing and also features.
www.uktrail.com Provides comprehensive information on transport and hostels.
www.travelscotland.co.uk Run in conjunction with the Scottish Tourist Board, with magazine-style features and reviews.
www.whatsonwhen.com Has a huge range of upcoming events around the world.

Outdoors

www.golfscotland.co.uk Everything you need to know about golf in Scotland.
www.goodbeachguide.co.uk How to check your kids won't be bathing in sewage. Lists facilities and activities for over 400 recommended UK beaches.
www.skiscotland.net Information on ski conditions at all centres, updated daily.
www.sustrans.org.uk Official site of the charity that co-ordinates the National Cycle Network. The clickable map lets you zoom in on sections of the route.
www.visitscotland.com/cycling Excellent site; even shows how steep the climbs are.
www.walkscotland.com Suggested walks, contacts and practical information for hikers and climbers.
www.walkingworld.com Perhaps the best directory of British walks, though you have to pay to download their detailed maps.

History, politics and culture

www.ceolas.org Celtic music site with lots of information and sounds.
www.electricscotland.com Massive directory with lots of information on clans, travel etc. In-depth history pages.
www.scotchwhisky.net Everything you ever wanted to know about the 'water of life'.
www.scotland.gov.uk Updates on government affairs in Scotland.
www.scottish.parliament.uk Easy to use guide to the Scottish Parliament.

Language

Though the vast majority of Scots speak English, to the untutored ear the Scottish dialect can be hard to understand, as many words and expressions are derived not from English but from Lowland Scots, or lallan, which is now recognized as a separate language as opposed to simply a regional dialect. In the Highlands and Islands, however, the accent is very clear and easy to understand.

Scotland's oldest surviving language is Scottish Gaelic (*Gaidhlig*, pronounced 'Gallic'), spoken by only about 2% of the population. This is in the Gaidhealtachd, the Gaelic-speaking areas of the Outer Hebrides, parts of Skye, and a few of the smaller Hebridean islands, where road signs are predominantly in Gaelic. Those wishing to teach themselves Gaelic could start with the BBC *CanSeo* cassette and book. A good phrasebook is *Everyday Gaelic* by Morag MacNeill (Gairm). Also, the Celtic Heritage Centre, based on Arran, has a great store of Gaelic and Celtic information and documents; they publish a quarterly newsletter. *Macbain's Etymological Dictionary of the Gaelic language* contains a wealth of words and information. ▸▸ *For more on the history of Gaelic, see page 409, and for a glossary of Gaelic words, see page 420.*

Disabled travellers

For travellers with disabilities, visiting Scotland independently can be a difficult business. While most theatres, cinemas and modern tourist attractions are accessible to wheelchairs, accommodation is more problematic. Many large, new hotels do have disabled suites, but will charge more, and most B&Bs, guesthouses and smaller hotels are not designed to cater for people with disabilities. Public transport is just as bad, though newer buses have lower steps for easier access and some **ScotRail** intercity services now accommodate wheelchair-users in comfort. Taxis, as opposed to minicabs, all carry wheelchair ramps, and if a driver says he or she can't take a wheelchair, it's because they're too lazy to fetch the ramp.

Wheelchair users, and blind or partially sighted people are automatically given 30-50% discount on train fares, and those with other disabilities are eligible for the Disabled Person's Railcard, which costs £14 per year and gives a third off most tickets. There are no reductions on buses however.

If you are disabled you should contact the travel officer of your national support organization. They can provide literature or put you in touch with travel agents specializing in tours for the disabled. The **Scottish Tourist Board** produces a guide, *Accessible Scotland*, for disabled travellers, and many local tourist offices can provide accessibility details for their area. A useful website is www.atlholidays.com which specializes in organizing holidays for disabled travellers, recommends hotels with good facilities and can also arrange rental cars and taxis.

Useful organizations include: **Disability Scotland**, Princes House, 5 Shandwick Place, Edinburgh EH2 4RG, T0131-229 8632; **The Royal Association for Disability and Rehabilitation (RADAR)**, Unit 12, City Forum, 250 City Road, London, EC1V 8AF, T020-7250 3222, www.radar.org.uk, is a good source of advice and information, and produces an annual guide on travelling in the UK (£7.50 including P&P); and **The Holiday Care Service**, second floor, Imperial Building, Victoria Road, Horley, Surrey RH6 7PZ, T01293-774 535, provides free lists of accessible accommodation and travel in the UK.

Gay and lesbian travellers

Don't assume that because men are wearing skirts in the Highlands that people take a relaxed attitude to homosexuality. The same prejudices apply as elsewhere in rural parts of the UK. Though Scotland is generally tolerant of homosexuality, overt displays of affection are not advised. Gay couples may also come up against subtle forms of discrimination, such as B&Bs spontaneously 'losing' bookings for a double room and being left with the option of taking two singles. The magazine, *Gay Scotland*, is a good source of information, as is the **Gay Switchboard**, T0131-556 4049, or the **Lesbian Line**, T0131-557 0751. For a good selection of gay events and venues, check out www.whatsonwhen.com. Other good sites include: www.gaybritain.co.uk and www.gaytravel.co.uk.

Student travellers

Discount passes

There are various official youth/student ID cards available. The most useful is the **International Student ID Card (ISIC)**. For a mere £6 the ISIC card gains you access to the exclusive world of student travel with a series of discounts, including most forms of local transport, up to 30% off international airfares, cheap or free admission to museums, theatres and other attractions, and cheap meals in some restaurants. There's also free or discounted internet access, and a website, www.usitworld.com, where you can check the latest student travel deals. You'll also receive the ISIC handbook, which ensures you get the most out of services available. ISIC cards are available at student travel centres, see page 29. US and Canadian citizens are also entitled to emergency medical coverage, and there's a 24-hour hotline to call in the event of medical, legal or financial emergencies.

If you're aged under 26 but not a student, you can apply for a **Federation of International Youth Travel Organisations (FIYTO)** card, or a **Euro 26 Card,** which give you much the same discounts. If you're 25 or younger you can qualify for a **Go-25 Card,** which gives you the same benefits as an ISIC card. These discount cards are issued by student travel agencies and hostelling organizations, see page 42.

Studying in Scotland

If you want to study in Scotland you must first prove you can support and accommodate yourself without working and without recourse to public support. Your studies should take up at least 15 hours a week for a minimum of six months. Once you are studying, you are allowed to do 20 hours of casual work per week in the term time and you can work full-time during the holidays. In North America full-time students can obtain temporary work or study permits through the **Council of International Education Exchange** (CIEE), 205 E 42nd Street, New York, NY 10017, T212-822 2600, www.ciee.org. For more details, contact your nearest British embassy, consulate or high commission, or the **Foreign and Commonwealth Office** in London, T020-7270 1500.

Travelling with children

Visiting the Scottish Highlands with kids is no different from other parts of the UK, though you may find that the locals are just that little bit more tolerant and helpful. If you're near a beach, toddlers will be in rock pool heaven, rooting around to their little heart's content as you sit nearby, shivering in the rain. Even teenagers should have no reason to moan as there are all manner of thrill-a-minute adventure sports to try, see Activities and sports on page 50 for more details.

If you're travelling with babies and/or toddlers you may find eating out a frustrating experience in some establishments, though the days of families being banished to some grubby room at the back, well out of the way of other diners, are, thankfully, a thing of the past in most places. The attitude to breastfeeding, while some way behind the likes of Scandinavia, is more relaxed than the US and becoming ever more civilized and progressive. In major towns and cities, Italian restaurants are generally more child-friendly. The child may not be quite be king here, but at least they are allowed to be seen and heard.

If you are flying, inform the airline in advance that you're travelling with a baby or toddler, and check out the facilities when booking as these vary with each aircraft. **British Airways** now has a special seat for under 2s; check which aircraft have been fitted with them when booking. Pushchairs can be taken on as hand luggage or stored in the hold. Skycots are available on long-haul flights. Take snacks and toys for in-flight entertainment, and remember that swallowing food or drinks during take-off and landing will help prevent ear problems.

A recommended website is www.babygoes2.com, while www.mumsnet.com/bigissues/travel.html, is useful for parents with older kids.

Women travellers

Travelling in Scotland is neither easier nor more difficult for women than travelling in other parts of the UK. Generally speaking, Scots are friendly and courteous and even lone women travellers should experience nothing unpleasant. However, common sense dictates that single women would do well to avoid hitching on their own in the middle of nowhere. In the main cities and larger towns, the usual precautions need to be taken and you should avoid walking in quiet, unlit streets and parks at night.

Working in Scotland

Citizens of European Union (EU) countries can live and work in Britain freely without a visa, but non-EU residents need a permit to work legally. This can be difficult to obtain without the backing of an established company or employer in the UK. Also, visitors from Commonwealth countries who are aged between 17 and 27 may apply for a working holidaymaker's visa which permits them to stay in the UK for up to two years and work on a casual basis (ie non-career oriented). These certificates are only available from British embassies and consulates abroad and you must have proof of a valid return or onward ticket, as well as means of support during your stay. Commonwealth citizens with a parent or grandparent born in the UK can apply for a Certificate of Entitlement to the Right of Abode, allowing them to work in Britain.

Pick up a copy of What Scotland, *a free guide for independent travellers living and working in Scotland; T020-7384 9330.*

An option for citizens of some non-Commonwealth countries is to visit on an au pair placement to learn English by living with an English-speaking family for a maximum of two years. Au pairs must be aged between 17 and 27, and come from one of the following countries: Andorra, Bosnia-Herzegovina, Croatia, Cyprus, the Czech Republic, The Faroe Islands, Greenland, Hungary, Macedonia, Malta, Monaco, San Marino, the Slovak Republic, Slovenia, Switzerland or Turkey. This can be a good way to learn English, but check out the precise conditions of your placement before taking it up.

Those wishing to devote their time helping the environment, or simply gain some valuable experience can begin their search with the following organizations: **The British Trust for Conservation Volunteers** ⓘ *33 St Mary's St, Wallingford, Oxon, OX10 OEU, T01491-821600, www.btcv.org*, get fit in the 'green gym', planting hedges, creating wildlife gardens or improving footpaths; **Earthwatch** ⓘ *57 Woodstock Rd, Oxford, OX2 6HJ, T01865-318 838*, team up with scientists studying our furry friends; **Jubilee Sailing Trust** ⓘ *Hazel Rd, Southampton, T023-8044 9108, www.jst.org.uk*, work on deck on an adventure holiday; and **Waterway Recovery Group** ⓘ *PO Box 114, Rickmansworth, WD3 1ZY, T01923-711 114, www.wrg.org.uk*, help restore a derelict canal.

Also check out the organizations listed on page 59, as well as the Scottish Youth Hostel Association (SYHA), see page 42.

Before you travel

Getting in

Visas

Visa regulations are subject to change, so it is essential to check with your local British embassy, high commission or consulate before leaving home. Citizens of EU member states, as well as citizens of Iceland, Liechtenstein, Norway and Switzerland, only need a passport (valid for at least six months) or an approved and valid national ID card for travel to the United Kingdom. Non-EU passport holders need to check whether they are among the 33 countries whose nationals do NOT need a visa to visit the EU for 90 days. These include Bulgaria, Croatia and Romania, as well as Australia,

 Canada, Japan, New Zealand and the United States. All other visitors require a visa and should contact the relevant embassy or consulate in their home country.

The **Foreign Office**'s excellent website, www.fco.gov.uk, provides details of British immigration and visa requirements and also has a directory of all British Embassies overseas. Also the **Immigration Advisory Service (IAS)** ⓘ *County House, 190 Great Dover St, London SE1 4YB, T020-7357 6917, www.vois.org.uk*, offers free and confidential advice to anyone applying for entry clearance into the UK.

For visa extensions contact the **Home Office, Immigration and Nationality Department** ⓘ *Lunar House, Wellesley Rd, Croydon, London CR9, T020-8686 0688*, before your existing visa expires. Citizens of Australia, Canada, New Zealand, South Africa or the USA wishing to stay longer than six months will need an Entry Clearance Certificate from the British High Commission in their country. For more details, contact your nearest British embassy, consulate or high commission, or the Foreign and Commonwealth Office in London, T020-7270 1500.

Customs

Visitors from EU countries do not have to make a declaration to customs on entry into the UK. The limits for duty-paid goods from within the EU are 800 cigarettes, or 1 kg of tobacco, 10 litres of spirits, 20 litres of fortified wine, 90 litres of wine and 110 litres of beer. There is no longer any duty-free shopping. Visitors from non-EU countries are allowed to import 200 cigarettes, or 250 grams of tobacco, two litres of wine, and two litres of fortified wine or one litre of spirits. There are various import restrictions, most of which should not affect the average tourist. There are tight quarantine restrictions which apply to animals brought from overseas (except for Ireland). For more information on British import regulations, contact **HM Customs and Excise** ⓘ *Dorset House, Stamford St, London SE1 9PJ, T020-7928 3344, www.hmce.gov.uk.*

Many goods in Britain are subject to a Value Added Tax (VAT) of 17.5%, with the major exception of books and food. Visitors from non-EU countries can save money through the Retail Export Scheme, which allows a refund of VAT on goods to be taken out of the country. Note that not all shops are participants in the scheme and that VAT cannot be reclaimed on hotel bills or other services.

What to take

You'll be able to find everything you could possibly need for your trip in Scottish cities, so if you wish you can pack light and buy stuff as you go along. Given the climate, you will more than likely need warm and waterproof clothing, whatever the time of year. Also bring light clothes in the summer, preferably long-sleeved to protect you from the midges, see page 62. If you're planning on doing some hillwalking you should come properly prepared, as the weather can change rapidly in the mountains, see also page 51. It's worth treating your boots with a waterproofing agent as some of the trails cross boggy ground.

If you are backpacking, a sleeping bag is useful in hostels, and a sleeping sheet with a pillow cover is needed if staying in Scottish Youth Hostel Association (SYHA) hostels (or you can hire one there). A padlock can also be handy for locking your bag if it has to be stored in a hostel for any length of time. Other useful items include an alarm clock (for those early ferry departures), an adaptor plug for electrical appliances, an elastic clothes line and, if you're hillwalking or camping, a Swiss Army knife, torch (flashlight) and compass are essential.

Insurance

It's a good idea to take out some form of travel insurance, wherever you're travelling from. This should cover you for theft or loss of possessions and money, the cost of all medical and dental treatment, cancellation of flights, delays in travel arrangements, accidents, missed departures, lost baggage, lost passport, and personal liability and legal expenses. There are a variety of policies to choose from, so it's best to shop around to get the best price. Your travel agent can also advise you on the best deals available. **STA Travel**, www.statravel.co.uk, with branches nationwide, and other reputable student travel organizations often offer good-value travel policies. Another company worth calling for a quote is **Columbus Direct**, T020-7375 0011. Older travellers should note that some companies won't cover people over 65 years old, or may charge high premiums. The best policies for older travellers are offered by **Age Concern**, T01883-346 964. Travellers from North America can try the **International Student Insurance Service (ISIS)**, which is available through **STA Travel**, T1-800-777 0112, www.sta-travel.com. Some other recommended travel insurance companies in North America include **Travel Guard**, T1-800-826 1300, www.noelgroup. com; **Access America**, T1-800-284 8300; **Travel Insurance Services**, T1-800-937 1387; and **Travel Assistance International**, T1-800-821 2828.

Points to note: you should always read the small print carefully. Some policies exclude 'dangerous activities' such as scuba diving, skiing, horse riding or even trekking. Not all policies cover ambulance, helicopter rescue or emergency flights home. Find out if your policy pays medical expenses direct to the hospital or doctor, or if you have to pay and then claim the money back later. If the latter applies, make sure you keep all records. Whatever your policy, if you are unfortunate enough to have something stolen, make sure you get a copy of the police report, as you will need this to substantiate your claim. See page 63 for details of medical insurance.

Money

The British currency is the pound sterling (£), divided into 100 pence (p). Coins come in denominations of 1p, 2p, 5p, 10p, 20p, 50p, £1 and £2. Bank of England banknotes are legal tender in Scotland, in addition to those issued by the Bank of Scotland, Royal Bank of Scotland and Clydesdale Bank. These Scottish banknotes (bills) come in denominations of £5, £10, £20, £50 and £100 and are legal tender in the rest of Britain, though less helpful shopkeepers south of the border may be reluctant to accept them.

Banks

The larger towns and villages have a branch of at least one of the big four high street banks – **Bank of Scotland, Royal Bank of Scotland, Clydesdale** and **TSB Scotland**. Bank opening hours are Monday to Friday from 0930 to between 1600 and 1700. Some larger branches may also be open later on Thursdays and on Saturday mornings. Banks are usually the best places to change money and cheques. You can withdraw cash from selected banks and ATMs (or cashpoints as they are called in Britain) with your cash card. In more remote parts, and especially on the islands, ATMs are few and far between and it is important to keep a ready supply of cash on you at all times. Outside the ferry ports on most of the smaller islands, you won't find an ATM. Your bank will give you a list of locations where you can use your card. **Bank of Scotland** and **Royal Bank** take **Lloyds** and **Barclays** cash cards; **Clydesdale**

In small and remote places, and on some islands, there may only be a mobile bank which runs to a set timetable. This timetable will be available from the local post office.

 takes **HSBC** and **National Westminster** cards. **Bank of Scotland, Clydesdale** and most building society cashpoints are part of the Link network and accept all affiliated cards. See also Credit cards, below. In addition to ATMs, bureaux de change can be used outside banking hours. These can be found in most city centres and also at the main airports and train stations. Note that some charge high commissions for changing cheques. Those at international airports, however, often charge less than banks and will change pound sterling cheques for free. Avoid changing money or cheques in hotels, as the rates are usually very poor.

Credit cards

Most hotels, shops and restaurants accept the major credit cards such as MasterCard and Visa and, less frequently, Amex, though some places may charge for using them. They may be less useful in more remote rural areas and smaller establishments such as B&Bs which will often only accept cash or cheques.

Visa card holders can use the **Bank of Scotland, Clydesdale Bank, Royal Bank of Scotland** and **TSB** ATMs; Access/MasterCard holders can use the Royal Bank and Clydesdale; Amex card holders can use the Bank of Scotland.

Traveller's cheques

The safest way to carry money is in traveller's cheques. These are available for a small commission from all major banks. **American Express (Amex), Visa** and **Thomas Cook** cheques are widely accepted and are the most commonly issued by banks. You'll normally have to pay commission again when you cash each cheque. This will usually be 1%, or a flat rate. No commission is payable on Amex cheques cashed at Amex offices. Make sure you keep a record of the cheque numbers and the cheques you've cashed separate from the cheques themselves, so that you can get a full refund of all uncashed cheques should you lose them. It's best to bring sterling cheques to avoid changing currencies twice. Also note that in Britain traveller's cheques are rarely accepted outside banks, so you'll need to cash them in advance and keep a good supply of ready cash.

Money transfers

If you need money urgently, the quickest way to have it sent to you is to have it wired to the nearest bank via **Western Union**, T0800-833 833, or **Moneygram**, T0800-894 887. Charges are on a sliding scale; ie it will cost proportionately less to wire out more money. Money can also be wired by **Thomas Cook** or **American Express**, though this may take a day or two, or transferred via a bank draft, but this can take up to a week.

Cost of travelling

The Highlands and Islands of Scotland can be an expensive place to visit, and prices are higher in more remote parts, but there is plenty of budget accommodation available and backpackers will be able to keep their costs down. Petrol is a major expense and won't just cost an arm and a leg but also the limbs of all remaining family members. Expect to pay up to 10p per litre more than in central and southern parts of Scotland. Accommodation and restaurant prices also tend to be higher in more popular destinations and during the busy summer months.

The minimum daily budget required, if you're staying in hostels or cheap B&Bs, cycling or hitching, and cooking your own meals, will be around £25-30 per person per day. If you start using public transport and eating out occasionally that will rise to around £35-40. Those staying in slightly more upmarket B&Bs or guesthouses, eating out every evening at pubs or modest restaurants and visiting tourist attractions, such as

Though using a credit/debit card is by far the easiest way of keeping in funds, you must check with your bank what the total charges will be; this can be as high as 4-5 % in some cases.

castles or museums, can expect to pay around £50-60 per day. If you also want to hire a car and use ferries to visit the islands, and eat well, then costs will rise considerably and you'll be looking at least £75-80 per person per day. Single travellers will have to pay more than half the cost of a double room in most places, and should budget on spending around 60% of what a couple would spend.

Getting there

Air

Generally speaking, the cheapest and quickest way to travel to Scotland from outside the UK is by air. There are good links to Edinburgh and Glasgow, with direct flights from many European cities, and direct flights from North America to Glasgow. There are also flights from a few European cities to Aberdeen and Inverness. There are no direct flights from North America to Edinburgh; these are usually routed via London or Dublin. There are also daily flights from Ireland and regular flights to most Scottish airports from other parts of the UK. There are no direct flights to Scotland from Australia, New Zealand, South Africa or Japan. You will have to get a connection from London. Those wishing to visit England as well should note that it is generally cheaper to fly to Scotland from the rest of Britain if you use an Airpass bought in your own country. This is offered by **British Airways** and **British Midland**. Airpasses are valid only with an international scheduled flight ticket.

From the UK and Ireland

There are direct flights to Scotland's three main airports – Glasgow, Edinburgh and Aberdeen – almost hourly from London Heathrow, Gatwick, Stansted and Luton airports. There are also daily flights from provincial UK airports and from Dublin. To fly on to the smaller airports, you'll need to change planes, see page 36 for domestic flights. The cheapest flights leave from London Luton or Stansted, plus a few provincial airports, with **Ryanair** and **easyJet**. If you book on-line, fares can be as little as £5 one-way during promotions, but you can often fly for under £50 return. These tickets may be subject to rigid restrictions, but the savings can make the extra effort worthwhile. Cheaper tickets usually have to be bought at least a week in advance, apply to only a few midweek flights, and must include a Saturday night stayover. They are also non-refundable, or only partly refundable, and non-transferable. A standard flexible and refundable fare from London to Glasgow or Edinburgh will cost at least £150-200 return. London to Glasgow and Edinburgh is roughly one hour.

There are also flights to Inverness from London and from many regional UK airports, including new services from Belfast City, Southampton and Nottingham. There are also flights from several UK airports to Wick, Kirkwall (Orkney) and Sumburgh (Shetland), including the recently launched **Atlantic Airways** service from London Stansted to Sumburgh. For full details of all flights to Highlands and Islands airports from the rest of the UK, visit the Highlands and Islands Airports Ltd website: www.hial.co.uk.

From the rest of Europe

There are direct flights to **Glasgow International** from many European capitals, including Copenhagen, Amsterdam, Paris (Beauvais), Dublin, Frankfurt Hahn, Stockholm, Brussels, Milan, Oslo and Barcelona. To **Edinburgh** from Paris (CDG), Zurich, Amsterdam, Brussels, Copenhagen and Frankfurt. There are direct flights to **Aberdeen** from Amsterdam, Copenhagen and Stavanger, and to **Inverness** from Amsterdam and Zurich.

From North America

Because of the much larger number of flights to London, it is generally cheaper to fly there first and get an onward flight, see above for the best deals. For low-season Apex fares expect to pay around US$400-600 from New York and other East Coast cities, and around US$500-700 from the West Coast. Prices rise to around US$700-900 from New York, and up to US$1000 from the West Coast in the summer months. Low-season Apex fares from Toronto and Montreal cost around CAN$600-700, and from Vancouver around CAN$800-900, rising to CAN$750-950 and CAN$950-1150 respectively during the summer. East Coast USA to Glasgow takes around six to seven hours direct. To London it takes seven hours. From the West Coast it takes an additional four hours.

To Glasgow International Continental Airlines fly from New York, **American Airlines** fly from Chicago and **Air Canada** from Toronto.

Airline contact details

Aer Arran, www.skyroad.com.
Aer Lingus, www.aerlingus.com.
Air Canada, www.aircanada.ca.
Air France, www.airfrance.com.
American Airlines, www.americanair.com.
Atlantic Airways, www.flyshetland.com.
BMI, www.flybmi.com.
British Airways, www.britishairways.com.
British European, www.flybe.com.
Continental, www.flycontinental.com.
Eastern Airways, www.easternairways.com.
easyJet, www.easyjet.com.
Euromanx, www.euromanx.com.
Icelandair, www.icelandair.com.
KLMUK, www.klm.com.
Lufthansa, www.lufthansa.com.
Ryanair, www.ryanair.com.
ScotAirways, www.scotairways.com.

Rail

There are fast and frequent rail services from London and other main towns and cities in England to Glasgow, Edinburgh, Aberdeen and Inverness. Journey time from London is about 4½ hours to Edinburgh, five hours to Glasgow, seven hours to Aberdeen and eight hours to Inverness. Two companies operate direct services from London to Scotland: **GNER** trains leave from Kings' Cross and run up the east coast to Edinburgh, Aberdeen and Inverness; and **Virgin** trains leave from Euston and run up the west coast to Glasgow. **Scotrail** operate the *Caledonian Sleeper* service if you wish to travel overnight from London Euston to Aberdeen, Edinburgh, Glasgow, Inverness and Fort William. This runs nightly from Sunday to Friday.

Eurostar ⓣ *T08705-186 186, www.eurostar.com*, operates high-speed trains through the Channel Tunnel to London Waterloo from Paris (three hours), Brussels (two hours 40 minutes) and Lille (two hours). You then have to change trains, and stations, for the onward journey to Scotland. If you're driving from continental Europe you could take Le Shuttle ⓣ *T08705-353 535, for bookings*, which runs 24 hours a day, 365 days a year, and takes you and your car from Calais to Folkestone in 35-45 minutes. Fares range from £84 to £165 per carload, depending on how far in advance you book or when you travel.

Enquiries and booking

National Rail Enquiries, T08457-484950, are quick and courteous with information on rail services and fares but not always accurate, so double check. They can't book tickets but will provide you with the relevant telephone number, see also below. The website **www.qjump.co.uk** is a bit hit-and-miss but generally fast and efficient and shows you all the various options on any selected journey, while **www.thetrainline.co.uk** also has its idiosyncrasies but shows prices clearly. For advance credit/debit card bookings, T08457-550 033. **GNER,** T08457-225 225, www.gner.co.uk; **Virgin,** T08457-222 333; and **ScotRail,** T08457-550 033, www.scotrail.co.uk.

Fares

To describe the system of rail ticket pricing as complicated is a huge understatement and impossible to explain here. There are many and various discounted fares, but restrictions are often prohibitive, which explains the long queues and delays at ticket counters in railway stations. The cheapest ticket is a **Super Apex**, which must be booked at least two weeks in advance, though this is not available on all journeys. Next cheapest is an **Apex** ticket which has to be booked at least seven days before travelling, and again tickets are restricted in number. Other discount tickets include a **Saver return**, which can be used on all trains, and a **Super Saver**, which costs slightly less but cannot be used on a Friday or during peak times. For example, a **GNER** London–Edinburgh Saver return costs £82.50, while an Apex is £51. A standard return with **Scotrail** on this route is £65. All discount tickets should be booked as quickly as possible as they are often sold out weeks, or even months, in advance, especially Apex and Super Apex tickets. The latter tickets guarantee seat reservations, but Saver and Super Saver tickets do not. These can be secured by paying an extra £1. A **Caledonian Sleeper Apex return** ticket from London to Edinburgh or Glasgow costs £89, while an open return is £125.

Railcards

There are a variety of railcards which give discounts on fares for certain groups. Cards are valid for one year and most are available from main stations. You need two passport photos and proof of age or status.

Young Person's Railcard For those aged 16-25 or full-time students in the UK. Costs £20 and gives 33% discount on most train tickets and some ferry services.

Senior Citizen's Railcard For those aged over 60. Same price and discount as above.

Disabled Person's Railcard Costs £18 and gives 33% discount to a disabled person and one other. Pick up application form from stations and send it to **Disabled Person's Railcard Office**, PO Box 1YT, Newcastle-upon-Tyne, NE99 1YT. It may take up to 21 days to process, so apply in advance.

Family Railcard Costs £20 and gives 33% discount on most tickets (20% on others) for up to four adults travelling together, and 60% discount for up to four children.

Road

Bus/coach

Road links to Scotland are excellent, and a number of companies offer express coach services day and night. This is the cheapest form of travel to Scotland. The main operator between England and Scotland is **National Express**, T08705-808080, www.nationalexpress.com. There are direct buses from most British cities to Edinburgh, Glasgow, Aberdeen and Inverness. Tickets can be bought at bus stations or from a huge number of agents throughout the country. Fares from London to Glasgow and Edinburgh with **National Express** start at around £20 return for an economy advance return. Fares to Aberdeen and Inverness are a little higher. The London to Glasgow/Edinburgh journey takes around eight hours, while it takes around 11 or 12 hours for the trip to Aberdeen and Inverness. From Manchester to Glasgow takes around 6½ hours.

Car

There are two main routes to Scotland from the south. In the east the A1 runs to Edinburgh and in the west the M6 and A74(M) runs to Glasgow. The journey north from London to either city takes around eight to 10 hours. The A74(M) route to Glasgow is dual carriageway all the way. A slower and more scenic route is to head off the A1 and take the A68 through the Borders to Edinburgh. There's an **Autoshuttle**

 Express service to transport your car overnight between England and Scotland and vice versa while you travel by rail or air. For further information T08705-133714; reservations T08705-502 309. See also Getting around, page 37.

Sea

There are direct routes to Scotland from Europe on the **Smyril Line** (Aberdeen, T01224-572 615; Lerwick, T01595-690 845, www.smyril-line.com) service to Lerwick (Shetland) from Norway (Bergen), Iceland (Seydisfjordur) and the Faroe Islands (Torshavn). It sails from mid-May to early September only once a week and takes 12 hours. A sleeping berth one way from Norway and Faroe Islands costs from £68 in high season. You then have to get from Lerwick to Aberdeen. **Northlink Ferries**, www.northlinkferries.co.uk, sail from Lerwick to Aberdeen, see page 382.

P&O Irish Sea (T0870-242 4777, www.poirishsea.com), has several crossings daily from Larne to Cairnryan (one hour) fares from £60 single for car and driver, and from Belfast to Troon (2½ hours) fares from £70 singles for car and driver. **Stena Line**, T0870-707 070, www.stenaline.co.uk, run numerous ferries (three hours) and high-speed catamarans (1½ hours) from Belfast to Stranraer, fares from £90 single for car and driver. **Seacat Scotland** (T0870-552 3523, www.seacat.co.uk) run daily services from Belfast to Troon (2½ hours; £250 for two adults and a car).

Touching down

Airport information

Glasgow International, T0141-887 1111, is eight miles west of the city, at junction 28 on the M8. It handles domestic and international flights. Terminal facilities include car hire, bank ATMs, currency exchange, left luggage, tourist information (T0141-848 4440) and shops, restaurants and bars. There's also a **Travel Centre** ⓘ *T0141-848 4330, daily 0800-2200 in summer, 0800-1800 in winter*, in the UK Arrivals concourse, and a **First Options Hotel and Travel Reservations** desk in the International Arrivals concourse, T0141-848 4731. **Edinburgh airport**, T0131-333 1000, has all facilities, including a tourist information desk, currency exchange, ATMs, restaurants and bars (first floor), shops (ground floor and first floor) and car hire desks in the terminal in the main UK arrivals area. For details of all facilities and amenities at all Highlands and Islands airports, visit www.hial.co.uk.

Tourist information

Tourist Information Centres

Tourist offices – called tourist information centres (TICs) – can be found in most Scottish towns. Their addresses, phone numbers and opening hours are listed in the relevant sections of this book. Opening hours vary depending on the time of year, and many of the smaller offices are closed during the winter months. All tourist offices provide information on accommodation, public transport, local attractions and restaurants, as well as selling books, local guides, maps and souvenirs. Many also have free street plans and leaflets describing local walks. They can also book accommodation for you, see page 40, for a small fee. Addresses of the main office of the Scottish Tourist Board – now called **Visit Scotland** – and the various Visit Scotland regional offices are given on page 21.

Touching down

Business hours 0900-1700.
Electricity The current in Britain is 240V AC. Plugs have three square pins and adapters are widely available.
Emergencies For police, fire brigade, ambulance and, in certain areas, mountain rescue or coastguard, dial 999.
Laundry Most towns have coin-operated launderettes. The average cost for a wash and tumble dry is about £3. A service wash, where someone will do your washing for you, costs around £4-5. In more remote areas, you'll have to rely on hostel and campsite facilities.
Time Greenwich Mean Time (GMT) is used from late October to late March, after which time the clocks go forward an hour to British Summer Time (BST). GMT is five hours ahead of US Eastern Standard Time and 10 hours behind Australian Eastern Standard Time.
Telephone To call Scotland from overseas, dial 011 from USA and Canada, 0011 from Australia and 00 from New Zealand, followed by 44, then the area code, minus the first zero, then the number.
Useful numbers: operator T100; international operator T155; directory enquiries T192; overseas directory enquiries T153.
Toilets Public toilets are found at all train and bus stations and motorway service stations. They may charge 20p, but are generally clean, with disabled and baby-changing facilities. Those in town centres are often pretty grim.
Weights and measures Imperial and metric systems are both in use. Distances on roads are measured in miles and yards, drinks poured in pints and gills, but generally, the metric system is used elsewhere.

Museums, galleries and historic houses

Most of Scotland's tourist attractions, apart from the large museums and art galleries in the main cities, are open only from Easter to October. Full details of opening hours and admission charges are given in the relevant sections of this guide.

Over 100 of the country's most prestigious sights, and 185,000 acres of beautiful countryside, are cared for by the **National Trust for Scotland (NTS)** ⓘ *26-31 Charlotte Square, Edinburgh EH2 4ET, T0131-2439300, www.nts.org.uk.* National Trust properties are indicated in this guide as 'NTS', and entry charges and opening hours are given for each property. If you're going to be visiting several sights during your stay, then it's worth buying a **Discovery ticket** for three, seven and 14 days: a 14-day pass costs £24 for an adult. YHA and HI members and student-card holders get 50% discount on NTS admission charges.

Historic Scotland (HS) ⓘ *Longmore House, Salisbury Place, Edinburgh EH9 1SH, T0131-668 8800, www.historic-scotland.gov.uk,* manages more than 330 of Scotland's most important castles, monuments and other historic sites. Historic Scotland properties are indicated as 'HS', and admission charges and opening hours are also given in this guide. **Historic Scotland** offer an Explorer Ticket which allows free entry to 70 of their properties including Edinburgh and Stirling castles. A three-day pass (can be used over five consecutive days) costs £18 adult, £13.50 concession, family £36, seven-day pass (valid for 14 days) £25.50/19/51, 10-day pass (valid for 30 days) £30/22.50/60. It can save a lot of money, especially in Orkney, where most of the monuments are managed by Historic Scotland.

Many other historic buildings are owned by local authorities, and admission is cheap, or in many cases free. Most fee-paying attractions give a discount or concession for senior citizens, the unemployed, full-time students and children

The Countryside Code

1. Drive carefully and behave courteously to other motorists and cyclists on narrow, winding island roads. Park vehicles where they will not be a hazard or disruption to other motorists, residents or businesses.
2. Keep to public paths through farmland to minimize crop damage, and avoid 'short-cuts' on steep terrain to prevent soil erosion and damage to natural vegetation.
3. Litter is an eye-sore, harmful to farm animals, wildlife and the water supply – leave no waste and take all your rubbish home.
4. Protect wildlife, plants and trees.
5. Respect ancient monuments, buildings and sites of religious importance – do not vandalize or cause graffiti.
6. Many of the abandoned crofts are derelict and dangerous – keep out for your own safety.
7. Avoid damaging crops, walls, fences and farm equipment; fasten all gates.
8. Do not collect wildflowers, seabird eggs or historical artefacts.
9. Avoid pollution of water supplies – there are few toilets outside of villages so when walking in the countryside bury human waste and toilet paper in the ground and at least 30 m from water courses.
10. Guard against risk of fire from matches, cigarettes, stoves and campfires.
11. Keep dogs under careful control, especially when near to sheep at lambing-time and seabird nesting sites at cliff edges, and avoid dog-fouling in public places.
12. Respect the peace, solitude and tranquillity of the islands for others to enjoy – keep noise to a minimum.
13. The landscape can be spectacular but dangerous – take particular care along precipitous cliff edges, hilltops and slippery coastal rocks.
14. Stay away from working areas on the moors and hills during grouse-shooting, lambing season, deer culling and heather burning, and respect other locally or nationally imposed access restrictions.
15. Report any damage or environmental concerns to the landowner or the Scottish Environment Protection Agency (SEPA), T01851-706 477.
16. Be adequately prepared when you walk in the hills – check the weather forecast, carry warm, waterproof clothing and adequate food and water supplies, and know how to use a map and compass.

under 16 (those under five are admitted free everywhere). Proof of age or status must be shown. Many of Scotland's stately homes are still owned and occupied by the landed gentry, and admission charges are usually between £4 and £8.

Local customs and laws

Visitors will generally find their Scottish hosts to be friendly and obliging; pathologically so. Friends of friends you met for 10 minutes six months ago will put you up in their house, fill you to bursting with food and drink and then lend you their new car to tour the region. This level of hospitality will be a significant part of the enjoyment of your trip. Those visiting the Outer Hebrides need to be aware of the strict observance of the Sabbath on those islands.

Tipping

Believe it or not, people in Scotland do leave tips. In a restaurant you should leave a tip of 10-15% if you are satisfied with the service. If the bill already includes a service charge, you needn't add a further tip. Tipping is not normal in pubs or bars. Taxi drivers will expect a tip for longer journeys, usually of around 10%; and most hairdressers will also expect a tip. As in most other countries, porters, bellboys and waiters in more upmarket hotels rely on tips to supplement their meagre wages.

Responsible tourism

The Highlands and Islands of Scotland are beautiful, dramatic and wild, but also a living, working landscape and a fragile and vulnerable place. By adhering to the Countryside Code (see box, opposite), you can help to minimize your impact and protect the natural and cultural heritage of this unique environment so that it can continue to be appreciated by other visitors. For further information on what action is being taken either in Scotland, throughout UK or across the world to control the negative effects of tourism on the natural environment and traditional cultures, contact **Tourism Concern** ① *T020-7753 3330, or the Tourism and Environment Forum, www.greentourism.org.uk.*

Safety

Incidences of serious crime in Highlands and Islands tend to be the exception rather than the rule and indeed are so rare that they always make front-page news. In fact, if someone failed to say 'good morning' – heaven forfend – it would provoke such an outrage that locals would be talking about little else for weeks to come. Orkney, for example, has the lowest crime rate in the UK (though there was one reported drive-by shouting back in the 1980s). In most island communities, even sizeable ones such as Tobermory on Mull, people don't even lock their doors at night, and will even leave their car keys still in the lock. The major safety issue when visiting the Highlands and more remote parts relates to the unpredictable weather conditions. Everyone should be aware of the need for caution and proper preparation when walking or climbing in the mountains. For more information on mountain safety, see page 52.

Getting around

It is easy to visit the main towns and tourist sights by bus or train, but getting off the beaten track without your own transport requires careful planning and an intimate knowledge of rural bus timetables. Public transport can also be expensive, though there's a whole raft of discount passes and tickets which can save you a lot of money. Hiring a car can work out as a more economical, and certainly more flexible, option, especially for more than two people travelling together. It will also enable you to get off the beaten track and see more of the country. Even if you're driving, however, getting around the remote Highlands and Islands can be a time-consuming business as much of the region is accessed only by a sparse network of tortuous, twisting single-track roads. Be sure to allow plenty of time for getting around and book ferries in advance during the busy summer season.

Air

As well as the main airports of Glasgow, Edinburgh, Aberdeen and Inverness, there are also numerous small airports, many of them on islands (one of them, on Barra, uses the beach as an airstrip). Internal flights are relatively expensive, however, and not really necessary in such a small country, unless you are short of time. For example a return flight from Edinburgh or Glasgow to Shetland can cost over £200. There are discounted tickets available, such as Apex fares, which must be booked at least 14 days in advance, and special offers on some services. There is no departure tax on flights from Highlands and Islands airports.

Offset your flight's carbon emissions by paying to have the appropriate number of trees planted in sustainable forests through Future Forests, www.futureforests.com.

The majority of flights are operated by **British Airways/ Loganair**, T0870-850 9850, www.britishairways.com/www.loganair.co.uk. For inter-island flights in Shetland, you should book direct through **Loganair**, T01595-840246. For information on flight schedules, call the airports listed on page 32, or **British Airways**. The British Airports Authority (BAA) publishes a free Scheduled Flight Guide.

Rail

The rail network in Scotland is limited and train travel is comparatively expensive, but trains are a fast and effective way to get around and also provide some beautifully scenic journeys. The West Highland line to Fort William and Mallaig and the journey from Inverness to Kyle of Lochalsh are among the most beautiful rail journeys in the world and well worth doing. Services between Glasgow, Edinburgh, Stirling, Perth, Dundee and Aberdeen are fast and frequent, and there are frequent trains to and from Inverness.

ScotRail operates most train services. You can buy train tickets at the stations, from major travel agents, or over the phone with a credit/debit card. For train times, call TT0871-2004950. For information and advance credit/debit card bookings call T08457-550033, or visit www.scotrail.co.uk. Details of services are given throughout the guide. For busy long-distance routes it's best to reserve a seat. Seat reservations to Edinburgh, Glasgow, Aberdeen or Inverness are included in the price of the ticket when you book in advance. If the ticket office is closed, there's usually a machine on the platform. If this isn't working, you can buy a ticket on the train. Cyclists should note that although train companies have a more relaxed attitude to taking bikes on trains, reservations for bikes (£3.50) are still required on some services.

Eurorail passes are not recognized in Britain, but **ScotRail** offers a couple of worthwhile travel passes. The most flexible is the **Freedom of Scotland Travelpass**, which gives unlimited rail travel within Scotland. It is also valid on all **CalMac** ferries on the west coast, many **Citylink** bus services in the Highlands, some regional buses, and Glasgow Underground. It also gives 20% discount on **Northlink Ferries** from Aberdeen to Orkney and Shetland. It costs £89 for four days' travel out of eight consecutive days, £119 for eight days travel over 15 consecutive days. The **Highland Rover** is more limited. It allows unlimited rail travel in the Highlands region, plus the West Highland line from Glasgow, and travel between Aberdeen and Aviemore. It also allows free travel on **Citylink** buses between Oban, Fort William and Inverness. It costs £59 for any four out of eight consecutive days.

Road

Bus and coach

Travelling around Scotland by bus takes longer than the train but is much cheaper. There are numerous local bus companies, but the main operator is **Scottish Citylink**, T08705-505 050, www.citylink.co.uk. Bus services between towns and cities are good, but far less frequent in more remote rural areas. Note that long-distance express buses are called coaches. There are a number of discount and flexible tickets available and details of these are given on the **Citylink** website which is fast and easy to use.

The **Brit Xplorer Pass** offers unlimited travel on all **Scottish Citylink** and **National Express** services throughout Britain. Passes cost from £79 for seven days, up to £139 for 14 days. They can be bought from major travel agents, at Gatwick and Heathrow airports, as well as from bus stations in Scottish towns and cities. **National Express Explorer Pass** offers unlimited travel within a specified period on **Scottish Citylink** buses. It is available to overseas visitors but must be bought outside Britain. **Smart Card** and **Discount Coach Card** holders can get a 30% discount on these prices. In North America these passes are available from **British Travel International**, T1-800-327 6097, www.britishtravel.com, or from **US National Express**, T502-298 1395.

Many parts of the Highlands and Islands can only be reached by Royal Mail **postbuses**. These are minibuses that follow postal delivery routes and carry up to 14 fare-paying passengers. They set off early in the morning from the main post office and follow a circuitous route as they deliver and collect mail in the most far-flung places. They are often very slow on the outward morning routes but quicker on the return routes in the afternoons. It can be a slow method of getting around, but you get to see some of the country's most spectacular scenery, and it is useful for walkers and those trying to reach remote hostels or B&Bs. There's a restricted service on Saturdays and none on Sundays. A free booklet of routes and timetables is usually available from local tourist information centres, or visit www.postbus.royalmail.com/RouteFinder.asp for a comprehensive route-planning service.

Car and campervan

Travelling with your own private transport is the ideal way to explore the country. This allows you to cover a lot of ground in a short space of time and to reach remote places. The main disadvantages are traffic congestion and parking, but this is only a problem in the main cities and on the motorways in the central belt. Roads in the Highlands and Islands are a lot less busy than those in England, and driving is relatively stress-free, especially on the B-roads and minor roads. In more remote parts of the country, on the islands in particular, many roads are single track, with passing places indicated by a diamond-shaped signpost. These should also be used to allow traffic behind you to overtake. Remember that you may want to take your time to enjoy the stupendous views all around you, but the driver behind may be a local doctor in a hurry. Don't park in passing places. A major driving hazard on single track roads are the huge numbers of sheep wandering around, blissfully unaware of your presence. When confronted by a flock of sheep, slow down and gently edge your way past. Be particularly careful at night, as many of them sleep by the side of the road (counting cars perhaps).

To drive in Scotland you must have a current **driving licence**. Foreign nationals also need an international **driving permit**, available from state and national motoring organizations for a small fee. Those importing their own vehicle should also have their vehicle registration or ownership document. Make sure you're adequately **insured**. In all of the UK you drive on the left. **Speed limits** are 30 miles per hour (mph) in built-up areas, 70 mph on motorways and dual carriageways, and 60 mph on most other roads.

It's advisable to join one of the main UK motoring organizations during your visit for their 24-hour breakdown assistance. The two main ones in Britain are the

 Automobile Association (AA), T0800-448866, www.theaa.co.uk, and the **Royal Automobile Club (RAC)**, T0800-550550, www.rac.co.uk. One year's membership of the AA starts at £46 and £39 for the RAC. They also provide many other services, including a reciprocal agreement for free assistance with many overseas motoring organizations. Check to see if your organization is included. Both companies can also extend their cover to include Europe. Their emergency numbers are: AA T0800-887 766; RAC T0800-828 282. You can call these numbers even if you're not a member, but you'll have to a pay a large fee. In remote areas you may have to wait a long time for assistance. Also note that in the Highlands and Islands you may be stranded for ages waiting for spare parts to arrive.

Note that petrol in the Highlands and Islands is a lot more expensive than in other parts of the UK, and that petrol stations and garages are few and far between.

Car hire can be expensive in Scotland and you may be better off making arrangements in your home country for a fly/drive deal through one of the main multinational companies. The minimum you can expect to pay is around £150-180 per week for a small car. Local hire companies often offer better deals than the larger multinationals, though **easyCar** can offer the best rates, at around £10 per day, if you book in advance and don't push up the charges with high mileage. They are based at Glasgow airport and there are plans to open a branch in Edinburgh. Some companies such as **Melvilles** offer the flexibility of picking up in Glasgow and leaving in Edinburgh, and vice versa. Most companies prefer payment with a credit card, otherwise you'll have to leave a large deposit (£100 or more). You'll need a full driver's licence (one or two years) and be aged over 21 (23 in some cases).

Alternatively, why not hire your own transport and accommodation at the same time by renting a campervan. Campervans can be rented from a number of companies and it's best to arrange this before arriving as everything gets booked up in the high season (June-August). The largest operator is **Freedom Campervans** (see below). Prices range from £400 per week for a two-berth van up to around £900 for a six-berth in summer. They also offer a Go-POD for budget travellers, which works out around the same price as staying in hostels and taking a backpacker bus tour.

Car/campervan hire companies

Arnold Clark, T0131-228 4747 (Edinburgh); T0141-339 9886 (Glasgow), www.arnoldclark.co.uk.
Avis, T08705-900 500, www.avis.co.uk, in the US T800-331 1084.
Budget, T0800-181 181, www.budgetrentacar.co.uk, in the US T800-527 0700.
Discount Car Hire Scotland, T0870-243 0733, www.discount-car-hire- scotland.co.uk.
easyCar, T0906-333 333 (60p per min) www.easycar.com.
Europcar, T08457-222 525, www.europcar.co.uk.
Freedom Campervans, T0870-285 6191, www.freedomcampervans.co.uk.
Hertz, T08705-996 699, www.hertz.co.uk, in the US T800-654 3001.
Holiday Autos, T8705-300 400, www.holidayautos.co.uk, in the US T800-422 7737, www.holiday/colauto.com.
National Car Rental, T08705-365 365, in the US T800-CAR-RENT, www.nationalcar.com.
Thrifty, T0131-337 1319 (Edinburgh), T0141-445 4440 (Glasgow), in the US T800-367 2277, www.thrifty.com.

Hitching

As in the rest of the UK, hitching is never entirely safe, and is certainly not advised for anyone travelling alone, particularly women travellers. Those prepared to take the risk should not find it too difficult to get a lift in the Highlands and Islands, where people are far more willing to stop for you. Bear in mind, though, that you will probably have to wait a while even to see a vehicle in some parts.

Sea

There are around 60 or so inhabited islands off the coast of Scotland, and nearly 50 of them can be reached by a scheduled ferry service. Most ferries carry vehicles and can be booked in advance. If you're travelling to the islands by car, it's a good idea to book ferries in advance whatever the time of year, particularly to the more popular islands.

The majority of ferry services on the west coast are operated by **Caledonian MacBrayne**, T08705-650000, www.calmac.co.uk, or **CalMac** as they're more commonly known. They sail from Oban, Mallaig and Ullapool to over 20 islands in the Inner and Outer Hebrides. They also run services on the Firth of Clyde. Fares are expensive, especially with a car, but if you're planning on using ferries a lot, you can save a lot of money with an **Island Hopscotch ticket**, which offers reduced fares on 17 set routes. The ticket is valid for one month and you need to follow your set itinerary, though this can be changed en route without too much fuss. For more details and some sample fares, see under the relevant destination. A more flexible option is the **Island Rover**, which offers unlimited travel on **CalMac** ferries for a set period, though you still need to make reservations. An eight-day pass costs £49.50 per passenger and £238 for a car, and a 15-day pass costs £72 per passenger and £357 for a car. **CalMac** schedules are complicated, but details of sailings are given under each relevant destination in this guide. **Western Ferries**, T0141-332 9766, runs services between Gourock and Dunoon and Islay and Jura.

Northlink Ferries, T01856-851 144, www.northlinkferries.co.uk, run car ferries to Orkney and Shetland. Ferries to Orkney depart from Aberdeen or from Scrabster, near Thurso. There are also car and passenger ferries to Orkney with **Pentland Ferries**, www.pentlandferries.co.uk, and a passenger-only ferry (summer only) with **John O' Groats Ferries**, www,jogferry.co.uk. See pages 340 and 364 for details of these. Ferries to Shetland sail from Aberdeen.

The Orkney islands are linked by services run by **Orkney Ferries**, www.orkneyferries.co.uk, while Shetland's heavily subsidized inter-island ferries are run by **Shetland Islands Council**, www.shetland.gov.uk. There are also numerous small operators offering day-trips to various islands. Details of these are given in the relevant chapters.

Maps

You'll find a good selection of maps of Scotland in many bookshops and at the main tourist offices. Road atlases can be bought at most service stations. The best of these are the large-format ones produced by the AA, Collins and Ordnance Survey which cover all of Britain at a scale of around three miles to one inch and include plans of the major towns and cities. The Michelin and Bartholomew fold-out maps are also excellent, as are the official regional tourist maps published by Estate Publications, which are ideal for driving and are available from most tourist offices.

The best detailed maps for walking are the Ordnance Survey maps, which are unsurpassed for accuracy and clarity. These are available at different scales. The Landranger series at 1:50,000 (1¼ inches to a mile) covers the whole of Britain and is good for most walkers. The new Explorer and Outdoor Leisure series are 1:25,000 and offer better value for walkers and cyclists. An excellent source of maps is **Stanfords** at 12-14 Longacre, London WC2E 9LP. There are branches of Stanfords in Bristol and Manchester too.

Sleeping

Staying in the Highlands and Islands of Scotland can mean anything from being pampered to within an inch of your life in a baronial mansion to roughing it in a tiny island bothy with no electricity. If you have the money, then the sky is very much the limit in terms of sheer splendour and excess. We have listed many of the top-class establishments in this book, with a bias towards those that offer that little bit extra in terms of character. Those spending less may have to forego the four-posters and Egyptian cotton sheets but there are still many good-value small hotels and guesthouses with that essential wow factor – especially when it comes to the views. At the bottom end of the scale, there are also some excellent hostels in some pretty special locations.

We have tried to give as broad a selection as possible to cater for all tastes and budgets but if you can't find what you're after, or if someone else has beaten you to the draw, then the tourist information centres (TICs) will help find accommodation for you. They can recommend a place within your particular budget and give you the number to phone up and book yourself, or will book a room for you. Some offices charge a small fee (usually £1) for booking a room, while others ask you to pay a deposit of 10% which is deducted from your first night's bill. Most tourist offices also offer a **Book-a-Bed-Ahead** service, which reserves accommodation for you at your next destination. This costs £3 per booking and is particularly useful in July and August, or if you'll be arriving in a town late. Details of town and city TICs are given throughout the guide. There are also several websites that you can browse and book accommodation. Try visitscotland.com, www.scottishaccommodationindex.com, www.aboutscotland.com and www.scotland200.com.

Accommodation in Scotland will be your greatest expense, particularly if you are travelling on your own. Single rooms are in short supply and many places are reluctant to let a double room to one person, even when they're not busy. Single rooms are usually more than the cost per person for a double room and in some cases cost the same as two people sharing a double room.

Hotels, guesthouses and B&Bs

Area tourist boards publish accommodation lists which include campsites, hostels, self-catering accommodation and VisitScotland-approved hotels, guesthouses and bed and breakfasts (B&Bs). Places participating in the **VisitScotland** system will have a plaque displayed outside which shows their grading, determined by a number of stars ranging from one to five. These reflect the level of facilities, as well as the quality of hospitality and service. However, do not assume that a B&B, guesthouse or hotel is no good because it is not listed by the tourist board. They simply don't want to pay to be included in the system, and some of them may offer better value.

Hotels

At the top end of the scale, there are some fabulously luxurious hotels, often in spectacular locations. Many of them are converted baronial mansions or castles and offer a chance to enjoy a taste of aristocratic grandeur and style. At the lower end of the scale, there is often little to choose between cheaper hotels and guesthouses or B&Bs. The latter often offer higher standards of comfort and a more personal service, but many smaller hotels are really just guesthouses, and are often family-run and every bit as friendly. Note that some hotels, especially in town centres or in fishing ports, may also be rather noisy, as the bar can often be the social hub. Rooms in most

Hotel price codes explained

Accommodation prices in this book are graded with the letters below and are based on the cost for two people sharing a double room with en suite bathroom during the high season. Cheaper rooms with shared bathrooms are available in many hotels, guesthouses and B&Bs. Many places, particularly larger hotels, offer substantial discounts during the low season and at weekends. All places listed are recommended as providing good quality and value within their respective price category. Note that youth hostels all cost under £15 per person per night.

L £160 plus
A £130-159
B £90-129
C £70-89
D £50-69
E £30-49
F £29 and under

mid-range to expensive hotels almost always have bathrooms en suite. Many upmarket hotels offer excellent room-only deals in the low season. An efficient last-minute hotel booking service is www.laterooms.com, which specializes in weekend breaks. Also note that many hotels offer cheaper rates for online booking through agencies such as www.lastminute.com.

If you'd like to stay in a Scottish castle as a paying guest of the owner, contact Scotts Castle Holidays, T0131-229 7111, www.scottscastles.com.

Guesthouses

Guesthouses are often large, converted family homes with up to five or six rooms. They tend to be slightly more expensive than B&Bs, charging between £25 and £40 per person per night, and though they are often less personal, usually provide better facilities, such as en suite bathroom, colour TV in each room and private parking. In many instances they are more like small budget hotels. Many guesthouses offer evening meals, though this may have to be requested in advance.

Bed and breakfasts (B&Bs)

B&Bs provide the cheapest private accommodation. At the bottom end of the scale you can get a bedroom in a private house, a shared bathroom and a huge cooked breakfast for around £20-25 per person per night. Small B&Bs may only have one or two rooms to let, so it's important to book in advance during the summer season and on the islands where accommodation options are more limited. More upmarket B&Bs have en suite bathrooms and TVs in each room and usually charge from £25-35 per person per night. In general, B&Bs are more hospitable, informal, friendlier and offer better value than hotels. Many B&B owners are also a great source of local knowledge and can even provide OS maps for local walks. B&Bs in the Outer Hebrides also offer dinner, bed and breakfast, which is useful as eating options are limited, especially on a Sunday.

Some places, especially in ferry ports, charge room-only rates, which are slightly cheaper and allow you to get up in time to catch an early morning ferry. However, this means that you miss out on a huge cooked breakfast. If you're travelling on a tight budget, you can eat as much as you can at breakfast time and save on lunch as you won't need to eat again until evening. This is particularly useful if you're heading into the hills, as you won't have to carry so much food. Many B&B owners will even make up a packed lunch for you at a small extra cost.

Hostels

For those travelling on a tight budget, there is a large network of hostels offering cheap accommodation. These are also popular centres for backpackers and provide a great opportunity for meeting fellow travellers. Hostels have kitchen facilities for self-catering, and some include a continental breakfast in the price or provide cheap breakfasts and evening meals. Advance booking is recommended at all times, and particularly from May to September and on public holidays, and a credit card is often useful.

Scottish Youth Hostel Association (SYHA)

The **Scottish Youth Hostel Association (SYHA)** ⓘ *7 Glebe Crescent, Stirling FK8 2JA, T01786-451 181, www.syha.org.uk*, is separate from the YHA in England and Wales. It has a network of over 60 hostels, which are often better and cheaper than those in other countries. They offer bunk-bed accommodation in single-sex dormitories or smaller rooms, kitchen and laundry facilities. The average cost is £10-15 per person per night. Though some rural hostels are still strict on discipline and impose a 2300 curfew, those in larger towns and cities tend to be more relaxed and doors are closed as late as 0200. Some larger hostels provide breakfasts for around £2.50 and three-course evening meals for £4-5. For all EU residents, adult membership costs £8, and can be obtained at the SYHA National Office, or at the first SYHA hostel you stay at. SYHA membership gives automatic membership of Hostelling International (HI). The SYHA produces a handbook (free with membership) giving details of all their youth hostels, including transport links. This can be useful as some hostels are difficult to get to without your own transport. You should always phone ahead, as many hostels are closed during the day. Phone numbers are listed in this guide. Many hostels are closed during the winter. Details are given in the SYHA Handbook. Youth hostel members are entitled to half-price entry to all National Trust for Scotland properties. The SYHA also offers an **Explore Scotland** and **Scottish Wayfarer** ticket, which can save a lot of money on transport and accommodation, especially if you're not a student, see page 37.

Independent hostels

The Independent Backpackers Hostels of Scotland is an association of nearly 100 independent hostels/bunkhouses throughout Scotland. They charge between £6 and £15 per person per night, though the average is around £8-10. They tend to be more laid-back, with fewer rules and no curfew, and no membership is required. They all have dormitories, hot showers and self-catering kitchens. Some include continental breakfast, or provide cheap breakfasts. All these hostels are listed on their excellent website, www.hostel-scotland.co.uk.

Campsites and self-catering

Campsites

There are hundreds of campsites around Scotland. They are mostly geared to caravans, and vary greatly in quality and level of facilities. The most expensive sites, which charge up to £10 to pitch a tent, are usually well-equipped. Sites are usually only open from April to October. If you plan to do a lot of camping, you should check out www.scottishcamping.com, which is the most comprehensive service with over 500 sites, many with pictures and reviews from punters. North Americans planning on camping should invest in an international camping carnet, which is available from home motoring organizations, or from **Family Campers and RVers** (FCRV), 4804 Transit Road, Building 2, Depew, NY 14043, T1-800-245 9755. It gives you discounts at member sites.

Pitch a tent on the wild side

The Land Reform (Scotland) Act 2003, which became law in 2005, established a statutory right to camp anywhere in the country, even without the consent of the owner or occupier. Obviously, such rights come with their own responsibilities and people should visit www.outdooraccess-scotland.com, or read *Wild Camping: a guide to good practice*, which is published by the Mountaineering Council of Scotland.

Self-catering

One of the most cost-effective ways to holiday in the Highlands and Islands is to hire a cottage with a group of friends. There are lots of different types of accommodation to choose from, to suit all budgets, ranging from luxury lodges, castles and lighthouses to basic bothies with no electricity.

The minimum stay is usually one week in the summer peak season, though many offer shorter stays of two, three or four nights, especially outside the peak season. Expect to pay at least £200-250 per week for a two-bedroom cottage in the winter, rising to £350-600 in the high season, or more if it's a particularly nice place. A good source of self-catering accommodation is the **VisitScotland**'s guide, which lists over 1200 properties and is available to buy from any tourist office, but there are also dozens of excellent websites to browse. Amongst the best of many websites are the following: www.cottages-and-castles.co.uk; www.scottish-country-cottages.co.uk; www.cottages4you.co.uk; and www.ruralretreats.co.uk. If you want to tickle a trout or feed a pet lamb, www.farmstay.co.uk, offer over a thousand good-value rural places to stay around the UK, all clearly listed on a clickable map. **Highland Hideaways** has a range of more individual self-catering properties, mainly in the Highlands and Islands. For a free brochure write to them at 5-7 Stafford Street, Oban, Argyll PA34 5NJ, T01631-526 056.

The **National Trust for Scotland** owns many historic properties which are available for self-catering holidays. Prices start at around £250 per week in high season rising to £1000 for the top of the range lodges. Contact them at 5 Charlotte Square, Edinburgh EH2 4DU, T0131-226 5922, www.nts.org.uk.

Eating

While Scotland's national drink is loved the world over, Scottish cooking hasn't exactly had a good press over the years. This is perhaps not too surprising, as the national dish, haggis, consists of a stomach stuffed with diced innards and served with mashed *tatties* (potatoes) and *neeps* (turnips). Not a great start. And things got even worse when the Scots discovered the notorious deep-fried Mars bar.

But Scottish cuisine has undergone a dramatic transformation in recent years and Scotland now boasts some of the most talented chefs, creating some of the best food in Britain. The heart of Scottish cooking is local produce, which includes the finest fish, shellfish, game, lamb, beef and vegetables, and a vast selection of traditionally-made cheeses. What makes Scottish cooking so special is ready access to these foods. What could be better than enjoying an aperitif whilst watching your dinner being delivered by a local fisherman, knowing that an hour later you'll be enjoying the most delicious seafood?

Modern Scottish cuisine is now a feature of many of the top restaurants in the country. This generally means the use of local ingredients with foreign-influenced culinary styles, in particular French. International cuisine is also now a major feature on

Restaurant price codes explained

The price ranges in this book are based on a two-course meal (main course plus starter or dessert) without drinks. We have tried to include an equal number of choices in each category, though this is not always possible. All places listed are recommended as offering relatively good value, quality and standards of service within their respective price category.

ΨΨΨ	over £20 a head
ΨΨ	£10-20 a head
Ψ	under £10 a head

menus all over the country, influenced by the rise of Indian and Chinese restaurants in recent decades. In fact, so prevalent are exotic Asian and Oriental flavours that curry has now replaced fish and chips (fish supper) as the nation's favourite food.

Food

Fish, meat and game form the base of many of the country's finest dishes. Scottish beef, particularly Aberdeen Angus, is the most famous in the world. This will, or should, usually be hung for at least four weeks and sliced thick. Game is also a regular feature of Scottish menus, though it can be expensive (dear), especially venison (deer), but delicious and low in cholesterol. Pheasant and hare are also tasty, but grouse is, quite frankly, overrated.

Fish and seafood are fresh and plentiful, and if you're travelling around the northwest coast you must not miss the chance to savour local mussels, prawns, oysters, scallops, langoustines (called prawns here), lobster or crab. Salmon is, of course, the most famous of Scottish fish, but you're more likely to be served the fish-farmed variety than 'wild' salmon, which has a more delicate flavour. Trout is also farmed extensively, but the standard of both remains high. Kippers are also a favourite delicacy, the best of which come from Loch Fyne or the Achiltibuie smokery, see page 244.

Haggis has made something of a comeback, and small portions are often served as starters in fashionable restaurants. Haggis is traditionally eaten on Burns Night (25 January) in celebration of the great poet's birthday, when it is piped to the table and then slashed open with a sword at the end of a recital of Robert Burns' *Address to the Haggis*. Other national favourites feature names to relish: **cock-a-leekie** is a soup made from chicken, leeks and prunes; **cullen skink** is a delicious concoction of smoked haddock and potatoes; while at the other end of the scale of appeal is **hugga-muggie**, a Shetland dish using fish's stomach. There's also the delightfully named **crappit heids** (haddock heads stuffed with lobster) and **partan bree** (a soup made form giant crab's claws, cooked with rice). Rather more mundane is the ubiquitous **Scotch broth**, made with mutton stock, vegetables, barley, lentils and split peas, and **stovies**, which is a mash of potato, onion and minced beef.

Waist-expanding puddings or desserts are a very important part of Scottish cooking and often smothered in butterscotch sauce or syrup in order to satisfy a sweet-toothed nation. There is a huge variety, including **cranachan**, a mouth-watering mix of toasted oatmeal steeped in whisky, cream and fresh raspberries, and **Atholl Brose**, a similar confection of oatmeal, whisky and cream.

Eaten before pudding, in the French style, or afterwards, are Scotland's many home-produced cheeses, which have made a successful comeback in the face of

In Scotland, proper fish and chips use only haddock – cod is for Sassenachs and cats.

mass-produced varieties. Many of the finest cheeses are produced on the islands, especially Arran, Mull, Islay and Orkney. **Caboc** is a creamy soft cheese rolled in oatmeal and is made in the Highlands.

Anyone staying at a hotel, guesthouse or B&B will experience the hearty **Scottish breakfast**, which includes bacon, egg, sausage and black pudding (a type of sausage made with blood), all washed down with copious quantities of tea, Scotland's staple drink. Although coffee is readily available everywhere, do not expect cappuccinos and café lattes: filter coffee is the staple 'tea-substitute' in most hotels and B&Bs. You may also be served kippers (smoked herring) or porridge, an erstwhile Scottish staple, which is now eaten by few people. Made with oatmeal and has the consistency of Italian polenta, it is traditionally eaten with salt, though heretics are offered sugar instead. Oatcakes (oatmeal biscuits) may also be on offer, as well as potato scones, baps (bread rolls) or bannocks (a sort of large oatcake). After such a huge cooked breakfast you probably won't feel like eating again until dinner.

Drink

Beer

Beer is the staple alcoholic drink in Scotland. The most popular type of beer is lager, which is generally brewed in the UK even when it bears the name of an overseas brand and is almost always weaker than in both strength and character than the lagers in mainland Europe. However, examples of the older and usually darker type of beers, known as ales, are still widely available, and connoisseurs should try some of these as they are far more rewarding. Indeed, the best of them rival Scotland's whiskies as gourmet treats.

Traditionally, Scottish ales were graded by the shilling, an old unit of currency written as /-, according to strength. This system is still widely used by the older established breweries, though many of the newer independents and 'micros' have departed from it. 70/- beers at around 3.5% ABV (alcohol by volume), known as 'heavy', and 80/- beers (4.5%) sometimes known as 'export', are the most popular, while 60/-, 'light' (3-3.5%) is harder to find. Very strong 90/- beers (6.5%+ ABV), known as 'wee heavies', are also brewed, mainly for bottling.

The market is dominated by the giant international brewers: Scottish Courage with its **McEwans** and **Youngers** brands; Interbrew with **Calders** and **Carslberg**; and Tetley with **Tennents** lagers. Tennents, the first British brewery to produce a continental-style lager commercially back in the 19th century, is today best known for its bland but very strong canned lagers popular with winos and those who like to get drunk very quickly and cheaply.

Much better are the ales from smaller independent breweries. Edinburgh's Caledonian is a world-class brewer producing many excellent beers, including a popular 80/- and a renowned golden hoppy ale, **Deuchars IPA. Belhaven**, an old, established family brewery in Dunbar, has some superb traditional beers including a malty 80/-, once marketed as the Burgundy of Scotland. Broughton, a microbrewery in the Borders, produces the fruity **Greenmantle** and an oatmeal stout. Another micro, Harvieston of Clackmannanshire (once an important brewing country) offers a wide and adventurous range of specialities, including **Ptarmigan** 80/- and a naturally brewed cask lager, **Schiehallion**. The Heather Ale Company, near Glasgow, has the spicy and unusual **Fraoch** (pronounced 'Frooch') which is flavoured with real heather as well as hops.

Draught beer in pubs and bars is served in pints, or half pints, and you'll pay between £2 and £3 for a pint. In many pubs the basic ales are chilled under gas pressure like lagers, but the best ales, such as those from the independents, are 'real ales', still fermenting in the cask and served cool but not chilled (around 12°C) under

Turn water into whisky

Malt whisky is made by first soaking dry barley in tanks of local water for two to three days. Then the barley is spread out on a concrete floor or placed in cylindrical drums and allowed to germinate for between eight and 12 days, after which it is dried in a kiln, heated by a peat fire. Next, the dried malt is ground and mixed with hot water in a huge circular vat called a 'mash tun'. A sugary liquid called 'wort' is then drawn from the porridge-like result and piped into huge containers where living yeast is stirred into the mix in order to convert the sugar in the wort into alcohol. After about 48 hours the 'wash' is transferred to copper pot stills and heated till the alcohol vaporizes and is then condensed by a cooling plant into distilled alcohol which is passed through a second still. Once distilled, the liquid is poured into oak casks and left to age for a minimum of three years, though a good malt will stay casked for at least eight years.

natural pressure from a handpump, electric pump or air pressure fount. All Scottish beers are traditionally served with a full, creamy head.

Whisky

No visit to the Scottish Highlands would be complete without availing oneself of a 'wee dram'. There is no greater pleasure on an inclement evening than enjoying a malt whisky in front of a roaring log fire whilst watching the rain outside pelt down relentlessly. The roots of Scotland's national drink (*uisge beatha*, or 'water of life' in Gaelic) go back to the late 15th century, but it wasn't until the invention of a patent still in the early 19th century that distilling began to develop from small family-run operations to the large manufacturing business it has become today. Now more than 700 million bottles a year are exported, mainly to the United States, France, Japan and Spain.

There are two types of whisky: single malt, made only from malted barley; and grain, which is made from malted barley together with unmalted barley, maize or other cereals, and is faster and cheaper to produce. Most of the popular brands are blends of both types of whisky – usually 60-70% grain to 30-40% malt. These blended whiskies account for over 90% of all sales worldwide, and most of the production of single malts is used to add flavour to a blended whisky. Amongst the best-known brands of blended whisky are **Johnnie Walker**, **Bells**, **Teachers** and **Famous Grouse**. There's not much between them in terms of flavour and they are usually drunk with a mixer, such as water or soda.

Single malts are a different matter altogether. Each is distinctive and should be drunk neat to appreciate fully its subtle flavours, though some believe that the addition of water helps free the flavours. Single malts vary enormously. Their distinctive flavours and aromas are derived from the peat used for drying, the water used for mashing, the type of oak cask used and the location of the distillery. Single malts fall into four groups: Highland, Lowland, Campbeltown and Islay. There are over 40 distilleries to choose from, most offering guided tours. The majority are located around Speyside, in the northeast. The region's many distilleries include that perennial favourite, **Glenfiddich**, which is sold in 185 countries. A recommended alternative is the produce of the beautiful and peaceful Isle of Islay, whose malts are lovingly described in terms of their peaty quality. Scots tend to favour the 10 year-old **Glenmorangie**, while the most popular in the USA is **The Macallan**.

Which whisky?

Opinions vary as to what are the best single malts and as to when you should drink them. As a rough guide, we would recommend a Speyside malt such as Glenmorangie or Glenlivet before dinner and one of the Islay malts – Ardbeg, Bowmore, Bunnahabhain (pronounced 'bun-a-haven'), Lagavulin, or the very wonderful Laphroaig (pronounced 'la-froig') – after dinner.

If the Islays are not to your taste, then you could try instead the versatile Highland Park from Orkney or perhaps Tamdhu or Aberlour from Speyside. Those eternal favourites, Glenfiddich and The Macallan, can be enjoyed at any time.

Eating out

There are places to suit every taste and budget. In the large towns and cities you'll find a vast selection of eating places, including Indian, Chinese, Italian and French restaurants, as well as Thai, Japanese, Mexican, Spanish and, of course Scottish, but beyond the main cities, choice is much more limited. More and more restaurants are moving away from national culinary boundaries and offering a wide range of international dishes and flavours, so you'll often find Latin American, Oriental and Pacific Rim dishes all on the same menu. This is particularly the case in the many continental-style bistros, brasseries and café-bars, which now offer a more informal alternative to traditional restaurants. Vegetarians are increasingly well catered for, especially in the large cities, where exclusively vegetarian/vegan restaurants and cafés are often the cheapest places to eat. Outside the cities, vegetarian restaurants are thin on the ground, though better-quality eating places will normally offer a reasonable vegetarian selection.

For a cheap meal, your best bet is a pub, hotel bar or café, where you can have a one-course meal for around £5-7 or less, though don't expect gourmet food. The best value is often at lunchtime, when many restaurants offer three-course set lunches or business lunches for less than £10. You'll need a pretty huge appetite to feel like eating a three-course lunch after your gigantic cooked breakfast, however. Also good value are the pre-theatre dinners offered by many restaurants in the larger towns and cities (you don't need to have a theatre ticket to take advantage). These are usually available from around 1730-1800 till 1900-1930, so you could get away with just a sandwich for lunch. At the other end of the price scale are many excellent restaurants where you can enjoy the finest of Scottish cuisine, often with a continental influence, and these are often found in hotels. You can expect to pay from around £25 a head up to £40 or £50 in the very top establishments.

The biggest problem with eating out in Scotland, as in the rest of the UK, is the ludicrously limited serving hours in most pubs and hotels. These places only serve food between 1230 and 1400 and 1700 and 1900, seemingly ignorant of the eating habits of foreign visitors, or those who would prefer a bit more flexibility during their holiday. In small places especially it can be difficult finding food outside these strictly enforced times. Places which serve food all day till 2100 or later are restaurants, fast-food outlets and the many chic bistros and café-bars, which can be found not only in the main cities but increasingly in smaller towns. The latter often offer very good value and above-average quality.

Entertainment

Bars and clubs

As in the rest of Britain, pubs are the main focus of social life and entertainment for most Scots. These vary greatly, from traditional old inns full of character (and often full of characters) to chic and trendy bars where you can order focaccia bread with sun-dried tomatoes washed down with your bottle of continental lager. Many pubs in large towns are owned by the large breweries and only serve their own particular beers, while in more remote parts the local hotel bar is often the only watering hole for miles around. Visitors should also note that the Scottish Parliament recently passed a law banning smoking in pubs and bars, which means that those wishing to light up will have to step outside into a cold, wet and hostile environment, knee-deep in ciggie butts – in other words, the north of England. Pubs generally are open from 1100 till 2300 Monday-Saturday and Sunday from 1100-1200 till 2230, though many close for a couple of hours between 1400 and 1600, which can be very annoying on a wet afternoon. In towns and cities many pubs are open till 2400 or 0100 on Friday and Saturday nights.

Cinema

Scotland, like the rest of the UK, has succumbed to the rise of home entertainment and many of the finest cinemas have long gone, replaced by bingo halls and out-of-town leisure and entertainment complexes showing a vast array of Hollywood blockbusters and little else. That's not to say that independent cinema is dead. Inverness, Perth and Oban all have independent cinemas showing the occasional arthouse film.

Dance

One of the most vibrant expressions of Celtic culture is the ceilidh (pronounced 'kay-lee') an evening of Scottish music and dance, the music provided by a ceilidh band, which normally consists of a fiddler, an accordionist, a drummer and a singer. Here you can spend the evening sampling the delights of Gay Gordons or Dashing White Sergeants. In case you're wondering, these aren't people who frequent these events – they are actually Scottish country dances which, along with eightsome reels, figure prominently in the ceilidh dance-band repertoire. Beware the well-meaning local lad or lassie bearing gifts of whisky, however – an excellent evening enjoying the music can often lead to a spectacular hangover the following morning. The local TIC, or newspaper, will have details of what's on where.

Music

Folk music clubs still thrive in Scotland although, sadly, seem to be restricted to an 'early-in-the-week' slot of a Monday or Tuesday evening in bars, as landlords attempt to bring in customers on what are generally quieter nights for business. Even the Scots, with their fearsome (and well-earned) reputation for partying, can't do it every night of the week. Look out for boards outside pubs which proclaim 'Live Music Tonight' or 'Folk Music Session – All Welcome', when the normally funereal atmosphere of the local pub is transformed into something resembling one of those Hollywood film scenes featuring Julia Roberts or Andie McDowell in an Aran jumper.

Theatre

The main focal points of Scottish theatre are, not surprisingly, the cities of Edinburgh and Glasgow. The latter in particular stages some of the UK's most exciting and innovative drama in its Citizens' and Tramway Theatres. Outside the big two, Perth, Pitlochry and Inverness all have thriving summer programmes.

Festivals and events

There is a huge range of organized events held throughout Scotland every year, ranging in size and spectacle from the Edinburgh Festival, the largest arts festival in the world, to more obscure traditional events featuring ancient customs dating back many centuries. The Scottish Tourist Board publishes a comprehensive list, *Events in Scotland*, twice a year. It's free and is available from the main tourist offices. The most popular tourist events are the **Highland Games** (or **Gatherings**), a series of competitions involving lots of kilts, bagpipes and caber-tossing, which are held across the Highlands and Islands, the northeast and Argyll from June to September. The best known is the **Braemar Gathering**, see page 92, which is attended by various members of the Royal Family. Those at Oban and Dunoon are large events, but smaller gatherings are often more enjoyable and 'authentic'. Details of Highland Gatherings are listed throughout the guide.

Details of local festivals are given in the listings sections of individual towns and cities; also visit www.whatsonwhen.com.

Folk festivals take place all over the country, from Arran to Shetland, and are great fun. Musicians from all over Scotland gather to play the tunes, sing the songs and maybe, just maybe, drink the odd beer or two. Among the best of the folk festivals is the **Shetland Folk Festival**, held over a long weekend in mid-April. Also recommended are those held in Inverness in July and August, Killin at the end of June, Islay during the last two weeks in May, Arran in early June, Skye at the end of July and Kirriemuir on the first weekend in September. Details of these festivals, and many others, are available from the **VisitScotland** regional office, see page 32.

Festivals

January

New Year's Day A variety of ancient local celebrations take place, including the Kirkwall Ba' Game, a mixture of football and mud wrestling.

Up Helly-Aa Re-enactment of the ancient Viking fire festival held on Shetland on the last Tue in Jan, see page 369.

Burns Night Burns suppers held on 25 Jan all over the country to celebrate the poet's birthday. Lots of haggis, whisky and poetry recitals.

May

Spirit of Speyside Whisky Festival: Held on Speyside in May.

The Highland Festival Held over 2 weeks from late May till early Jun at venues throughout the Highland region. For details, T01463-719000, www.highlandfestival.org.uk.

September

Braemar Highland Gathering Attended by the Royal Family in Sep.

October

National Mod Competitive Gaelic music festival held at various locations.

Tour of Mull Rally The highlight of the Scottish rally season, run over the island's public roads.

December-January

Hogmanay Old year's night, and the most important national celebration. Possible derivations of the word include Holag Monath, Anglo Saxon for 'holy month', and Hoog min dag, which is Dutch for 'great love day'. Edinburgh's huge street party is the largest in the northern hemisphere.

Bank holidays

New Year's Day and **2 Jan**, **Good Fri** and **Easter Mon**, **May Day** (1st Mon in May), **Victoria Day** (the last Mon in May), **Christmas Day**and **Boxing Day**. There are also local public holidays in spring and autumn. Dates vary from place to place. Banks are closed during these holidays, and sights and shops may be affected. Contact the relevant Area Tourist Board for more details.

Shopping

Scottish textiles, especially the **tartan** variety, are popular and worth buying. You can get hold of everything from a travelling rug to your own kilt outfit. Shops up and down the country, and especially in Inverness, can tell which clan your family belongs to and make you a kilt in that particular tartan. For the full outfit, including kilt, sporran, jacket, shoes and *skeann dhu* dagger, expect to pay in the region of £600, or more if you want more elaborate accessories. **Harris Tweed** is also a good buy and you can watch your cloth being woven on the Hebridean islands of Harris and Lewis (see box on page 318).

Knitwear is also good value and sold throughout Scotland. Shetland is a good place to find high-quality wool products. Note that Aran jumpers are not from the island of Arran, but from Aran (with one 'r') in Ireland. **Jewellery** is another popular souvenir and there are many excellent craft shops throughout the Highlands and Islands making beautiful jewellery with Celtic designs. **Glassware** is also popular, particularly Edinburgh crystal and Caithness glass, as well as pottery.

Food is another good souvenir and not just the ubiquitous shortbread sold in tartan tins. If you haven't far to travel home, smoked salmon, or any other smoked product, is good value. One of the best places for food products is the island of Arran, where you can buy their delicious local mustards and preserves, smoked fish and game, and cheeses. And, of course, there's **whisky**. Most distilleries will refund the cost of their guided tour in the form of a discount voucher on a bottle of their brand whisky.

Shop hours in Scotland are generally Monday to Saturday from 0900-1730 or 1800. In larger towns and cities, many shops also open on Sundays and late at night, usually on a Thursday and Friday. Large supermarkets and retail complexes found outside large towns are open till 2000 or later Monday to Saturday and till 1600 on Sunday. In the Highlands and Islands, few shops are open on Sunday, most notably in the Outer Hebrides where nothing is open on a Sunday. Also note that in many rural areas there is an early-closing day when shops close at 1300. This varies from region to region, but the most common day is Wednesday.

Sport and activities

Blessed with wild, rugged mountains, windswept lochs, idyllic islands and miles of remote coastline, Scotland is paradise for the visitor who comes to unwind or in search of adventure amidst breathtaking scenery. Indeed, enlightened (2005) access legislation (www.outdooraccess-scotland.com) now provides almost limitless opportunities for the responsible tourist to freely roam through the countryside, cycle miles of forest, paddle tumbling rivers or scramble up mountains to bag Munros (mountains over 3000 ft). Furthermore, come rain, hail or shine, operators now offer a vast array thrilling, adrenaline-packed activities; from canyoning, fun-yakking and whitewater rafting, to telemark skiing, skydiving and surfing, demonstrating that Scotland's growing reputation as an adventure sports' paradise is no idle boast. Of course, as the following pages highlight, Scotland also enjoys world-class salmon fishing, golf and hillwalking; there are now almost a dozen long-distance footpaths such as the 90-mile West Highland Way. But if you'd rather enjoy your adventure indoors, there's Ice Factor, the world's largest ice-climbing facility in Kinlochleven, Edinburgh's gargantuan (120-ft high) rock-climbing wall at Ratho and even year-round snow-skiing at Braehead near Glasgow! At the end of this section is a list of organizations that are able to provide further information on sports and activities in Scotland, see page 59.

Munros, Corbetts and Grahams

There are 284 mountains over 3000 ft (914 m) in Scotland, known as 'Munros', after Sir Hugh Munro, first president of the Scottish Mountaineering Club (SMC), who published the first comprehensive list of these mountains in 1891. In the 1920s a further list was published, of the 221 summits between 2500 and 3000 ft, by J Rooke Corbett, and these became known as 'Corbetts'. A third list, of summits between 2000 and 2500 ft was compiled by Fiona Graham and published in 1992. This list was subsequently revised and corrected and now all peaks that are between 2000-2500 ft are called 'Grahams'.

This is where the term 'Munro-bagging' comes from – one of Scotland's favourite pastimes – climbing as many peaks over 3000 ft as possible.

Canoeing, kayaking and rafting

Scotland's rivers, lochs and deeply indented coastline offer great opportunities for canoeing, surf-kayaking, sea kayaking and careering down rivers in inflatable two-man fun-yaks and whitewater rafts. Perthshire, served by the Tummel, Garry and Tay is arguably Scotland's kayaking hub and where to find adventure operators such as **Nae Limits** and **Splash**. However, whilst legions of river kayakers head for the slalom gates of Grandtully, it's the azure waters of the Inner and Outer Hebrides and operators including **Skyak Adventures** and **Wilderness Scotland** which have helped establish Scotland as one of Europe's top sea-kayaking destinations. Meanwhile, budding surf-kayakers can join the likes of **Hebridean Pursuits** for a roller-coaster ride down the powerful waves that pound the sands off Tiree and Thurso. » *See page 59 for details of organizations and companies offering information, courses and trips.*

Canyoning

This involves heading downriver in a gorge and dropping several hundred feet by swimming, jumping into plunge pools, sliding down log flumes and abseiling. In Perthshire and Lochaber you can also go cliff-jumping from heights of up to 60 ft into rock pools combined with headfirst descents of waterfalls. If that's too tame then try the Tyrolean Traverse, which involves crossing a gorge at a height of 300 ft. » *See page 59 for companies offering canyoning trips.*

Climbing

With hundreds of summer and winter climbing routes, rock climbers and winter mountaineers alike are spoilt for choice. From Glencoe and Lochaber to the Cuillin ridge on Skye, the Cairngorms and majestic hills of Torridon and Assynt, there's no lack of opportunity to test one's nerve. In addition, Glasgow, Edinburgh and Aberdeen are among the major centres with spectacular indoor walls so there's plenty of opportunity to grab some vertical action. Some useful websites are: www.glenmorelodge.org.uk, www.mountaineering-scotland.org.uk, www.alienrock.co.uk. Scotland is a great place to try rock climbing and its arduous winter cousin, ice climbing. The Cairngorms and Cuillins offer challenging climbing, as do Glencoe and Torridon. Most mountaineering clubs have regular weekend meets in the hills as well as social

Mountain safety

Visitors to Scotland should be aware of the need for caution and safety preparations when walking or climbing in the mountains. The nature of Scottish weather is such that a fine sunny day can turn into driving rain or snow in a matter of minutes. Remember that a blizzard can be raging on the summit when the car park at the foot of the mountain is bathed in sunshine. It is essential to get an up to date weather forecast before setting off on any walk or climb. Whatever the time of year, or conditions when you set off, you should always carry or wear essential items of clothing. A basic list for summer conditions would be: boots with a good tread and ankle support and a thick pair of socks; waterproof jacket and trousers, even on a sunny day; hat and gloves are important if the weather turns bad; warm trousers should be worn or carried, tracksuit bottoms are okay if you also have waterproof trousers; spare woolly jumper or fleece jacket will provide an extra layer; map and compass are essential to carry and to know how to use. Other essentials are food and drink, a simple first-aid kit, a whistle and a torch. A small 25-30 litre rucksack should be adequate for carrying the above items. Also remember to leave details of your route and expected time of return with someone, and remember to inform them on your return.

In the winter extra warm clothing is needed, as well as an ice axe and crampons, and the ability to use them. The skills required for moving over ice or snow should be practised with an experienced and qualified mountain guide/instructor.

gatherings closer to home. Some useful websites are: www.winternetscotland.co.uk, www.scotclimb.org.uk and www.nae-limits.com.

Cycling

The bicycle was invented in Scotland, so it seems appropriate that travelling by bike is one of the best ways to explore the country. Thanks to SUSTRANS (www.sustrans.org.uk) and other hard-working voluntary organizations, Scotland has a growing number of traffic-free cycle routes – though it can still be a nerve-wracking experience negotiating Edinburgh and Glasgow city centre by bike!

Though Scotland's apparent love affair with the car continues, the sport of cycling and particularly cross-country and downhill mountain-biking has really taken off over the past decade. Indeed, today Scotland is regarded, by no less than the **International Mountain Biking Association** as one of the world's top mountain biking destinations. Surprised? You shouldn't be. This country has no less than a dozen dedicated mountain bike trail centres from Kirroughtree in Galloway (which forms part of the magnificent 7 Stanes project, www.7stanes.gov.uk) to the Cairngorms (www.mountainbikers.org.uk) and Learnie Forest in the Black Isle (www.himba.org.uk). These are hot mountain bike destinations but, arguably, the most famous is to be found at Fort William where the 'Witch's Trail' and nerve-wracking 2.4km 'black' run downhill track annually attracts the world's best riders for a stage of the UCI MTB World Cup (www.ridefortwilliam.co.uk). The Fort William downhill track (May to September) is accessed by rider and bike being carried up the gondola system (1000-1700 core hours). An adult multi-trip ticket costs £18.50 per day and all participants under 16 years-of-age must have their parent/guardian sign a special participation form before purchasing a ticket. Bike hire is available from the Nevis Range centre or at Off Beat Bikes in Fort William, www.offbeatbikes.co.uk.

Wherever you choose to exercise your pedal power, it's worth noting that many of these innovative and mammoth family-friendly trails, designed to cater for the beginner and expert alike, have been created with the support of **Forestry Commission Scotland** (www.forestry.gov.uk/scotland).

If road and touring is more your thing, Scotland's miles of rural roads are a delight to explore with routes using disused railway tracks and upgraded canal towpaths including the Glasgow to Edinburgh (Clyde and Forth Canal) cycleway, Loch Lomondside and dedicated tracks on the Isle of Arran. The wild and remote Highlands are very popular with cycle tourers. Routes such as Torridon and Applecross provide challenging climbs and exhilarating descents. However, many off-road routes are shared with walkers and horse-riders so caution and consideration should be exercised at all times.

You can cut down on the amount of pedalling you have to do by transporting your bike by train. Bikes can be taken free all **Firstscotrail** services including the sleeper rail services on a first come, first served basis (call **ScotRail** bookings, T08457-550033; www.firstscotrail.com). However, check with **Virgin Rail** and **GNER** for their conditions of carriage. Regardless, space is always limited on trains so it's a good idea to book as far in advance as possible. With few exceptions, such as the **Dearman** coach between Ullapool and Durness, buses are unable to carry bikes unless they are dismantled and boxed. Ferries transport bikes for a small fee and airlines will often accept them as part of your baggage allowance. Check with the ferry company or airline about any restrictions.

Bike rental is available at cycle shops in most large towns and tourist centres. Expect to pay from around £15 per day, or from £60 a week, plus a refundable deposit. Expect to pay more at dedicated mountain bike trail centres for a full suspension 'downhill' bike. There's also the option of a cycling holiday package, which includes transport of your luggage, pre-booked accommodation, route instructions and food and backup support.

Whatever your cycling interest, ask your local **Visitscotland** tourist office for maps and details of cycle routes in their area or log onto www.visitscotland for further information about cycling. Visitscotland also publish an excellent resource guide (free) entitled *Cycling in Scotland* which includes a listing of bike repair shops and operators (see also www.spokes.org.uk). ▸▸ *See also Books, page 416, for cycling guidebooks.*

Diving

Scotland may not have the Great Barrier Reef but it does have some of the finest diving locations in the world, featuring shipwrecks, reefs, sheer underwater cliffs, soft corals and abundant sea life. The west coast offers the best diving, as the water is warmed by the effects of the Gulf Stream and is not cold, even without a dry suit. Among the best sites are the west coast of **Harris**, the **Summer Isles** and the remote island of **St Kilda**. There are lots of wrecks in the **Sound of Mull**, and the chance to find a Spanish Galleon off **Tobermory**. **Scapa Flow** in Orkney is world-renowned as the burial site of the German First World War fleet. ▸▸ *For a list of operators and organizations, see page 59.*

Fishing

Scotland's rivers, streams, lochs and estuaries are among the cleanest waters in Europe and are filled with salmon, trout (sea, brown and rainbow) and pike. Not surprisingly, then, fishing (coarse, game and sea) is hugely popular in Scotland.

There is no close season for coarse fishing or sea angling. For wild brown trout the close season is early October to mid-March. The close season for salmon and sea trout varies from area to area and between net and rod fishing. It is generally from late

 August to early February for net fishing, and from early November to early February for rod fishing. No licence is required to fish in Scotland, but most of the land and rivers are privately owned so you must obtain a permit from the owners or their agents. These are often readily available at the local fishing tackle shop and usually cost from around £15, though some rivers can be far more expensive.

Visitscotland's booklet, *Fishing in Scotland* is a good introduction and can be picked up at its local offices. It's also worthwhile checking out www.fishscotland.co.uk which is packed with all kinds of sea and freshwater fishing information. For a list of organizations, see page 59.

Golf

Scotland has over 400 golf courses, with more being built all the time, and therefore has more courses per head of population than any other country in the world. Any decent-sized town in Scotland will have a golf course nearby and most, if not all, are available for play. There are many public courses, which tend to be both cheap and extremely busy, often have excellent layouts. The majority of private clubs allow visitors, although many have restrictions as to what days these visitors can play. Weekends are usually reserved for club competitions for the members so it is best to try to play on a weekday. All private clubs have a dress code and it is inadvisable to turn up for a round in a t-shirt and jeans. These minor caveats aside, you are more than likely to receive a warm and courteous welcome. To arrange golfing holidays visit www.scotland-golf-tours.co.uk.

Many clubs offer a daily or weekly ticket with the cost varying depending on the course and area. For example, a **Perthshire Highlands Ticket** (T01577-861186) costs £35 for three days and allows up to 27 holes to be played per day on courses including Blair Atholl and Killin. The **Carnoustie Country Dream Ticket** (T0800-975 5955) provides access to four of the world's classic links courses for £195 (April to October) whilst it's best to call T01334-466666 for details of the coveted St Andrews Links Trust Golf Passes. **Visitscotland**'s *Golfing in Scotland* brochure (www.visitscotland.com) provides a comprehensive break-down of prices and courses across the country plus lists of accommodation providers. **Visitscotland** addresses are given on page 21. For a list of recommended golf books, see page 416. For a list of organizations, see page 59.

Health and beauty

Nothing can be more relaxing after a hard day's walking or sightseeing than spending an hour or two being preened and pampered in a spa. If your feeling flush, one hotel that really know how to do it style is the world renowned **Gleneagles Hotel Spa**, see page 76.The location for world leaders during their G8 summit pow-wow in 2005 and boasting world-class equestrian, shooting and golfing facilities (and a five-star restaurant), this is also where therapists and masseurs will pamper away your worries (and those of your partner) for £570 per night including an 80-minute spa session, dinner, bed and breakfast. Of course, there are more modestly priced breaks. Check out www.visitscotland.com for details.

Hillwalking

Scotland is a walker's paradise. Throughout the country there are numerous marked trails, ranging from short walks to long-distance treks from one side of the country to the other. Whatever your taste or level of fitness and experience, you'll find plenty of opportunities to get off the beaten track and explore the countryside.

The best time for hiking in the mountains is usually from May to September, though in the more low-lying parts, April to October should be safe. Winter walking in the Highlands requires technical equipment such as ice axes and crampons and a lot of experience. July and August are the busiest times, though only the most popular routes, such as Ben Nevis, get really crowded. Another problem during these months are midges, see page 62. May to mid-June is probably the most pleasant time overall, as the weather can often be fine and the midges have yet to appear. September is also a good time, though it can be a lot colder. For a list of helpful organizations, see page 59.

Access

Scotland has a long tradition of enabling access to mountain and moorland. This free access, of course, relies on walkers behaving responsibly and recognizing that the countryside is a place of work as well as recreation. It's the Land Reform (Scotland) Act 2003 that underpins one's right to roam in Scotland but with the proviso that it's undertaken responsibly and in accordance with the Outdoor Access Code. In particular, it's the individual walker's responsibility to ensure he or she doesn't damage fences, crops or worry livestock. By adhering to these commonsense rules, all who come to enjoy Scotland's countryside will be helping to maintain access that is the envy of every other country in the UK. However, most land in Scotland remains privately owned and at certain times of the year, such as the main shooting seasons, walkers may be asked to respect certain restrictions on access. The main deer-stalking season runs from mid-August to 20 October and the grouse shooting season is between 12 August (referred to as the 'Glorious Twelfth') and 10 December. For more information on this, see *Heading for the Scottish Hills* which is published by the Mountaineering Council of Scotland, see page 51, and the Scottish Landowners Federation and gives estate maps and telephone numbers to call for local advice. There may also be restricted access during the lambing season from March to May.

Walking routes, ranging from a coastal stroll to an arduous mountain trek, are denoted throughout the guide by ▲.

It is not an offence to walk over someone's land in Scotland (on the condition no crops are damaged or livestock disturbed) but, especially during the stalking and shooting seasons, you may be asked to take a different route, though this rarely happens. Scotland's first national parks opened in recent years: **Loch Lomond and the Trossachs National Park** (www.lochlomond-trossachs.org) in 2002 and **Cairngorms National Park** (www.cairngorms.co.uk) in 2003. There is free access at all times of the year to areas owned by the **National Trust for Scotland**. These areas include Torridon and Glencoe. There is also free access to most land owned by the **Forestry Commission**, and there is good public access to land owned by the **John Muir Trust**, **Scottish Natural Heritage**, the **Royal Society for the Protection of Birds** and the **Woodland Trust**, though these areas are not marked on Ordnance Survey (OS) maps. Also not shown on OS maps are Rights of Way, which are signposted by the Scottish Rights of Way Society's green metal signs. The society publishes maps of rights of way, many of which follow ancient 'drove roads' through the hills.

Information and advice

Visitscotland, the national tourist agency, is a useful source of information for walkers and local TICs have details of interesting local walks. Many walk descriptions and maps are given in this guidebook, but these should ideally be used in conjunction with a good map, such as the Ordnance Survey (OS) Landranger series. The relevant map numbers have been listed, where possible, with the route description. OS maps can be found at TICs and also at outdoor shops, which are usually staffed by experienced climbers and walkers who can give good advice about the right equipment. The best-equipped shops are **Tiso**, www.tiso.co.uk, who have branches in the main towns and cities, and **Nevisport**, in Fort William. For a list of recommended walking guidebooks and maps, see page 416.

Long-distance walks

Scotland also boasts a network of 18 (at the last count) fantastic long-distance walking trails including the Speyside Way, West Highland Way, recently opened 89-mile Kintyre Way, the Isle of Arran Coastal Way (www.coastalway.co.uk) and the spectacular Cape Wrath Trail (www.capewrathtrail.co.uk). Whichever you choose to amble or stroll, you are guaranteed ever-changing landscapes of woodland, rugged mountainsides and serene lochs. Well signposted, most also offer sufficient places for accommodation and supplies en route. These walks can be attempted in full, or sampled in part by less experienced walkers. Area tourist offices can provide information and advice for their own particular sections. One of the main trails, the **Speyside Way**, see page 102, is covered in the relevant section of this guide.

The best-known, and busiest, long-distance trail is the **West Highland Way**, which runs for 95 miles from Milngavie (pronounced 'mull-guy'), just north of Glasgow, to Fort William. The route progresses steadily from the Lowlands, along the eastern shore of Loch Lomond and the traverse of the western edge of Rannoch Moor, to enter Glencoe at White Corries. It continues over the Devil's Staircase, past Kinlochleven, and through Glen Nevis to Fort William. Many walkers finish off with an ascent of Ben Nevis (4406 ft), the highest mountain in Britain, see page 203. Further information, including a trail leaflet with accommodation and facilities guide, is available from **West Highland Way Ranger Service**, Balloch Castle, Balloch G53 8LX, T01389-758216.

Short walks

Many of the most popular short walks, including the ascent of Ben Nevis, are described in this guidebook. These range from gentle strolls through forest glades to strenuous hikes, steep hills and mountains, and also include some beautiful coastal trails. One of the most popular pastimes in Scotland is Munro-bagging, see also box, page 51, which involves climbing as many peaks over 3000 ft as possible. The best area for this is the Highlands, which provide many challenging peaks, and it's possible to climb several in a day. Many of these hills are straightforward climbs, but many also require a high level of fitness and experience, and all require proper clothing, see page 52. You should never attempt walks beyond your abilities.

Other good areas for walking include the Isles of Arran, Mull, Islay and Skye, and Perthshire and the Trossachs. The mighty Cairngorms are better known as a winter ski area, but provide excellent year-round hillwalking and climbing. This is extremely wild terrain, however, and suitable only for experienced walkers. If wishing to explore such places it's worth considering booking a walking or climbing holiday with such operators as **Wilderness Scotland** ⓘ *T0131 6256635, www.wildernessscotland.com.* There are many opportunities for less-experienced walkers in Rothiemurchus Estate and Glenmore Forest Park around Aviemore. Other areas which are best left to serious climbers are Torridon, Kintail and Glencoe, though the latter also offers a few more straightforward walks through spectacular scenery, see page 210.

Kite surfing and windsurfing

Kite-surfing, which involves whizzing over the sea with a tiny board strapped to your feet and body harnessed to a powerful kite, is growing in popularity in Scotland with Troon, St Andrews and Tiree all popular locations for 'grabbing air'. However, windsurfing and particularly wave-sailing amidst the powerful surf of Tiree and Machrihanish remains extremely popular with the former hosting the annual Tiree Wave Classic every October. ▸▸ *See page 59 for details of companies offering flights.*

Paragliding

If you fancy getting high during your visit, you can try your hand at the exciting sport of paragliding. **Cloudbusters** south of Glasgow and **Flying Fever** on the Isle of Arran offer tandem and solo paragliding lessons, courses and hire from beginner to advanced. ▸▸ *See page 59 for details of companies offering flights.*

Pony trekking and horse riding

Pony trekking is a long-established activity in Scotland and miles of beautiful coastline, lochsides, and moorland are accessible on horseback. There are numerous equestrian centres around the country catering to all levels of riders. **Visitscotland** produces a *Trekking & Riding* brochure listing riding centres around the country, all of them approved by the **Trekking and Riding Society of Scotland** (**TRSS**) or the **British Horse Society** (**BHS**). Centres offer pony trekking (leisurely strolls at walking pace for novices), hacks (short rides at a fast pace for experienced riders) and trail riding (long-distance rides at no more than a canter). For general information contact the TRSS. ▸▸ *For a list of organizations, see page 59.*

Skiing

Conditions in Scotland are not as reliable as the Alps, but with short, steep descents off piste, dozens of beginner/intermediate groomed piste and breathtaking mountain scenery, snowboarders, skiers and telemark skiers are handsomely rewarded when the snow falls and the sun shines. The core season is from January to April, but it is possible to ski from as early as November to as late as May. Ski packages and lessons are available, though it's easy to arrange everything yourself and there's plentiful accommodation and facilities in and around the ski centres.

Check out www.born2ski.com for everything from snow reports to après ski ratings.

Ski centres

There are five ski centres in Scotland – well, six if you include the recently opened 200-m real snow indoor slope at **XScape Braehead** outside Glasgow (www.xscapebraehead.com). The largest are **Glenshee**, which has the most extensive network of lifts and selection of runs and **Cairngorm**, which has over 30 runs spread over an extensive area. **Glencoe** is the oldest of the ski resorts and with runs like the 'flypaper' offers some tremendous skiing for experts. **Nevis Range** Aonach Mor near Fort William, has the highest ski runs and only gondola in Scotland. The Lecht is ideal for beginner and intermediate skiers/boarders and also has a fun 'tubing' piste. Access to all five centres (and Braehead) is easiest by car. Each resort has a ski patrol, cafe and hire/lesson facilities.

Costs

Ski equipment and clothing can be hired at all resorts, but lessons should be booked in advance. Prices vary from centre to centre, but on average expect to pay around £15-20 per day for hire of skis, sticks and boots. Snowboard hire is around £17 per day for board and boots. Lift passes cost around £22-26 per day with five-day packages around £90-100. Ski lessons are around £25-30 for half-a-day. Packages including ski hire, tuition and lift pass vary in cost according to location. At Nevis Range, an adult can expect to pay from £85 for the complete 48-hour package including lift pass. A peak time ski pass at Braehead is around £31 for two hours.

Information

Details for each of the five resorts, including phone numbers, are given in the appropriate place in the main text. For further general information contact **Visitscotland** for its *Ski Scotland* brochure and accommodation list, or visit their website, www.visitscotland.com/adventure, which is updated daily. Or you can contact **Snowstorm Scotland**, T0131 445 4151, www.snowsportscotland.org. The easiest way to keep abreast of snow and weather conditions at all of Scotland's mountain resorts is to log onto their respective websites where, during the season, detailed daily reports are posted, including the number of pistes open, their locations and the forecast for the next 24 hours.

Surfing

Scotland has some of the best surfing beaches in Europe, a fact recognized by its hosting of a **World Pro Surf Tour** (qualifying) competition in 2006. But despite the clean coral and beach breaks, powerful waves and pristine (island) beaches, this is no sun-drenched Hawaii. Surfing in Scotland is decidedly chillier with temperatures in the spring and autumn as low as 4-5°C! However, you could be pleasantly surprised at the temperature (when wearing a wetsuit) between July and October. A good wetsuit is therefore essential.

The best beaches on the West Coast are to be found at the northern tip of the Isle of Lewis, on North and South List, the north coast of Scotland (including Thurso), Machrihanish at the southwestern tip of the Mull of Kintyre and all along the coast east of Edinburgh. On the north coast the top spot is Thurso, home to the world-class Thurso east break (strictly for experts). In recent years, a host of reputable surf schools have sprung up including **Coast 2 Coast** operated east of Edinburgh at Belhaven beach (see Operators and useful organizations, below). Also try the surf shops, which sell equipment and provide information on the best breaks. Useful websites, www.sas.org.uk and www.hebrideansurf.co.uk.

Wildlife watching

Almost anywhere around the western and northern coasts of Scotland there is a chance to see bottlenose dolphins, white-beaked dolphins, Rissa's dolphins, common dolphins, white-sided dolphins, pilot whales, minke whales, porpoises, seals and, occasionally orcas (killer whales). The best places to see **dolphins** (bottlenose) are at Cromarty and Chanonry Point, both on the Moray Firth. Other good places to catch glimpses of bottlenose and other dolphins, as well as porpoises and minke whales, are the westerly tip of Ardnamurchan (page 218), Mull, Neist Point on Skye (page 281), Gairloch and Rubha Reidh lighthouse (page 234), Stoer Head (page 245), Handa Island (page 246), Cape Wrath (page 253), Strathy Point (page 253), Dunnet Head (page 254), Duncansby Head (page 255), Lybster (page 266), Brora and Golspie (page 265), Tarbat Ness (page 262) and off the Isle of Mull (T01688 302916, www.sealifesurveys.com). The **Dolphin Centre** at North Kessock, near Inverness (see page 259) has more information on where to see dolphins and seals locally. Generally speaking, the best time to see the various species of marine mammals (cetaceans) is late summer, from late July to early September. The **Hebridean Whale and Dolphin Trust** promotes a greater understanding of marine mammals off the west coast of Scotland, see page 156 for details, or contact the **Sea Watch Foundation**, www.seawatchfoundation.org.uk. Also contact the local **Ranger Services**: Caithness, T01847-821531; Sutherland, T01571-844654; Wester Ross, T01854-633350; Skye and Lochalsh, T01471-822905; Lochaber, T01397-705922; Inverness and Nairn, T01463-724260.

Seals can be seen in abundance, particularly in the wonderfully serene Lochranza Bay in the north of Arran. They can often be observed lolling about on sandbanks when the tide is out, and there are plenty of seal-spotting boat trips on offer from spring to autumn. To be guaranteed to spot seals, visit the **Scottish Sea Life Sanctuary**, T01631-720386, www.sealsanctuary.co.uk, north of Oban. **Otters** are more elusive. They tend to live on undisturbed remote stretches of the seashore or quiet areas of a river. If you are determined to spot the creatures, contact **Skye Environmental Centre**, home to the **International Otter Survival Fund**, T01471-822487, www,otter.org, for further information.

Scotland is great for **birdwatching**. Over 450 species have been recorded, including vast colonies of seabirds, birds of prey and many rare species. Among the best places in Scotland to see birds are Handa Island off the coast of Sutherland, and the Treshnish Islands, off Mull, where you'll see colonies of shags, razorbills, guillemots and puffins. Details of how to get there are given in the relevant sections. Another excellent place for birdwatching is Loch Garten by Boat of Garten, where you can see ospreys. Many of the Hebridean islands, such as Islay, Mull and Tiree, are home to a rich variety of seabirds and you can also see golden eagles. Orkney and Shetland are famous for their varied birdlife and are home to large colonies of seabirds and migratory birds. There are puffins, kittiwakes, fulmars, shags, razorbills, guillemots and even auks.

Operators and useful organizations

Birdwatching

Royal Society for the Protection of Birds, 17 Regent Terr, Edinburgh EH7 5BT, T0131-5573136.

Scottish Ornithologists Club, 21 Regent Terr, Edinburgh EH7 5BT, T0131-5566042.

Scottish Wildlife Trust, Cramond House, Cramond Glebe Rd, Edinburgh EH4 6NS, T0131-3127765, www.swt.org.uk, which owns and runs over 100 nature reserves.

Canoeing and sea kayaking

Canoe Hebrides, T01851-820726, www.canoehebrides.com.

Canoe Scotland, T0131-3177314, www.scot-canoe.org. For details of clubs and events throughout Scotland.

Hebridean Pursuits, www.hebrideanpursuits.com.

National Kayak School, Weem, Aberfeldy, T01887-820498, www.nationalkayak school.com. Whitewater kayaking lessons from £25 per half-day.

Sea Kayak Shetland, T01595-859647, www.seakayakshetland.co.uk

Skyak Adventures, Isle of Skye, www.skyakadventures.com.

Canyoning

Nae Limits, Dunkeld, Perthshire, T0771-8918275, www.nae-limits.com. Half-day canyoning for £40 and a host of other adrenaline activities.

Vertical Descents, 8 miles south of Fort William, T01855-821593, www.vertical descents.com, is also recommended and offers canyoning from £40 per half-day up to £70.

Climbing

Mountaineering Council of Scotland, The Old Granary, West Mill St, Perth, T01738-638227, www.mountaineering-scotland.org.uk. See also www.glenmore lodge.org.uk, T01479-861256.

Cycling

Cyclists' Touring Club (**CTC**), Cotterell House, 69 Meadrow, Godalming, Surrey GU7 3HS, T01483-417217, www.ctc.org.uk, is the largest cycling organization in the UK, providing a wide range of services and information on transport, cycle hire and routes including day rides and longer tours.

Scottish Cyclists' Union (**SCU**), The Velodrome, Meadowbank Stadium, London Rd, Edinburgh EH7 6AY, T0131-6520187, www.btinternet.com/~scottish.cycling, produces an annual handbook and calendar of events for road racing, time trialling and mountain biking. There's an excellent website packed with information to keep your road and mountain bike wheels turning: www.scuonline.org. It's also worthwhile picking up a copy of *Scottish Mountain Biking Trails Guide*; www.visit scotland.com/adventure which provides a good description of the key mountain bike centres and trails across Scotland. In addition, see also www.forestry.gov.uk for details of Forestry Commission Scotland sites with mountain biking trails.

SUSTRANS, T0845-1130065, www.sustrans.org.uk, is the UK's leading sustainable transport charity and among its many activities is the co-ordinator of the UK's 10,000 miles of traffic-free walking and cycling **National Cycle Network**.

Diving

The Puffin Dive Centre, see page 123, www.puffin.org.uk, is the UK's most comprehensive diving facility and runs intensive PADI courses.

Scottish Sub Aqua Club, 40 Bogmoor Pl, Glasgow, G51 47Q, T0141-4251021, www.scotsac.com.

Fishing

Scottish Federation of Sea Anglers, Brian Burn, Flat 2, 16 Bellevue Rd, Ayr, KA7 2SA, T01292-264735. See also; www.visitscotland.com/fish; www.fishscotland.co.uk (for a complete listing and key information about locations in Scotland); www.fishhebrides.co.uk; and www.fishtweed.co.uk.

General

Forestry Commission Scotland, 231 Corstorphine Rd, Edinburgh EH12 7AT, T0131-3340303, www.forestry.gov.uk (and click on Scotland). Ideal starting point to gleen walking, cycling and wildlife information/routes across Scotland. See also www.forestholidays.co.uk for accommodation in woodland areas.

John Muir Trust, 41 Commercial St, Edinburgh EH6 6JD, T0845-4582910, www.johnmuiraward.org/www.jmt.org.

National Trust for Scotland (NTS), 26-31 Charlotte Sq, Edinburgh EH2 4ET, T0131-2439300, www.nts.org.uk.

Scottish Natural Heritage, Great Glen House, Leachkin Rd, Inverness, T01463-725000, www.snh.org.uk.

Scottish Rights of Way Society www.scotways.com.

Visitscotland, 23 Ravelston Terr, Edinburgh EH4 3EU, T0845-2255121, www.visit scotland.com; and 19 Cockspur St, London SW1 5BL, T020-7930 2812.

Woodland Trust, Glenruthven Mill, Abbey Rd, Auchterarder, Perthshire PH3 1DP.

Horse riding

British Horse Society Scotland, Woodburn Farm, Crieff, T01764-656334, www.bhs.org.uk. The BHS website provides a full listing of all BHS-approved riding schools in Scotland and details of forthcoming major events.

Trekking and Riding Society of Scotland (TRRS), Horse Trials Office, Blair Atholl, Perthshire, T01796-481543.

Kitesurfing

Kite Sports Scotland (KSS) in St Andrews (also Dunbar and Gullane in East Lothian) are also recommended for lessons and advice T07875-773346, www.kss.uk.com.

Wild Diamond, T01879-220399, www.surf schoolscotland.co.uk, www.wild diamondsurf.co.uk, offers windsurfing, kite-surfing and surfing lessons and hire.

The Wind Wizard, Glasgow, T0141-332 8407, www.windspells.com, runs courses.

Paragliding

Flying Fever, Isle of Arran, T01770-303899, www.flyingfever.net. Daily May-Oct, offers a tandem flight as part of a Funday for £95.

Cloudbusters, T07899-878509. Another reputable company that offers lessons, hire and tandems just south of Glasgow.

Skiing

Snowstorm Scotland, T0131-445 4151, www.snowsportscotland.org. Contact for information on all aspects of Scottish skiing and snowsports.

Surfing

British Surfing Association, Champions Yard, Causewayhead, Penzance, Cornwall, T01736-360250.

Scottish Surfing Federation, www.scottishsurfingfederation.com. From the famous Thurso East break and surf competitions in northeast Scotland, to the massive waves on the Isle of Lewis and Tiree, to instruction and hire on a string of East Lothian beaches, Scottish surfing is really taking off. Good shops include:

Boardwise, 1146 Argyle St, Glasgow, T0141-3345559.

Clan Surf, 45 Hyndland St, Partick, Glasgow, T0141-3396523.

Coast 2 Coast Surf School,T07971-990361 www.c2csurfschool.com, Belhaven Bay, East Lothian (and 'surf safaris') throughout Scotland). 2- to 3-hr lesson with equipment from £35 year-round.

Granite Reef, 45 Justice St, Aberdeen, T01224-621193.

Great Escape, 57 High St, North Berwick T01620-893793.

Whitewater rafting

Monster Activities, T01809-501340, www.monsteractivities.com.

Nae Limits, Dunkeld, Perthshire, T01350-727242, www.naelimits.co.uk (from £35 per person).

Splash, T01887-829706, www.rafting.co.uk.

Spectator sports

Curling

Curling is nothing to do with hairdressing, but is in fact a winter game which involves sliding smooth circular granite stones across the ice as close to the centre of a target as possible, while your team-mates use brooms to sweep away the loose white flakes (a bit like hairdressing, in fact). It is still played occasionally on frozen ponds but more commonly you'll see it played on indoor ice rinks.

Football

Football (soccer) is Scotland's most popular spectator sport. The **Scottish Football League**, established in 1874, is the main competition, with three divisions of 10 teams and one of 12. Scottish football is dominated, and always has been, by the two main Glasgow teams, **Rangers** and **Celtic**, known collectively as the 'Old Firm', who regularly attract crowds of over 50,000. For a brief period in the 1980s this stranglehold was broken by **Aberdeen** and **Dundee United**, but events since (Hearts brief flurry in 2004-2005 notwithstanding) have proved this an aberration rather than a trend. Money is the main reason for this and the Old Firm have seemingly endless pots of the stuff, which is why they have been able to fill their team with expensive foreign imports and win most of the domestic competitions. Though neither side has fared too well in European competition in recent years, Celtic were the first British side to win the **European Cup**, in 1967.

Scotland's top 12 teams make up the **Premier League**, which has become a battle between the big two for the championship. The only Highland team in the Premier League is Inverness Caledonian Thistle (www.caleythistleonline.com). The domestic football season runs from early August to mid-May. Most matches are played on Saturdays at 1500, and there are often games through the week, on Tuesday and Wednesday evenings at 1930. There is usually a match on a Sunday afternoon, which is broadcast live on satellite TV. Tickets range from £10 up to £20 for big games.

The national team play at the recently renovated Hampden Park in Glasgow. Their passionate supporters, known as the 'Tartan Army', have gained something of an international reputation for their fun-loving attitude and self-deprecating humour in the face of defeat. This has stood them in good stead over the years for, despite qualifying for most **World Cup Finals** since 1974, Scotland have never managed to reach the second round, failing against such footballing giants as Iran and Costa Rica along the way. But though the patience of the Tartan Army has been severely tested in recent times, things are beginning to look up for the Scots, under the steady hand of Walter Smith. A win over France in 2006 served notice that Scotland are back.

Once bitten, twice shy

The major problem facing visitors to the Highlands and Islands of Scotland during the summer months is *Culicoides Impunctatus* – or the midge, as it's more commonly known. These tiny flying creatures are savage and merciless in the extreme and hunt in huge packs. Indeed, it is estimated that midges cost the Scottish tourist industry some £286 million in lost revenue. No sooner have you left your B&B for a pleasant evening stroll, than a cloud of these bloodthirsty little devils will descend, getting into your eyes, ears, nose and mouth – and a few places you forgot you even had. The only way to avoid them is to take refuge indoors, or to hide in the nearest loch.

Midges are at their worst in the evening and in damp, shaded or overcast conditions, and between late May and September, but they don't like direct sunlight, heavy rain, smoke and wind. Make sure you're well covered up and wear light-coloured clothing (they're attracted to dark colours). Most effective is a midge net, if you don't mind everyone pointing and laughing at you. Insect repellents have some effect, particularly those with DEET, but those who don't fancy putting chemicals on their skin can try Mozzy Off (www.mozzyoff.com), which comprises 100% plant oils, while the Thurso-made Essential Spirit (www.essentialspirit.co.uk) is also made from natural ingredients. A more radical approach is the Midegeater, a trap which emits carbon dioxide to lure the little blighters within range and then sucks them in at high speed. Those who see prevention as the best form of cure can log on to www.midgeforecast.co.uk, a new online midge forecast service that gives five-day predictions of midge movements.

If you do get bitten, spare a thought for the gravedigger from Rùm. According to legend, as punishment for not burying a body properly he was stripped naked, tied to a post and left outside with only the midges for company. The poor chap eventually died of the countless bites.

Rugby Union

Rugby is one of the major sports of the country but lags a long, long way behind football in terms of popularity. The national team plays at Murrayfield in Edinburgh, and during match weekends there's always a great atmosphere in the city. Every year, in February and March, Scotland takes part in the **Six Nations Championship**, along with the other home teams, plus France and Italy. The most important game, though, is the clash with the 'Auld enemy', England. Tickets for games are hard to come by, but you can contact the **Scottish Rugby Union (SRU)**, T0131-3465000, for details of upcoming home fixtures and where to find tickets. The club rugby season runs from September to May.

The game in Scotland has been in a state of disarray ever since the advent of professionalism, but since the nadir of the 2004 Six Nations championship, the team have been faring better, managing famous victories over the Auld Enemy and France in the 2006 competition.

Shinty

Shinty (or *camanachd* in Gaelic) is an amateur sport similar to Ireland's hurling. It's a physical game played at a fast and furious pace, and is a bit like hockey, but with more blood. The game is played mostly in the Highlands, and the highlight of the season is the **Camanachd Cup Final**, which attracts a large crowd and is televised on STV.

Health

No vaccinations are required for entry into Britain. Citizens of EU countries are entitled to free medical treatment at National Health Service hospitals. The UK adopted the European Health Insurance Card (EHIC) in 2005. For details, see the Department of Health website, www.dh.gov.uk/travellers. Also, Australia, New Zealand and several other non-EU European countries have reciprocal health-care arrangements with Britain. Citizens of other countries will have to pay for all medical services, except accident and emergency care given at Accident and Emergency Units (A&E) at most (but not all) National Health hospitals. Health insurance is therefore strongly advised for citizens of non-EU countries.

Medical emergency: dial T999 or T112 (both free) for an ambulance.

Pharmacists can dispense only a limited range of drugs without a doctor's prescription. Most are open for normal shop hours, though some are open late, especially in larger towns. Local newspapers will carry lists of which are open late. Doctors' surgeries are usually open from around 0830-0900 till 1730-1800, though times vary. Outside surgery hours you can go to the casualty department of the local hospital for any complaint requiring urgent attention. For the address of the nearest hospital or doctors' surgery, T0800-665544. See also individual town and city directories throughout the book for details of local medical services.

You should encounter no major problems or irritations during your visit to Scotland. The only exceptions are the risk of hypothermia if you're walking in the mountains in difficult conditions, see box, page 52, and the dreaded midge, see box, page 62.

Keeping in touch

Communications

Internet

Even in the Highlands of Scotland, internet access is extensive. Every major town now has at least one internet café, with more springing up daily. Email works out much, much cheaper than phoning home and is also useful for booking hotels and tours and for checking out information on the web. Many hotels now have Wi-Fi access and many hostels also offer internet access to their guests. Websites and email addresses are listed where appropriate in this guide. **VisitScotland** and area tourist boards have their own websites and these are given on page 21. Internet cafés are also listed under each relevant section. In the absence of any listed under a particular town try the public library or ask at the TIC.

Post

Most post offices are open Monday to Friday 0900 to 1730 and Saturday 0900 to 1230 or 1300. Smaller sub-post offices are closed for an hour at lunch (1300-1400) and many of them operate out of a shop. Post offices keep the same half-day closing times as shops.

Stamps can be bought at post offices, but also from vending machines outside, and also at many newsagents. A first-class letter to anywhere in the UK costs £0.32 and should arrive the following day, while second-class letters cost £0.23 and take between two to four days. For more information about Royal Mail postal services, call T08457-740740 or www.royalmail.com.

Telephone

Most public payphones are operated by British Telecom (BT) and are fairly widespread in towns and cities, though less so in rural areas. BT payphones take either coins (20p, 50p and £1) or phonecards, which are available at newsagents and post offices displaying the BT logo. These cards come in denominations of £2, £3, £5 and £10. Some payphones also accept credit cards.

For most countries (including Europe, USA and Canada) calls are cheapest between 1800 and 0800 Monday-Friday and all day Saturday and Sunday. For Australia and New Zealand it's cheapest to call from 1430 to 1930 and from midnight to 0700 every day. Area codes are not needed if calling from within the same area. Any number prefixed by 0800 or 0500 is free to the caller; 08457 numbers are charged at local rates and 08705 numbers at the national rate. To call Scotland from overseas, dial 011 from USA and Canada, 0011 from Australia and 00 from New Zealand, followed by 44, then the area code, minus the first zero, then the number. To call overseas from Scotland dial 00 followed by the country code. Country codes include: Australia 61; Ireland 353; New Zealand 64; South Africa 27; USA and Canada 1.

Useful numbers include: operator T100, international operator T155.

Visitors from the US can buy a Mobile World SIM card from www.cellularabroad.com (US$49 for 100 minutes), or an unlocked World Phone and then buy a UK SIM card from any supermarket. Note that mobile reception can be patchy in the Highlands and Islands of Scotland and that cellphones are called mobile phones in the UK.

Media

Newspapers and magazines

The main British daily and Sunday newspapers are widely available in Scotland and some of them publish special Scottish editions, among them the *Scottish Daily Mail*, *Scottish Daily Express* and Rupert Murdoch's notorious scandal sheet, *The Sun*.

The Scottish press produces two main 'quality' newspapers, *The Scotsman*, published in Edinburgh, and *The Herald*, published in Glasgow, which is the oldest daily newspaper in the English-speaking world, dating from 1783. The biggest-selling daily is the *Daily Record*, a tabloid paper (or red top as they are known). The Sunday equivalents of the dailies are *Scotland on Sunday* from the Scotsman stable, the *Sunday Herald* and the *Sunday Mail*, published by the Daily Record, while the rather couthy *The Sunday Post*, is popular with wrinklies. Provincial newspapers are widely read in Scotland. The main Highlands varieties are the weekly *Oban Times* and the radical, crusading *West Highland Free Press* published on Skye.

TV and radio

There are five main television channels in Scotland; the publicly funded BBC 1 and 2, and the independent commercial stations, Channel 4, Channel 5 and ITV. The ITV network in Scotland is formed by STV, which serves central Scotland and parts of the West Highlands, as well as the Aberdeen-based Grampian TV which produces a lot of Gaelic programmes.

The BBC network also broadcasts several radio channels, most of which are based in London. These include: Radio 1 aimed at a young audience; Radio 2 targeting a more mature audience; Radio 3 which plays mostly classical music; Radio 4 which is talk-based and features arts, drama and current affairs; and Radio 5 Live which is a mix of sport and news. Radio Scotland (92-95FM, 810MW) provides a Scottish-based diet of news, sport, current affairs, travel and music. It also provides a Gaelic network in the northwest, and local programmes in Orkney and Shetland. There are also a large number of local commercial radio stations, stretching from Shetland in the north to the Borders.

Central Highlands

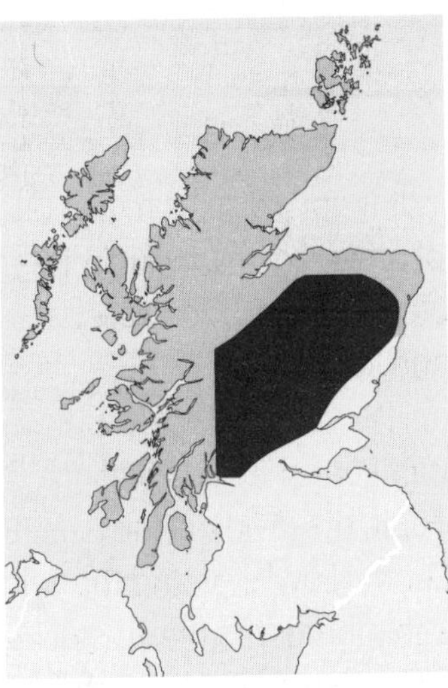

Footprint features

Introduction

The vast swathe of Central Highlands is not a distinct region but rather the sum of disparate parts of other regions, including Perthshire, the Trossachs, Angus Glens, Deeside, Don Valley, the Grampians, Speyside, Strathspey and Loch Lomond .

The historically important regions of Perthshire and Stirling straddle the Highland Boundary Fault, the dividing line between the heavily populated Central Lowlands and the wild and empty Highlands. Just across this 'border' is the Trossachs, a picture-postcard area of mountains, forests and lochs that stretches west from Callander to the eastern shore of Loch Lomond, and the glens of Perthshire, whose atmospheric lochs and mountains are rich in history.

The spectacular and varied landscape ranges from the gentle pleasures of Loch Tay to the rugged peaks of the Grampian Mountains, where there are Munros aplenty for the bagging and decent winter skiing. On the eastern shores of Loch Lomond is the West Highland Way, Scotland's most popular long-distance hike. In the northeast, in the Spey Valley, are the tasty staples of a Highland tourist diet – whisky and salmon – while, nearby, stand many of Scotland's most notable castles, one of which is the holiday home of the most famous family in the UK.

★ Don't miss...

1 **Fortingall** Find the Roman in the gloamin' in this bonny wee Perthshire village, said to be the birthplace of Pontius Pilate, page 75.
2 **Glen Lyon** Take a picnic to this glorious glen and try, if you can, to imagine a more perfect place, page 75.
3 **Duke's Pass** Travel the road from Aberfoyle to Callander, and capture the special appeal of the Trossachs, page 83.
4 **Drover's Inn** Spend an evening in the archetypal Highland watering hole, sampling the finest single malts, page 88.
5 **Boat of Garten** Catch a glimpse of the elusive osprey, Britain's most famous bird of prey, page 106.

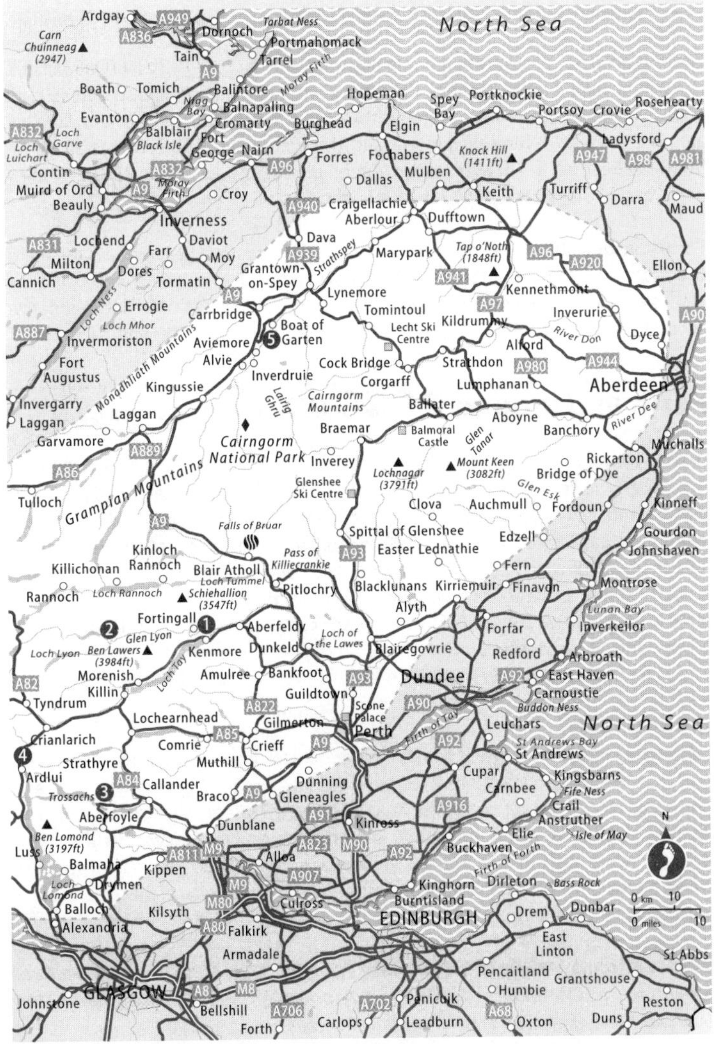

Perthshire

Perth, where the rural and urban intertwine, is the main gateway to the eastern side of the Highlands and the A9, the road north, is a gentle introduction to the wild northern reaches of Scotland. The Perthshire Highlands may lack the sheer magisterial grandeur of the northwest but they have their own serene beauty. Numerous remnants from the highland's troubled past are scattered around the glens of Perthshire, including Blair Castle and Scone Palace. » *For Sleeping, Eating and other listings, see pages 76-80.*

Ins and outs

Getting there Perth is accessible from almost anywhere in the country. It's only 1½ hours from Edinburgh or Glasgow, and half an hour from Dundee by road, and is on the main train lines to these cities, as well as on the main lines north to Aberdeen and Inverness. » *For further details, see Transport page 80.*

Getting around Though the more remote northerly parts of Perthshire are difficult to reach by public transport, much of the region is easily accessible. The main road north to Inverness, the A9, runs through the heart of the region. Dunkeld and Pitlochry are on the Perth–Inverness rail line and there are several daily trains to Perth. **Strathtay Scottish** ⓘ *T01382-228345*, run hourly buses (less frequently on Sunday) from Perth to Blairgowrie and Glenshee on the A93.

Tourist information The region, from Kinross in the south to Blair Atholl in the north and from Glenshee in the east to Rannoch Moor in the west, is covered by **Visitscotland Perthshire** ⓘ *www.perthshire.co.uk*, with tourist offices in Aberfeldy, Auchterarder, Blairgowrie, Crieff, Dunkeld, Kinross, Perth and Pitlochry.

Perth and around » *pp76-80. Colour map 4, C3.*

→ *Phone code: 01738. Population: 48,000.*

'The Fair City' of Perth is aptly named. Situated on the banks of Scotland's longest river, the Tay, Perth and its surrounding area boasts some of the most beautiful scenery in the country. A pleasant, compact town, Perth was once the capital of Scotland. Awash with 'scone shops' of which Scottish comedian Billy Connolly would be proud, there are several notable sights to visit, from its ultra-modern Concert Hall to the fascinating jewel in Perth's crown, Scone Palace. For nearly 500 years Scone was the home of the Stone of Destiny and the site where every Scottish king was crowned. The city is well placed for outdoor activities such as walking, fishing, cycling and skiing.

Ins and outs

Getting around The train and bus stations are almost opposite each other at the west end of town, where Leonard Street meets Kings Place. The town centre is compact and easy to get around on foot, but Scone Palace and many B&Bs are on the eastern bank of the river, so you may wish to take a bus. Local buses are run by **Stagecoach** ⓘ *T01738-629339*, which also runs a **Sunday Vintage Bus Tour** of the key historical sights including Scone Palace and Balhousie Castle – the spiritual home of the famous Black Watch regiment (July to August only, every 6 minutes, 1200-1725, £1.25, children £0.65).

Tourist information **Perth TIC** ⓘ *Lower City Mills, West Mill St, T01738-450600. Apr-Jun, Sep and Oct Mon-Fri 0900-1700, Sat 1000-1600, Sun 1100-1600, Jul and Aug Mon-Sat 0900-1830, Sun 1100-1700, Nov-Mar Mon-Sat 0900-1600.*

Sights

North of the High Street, on North Port, is the **Fair Maid's House** (closed to the public) the fictional home of Sir Walter Scott's virginal heroine in his novel, *The Fair Maid of Perth*. Close by, at the corner of Charlotte Street and George Street, is the **Museum and Art Gallery** ⓘ *T01738-632488, Mon-Sat 1000-1700, free*, with displays on local history, art, archaeology, natural history and whisky.

In the 18th century the world-famous Black Watch regiment was raised in Perth, and the **Black Watch Museum** ⓘ *Hay St, T0131-3108530, May-Sep Mon-Sat 1000-1630, Oct-Apr Mon-Fri 1000-1530, free*, housed in the 15th-century Balhousie Castle, is well worth a visit even to the most un-military minded. The museum is on the edge of the North Inch, to the north of the town centre. It's also worth perusing the work of the renowned Scottish colourist, John Duncan Fergusson, within the **Fergusson Gallery** ⓘ *T01738-441944, Mon-Sat 1000-1700, free*, former site of Perth's waterworks.

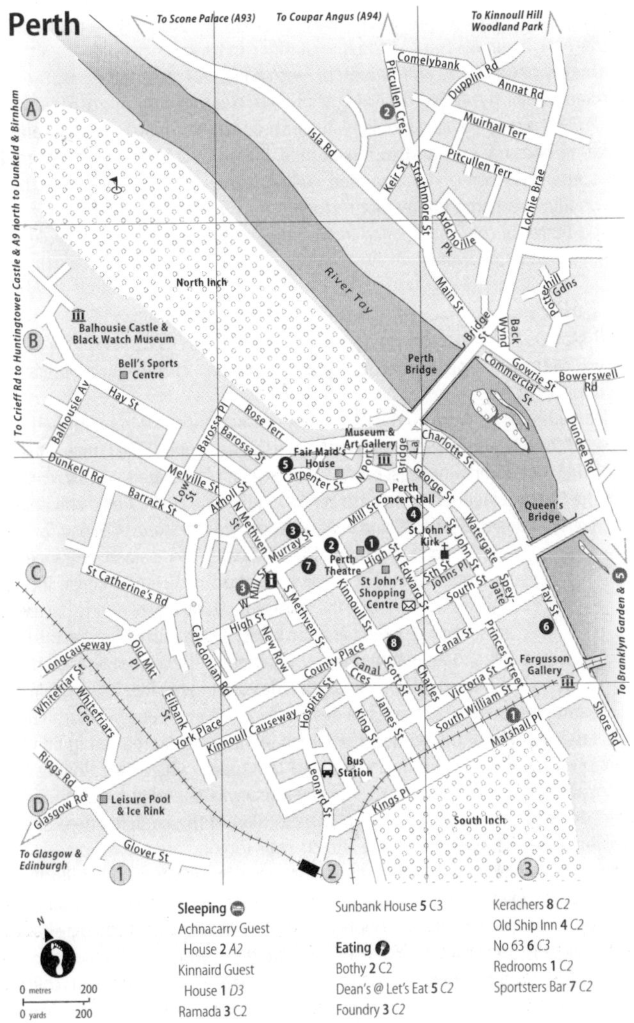

For those with more horticultural leanings, **Branklyn Garden** ⓘ *116 Dundee Rd, T01738-625535 (NTS), 1 Apr-Oct daily 1000-1700, £5, £4 concession*, has been described as "the finest two acres of private garden in the country". With an impressive collection of rare and unusual plants, it includes superb examples of Himalayan poppies. Well worth a visit at any time of year, many of the plants grown there are on sale in the shop.

Kinnoull Hill Woodland Park is a beautiful wooded area on the outskirts of the city. The trip to the top of Kinnoull Hill (783 ft) itself affords an astounding view across Perth, down to the Tay estuary and through Fife to the Lomond hills. To the north, the views stretch from Ben More in the west to Lochnagar in the northeast. There are four walks through the Woodland Park – Nature Walk, Tower Walk, Jubilee Walk and Squirrel Walk – and each of these is graded according to how difficult it is and what type of conditions the walker can expect. However, none of the walks are extremely strenuous, though the Squirrel Walk is most suitable for the less able. If you're feeling particularly energetic, cycling and horse riding take place in specific zones in the park, principally in the Deuchny Wood area. There is a Countryside Ranger Service in the park and they will be happy to answer any questions you may have about their work or the park itself. Also ask at the tourist office in town for details.

Huntingtower Castle ⓘ *3 miles west of Perth on the A85 to Crieff, T01738-627231 (HS) Apr-Sep daily 0930-1830, Oct-Mar Mon-Wed, Sat and Sun 0930-1630 (closed Thu and Fri) £3, £2.50 concession*, is also worth a visit. It consists of two complete towers dating from the 15th and 16th centuries, linked by a 17th-century range, and features some fine 16th-century painted ceilings. The castle, once owned by the Ruthven family, has some interesting history of its own. Prior to the building of the range, a daughter of the house once leapt between the two towers to avoid being caught in her lover's bedroom.

Scone Palace

ⓘ *T01738-552300, www.scone-palace.co.uk, 24 Mar-31 Oct 0930-1730 (last admission 1645), £7.20, £6.20 concession, £4.20 children, grounds only £3.80/£3.50/£2.50*

Three miles northeast of Perth on the A93 Braemar road, is the not-to-be-missed Scone Palace, one of the most historically important places in the country. The home of the Earls of Mansfield, Scone (pronounced 'scoon') has a long and fascinating history. It was the capital of the Pictish Kingdom in the sixth century and home of the Celtic church. Here, Kenneth MacAlpin united Scotland, and in AD 838, placed the stone of Scone (or 'Stone of Destiny') on Moot Hill, opposite the palace entrance. This became the ancient crowning place of Scottish kings, including Macbeth and Robert the Bruce. The Royal City of Scone became the seat of government, and the kings of Scotland resided at the Palace of Scone before their coronations. The coronation stone was removed to Westminster by that most hated foe, Edward I, in 1296, and only recently returned to Scotland in a desperate, but failed, Conservative attempt to win back support north of the border. The famed stone currently resides in Edinburgh Castle. In 1651, the last coronation in Scotland took place when King Charles II was crowned by the Scots on the Moot Hill. The ceremony was attended by Lord Stormont, forefather of the present occupier, Lord Mansfield. Part of the church where this took place still remains. Today, Scone Palace attracts over 100,000 annual visitors.

Though historically important, much of the present palace building only dates from the 19th century.

Aside from its impressive history, the palace also houses beautiful collections of porcelain, needlework, royal furniture, clocks, ivories and many other absorbing artefacts. You could also spend a few hours walking in the magnificent 100-acre gardens, filled with bluebells, rhododendrons, roses and rare trees, with strutting peacocks and Highland cattle roaming around. There's also a maze, picnic park and children's adventure playground, plus a gift shop and coffee shop with delicious home baking.

Dunkeld and Birnam

Twelve miles north of Perth is the attractive village of **Dunkeld**, standing right on the Highland line. It's definitely worth making a stop here, if only to admire the **cathedral** ⓘ *Apr-Sep 0930-1830, free*, in the most idyllic situation on the banks of the fast-flowing, silvery Tay. Half of it is still in use as a church and the other half is in ruins. The oldest part of the cathedral is the 14th-century choir, which now forms the parish church, while the 15th-century nave and tower are also still standing. Much of the original was damaged during the orgy of ecclesiastical destruction that accompanied the Reformation. It was damaged again in the Battle of Dunkeld in 1689, fought between supporters of the protestant William of Orange and the Stuart monarch James VII. Dunkeld offers excellent walking opportunities, details of which are available from the **TIC** ⓘ *at The Cross, T01350-727688*.

Across the bridge from Dunkeld is **Birnam**, made famous in Shakespeare's *Macbeth*. Birnam was the inspiration for another famous literary figure, Beatrix Potter, who spent her childhood summers here. Visitors can explore the origins of Peter Rabbit at the **Beatrix Potter Exhibition** ⓘ *T01350-727674, daily 1000-1700, free*.

A short distance north of Dunkeld on the A9 is the turning to **The Hermitage**. A marked woodland walk starts from the car park and follows the River Braan to the Black Linn Falls, overlooked by Ossian's Hall, an 18th-century folly built by the Duke of Atholl. It's a beautifully serene spot, which has inspired the likes of Wordsworth and Mendelssohn. Further on is **Ossian's Cave**. Buses to Pitlochry stop at the turning for The Hermitage.

A few miles northeast of Dunkeld, off the A923 to Blairgowrie, is the **Loch of the Lowes Visitor Centre** ⓘ *Apr-Sep daily 1000-1700; £2.50, £1.50 concession*, managed by the Scottish Wildlife Trust. There's a hide with binoculars for viewing ospreys which breed here and which can sometimes be seen over the loch. There's also a 'nest-cam' and shop.

Pitlochry and around

» *pp76-80. Colour map 4, B3.*

→ *Phone code: 01796.*

Despite being one of the busiest Highland tourist towns in the summer, Pitlochry's setting on the shores of the River Tummel, overlooked by Ben y Vrackie, makes it a pleasant enough base for exploring the area, especially out of season. The town also has a few attractions of its own.

Sights

Pitlochry's main attraction is the **fish ladder**, part of the power station and dam which formed man-made **Loch Faskally** when it was constructed on the River Tummel. The ladder allows salmon to swim up to their spawning grounds and you can watch them leaping spectacularly in the spring and summer. The best months are May and June. The fish ladder is across the river, a short distance from the **Pitlochry Festival Theatre**, see Entertainment, page 79.

Also here is **Explorers – The Scottish Plant Hunters' Garden** ⓘ *T01796-484600, www.explorersgarden.com, Apr-Oct daily 1000-1700, £3, concession £2.50, children £1*. This fascinating garden containing diverse plant species and trails pays tribute to the story of Scotland's 18th- and 19th-century botanists and explorers.

There are two whisky distilleries to visit. The larger, though less inspiring, of the two is Bell's **Blair Atholl Distillery** ⓘ *T01796-482003, Easter-Sep Mon-Sat 0930-1700, Sun 1200-1700, Oct Mon-Fri 1000-1600, Nov-Easter Mon-Fri 1100-1600, £4, redeemable in shop*, at the southern end of town, heading towards the A9 to Perth. A couple of miles east of town, on the A924, is the **Edradour Distillery** ⓘ *T01796-T472095, www.edradour.co.uk, Jan and Feb Mon-Sat 1000-1600, Sun*

 1200-1600, Mar-Oct Mon-Sat 0930-1800, Sun 1130-1700, Nov and Dec Mon-Sat 0930-1700, Sun 1200-1700, free, the smallest in Scotland, which can be a blessing or a curse, depending on how busy it is.

▲ The tourist office sells a useful leaflet, *Pitlochry Walks* (£0.80), which describes several long local walks, and there are many other fine walks in the surrounding area. The greatest walking attraction is **Ben y Vrackie** (2758 ft), a steep 6-mile walk (there and back) from the tiny hamlet of Moulin, a mile north of Pitlochry on the A924 (turn left at the **Moulin Inn**). The path is well trodden and the going is relatively easy, across bleak moorland, until the steep final ascent on scree. On a clear day the views across Perthshire and towards the Trossachs from the summit are wonderful. Don't attempt this on a cloudy day. In spite of its proximity to Pitlochry, you need to be properly equipped and take the usual safety precautions, see page 52.

OS Landranger maps Nos 43 and 52 cover all the walks, and the OS Explorer map No 21 (Pitlochry and Loch Tummel) covers them in greater detail.

Another excellent walk from Pitlochry, described in the tourist office leaflet, leaves town on the north road and turns left past the boat station. It then crosses the Cluanie footbridge and follows the road to Loch Faskally and up the River Garry to Garry Bridge over the Pass of Killiecrankie, see below. The path returns to Pitlochry along the west bank of the River Garry, before turning west up the River Tummel, passing close by the Linn of Tummel, then crossing the Tummel and following the west shore of Loch Faskally to the dam and fish ladder.

Pass of Killiecrankie

Four miles north of Pitlochry the A9 cuts through the Pass of Killiecrankie, a spectacular wooded gorge which was the dramatic setting for the Battle of Killiecrankie in 1689, when a Jacobite army led by Graham of Claverhouse, Viscount 'Bonnie Dundee', defeated the government forces under General Hugh Mackay. One government soldier allegedly evaded capture by making a jump of Olympic gold medal-winning proportions across the River Garry at **Soldier's Leap**. The **NTS visitor centre** ⓘ *T01796-473233, Apr-Oct daily 1000-1730, free (honesty box £1 donation advised)*, tells the story of the battle and features interactive displays on the area's natural history.

▲ A 3-mile waymarked trail around the **RSPB Killiecrankie Nature Reserve** starts from the Balrobbie Farm car park. Follow the signs for the reserve from Killiecrankie village, take the minor road over the River Garry, then take the left fork up a steep hill. Turn right at the sharp bend into the farm car park. Access to the reserve is free, but there's a cairn for donations and a parking charge.

Head down the driveway, then turn right along the road which climbs uphill below wooded crags. Turn right through a gate, opposite a cottage and follow a grassy track to a gate in a stone wall. Through the gate, the path climbs diagonally under the crags to an iron gate beside a bench. Go through the gate and the path zigzags steeply up to an area of open marsh. The path curves right and continues to climb across a heather moor and past a ruin.

At the crest of the hill, from where there are wonderful views down to Blair Atholl, go downhill, over a stile and enter woodland. Beyond the trees is another bench, then the trail turns to the right. After another two stiles the path heads left downhill, then zigzags down a rocky slope, before heading diagonally downhill to the right to an iron gate. Pick up the path again by a stone wall and follow it back to the car park.

Blair Castle

ⓘ *www.blair-castle.co.uk, T01796-481207, Apr-Jun, Sep and Oct 1000-1800, Jul and Aug 0930-1800, house and grounds £7.20, £6.20 concession, £4.20 children.*

Seven miles from Pitlochry, and a mile from the village of Blair Atholl, is Blair Castle, the traditional seat of the Earls and Dukes of Atholl. This whitewashed, turreted castle dates from 1269 and presents an impressive picture on first sight. This is the headquarters of Britain's only private army, the Atholl Highlanders. Thirty rooms in the castle are open for public viewing and are packed full of paintings, furniture, armour, porcelain and much else besides, presenting a startling picture of aristocratic Highland life in previous centuries. The surrounding landscaped grounds are home to peacocks and Highland cattle, and there are woodland walks and a walled Japanese water garden to enjoy. A handy camping site is immediately adjacent to the castle grounds.

▲ Falls of Bruar

Eight miles from Blair Atholl, just off the A9, are the dramatic Falls of Bruar. A well-maintained path leads from the lower falls along the deep gorge of the Bruar River to the upper falls and back down the other side. It's a 1½-mile round trip.

From the House of Bruar (see below), turn right by the adventure playground, then left up the river bank. The path passes under a railway arch and through a kissing gate. It then heads through open forest to a rocky outcrop, from where you can see the lower falls. A series of wooden steps leads down from the outcrop, then a path climbs up till it forks. Go right, then cross the bridge, from where there's a good view of the lower falls. From here a clear path leads up the far side till it reaches a deer fence. Climb up to the gate, go through it and continue uphill through trees till the path levels out high above the gorge. Further on there's a picnic area, then the path curves left down to the upper bridge, which is a great vantage point from which to admire the stunning view. The path heads left through more trees. It then crosses a stream before descending to the lower bridge and then back to the car park. Take extreme care with children.

By the car park is the tourist-trap of the **House of Bruar**, a huge shopping emporium designed like a Victorian hunting lodge where you can buy all kinds of souvenirs and enjoy some very fine, though pricey, Scottish cooking.

From Blair Atholl to Kinloch Rannoch

The B8019 turns off the B8079 road from Pitlochry to Blair Atholl and runs west along the shores of beautiful lochs Tummel and Rannoch, best seen in the autumn when the trees change their colours. At the eastern end of Loch Tummel is **Queen's View**, a spectacular viewpoint which looks down the loch and across to Schiehallion. Here, there's a **Forestry Commission Scotland visitor centre** ⓘ *T01796-473123, Apr-Oct daily 1000-1800, free, £1 parking charge* with displays and audio-visual programmes about the area and maps for sale outlining locals walks and climbs. There's also a cosy tearoom.

▲ Schiehallion (3547 ft) is one of Scotland's best-loved mountains, whose distinctive conical peak made it ideal for use in early experiments in 1774 to judge

Blair Atholl to Glen Fincastle walk

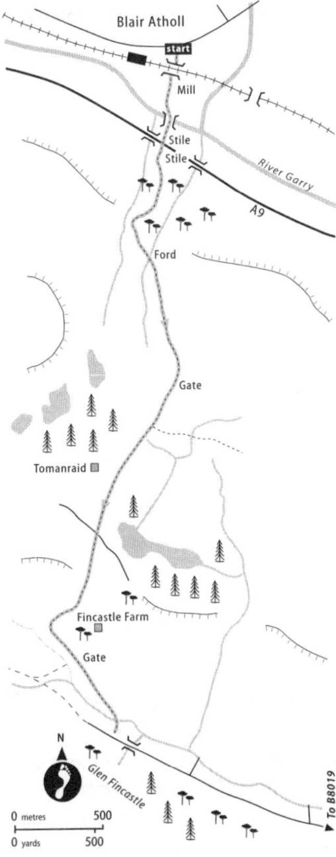

the weight of the earth. These were not an unqualified success, but led to the invention of contour lines as an aid to surveying the mountain. The walk to the summit is fairly straightforward, except for the very rocky final stretch. You'll need to be properly clothed and equipped and take a map and compass. The route to the summit starts at the car park on the B846 Kinloch Rannoch to Aberfeldy road, near Braes of Foss. OS sheet No 51 covers the route.

Beyond Loch Tummel is the village of **Kinloch Rannoch**, where hikers can stock up on supplies before heading into the hills. Sixteen miles west of the village the road ends at the very remote Rannoch station, where tired hikers can catch trains north to Fort William or south to Glasgow.

Blair Atholl to Glen Fincastle walk

A lovely 3-mile linear walk leads from Blair Atholl village to Glen Fincastle, passing through woodland and across moorland and pasture. Starting in the village, head down past the watermill and stay on the road until it ends at the river. Then follow a path left till it takes you to a footbridge over the River Garry. Cross the footbridge and then over two stiles till you reach the main A9. Cross the road, taking care as it's usually busy, to another stile, then continue through trees to a gate with a footprint sign. On the other side of the gate, the path zigzags up through a wood which thins out as you reach the top of the hill.

Here, the path fords a stream then continues across open moorland to the other side of the hilltop, where there's a gate. Go through the gate and follow the grassy track down to Tomanraid cottage. From here you can see down into Glen Fincastle. Before the cottage go left over a stile and then down to a gate. Through the gate, head straight along the track till you reach a junction. Go through the gate ahead and down a grassy lane to another gate. Then the path curves diagonally to the left down to a metal gate at the end of a public road. To return to Blair Atholl simply retrace your steps.

Aberfeldy and Loch Tay

» *pp76-80. Colour map 4, B2.*

→ *Phone code: 01887.*

The quaint town of Aberfeldy stands on the banks of the River Tay, on the A827 which runs between the A9 and Loch Tay. Popular with kayakers who brave the rapids in nearby Grandtully, the village is well placed geographically for exploring the northern part of Perthshire and less crowded than Pitlochry. The 14-mile-long Loch Tay is surrounded by some of the loveliest scenery in Perthshire and is well worth exploring.

Aberfeldy

The River Tay is spanned by Wade's Bridge, built by General Wade in 1773 during his campaign to pacify the Highlands.

Dewar's World of Whisky ⓘ *T01887-822010, www.dewarsworldof whisky.com, Apr-end Oct Mon-Sat 1000- 1800, Sun 1200-1600, Nov-Mar Mon-Sat 1000-1600, £5.50, concession £4, children £3*, just outside Aberfeldy, is another of Scotland's many distillery visitor centres now offering a tour, dram and history of the water of life.

A mile west of Aberfeldy, across the Tay at Weem, is **Castle Menzies** ⓘ *T01887-820982, Apr to mid-Oct Mon-Sat 1030-1700, Sun 1400-1700, £4, £3.50 concession, £2 children*, an impressive, restored 16th-century 'Z-plan' fortified tower house, the former seat of the chief of Clan Menzies.

A popular local walk is to the **Falls of Moness**, through the famous **Birks of Aberfeldy**, forever associated with the poet Robert Burns whom in 1787 was inspired by the *birks* (birch trees) to write his eponymous song. It's a fairly easy walk along a marked trail lined with oak, elm, ash and birch trees up to the falls where there are lovely views of Strathtay and the surrounding hills. It's about 4 miles there and back.

“” On a summer's day there can be few lovelier places on earth, as the River Lyon tumbles through corries and gorges and through flowering meadows, with high mountain peaks on either side and eagles soaring overhead...

Loch Tay and around

At the northeast end of Loch Tay is **Kenmore**, a neat little village of whitewashed cottages dominated by a huge archway which stands at the gateway to Taymouth Castle, built by the Campbells of Glenorchy in the early 19th century. Now a **golf course** ⓘ *T01887-830228*, with stunning views, the course is being revamped and expected to reopen in early 2008. Near the village, on the southern bank of the loch, is the informative **Scottish Crannog Centre** ⓘ *T01887-830583, mid-March to end Oct 1000-1730, Nov, Sat/Sun 1000-1600, £4.95, concession £4.25, £3.25*, an authentic reconstruction of a *crannog*, an artificial Bronze Age island-house built for the purpose of defence.

Loch Tay is a major watersports centre, see Activities and tours page 79, for details.

For those with their own transport, two of the least-known and loveliest routes in the country are at hand. The first is the spectacular road which winds its way south from Kenmore high up into the mountains, across a bleak and barren plateau and down the other side to the tiny hamlet of **Amulree**. This road is often closed in the winter and there are gates at either end. From Amulree you can continue south to Crieff, through the gentler, but equally stunning scenery of the **Sma' Glen**. Alternatively, you could head north to Aberfeldy and then complete the circuit back to Kenmore.

A few miles west of Kenmore a minor road turns off the A827, which runs along the north bank of the loch, and heads to **Fortingall**, a tiny village of classic beauty which features on many a calendar. It's little more than a row of thatched cottages which wouldn't even get a mention were it not for two amazing claims. The 3000-year-old yew tree in the churchyard is said to be the oldest living thing in Europe. Even more astonishing is the claim that this is the birthplace of **Pontius Pilate**, said to be the son of a Roman officer who was stationed here. Furthermore, it is believed that Pilate returned here to be buried, and a gravestone in the churchyard bears the initials 'PP'. If you have your own transport, make a detour up **Glen Lyon**, one of the most beautiful of all Scottish glens. On a summer's day there can be few lovelier places on earth, as the River Lyon tumbles through corries and gorges and through flowering meadows, with high mountain peaks on either side and eagles soaring overhead. It's no surprise that Wordsworth and Tennyson waxed lyrical over its qualities. The road from Fortingall runs all the way to the head of the glen, at Loch Lyon. This is walking and fishing paradise. There are several Munros to 'bag' and fishing permits are available at the **Fortingall Hotel**, see Sleeping, page 76.

Ben Lawers → *OS sheet No 51 covers the area.*

The highest mountain in Perthshire, Ben Lawers (3984 ft), dominates the north side of Loch Tay. Its massif of seven summits includes six Munros which are linked by an 8-mile ridge which can be walked in one day by fit and experienced hillwalkers. The best access to the ridge is from Glen Lyon. The trek to the main summit starts from the **NTS Visitor Centre** ⓘ *T01567-820397*, 2 miles along a track which turns off the main

 A827 about halfway between Kenmore and Killin. This track continues over a wild pass to Bridge of Balgie in Glen Lyon. Leaflets describing the climb are available from the visitor centre. It's a 7-mile walk there and back, and though the route is straightforward and easy to follow, it's a very steep, tough climb of 2700 ft from the centre to the summit. Allow five to six hours. You should be fit, properly clothed, see page 52, and have some previous hillwalking experience; but the views from the top on a clear day are amazing, across to the North Sea in the east and the Atlantic Ocean in the west. Information about an easier 1-mile trail and the flora and fauna in the area is available from the visitor centre.

Blairgowrie and Glenshee

» *pp76-80. Colour map 4, B3.*

→ *Phone code: 01250.*

The other major road running north from Perth is the A93, soon reaching the respectable town of **Blairgowrie**, or Blairgowrie and Rattray to give it its full title. It lies amidst the raspberry fields of Strathmore and is conveniently placed to serve as an accommodation centre for **Glenshee Ski Centre**, see Activities and tours, page 79. The **TIC** ⓘ *26 Wellmeadow, T01250-872960, daily*. A quiet agricultural town, Blairgowrie boasts several good restaurants and tea-rooms including Cargills by the river whilst **Strathmore Golf Centre** ⓘ *T01828-633322* or **James Crockart and Son** ⓘ *T01250-872056*, will appeal to golf and fishing fanatics respectively. However, for many, Blairgowrie is a convenient sandwich stop before driving south towards Perth or following the twisty A93 road north to the Spittal of Glenshee, the ski centre and the stunning scenery of Braemar and Deeside beyond.

Sleeping

Perth and around *p68, map p69*

L Hilton Dunkeld, Dunkeld, T01796-727771, www.dunkeld.hilton.com. Luxurious former summer residence for the wife of the 7th Duke of Atholl, now an impressive hotel with full leisure and outdoor activity facilities.

L Kinnaird House, Dalguise, about 7 miles north of Dunkeld via the A9 and the B898, T01796-482440. Beautiful situation on 9000 acre estate boasting fine food (ΨΨΨ-ΨΨ) and accommodation.

L-A Ballathie House Hotel, Kinclaven, near Stanley, 9 miles north of Perth, just off the A9, T01250-883268, www.ballathiehouse hotel.com. 43 rooms. Another elegant, 19th-century former hunting lodge serving up delicious traditional Scottish cuisine in beautiful surroundings (ΨΨΨ). Renowned as a base for traditional field sports, the estate also offers self-catering and B&B options in its 2003-opened Sportsman's Lodge (from £40 per person).

B The Pend, 5 Brae St, Dunkeld, T01796-727586, www.thepend.com. Beautifully appointed luxury guesthouse boasting terrific ambience and food.

B Tormaukin Inn, Glendevon, 10 miles south of Crieff. T01259-781252. Atmospheric 250-year-old inn with comfortable rooms, real ales and a terrific restaurant (ΨΨΨ-ΨΨ) including steak and ale pie and baked hare.

B-C Huntingtower Hotel, 1 mile west of Perth off the A85 to Crieff, T01738-583771, www.huntingtowerhotel.co.uk. Elegant Tudor-style country house hotel with 34 rooms in landscaped gardens serving good food (ΨΨΨ-ΨΨ) and able to organize many outdoor activities.

C Sunbank House Hotel, 50 Dundee Rd, Perth, T01738-624882, 9 rooms. A lovely little traditional sandstone hotel overlooking the Tay and close to Branklyn Garden and Kinnoull Hill.

Three miles south of Blairgowrie, just off the A93 by Meikleour, is a 100-ft-high beech hedge – the highest hedge in the world!

C-D Ramada Hotel, West Mill St, Perth, T01738-628281. Almost opposite the TIC and beautifully converted from its origins as a 15th-century water mill, guests are assured of comfort, reasonable food and a central location for the key town sites.

D Achnacarry Guest House, 3 Pitcullen Cres, on the A94 Coupar Angus road, 10 mins' walk from Perth town centre, T01738-621421, www.achnacarry.co.uk. Comfortable Victorian residence.

D The Millhouse, Guildtown, Newmiln Country Estate by Scone Palace, T01738-553248. A 100-year-old renovated millhouse in peaceful grounds and just minutes from Scone Palace.

D-E Birnam Wood House, Perth Rd, Birnam by Dunkeld, T01350-727782, www.birnam woodhouse.co.uk. This small, friendly guesthouse is finely appointed and cooks up terrific breakfasts.

D-E Kinnaird Guest House, 5 Marshall Pl, T01738-6280121, www.kinnaird-guesthouse.co.uk. Part of an 1806 Georgian terrace, built on the site of an ancient fort and overlooking the South Inch, Perth.

F Comrie Croft, Cromrie Rd by Crieff T01764-670140. Open all year, comfortable backpackers' hostel with private loch.

F Gulabin Lodge, Cairnwell Mountain Sports, Spittal of Glenshee, by Blairgowrie. T01250-885255. Excellent hostel handy for ski area, post bus and outdoor adventure.

F Wester Caputh Independent Hostel, at Caputh, 5 miles east of Dunkeld, on the A984 to Coupar Angus, T01738-710449. It has 18 beds, is open all year and, although it's a 3-mile walk to the pub, it's 300 yds from public transport.

Camping and self-catering

Finegand Holiday Cottages, by Blairgowrie, T01250-885234. Four rustic, modestly equipped cottages (sleep 4-7) on a quiet upland farm (from £173 per week).

Cleeve Caravan Park, on the Glasgow road, near the ring road, about 2 miles from town, T01738-639521. Open Apr-Oct.

Scone Palace Camping & Caravan Club Site, T01738-552323. Mar-Oct.

Pitlochry and around *p71*

There are too many guesthouses and B&Bs in Pitlochry to list here. The tourist office, T01796-472215, will provide a full list.

L Killiecrankie Hotel, 3 miles north of town, in the village of Killiecrankie, T01796-473220, www.killiecrankiehotel.co.uk. Open Mar-Nov. 10 rooms. A cosy country house that prides itself on its choice of wines, gourmet dinners (ΨΨΨ-ΨΨ) and fine malts.

A-B The Atholl Palace Hotel, T01796-472400, www.athollpalace.com. With its conical towers, this grand hotel with new pool and spa is arguably the most distinctive hotel in the area.

B-D Pine Trees Hotel, Strathview Terr, T01796-472121, wwwpinetrees hotel.co.uk. Comfortable, large Victorian country house set in 10 acres of gardens away from the tourist bustle.

C Easter Dunfallandy Country House , T01796-474128, dunfallandy.co.uk. Home-made bread and preserves, afternoon tea on arrival and a fine rural location ensure a rewarding stay.

C-D Craigatin House & Courtyard, 165 Atholl Rd, T1796-472478. Good value B&B.

C-D East Haugh House, 1½ miles southeast of town, off the old A9, T01796-473121. Set in beautiful gardens, this charming 2005 Country Sports Hotel of the Year offers a warm welcome, excellent restaurant dining (ΨΨΨ-ΨΨ) and can arrange a multitude of outdoor sports.

E Bunrannoch House, Kinloch Rannoch, T01882-632407, www.bunrannoch.co.uk. A former Victorian shooting lodge providing a warm welcome and terrific views of the loch.

E Dalshian House, Old Perth Rd, T01796-472173. An impressive, long-standing B&B in rural location just 5 mins from the town.

F Pitlochry Backpackers, 134 Atholl Rd, T01796-470044. Accommodation and 'vibe' that will appeal to the younger crowd and 'young at heart' seeking a welcoming, low-budget stay.

F SYHA Youth Hostel, on Knockard Rd overlooking the town centre, T1796-472308. Open all year.

Aberfeldy and Loch Tay *p74*

L-A Ardeonaig House Hotel, south Loch Tay by Aberfeldy, T01567-820400. Charming, fantastic location, a terrific (South African) wine list and food to die for (ΨΨΨ). Recommended.

A Guinach House, Aberfeldy, T01887-820251. Another rural treat in a lovely setting by the Birks (ΨΨΨ).

C **Ailean Chraggan**, Weem, a mile or so west from Aberfeldy, T01887-820346. Serves good food in the bar (ΨΨ).

C **Fortingall Hotel**, next to the churchyard in Fortingall, T01887-830367, www.fortingallhotel.com. Peaceful hotel boasting fine food and 10 tastefully refurbished en suite rooms.

C-D **Kenmore Hotel**, Kenmore, T01887-830205. Claims to be Scotland's oldest coaching inn, dating from 1572. True or not, the snug bar certainly oozes character and serves hearty meals (ΨΨ-Ψ). The modest bedrooms are reasonable whilst the somewhat characterless main restaurant provides excellent views over the surrounding area (ΨΨ).

F **Adventurer's Escape**, Weem by Aberfeldy, T01887-820498. Ideal for canoeing and mountaineering instruction.

F **The Bunkhouse**, Glassie Farm Aberfeldy, T01887-820265. Cheap and basic.

Self-catering

Mains of Taymouth Cottages , Kenmore T01887-830226. £250-£2700 per week. Luxury appointed cottages sleeping 2-10 on 120-acre estate by Tay Forest Park.

Rannoch Lodge by Kinloch Rannoch, T01882-633204. £250-£525 per week. Secluded in 30 acres of wood and parkland, 4 traditional stone cottages (sleep 4-7) boast ½ mile of secluded beach at the head of Loch Rannoch.

Eating

Perth and around *p68, map p69*

ΨΨ **The Bothy Restaurant and Bar**, 33 Kinnoull St, T01738-449792. Pleasant ambience with surf-n-turf and duck amongst the treats.

ΨΨ **Dean's @Let's Eat** , Kinnoull St, T01738-643377. Tue-Sat 1200-1400, 1830-2130. Tasty contemporary Scottish cuisine, cooked fresh to order with a smile.

ΨΨ **Kerachers**, 168 South St, T01738-449777. Serves up excellent seafood, game and vegetarian dishes.

ΨΨ **No 63**, 63 Tay St, T01738-441451. Tue-Sat 1200-1400, 1830-2100. Stylish restaurant down by the river. Delicious!

ΨΨ **Redrooms**, Perth Theatre, 185 High St, T01738-472709. Daily 1000-1700 (and theatre nights). Good selection of dishes served in a relaxing ambience that attracts an older and post-theatre clientele.

Ψ **The Old Ship Inn**, Skinners Lane. Est 1665, one of Perth's oldest licensed premises. For hearty pub grub, old-world charm and banter of local worthies.

On Murray St, a younger crowd will find pub grub and beer in Sportsters Bar and The Foundry.

Pitlochry and around *p71*

House of Bruar, see page 73, is a good place to stop for a bowl of soup or some fudge along the A9.

ΨΨΨ **East Haugh Country House Hotel & Restaurant**, a couple of miles south of Pitlochry on the old A9 road, T01796-473121, www.easthaugh.com. A 17th-century country house with excellent and elegant dining and great bar lunches.

ΨΨΨ-ΨΨ **Loft**, Golf Course Rd, Blair Atholl, T01796-481377, www.theloftrestaurant.co.uk. Thoughtfully prepared, tasty menu. Lovely ambience and value for money.

ΨΨΨ-Ψ **Killiecrankie Hotel**, see Sleeping, above. Excellent bar meals and lovely dinners. The bar is less formal and cheaper than the restaurant.

ΨΨ **Port-na-Craig Inn & Restaurant**, T01796-472777, just below the Festival Theatre on the banks of the River Tummel. Good hearty, moderately priced lunches and bar meals.

ΨΨ-Ψ **Moulin Inn**, a few miles north of Pitlochry, at Moulin on the A924, T01796-472196, www.moulinhotel.co.uk. Food daily till 2200. Serves good, cheap pub food and fine real ales from its own microbrewery (try their 'Braveheart').

Ψ **Food for Thought**on Moulin St, Pitlochry. An excellent delicatessen and coffee shop.

Aberfeldy and Loch Tay *p74*

ΨΨΨ **Ardeonaig House Hotel**, south Loch Tay by Aberfeldy, T01567-820400. Recently voted

For an explanation of sleeping and eating price codes used in this guide, see inside the front cover. Other relevant information is found in Essentials, see pages 40-47.

one of the best inns in Britain and one of the most romantic small hotels in Scotland, this charming retreat boasts a terrific South African wine list and 3 dinner menus including a £65, 6-course, mouthwatering gourmet tasting menu. Local grouse, Glen Almond hare and fresh langoustine are among the many treats. Recommended.

Entertainment

Perth and around *p68, map p69*

Famous Grouse Experience, Crieff, T01764-656565, daily, year-round, 0900-1630, £7.50, £5. Tour Scotland's oldest distillery and sample the **Famous Grouse** and several single malts on a 60-min tour incorporating a BAFTA award-winning interactive show. There's even a dancing grouse and a floor of 'ice'. Recommended.

Perth Concert Hall, Mill St, T0845-6126319, is a striking £20 million arts and rock concert venue complete with minimalist café.

Perth Theatre, 185 High St, Perth, T01738-621031, is a beautiful Victorian-era theatre with an excellent reputation for high-class productions.

Playhouse, 6 Murray St, Perth, T01738-623126, offers a dose of escapism on the big screen.

Pitlochry and around *p71*

Pitlochry Festival Theatre, across the river from the town centre, T01796-484626, www.pitlochry.org.uk, stages a different play every night 6 nights a week May-Oct and other shows throughout the year.

Festivals and events

Perth and around *p68, map p69*

May Blair Atholl Gathering and Highland Games is a spectacular open-air event held in the grounds of Blair Castle.

Jul **T in the Park Balado**, Kinross, one of Britain's biggest open-air music festivals attracting 'A-list' rock and pop acts from around the UK.

Aug Perth Highland Games is held on the 2nd Sun in Aug, the week after the **Perth** Show, which also take place in South Inch.

Sep Blairgowrie and East Perthshire Walking Festival.

Activities and tours

Perth and around *p68, map p69*

Cycling

Perthshire. Three national cycle routes pass through Perthshire using quiet country roads and off-road track. Ask at the local tourist office or see www.sustrans.org.uk for details.

Fishing

Gordonian Fishings, Old Carpow, Newburgh, T01738-850757. Open 15 Jan-15 Oct this facility provides tuition and permits for salmon, trout and grayling fishing on the River Tay. Trout permits are £20 per day, salmon permits £35-£90 per day. Details of all the Perthshire fisheries are available from the TIC.

Golf

King James VI Golf Club, Moncreiffe Island, Perth. T01738-632460. 18-hole golf-course near town centre. See www.perthshire.co.uk for a full listing of the area's many courses.

Horse racing

Perth Racecourse, near Scone Palace, T01738-551597, has regular jump racing events during the summer.

Leisure centres

Bell's Sports Centre, Hay St, T01738-622301, daily 0900-2200, covers virtually every sport and leisure activity imaginable.

Dewar's Centre, Glover St and next door to the pool, T01738-624188, where the visitor can curl, ice skate or bowl.

Perth Leisure Pool, T01738-492410, open daily 1000-2200, west of the town centre on the Glasgow road, claims to have the best leisure swimming pool in Scotland.

Pitlochry and around *p71*

Cycling

Basecamp Bikes, The Firs, Blair Atholl, T01796-T481256, www.basecamp-bikes.co.uk, have well-mapped off-road routes and hire bikes from £10 per ½ day. See also www.scotcycle.co.uk.

Escape Route, 3 Atholl Rd, Pitlochry, T/F01796-473859. Hire, sell and repair touring and off-road bikes.

Walking
Atholl Estates Ranger Service, T01796-481646. Offer advice, guided walks and leaflets on 9 waymarked walking and bike trails (30 miles) in the Blair Atholl area.

Aberfeldy and Loch Tay *p74*
Aberfeldy, Weem and Kenmore boast several notable centres offering river-kayaking, whitewater rafting and canyoning. Try **Nae Limits**, Dunkeld, T01350-727242, www.naelimits.com; **National Kayak School**, Weem, T01887-820498; **Splash**, Aberfeldy, T01887-829706, www.rafting.co.uk. **Highland Adventure Safaris**, Aberfeldy, T01887-820071, www.highlandadventuresafaris.co.uk. Wildlife spot from landrovers (from £35) or take to the wheel yourself for some memorable off-road adventure (from £55). **Loch Tay Boating Centre**, Kenmore, T01887-830291, Apr-Oct daily 0900-1900. Hires speedboats, fishing boats and canoes, as well as bicycles.

Blairgowrie and Glenshee *p76*
Glenshee ski centre, T01339-741320, www.glenshee.co.uk, is at the crest of the Cairnwell Pass (2199 ft). The most extensive ski area in Scotland, Glenshee is ideal for telemark and alpine skiing. Lessons, ski and snowboard rental also available from Glenshee Ski School, Spittal of Glenshee, T01250-885216. Adult day lift pass from £23; child £14. Call the centre to check weather forecast.

Transport

Perth and around *p68, map p69*
Bus Strathtay Scottish, T01250-872772, www.strathtaybuses.com, run regular buses to **Blairgowrie**, **Dunkeld**, **Aberfeldy, Alyth**, **Scone** and **Dundee**. **Citylink** buses running between **Perth** and **Inverness** stop at the train station by **Birnam** several times daily. **Scottish Citylink** buses, T08705-505050, run frequently to **Glasgow** (1 hr 25 mins), **Edinburgh** (1½ hrs), **Dundee** (35 mins), **Aberdeen** (2½ hrs) and **Inverness** (2½ hrs).

Car hire Arnold Clark, St Leonard's Bank, Perth, T01738-442202, hires cars.

Train There are also hourly trains to **Stirling** (30 mins), **Dundee** (25 mins) and **Aberdeen** (1 hr 40 mins), and several daily to **Inverness** via **Pitlochry** (30 mins) and **Aviemore**. There's an hourly train service (Mon-Sat; 2-hourly on Sun) to **Glasgow Queen St** (1 hr); and frequent trains to **Edinburgh** (1 hr 20 mins).

Pitlochry and around *p71*
Bus Elizabeth Yule **Transport**, T01796-472290, runs a (Mon-Sat only) service between Pitlochry and Calvine via **Blair Atholl** and Killiecrankie with buses leaving Pitlochry at the following times; 0750, 1000, 1300, 1540, 1625 and 1740.
Train From Pitlochry not all trains stop at Blair Atholl.

Blairgowrie and Glenshee *p76*
Bus The only public transport to the ski resort is a daily postbus service (Mon-Sat only) from **Blairgowrie** to **Spittal of Glenshee**, call T01250-872766 or see www.royalmail.com/postbus, or from **Braemar** and **Ballater**.

The Trossachs and Loch Lomond

Strictly speaking, the Trossachs (derived from the Gaelic, 'Na Troiseachan' meaning 'the crossing place') is the narrow wooded glen between Loch Katrine and Loch Achray, but the name is now used to describe a much larger area between Argyll and Perthshire, stretching north from the Campsies and west from Callander to the eastern shore of Loch Lomond. It's a very beautiful and diverse area of sparkling lochs, over 20 craggy Munros (mountains of over 3000 feet) and deep, forested glens. For this reason, it's often called the 'Highlands in miniature', best visited in the autumn when the hills are purple and the trees are a thousand luminous hues, from lustrous gold to flaming scarlet and blazing orange. The Trossachs was one of the country's first holiday regions, and remains a major tourist destination. Its enduring appeal is due in no small measure to Sir Walter Scott, who eulogized its great natural beauty in his epic poem, Lady of the Lake, *and whose historical novel,* Rob Roy, *immortalized the region's most famous (and arguably infamous) 17th-century clan chief who ruled the lands west of Balquhidder.*

West of the Trossachs is Loch Lomond, Britain's largest inland waterway, measuring 22 miles long and up to 5 miles wide. Though still 'bonnie', its western banks now reverberate to the noise of traffic heading north from nearby Glasgow (20 miles) to Fort William on the busy A82. In spite of being part of the 720-square-mile Loch Lomond and Trossachs National Park, Scotland's first, the loch's western shores still teem with speedboats and jet-skis in summer. Thankfully, though the massif of Ben Lomond (allow five hours return) attracts many a hiker at Rowardennan's road end, the eastern shore remains distinctly quieter. ›› *For Sleeping, Eating and other listings, see pages 86-89.*

Ins and outs

Getting there There are regular (Monday to Saturday) buses from Stirling to Aberfoyle and Callander (T0870-6082608). There are also daily services to Aberfoyle from Glasgow, via Balfron. There's a daily **Scottish Citylink** service between Edinburgh and the Isle of Skye which stops in Callander and links with buses to Killin. There's a **postbus service** ⓘ *T01752-494527, www.royalmail.com/postbus*, from Aberfoyle to Inversnaid on Loch Lomond. It leaves Aberfoyle post office daily, except Sunday, at 0900 and arrives at Inversnaid at 1325. You'd be quicker hiring a bike and cycling the route! ›› *For further details, see Transport page 88.*

Getting around The **Trossachs Trundler** is an alternative for those wanting to make the journey from Callander to Aberfoyle via the *SS Sir Walter Scott* on Loch Katrine before winding over the Duke's Pass into Aberfoyle. Running four times a day between May and early October, the minibus can carry two bikes and wheelchairs. Current prices are £5 for a day-pass or £12 for a family of four. Contact the local TIC for details, see below.

Tourist information **Aberfoyle TIC** ⓘ *on the main street, T01877-382352, www.visitscottishheartlands.com, Apr-Jun and Sep-Oct 1000-1700; July and Aug 0900-1800, Nov-Mar weekend only, 1000-1600.* **Callander TIC** ⓘ *Ancaster Sq, T01877-330342, daily, Apr-May, 1000-1700; Jun-Sep 1000-1800; winter 1000-1700*, shares the same building as the Rob Roy and Trossachs Visitor Centre. Fifteen miles southwest of Aberfoyle in Balloch, the southernmost end of Loch Lomond and terminus for trains from Glasgow, is the **Loch Lomond National Park Gateway Centre** ⓘ *T01389-722199, www.lochlomond-trossachs.org*. Here you'll find a large **tourist information office** ⓘ *daily 1000-1700*, and details about ferry and bus transport in the entire park area. Adjacent to the modern Gateway Centre is the retail crescent of **Loch Lomond Shores**, with attractions including the recently opened **Loch Lomond Aquarium** ⓘ *T01389-721500, daily 1000-1700, £7.95, £6.95 concession, £5.50 children*, as well as the watersport, walking and cycling operator, **Can You Experience** and a café aboard the restored steamer *Maid of the Loch*. **Tarbet TIC** ⓘ *T01301-702260, Apr-Oct.*

The Trossachs ›› *pp86-89. Colour map 4, C1-2.*

Walking in the Trossachs → *OS Landranger maps 56 and 57 covers these routes.*

Loch Lomond and the Trossachs is superb walking country. East of Loch Lomond itself, the two most challenging peaks are Ben Venue and Ben A'an, respectively 3 and 5 miles north of Aberfoyle. **Ben Venue** (2385 ft) is a fairly strenuous climb that begins with a steady waymarked ascent (dress and equip yourself appropriately for the climb) from behind the **Loch Achray Hotel**. Allow about four hours for the return

Better red than dead

As the tourist board never tires of reminding us, the Trossachs is Rob Roy country. Rob Roy ('Red Robert' in Gaelic) was one of Scotland's most notorious outlaws or one of the bravest Highland heroes, depending on your point of view. It is true that he was a freebooter, but he was also defending Highland clan culture and more specifically fighting for the very survival of his own clan against proscription and persecution by the government and its supporters.

Rob Roy MacGregor (1671-1734) was born in Glengyle, to the north-west of Loch Katrine. The MacGregors' lands included those previously owned by the rival Campbells but bestowed on the MacGregors for services rendered to Alexander II in his conquest of Argyll. For a long time the clan kept possession of their lands by right of the sword, but the constant attempts by neighbouring clans to displace them led to retaliation by the MacGregors and earned them a reputation for being aggressive. Rob Roy did little to change this image, and his bitter feud with the powerful Duke of Montrose led to his being outlawed and eventually captured and sentenced to transportation. He was pardoned and returned to Balquhidder, where he stayed for the rest of his life. He now lies buried in the churchyard.

The Rob Roy story was first popularized by Sir Walter Scott's eponymous 19th-century novel, and his life continues to be romanticized, most recently in the 1995 film starring Liam Neeson and Tim Roth. Like Robin Hood before him, his courage in refusing to bow to the forces of authority seems to strike a chord with people.

trip. Though **Ben A'an** (1520 ft) isn't a giant of a hill, it's a steep, unrelenting climb from the moment you begin at the car park 500 yards west of the former grand **Trossachs Hotel** on the north bank of Loch Achray. You should reach the summit within 1½ hours. Whichever ascent you choose, spectacular views await westwards towards Loch Lomond and southwards to the Campsie Hills and Glasgow. Before you go, pack a picnic to enjoy the views over Loch Katrine. On a still day, it's possible to hear the commentary from the deck of the toy-like *SS Walter Scott* far below Ben A'an. All local TICs sell detailed maps of the area.

Both these mountains lie within the **Queen Elizabeth Forest Park**. This vast and spectacular wilderness of 75,000 acres borders Loch Lomond to the west and incorporates Loch Ard, Loch Achray and Loch Lubnaig, as well as Ben Venue, Ben A'An and **Ben Ledi**, which overlooks Callander. The park is run by the Forestry Commission and is criss-crossed by a network of less difficult waymarked trails and cycling paths which start from the David Marshall Lodge, **Queen Elizabeth Park Visitor Centre** ⓘ *T01877-382258, Mar-Jun, Sep-Oct daily 1000-1700; Jul-Aug 1000-1800; Nov-Feb 1000-1600, parking £1*, about half a mile north of Aberfoyle on the A821. The centre incorporates audio-visual displays on the park's flora and fauna, information on the area's numerous walks and cycle routes, a restaurant and children's play area.

Aberfoyle

The sleepy village of Aberfoyle suddenly bursts into life in the summer with the arrival of hordes of tourists. It lies on the edge of the Queen Elizabeth Forest Park and like Callander to the east, is a major tourist hub providing an ideal base for golf and walking and cycling in the surrounding hills. There's an abundance of guesthouse accommodation, though it's advisable to book ahead during the busy summer season.

Three miles east of Aberfoyle is the **Lake of Menteith**, the only lake in Scotland (as opposed to loch). On **Inchmahome Island** in the middle of the lake are the beautiful and substantial ruins of **Inchmahome Priory** ⓘ *T01877-385294 (HS), Apr-Sep daily 0930-1830, £4*, the 13th-century Augustinian priory where the four-year-old Mary, Queen of Scots was sent in 1547, safe from the clutches of Henry VIII. A ferry takes visitors over to the island from **Port of Menteith**.

To the north of Aberfoyle is Doon Hill, better known as the **Fairy Knowe**. The tree at the top is said to be the home of the 'People of Quietness', and in 1692 a local minister was less than discreet in telling the world of their secrets. As punishment he was taken away to fairyland, and his spirit has languished there ever since. If you go round the tree seven times, your wish will be granted, but go round it backwards and... well, we won't be held responsible. It's about 1½ hours up and back. Follow the road across the bridge south of the car park by the Vistitor Centre, then continue until it forks; take the left fork, a waymarked path, to the hilltop.

Aberfoyle to Callander

The A821 route north from Aberfoyle, through the spectacular **Duke's Pass**, and then east past Loch Achray and Loch Vennachar, is a beautiful route and not to be missed. There are a couple of worthwhile diversions along the way. About 5 miles north of Aberfoyle, a forest track branches to the right and runs through Achray Forest and along the shores of **Loch Drunkie**, before rejoining the A821 further north. A few miles further on, a road turns left to **Trossachs Pier** on the southern shore of **Loch Katrine**. This is the departure point for cruises (April to October) on the *SS Sir Walter Scott*, see Activities and tours, page 88. At 1100 daily (£7.50 return) it sails to the remote settlement of **Stronachlachar** on the far western shores of the loch and back. There is also a one-hour afternoon cruise (£6.25) that makes a short, non-stop loop of the southern section of the freshwater loch. There's a cycle path around the loch as far as Stronachlachar so it's possible to take the morning cruise and cycle back to the pier. Bikes are available for hire at the pier. » *See Transport, page 88.*

Callander and around

At the eastern end of the Trossachs and 14 miles northwest of Stirling is Callander, a tourist honey-pot whose Main Street sadly boasts all too many tartan-tack shops. Yet look closely and you'll also find several excellent restaurants, delightful corner shops selling home-made fudge and at **Deli Ecosse** by the TIC, a superb range of takeaway or eat-in Scottish and continental sandwiches, wines and fresh coffee. With the

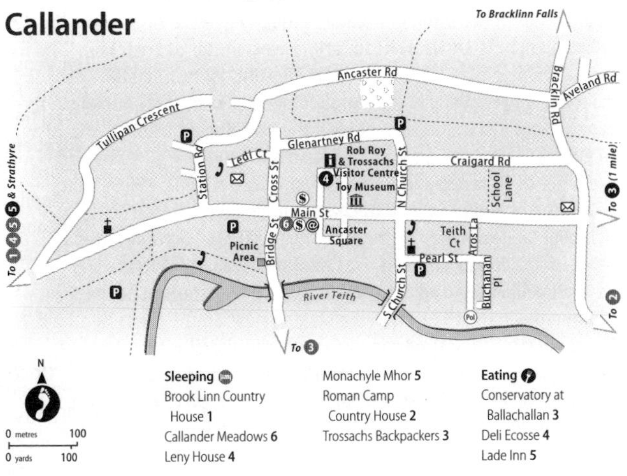

Ben Ledi Café also serving up affordable mouth-watering treats, it's just as well there are many walks and cycling trails (including Route 7 to Balquhidder) to burn off those holiday calories. The overworked **TIC** ⓘ *Apr-May and Oct-Mar daily 1000-1700; Jun-end Sep 1000-1800,* shares the same building and times as the **Rob Roy and Trossachs Visitor Centre** ⓘ *£3.85*. Though rumours persist that it will close, the interactive displays and film clips continue to provide an entertaining account of the life of Rob Roy MacGregor.

Opened in 1995, Callander's family-run **Toy Museum** ⓘ *111 Main St, T01877-330004, Apr-Oct daily*, is a true Aladdin's Cave, crammed with toys from the past 100 years. Step into the modest shop, pay the £2 entry fee and whatever your age, take a fascinating trip down memory lane. There are over 100 original Action Men, Victorian-era tin soldiers, Hot Wheels and Dinky Toys from the 1930s. You will also find bisque dolls dating back to the 1880s, 1930s dolls houses and over 100 vintage teddy bears, including the loveable Paddington Bear.

▲ A recommended local walk is to **Bracklinn Falls**, reached by a woodland trail which leads from Bracklinn Road. At the time of writing this is not a circular walk as a wooden bridge has been washed away. Normally, it's about 30 minutes' walk each way. Another trail from Bracklinn Road leads up to **Callander Crags**, from where there are great views of the surrounding area. Allow 1½ hours there and back. The most challenging walk in the area is to the summit of **Ben Ledi** (2857 ft), but it's a tough climb and you'll need to be fit, experienced and prepared. Ask at the TIC for further information and for maps.

Two miles north of Callander, on the A84 route to the Highlands, are the **Falls of Leny**, in the narrow and dramatic Pass of Leny. The falls are accessible from the car park by the roadside or via the **Callander to Strathyre Cycleway** (Route 7), which follows the old train line to Oban, from Callander north along the west bank of **Loch Lubnaig**. This forms part of the **Glasgow to Killin Cycleway**, which runs from the centre of Glasgow, via Balloch, Aberfoyle, Callander, Balquhidder and Lochearnhead, to Killin. For the fit, this is the best way to see the Trossachs.

The A84 heads north from Callander along the east bank of Loch Lubnaig, and beyond towards **Loch Earn**. A few miles further north, a side road branches left to the tiny village of **Balquhidder**, famous as the burial place of Rob Roy. His grave in the churchyard, by his wife and two of his sons, is thankfully understated. In the nearby converted village library, there's a fabulous cosy tea-room with delicious sandwiches (March to October, times vary).

North of Callander to Lochearnhead and Killin

A few miles north of the turning to Balquhidder, where the A84 meets the A85 from Crieff to Crianlarich, is **Lochearnhead**, at the western tip of Loch Earn. The loch is a highly popular watersports centre, see Activities and tours, page 88. Lochearnhead is also a good base for walking in the surrounding hills. In the far northwestern corner of the Stirling region, just to the west of Loch Tay, is **Killin**, a pleasant little village which makes a good base for walkers wishing to explore the wild mountains and glens of the ancient district of **Breadalbane** (pronounced *Bread-albinn*). Killin's picture-postcard setting, with the beautiful **Falls of Dochart** tumbling through the centre of the village, makes it a popular destination for tourists. The **TIC** ⓘ *Mar-Oct daily*, overlooks the falls.

Twelve miles west of Killin is **Crianlarich**, at the crossroads of the A82 Glasgow–Fort William road and the A85 to Perth, and at the junction of the Glasgow to Fort William and Oban rail lines. It is a staging post on the **West Highland Way**. Six miles further north is tiny **Tyndrum**, which shot to prominence almost 20 years ago after the discovery of gold in the surrounding hills. There's a seasonal **TIC** ⓘ *main road, T01838-400246, Apr-Jun and Sep-Oct 1000-1700; Jul and Aug 1000-1800.* Adjacent to the TIC is **Real Food Café**, an award-winning organic fast-food stop that's not cheap – but worth it!

Loch Lomond » pp86-89. Colour map 4, C1.

Britain's largest inland waterway is one of Scotland's most famous lochs, thanks to the Jacobite ballad about its 'bonnie banks'. These same banks are now one of the busiest parts of the Highlands, due to their proximity to Glasgow (only 20 miles south along the congested A82). During the summer the loch becomes a playground for day-trippers who tear up and down the loch in speedboats and on jet skis, obliterating any notion visitors may have of a little peace and quiet.

At the southern end of the loch is the resort town of **Balloch**, packed full of hotels, B&Bs, caravan parks and any number of operators offering boat trips around the loch's southern waters. At the northern end of the town is **Loch Lomond Shores** ⓘ *T01389-722199, daily year round*, a huge visitor centre-cum-shopping mall, adjacent to which is the **TIC** and **National Park Gateway Centre**, as well as shops and cafés. Here you can pick up all the information you need on the national park, as well as book a loch cruise, hire bikes, kayaks or sailing dinghies, or simply enjoy the views from the café in the Drumkinnon Tower (see Activities and tours, page 88, for further information). The **Loch Lomond Aquarium** ⓘ *daily 1000-1700, £7.95, concessions £6.95, children £5.50, U-15s must be accompanied by an adult*, Balloch, opened in 2005 in the Drumkinnon Tower on the banks of Loch Lomond. It's a fun educational experience that takes you on an 'underwater journey' to understand the abundant and diverse marine creatures that live in Loch Lomond, the Clyde Estuary and in the ocean. Giant fish tanks, touch pools, a sunken boat, rare otters and interactive displays are all part of the attraction. There is also a café.

The west bank of the loch, from Balloch north to Tarbet, is one long, almost uninterrupted development of marinas, holiday homes, caravan parks and exclusive golf clubs. The most picturesque village here is **Luss**, though it is more of a theme park than a real village. It is to the genuine Highland experience what Ozzy Osbourne is to philosophical debate. One-and-a-half-hour boat trips leave from Luss pier. Further north, things begin to quieten down a bit. At Tarbet, it's worthwhile jumping aboard one of the boats run by **Loch Lomond Cruises** ⓘ *T01301-702356, www.cruiseloch lomond.co.uk*. There are a number of cruise options (from £7.50) but surely the most innovative is The 'West Highland Way Rambler', whereby hikers first enjoy a 45-minute cruise under Ben Lomond before disembarking at Rowardennan and hiking 6 miles north along the famous West Highland Way to Inversnaid before being picked up again by the boat. Still further north, the loch gets deeper, quieter and narrower en route to **Ardlui** and the famously cosy and rustic **Inverarnan Inn**, beyond which the A82 meets the A85 at **Crianlarich**.

The tranquil east bank of Loch Lomond is a great place for walking. The **West Highland Way** follows the east bank all the way from **Drymen**, through **Balmaha**, **Rowardennan** and **Inversnaid**. Beyond Rowardennan this is the only access to the loch's east bank, except for the road to Inversnaid from the Trossachs. From Rowardennan you can climb **Ben Lomond** (3192 ft), the most southerly of the Munros. It's deceptively long though not too difficult and the views from the top, in good weather, are astounding. An easier climb is **Conic Hill**, on the Highland fault line and very close to Glasgow. The route starts from the Forestry Commission interpretative and ranger post in the car park at Balmaha. It takes about 1½ hours to reach the top, from where the views of the loch are stunning. Across the road, it's worthwhile hopping aboard the **MacFarlane and Son**-operated mail-boat cruise (£8)

Finish off the walk to Conic Hill with a pint and a meal at the Oak Tree Inn (see Eating, page 88).

Loch Lomond, along with a large chunk of the Cowal Peninsula, the Campsies and the Trossachs, are all part of the Loch Lomond and the Trossachs National Park, which become Scotland's first national park, as late as 2002.

 that leaves from the pier and delivers post to the offshore islands. Alternatively, there's a ferry to explore the beautiful isle of **Inchcailloch** with its nature trails and ancient ruins. In both cases, times vary so it's best to call ahead (T01360-870214, www.balmahaboatyard.co.uk).

Sleeping

The Trossachs *p81*

L-B Monachyle Mhor Hotel, Balquhidder, on the road to Inverlochlarig, T01877-384622, www.monachylemhor.com. Renowned for its culinary delights and warm welcome, this family-run hotel boasts terrific views over the loch in a peaceful, rural setting. There's also a **Coach House Cottage** available to let (£350-£750 per week). One of the UK's top 200 restaurants, the hotel's organic garden provides fresh herbs whilst much of the produce is sourced in the local area. It's fabulous, though dinner starts at £44 per head (¶¶¶). Recommended.

A MacDonald Forest Hills Hotel, Loch Ard, on the B829 from Aberfoyle, T01877-387277, www.macdonald-hotels.co.uk. 54 rooms. Graceful 19th-century country house converted into a family-friendly hotel offering multitudinous facilities and activities such as indoor pool with sauna, steam room and fully equipped gym, sailing courses, pony trekking, kayaking, canoeing, windsurfing, fly fishing and curling on their indoor rink. Reasonably priced restaurant (¶¶¶-¶¶) and option of bar meals (¶¶).

A-B Lake Hotel, in Port of Menteith, on the lakeshore overlooking Inchmahome, T01877-385258, www.lake-of-menteith-hotel.com. A discerning hotel in a beautiful location that cooks up many memorable treats in the restaurant ¶¶¶-¶¶).

A-B Roman Camp Country House Hotel, Callander, T01877-330003, www.roman-camp-hotel.co.uk. An exquisite16th-century former hunting lodge set in extensive grounds by the river, away from the hoi polloi. Oozes character and Queen Victoria was quite taken with the place. Good Scottish cuisine (¶¶¶-¶¶).

B Creagan House, at the northern end of Loch Lubnaig, in Strathyre, T01877-384638, an atmospheric family-run 17th-century farmhouse consistently providing award-winning service combined with fine food, an impressive wine list and over 50 drams in its cosy restaurant (¶¶¶-¶¶).

B The Four Seasons, in the village of St Fillans, a few miles east of Lochearnhead, T01764-685333, www.thefourseasonshotel.co.uk. Spectacular setting on the shores of Loch Earn, this 12 bedroom 19th-century house boasts 2 fine restaurants (¶¶¶-¶¶) serving traditional Scottish cuisine. There are also **chalets** (**C**) within the wooded grounds.

B Leny House, Callander, T01877-331078, www.lenyestate.com. Stay in the baronial north wing of historic Leny House and enjoy 5-star self-catering (£900-£1160 per week) or 4 guests can enjoy a luxurious stay in the estate **cottages** (£500-£750) and **chalets**.

C Creag-Ard House, in Milton, 2 miles west of Aberfoyle overlooking Loch Ard, T01877-382297. Easter-Oct. Beautiful location, a warm welcome, a hearty breakfast and even the chance to trout fish on the loch outside your window. Recommended.

D Brook Linn Country House, Callander, T01877-330103, www.brooklinn-scotland.co.uk, all year. B&B (and dinner) is available in this fine Victorian house where the secluded walled garden and grounds include a small cottage (£150-£420 per week).

D Callander Meadows, 24 Main St Callander, T01877-330181, www.callandermeadows.co.uk. Simplicity is the key to this 18th-century townhouse offering 3 delightful en suite bedrooms and a wonderful restaurant menu (¶¶¶-¶¶) including desserts to die for. Recommended.

F Braveheart Backpackers, Lochay Lodge and Steading by the **Killin Hotel**, T0131-556 5560. Basic accommodation in this pretty village. Bike and canoe hire available.

F Trossachs Backpackers, a couple of miles out of Callander, along the Invertrossachs Rd which turns off the A81, T01877-331200, Scottish-hostel.co.uk. Over 30 beds, with dorms and family rooms. Relaxed and peaceful independent hostel with bike rental available next door.

Self-catering

Altskeith House, by Loch Ard, T01877-382878, www.altskeith.com. £2200-£4500 per week. This historic, sandstone house, blessed with breathtaking views over Loch Ard towards Ben Lomond, promises and delivers a heavenly luxury stay for the discerning traveller and up to 21 other guests. A home from home, every room oozes character, including the huge rustic living room with roaring fire, gargantuan dining room, tastefully appointed bedrooms and a kitchen fit for Jamie Oliver. There are also endless outdoor pursuits to enjoy, from windsurfing, biking and kayaking to walking in the nearby Loch Ard Forest. Glasgow is 45 mins' drive away, Edinburgh 60 mins.

Camping

Cobeland Campsite, 2 miles south of Aberfoyle on the edge of the Queen Elizabeth Forest Park, T01877-382392. Open Apr-Oct.
Trossachs Holiday Park, 3 miles south of Aberfoyle, off the A81, T01877-382614. Open Mar-Oct. An excellent site set in 40 acres with mountain bike hire.

Loch Lomond *p85*

L Cameron House Hotel, 2 miles north of Balloch, T01389-755565, www.cameronhouse.co.uk. This exclusive lochside hotel comes complete with spa, 3 restaurants (ΨΨΨ-ΨΨ) and a marina.
C Rowardennan Hotel, Rowardennan, T01360-870273. Comfortable choice, serves bar meals.
F Inversnaid Bunkhouse, Inversnaid, T01301-702870. Hikers on the West Highland Way who reach Inversnaid on the remote banks of Loch Lomond are highly recommended to stay overnight at the bunkhouse (call ahead for the van to pick you up from the soulless Inversnaid hotel. The bunkhouse even has an outdoor hot tub and bar! Recommended.
F Loch Lomond SYHA Youth Hostel, Arden, T01389-850226, www.syha.org.uk. Grand 19th-century turreted mansion complete with the obligatory ghost and outstanding lochside location close to Ben Lomond footpath.

Camping

Milarrochy Bay, Balmaha, 5 miles north of Drymen, T01360-870236. A very good campsite with stunning views over Loch Lomond.
Lomond Woods Holiday Park, Tullichewan, on the Old Luss Rd, T01389-755000. A good campsite where you can hire mountain bikes.

Eating

The Trossachs *p81*

ΨΨΨ **Monachyle Mhor Hotel**, see Sleeping, above. This renowned restaurant makes stylish and imaginative use of superb local ingredients. Outstanding service and food as you'd expect for a dinner that starts at £44 per head. Book ahead. Recommended.
ΨΨΨ-ΨΨ **Callander Meadows**, Main St, Callander, T01877-330181. Another great restaurant that prides itself on its imaginative menu, fresh, locally sourced produce and irresistible desserts.
ΨΨΨ-ΨΨ **The Conservatory at Ballachallan**, 1 mile south of Callander off the main road, T01877-339190. Mar-Oct. A farm-steading restaurant specializing in Scottish cuisine including seafood such as delicious cullen skink soup and scallops. Welcoming and reasonably priced. Also lunches and home-baking. Recommended.
ΨΨΨ-ΨΨ **Roman Camp Hotel**, Callander, see Sleeping, above. Lovely restaurant and reasonably priced for lunch or dinner.
ΨΨ **Brig O' Turk Tearoom**, Brig O' Turk, Callander. Look out for the shabby green hut with peeling paint and tired-looking hanging baskets outside. Inside it's like a scout hut with higgledy-piggeldy chairs and mismatching crockery and tablecloths. Informal and very good food – when it's open!
ΨΨ **The Lade Inn**, Kilmahog, 1 mile north of Callander. T01877-330152. In a rustic setting enjoy the real ales from the microbrewery and delicious restaurant/bar meals (ΨΨ-Ψ) prepared using locally sourced produce including trout and beef. Terrific atmosphere.
Ψ **Deli Ecosse**, Callander, T01877-331220. Mar-Oct daily 0900-1700; Nov-Feb weekends only. For hearty, freshly prepared sandwiches, freshly brewed coffee and an excellent choice of Scottish food and wines, pop in and share your banter with Sandy, the friendly owner.

Loch Lomond *p85*

ΨΨΨ **Cameron House Hotel**, 2 miles north of Balloch, T01389-755565, www.cameronhouse.co.uk. 3 lovely restaurants and a beautiful lochside setting. Dress to impress.

🍴🍴 **Inverbeg Inn**, a few miles north of Luss, at Inverbeg, T01436-860678. Good food including grilled venison sausages and seafood chowder, though lacking atmosphere.

🍴🍴 **Oak Tree Inn**, Balmaha, On the east side of the loch, T01360-870357. Excellent pub food served with a touch of finesse. Busy in summer though great atmosphere. Has double rooms for B&B (**D**), should lunch become dinner.

🍴 **Tarbet Tea room**, Tarbet, T01301-702200. Daily 0830-1700 year-round. Tucked just off the main road as the road forks to Arrochar, this humble dwelling that served as a school in WW2 is where weekend walkers and cyclists come in their droves for a hearty cooked breakfast, toasties or cream tea (£3). Fantastic value and very friendly; just don't expect silver service. Recommended.

Bars and clubs

Loch Lomond *p85*

The Clachan Inn, Drymen, T01360-660824. Established in 1734, this whitewashed, croft-like, cosy pub serving heart bar meals (🍴🍴-🍴) and fine ales may well be Scotland's oldest registered pub.

Drover's Inn, Inverarnan, T01301-704234. The famous Highland watering hole, with smoke-blackened walls, low ceilings, bare floors, open fires, a hall filled with stuffed animals, barman in kilt and a great selection of single malts. The perfect place for a wild night of drinking in the wilderness. The **Stagger Inn** across the road is a handy back packers' hostel should you fail to leave the bar.

Activities and tours

The Trossachs *p81*

For detailed advice on the many cycling, fishing, walking and hiking possibilities within the Loch Lomond and Trossachs National Park contact the **National Park Gateway Centre**, www.lochlomond-trossachs.org, T01389-722199. Alternatively, call 08707-200642 and ask for the GO Outdoors leaflet, www.gosmileoutdoors.co.uk.

Lochearnhead Watersports, T01567-830330, has water-skiing, canoeing, kayaking and wake-boarding on the loch.

SS Sir Walter Scott, T01877-376316, Loch Katrine. 5 miles north of Aberfoyle over the Duke's Pass, you'll find a turn-off to the Trossachs pier. From Apr-Oct at 1100 daily (£7.50 return) the cruise boat sails to the remote settlement of **Stronachlachar** on the far western shores of the loch and back. There is also a 1-hr afternoon cruise (£6.25) that makes a short, non-stop loop of the southern section of the freshwater loch. There's a cycle path around the loch as far as Stronachlachar so it's possible to take the morning cruise and cycle back to the pier. Bikes are available for hire at the pier with **Katrinewheels**, T01877-376316.

Loch Lomond *p85*

Can You Experience, T01389-602576, www.canyouexperience.com. Based beside Lomond Shores at Balloch, this operator offers guided walks around Loch Lomond including excursions to the offshore islands, hires mountain bikes by the day (£15), kayaks and even pedalos (£10 for 30 mins). Also guided canoe trips.

Cruise Loch Lomond, Tarbet, T01301-702356, www.cruiselochlomond.co.uk. Operating from Tarbet since 1973, its modern cruise boats run a host of excellent year-round excursions with commentary, including the **West Highland Way Explorer** (from £14.50), **Inversnaid Explorer** (from £7.50) and **Rob Roy Discovery** (from £12.50).

Loch Lomond Waterski Club, by Balloch, T01436-860632, offers tuition and water-ski hire (Apr-Sep).

Lomond Activities, Drymen. T01360-660066. Individual and family bike hire including child seats and helmets.

Lomond Adventure, Balmaha, T01360-870218. Easter-Oct. Offers instruction and hire for kayaks, canoes, power boats, dinghy sailing and waterskiing.

Sweeney's Tours, T01389-722406, run cruises from Balloch and Luss.

Transport

The Trossachs *p81*

Pick up a free copy of *Loch Lomond and the Trossachs – exploring the park by ferry, bus or train*, from any TIC.

Bus The **Citylink** (T08705-505050) Oban to Dundee bus runs twice daily through Perthshire villages including **Comrie**, **St**

Fillans, **Lochearnhead** and **Killin**. The same operator also runs a once daily service (Mon-Sat) from **Edinburgh** via **Stirling** to **Fort William** that passes through **Callander**, **Strathyre**, **Lochearnhead** (No 25 post bus connects with Killin), **Crianlarich** and **Tyndrum**. Caber Coaches (T01887-820090) (No 893) and the postbus (No 213) operate a service (Mon-Sat) between **Aberfeldy** and **Killinvia Kenmore**. There's also a postbus service (No 25) between **Crianlarich** and **Tyndrum** and **Killin** (Mon-Sat). First run leaves Crianlarich 1026 and arrives Killin 1100. Caber Coaches also run a service (Tue and Sat) between **Aberfeldy** and **Killin** stopping en route at **Loch Tay Crannog**, **Kenmore** and **Fortingall**.

Cycle Cycle hire from Wheels, Invertrossachs Rd, Callander, T01887-331100. Katrine Wheels, at Loch Katrine, T01877-376316, Apr-Oct daily 0900-1700, £10 per ½ day, tandems and trailers available.

Train There are 2 train stations at **Tyndrum** and **Crianlarich**. One serves the **Glasgow** to **Oban** line and the other the **Glasgow** to **Fort William** line.

Loch Lomond *p85*
Bus Scottish Citylink buses run regularly from Glasgow to **Balloch** (45 mins), and on to **Luss** and **Tarbet** (1 hr 10 mins). Some go to **Ardlui** (1 hr 20 mins) and on to **Crianlarich**.

First buses run a 4 times daily (Mon-Fri) service (No10 and 11A) between Glasgow and Aberfoyle via Drymen. First also operate a service (Mon-Sat) to **Balloch** that stops in **Drymen**, and an Aberfoyle to Stirling service (Mon-Sat) (Nos 11 and 11A), which stops at Port of Menteith.

Ferry In addition to cruise companies there are several small ferry operators who provide a convenient means for (foot passengers only) to cross Loch Lomond. There's a passenger ferry service across the loch between **Inverbeg** and **Rowardennan**, T01360-870273, Apr-Sep 3 times daily. Leave Inverbeg at 1030, 1430, 1800; return 1000, 1400, 1730. Another service crosses the loch between **Inveruglas** and **Inversnaid**, T01877-386223, operated by Inversnaid Hotel. No fixed timetable. Call for details. There's also a ferry between **Ardlui** and **Ardleish**, T01301-704243, operated by Ardlui Hotel. This operates on demand between 0900-2000. Raise the signal ball at either side to call the ferryman.

Train There are 2 rail lines from **Glasgow** to **Loch Lomond**. One runs to **Balloch** every 30 mins (35 mins) the other is the West Highland line to **Fort William** and **Mallaig**, with a branch line to **Oban**. It reaches Loch Lomond at **Tarbet** and there's another station further north at **Ardlui**.

Deeside

→ *Colour map 4, A4-6.*

The River Dee rises in the Cairngorms and flows down through the surrounding hills, eastwards to the sea at Aberdeen. The valley of the Dee is known as Deeside, or rather Royal Deeside, for its connections with the royal family who have holidayed here, at Balmoral, since Queen Victoria first arrived in 1848. Originally, Queen Victoria and Prince Albert were looking for an estate further west, but were advised that the Deeside climate would be better for Albert's delicate constitution. The queen fell in love with this area and its people, and following Albert's death she sought out the company of straight-talking northerners, preferring their down-to-earth honesty to the two-faced toadies she endured at court.

Today, Deeside's royal associations have made it the tourist honeypot of the northeast, but the royal presence has also saved it from mass development. There's an air of understated affluence and refinement in the villages strung out along the A93 that runs along the north bank of the Dee and, as well as the obvious attraction of Balmoral, there are many other fine examples of baronial castles. Deeside is also a great area for outdoor activities, such as hiking in the surrounding mountains, fishing, stalking, mountain biking, canoeing and skiing. ▸▸ *For Sleeping, Eating and other listings, see pages 94-96.*

Ins and outs

Getting there

Aberdeen airport is 7 miles northwest of the city centre, at Dyce, off the A96 to Inverness. There are regular domestic flights to Scottish and UK destinations, including Orkney and Shetland, as well as international flights to several European destinations. For **airport information** ⓘ *T01224-722331*. There's car hire and currency exchange at the airport. **First Aberdeen** ⓘ *T01224-650065*, buses run regular daily services to and from the city centre (35 minutes, £1.30 single). Alternatively, take a train to Dyce station and a bus or taxi from there. A **taxi** ⓘ *T01224-725500/728*, from the airport to Dyce railway station costs around £7, and £17 to the city centre. ▸▸ *For further details see Transport, page 96.*

Aberdeen is linked to Lerwick in Shetland and Kirkwall in Orkney by **Northlink ferries** ⓘ *T0845-6000449, www.northlinkferries.co.uk*. There are regular sailings from the passenger terminal in the harbour, a short walk east of the train and bus stations.

Tourist information

The regional **Visitscotland** website is a good starting point: www.aberdeen-grampian.com. For details of the Castle Trail, Victorian Heritage Trail and Deeside Tourist Route, contact the TIC in Aberdeen, or in any of the towns along the way. **Banchory TIC** ⓘ *in the local museum, Bridge St, behind the High St, Apr-late Oct*, can provide information on walking and fishing in the area. **Ballater TIC** ⓘ *in the Old Royal Station, T01339-755306, www.ballaterscotland.com, Oct-May daily 1000-1700, Jun-Sep 0900-1800*. Unsurprisingly, it is complemented by a small, informative railway museum (same opening hours as the TIC). **Braemar TIC** ⓘ *Balmoral Mews, on Mar Rd, T01339-741600, Nov-May Mon-Sat 1030-1330, 1400-1700, Sun 1300-1600; Jun-Oct daily 0900-1700.*

Around Deeside ▸▸ *pp94-96.*

Aberdeen to Banchory → *Colour map 4, A5-6.*

The first sight of interest heading west from Aberdeen is **Drum Castle** ⓘ *T01330-811204, www.drum-castle.org.uk, Easter-Jun and Sep Sat-Mon, Wed and Thu 1230-1700; Jul and Aug daily 1100-1700; gardens Easter-end Sep daily 1100-1800; grounds open dail all year. Castle, gardens and grounds £8, £5 concession, car park £2*. Three miles west of **Peterculter** (pronounced 'Petercooter') Drum Castle is a combination of a 13th-century square tower, Jacobean mansion house and later Victorian additions. It was given to one William de Irvine by Robert the Bruce for service rendered at Bannockburn and was in the family's hands for over 650 years, until it was taken over by the National Trust for Scotland in 1976. There's a beautiful walled garden and a trail through the 100-acre ancient **Wood of Drum** which forms part of the castle grounds.

A few miles southeast of Peterculter is its sister village, **Maryculter** (pronounced 'Marycooter'), where you'll find **Storybook Glen** ⓘ *T01224-732941, www.storybookglenaberdeen.co.uk, Mar-Oct daily 1000-1800, Nov-Feb 1000-1600, £4.85, children £3.50*, the northeast's answer to Disneyland. This very attractive and tasteful 'theme park' is a great place to take the kids. There are over 100 nursery rhyme and fairytale characters, secret waterfalls and even fairytale castles!

Fifteen miles west of Aberdeen, where the A93 meets the A957 from Stonehaven, is **Crathes Castle** ⓘ *T01330-844525, castle Apr-Sep daily 1030-1730, Oct daily 1030-1630 (last admission to castle 45 mins before closing); licensed restaurant Apr-Oct daily 1030-1730, Nov-Mar Thu-Sun 1030-1545; grounds and garden daily 0900-sunset; castle and grounds combined £10, concession £7*. It's a perfect 'fairytale' castle built over 40 years in the mid-16th century. The turreted tower house is still furnished with many period pieces and wall hangings, and is notable for its superb painted ceilings. There are narrow spiral staircases leading to tiny rooms, one of which is said to be inhabited by an obligatory ghost. The castle is well worth exploring but is almost overshadowed by the exceptional gardens, which shouldn't be missed. There are no fewer than eight of them, so take your time. There's also a visitor centre, restaurant and shop. It's also worth taking one of several waymarked trails into surrounding countryside inhabited by roe deer and red squirrels.

Banchory to Alford → *Phone code: 01330. Colour map 4, A5.*

Banchory, with the River Dee burbling through, makes a very pleasant base for exploring Deeside though aside from salmon and trout fishing in the area, there's little in the town itself to hold the visitor. You can watch salmon leaping spectacularly at the Bridge of Feugh, to the south of town. There is a sad tale, though, of a lady-in-waiting who was staying at Balmoral when the royal family were in residence some years ago. She was standing fishing in the river, in quite deep water, and wearing chest-height waders, when the sovereign rode by. Seeing the king, she curtsied, whereupon the water flowed quickly into her waders and she sank beneath the water and drowned.

From Banchory, head northwest on the A980 to Alford, in the Don Valley, see page 96. Roughly halfway is the village of **Lumphanan**, once thought to be the burial place of Macbeth, the Scottish king so misrepresented by Shakespeare (he is actually buried on Iona). Macbeth's Cairn is instead a prehistoric cairn. Just to the south of the village is the **Peel Ring**, a 12th-century Motte, and one of Scotland's earliest medieval sites.

West of Banchory → *Colour map 4, A5.*

The attractive little village of Aboyne is 30 miles west of Banchory on the A93. A few miles further on is Dinnet. In the Muir of Dinnet National Nature Reserve you can explore the Burn o' Vat, a sheltered valley which attracts many butterflies and dragonflies. During the walk, you'll come to a huge circular stone chamber and, in nearby Loch Kinord, there are crannogs, which are ancient man-made islands.

Ballater and Balmoral → *Colour map 4, A4.*

The neat little town of Ballater is proud of its royal connections. You can buy meat from the butcher with his 'By Royal Appointment' sign, or clothes from royal outfitters. This is where Lizzie and Phil pop down to the shops for a pint of milk or perhaps to choose a DVD for a quiet night in. Ever since Queen Victoria first arrived by train from Aberdeen in 1848, the royal family have been spending their holidays here in their summer residence, Balmoral. She was not amused at the prospect of having an unsightly rail station on her doorstep, so the line ended 8 miles east, at Ballater. The line has been closed for some time, but you can still visit the TIC which is within the old train station.

The royals are not the only famous summer visitors. The poet **Byron** (who attended Aberdeen Grammar School) spent many childhood summer holidays at Ballaterach, a few miles east of Ballater. He had a narrow escape when he slipped and nearly fell into the fast flowing stream at the Linn of Dee, beyond Braemar. He was rescued just in time and went on to wax poetic about the beautiful hills which are Ballater's other great attraction. The town makes the ideal base for hiking (see below) as well as a number of other outdoor activities. Many of the walks set off from within the 6000 acre **Loch Muick** (pronounced 'Mick') and **Lochnagar Wildlife Reserve**, nine miles southwest of Ballater, at the head of Glen Muick. There's a visitor centre and car park at Spittal of Glenmuick. From here a track leads along the west shore of the loch to the lodge where Queen Victoria met John Brown. You may spot birds of prey and deer. For guides and equipment for canoeing, climbing, mountain biking and skiing, contact **Adventure Scotland**, T0870-2402676, see page 95.

We are most certainly amused

There has been a gathering of some sort at Braemar for 900 years, ever since Malcolm Canmore set contests for the local clans so that he could pick the strongest and bravest of men for his army. These events take place up and down the country throughout the summer, but none is as famous, or well attended, as Braemar's. Queen Victoria attended in 1848 and the gathering is still patronized by the royal family. Crowds come from all over the world to proclaim the monarch as Chieftain of the Braemar Gathering.

At the gathering the visitor will see contests in traditional Scottish events, such as tossing the caber, Highland dancing and bagpipe competitions and displays. There is an inter-services tug o' war championship, a medley relay race and a hill race up Morrone. The sound of the massed pipes echoing around the encircling heather-clad hills and a plethora of tartan also help to make this a real tourist highlight. The royal connection (and the crowds) apart, many other local communities hold similar games.

Balmoral Castle → *Colour map 4, A4.*

ⓘ *T01339-742534, www.balmoralcastle.com, Apr-Jul 1000-1700, £6, concessions £5, children £1.*

Eight miles west of Ballater is the area's main attraction, Balmoral Castle. The 16th-century tower house, formerly owned by the local Gordon family, was bought for Queen Victoria by Prince Albert in 1852 and converted into today's baronial mansion. It has been the royal family's summer retreat ever since. Only the ballroom and the grounds are open to the likes of you and me, and only for three months of the year. Pony trekking and pony cart rides are available around the grounds and are favourite ways of enjoying the wonderful scenery. Opposite the castle gates is **Crathie Church**, which is used by the family when they're in residence. There's a small souvenir shop next to the main gates and a visitor centre which gives a lot of information on the castle and its owners.

Braemar → *Colour map 4, A3.*

Nine miles west of Balmoral, is Braemar, the final town on Deeside, lying at the foot of the awesome, brooding **Cairngorm Massif**, which dominates the Eastern Highlands. Even at the height of summer you can see a dab of snow still lying in a hollow in the surrounding mountains, and Braemar is an excellent base for hiking, see below, and winter skiing at Glenshee, see page 76. It's an attractive little place, much loved by Queen Victoria and much visited during its annual **Braemar Gathering** (or games, see box, page 92), which attracts tens of thousands of visitors each year, amongst them members of the royal family. **Braemar Highland Heritage Centre** ⓘ *Balmoral Mews by the tourist office, T01339-741944, Apr-Sep 0900-1800 (Jul-Aug till 2000), Oct-Mar 1000-1700, free*, with a small exhibition including a 12-minute audio-visual presentation.

Just north of the village is **Braemar Castle** ⓘ *T01339-741219*, dating from 1628. This impressive fortress was used by Hanoverian troops after the Jacobite Rising of 1745. It is L-shaped, with a star-shaped defensive wall and a central round tower with a spiral stair. There are barrel-vaulted ceilings and an underground prison. Its owner also possesses the world's largest cairngorm – a semi-precious stone, a variety of quartz, which is yellow, grey or brown in colour – weighing 52 lbs. Unfortunately, at the time of writing the castle is closed and there's uncertainty as to whether it will reopen to the public. Call the TICs in Ballater or Braemar for the latest information.

A very scenic side trip from Braemar is to the **Linn of Dee**, 6 miles west of the village, at the end of the road. Here, the river thunders through a narrow gorge to spectacular effect. There are numerous walks from here along the river, or for the more adventurous, the famous **Lairig Ghru**, which runs through the Cairngorms to Aviemore, see page 104. Between the Linn of Dee and the tiny settlement of **Inverey**, a mile to the east, there's a very basic youth hostel (open early May to end September), which has no showers and no phone, so book through **Braemar youth hostel**, see page 94. The postbus from Ballater post office (Route 072) leaves at 0845 (Monday to Saturday) for Linn of Dee via Glenshee and the Inverey hostel.

Walks in Deeside

Ballater and Braemar are ideal bases for walking in the surrounding Grampian Mountains, and if you feel like 'bagging a Munro' (ie climbing a mountain over 3000 ft), there are some close at hand. All of this area, that's also reportedly home to 25% of Britain's endangered species, is included in the new **Cairngorms National Park** ⓘ *www.cairngorm.co.uk*, which opened in 2003. This is the largest national park in Britain, covering a vast 4500 sq km, from Aboyne in the east to Dalwhinnie in the west, and from Blair Atholl north to Grantown-on-Spey.

Lochnagar → *OS Landranger No 44.*

The best walk in the area is to the summit of Lochnagar (3786 ft), made famous by Prince Charles in the book he wrote for his brothers when young, *The Old Man of Lochnagar*. The noble and mysterious mountain dominates the **Royal Forest of Balmoral** and takes its name from a small loch at its foot (it's also known as the White Mounth). This fine granite mass is approached from the car park by the Rangers' Visitor Centre at Spittal of Glen Muick. The path to the top is well trodden and well marked, though steep as you near the summit. It's 10 miles there and back, so allow a full day for the climb. You'll need to be properly equipped and take a map.

Cambus o' May and Morrone → *OS Landranger No 43.*

An easier walk is to Cambus o' May, on the river, about 4 miles east of Ballater. It's a great spot for a picnic, or to swim in the river, or to enjoy a stroll along the riverbank. A good walk from Braemar is to the summit of Morrone (2818 ft), the mountain to the southwest. The walk takes about four hours in total.

Glen Tanar to Glen Esk → *OS Landranger No 44.*

Another good climb is the route up **Mount Keen** (3077 ft), the most easterly Munro, which lies between Deeside and Glen Esk, the loveliest of the Angus glens. Again, you should allow a whole day for this expedition. It can be approached from the visitor centre in Glen Tanar, at the end of the little road that runs southwest off the B976, across the river from Aboyne. You can climb to the summit and return by the same route but, if your party has two cars, it is well worth walking over to Glen Esk, 14 miles away. Drive around to the Invermark car park at the head of Glen Esk and park your car there. From Glen Tanar follow the old drove road which at times runs with the Mounth road. Skirting the **Home Farm** with its Arboretum and its dammed lake, the fairly flat track winds along Glen Tanar through the forest for about 4 miles. Then comes the Halfway Hut, used for rest by former shooting parties. You pass shooting butts en route. The next stretch is through open country with the **Clachan Yell** (626 ft) on the left.

The walk proper then begins to take shape. Cross the stone bridge of **Etnach**, and then the path begins to lead up to the **Shiel of Glentanar**. The second bridge forks left and the track heads for the summit. The rough path continues along a ridge, the shoulder of Mount Keen. From the summit with its stone marker, **Dinnet**, see page 91, and its two lakes are visible to the north, and the River Esk glints its way down the valley to the south. Watch out for adders around here. On the descent, you'll pass the

 Queen's Well, used by Queen Victoria when she and her party went down to Fettercairn posing as a wedding party. The well is decorated with a graceful granite crown which was erected in 1861. The royal party covered much of the climb on hill ponies. The stone arch at Fettercairn commemorates this visit.

Sleeping

Banchory *p91*
There are some very fine places to stay in and around Banchory.
A Banchory Lodge Hotel, T01330-822625, www.banchorylodgehotel.co.uk. The roaring open fires, 4-poster beds and views over the River Feugh and Dee whilst fine dining (ΨΨΨ-ΨΨ) on locally sourced beef and salmon make this one of Deeside's rewarding escapes.
A Raemoir House Hotel, 3 miles north of town on the A980, T01330-824884, www.raemoir.com. This fabulous, Georgian country mansion hotel is set in acres of stunning wood and parkland. Boasting award-winning cuisine including its specially reared Tamworth pork, the Raemoir is a popular lunch stop (ΨΨ) whilst, for £35 per head, guests are treated to a 4-course formal dinner (ΨΨΨ).
B Tor-na-Coille Hotel, outside town on the Inchmarlo Rd, T01330-822242, www.tornacoille.com. This tastefully furnished 23-bedroom Victorian country house hotel is set in lovely grounds and boasts a considerable reputation for its modern Scottish cooking (ΨΨΨ-ΨΨ).
D The Old West Manse, 71 Station Rd, T01330-822202. Well-appointed, friendly, 3-bedroom guesthouse where golf, or even a babysitting service, can be arranged for guests.
E June Little, 73 High St, T01330-824666. An excellent choice.

Self-catering
Mill of Tilquhillie, Banchory, T01330-844616. £245-£495 per week. A charming self-catering option. A 2-bedroom, granite stone, former watermill complete with wood-burning stove and wildlife pond nearby. Sleeps 4.

Camping
Silver Ladies Caravan Park, Strachan, just outside Banchory, T01330-822800.

Ballater and Balmoral *p91*
There's plenty of accommodation in Ballater, from expensive hotels to reasonable B&Bs.
A Balgonie Country House Hotel, on the western outskirts of town, off the A93 T/F01339-755482. 9 rooms, open Feb-Dec. Friendly and comfortable country house hotel with a very good restaurant (ΨΨΨ).
A-B Hilton Craigendarroch, Braemar Rd, T01339-755858, www.hilton.com. Victorian country house converted into a modern resort hotel with full leisure and sports facilities. Lovely restaurants (ΨΨΨ).
B Darroch Learg Hotel, ½ mile from town, off the A93 heading west to Braemar, T01339-755443, www.darrochlearg.co.uk. 18 rooms, open Feb-Dec. Pick of the bunch. Friendly country house hotel with fine views and a reputation for superb food (ΨΨΨ) and an excellent wine list.
B-C The Green Inn, Ballater town centre T/F01339-755701. Renowned for its cuisine but there are also 3 well-appointed bedrooms upstairs.
C Deeside Hotel, set back from the A93 heading out of town towards Braemar, T01339-755420, www.deesidehotel.co.uk. Friendly, good value and good food (ΨΨ).
C Glen Lui Hotel, Invercauld Rd, T01339-755402, www.glen-lui-hotel.co.uk. 19 rooms. With new owners, this comfortable hotel offers fine food (ΨΨ-Ψ) and views over the golf course to Lochnagar.
C Inverdeen House, 11 Bridge Sq, T01339-755759, www.inverdeen.com. Among the many B&Bs, this one is recommended. French, German and Polish spoken, great breakfasts, no smoking.

Camping
Anderson Road Caravan Park, T01339-755727, Apr-Oct.

Self-catering
Royal Deeside Holiday Cottages, Ballater, T/F01339-885341. £290-£430 per week. Managed by the Dinnet Estate, there are 8 traditional stone cottages in peaceful surroundings. Sleep 4-8.

Braemar *p92*
Accommodation is hard to find before and during the Braemar Gathering, but at other times of the year there's plenty to choose from including many B&Bs and guesthouses.
A-F Braemar Lodge Hotel, on the outskirts of the village on the road south to Glenshee and Blairgowrie, T01339-741627, www.braemarlodge.co.uk. A lovely hotel with the option of **log-cabin** (**D**) and **bunkhouse** accommodation (**F**) in the hotel grounds.
D Callater Lodge Hotel, Glenshee Rd, T01339-741275, www.hotel-braemar.co.uk. Charming and comfortable guesthouse with self-catering, **chalet-style option** (£260 per week) in the grounds. Sleeps 2.
D Clunie Lodge, Cluniebank Rd, T01339-741330. 5 rooms, 3 en suite. Good-value guesthouse with fine views.
D Schiehallion House, Glenshee Rd, T01339-741679. Open Jan-Oct. 6 rooms, 5 en suite. Traditional Highland welcome in this friendly guesthouse.
F Braemar Lodge Bunkhouse, 6 Glenshee Rd, T01339-741627, www.braemarlodge.co.uk. Another good choice.
F Rucksacks, 15 Mar Rd, T01339-741517. A cheap and friendly bunkhouse complete with sauna that's popular with hikers and rents out mountain bikes.
F SYHA Youth Hostel, Corrie Feragie on Glenshee Rd, T01339-741659. Open all year.

Camping
Invercauld Caravan Site, Glenshee Rd, T01339-741373. Open Dec-Oct.

Eating

Banchory *p91*
TTT-TT The Milton Restaurant, opposite the gates of Drum Castle, T01330-844566. With BBQs, hearty breakfasts and delights such as Cruden Bay crab bisque and loin of venison on its dinner menu this restaurant has a growing reputation in the northeast of Scotland; guests even fly in by helicopter.
TT-T Burnett Arms Hotel, High St, T01330-824944. Aside from the hotels listed above, this former coaching inn is one of the better eateries in Banchory.
T The Shieling Coffee Shop, 18 Dee St, T01330-823278. Mon-Sat 0900-1730. A terrific stop for a traditional tea and scone.

Ballater and Balmoral *p91*
See also Sleeping, above.
TTT The Green Inn, on the green in the town centre, T/F01339-755701. You'll find many a local dining in what has become one of the best restaurants for lunch or dinner in the area. It's not the cheapest option but the food is terrific. Recommended.
TT Inver, Crathie, T01339-742345. An 18th-century inn with a roaring fire and views over the Balmoral Estate which serves good, honest food. Also accommodation (**B**).
TT La Mangiatoia, Bridge Sq, T/F01339-755999. Serves primarily Italian fare in its family-friendly restaurant.

Braemar *p92*
A quiet town, Braemar isn't teeming with café-bars and restaurants.
TTT-TT Braemar Lodge, see Sleeping, above. Serves daily lunches and dinners with the dinner menu including staples such as Aberdeen Angus beef and game.
TT-T The Gathering Place, Invercauld Rd, T01339-741234. Tue-Sun 1830-2030. Tucked beside **Braemar Mountain Sports** and close to the bank, this lovely, cosy restaurant boasts fine Scottish cuisine with a Mediterranean twist, a roaring open fire and walls adorned with Scottish artworks. Recommended.

Activities and tours

Deeside *p96*
For ski and telemark rental and advice on mountain conditions, pop into **Braemar Mountain Sports**, 5 Invercauld Rd, Braemar, T013397-41242.
Adventure Scotland, T0870-2402676, www.adventure-scotland.com, offers a wide range of adventure activities, including whitewater rafting, mountain biking, skiing and hiking.
Fishing Feb-Sep there are many places to fish on the River Dee for salmon. For a full reference of locations and operators visit www.fishdee.co.uk, or T01573-470612, to request a booklet.
Glen Tanar Equestrian Centre, south of Aboyne, in Glen Tanar (see Walks, page 93), T01339-886448, offers riding in the forests and hills.

❂ Festivals and events

Deeside *p96*
Sep Braemar Games are held on the first Sat in Sep. Booking is highly recommended. For details visit the comprehensive website, www.braemargathering.org, or contact the Secretary, BRHS, Coilacreich, Ballater, AB35 5UH, T01339-755377.

Transport

Deeside *p96*
Bus From Aberdeen, all the main tourist attractions in Deeside can be reached by bus. To reach **Balmoral** by bus from Aberdeen catch the one destined for **Braemar**. Contact Bluebird Northern, T01224-212266, or Traveline, T0870-6082608, for information.

If you wish to explore Deeside along a less popular route (though even in the summer, crowds are never great) take the B976 along the south bank of the River Dee. Fortunately, the Heather Hopper, operated by Stagecoach Bluebird (T01343-544222) and D&E Coaches (T01463-222444), provides the link between the many rural outposts of Deeside and key Speyside destinations (see www.cairngorms.co.uk). From Jul-Sep the morning 501 bus runs (Mon-Sat) from **Ballater** via **Strathdon** and **Tomintoul** to **Grantown**. The afternoon bus continues on to **Dulnain Bridge**, **Carrbridge** and **Inverness**. Alternatively, for passengers travelling between **Aberdeen** and **Perth** the 502 bus (Jul-Sep, Mon-Sat only) leaves **Strathdon** at 1035 and travels via **Ballater**, **Crathie**, **Braemar** and **Cairnwell** to **Pitlochry**.

The Don Valley → *Colour map 4, A4-5.*

North of Royal Deeside is the lesser-known valley of the Don, Aberdeen's second river and regarded by enthusiasts as one of the finest trout-fishing rivers in Europe. This relatively little-visited corner of the northeast is a historian's and archaeologist's dream, littered with medieval castles, Pictish stone circles and Iron Age hillforts. A quarter of all Britain's stone circles can be found here (if you look hard enough). Local tourist offices have free leaflets on the region's archaeological sites, with background information and details of how to find them. The main sites are included in the tourist board's 'Stone Circle Trail'. There's also a well-signposted 'Castle Trail', which includes the area's main castles. One of these castles, Corgarff, stands at the southern end of the notoriously steep Lecht Road, which runs from Cock Bridge to Tomintoul. This area, which will test the mettle of even the fittest cyclist, is known as the Lecht and incorporates Scotland's smallesr ski centre. ▸▸ *For Sleeping, Eating and other listings, see page 99.*

Inverurie and around → *Colour map 4, A5.*

The solid farming town of Inverurie is 17 miles northwest of Aberdeen on the A96 to Inverness. It makes a useful base for visiting the numerous castles and ancient relics dotted around the area. The **Thainstone Mart**, south of town just off the A96, is one of the largest livestock markets in the country, and interesting if you like that sort of thing. It's held Monday, Wednesday and Friday around 1000. There's a **TIC** ⓘ *18 High St, T01467-625800, Apr-Sep 0900-1700.*

About 6 miles southwest of Inverurie, off the B993 (turn first left after the village of Kemnay), is the magnificent **Castle Fraser** ⓘ *T01330-833463, castle, shop and tea-room, Apr-June and Sep Fri-Tue 1200-1700, Jul-Aug daily 1100-1700; garden and grounds all year daily 0800 till dusk, castle, garden and grounds £8 concession £5.* Built in 1575 by the Sixth Earl of Mar, it is similar in style to Crathes and Craigievar. The interior was remodelled in 1838 and many of the furnishings date from that period. There's a walled garden and trails through the estate. A 'Woodland Secrets' area has recently been created where children can play amongst wooden sculptures, there's a bamboo snake, tepees and even a tree-house.

▲ Close by, and signed off the B993, is the 4000-year-old **Easter Aquhorthies Stone Circle**. This archaeological site is overshadowed by Bennachie (1732 ft), by far the best hill in the area and thought to be the site of Mons Graupius, in 83 AD, when the Romans defeated the Picts. It's a straightforward two-hour walk to the summit and the views from the top are great. There are various trails, though the most commonly used route starts from the **Bennachie Centre** ⓘ *1 mile beyond Chapel of Garioch, signposted off the A96 at Pitcaple, 5 miles northwest of Inverurie, T01467-681470, Apr-Oct Tue-Sun 1030-1700, Nov-Mar Wed-Sun 1000-1600*. Near here is the **Maiden Stone**, a 10-ft-high Pictish gravestone with relief carvings showing what looks like an elephant, along with other creatures not normally found around these parts.

A few miles west of the turn-off to Chapel of Garioch, the B9002 heads west off the A96 to the village of Oyne, site of the **Archaeolink Prehistory Park** ⓘ *T01464-851500, www.archaeolink.co.uk, Mar-Oct daily 1000-1700, Nov-Feb 1000-1600 (last entry 1500), £5, concession £4.50, children £3.40*. In just one day this fantastic, state-of-the-art interpretative centre takes you on a 10,000-year journey back in time. It's a great introduction to the numerous ancient sites in the area and explains why the stone circles were built and what the various carved symbols mean. The 40-acre park includes various interesting features such as a reconstructed Iron Age farm, Stone Age settlement and Roman camp, as well as a hilltop Iron Age fort. The Archeodrome features audio-visual presentations which bring to life the ancient history of the area. There are even prehistoric craft workshops – and thankfully, a modern tea-room!

Near the village of Daviot, north of the A96 off the B9001 from Inverurie, or via the A920 west of Oldmeldrum, is the **Loanhead of Daviot Stone Circle**. This impressive 6000-year-old site is 500 yards from the village and consists of two stone circles, the smaller of which encloses a cremation cemetery dating from 1500 BC. Thirteen miles north of Inverurie is **Fyvie Castle** ⓘ *off the A947 between Oldmeldrum and Turriff, T01651-891266, (NTS) Apr-Jun and Sep Fri-Tue 1200-1700, Jul and Aug daily 1100-1730, grounds open all year daily 0930-dusk, £7, concessions/children £5.25*. This grandest of Scottish baronial piles is a major feature on the 'Castle Trail'. The oldest part of the castle dates from the 13th century, although the extravagantly opulent interior is mostly Edwardian. Each of the castle's five towers is named after one of the five families who have had the pleasure of living here over the centuries. The landscaped grounds and Fuyvie Loch are also worth exploring and even the tearoom is great.

Alford → *Colour map 4, A5.*

The main tourist centre on Donside is the little country town of Alford (pronounced 'Ah-ford'), 25 miles west of Aberdeen. The principal point of interest in town is the **Grampian Transport Museum** ⓘ *T01975-562292, end Mar-end Oct daily 1000-1700, £5.20, £4.40 concessions, £2.60 children*, which features a comprehensive and fascinating display of transport history, with collections of cars, buses, trams, steam engines and some more unusual exhibits. Almost next door is the terminus for the **Alford Valley Railway** ⓘ *T07879-293934, Apr-May and Sep weekends only, 30-min service 1330-1630; Jun, Jul, Aug daily 1030-1630*. Pulled along a narrow-gauge railway line between Haughton park and back (one hour) this family-orientated attraction run by train enthusiasts boasts restored diesel locomotives, a 50-seat 'Silver Jubilee' carriage and a restored 1895 former Aberdeen tram car; double check timetable and prices. The railway station is also where you'll find the **TIC** ⓘ *T01975-562052, daily Apr-Sep*. Also in town is the **Alford Heritage Centre** ⓘ *Mart Rd, T01975-562906, Apr-Oct Mon-Sat 1000-1700, Sun 1300-1700, £3.50, concession £1*, a charitable organization run by volunteers with a large display of the area's agricultural past and bygone era including a school-room, farmhouse and shoemakers. Alford is close to Lecht Ski Centre, see page 102, but you can ski here year round on the local dry ski slope at **Alford Ski Centre** ⓘ *Greystone Rd, T01975-563024*. There's also snowboarding, instruction and equipment hire.

Craigievar Castle

ⓘ *T01339-883635, castle open mid-Apr to 30 Sep Fri-Tue 1200-1730 (last admission 1645); grounds open all year daily 0930-dusk, £10, £7 concession.*

Six miles south of Alford is one of the northeast's most gorgeous castles, the classic tower house of Craigievar, with its impressive turrets, balustrades and cupolas. The castle remains much as it was when it was built in 1626 by wealthy local merchant, William Forbes. Unfortunately, though, its popularity led to its deterioration and the NTS now restricts entry to only a small number of visitors at a time to prevent further damage. Restoration work is ongoing on a castle that stands in extensive parkland with a waymarked path.

Kildrummy Castle

ⓘ *T01975-571331, Apr-Sep daily 0930-1830, £2.50, £1.60 concessions, £0.75 children.*

Six miles west of Alford, the A944 meets the A97 which heads north towards the town of Huntly on Speyside, see page 101. A few miles south of the junction stand the extensive and impressive ruins of Kildrummy Castle, Scotland's most complete 13th-century castle. Amongst the most infamous events in the castle's long and bloody history was the treacherous betrayal of Robert the Bruce's family to the English during the Wars of Independence. It was the seat of the Earls of Mar and used as an HQ for the Jacobite rebellion of 1715, after which the Sixth Earl of Mar ('Bobbing John') fled to exile in France and the castle fell into ruin. The Kildrummy Castle Gardens (opening times as castle, above) are also worth a visit.

Strathdon and Corgarff Castle

The tiny village of Strathdon, 10 miles southwest of Kildrummy, is famous for the **Lonach Highland Gathering**. Held on the third Saturday in August, it has a healthy blast of authenticity in comparison to the more glitzy affair in Braemar on Deeside. The Scottish comedian, Billy Connolly owns a house in the area.

Five miles west of Strathdon the A944 meets the A939 Ballater–Tomintoul road. A few miles beyond the junction is the austere **Corgarff Castle** ⓘ *Apr-Sep daily 0930-1830, Oct-Mar Sat-Sun 0930-1630, £3.50*, a 16th-century tower house, later turned into a garrison post, with an eventful and gruesome history. Here Margaret Forbes and her family were burned alive by the Gordons in 1571 during the bitter feud between the two families. In the wake of the ill-fated 1745 rebellion the government remodelled the castle, building a star-shaped defensive wall, and garrisoned 60 men to maintain order and communications in this part of the Highlands. Corgarff continued in use into the 19th century when English Redcoats were stationed here in order to try and prevent whisky smuggling.

Tomintoul → *Colour map 4, A4. Altitude: 1600 ft.*

Beside Corgarff is the hamlet of **Cock Bridge**, standing at the end of one the most beautiful and notorious stretches of road in the country. In winter, the Tomintoul to Cock Bridge road is almost always the first road in Scotland to be blocked by snow (you have been warned!). From Cock Bridge the A939 rises steeply to the Lecht Pass (2089 ft) before dropping dramatically to Tomintoul, the highest village in the Highlands. Tomintoul is well placed for both the Whisky and Castle Trails. It is also the nearest settlement of any size to the Lecht, one of Scotland's top five ski resorts (see below), and it marks the end of the long-distance Speyside Way (see page 102), so is popular with walkers and skiers. The **TIC** ⓘ *T01807-580285*, is on the village square, as is the **Museum and Visitor Centre** ⓘ *T01807-673701, Apr-Aug Mon-Sat 0930-1200, 1400-1630; Sep Mon-Sat 0930-1200, 1400-1600; Oct Mon-Fri 1400-1600, free*, which has a display of local history, wildlife, landscape and outdoor activities. Ten miles north of Tomintoul on the B9008 is the **Glenlivet Crown Estate** ⓘ *T01807-580283, www.crownestate.co.uk/glenlivet*, with a network of hiking paths and cycle trails, as well as lots of wildlife, including reindeer.

Sleeping

Inverurie and around *p96*

A-B Pittodrie House Hotel, near Chapel of Garioch, T01467-681444, www.macdonaldhotels.co.uk. 27 rooms. This magnificent baronial mansion, originally belonged to the Earls of Mar. The 2000-acre estate was granted to them by Robert the Bruce for their loyalty at the Battle of Bannockburn. The opulent surroundings are matched by superb cuisine. After dinner, take your dram down to the billiard room and relax in style.

A-B Thainstone House Hotel, to the south of Inverurie off the A96, T01467-621643. A luxurious country mansion offering excellent cuisine and leisure facilities.

D Breaslann Guest House, Old Chapel Rd, T01467-621608. One of a decent selection.

D Fridayhill, Kinmuck, Inverurie, T01651-882252. A small, comfortable B&B.

Alford *p97*

B-C Carriages Hotel, Commercial Rd, Insch, T01464-820604. Comfortable with good food (ΨΨ).

C-D Frog Marsh, Mossat, Alford, T01975-571355, www.frogmarsh.com. Open year-round. A well-appointed, very friendly guesthouse that has a fine reputation for its delicious breakfasts and evening meals. The owners also offer their delightful **Meadowsweet Cottage** as a self-catering option (£375). Recommended.

D Forbes Arms Hotel, 1 mile west of town, Bridge of Alford, T01975-562108. Comfortable B&B with dinner option and good bar food (ΨΨ-Ψ).

Kildrummy Castle *p98*

L Kildrummy Castle Hotel, T01975-571288, www.kildrummycastlehotel.co.uk. A baronial country mansion spectacularly set in beautiful grounds across the river from the 13th-century castle ruins. 16 superbly appointed bedrooms, with 4-poster beds in the master bedrooms. In the restaurant you'll find a mouth-watering menu (ΨΨΨ-ΨΨ).

Corgarff Castle *p98*

D-F Allargue Arms Hotel, by Corgarff, T01975-651410. Includes both B&B and bunkhouse accommodation.

F Jenny's Bothy, just before the castle, turn onto an old military road for about 1 mile, T01975-651449. This basic but wonderfully remote bunkhouse is open all year.

Tomintoul *p98*

C Glenavon Hotel, main square, T01807-580218. There are a few hotels around the main square, the best of which is this family-run hotel. It's also where to find hearty bar meals and a real ale. Popular with après-skiers, tired walkers and locals.

D Livet House, Main St, T01807-580205. A pleasant B&B that's handy for the pub and outdoor pursuits alike!

F SYHA Hostel, Main St, T0870-0041152. Apr-end Sep.

Transport

The Don Valley *p96*

Bus Travelling around the Don Valley without your own transport is not easy. There are regular trains and buses to **Inverurie** from **Aberdeen** and **Inverness**. Bluebird Northern, T01224-212266, No 220 runs regularly every day from **Aberdeen** to **Alford** (1¼ hrs). Bus No 219 runs from **Alford** to **Strathdon Bellabeg** (Mon-Sat) at least once a day. The **Heather Hopper**, operated by Stagecoach Bluebird (T01343-544222) and D&E Coaches (T01463-222444) provides the link between the many rural outposts of Deeside and key Speyside destinations (see www.cairngorms.co.uk). From Jul-Sep (Mon- Sat) the morning 501 bus runs from **Ballater** via **Strathdon** and **Tomintoul** to **Grantown**. The afternoon bus continues on to **Dulnain Bridge**, **Carrbridge** and **Inverness**. Alternatively, for passengers travelling between **Aberdeen and Perth**, the 502 bus (Jul-Sep, Mon-Sat only) leaves **Strathdon** at 1035 and travels via **Ballater**, **Crathie**, **Braemar** and **Cairnwell** to **Pitlochry**.

There is an 0835 bus from **Dufftown** (Sat only) to **Tomintoul** arriving 0915 and returning to Dufftown at 0958. Call Roberts of Rothiemay, T01466-711213. From Tomintoul, Central Coaches (Smith's) run a bus to **Keith** (Tue only) and **Elgin** (Thu only). Hayf buses of Huntly run a **Tomintoul** to **Aberlour** service (Mon-Fri only).

Speyside

→ Colour map 2, C3-4.

The River Spey is Scotland's second longest river, rising in the hills above Loch Laggan and making its way northeast to where it debouches at Spey Bay, on the Moray Coast. Speyside is one of Scotland's loveliest valleys and is synonymous with two of Scotland's greatest products, salmon and whisky. The upper part, Strathspey, is equally famous for its hiking, skiing and watersports. It is covered in the Highlands chapter. This section covers the lower part of the valley and comprises the famous Malt Whisky Trail. There are more malt whisky distilleries in this small area than in any other part of the country, including some famous brands such as Glenlivet and Glenfiddich. However, it's not all whisky in these parts: there's also some fine walking along the Speyside Way which runs from Spey Bay south to Tomintoul. ▸▸ *For Sleeping, Eating and other listings, see pages 103-104.*

Dufftown and around

→ Colour map 2, C4.

A good place to start your whisky tour is Dufftown, founded in 1817 by James Duff, the fourth Earl of Fife, and the self-proclaimed 'Malt Whisky Capital of the World'. There's more than a grain of truth in that assertion, for there are no fewer than seven working distilleries here. This is indeed the town that was built on seven stills.

Just outside of town, on the A941 to Craigellachie, is the **Glenfiddich Distillery**, the town's most famous distillery and one of the best known of all malt whiskies, see box, page 101. Behind the distillery are the 13th-century ruins of **Balvenie Castle** ⓘ *T01340-820121, www.historic-scotland.gov.uk, Apr-Sep Sat-Wed 0930-1630 (closed Thu and Fri), £3, concession £2.30, children £1.30*, built by Alexander 'Black' Comyn, then added to in the 15th and 16th centuries, and visited by Mary, Queen of Scots in 1562. Four miles north of Dufftown, at the junction of the A941 and A95, is the little village of Craigellachie, site of the Speyside Cooperage, see box, page 101, and where you can see Thomas Telford's beautiful bridge over the River Spey.

The nearby village of **Aberlour** is the home of the famous **Walkers Shortbread** ⓘ *T01340-871555*. Also here is the expensive but superb **Aberlour Distillery** ⓘ *T01340-881249, www.aberlour.com, tours at 1030 and 1400 Apr-Nov daily; Jan-Mar Mon-Fri 1000-1600, £7.50*. Close by and in the Easter Elchies Estate is the exclusive **Macallan Distillery** ⓘ *T01340-872280, www.themacallan.com, tours every hour Mar-Oct Mon-Sat 0930-1630, Nov-Easter Mon-Fri 1100-1500, booking essential, free (incredibly)*. Only accompanied children over the age of 8 are permitted on the guided tours.

About 8 miles southwest of Craigellachie, on the A95 to Grantown-on-Spey, is the 'pearl of the north' **Ballindalloch Castle** ⓘ *T01807-500205, Easter-end Sep Sun-Fri 1000-1700, £7 entry, concessions £6, children £3.50*, a mile west of the village of **Marypark**. The castle is one of the loveliest in the northeast and has been lived in continuously by its original family, the Macpherson-Grants, since 1546. It houses a fine collection of Spanish paintings and the extensive grounds are home to the famous Aberdeen-Angus herd of cattle, which have been bred here since 1860. Also in Ballindalloch is the **Glenfarclas Distillery** ⓘ *T01807-500257, www.glenfarclas.co.uk, tours Apr-Sep Mon-Fri 1000-1700, Jul-Sep Mon-Sat 1000-1600, Oct-Mar Mon-Fri 1000-1600, £3.50, children free*, which, despite the relatively high entrance fee, is a worthwhile experience.

Dufftown TIC ⓘ *clock tower, centre of the main square, T01340-820501, Apr-Oct*, has maps and information on the Whisky Trail.

Whisky-a-go-go

Speyside is Scotland's most prolific whisky-producing region and the Malt Whisky Trail is a well-signposted 70-mile tour around seven of the most famous distilleries, plus the Speyside Cooperage. Most of the distilleries offer guided tours, and most (with the exception of Glenfiddich) charge an entry fee, which can then be discounted, in full or in part, from the cost of a bottle of whisky in the distillery shop. Tours also include a free dram. Those listed below are the most interesting. See also www.maltwhiskytrail.com.

Strathisla, *Keith, T01542-783044. Apr-Nov Mon-Sat 0930-1600, Sun 1200-1600. Adults £5, under 18s free*, is the oldest working distillery in the Highlands (1786) and perhaps the most atmospheric, in a beautiful setting on the River Isla. This is a relatively rare malt, which is also used in the better-known Chivas Regal blend.

Speyside Cooperage, *T01340-871108, all year Mon-Fri 0930-1600, £3.10, concessions £2.50, children £1.80*, is near Craigellachie, 4 miles north of Dufftown. You can watch the oak casks for whisky being made.

Cardhu, *T01340-872555, Mar-Jun and Oct-Nov Mon-Fri 0930-1630, Jul-Sep Mon-Sat 0930-1630, Sun 1100-1600, Dec-Feb Mon-Fri 1100-1500, £4*, is 7 miles west of Craigellachie, at Knockando on the B9102. This lovely little distillery is the only malt distillery pioneered by a woman. Their fine malt is one of many used in the famous Johnnie Walker blend.

Glen Grant, *T01340-832118, Apr-Nov Mon-Sat 0930-1600, Sun 1200-1600, free*, is in Rothes, on the A941 to Elgin. Stroll through the garden to the heather-thatched dram pavilion.

Glenfiddich, *T01340-820373, www.glenfiddich.com, Apr-Oct Mon-Sat 0930-1630 and Sun 1200-1630, Nov-Mar Mon-Fri 0930-1630, original tour free, connoisseurs' tour £15, including a tutored nosing*, is just north of Dufftown, on the A941. Probably the best known of all the malts and the most professionally run operation. It's the only distillery where you can see the whisky being bottled on the premises, and the only major distillery that's free, including the obligatory dram. It's also one of few Scotch whisky companies still to be in the hands of its founding family.

Glenlivet, *T01340-821720, www.theglenlivet.com, Apr-3 Nov Mon-Sat 0930-1600, Sun 1200-1600, free*, is 10 miles north of Tomintoul on the B9008. This was an illicit whisky until it was licensed in 1824. The distillery was later founded in 1858 and this malt has gone on to become one of the world's favourites.

Huntly and around → *Colour map 2, C5.*

Ten miles east of Dufftown is the pleasant and prosperous-looking little town of Huntly. Close to the Whisky Trail and on the main Aberdeen to Inverness train route, it makes a convenient base from which to explore this area. The town also boasts a lovely little castle all of its own. The 16th-century **Huntly Castle** ⓘ *T01466-793191, Apr-Sep daily 0930-1830, Oct-Mar Sat-Wed 0930-1630, £3.30, £2.50 concession, children £1.30*, stands in a beautiful setting on the banks of the River Deveron, on the northern edge of town. It was built by the powerful Gordon family and is notable for its fine heraldic sculpture and inscribed stone friezes, particularly over the main door. Near the castle is the **Nordic Ski Centre** ⓘ *T01466-794428*, the only year-round cross-country ski centre in the UK. The centre also hires out ski equipment and mountain bikes. **Huntly TIC** ⓘ *T01466-792255, Apr-Oct.*

Seven miles south of town, near the village of Kennethmont, is **Leith Hall** ⓘ *T01464-831216, Easter and May-Sep daily 1200-1700, garden and grounds open all year, £8, concession £5, children £1.90*, an unprepossessing mid-17th-century mansion house. The house contains the personal possessions of successive Leith lairds, most of whom saw military service overseas, but more interesting are the extensive grounds which include a 6-acre garden, 18th-century stables and ice house, two ponds, a bird observation hide and countryside walks.

The Tap o' Noth walk → *Colour map 4, A5. OS Landranger No 37.*

Eight miles south of Huntly on the A97 is the village of Rhynie, where you turn off for one of the best walks in the northeast. The Tap o' Noth (1851 ft) dominates this part of rural Aberdeenshire and the panoramic views from the top make it a worthwhile climb. It's also a fairly easy walk to the conical summit, where there's a vitrified fort. The total distance is of this walk is 3 miles. Allow at least two hours there and back.

Start the walk from the car park at **Scurdargue**, a few miles west of Rhynie, off the A941. Leave the car park and head straight up the track to a gate. Go through the gate and cross some rough pasture into woodland. At the northwest corner of the wood, go through another gate and turn left onto a track. Follow this grassy track uphill beside a fence until you see another area of forestry ahead, with rough pastureland on the right. Follow the faint track across the pasture to the broad track which then climbs up the Tap's western slopes. Follow this all the way to the top, up the tight zigzag on the southern flank and through the eastern entry to the hillfort, into a large enclosure. On the way back down look out for a subsidiary path under the fort's western ramparts. This path descends steeply to the left, south of the main track. It then joins the main track and you can retrace your steps back to the car park.

The Speyside Way → *www.moray.gov.uk.*

The Speyside Way follows the River Spey from its mouth at Spey Bay inland as far as Ballindalloch, then crosses high moorland to Tomintoul and Aviemore. Currently, there is a public consultation on plans to extend the route southwards from Aviemore to Newtonmore. The 84-mile route takes five to seven days to complete. Much of it is on an old railway line and passes close to several small villages, meaning that it can easily be broken down into shorter walks. It also passes several distilleries along the way.

Rucksack Reader produce a guide to the Speyside Way and there is also a very good Harvey map of the route (£9.95) available from TICs, good bookshops and **Moray Council Ranger Service** ⓘ *Boat of Fiddich, Craigellachie, T01340-881266.*

Lecht Ski Centre → *Colour map 4, A5.*

ⓘ *Day ticket £22 adults, £11.25 for children; half-day ticket £17 and £8.50 children. There's ski school and equipment hire (adult ski £15.75, snowboard £17) and tubing hire (for £8 per hr scoot down the piste on a super-fast tyre-like sledge!) at the base station, T01975-651440, www.lecht.co.uk; phone or check website for latest weather conditions.* The Lecht is a ski resort for all seasons. It offers dry-slope skiing throughout the year and its snowmaking facilities mean that the winter season can be extended beyond January and March. The Lecht's gentler slopes make it ideal for beginners and intermediates and the emphasis is on family skiing. There's a snowboard fun park with half pipe, log slide, gap jump and table top. However, there are also more difficult runs for the more experienced skier, and extensive off-piste skiing. In addition, there's a summer activity area with quad bikes and fun-karts.

It's believed that the name, Tap o' Noth, derives from the Gaelic taip a'nochd, *which translates as 'look-out top'. But there's also a local legend that the hill's giant, Jack o'Noth, stole the sweetheart of his neighbour, Jack o'Bennachie. In retaliation, the cuckolded neighbour hurled a huge boulder and flattened Jack on his own hilltop.*

Sleeping

Dufftown and around *p100*

A Craigellachie Hotel, Craigellachie, T01340-881204, www.craigellachie.com. 25 en suite rooms are to be found in this superb country hotel which oozes style and comfort and a commendable Ben Aigen restaurant (¥¥¥).

B Minmore House Hotel, 10 miles southwest of Dufftown, in the village of Glenlivet, T01807-590378, www.minmorehousehotel.com. May-end Jan. Right beside the distillery this is the former home of the owner. Whether scoffing on the delicious afternoon tea (¥¥) or tucking into award-winning lunch and dinner (¥¥¥) it's a delight to eat here. Shooting and fishing can also be arranged – or choose from a selection of over 100 malt whiskies. Recommended.

C-D Highlander Inn, on Victoria St, Craigellachie, T/F01340-881446. Modest accommodation with a reputation for serving up hearty bar meals (¥¥).

D Tannoch Brae, Dufftown, T01340-820541, www.tannochbrae.co.uk. 6 en suite rooms in a very comfortable guesthouse with a reputation for fine food (¥¥).

D-E Mrs Souter's B&B, 43 Fife St. Provides a warm welcome, fine hospitality and an excellent breakfast.

Self-catering

Pitchroy Cottage, Ballindalloch Castle Estate, T01807-500205. £300-£600 per week. Captain WE Jones, the creator of Biggles, wrote his novel in this delightful estate cottage. Aside from the open fire and peacefulness, guests can enjoy many activities on the estate including stalking, fishing and golf (£10 day ticket). The estate also has several other self-catering options. Visit www.ballindallochcastle.co.uk

Huntly and around *p101*

C The Castle Hotel, T01466-792696, www.castlehotel.uk.com. Standing in extensive private grounds, this former home of the Duke of Gordon is now an impressive hotel with tastefully furnished rooms complemented by thoughtfully prepared food from the restaurant (¥¥¥-¥¥).

D-E Greenmount Guesthouse, 43 Gordon St, T01340-792482. Welcoming B&B in this modest, former 1854 townhouse.

E New Marnoch, 48 King St, T01340-792018. Complement their hospitable B&B with their **Rose Cottage** self-catering option (£230-350 per week; sleeps 4).

E Strathlene, MacDonald St, T01340-792664. Well located near town centre, friendly and comfortable B&B in traditional granite house.

Eating

Dufftown and around *p100*

In addition to the restaurants in the hotels, it's worthwhile considering the following:

¥¥¥-¥¥ La Faisandarie, Dufftown, T01340-821273. Has a good reputation, book first.

¥¥ A Taste of Speyside, Balvenie St, Dufftown, T01340-820860. A good choice.

¥¥-¥ The Mash Tun, 7 Broomfield Sq, Aberlour, T01340-881771. Best known for its superb real ales, but also serves pretty fine pub grub. Sitting on the banks of the Spey with play ground to keep the saucepan lids entertained.

Bars and clubs

Huntly and around *p101*

Auld Pit, Bogie St, Huntly. Lively pub with some great folk music nights.

Entertainment

Dufftown and around *p100*

Commercial Hotel, Church St, T01340-820313, has ceilidhs during the summer.

Festivals and events

Speyside *p100*

May Spirit of Speyside Whisky Festival, a celebration of 'the water of life' with various whisky-related events taking place throughout the region. For details T01343-542666 or visit www.spiritofspeyside.com.

Transport

Speyside *p100*

Bus Bluebird Buses, T01224-212266, run a daily service from **Elgin** (No 336). There's also a service (Nos 360 and 361) which connects **Dufftown** with **Keith** and **Aberlour**

(Mon-Fri). The No 230 connects Dufftown with Huntly (Mon-Sat). For details call **Bluebird and WW Smith**, T01542-882113.

Train A restored old train powered by a diesel engine runs from Dufftown to Drummuir (5 miles) and on to Keith (10 miles). May-Sep Sat and Sun; Easter, Jun-Aug Fri-Sun £8, concession £6, £4 children. Call ahead (Sat, Tue, Thu only) on T01340- 821181, or visit www.keith-dufftown.org.uk, for the timetable.

Strathspey and the Cairngorms

One of Scotland's busiest tourist areas is Strathspey, the broad valley of the River Spey, Scotland's second longest river, which rises high in the hills above Loch Laggan and flows northeast to its mouth on the Moray Firth. The lower reaches are famous for salmon fishing and whisky and are covered in the Speyside section of this guide (see page 100), while the upper reaches attract outdoor sports enthusiasts in droves. Hemmed in between the mighty Monadhliath Mountains to the north and the magnificent Cairngorms, Britain's second highest range, to the south, this is an area which offers excellent hiking, watersports, mountain biking and above all, winter skiing. In September 2003, the Cairngorms were officially declared a national park, the largest in Britain. » *For Sleeping, Eating and other listings, see pages 107-112.*

Ins and outs

Getting there and around This part of the Highland region is easily accessible by public transport as Aviemore is one of the main hubs, with regular buses and trains to and from Inverness, Perth, Edinburgh and Glasgow. » *For further details, see page 111.*

Tourist information **Aviemore TIC** ⓘ *Grampian Rd, about 400 yds south of the train station, T01479-810930/810363, Sep-Jun Mon-Sat 0900-1700, Jul-Aug Mon-Sat 0900-1900, Sun 0900-1700; phone to check times*, will book accommodation as well as provide free maps and leaflets on local attractions and change foreign currency. The train station, banks, supermarket, restaurants and pretty much everything else are all found along the rather work-a-day Grampian Road. Buses, including those to the ski centre and **Scottish Citylink**'s Inverness/Glasgow/Edinburgh services, stop here too.

Aviemore and around → *Phone code: 01479. Colour map 4, A3. Population: 2500.*

The main focus of the area is the tourist resort of Aviemore, a name synonymous with winter sports. In the 1960s Aviemore was transformed from a sleepy Highland village into, until very recently, a jumble of concrete buildings, tacky gift shops and sprawling coach parks. Today, the creation of the **Macdonald Aviemore Highland Resort** ⓘ *www.aviemorehighlandresort.com*, complete with retail complex, food court, restaurants, golf course, swimming pool and beauty spa has arguably helped Aviemore rectify the worst excesses of its early mistakes. However, it remains a 'tourist honey-pot' with a rash of 'trendy' bars and run-of-the-mill restaurants that are a magnet for the stag, hen and après-ski crowds. That said, gastronomes will not be disappointed (see Sleeping and Eating, pages 107 and 109).

Aside from acting as a base to hire outdoor equipment, collate information or hop on the Strathspey Railway, see page 111) there's little of real interest in Aviemore itself. The real fun and places of interest are in the surrounding mountains, forests, rivers and villages. A great place for kids is the **Cairngorm Reindeer Centre** ⓘ *Glenmore Forest Park, on the road from Coylumbridge, 7 miles from Aviemore, T01479-861228, www.reindeer-company.demon.co.uk, £7, children £4*, where adults and kids can join the reindeer herder on the hillside (1100 and 1430 May to September and 1100 year-round) and even feed the stags and hinds of the glen.

Families will also enjoy the **Cairngorm Sled-dog Adventure Centre** ⓘ *T07767-270526, year-round*, just 3 miles east of Aviemore on the 'ski road' and 500 yards past the Clay Pigeon Shooting range in Rothiemurchus Estate. A range of daily tours are offered including the kennel visit (60 minutes, £8 and £4 child) where visitors can see the 30 huskies being fed and trained and also learn about the fascinating history of dog-sledding. However, for some 'Yukon trail' adrenaline fun, there are also two-day sled-dog 'musher' courses (£245) when you take the reins on a dog-sled buggy (or on snow) and drive your dog team. There are also two- to three-hour trips on the snowy/muddy forest tracks whilst being pulled along on the sled-buggy by the dog teams (£50 adult, £35 child).

From mountaineering in the Cairngorm massif to fishing the Spey, cycling through Rothiemurchus Estate or careering down Cairngorm mountain on a snowboard, this is a land of action.

The **Rothiemurchus visitor centre** ⓘ *Inverdruie, www.rothiemurchus.net, T01479-812345*, is definitely worth a visit. In addition to being packed with information on the walks, nature trails, stalking, fishing, pony trekking and cycling options on the huge estate, the centre boasts a fantastic delicatessen and high- quality arts and crafts shop whilst directly next door await tasty, great-value lunches and dinners (🍴🍴-🍴) in the **Einich** (T01479-812334).

The area around Aviemore is blessed with an abundance of craggy peaks, lochs, rivers and acres of forest including pockets of the ancient and native Caledonian pine forest. Subsequently, much of Speyside is home to rare wildlife including to pine martens, wildcats, red squirrels, ospreys and capercaillie, and Britain's only herd of wild reindeer. Most of upper Strathspey is owned by the Forestry Commission and Rothiemurchus Estate which has been in the possession of the Grant family since the 16th century. Fortunately, the owners enthusiastically support access to these lands that form part of the Cairngorm National Park and which, among the opportunities for outdoor adventure and inhaling fresh air, boast miles of waymarked trails.

▲An easy circular walk of about two hours around **Loch an Eilean** in Rothiemurchus Estate starts from the end of the side road which turns east off the B970, 2 miles south of Aviemore. From the car park at the end of the road head for the lochside. The route around the loch is clearly marked and it's difficult to lose your way as it follows the loch shore. It's a very pleasant walk through woodland with views of a 14th-century castle ruin on an island in the middle of the loch. The views and change of light here are breathtaking whilst it's a magical experience to hear one's call echo across the loch and through the silent forest. You can extend the walk by around a mile by including the circuit around **Loch Gamhna**. The paths around Loch an Eilein are also connected with the massive network of trails around Rothiemurchus. OS Sheet 36 covers the route. There's a small visitor centre and shop in a croft by the car park.

Cairngorm National Park

The area around Aviemore is only a small part of the Cairngorms National Park, whose boundaries extend from Grantown on Spey to the heads of the Angus Glens, and from Ballater on Deeside to Loch Laggan. Scotland's second national park is also the UK's largest at 1400 square miles. It is home to 25% of Scotland's native woodland and is a refuge for many rare plants and animals, including 25% of the UK's threatened species. Probably the most famous of the park's wild residents is the osprey, but you'll also see golden eagles, ptarmigan, the extremely rare crossbill, red deer, red squirrel and pine marten. As well as the park's natural attractions, there are also countless outdoor activities on offer for the Cairngorms is one the UK's prime climbing and hiking areas and now home to an increasing number of outdoor adventure operators. Whether you seek excellent mountain biking, watersports, winter sports (at Cairngorm, the Lecht, see page 102, and Glenshee, see page 80), horse riding, fishing or stalking, this is where to come.

The Cairngorms provide some of Scotland's most challenging walking, with no fewer than 49 Munros and half of Britain's 8 mountains over 4000 ft (Ben MacDrui, Braeriach, Cairn Toul and Cairn Gorm). These mountains come into their own in winter, providing experienced climbers with a wide range of classic ice climbs. However, in light of the sub-Arctic weather conditions which can produce frightening and disorientating white-outs, forays onto these summits should not be taken lightly. They require a high degree of fitness, experience and preparation (see page 52).

Walking in the Cairngorms

The summit of **Cairn Gorm** (4084 ft) is readily accessible as you take the mountain railway up to the **Ptarmigan** restaurant. However the railway cannot be used to access the high mountain plateau beyond the ski area and mountain walkers may not use the railway for their return journey.

There are over 50 miles of footpath through this area, including many peaceful walks through the **Rothiemurchus Forest**. There are also ranger-led guided walks. You can find out more at the excellent **Rothiemurchus Estate Visitor Centre** ⓘ *T01479-810858, daily 0900-1700*, which is a mile from Aviemore along the ski road and can provide a free *Visitor Guide and Footpath Map*.

Another good area for walking is around **Glenmore Forest Park**. The visitor centre, T01479-861220, near Loch Morlich, has a *Glen More Forest Guide Map* which details the many local walks.

The best known of the long-distance trails is the famous **Lairig Ghru**, a 25-mile hike from Aviemore over the Lairig Ghru Pass to Braemar. The trail is well marked but can easily take over eight hours and is very tough in parts. Note that the weather in this part of the world can be very unforgiving for the ill-equipped and unprepared. Do not underestimate this walk.

An easier proposition is a 12-mile loop which leads to the start of the Lairig Ghru pass, starting from Loch Morlich. To reach **Loch Morlich** take the B970 east from the southern end of Aviemore, beyond Coylumbridge. The route starts at the western end of Loch Morlich where a forestry track runs south from the road. It leads to a bridge over the River Luineag. Cross the bridge and continue along the track, keeping straight on where another track heads off left. About a mile further on, another track heads off to the right, but keep to the left fork, signposted for **Rothiemurchus Lodge**.

The track climbs up towards the lodge. Just before it, turn right on to a clear track which leads up to a reservoir. Soon another track heads off to the right signposted for the Lairig Ghru. Follow this path through heather moorland. The path then heads left, climbing up through open moorland to the lip of the glen. The entrance to the Lairig Ghru is straight ahead.

After about a mile, as the hills begin to encroach on either side, a rough path almost doubles back to the left. Follow this path up the slope to the gap between Creag a' Chalamain and Creag an Leith-Choin. The deep gully, the Chalamain Gap, is filled with huge boulders and requires great care when clambering through it. Beyond the gully a path leads through heather and pine saplings, dropping down to the side of a burn, then climbing up on the other side of the burn. Continue on this path, which then drops steeply down to the side of the burn. Cross the footbridge and climb the slope beyond to reach the main road. Turn left along the road to return to the start of the route.

Boat of Garten → *Phone code: 01479. Colour map 4, A3.*

Eight miles northeast of Aviemore is the quiet village of Boat of Garten, home to breeding pairs of rare ospreys on Loch Garten, 2 miles east of the village. **Abernethy Forest RSPB Reserve** ⓘ *T01479-821409, daily 1000-1800, £3, concession £2 , children £0.50*, on the shore of Loch Garten, is best visited during the nesting season, between late April and August, when the RSPB opens an observation centre. This is also one of few places in the world to see Scottish crossbills. You may also see ospreys at the Rothiemurchus trout loch at Inverdruie, and maybe even on Loch Morlich and Loch Insh. The Abernethy reserve is also home to several other rare species such as capercaillie, whooper swans and red squirrels. 'Caperwatch' takes place from April to mid-May 0530 to 0800.

Carrbridge → *Phone code: 01479. Colour map 4, A3.*

At Carrbridge, a pleasant little village 7 miles north of Aviemore, is the **Landmark Forest Theme Park** ⓘ *T01479-841613, Apr to mid-Jul daily 1000-1800, mid-Jul to Aug 1000-1900, Sep-Mar 1000-1700, £9.75, concessions £7.10, children £7.60, www.landmark-centre.co.uk*, a woodland park which combines entertainment, education and shopping. This is where kids can really let off steam as they explore the raised Treetop Trail for viewing wildlife, a maze, fire tower and the highly popular Water Coaster. It's far from tacky and brilliant fun. In the village itself is the decidedly fragile-looking 17th-century stone arch of the **Bridge of Carr**, which is definitely not for vertigo sufferers. The nine-hole 2623-yard **Carrbridge Golf Course** ⓘ *T01479-841623*, is also worth a hit.

Kingussie → *Phone code: 01540. Colour map 4, A2. Population: 1500.*

The quiet village of Kingussie (pronounced *King-yoosie*) lies 12 miles southwest of Aviemore and makes a pleasant alternative as a place to stay. The main attraction here is the excellent **Highland Folk Museum** ⓘ *T01540-661307, Apr-end Sep, Mon-Sat 0930-1730, Oct Mon-Fri 0930-1630, winter guided tours only, £2 adult, children and concessions £1*, which contains a fascinating collection of traditional Highland artefacts, as well as a farming museum, an old smokehouse, a water mill and traditional Hebridean blackhouse. During the summer there are also demonstrations of spinning, woodcarving and peat-fire baking. The **TIC** ⓘ *T01540-661297*, is housed in the museum and has the same opening hours.

Another worthwhile attraction is **Ruthven Barracks**, standing on a hillock across the river. This former barracks was built by the English Redcoats as part of their campaign to tame the Highlands after the first Jacobite rising in 1715. It was destroyed by the Jacobites in the wake of defeat at Culloden to prevent it from falling into enemy hands, and it was from here that Bonnie Prince Charlie sent his final order which signalled the end of his doomed cause. Access is free and the ruins are particularly attractive at night when floodlit.

At nearby Kincraig village, between Kingussie and Aviemore, is the **Highland Wildlife Park** ⓘ *T01540-651270, Apr, May, Sep and Oct daily 1000-1800, Jun-Aug 1000-1900, Nov-Mar 1000-1600, park tours £9.50, concession £8.50, children £6.75*, which has a captive collection of rare native animals including wildcat plus European bison and over 60 red deer.

Grantown-on-Spey → *Phone code: 01479. Colour map 4, A3. Population: 3250.*

This genteel Georgian holiday town is 15 miles northeast of Aviemore and attracts the more mature tourist by the coach load. Everything here is geared towards fishing, and anyone wishing to get kitted out in proper style should get themselves down to either **Mortimers** or **Ritchies** on the High Street. The tourist information centre ⓘ *T01479-872773, Apr-Oct 0900-1800*, is also here.

Sleeping

Aviemore *p104*

A-D The Macdonald Aviemore Highland Resort, T0845-6083734, T01479-815300, www.aviemorehighlandresort.com. Huge leisure and conference complex featuring 4 hotel options: the luxurious **Macdonald Highland Hotel** (**A**), the family-orientated **Academy Hotel** (**B**), the **Four Seasons** (**A**) and the **Aviemore Inn** (**B**). Also has deluxe (3-bedroomed, en suite) wooden lodges (3 nights £700/7 nights £1500) plus a fine-dining restaurant **Aspects** (TTT-TT). This village within a village also comes complete with 1st-class leisure facilities, including the 18-hole **Spey valley golf course** (£69 a round), and swimming pool (free to guests).

C Cairngorm Hotel, Grampian Rd, T01479-810233, www.cairngorm.com. Slap bang in the midst of Aviemore, this is where to combine a comfortable stay with good craic in the bar among the locals whilst dining on hearty bar meals (T) and freshly prepared game and seafood in the restaurant (TTT-TT).

D Ravenscraig Guest House, T01479-810278, www.aviemoreonline.com. 12 rooms. Open all year. Very good-quality guesthouse, worth the wee bit extra.

F Aviemore Independent Bunkhouse & Backpackers Hostel, Dalfaber Rd, T01479-811137. 40 beds. Very cosy and high-quality facilities.

F SYHA hostel, Grampian Rd, near the tourist office, T01479-810345. Open all year.

Around Aviemore

L-B Hilton Coylumbridge Hotel, Coylumbridge by Aviemore, T01479-810661, www.hilton.co.uk/coylumbridge. Set in 65 acres of woodland by Rothiemurchus Estate, the family-friendly credential of this luxury hotel include a dedicated Fun House, dry ski slope and climbing wall, whilst the parents can relax by the pool and enjoy fine dining (TTT-TT) just 15 mins' walk from Aviemore town centre.

B-C Corrour House Hotel, Inverdruie, 2 miles southeast of Aviemore, T01479-810220, www.corrourhouse.co.uk. Open Dec-Oct. This Victorian country house oozes charm, enjoys wonderful views and offers superb cuisine (TTT-TT). With breathtaking views over the Rothiemurchus Estate towards the Lairig Ghru and Cairngorm massif, this is arguably the best small hotel in the area. Recommended.

B-D Glenmore Lodge, Glenmore, T01479-861256, www.glenmorelodge.org.uk. Britain's top outdoor training centre, patronized by many British Winter Olympians. Equipped with a pool, gym and even a roller-ski cross-country track within the forest, there's twin-room and chalet accommodation at this ideal base for those seeking a rural retreat with top-class instruction in climbing, mountaineering and kayaking.

C Rowan Tree Restaurant & Guest House, Loch Alvie, 1½ miles south of Aviemore on the B9152, T01479-810207, www.rowantreehotel.com. Like the **Corrour**, a tasteful, friendly hotel that goes the extra mile for guests. This is one of the oldest hotels in the area and serves excellent food (lunch TT, dinner TTT).

Camping

Forest Enterprise site, Glenmore, T01479-861271.

Aviemore, Dalraddy Holiday Park, T01479-810330, www.alvie-estate.co.uk. Quiet family park set in 25 acres of birch woodland.

Rothiemurchus Camping & Caravan Park, Coylumbridge, T01479-812800. Very good campsite.

Boat of Garten *p106*

B Boat Hotel, T01479-831258, www.boathotel.co.uk. A lovely traditional hotel located at the northern end of the village with its **Caipercaillie** restaurant serving delicious lunches and evening meals (TTT-TT).

C Glenavon House, Kinchurdy Rd, T01479-831213. A lovely guesthouse.

D-E Heathbank House, T01479-831234, www.heathbankhotel.co.uk. Retaining many original 18th-century features, Heathbank House serves tasty dinner and breakfast in the Charles Rennie Mackintosh-style dining room whilst the golf course is only 100 yds away!

Camping

Boat of Garten Caravan and Camping Park, T01479-831652. Quiet and child-friendly within easy walking of **Boat Hotel**, golf course and attractions.

Carrbridge *p107*

B Dalrachney Lodge Hotel, T01479-841252, www.dalrachney.co.uk. A former Victorian hunting lodge with tastefully furnished rooms, a lovely restaurant and bar (TT) and infinite outdoor pursuits at its doorstep, including options on salmon fishing and extensive grounds for landing your helicopter.

C-D The Mellon Patch B&B, Carrbridge, T01479-841592, www.mellonpatch.com. 3 double, en suite rooms, very hospitable hosts and a terrific breakfast make this a great patch in which to stay.

D Cairn Hotel, T01479-841212, cairnhotel.co.uk. Oozing 'old world' charm, this is where to join the local worthies for some après-ski banter in the atmospheric bar over terrific, good-value bar food (¶) or an informal evening meal (¶¶).

F Carrbridge Bunkhouse Hostel, T01479-841250, www.carrbridge-bunkhouse.co.uk. It's ½ mile out of the village towards Dalrachney – but worth the walk.

Kingussie *p107*

D Glengarry, East Terrace, T01540-661386, www.scot89.freeserve.co.uk. A beautifully appointed B&B serving delicious breakfasts.

D Greystones, on Acres Rd, T01540-661052. A modest and comfortable B&B with a roaring open fire and which featured in the TV series *Monarch of the Glen*.

D Monadhliath Hotel, Laggan by Newtonmore, T01528-544276. A former manse (the church still stands in the grounds), this modest hotel with a cosy bar is ideal for those seeking to explore the nearby **Laggan Wolftrax Mountain Bike Centre**, fish (permits available), pony-trek or walk.

D-E The Auld Poor House, Kingussie, T01540-661558. Built in 1880 as the paupers house, this award-winning B&B combines rustic charm with a terrific breakfast and the chance to enjoy some in-house reiki and massage after a long day in the hills.

E Eagle View Guesthouse, Perth Rd, T01540-673675, www.eagleviewguesthouse.co.uk. Opened in 2005, this friendly B&B delivers a touch of class and includes a hearty full Scottish breakfast.

F Croftdhu Hostel, Strone Rd, Newtonmore, T01540-673504, www.hostel-scotland.co.uk. Another good, friendly hostel in the heart of traditional shinty country.

F Glen Feshie Hostel, Ballachroick, by Kincraig, T01540-651323. Peaceful with the forests and mountains on your doorstep.

F Happy Days Hostel, 65 High St, Kingussie, T01540-661175 www.happydayshostel.co.uk. Eat, sleep and enjoy.

F The Laird's Bothy, High St, Kingussie next to **Tipsy Laird** pub, T01540-661334, www.thetipsylaird.co.uk. A decent hostel.

Grantown-on-Spey *p107*

As you'd expect in such a respectable place, there's a wide range of upmarket accommodation and a number of very good places to eat. Some of the best places in town are on Woodland Terr.

A Muckrach Lodge Hotel & Restaurant, a few miles southwest of town at Dulnain Bridge, T01479-851257, www.muckrach.co.uk. Another delightful, high-class small hotel and one with an enviable reputation for its cuisine (¶¶¶).

A-B Culdearn House, Woodlands Terr, T01479-872106, www.culdearn.com. Arguably the best place to stay, with its attention to detail, beautifully appointed traditional rooms and award-winning fine dining (¶¶¶).

B-C Auchendean Lodge Hotel, a few miles southwest of town, T01479-851347, www.auchendean.com. An elegant hotel at Dulnain Bridge with a superb restaurant (¶¶¶-¶¶).

C-D The Garth Hotel, Castle Rd, T01479-872836. This is where to combine a comfortable stay with freshly prepared dinners (¶¶¶-¶¶) before choosing from among the hotel's excellent selection of whiskies.

F Ardenbeg Bunkhouse & Outdoor Centre, T01479-872824, www.ardenbeg.co.uk. A good-value, budget option that's fully geared up to quickly have you enjoying the outdoors.

Self-catering

Cragganmore Lodge, by Cragganmore Distillery, mid-way between Grantown and Aberlour, T01324-861635. £320-£510 per week, modern chalet-style self-catering (sleeps 5-6) that's ideal for guests seeking quick access to rural walks including the Speyside Way.

Eating

Aviemore and around *p104*

¶¶¶-¶ Aspects, T01479-815300 www.aviemorehighlandresort.com. Within the resort complex, Aspects prides itself on offering freshly produced Scottish-based cuisine in a stylish setting (daily 1930-2130). The **Steakhouse** (**¥¥¥-¥¥**) at Dalfaber (phone number as above), less formal, is the place to enjoy tender Scotch beef, whilst, during the day, all the family can tuck in at the **food court**.

¥¥¥-¥ Cairngorm Hotel, T01479-810233, see Sleeping, above. Has a good reputation for serving up tasty Scottish dinner classics as well as your favourite pub-grub.

¥¥ Old Bridge Inn, T01479-811137, Dalfaber Rd. Tucked away on the old road below the main street, this atmospheric inn remains a high-quality eating establishment favoured by many a local. Ceilidhs and Highland dinner dances are hosted and, for less formal eating, diners can sit by the bar to enjoy a pint of real ale with some hearty pub-grub (**¥¥-¥**). Recommended.

Around Aviemore

¥¥¥-¥ The Einich, Inverdruie, 2 miles along the 'ski road' serves fantastic, wholesome sandwiches, soups and home-baked food during the day, whilst the dinners (including divine desserts) are delicious. Recommended.

¥¥-¥ Loch Insh Watersports Centre, Kincraig, between Aviemore and Kingussie.
A good lochside restaurant which doubles as a café during the day.

Kingussie *p107*

¥¥¥-¥¥ The Cross, Tweed Mill Brae, a private drive leading off Ardbroilach Rd, T01540-661166. This is a good place to eat freshly prepared local produce. They also have rooms (**A-C** for dinner, B&B).

¥¥ Osprey Hotel and **¥¥ Scot House Hotel** both have reasonable restaurants, whilst the **¥¥-¥ Glen Hotel** is recognized by CAMRA for its quality of fine ales.

¥ Tipsy Laird pub serves good meals and real ales, or try the **¥ Gilly's Kitchen** on the main street.

Activities and tours

Strathspey & the Cairngorms *p104*

Fishing

Fishing is a major pursuit in the area. Armed with a permit, you can fish for trout and salmon on the River Spey (from £20 per day). The Rothiemurchus Estate also offers rainbow trout fishing and equipment hire for its stocked loch at Inverdruie (day, £25 and £5 tackle hire). There's even a 'novice loch' where, with rod and tackle provided, beginners can benefit from an hour's instruction for £12.50. For further information about fishing at Rothiemurchus and on the Spey call T01479-810703 or T01479-812345, or pop into **Speyside Sports** in Aviemore, for rods and tackle. Alternatively, log onto www.fishspey.co.uk, fishfindhorn.co.uk or www.visitscotland.com/fish for a full listing of stockists and hire outlets.

Horse riding

Horse riding and pony trekking are on offer at various places throughout Strathspey.

Alvie Stables, Alvie, near Kincraig, T01540-651409, T0831-495397 (mob) is excellent.

Carrbridge Trekking Centre, Station Rd, Carrbridge, T01479-841602.

Mountain biking

From Rothiemurchus Estate and Glenmore Forest to the tough 'Burma Road' connecting Carrbridge with Aviemore and the Ryvoan route, Cairngorm National Park and outlying areas make perfect mountain bike country for novices and experts.

Bothy Bikes, Unit 7, Grampian Rd, Aviemore T01479-810111. Daily 0900-1700. They also have a hire facility beside the Rothiemurchus Visitor Centre at Inverdruie. £12 half-day/£17 full day for well-maintained suspension mountain bike including helmet, tool kit, map and route advice. Kids' bikes £6/£8. Child seat free with bike hire. Excellent, knowledgeable MTB guide and local operator to ensure you are quickly pedalling on your way.

You can also hire bikes at Loch Insh Watersports (see Watersports, below).

Multi-sport adventure

As one of Scotland's primary outdoor adventure locations, there are a host of operators offering all kinds of adrenaline activities and professional coaching. Among reputable operators are the following:

G2 Outdoor, T07946-285612, www.g2outdoor.co.uk. From gorge walking to mountaineering, telemark skiing and river kayaking (£45), this is a highly professional, fun-orientated outfit.

Glenmore Lodge, T01479-861256, www.glenmorelodge.org.uk. Arguably

Britain's top outdoor training centre with a rash of expert mountain and kayaking guides available to coach those who want to learn or improve their kayaking, winter mountaineering and/or rock climbing skills. , **Rothiemurchus Estate**, T01479-812345. Amongst its host of outdoor activities the estate runs an excellent 'Behind the Scenes' tour (£15 per person, 3 hrs, max 7 persons) designed to provide photo opportunities and an insight into the wildlife, ancient Caledonian forest and history of the land as you explore the vast estate by 4WD.

Skiing

Cairngorm is Scotland's longest-established ski resort and remains Scotland's largest ski area, with almost 30 runs and over 20 miles of pistes. This is where many of Britain's leading ski racers have first learnt the arts of skiing and snowboarding. When the sun shines, the snowfall is good and the crowds are few it can be a very satisfying experience. The season normally runs from Jan until the snow disappears, which can be as late as May. **Cairngorm Ski Area**, www.cairngorm mountain.org. 9 miles southeast of Aviemore and starting over 2500 ft above Loch Morlich, is reached by a frequent bus service (Nos 34 and 36) from Aviemore. One of Scotland's most extensive ski areas, visitors can rent skis and snowboards, book lessons and purchase day and half-day ski passes from the busy **Day Lodge**, T01479-861261, at the foot of the ski area. A full breakdown of prices can be accessed on their website. Aside from dozens of pistes, Cairngorm also boasts Scotland's only funicular mountain railway. This runs to the **Ptarmigan** restaurant/café and gift shop near the summit of Cairn Gorm. The funicular (information T01479-861341) runs Apr-Oct daily 1000-1630, Nov-Mar from 0900, £8.75, concession £7.50, child £5.50. The **Aviemore TIC** and the **Cairngorm Day Lodge** ticket office provide free piste maps of the Cairngorm ski area

Loch Morlich and Rothiemurchus Estate and around provide good cross-country skiing if there's enough snow, though in recent years snowfall has been below average.

Walking

The walks around Strathspey are covered by OS Landranger map No 36 (1:50,000 scale) or OS Outdoor Leisure Map No 3 (1:25,000 scale). See page 106.

Watersports

In summer, the main activities are water-sports, and there are 2 centres which offer sailing, canoeing and windsurfing tuition and equipment hire.

Loch Morlich Watersports Centre, 8 miles east of Aviemore, T01479-861221. Open May-Sep.

Loch Insh Watersports Centre, T01540-651272, www.lochinsh.com. Open year-round. the centre has been running for over 40 years and offers a whole host of activities including kayaking, sailing, windsurfing in addition to mountain bike hire. There's also a fabulous boathouse café/restaurant with views across the loch (ΨΨ-Ψ) and chalet options (from £168 for 2 nights) with loch views.

Transport

Aviemore *p104*

Bus There are **Scottish Citylink** buses, T08705-505050, www.citylink.co.uk, between Aviemore and **Inverness** (45 mins), **Kingussie** (20 mins), **Pitlochry** (1¼ hrs), **Perth** (2 hrs), **Glasgow** (3½ hrs) and **Edinburgh** (3½ hrs). For **Aberdeen**, change at Inverness.

Car hire Northern Vehicle Hire, agents for Europcar, T01479-811463.

Train There are direct trains to and from **Glasgow** and **Edinburgh** (3 hrs) and **Inverness** (40 mins). **Strathspey Steam Railway**, T01479-810725, www.strathspey railway.co.uk (Apr-Oct and 'Santa' and 'New Year' specials) is a fabulous 'old world' experience that runs between **Aviemore**, **Boat of Garten** and **Broomhill**. The station is just to the east of the main train station. £9.50, £4.75 child, £24 family return.

Boat of Garten *p106*

Train The most unusual way to get to Boat of Garten is on the **Strathspey Steam Railway** which runs regularly in summer from **Aviemore**, T01479- 810725. **Loch Garten** is not easy to reach without your own transport, check with TICs for tours.

Carrbridge *p107*

Bus There are several buses (Mon-Sat) from **Inverness** to **Grantown-on-Spey** and Aviemore with Highland Country Buses, T01463-710555, T01479-811211. There are regular buses daily between **Cairngorm Mountain** and **Aviemore Highland Resort** via **Glenmore** and **Coylumbridge**. Highland Country Buses also operate 3 buses a day (Mon-Sat) **Inverness** to **Newtonmore** via **Carrbridge**, **Aviemore** and **Kingussie**.

Kingussie *p107*

Bus Kingussie is on the main **Inverness** to **Perth/Glasgow/Edinburgh** routes. All Perth–Inverness trains stop here as do most Citylink buses. There's also an infrequent school bus service run by Highland Country Buses between **Kingussie**, **Aviemore**, **Newtonmore** and **Dalwhinnie**.

Grantown-on-Spey *p107*

Bus There are several buses (Mon-Sat) between Grantown and **Aviemore** (35 mins); 2-3 buses a day (Mon-Sat) to/from **Inverness** (1¼ hrs).

Argyll & Inner Hebrides

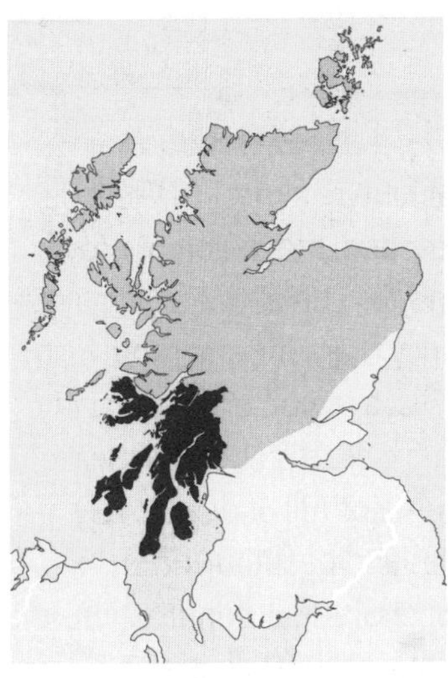

Footprint features

Introduction

Stretching north from the Mull of Kintyre almost to Glencoe and east to the shores of Loch Lomond, the region of Argyll marks the transition from Lowland to Highland. Argyll may be Highlands-lite to some – less starkly dramatic and more lush – but it has its own special beauty. It's a region of great variety, with all the ingredients of the classic Scottish holiday: peaceful wooded glens, heather-clad mountains full of deer, lovely wee fishing ports, romantic castles and beautiful lochs. Despite its proximity to the massive Glasgow conurbation, Argyll is sparsely populated. The main tourist centre and second largest town, Oban, has only 8000 inhabitants. Oban is also the main ferry port for Argyll's Hebridean islands.

The Inner Hebrides comprise the great swathe of islands lying off the western coast of Argyll, each with its own distinct appeal. The most accessible and most popular is Mull, a short ferry ride from Oban. The variety of scenery on offer is astounding and its capital, Tobermory, is the most attractive port in western Scotland. A stone's throw from Mull is tiny Iona, one of the most important religious sites in Europe, with some divine beaches. Boat trips can be made to the dramatic island of Staffa, looming out of the sea like a great cathedral and the inspiration for Mendelssohn's *Hebrides Overture*. Further west, windswept Coll and Tiree offer miles of unspoilt beaches and great windsurfing and, to the south, Colonsay is a stress-free zone that makes Mull seem hectic. Those who enjoy a good malt whisky should head for Islay, famed for its distilleries, while neighbouring Jura is a wild and beautiful place, perfect for some off-the-beaten-track hiking. If you're after some peace and quiet on Jura then you're in good company, for this is where George Orwell came to write *Nineteen Eighty-Four*.

★ Don't miss...

1 **Loch Etive** Take a cruise on this hidden treasure, inaccessible except by boat, page 125.
2 **Inverawe Fisheries and Smokery** Sample the finest of piscine cuisine, preferably to take away for a picnic, page 125.
3 **Kilmartin Glen** Explore the archaeological wonders of Argyll's very own prehistoric park, page 127.
4 **Tighnabruaich** Best seen at the end of a drive down the southwest coast of Cowal, with wonderful views across the Kyles of Bute, page 133.
5 **Mount Stuart** Take a look around this magnificent Gothic fantasy, page 134.
6 **Staffa** Take a boat to this spectacular island and witness the cathedral-like Fingal's Cave, which inspired Mendelssohn, page 149.
7 **Iona** Hire a bike and explore the most spiritual, and one of the loveliest, Hebridean islands, page 151.
8 **Jura** Follow in the footsteps of George Orwell on one of Scotland's most remote islands, page 166.

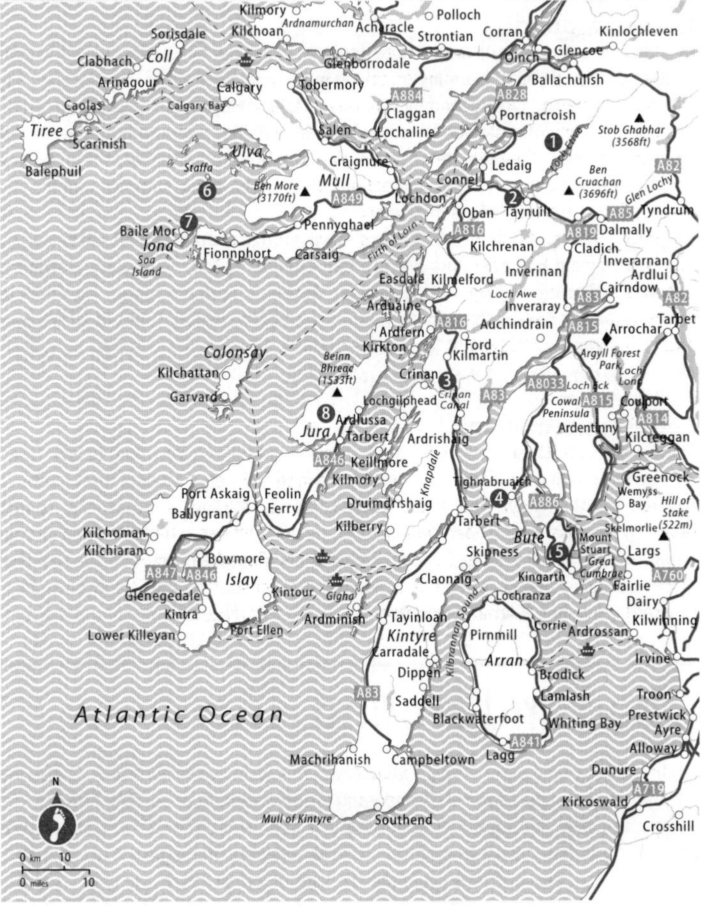

Ins and outs

Getting there

There are plenty of buses and trains from Glasgow and Fort William to Oban. For full details of bus connections contact **Scottish Citylink** ⓘ *T08705-505050*, or contact the **Oban TIC** ⓘ *T01631-563122*. Bus, train and ferry times can be found in Argyll and Bute Council's free *Area Transport Guides* to Lorn, Mull and Islay and Jura, available at Oban tourist office. There are flights from Glasgow to Port Ellen (Islay) and to Tiree. For full details of flight times and prices call **British Airways** ⓘ *T0870-8509850*, the local TICs, or **Port Ellen airport** ⓘ *T01496-302022*, and **Tiree airport** ⓘ *T01879-220309*.

CalMac car and passenger ferries sail to and from Mull, Islay, Coll, Tiree, Colonsay and Gigha, and passenger-only ferries sail to Iona (and to the Small Isles, see page 293). The departure point for ferries to Mull, Coll, Tiree and Colonsay is Oban. Ferry times change according to the day of the week and time of year. Services listed in the Transport sections for each separate island are for the summer period (end March to end October). For full details see the *CalMac Ferry Guide* or call **CalMac** ⓘ *T08705-650000, www.calmac.co.uk (general enquiries)*. The departure point for ferries to Islay (and on to Jura), and some ferries to Colonsay, is Kennacraig. » *For further details, see the Transport sections: Mull, page 157; Coll, page 160; Tiree, page 160; Colonsay, page 161; Islay and Jura, page 168.*

Getting around

Most ferries to the islands and remote peninsulas are run by **CalMac**, see above for contact details. If you're planning on taking more than a couple of ferries, especially with a car, it may be more economical to buy an **Island Hopscotch** ticket. They can be used on a variety of route combinations and are valid for a month from the date of your first journey. They require advance planning but are better value than buying single tickets. Contact **CalMac** for details. During the peak summer months it's essential to book ferry tickets in advance.

Public transport is limited in much of Argyll, though the main towns are served by buses. The main bus operators are **Scottish Citylink** ⓘ *T08705-505050*, **Bowmans Coaches** ⓘ *T01680-812313*, and **Westcoast Motors** ⓘ *T01631-570500*. The Oban to Glasgow rail line passes through the northern part of the region. Times of local buses and trains can be checked at local tourist offices. » *For further details, see the relevant Transport sections, pages 123, 138, 145, 156, 160 and 168.*

Tourist information

There are TICs in Oban, Craignure and Tobermory (Mull) and Bowmore (Islay). Oban TIC has information on all the islands covered in this chapter. Most of this chapter is covered by the **Argyll the Isles, Loch Lomond, Stirling & Trossachs Tourist** Board ⓘ *www.visitscottishheartlands.com*. The main offices, which are open all year round, are in Oban, Inveraray, Dunoon, Rothesay and Campbeltown. There are seasonal offices in Lochgilphead, Tarbert, Ardgarten and Helensburgh. The island of Arran is covered by **Ayrshire & Arran Tourist Board** ⓘ *T01292-470700, www.ayrshire-arran.com*.

Oban and around

Oban is a busy little place. Argyll's tourist hub, this Victorian seaside town is also the largest west coast port north of Glasgow and the main departure point for ferries to the Inner and Outer Hebrides. Not surprisingly, it gets very crowded in summer, with passing traffic and people using it as a base for exploring the region. A working port, Oban's main streets narrowly avoid the excesses of tourist kitsch and offer visitors a wide range of hotels, guesthouses, B&Bs, restaurants and shops. Note that many restaurants stop serving by 2200. There are also several tourist attractions of note if stuck here in bad weather. The town itself lies in the beautiful setting of a wide, crescent-shaped bay backed by steep hills, with the tiny, idyllic island of Kerrera, just offshore, providing a natural shelter. Oban is at the centre of the northerly part of Argyll, known as Lorn, which comprises several relatively peaceful islands including Lismore, Kerrera, Seil and Luing. »» *For Sleeping, Eating and other listings, see pages 121-124.*

Ins and outs

Getting there and around Oban is reasonably well served by buses and trains from Glasgow, Fort William and Inverness, and there are a number of west coast local bus services to and from Lochgilphead and Kilmartin. There are regular local buses around town and around Lorn, including to Ellenabeich and North Cuan on Seil, Isle of Luing, North Connel, Dalavich, Bonawe and Ganavan Sands. These are mostly operated by **West Coast Motors** ⓘ *T01586-552319.* »» *For further details, see Transport, page 123.*
Tourist information Oban TIC ⓘ *Argyll Sq, T01631-563122, year round daily Mar-Oct 0900-1700, Nov-Feb 0930-1700,* has coin-operated internet access.

Oban »» *pp121-124. Colour map 3, B5.*

→ *Phone code: 01631.*

The town's great landmark is **McCaig's Tower**, an incongruous structure that resembles Rome's Coliseum and which dominates the skyline. The tower was built by local banker John Stuart McCaig in the late 19th century, as a means of providing work for unemployed stonemasons. Unfortunately, McCaig died before the project was complete, and to this day no one is quite sure of his intentions. There's not much to see, apart from the exterior walls, but the views of the town and bay are quite magnificent and well worth the climb up. There are various routes on foot, but the most direct is to go up Argyll Street and on the left beside the church climb the set of steps known as **Jacob's Ladder**, which lead to Ardconnel Terrace. Turn left here and the tower soon comes into view and is well signposted.

Don't leave town without a visit to Sweeties, a glorious, old-fashioned sweet shop with over 350 varieties to choose from, most of them handmade in Scotland.

Another good walk is to the ruins of seventh-century **Dunollie Castle**, north of town on the Corran Esplanade towards Ganavan, from where there are also wonderful views. The castle was built on the site of an ancient stronghold of the King of Scots, and was then taken over in the 13th century by the MacDougalls, Lords of Lorn. Continue round the corner to **Ganavan Sands**, a long, safe sandy beach about 1½ miles north of the town, for a romantic west coast sunset.

If the weather's bad you can take a tour round the excellent **Oban Distillery** ⓘ *Stafford St, opposite North Pier, T01631-562110, Easter-Jun Mon-Sat 0930-1700, Jul-Sep Mon-Fri 0930-1930, Sat 0930-1700, Sun 1200-1700, Oct Mon-Sat 0930-1700, Nov Mon-Fri 1000-1700, Dec-Feb Mon-Fri 1230-1600, Mar Mon-Fri 1000-1700. £5.* The **War and Peace Museum** ⓘ *01631-570007, Mon-Sat 1000-1800, Sun 1000-1600, free,* has expanded and is worth a look. Staffed by enthusiastic volunteers, it tells the story of Oban's role in the Second World War through a fascinating display of old photos and memorabilia.

Dunstaffnage Castle ⓘ *T01631-562465, Apr-Sep daily 0930-1830, Oct daily 0930-1630, Nov-Mar Sat-Wed 0930-1630, castle grounds open all year, £3, concession £2.30, children £1.30,* 3 miles north of Oban, off the A85, is an impressive 13th-century fort with much of its towering curtain wall still intact. The ruins of the little chapel nearby are worth a look. Long before this castle served as a temporary prison for Flora MacDonald, it's believed the site was used to keep the original Stone of Destiny.

Two miles east of Oban along the Glencruitten Road is the **Rare Breeds Farm Park** ⓘ *T01631-770608, mid-Mar to late Oct daily 1000-1800, £6, concession £5, children £4.* Part of a working livestock farm and complete with tea-room, it's a fun place for kids, with strange-looking goats mingling with sheep, highland cows, deer and pigs. Regular buses run to the farm from Oban train station.

Around Oban » pp121-124.

Isle of Kerrera → *Phone code: 01631. Colour map 3, B-C5.*

Boasting arguably one of the best short (6-mile) coastal walks in the UK, the tranquil isle of Kerrera lying half a mile offshore and a five-minute ferry ride (£4 return) from Oban, provides the perfect antidote to the bustle of Oban. Walkers or cyclists to this

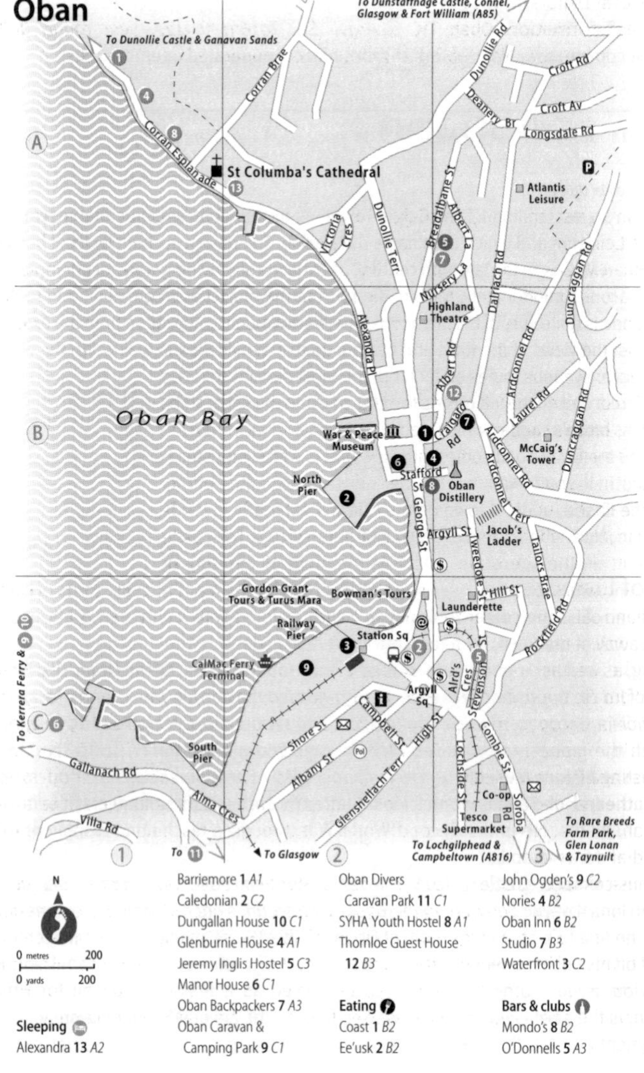

'dry' isle that supports just 35 inhabitants may spot sea eagles and seals or even porpoise offshore. Five minutes' walk south of the welcoming Kerrera bunkhouse and tea-room visitors are rewarded with the imposing ruins of Gylen Castle and views across to Mull, the Slate Islands, Lismore and Jura. Built by the MacDougall's in 1587 **Gylen Castle** sits proudly on a clifftop looking down the Firth of Lorn. A mile northwest of the ferry jetty is **Slatrach Bay**, a sandy beach providing a terrific place for a family picnic. However, there are no shops so arrive with provisions.

Connel to Barcaldine Castle → *Phone code: 01631. Colour map 3, B5.*

Five miles north of Oban an impressive steel cantilever bridge carries the A828 across the mouth of Loch Etive at Connel. It's worth stopping here to see the **Falls of Lora**, a wild tide-race created by the narrow mouth of the sea loch and the reef that spans most of it, thus restricting the flow of water. The result is the impressive rapids, which are best seen from the shore in the village or from halfway across the bridge.

Ten miles north up this road on the shore of Loch Creran and past the turn-off to 16th-century Barcaldine Castle, a most atmospheric B&B option awaits (see Sleeping, page 121). **Oban Sealife Centre** ⓘ *T01631-720386, Apr-Oct daily 1000-1700 (ring for winter opening hours), £10.50, children £7.50; bus No 405 runs regularly from Oban to the Sealife Centre (see Transport, page 123).* Enormous fun, this environmentally friendly facility rescues seals and other aquatic creatures which are then released back into the wild at the end of the season. Aside from over 30 displays, there's a touch pool, an underwater observatory and a terrific forest adventure trail. Parents can rest their tired feet in the coffee shop.

Appin → *Phone code: 01631. Colour map 3, B5.*

The road runs around Loch Creran and enters the district of Appin, made famous in Robert Louis Stevenson's *Kidnapped*, which was based on the 'Appin Murder' of 1752 (see Activities and tours, page 123). A road turns southwest off the main Fort William road to **Port Appin**, on the western tip of the peninsula, the departure point for the passenger ferry to Lismore. To the north of Port Appin is the irresistibly photogenic **Castle Stalker**. Standing on its own tiny island with a background of islands and hills, it's probably second only to the famous Eilean Donan in its portrayal of Scotland's romantic image. It was built in the 16th century by the Stewarts of Appin before falling into Campbell hands after the ill-fated 1745 rebellion. The current owners open it to the public for a limited period in July and August. Check opening times at the tourist office in Oban.

Isle of Lismore → *Phone code: 01631. Colour map 3, B5.*

The island of Lismore lies only a few miles off the mainland, in Loch Linnhe, yet feels a world away. It makes an ideal day trip and offers great opportunities for walking and cycling, as well as wonderful views across to the mountains of Morvern and Mull, the Paps of Jura to the south and Ben Nevis to the north. It's a fertile little island (the name *leis mór* is Gaelic for the big garden) that once supported a population of 1400, though the present population is about a tenth of that. Lismore has a long and interesting history. It was the ecclesiastical capital of Argyll for several centuries and the **Cathedral of St Moluag** was founded here in the 12th century, just north of Clachan. All that remains is the choir, which is now used as the parish church. The cathedral occupies the site of a church founded by the Irish saint, who established a religious community on the island about the same time as St Columba was busy at work in Iona. Legend has it that the two saints were racing to the island, in an attempt to be the first to land and found a monastery. Such was Moluag's religious zeal that he cut off his finger and threw it on to the shore, thus claiming possession. This sort of behaviour is, of course, frowned upon in Olympic rowing events. Not far from the church, is the 2000-year-old **Broch of Tirefour**, one of the best-preserved prehistoric monuments in Argyll, with surviving circular walls up to 16-ft high. Other sights include **Castle Coeffin**, a 13th-century fortress built by the MacDougalls of Lorn on the site of an earlier Viking settlement. In the southwest of the island lies the 13th-century Achadun Castle, built for the Bishops of Argyll. It's a short walk from here to **Bernera Island**, which can be reached at low tide (but don't get stranded).

South Lorn and the Slate Islands → *Phone code: 01852. Colour map 3, C4-5.*

Eight miles south of Oban the B884 turns west off the A816 and wriggles its way round glassy lochs and knobbly, green hills studded with copper-coloured cattle to the tiny Slate Islands, so called because in the mid-19th century, the island's slate quarries exported millions of roofing slates every year. The quarrying industry has long since gone, leaving the area dotted with pretty little villages of whitewashed cottages once inhabited by slate workers.

The most northerly of the Slate Islands is **Seil** (or Clachan Seil), which is reached from the mainland across the seriously humpbacked Clachan Bridge. Better known as the 'Bridge over the Atlantic', it was built in 1792, with its high arch allowing ships to pass beneath. Beside the bridge is an old inn, **Tigh an Truish**, or 'House of the Trousers', where islanders once swapped their kilt for trousers in order to conform to the post-1745 ban on the wearing of Highland dress. There's also a petrol pump and souvenir shop here. Two miles south, at **Balvicar** (where there's a bank in the grocery store) the road turns right and climbs up and over to the harbour and attractive village of **Ellenabeich**, which is also, rather confusingly, known by the same name as the nearby island of Easdale. Ellenabeich is home to the Isle of Seil microbrewery (reputedly Scotland's smallest) since 2004. Before sinking a pint of their Corryveckan Ale, try the 130-yard, 12-hole Isle putting green. Apparently, if you beat the course par of 24, a bottle of Oban whisky is yours! The village is also the base for the excellent **Seafari Adventures** (see Activities and tours, page 123), and here too you'll find the **Scottish Slate Islands Heritage Trust Centre** ⓘ *T01852-300449, Apr-Oct daily 1030-1300, 1400-1700, £1.50, children £0.25*, with its fascinating insight into the area's history.

Seil is well worth a visit, for its walks and fascinating island history. It is also the departure point for exciting wildlife cruises, see page 123.

Endearingly tiny **Easdale** is separated from Seil by a 500-yard-wide channel which has to be dredged to keep it open. The island, only 800 yards by 700 yards, was the centre of the slate industry and, between 1842 and 1861 produced over 130 million roof slates. Now inhabited by just 71 residents, the island once supported over 450 people before the quarries were flooded in the great storm of 1881 and the industry collapsed. A few minutes' walk from the ferry pier you'll find the delightful folk museum run by island volunteers. If the museum is closed, wander past the whitewashed former slate workers' cottages to seek out island information over a pint at the cosy **Puffer Bar**. The island's lively social life also revolves around the community hall with one of the highlights of the year being the annual keenly contested world stone-skimming championships. See Festivals and events, page 123. For more information on the island, visit www.easdale.org.

Another road runs south from Balvicar to **North Cuan**, from where the car ferry sails across the treacherous Cuan Sound to the long, thin island of **Luing** (pronounced 'Ling'). The island once had a population of around 600 which was drastically reduced during the Clearances to make way for cattle. Luing is still well known for its beef, and is the home of a successful new breed named after it. The island is small, 6 by 2 miles, and mostly flat, making it ideal for exploring by bike. Bikes can be hired just 50 yards from the ferry slipway at the **Sunnybrae Caravan Park** ⓘ *T01852-314274*. A mile or so further south is the village of **Cullipool**, see Transport, page 123. The only other village is Toberonochy, 3 miles from Cullipool. Wildlife abounds with sightings of otters, seals, eagles and buzzards, whilst visitors can also enjoy a breathtaking panorama of the outlying isles of Mull, Shuna and Scarba.

South of the turn-off to the Slate Islands is **Arduaine Gardens** ⓘ *T01852-200366, Apr-end Sep, daily 0930-1630, £5, concession £4*, a beautiful place and an absolute must for all gardening enthusiasts. Gifted to the National Trust for Scotland in 1992, this 20-acre oasis boasts spectacular rhododendrons in early summer, Himalayan lilies, blue Tibetan poppies, a woodland garden, sweeping lawns and inspirational views across to Jura and the Slate Islands.

This is serious boating country, and just south of Arduaine, on the northern coast of the Craignish Peninsula, is surreal **Craobh Haven**, a yachting marina built in the style of a reproduction 18th-century fishing village. South of Craobh Haven is another yachting marina at **Ardfern**, where the **Galley of Lorn Hotel** and pub is invariably packed with yachties. You can arrange boat trips from Ardfern around Loch Craignish and to the offshore islands, see Activities and tours, page 123.

Sleeping

Oban *p117, map p118*
The main ferry port for the islands, Oban gets busy in the summer with traffic. It's often an idea to get the tourist office to find you a bed; it'll cost more, but saves time and effort.

L **Caledonian Hotel**, Station Sq, T01631-563133, www.swallowhotels.com. Impressive 18th-century former station building overlooking the ferry pier. For a touch of luxury try one of the Captain's rooms with views across Oban bay. Coffee connoisseurs will enjoy the menu in the brasserie.

L **Manor House Hotel**, Gallanach Rd, T01631-562087. 11 rooms, open year-round. Beautiful stone house in secluded location overlooking the bay on the road south towards the Kerrera ferry. Style and comfort assured.

B **Dungallan House Hotel**, Gallanach Rd, T01631-563799, www.dungallanhotel-oban.co.uk. Built in 1870 by the Duke of Argyll, this tastefully refurbished residence offers fine dining on locally sourced produce, over 100 malts and excellent views on the road south to the Kerrera ferry.

C **Alexandra Hotel**, Corran Esplanade, T01631-562381. Large hotel with well-equipped rooms and good facilities including pool and steam room.

C **Barriemore Hotel**, Corran Esplanade, T01631-566356, F01631-571084. 13 rooms, open Feb-Dec. A delightful, friendly, guesthouse with great views of Oban bay at the quieter end of the esplanade.

C **Glenburnie House**, Corran Esplanade, T/F01631-562089. 12 rooms, open Apr-Oct. A guesthouse renowned for tasteful rooms and excellent breakfasts including fresh fruit salad and salmon with scrambled eggs.

D **Thornloe Guest House**, Albert Rd, T/F01631-562879, www.thornloeoban.co.uk. 7 rooms. Quiet and centrally located guesthouse run by Alan and Valerie Bichener. Welcoming with good-sized en suite rooms and limited off-street parking. Enjoy the sea views with a bottle of wine in the conservatory.

F **Jeremy Inglis Hostel**, 21 Airds Cres, opposite the tourist office, T01631-565065. Handy for the train station and ferry, these small quirky rooms include continental breakfast.

F **Oban Backpackers**, Breadalbane St, T01631-562107. Open year-round and very popular. Book ahead.

F **SYHA Youth Hostel**, Corran Esplanade, just beyond St Columba's Cathedral, T01631-562025. Open all year.

Camping

Oban Caravan & Camping Park, Gallanach Rd, 3 miles south of town beyond the Kerrera ferry. T01631-562425, F01631-566624. Apr to mid-Oct. Beautiful setting but beware late-night revellers.

Oban Divers Caravan Park, on the Glenshellach Rd, 1½ miles south of the ferry terminal, T/F01631-562755. Mar-Nov. Very good campsite with good facilities for kids.

Around Oban *p118*

L **Airds Hotel**, Port Appin, T01631-730236, F01631-730535. Regarded as one of the UK's finest hotels, a personal touch pervades this classy establishment that boasts exquisite views, fine dining and delightful rooms.

L **Willowburn Hotel**, Seil, T01852-300276, www.willowburn.co.uk. Open Mar-Nov. 7 rooms. Delightful, peaceful setting with views over Sound of Seil. They smoke their own salmon, duck and cheeses and serve local produce.

A **Loch Melfort Hotel**, Arduaine, T01852-200233, www.lochmelfort.co.uk. Open all year. 23 rooms. Terrific seafood and game as you enjoy the views over Asknish Bay.

B **Barcaldine Castle**, Barcaldine Castle, Benderloch, T/F01631-720598. Year-round. 2 bedrooms. 9 miles north of Oban and the A828, this is a rare opportunity to reside in a 16th-century castle and home of the Campbells of Barcaldine. You'll even step over the dungeon en route to breakfast!

B-C **Pierhouse Hotel**, Port Appin, T01631-730302, www.pierhousehotel.co.uk. 12 en suite rooms. Open all year. Looking out to the tiny pier, this stylish little hotel has a reputation for excellent, moderately priced local seafood. Rooms are tidy and comfortable. Also bar and pool room.

F **Kerrera Bunkhouse**, Isle of Kerrera, T01631-570223. www.kerrerabunk house.co.uk. Year-round. 6 beds. Friendly accommodation complete with tea garden (Easter-Oct Wed-Sun 1000-1700).

Camping

F **Camping and Caravanning Club, Oban**, 12 miles north of Oban. T01631-720348. Apr-Oct. Clean and friendly.

Eating

Oban *p117, map p118*

¥¥¥ **The Waterfront**, Ferry Pier, T01631-563110. Excellent seafood restaurant that owns 2 fishing boats to land its daily catch. Pricey but the Waterfront Platter of langoustines, sea bass, scallops and garlic mussels is enticing. Daily 1130-1400 and 1800-late.

¥¥¥-¥¥ **Coast**, George St, T01631-569900. Its imaginative menu in stylish setting delivers mouth-watering vegetarian, meat and seafood dishes with a smile. Daily 1200-1400; 1730-2130.

¥¥ **Ee'usk**, North Pier, T01631-565666. Busy, glass-fronted trendy fish restaurant which prides itself on the quality of its seafood. Service with flair. Daily 1100-1600 and 1800-2130.

¥¥ **The Studio**, Craigard Rd, T01631-562030. A cosy restaurant away from the busy waterfront that serves a fine Stornoway black pudding starter and prime steaks in addition to its daily catch. Daily 1800-2200.

¥ **John Ogden's**, by the ferry terminal. After 15 years Ogden's bustling green shed remains Oban's best seafood haunt. For an inexpensive quality snack walk no further. Try a pot of squat lobster tails (£1.95), a fresh crab sandwich or the mouth-watering scallops in garlic (£4.95). Daily 0900-1800.

¥ **Nories**, George St. After 43 years it remains Oban's finest and friendliest chippie. Ask for it wrapped in newspaper.

¥ **The Oban Inn**, North Pier, T01631-562484. Atmospheric, old-world bar serving hearty bar food, not least an inexpensive plate of mussels. Lunch and dinner (until 2200) daily.

Around Oban *p118*

¥¥¥ **Airds Hotel**, Port Appin, T01631-730236, F01631-730535. Upmarket, award-winning fine dining based on 'modern French with a Scottish twist'.

¥¥ **The Oyster Inn**, Connel Bridge, T01631-710666, www.oysterinn.co.uk. Modern, child-friendly restaurant with wide-ranging menu, real ales and sea views.

¥¥-¥ **Oyster Brewery and Restaurant**, Ellenabeich pier, Seil, T01852-300121. www.oysterbrewery.com. Daily 1100-2100. Stars of Channel 4's *Life Begins* series, this harbourside hostelry is where to sample smooth real ales and a delicious seafood salad whilst bantering with the friendly locals. Enjoy.

Bars and clubs

Oban *p117, map p118*

The young crowd may head for **Mondo's**, but Oban is no party town.

Mondo's, George St. For those in search of drink promos, loud music and TV screens.

Oban Inn, by the North Pier, is by far the most atmospheric 'old-world' pub in town with real ales on tap, bar food and an intriguing eclectic mix of flags and memorabilia adorning the walls.

O'Donnells, Breadalbane St. Popular Irish theme bar.

Around Oban *p118*

You'll always find a pint and warm welcome at the **Galley of Lorn Hotel** in Ardfern, the **Puffer Bar** in Easdale, and **Oyster Brewery Bar and Restaurant**, in Ellenabeich.

Entertainment

Oban *p117, map p118*

The Highland Theatre, at the north end of George St, T01631-562444, is confusingly the local cinema. It shows most of the popular current releases.

Festivals and events

Oban *p117, map p118*

Apr-May Highlands & Islands Music & Dance Festival for Children is held at the end of Apr/beginning of May.

Aug Argyllshire Gathering (Oban Games) is held during the 4th week of Aug in Mossfield Park, www.obangames.com.

Sep World stone-skimming championships are held on Easdale in late Sep (and usually won by an Aussie – make of that what you will). Lots of drinking and merriment, see www.stoneskimming.com.

Activities and tours

Oban *p117, map p118*

Boat trips

Boat trips can be made from Oban to Mull, Iona, Staffa and The Treshnish Islands with a variety of companies.

Bowman's Tours, Queens Park Pl, T01631-566809; **Gordon Grant Tours**, T01681-700338; www.staffatours.com; **Turus Mara**, T08000-858786; **Argyll Charters**, T01631-563387, and **Allan's Seal Trips**, T01631 565059, offer a variety of island and wildlife cruises, ranging in price from £21.

Oban Sea Fishing, T07793-120958, Dunstaffnage Marina, www.obansea fishing.com. Offshore fishing for all standards.

Diving

Puffin Dive Centre, Gallanach Port, Gallanach Rd, T01631-566088, or booking office at George St, T01631-571190. Established in 1992, this dive centre offers a 2-hr beginner 'try-a-dive' (£57.50) and training for all standards including wreck diving.

Swimming

Atlantis Leisure, Dalriach Rd, T01631-566800, www.atlantisleisure.co.uk. Sports and leisure centre with pool.

Around Oban *p118*

Boat trips

Craignish Cruises, T01852-500540, www.craig nishcruises.co.uk, runs private charters and fishing trips from Ardfern Yacht Centre to the Sound of Jura, Corryvreckan and Garvellachs.

Kerrera Sea Adventures, T01631-563664/07786-963279, runs 1-hr wildlife trips around Kerrera on an fast, 7.6-m rigid inflatable boat (RIB).

Seafari Adventures, T01852-300003, www.seafari.co.uk, is based at Ellenabeich on Seil (also book at Oban TIC). Their 300 hp RIBS take you on a thrilling ride across the Corryvreckan whirlpool (see page 166), with opportunities to spot seals, porpoises and lots of seabirds. £27.50, children £20.50.

Horse riding

Ardfern Riding Centre, **Craobh Haven**, T01852-500632. Establisherd in 1972, they offer a variety of trails and pub rides, from £20 for 1 hr.

Lettershuna Riding, T01631-730227. For pony trekking.

Watersports

Linnhe Marine Watersports Centre, Lettershuna, just beyond Port Appin, T01631-730401. Hire motor boats (from £30 per hr), sailing dinghies and windsurfing boards (also lessons). May-Sep 0900-1800.

Transport

Oban *p117, map p118*

Bus There are regular daily buses to and from **Inverness** (4 hrs hrs) via **Fort William** (1¼ hrs) and **Benderloch** and **Appin** with Scottish Citylink, T08705-505050. Scottish Citylink Coaches also run a regular daily service to and from **Glasgow** (3 hrs). McGill's Bus , T01475-711122, also run to Glasgow (3 hrs) on Tue and Sat.

The West Highland Flyer minibus, T07780-724248, Easter-end Oct Mon, Wed and Sat, links the **Oban** (Mull) and **Mallaig** (Skye) ferries.

Regular daily buses run to and from **Dalmally**, via **Cruachan Power Station**, **Lochawe** and **Taynuilt Hotel**, operated by Scottish Citylink, T08705-505050, Awe Service Station, T01866-822612, and West Coast Motors, T01586-552319. Mon-Sat there are buses to **Ardrishaig**,via **Kilmartin** and **Lochgilphead** with West Coast Motors, T01586-552319 and **Scottish Citylink**. **West Coast Motors** also run (Mon-Sat) to **Ellenabeich** and **North Cuan**.

Car hire Flit Van & Car Hire, Glencruitten Rd, T/F01631-566553. From £35 per day.

Cycle You can rent adult, kids' and trailer bikes (from £14 per day) from **Liberty Cycless**, Unit 9, Mill Lane, T01631-564000. There are numerous cycling routes and walks in Argyll. Ask at the TIC for the leaflet, *Cycle the Forests of North Argyll*, or visit www.forestry.gov.uk/mtbscotland.

Ferry Oban is the main ferry port for many of the Hebridean islands. **CalMac** ferry terminal, T08705-650000, is on Railway Pier, to the south of the town centre. See the islands' Transport sections for details.

Train Only 100 yds away is the train station which is next to the bus terminal. There are 3 trains daily to **Glasgow**, via **Crianlarich**, where the Oban train connects with the Mallaig/Fort William–Glasgow train.

Around Oban *p118*
Cycle hire Isle of Luing Bike Hire, Isle of Luing, T01852-314274. £15 per day.

Ferry The departure point for ferries to **Kerrera** is 1½ miles along the Gallanach Rd. Regular intervals daily 0845-1800 (Sun 1030-1700) throughout the year. £4 return.

A passenger ferry leaves from **Port Appin** pier to the north point of **Lismore** island daily and throughout the year every hour (except 1300), 10 mins, £2.50 return. A tiny passenger ferry sails from **Ellenabeich** on Seil to **Easdale**, making the 3-min trip at regular intervals between 0745 and 2100 Mon-Sat, partly to schedule, partly on request. Ring the bell in the shelter on the pier. A daily car ferry to **Luing** (South Cuan), T01631-562125, sails from South Cuan on Seil (5 mins), every 15 mins from 0730 to 1820 (later in summer) and on Sun every 20 mins from 1100 to 1810. Return fare is £1.40 per passenger and £5.70 per car.

❻ Directory

Oban and around *p117, map p118*
Banks Several major banks have branches with ATMs in the centre and you can change foreign currency at the TIC. Note that some B&Bs and pubs on the islands will only take cash. **Internet** Oban Backpackers, but there's free access at **Oban Library**, 77 Albany St, T01631-571444.

Mid-Argyll, Kintyre, Cowal and Bute

Further south from Oban the long finger of Mid-Argyll extends past the offshore 'whisky isles' of Islay and Jura, pointing southwards into the remote Kintyre Peninsula where rolling hills protect the Isle of Arran from the wrath of the Atlantic Ocean. Packed with history, winding roads take visitors on a journey past attractive sea lochs and huge forests, revealing at Kilmartin Glen one of Europe's most important prehistoric sites. Mull of Kintyre is the lonely tip, a stone's throw from Northern Ireland. On the other side of Loch Fyne is the walking haven and giant claw of Cowal Peninsula, looking as if it's about to crush in its grasp the aptly named Isle of Bute, home to one of Scotland's most fantastical stately homes. ▸▸ *For Sleeping, Eating and other listings, see pages 136-139.*

Ins and outs

Cowal's main **TIC** ⓘ *Alexandra Parade, Dunoon, T01369-703785, all year*; **Helensburgh TIC** ⓘ *clock tower on the waterfront, T01436-672642, Apr-Oct*; **Bute TIC** ⓘ *Promenade, Rothesay, T01700-502151, all year*; **Inveraray TIC** ⓘ *Front St, T01499-302063*; **Lochgilphead TIC** ⓘ *Lochnell St, T01546-602344, Apr-Oct*; **Tarbert TIC** ⓘ *Harbour St, T01880-820429*; and **Campbeltown TIC** ⓘ *Old Quay, T01586-552056.*

Loch Awe and Loch Etive pp 136-139. Colour map 3, C5/B5-6.

Loch Awe is the longest freshwater loch in Scotland and, further north, is the beautiful Loch Etive. There's enough here to justify a couple of days' exploration, particularly the little visited west shore of Loch Awe, and there are plenty of other places to visit around Inveraray to the south.

At the northeastern tip of Loch Awe, between the villages of of **Dalmally** and **Lochawe**, is the romantic ruin of **Kilchurn Castle**, on a promontory jutting out into the loch. It can be visited by boat from **Ardanaiseig Hotel** ⓘ *T01866-833333*, on the east side of the loch. Also worth a look around here is the lovely, and rather bizarre, **St Conan's Church** ⓘ *free, donation requested,* just off the A85 by Lochawe village. Built in the late 19th century but not used until 1930, the church's serene atmosphere is striking. Inside is an effigy of Robert the Bruce, with one of his bones buried underneath. The exterior, especially the south side overlooking the loch, is a riot of eccentric detail.

Four miles west of Lochawe, and almost a mile inside Ben Cruachan (3695 ft) is the underground attraction of the **Cruachan Power Station** ⓘ *0930-1700, £5, children £2 (free if arrive by cycle)*, or 'Hollow Mountain'. From the visitor centre on the shores of Loch Awe, a bus trip takes you into the heart of the mountain through tunnels until you reach the giant steel doors and generating room. Whilst exploring this Bond-like subterranean warren, it's impossible to forget the millions of tonnes of rock above your head. Pray Loch Awe doesn't spring a leak!

Further west, and 12 miles east of Oban, is the tiny village of **Taynuilt**, near the shore of Loch Etive. Just before the village, at Bridge of Awe, is a sign for **Inverawe Fisheries Country Park** ⓘ *T01866-822808, www.smokedsalmon.co.uk, Apr-Dec daily 0830-1700*, where you can take fishing lessons (£28.50), learn about traditional smoking techniques, or wander along a series of nature trails. If the weather's fine, you can buy some of their delicious smoked products and have a picnic, see box, page 126. If you fancy some smoked salmon delivered to your home, make sure you sign up for their mailing list.

One mile north of the village on the shores of Loch Etive is **Bonawe Iron Furnace** ⓘ *T01866-822432, Apr-Sep daily 0930-1830, £3.50, concession £2.50, children £1.50*. Founded in 1753 by a group of Cumbrian ironmasters, Bonawe used the abundant woodlands of Argyll to make charcoal to fire its massive furnace. At its height, it produced 600-700 tons of pig-iron a year and provided cannonballs for Admiral Nelson at the Battle of Trafalgar. Iron production ceased at Bonawe in 1876 and it has now been restored as an industrial heritage site, with displays explaining the whole production process.

Beyond Bonawe is the tranquil pier from which **Loch Etive Cruises** depart (see page 138). Inaccessible except by boat, the 90-minute (£4.80) or three-hour (£8.80) cruise of one of Scotland's great hidden treasures is definitely worth it, see Activities and tours, page 138.

Running south from the village is the very lovely and very quiet Glen Lonan. Three miles along the Glen Lonan road is **Barguillean's Angus Garden** ⓘ *T01866-822335, daily 0900-1800, free*, one of Argyll's youngest and smallest gardens, but also one of the most peaceful and evocative, set around the shores of little Loch Angus. It was created in 1957, in memory of Angus MacDonald, a journalist and writer killed in Cyprus in 1956.

Between Loch Awe and Loch Etive runs the River Awe, which squeezes through the dark and ominous Pass of Brander. It is so steep and narrow that, according to legend, it was once held against an entire army by an old woman brandishing a scythe.

Piscine cuisine

At **Inverawe Fisheries and Smokery**, see page 125, they buy smaller farmed salmon because they believe the lower fat content makes them tastier than larger ones. Traditional methods prevail here. The fish are dry salted, washed, smoked over oak logs for anything from 16 to 24 hours, depending on conditions, and then hand-sliced. The result is a rich and freshly oaky taste. From a 100 g smoked salmon pack (£3.85) to a whole side of salmon (£26), as well as gravadlax, smoked trout, eel and halibut, there's a diverse range to choose from.

Knipoch Smokehouse, in South Lorn near Oban, T01852-316251, www.knipochsmokehouse.co.uk, on the other hand, believes that large salmon, weighing 6-7 kg, produce the best quality. Its approach involves a dry salt cure strengthened with sugar, whisky, juniper and rowan berries, plus a lengthy two- to three-day smoke. The fish comes out so black it has to be washed and trimmed to look presentable, and the taste is rather unusual: strong, sweet, sharp and almondy. A whole side costs £45, but it can be cut to any size: sliced at £17.60 per 500 g, unsliced at £15.95.

A single-track road runs southwest of Kilchrenan along the shores of Loch Awe to the tiny villages of **Dalavich** and **Ford**, through the very beautiful Inverinan Forest, a Forestry Commission property which has a series of undemanding marked trails running through the hills overlooking the loch. The first walk starts out from the little hamlet of **Inverinan**. Red waymarkers lead you from the car park into the woods surrounding the gorge of the River Inan. Part of the route follows the old drove road along which cattle were driven from the Highlands down to the markets in south and central Scotland. The walk is 3 miles long and should take around 1½ hours. Further along the road, half a mile north of Dalavich, is a car park at **Barnaline Lodge**, the starting point for a 9-mile bike route, a waymarked walk through the Caledonian Forest Reserve, and a couple of other woodland walks. The longest of the walks is the 5-mile route that leads along the **River Avich**, then along the shores of **Loch Avich** before returning to the lodge. Two and a half miles south of Dalavich is a car park, which marks the starting point for a blue waymarked walk along the shores of **Loch Awe**. The route passes through **Mackenzie's Grove**, a sheltered gorge containing some of the largest conifers on the west coast. The route then runs along the shores of the loch, from where you can see the remains of a *crannog*, one of over 40 of these Iron Age settlements on Loch Awe. The route then heads back to the car park; about 3 miles in total. These routes are all outlined, with accompanying maps, in the Forestry Commission leaflet, *A Guide to Forest Walks and Trails in North Argyll*, available at tourist offices. Alternatively visit www.forestry.gov.uk/recreation.

Inveraray and around » *pp 136-139. Colour map 3, C6.*

Inveraray → *Phone code: 01499.*

Inveraray is the classic 18th-century planned town (don't call it a village), with its straight, wide streets and dignified Georgian houses, and enjoys the most stunning of settings, on the shores of Loch Fyne. It was rebuilt by the third Duke of Argyll, head of the Campbell clan, at the same time as he restored the nearby family home, which now attracts hordes of summer visitors. As well as its natural beauty and elegance, and fine castle, Inveraray has several other attractions that make an overnight stay in the town worthwhile.

One of Argyll's most famous castles, **Inveraray Castle** ⓘ *T01499-302203, Apr-Oct, Mon-Sat 1000-1745, Sun 1200-1745 (last admission 1700), £6.30, concession £5.20, children £4.10*, has been the clan seat of the Campbells for centuries and is still the family home of the Duke of Argyll. The present neo-Gothic structure dates from 1745, and its main feature is the magnificent armoury hall, whose displays of weaponry were supplied to the Campbells by the British government to quell the Jacobite rebellion. The elaborately furnished rooms are also on display, as is the fascinating and troubled family history in the Clan room. For £1 from the TIC, the booklet *Five Walks on Inverary Estate* is a worthwhile investment.

Inveraray Jail ⓘ *T01499-302381, Apr-Oct daily 0930-1800, Nov-Mar daily 1000-1700, £6.25, concession £4.15, children £3.15, family £17.20*, the Georgian prison and courthouse in the centre of the town has been brilliantly restored as a fascinating museum that gives a vivid insight into life behind bars from medieval times up until the 19th century. You can sit in on an 1820 courtroom trial, then visit the cells below and learn all about some of the delightful prison pursuits, such as branding with a hot iron, ear nailing and public whipping. The whole experience is further enhanced by the guides, who are dressed as warders and prisoners. Makes you want to stay on the right side of the law, although, thankfully, conditions have improved – as you will see for yourself.

Another worthwhile diversion, especially if you've got kids in tow, the **Inveraray Maritime Museum** ⓘ *T01499-302213, Apr-Oct daily 1000-1800, Nov-Mar daily 1000-1700, £3.80, concession £2.80, children £2.20*, housed in the *SV Arctic Penguin*, one of the world's last iron sailing ships, which is moored at the lochside pier. Below decks are fascinating displays on Clyde shipbuilding, the Highland Clearances and footage from the maritime TV classic *Para Handy* as well as the chance to blow the foghorn and relax with an on-board cuppa.

A few miles southwest of town, on the A83 to Lochgilphead, is **Argyll Adventure** ⓘ *T01499-T302611, www.argylladventure.com, Apr-end Oct daily 1000-1700, from £4 per activity*. Here, by the banks of Loch Fyne, both children and the young at heart can indulge in laser clay-pigeon shooting, Laser Quest, bungee trampolining, climbing and horse riding (from £22).

Three miles beyond Argyll Adventure is **Auchindrain Township** ⓘ *T01499-500235, Apr-Oct daily 1000-1700 (last admission 1600) £4.50, concession £3.50, children £2.20*, a restored and authentic West Highland farming village with parts dating to the 1700s. Features include two perfectly restored thatched cottages and barns, furnished and equipped with dairy and household items to give a real insight into what rural life must have been like in centuries past. There's also an informative visitor centre and coffee-shop.

Four miles further down the A83 is **Crarae Gardens** ⓘ *T01546-886614, visitor centre, Easter-30 Sep, daily 1000-1700, gardens open all year, daily 0930-sunset, £5, concession £4*, one of Scotland's very best public gardens, dramatically set in a deep wooded glen on the shores of Loch Fyne. Initiated by Lady Campbell in 1912, there are marked woodland walks winding their way through a spectacular array of rhododendrons, azaleas and numerous other exotic plants towards the tumbling waterfalls of the 'Himalayan Gorge'. Any time of year is rewarding to visit including autumn when foliage is resplendent in rich tints.

Kilmartin and around → *Phone code: 01546. Colour map 3, C5.*

Much of this region was once part of the ancient Kingdom of Dalriada, established by the Irish Celts (known as the *Scotti*, hence Scotland) who settled here in the fifth century. North of Lochgilphead, on the A816 to Oban, is **Kilmartin Glen**, an area of Neolithic and Bronze Age chambered and round cairns, stone circles, rock carvings, Iron Age forts and duns, Early Christian sculptured stones and medieval castles. Before exploring this fascinating area, it's best to stop first at **Kilmartin House**

 Museum ⓘ *T01546-510278, Mar-Sep daily 1000-1730 (call for winter opening), £4.60, concession £3.90, children £1.70*. Housed in the old manse next to the parish church in the tiny village of **Kilmartin** the 15-minute audio-visual display, imaginative exhibits including Neolithic exhibits provide a fascinating and invaluable insight into the surrounding landscape. The café/restaurant is well worth a visit on its own (see Eating, page 137). Next door in the church graveyard are the **Kilmartin crosses**, dating from as far back as the ninth and 10th centuries. Also within the graveyard is one of the largest collections of medieval grave slabs in the West Highlands.

Two miles north of Kilmartin, sitting high above the A816, is **Carnasserie Castle** ⓘ *free, it's a little way from the car park*, an imposing 16th-century tower house built by John Carswell, Bishop of the Isles, who translated *The Book of the Common Order* in 1567, the first book to be printed in Gaelic.

Most notable of all is the **linear cemetery**, a line of burial cairns that stretch southward from Kilmartin village for over 2 miles. The largest and oldest of the group is the Neolithic cairn, Nether Largie South, which is over 5000 years old and big enough to enter. The other cairns, Nether Largie North, Mid Nether Largie and Ri Cruin, are Bronze Age, and the huge stone coffins show carvings on the grave slabs. Nearby are the Temple Wood Stone Circles, where burials took place from Neolithic times to the Bronze Age.

On the other side of the A816, and visible from the road, is a group of monuments which can all be reached from Dunchraigaig Cairn. This is a huge Bronze Age cairn with some of the covering stones removed to reveal three stone coffins. From here a path is signed to **Ballymeanoch Standing Stones**, the tallest of which is 12-ft high. Two of the stones are decorated with cup marks, prehistoric rock carvings that can be found at numerous locations throughout the Kilmartin area. There's also a henge monument in the same field. These were generally round or oval platforms with an internal ditch, and it's thought they were used for ceremonial purposes. The best example of rock carvings is at Achnabreck, near Cairnbaan village, the largest collection anywhere in Britain. The purpose and significance of these cup- and ring-marked rocks is still a matter of debate.

A few miles south of Kilmartin village is the Iron Age hill fort of **Dunadd**, which stands atop a rocky outcrop and dominates the surrounding flat expanse of **Moine Mhór** (Great Moss), one of the few remaining peat bogs in the country and now a nature reserve. **Dunadd Fort** became the capital of the ancient kingdom of Dalriada around AD 500 and is one of the most important Celtic sites in Scotland. The views from the top are wonderful and worth the visit alone, but you can also see carved out of the exposed rock, a basin and footprint, thought to have been used in the inauguration ceremonies of the ancient kings of Dalriada. There's also an inscription in *ogham* (a form of early writing from Ireland) and the faint outline of a boar, possibly of Pictish origin.

Crinan Canal → *Colour map 3, C5.*

Kilmartin Glen is bordered to the south by the Crinan Canal, a 9-mile stretch of waterway linking Loch Fyne at Ardrishaig with the Sound of Jura. It was designed and built by Sir John Rennie in 1801, with the assistance of the ubiquitous Thomas Telford, to allow shipping to avoid the long and often hazardous journey round the Mull of Kintyre and to help stimulate trade in the islands. These days you're more likely to see pleasure yachts and cruisers sailing on the canal than the cargo vessels which once transported coal and other goods to the islands and returned with livestock. You don't need to come in a boat to appreciate the canal. You can walk or cycle along the towpath that runs the entire length of the canal, from Ardrishaig to Crinan, and watch boats of all shapes and sizes negotiating a total of 15 locks. The best place to view the canal traffic is at **Crinan**, a pretty little fishing port on Loch Crinan at the western end of the canal, see Activities and tours, page 138.

Knapdale

Running south from the Crinan Canal down to Kintyre is Knapdale, a forested, hilly area that gets its name from its Gaelic description, *cnap* (hill) and *dall* (field). It's an area worth exploring, for there are many walking and cycling trails and superb views from the west coast across to the Paps of Jura. Immediately south of the canal is Knapdale Forest, which stretches from coast to coast over hills dotted with tiny lochs. Forestry Commission Scotland has marked out several lovely trails. Three fairly easy circular routes start from the B8025 which runs south from **Bellanoch**, just east of Crinan.

One trail sets out from the car park at the unmanned Barnluasgan Interpretation Centre and runs up to a point beyond **Loch Barnluasgan**, with great views over the forest and the many lochs. It's a mile in total. A second trail, also a mile long, starts from a car park a little further along the B8025 and heads through the forest to the deserted township of **Arichonan**. The third trail starts out from the car park between the starting points for the first and second trails. It runs right around **Loch Coille-Bharr** and is 3 miles long. A more strenuous walk starts from a car park about 100 yards into the forest, off the B841, about half a mile west of Cairnbaan, and climbs up to the peak of **Dunardy** (702 ft).

At the Barnluasgan Interpretation Centre a little side road turns south down the eastern shore of beautiful Loch Sween, past the village of Achnamara, to the 12th-century **Castle Sween**. First impressions of the castle, situated on the shores of the lovely loch with the forested hills all around, are tainted by the sprawling caravan park and self-catering chalets on a nearby 15,000-acre estate. Unfortunately, the caravans were not there when Robert the Bruce attacked the castle, otherwise he might have done us all a favour by razing them. Three miles south is the ruined 13th-century **Kilmory Knap Chapel**. A new glass roof protects the carved stones inside. Here, visitors will find an 8-ft-high, 15th-century **MacMillan's Cross**, which shows the Crucifixion on one side and a hunting scene on the other. There are also several unmarked graves, believed to be those of 13th-century Knights Templar who fled from France.

Lochgilphead

→ *Colour map 3, C5.*

The main town in the area of Mid-Argyll, and administrative centre for the entire Argyll and Bute region, is Lochgilphead, a sleepy little place at the head of Loch Gilp, an arm of Loch Fyne. Lochgilphead started life as a planned town, but the industries came and went, leaving it with the customary grid plan of wide streets but little else. Today it serves as a useful base for exploring the area, with accommodation options, a bank and supermarket. There's a nice easy walk from the car park at Kilmory Castle Gardens, about a mile east of town, up to Kilmory Loch. It takes about an hour there and back and is well marked. The gardens also make a pleasant stroll and there are other marked walks, including up to **Dun Mór** (360 ft).

Kintyre

» *pp 136-139. Colour map 5, A-B2.*

→ *Phone code: 01880.*

The long peninsula of Kintyre is probably best known as the inspiration for Paul McCartney's phenomenally successful 1970s dirge, *Mull of Kintyre*, but don't let that put you off. Historic Kintyre may be isolated but it's also packed with great scenery, wildlife and beaches which attract the experienced surfer and windsurfer alike. Hardy walkers also have the opportunity to explore a newly opened 89-mile **Kintyre Way coastal route** ⓘ *www.kintyreway.com*, stretching from Tarbert harbour to Dunaverty in the south. The peninsula would be an island, were it not for the mile-long isthmus between West and East Loch Tarbert, a fact not lost on King Magnus Barefoot of

Norway. In the 11th century he signed a treaty with the Scottish king, Malcolm Canmore, giving him all the land he could sail round, and promptly had his men drag his longboat across the narrow isthmus, thus adding Kintyre to his kingdom.

Ins and outs

Getting around Public transport on Kintyre has improved though still requires patience. On the west coast there's a regular (daily) bus service running between Campbeltown, Tarbert, Lochgilphead and Glasgow that also stops at the Kennacraig ferry terminal (for crossings to Islay). From Tarbert to Claonaig (for ferries to Lochranza on Arran) and Skipness there are buses at least three times daily (except Sunday). Four times daily a bus also covers the quiet east route between Campbeltown and Carradale. Details from **Argyll & Bute Council**, T01546-604695, or **Tarbert TIC** ⓘ *T01880-820429*. *» For further details, see Transport, page 138.*

Tarbert → *Colour map 5, A3.*

The fishing village of Tarbert sits at the head of East Loch Tarbert, in a sheltered bay backed by forested hills, and is one the most attractive ports on the west coast. Tarbert (the name derives from the Gaelic *An Tairbeart*, meaning 'isthmus') has a long tradition of fishing, and in the 18th and 19th centuries was a major herring port. Today, prawns and other shellfish are the main catch and though there is still a sizeable fleet, fishing has declined in importance to the local economy. Tourism is now a major source of income, with yachties in particular swelling local coffers when the **Scottish Series**, the second largest yacht race in the UK sails into the picturesque natural harbour. **TIC** ⓘ *Harbour St, T01880-820429, Apr-Oct.*

Overlooking the harbour is the dramatically sited ruin of **Robert the Bruce's 14th-century castle**. There's not much left to see, other than the five-storey 15th-century keep. It's unsafe to investigate the ruins too closely, but the view alone is worth the walk. There are steps leading up to the castle, next to the **Loch Fyne Gallery** on Harbour Street. Behind the castle there are several marked trails leading up into the hills, with great views over Loch Fyne and the islands. Less strenuous is the short walk at the end of Garvel Road, on the north side of the harbour, which leads to the beach. At the end of East Pier road, beyond the Cowal Ferry, is yet another good walk, to the **Shell Beaches**. One mile south, you can also explore the lovely gardens at **Stonefield Castle Hotel**, see Sleeping, page 136.

Gigha → *Colour map 5, A2.*

The small island of Gigha (pronounced *Gee-a* with a hard 'g'; www.isle-of-gigha.co.uk) translates from Norse as 'God's Island'. A grand claim, perhaps, but there's no question that this most accessible of islands is also one of the loveliest (and pretty much midge-free!). It's only a 20-minute ferry ride away, and is only 7 miles by 1 mile, so it can be visited easily in a day, which is just about enough time to appreciate why the Vikings loved it so much. Like so many of the Hebridean islands, Gigha has had a long list of owners, including various branches of the MacNeils and, more recently, in 1944, Sir James Horlick, he of bedtime drink fame. Now, though, the islanders are the proud owners of their own little piece of paradise, thanks to a successful buy-out in 2001.

It was Horlick who created the islanders self-proclaimed 'Jewel in the Crown'; the wonderful **Achamore Gardens** ⓘ *1 mile south of the ferry terminal, T01583-505254, all year daily 0900-dusk, £2*. Thanks to Gigha's mild climate, the 50-acre woodland garden has an amazing variety of tropical plants, including rhododendrons, azaleas and camellias. The sight of albino peacocks and palm trees may have you doubting this is a Scottish island at all. There are two marked walks, starting from the walled garden. Managed by the island's Heritage Trust, a three-year, £600,000 garden restoration project is now underway to ensure Gigha's 'jewel' continues to shine for years to come.

▲ The island's other delights include some good walks, white sandy beaches and fantastic views across to Jura on one side and Kintyre on the other. One of the best walks is to take the path left after the nine-hole golf course, signed Ardaily, past Mill Loch to the **Mill** on the west shore. The views from here are just magnificent. Another good idea is to walk, or cycle (see Transport, page 138) to the peninsula of **Eilean Garbh** at the north of the island. About half a mile beyond Kinererach Farm a path leads left to the peninsula where two crescent-shaped beaches are separated by a thin spit of land. And if the weather's good enough for a picnic, make sure you try some of the island's famously distinctive cheese.

Campbeltown and around → *Colour map 5, B2.*

At the southern end of the Kintyre Peninsula is **Campbeltown**, once home to 34 whisky distilleries and a large fishing fleet. Still the largest town in Kintyre, the two remaining distilleries hint at the town's decline in fortune, though the **Campbeltown Heritage Centre** ⓘ *T07733-485387, Easter-Oct, £2*, richly documents its history. Six miles west lies **Machrihanish** and a secretive military airbase beyond which miles of golden sands and gigantic Atlantic breakers beckon beachcombers and experienced wave-sailors alike. Nearby is a dramatic 18-hole championship golf course. The beach can be approached either by walking north from the village, or south from the car park on the main A83 to Tayinloan and Tarbert, where it leaves the coast.

▲ If the weather's good, it's worth taking a walk up to **Beinn Ghulean**, which overlooks the town and loch. Follow the signs for the A83 to Machrihanish until you reach Witchburn Road. After passing the creamery on your left, turn left into Tomaig Road and continue till you come to a wooden gate. Cross over the stile and follow the track through the fields, crossing two more stiles, before you reach the Forest Enterprise sign which marks the start of the walk. It's about 4 miles there and back from the end of Tomaig Road.

One of the most popular day trips is to the uninhabited **Davaar Island**, connected to the peninsula by a tidal breakwater. Here you can see the cave painting of the Crucifixion, completed in secret by a local artist in 1877. The island can be visited at low tide from Kildalloig Point, a couple of miles east of town. Check tide times at the tourist office before setting out.

It's only a short drive south from Campbeltown to the tip of the peninsula, the Mull of Kintyre, eulogized by one-time resident Paul McCartney in the irritating eponymous hit single. There's nothing much to see in this bleak, storm-battered place, apart from the coast of Ireland, a mere 12 miles away and clearly visible on a good day. The road out to the lighthouse, built in 1788 and remodelled by Robert Stevenson, grandfather of Robert Louis, is pretty hairy, to put it mildly. It's possible to walk from here up to Machrihanish (about 10 miles), past the ruined township of **Balmavicar** and the **Largiebaan Bird Reserve**. The views are great and there's a chance of seeing golden eagles.

The southernmost village on Kintyre is **Southend**, a bleak, windswept place with a wide sandy beach. At the east end of the beach, jutting out on a rocky promontory, are the scant remains of **Dunaverty Castle**, once a MacDonald stronghold, where 300 Royalists were brutally massacred in 1647 by the Covenanting army of the Earl of Argyll, despite having already surrendered. To the west of Southend, below the cliffs, is the ruined 13th-century **Keil Chapel**, which is said to mark the spot where St Columba first set foot on Scottish soil, before heading north to Iona. Close by is a pair of footprints carved into the rock, known as **Columba's footprints**.

The slow and winding single track B842 meanders up the east coast from Campbeltown to Skipness and **Claonaig**, departure point for the ferry to Arran, see page 139. The scenery en route is gentle and pleasant, with nice views of Arran, and there are some worthwhile places to stop.

Ten miles up the coast are the idyllic ruins of **Saddell Abbey**, a Cistercian establishment founded by Somerled in 1160. The abbey fell into ruin in the early 16th century and much of the stone was used in the building of 18th-century Saddell Castle for the Bishop of Argyll. Though little remains, there are some impressive medieval grave slabs, depicting knights, monks, ships, animals and other images.

A few miles further north is the village of **Carradale**, the only place of any size on the east coast, nestling in the sandy sweep of beautiful Carradale Bay. There are several pleasant marked walks through the woods between the B842 and the shore. The shortest of these walks (with green waymarkers) starts from the Network Centre (see below) and is a mile long. There's a 3-mile walk with red waymarkers which starts at the **Port Na Storm** car park and follows the forest road to the left. After 150 yards the route turns left again at the road junction. A mile further on, you turn right off the road and follow the track up to the summit of **Cnoc-nan Gabhor**, from where there are great views of Kintyre and across to Arran. A third walk (6 miles; blue waymarkers) also starts from the Port Na Storm car park. This time the route heads right at the junction 150 yards beyond the car park and then runs north along the shore, with a chance of seeing dolphins and basking shark. The path then swings west towards the road, then turns south with views of Carradale Glen.

Twelve miles north of Carradale the B842 ends at **Claonaig**, which is actually nothing more than a slipway for the ferry to Arran, see below. From here the B8001 heads west to meet the A83 near the Kennacraig ferry pier. A dead-end road runs north for a few miles to the tiny village of **Skipness**, where you can visit the substantial ruins of the 13th-century Skipness Castle and nearby chapel.

Cowal Peninsula and the Clyde Coast

» pp 136-139. Colour map 5, A3/4.

The Cowal Peninsula reaches out into the Firth of Clyde, framed by Loch Fyne and Loch Long. This is the most visited part of Argyll due to its proximity to Glasgow, but, despite the summer hordes, many of whom come for the **Cowal Highland Gathering** in late August, much of it is undisturbed. Most people head straight for the rather drab main ferry port and traditional Clyde seaside resort of Dunoon. More adventurous souls enjoy the forests and mountains of Argyll Forest Park in the north or the peace and tranquillity of the southwest coastline.

Argyll Forest Park

The northern part of the peninsula is largely covered by the sprawling Argyll Forest Park which extends from Loch Lomond south to Holy Loch. This area contains the most stunning scenery in Cowal, and includes the **Arrochar Alps**, a range of rugged peaks north of Glen Croe which offer some of the best climbing in Argyll. The most famous of these is anvil-like Ben Arthur (2891 ft), better known as **The Cobbler**. Less imposing are the hills south of Glen Croe, between Loch Goil and Loch Long, in an area known as Argyll's Bowling Green (not because it's flat, but an English corruption of the Gaelic *Baile na Greine*, meaning 'Sunny Hamlet'). There are many footpaths and cycle tracks threading their way through the park. Details of five are outlined in the excellent *Argyll Forest Park Guide* (£2), available from the Forestry Commission office in Ardgarten.

Arrochar to Dunoon

The gateway to Cowal, Arrochar, sits at the head of Loch Long on the main A83, only a few miles west of Tarbet and the shores of Loch Lomond. It's a small, uninspiring place but the setting is dramatic, with The Cobbler towering overhead. A few miles beyond Arrochar, on the shores of Loch Long, is **Ardgarten**, where there's an excellent **Forestry Commission visitor centre** ⓘ *T01863-702432, daily Apr-Oct 1000-1700*. This provides useful information on hillwalking and wildlife and is an excellent start-point for climbing The Cobbler (seven hours return trip). From Ardgarten the A83 climbs steeply up Glen Croe to reach one of Scotland's classic viewpoints at the top of the pass, the **Rest and be Thankful** (built under Major Caulfeild after the '45). The hordes of like-minded tourists, eager for that memorable photograph, cannot detract from the majestic views of the surrounding craggy peaks.

Here the road forks. The A83 continues towards **Inveraray**, see page 126, and the single-track B828 heads southwest to meet the B839, which runs down to the village of **Lochgoilhead**, in a beautiful setting on Loch Goil. There are several hotels and B&Bs as well as an unsightly village of self-catering holiday chalets next door. At the end of the road, several miles down the west side of Loch Goil, are the ruins of 15th-century **Carrick Castle**.

The A83 meanwhile runs down through **Glen Kinglas** to reach the village of **Cairndow**, at the head of Loch Fyne. Here, gastronomes must decide whether to drive south down the A815 and east side of Loch Fyne for Inver Cottage, by Castle Lachlan, or continue towards Inveraray and **Clachan**, to dine in the ever popular **Loch Fyne Oyster Bar**, see page 137. At the southern end of Loch Eck, at Benmore, is the **Younger Botanic Garden** ⓘ *T01369-706261, Apr-Sep daily 1000-1800, Mar and Oct 1000-1700, £3.50, concession £3, children £1*, a lovely woodland garden and offshoot of the Royal Botanic Garden in Edinburgh. Its 140 acres are laid out with over 250 species of rhododendrons and feature an avenue of giant redwoods.

Dunoon → *Colour map 5, A4.*

The largest town in Cowal, with around 8000 inhabitants, is Dunoon, one-time favourite holiday destination for Glaswegians, who came in their hordes on board the many paddle steamers that sailed "doon the watter" from Glasgow. Dunoon still attracts many visitors, but the town's economy has suffered following the closure of the Holy Loch US nuclear submarine in the 1990s. Nevertheless, Dunoon still comes to life during the **Cowal Highland Gathering**, see page 138. There's not much to detain you here, although the **Castle House Museum** ⓘ *Easter-Oct Mon-Sat 1030-1630, Sun 1400-1630, £1.50, concession £1, children free*, on Castle Hill overlooking the town, allows you to bone up on Cowal's often grisly past.

The southwest

One of the most beautiful parts of Argyll is the southwest of Cowal, particularly the route down to the little village of **Tighnabruaich**. The A8003 runs down the west side of Loch Riddon and there are few lovelier sights than the view from this road across the **Kyles of Bute**, the narrow straits that separate Cowal from the island of Bute. Tighnabruaich gets busy in the summer with visitors who come here to enjoy the best sailing on the west coast. A few miles southwest of Kames is **Portavadie**, on the west coast of Cowal. A **CalMac** car and passenger ferry sails from here to Tarbert, on the Kintyre Peninsula, saving a lot of time if you're heading for the islands of Islay, Jura or Colonsay.

Helensburgh → *Colour map 5, A4.*

Overlooking the Clyde is the town of Helensburgh, its wide, grid-plan streets lined with elegant Georgian houses. The town is most famously known for its connection with the great Glasgow architect, **Charles Rennie Mackintosh**. In the upper part of the town is **Hill House** ⓘ *Upper Colquhoun St, T01436-673900, Apr-Oct daily 1330-1730, £8, concession £6, tearoom open 1330-1630, trains from Glasgow Queen Street station to Helensburgh Central*, one of the best examples of Mackintosh's work. The

In 1799 an English traveller called Sarah Murray described the route over the Rest as "one of the most formidable [...] and gloomy passes in the Highlands".

house was designed for Glasgow publisher Walter Blackie in 1902-1904, and is managed by the National Trust for Scotland. In accordance with Blackie's wish to have a house with an individual feel, it is a masterpiece of balanced perfection and artistry with great attention to detail. The use of light and dark and the symbolism of the floral patterns – hallmarks of his personal art nouveau style – are in evidence. After exploring the house, you can visit the cosy tearoom in the converted kitchen.

Isle of Bute

» pp 136-139. Colour map 5, A3.

Barely a stone's throw off the south coast of Cowal is the island of Bute, another favourite holiday destination for people from Glasgow and Ayrshire, who come here in droves during the busy summer months. But though the island is small (15 miles long by 5 miles wide), it's deceptively easy to escape the hordes, who tend to congregate around the east coast resort of Rothesay, leaving the delights of the sparsely populated west coast free for those who enjoy a bit of peace and quiet.

Rothesay

The sole town on Bute is Rothesay, with its handsome period mansions lining the broad sweep of bay, its elegant promenade lined with palm trees and the distinctive 1920s **Winter Gardens**, now refurbished and housing a cinema and restaurant, as well as the TIC. **Rothesay Castle** ⓘ *T01700-502691, Apr-Sep daily 0930-1830, Oct-Mar Mon-Wed, Sat and Sun 0930-1630, £3.50, concession £2.50, children £1.50.* One thing men must do before leaving Rothesay is visit the palatial **Victorian public toilets** ⓘ *Easter-Sep 0800-2100, Oct-Mar 0900-1700, £0.20.* This architectural gem enables gents to 'spend a penny' in style.

Mount Stuart

ⓘ *T01700-503877, www.mountstuart.com, May-Sep Sun-Fri 1100-1700, Sat 1000-1430, gardens 1000-1800, house 1100-1700, £7.50, concession £6, children £3.50.*

One of Bute's main attractions is Mount Stuart, a unique Victorian Gothic house set in 300 acres of lush woodland gardens, 3 miles south of Rothesay. This magnificent architectural fantasy reflects the Third Marquess of Bute's passion for astrology, astronomy, mysticism and religion, and the sheer scale and grandeur of the place almost beggars belief. This is truly one of the great country houses of Scotland and displays breathtaking craftsmanship in marble and stained glass, as well as a fine collection of family portraits and Italian antiques. Much of the existing house dates from 1877, and was built following a terrible fire which destroyed the original, built in 1719 by the Second Earl of Bute. Equally impressive are the landscaped gardens and woodlands, established by the Third Earl of Bute (1713-1792), who advised on the foundation of Kew Gardens in London, and the stunning visitor centre complete with audio-visuals and restaurant. The present owner is Johnny

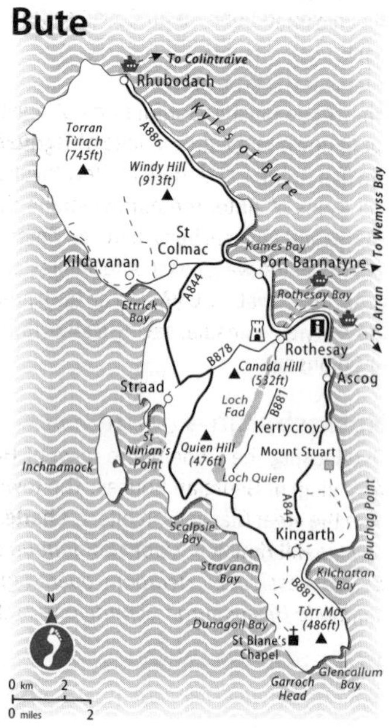

Dumfries (only the Daily Mail calls him the Seventh Marquess of Bute), former racing driver who won Le Mans in 1988 and who, famously, gave up his house for the headline-grabbing wedding of Stella McCartney, daughter of Paul, in 2003. It's worth spending a whole day here in order to take in the amazing splendour of the house and to explore the beautiful gardens. And if the weather's fine, why not bring a picnic and enjoy the wonderful sea views.

Other sights around the island

Just before Mount Stuart is the tidy little village of **Kerrycroy**, designed by the wife of the Second Marquess of Bute and featuring an interesting mix of building styles. South of Mount Stuart and the village of Kingarth is **Kilchattan Bay**, an attractive bay of pink sands and the start of a fine walk down to Glencallum Bay, in the southeastern corner of the island.

Southwest of Kilchattan Bay is **St Blane's Chapel**, a 12th-century ruin in a beautifully peaceful spot near the southern tip of the island. The medieval church stands on the site of an earlier monastery, established in the sixth century by St Blane, nephew of St Catan, after whom Kilchattan is named. The ruin can be reached by road from Rothesay, or as part of the walk from Kilchattan Bay. Four miles north of St Blane's, on the west coast, is **Scalpsie Bay**, the nicest beach on the island and a good place for seal spotting. A little further north is **St Ninian's Point**, looking across to the island of **Inchmarnock**. At the end of the beach are the ruins of a sixth-century chapel, dedicated to St Ninian.

The Highland-Lowland dividing line passes through the middle of Bute at Loch Fad, which separates the hilly and uninhabited northern half of the island and the rolling farmland of the south. The highest point on the island is **Windy Hill** (913 ft) in the north, from where there are great views across the island. A less strenuous walk is up **Canada Hill**, a few miles southwest of Rothesay, above Loch Fad. Walk along Craigmore promenade and turn off at the old pier to **Ardencraig Gardens**. Then continue uphill along the golf course to the top of the hill for great views of the Firth of Clyde.

▲ Kilchattan Bay to Glencallum Bay walk

A longer walk is the circular route from Kilchattan Bay south to Glencallum Bay and back, via St Blane's chapel. The bay was once a final staging point for boats bound for overseas. The walk is 5 miles in total. Allow about four hours. There are buses to and from Rothesay. The route is waymarked, but if you want to take a map, it's OS Landranger sheet 63 or Explorer 362. The Rothesay Discovery Centre (TIC) carries a full stock of maps.

Follow the signpost for 'Kelspoke Path' beside Kiln Villas and take the track which climbs steadily before turning sharply back on itself. Go through a gate and shortly before the next gate turn right. Follow the rough track, which swings right, then left over open ground to the ruins of Kelspoke Castle.

Continue along the grassy path, past a reservoir on your right, then cross the stile and go down and across a small burn. Turn left and follow the burn, before heading right to join the shore path and follow this past the lighthouse on your left and around the headland to **Glencallum Bay**. Continue round the shoreline and at the far end of the bay follow the waymarks as the path climbs to cross the headland. The path then levels out and from here there are great views across to the mountains of Arran.

The path then reaches the col above **Loch na Leighe**. Drop down to the loch and follow the waymarks south over open ground. Before reaching a farm called The Plan, go right over two footbridges, then left below a low ridge. Keep to the right of the buildings, following the waymarks across open ground to the stile that crosses to the ruins of St Blane's Chapel (see above). Leave the chapel by the gap in the boundary wall and go through a gate, turning left on a clear track which climbs steadily to a stile. Cross the stile and turn right, following the edge of the field down to a gate. Walk uphill on the left side of the field to Suidhe Hill. At the top of the field, cross the fence and keep going, turning right at the corner of the fence. Go through a gate at the next corner and look for a waymark about 100 yards downhill. Follow the path steeply downhill, passing through a kissing gate and staying close to the wall. You then reach a drying green at the foot of the hill; turn left and follow a path around the buildings and back onto the road at **Kilchattan**.

Sleeping

Loch Awe and Loch Etive *p125*

L **Ardanaiseig Hotel**, T01499-833333, www.ardanaiseig-hotel.com. 3 miles east of Kilchrenan village (12 miles from Taynuilt) on an unclassified road. Open Feb-Dec. A luxurious highland retreat serving a fabulous 7-course dinner (𝕐𝕐𝕐) and running trips to atmospheric Kilchurn Castle in its private boat.

C **Blarcreen Farm**, Archattan, T01631-750272, www.blarcreenfarm.com. Open Mar-Dec. A mile past Archattan Priory on the road from Oban to Bonawe. Elegant Victorian farmhouse standing on its own surrounded by lovely countryside. Individually styled rooms, superb cuisine and homely ambience.

Self-catering

Inistrynich, Lochaweside, Dalmally, T01838-200256, www.loch-awe.com/inistrynich. This delightful cottage (sleeps 4-8) is nestled by the loch with fishing, golf and walking nearby.

Inveraray and around *p126*

L **Crinan Hotel**, T01546-830261, www.crinanhotel.com. Nestled on the shores of Loch Crinan and by the famous Crinan Canal, guests are assured of fine dining and luxury in this acclaimed retreat. Fantastic views, pampering on a majestic scale and a sensational restaurant make a stay here well worthwhile.

A-D **George Hotel**, Main St, Inveraray, T01499-302111, www.thegeorgehotel.co.uk. Enjoy genuine hospitality and tasty local produce (see Eating, below) in this atmospheric late 18th-century hotel with cosy bar, real ales and a resident ghost. The Merchants Room with double jacuzzi is booked up to 12 months in advance.

D **Kilmartin Hotel**, opposite the church in Kilmartin village, T01546-510250. 4 en suite rooms. Handy, comfortable stop whilst exploring historic Kilmartin Glen.

D **Little Keills Guest House**, Tayvallich, T01546-870623, www.littlekeills.com. 11 miles from Lochgilphead and by 13th-century Keills Chapel, this small B&B enjoys stunning views over the Sound of Jura.

F **Inverary Youth Hostel**, Dalmally Rd, Inveraray, T0870-004 1125. Apr-end Oct The perfect budget base from which to explore the nearby castle and town.

Self-catering

The Paymaster's House, Inverary, T01499-302003, www.paymastershouse.co.uk. A delightful 1780s dated option, oozing character and history in the heart of Inverary.

Kintyre *p129*

L-A **Stonefield Castle Hotel**, 2 miles north of Tarbert, on the A82 to Lochgilphead, T01880-820836. This impressive 18th-century former castle home of the Campbells provides guests with comfort, eye-catching views of Loch Fyne and acres of garden to walk off that delicious 4-course dinner.

C **Achamore House**, Isle of Gigha, T01583-505400, www.isle-of-gigha.co.uk. Set in midst of famous Achamore Gardens this 18th-century mansion has 10 tastefully furnished bedrooms to let with the cosy island bar nearby.

C **Kilberry Inn**, west of Tarbert on the B8024, T01880-770223, www.kilberryinn.com. 3 rooms. Open Easter-Oct. Offers superb Scottish meat and seafood dishes (𝕐𝕐-𝕐), cosy comforts and perfect peace.

C-E **Post Office House**, Gigha, T01583-505251. 5 mins from the ferry, with B&B and self-catering option. Owners also run the Isle of Gigha post office and general store and rent out bikes (£6 per day).

D **Rhu House**, Tarbert, T/F01880-820231, Comfortable B&B looking out over west Loch Tarbert. Handy for Islay ferry.

Camping

Portban Holiday Park, Kilberry, Tarbert, T01880-770224. Majestic views towards Jura from the comfort of your tent.

Cowal Peninsula and the Clyde Coast *p132*

L-B **An Lauchin**, Tighnabruaich, T01700-811239. Formerly **The Royal**, this elegant hotel with its own moorings boasts exquisite fine dining (ΨΨΨ), beautiful decor and many a fine dram in the snug bar.

D **Kames Hotel**, Kames, T01700-811489/F01700-811283. 10 en suite rooms Terrific views down the Kyles and great food.

Self-catering

Cove Park, Rosneath Peninsula, Loch Long, T01436-850123, www.covepark.org. Very unusual and extremely restful place to stay, on the shore of Loch Long, 20 mins by car from Helensburgh. Accommodation in one of 2 'pods' or 3 'cubes'. The former are designed to blend in seamlessly with the surrounding landscape, with balconies overlooking the loch, and can sleep up to 4 in 2 en suite bedrooms; £100 per pod per night. The latter are designed for singles or couples and cost £30 per night each. If you're looking for something a bit different, or just to really get away from it all, this is where to come. It is also a centre for the creative arts and runs an annual programme of artists' residences. Highly recommended.

Camping

Glendaruel Caravan/Campsite, T01369-820267. Terrific secluded location, well maintained and close to amenities.

Isle of Bute *p134*

A **Balmory Hall**, 3 miles south of Rothesay, at Ascog, T/F01700-500669, www.balmoryhall.com. This Italianate mansion, set in 10 acres of grounds and once home to the 3rd Marquess of Bute, is now a superior guesthouse run by Tony and Beryl. A stay here is a memorable experience, the setting is idyllic and the suites are elegant and sumptuous (sample the Bute Suite for some serious indulgence). The 7-course breakfast is an event in itself – simply out of this world. There are also self-catering apartments for weekend breaks (£225-265 per person). Very highly recommended.

A-D **Cannon House Hotel**, Battery Pl, Rothesay, T01700-502819. A comfortable Georgian townhouse. Close to the ferry.

E **Kingarth Hotel**, in Kingarth, in the south of the island, T01700-831662, www.kingarthhotel.com. Quiet, cosy 1782 inn offering genuine hospitality, terrific seafood/steak platters (ΨΨ-Ψ) and the chance to banter with the locals.

Self-catering

Ardencraig House, Ardencraig Rd, Rothesay. T01700-505077. Luxury 4-apartment option in converted Victorian-era mansion with views of Clyde (£250-£475 per week).

Eating

Inveraray and around *p126*

ΨΨΨ-ΨΨ **Loch Fyne Oyster Bar**, at Cairndow on the A83 near Clachan. T01499-600236. Daily 0900-2030. Book ahead to reserve at this famous seafood restaurant known to attract heavyweight (in both senses of the word) politicians and gastronomes alike.

ΨΨ-Ψ **The George Hotel**, Main St, Inverary, T01499-302111. Real ales on tap, hearty bar meals and reasonably priced dinners using locally sourced meats and seafood. If staying, try the home-made jams.

ΨΨ-Ψ **Kilmartin House Café**, Kilmartin House, see Sleeping, above. Daily 1200-1700 and Thu-Sat evenings for dinner. Superb cooking, much better than you should expect and a lesson to many other visitor attractions in how to do things well. Wholesome and healthy soups, snacks, homemeade bread and excellent coffee.

Cowal Peninsula and the Clyde Coast *p132*

ΨΨΨ-ΨΨ **An Lauchin**, T01700-811239. Game terrine, venison with red onion marmalade, cranachan. The former **Royal Hotel** provides Scottish cuisine at its best.

ΨΨ-Ψ **Inver Cottage**, Strathlachlan on B8000, past Strachur T01369-860537. Mouth-watering starters, succulent game and hand-dived scallops; to-die-for desserts and homely ambience. A gem; book ahead.

Isle of Bute *p134*
West End Café, 1-3 Gallowgate, Rothesay, T01700-503596. It is a must while you are on Bute to sample the fish and chips at this award-winning chippie. It's open all year round except Mon. Phone ahead to avoid the massive queues in summer.

Festivals and events

Kintyre *p129*
Aug If you're around Campbeltown mid-Aug don't miss the **Mull of Kintyre Music Festival**, 3 days of the best in traditional Celtic music, held throughout the town.
Sep **Gigha Music Festival**, is held early in the month.

Cowal Peninsula and the Clyde Coast *p132*
Aug **Dunoon Highland Games**, held on the last weekend of the month, are the world's largest and culminate in a spectacular march of massed pipes and drums through the streets.
Oct **Cowalfest**, an action-packed week-long walking and arts festival in early Oct.

Isle of Bute *p134*
May The **Isle of Bute Jazz Festival** is held during the May Bank Holiday weekend.
Jul **Isle of Bute Dunoon Sheepdog Trials** and **Inverary Highland Games**.

Activities and tours

Loch Awe and Loch Etive *p125*
Boat trips **Loch Etive Cruises**, T01866-822430. Cruises depart at 1200 (1½-hr cruise; 4.80) and 1400 (3-hr cruise; £8.80), Easter-Oct Sun-Fri (Sat charters only). No booking necessary but arrive in plenty of time. The departure point is 1 mile from Taynuilt up road to the Bonawe Heritage Site.

Fishing **Lochawe Boats**, Arbrecknish by Dalavich, off the B840, T01866-833256. All year. £17 per day for rowing boat/canoe. £35 per day for outboard boat. Loch Awe fishing permits from £6 per day.

Inverary and around *p126*
Adventure and horse riding **Argyll Riding**, Dalchenna Farm, 2 miles south of Inveraray on A83, T01499-302611, www.horserides.co.uk. BHS-approved riding school and trekking (Easter-Oct). Also bungee trampolines, climbing walls and clay-pigeon shooting (year-round, daily from 1000).
Argyll Trail Riding, Brenfield Farm, Ardrishaig (2 miles), T01546-603274, www.brenfield.co.uk. Riding trails/beach gallops. Clay-pigeon shooting.

Boat trips **Gemini Cruises**, based at Crinan harbour, T/F01546-830238, www.gemini-crinan.co.uk. 2-hr wildlife-spotting cruises round Loch Craignish or longer trips to the Gulf of Corrievreckan. From £14 (£9 child) for 2-hr cruise.
River Rocket, T01369-707054, www.riverrocket.co.uk. Easter-Oct daily. Sea Tours, Holy Loch Marina, by Dunoon, also 'rocks n' wrecks, fjords, and the Kyles'. From £17.50 (£14 child).
Sanda Island, T01586-554667. All year, daily in summer. Spend 3 hrs on the privately owned historic island of Sanda (2 miles off Mull of Kintyre) with its cosy wee pub and ancient sites. Reached aboard the *Seren Las* £20, concession £18, children £14, from Campbeltown.

Transport

Inverary and around *p126*
Bus There are buses from **Lochgilphead** to **Cairnbaan**, **Crinan**, **Achnamara** and **Tayvallich** several times daily Mon-Fri; T01546-870330. There is at least 1 daily bus to **Oban** via **Kilmartin** (Mon-Sat) and several daily buses to **Inveraray**. There's a regular service to and from **Ardrishaig** and from Argyll to/from Glasgow.

Cycle Crinan Cycles, 34 Argyll St, Lochgilphead, T01546-603511. Bikes for rent from £12 per day, also parts and repairs and will advise on routes and provide maps. Mon-Sat 0930-1730.

Kintyre *p129*
Air There are 2 flights daily (35 mins), all year round from Glasgow to **Campbeltown (Machrihanish)** airport. For times and reservations, contact **British Airways**, T0141 842 7453, T0870-8509850.

There are several daily **Citylink** buses, T08705-505050, from **Glasgow** to **Campbeltown** (4½ hrs) via **Inveraray**, **Lochgilphead**, **Kennacraig** and **Tarbert**. There are 5 buses a day from Campbeltown to **Machrihanish Saddell** (25 mins) and **Carradale** (45 mins) (2 Sun) and **Southend** (3 Mon-Sat, 2 Sun, 25 mins). Ask at TIC for Area Transport Guide.

Ferry There is a car and passenger ferry from Portavadie on the Cowal Peninsula to **Tarbert** (25 mins, £3.15 per passenger, £14.35 per car), which leaves daily every hr from Apr-Oct; less frequently in winter. There is a ferry from **Lochranza** on Arran from **Claonaig** on the west coast of Kintyre (and east of Kennacraig) 9 times daily (30 mins, £4.55 per passenger, £20.35 per car). Ferries leave from **Kennacraig**, 5 miles south of Tarbert, to **Islay** (see page 168) and to **Colonsay** (see page 158). A small car and passenger ferry leaves from Tayinloan to the ferry pier at Ardminish on Gigha, daily all year round (hourly Mon-Sat 0800-1800, Sun 1100-1700), 20 mins, £5.40 per passenger, £20.25 per car.

Cowal Peninsula and the Clyde Coast *p132*

Ferry To Dunoon there are **CalMac** ferries every hr (0620-2020) from **Gourock**, with train connections to and from Gourock to **Glasgow Central**, 25 mins, £3.15 one way per person, £7.80 per car. There is also a ferry service from **McInroy's Point**, 2 miles from Gourock, with **Western Ferries**, www.western-ferries.co.uk. It leaves every 15-20 mins during peak times and runs daily from 0730-2400, £3.30 per passenger, £9.30 per car.

Isle of Bute *p134*

Bus The service provided by **West Coast Motors** is good, though limited on Sun. There are buses to Rothesay from **Tighnabruaich** in southwest Cowal at least once a day from Apr-Oct, daily (1 hr). For times, contact **West Coast Motors**, T0870-8506687.

Cycle The best way to see Bute is still by bike with roads fairly quiet and in good condition beyond Rothesay.

Ferry A car/passenger ferry makes the 5-min crossing from **Colintraive** to **Rhubodach**, at the northern end of Bute, daily every ½ hr or hr; Easter-end Aug Mon-Sat 0530-1955 and Sun 0900-1955. It costs £1.20 one way per person and £7.50 per car.

Train Bute is easily accessible from **Glasgow**. Take a train from Glasgow Central to the ferry terminal at **Wemyss Bay** (1 hr 10 mins), and from there it's a 35-min crossing to Rothesay. They leave every 45 mins from 0715 till 1945 (later on Fri, Sat and Sun), £3.70 one way per passenger, £14.90 per car. For times and fares T08705-650000.

Isle of Arran

→ *Phone code: 01770. Colour map A3/B3.*

In the wedge of sea between Ayrshire and Kintyre lies the oval-shaped, compact Isle of Arran. A land of beauty and contrast, the rugged, mountainous north is akin in hue and character to the northwest Highlands, whilst the fertile, forested south is lowland country. Unspoiled and alive with ancient history, myths and geological treasures, 25-mile-long Arran deserves its sobriquet, 'Scotland in Miniature'. Moreover, despite its popularity and accessibility from the Central Belt, outside Brodick you're as likely to spot a deer as a fellow tourist. ▸▸ *For Sleeping, Eating and other listings, see pages 136-139.*

Ins and outs

Getting there The main ferry route to Arran is from the distinctly unappealing Ayrshire town of Ardrossan to the island's main town, Brodick. There are train connections from Glasgow and bus connections from Edinburgh to Ardrossan. The other ferry route is from Claonaig, near Skipness, to Lochranza in the north of the island. ▸▸ *For further details, see Transport, page 145.*

 Getting around A reliable bus network makes using public transport feasible whilst many visitors choose to explore by bike.

Tourist information Brodick TIC ⓘ *beside the pier and bus terminal, T01770-303774, www.ayrshire-arran.com, Easter-Oct Mon-Sat 0900-1930, Sun 1000-1700; winter hours vary.*

Brodick

Whether coming to play golf (there are seven courses), walk, climb or sample the ales, whisky and cheese produced by proud Arranachs, the largest town and port of Brodick is where most visitors step ashore. Lying in a 'broad bay', (hence its Norse name *breidr vik*, Brodick offers up guesthouses, eateries and shops but little of the scenic charm that awaits along the outlying winding roads.

Two miles north of town and overlooking Brodick Bay is the impressive **Brodick Castle** ⓘ *T01770-302202; castle and restaurant, Easter-31 Oct daily 1100-1630 (castle closes 1530 in Oct), walled garden 1000-1630; country park open all year, castle, garden and country park £10, £7 concession.* The ancient seat of the Dukes of Hamilton, it is now a flagship NTS property. Parts of the castle date from the 13th century and extensions were added in the 16th, 17th and 19th centuries. With paintings, antiques and (apparently) ghosts aplenty, it's worth exploring the sumptuously furnished rooms and the beautiful walled garden. The surrounding country park incorporates 11 miles of marked trails and an adventure playground for the kids.

Halfway between the village and the castle is the excellent **Arran Heritage Museum** ⓘ *T01770-302636, www.arranmuseum.co.uk, Apr-Oct daily 1000-1630, £2.50, children £1.25.* Within a former croft and smiddy, visitors can discover a wealth of information about the island's archaeology, geology, social history before popping next door for delicious home-baking and freshly prepared lunches at **Café Rosaburn** (April to October).

Just over a mile north you'll discover **Arran Aromatics** where nature has been harvested to produce scented handmade soaps and oils. Continuing to Cladach by the castle, there's the chance to undertake a 45-minute sampling tour of real ales including a tasty Arran Blonde at the **Arran Brewery** ⓘ *T01770-302353, Apr-Sep Mon-Sat 1000-1700, Sun 1230-1700; Nov-Mar Wed-Sat and Mon 1000-1530, £2.*

South Arran

The south of Arran is a fertile landscape of rolling hills and pretty little seaside villages, where you'll find the bulk of the island's population and tourists. A few miles south of Brodick is **Lamlash**, a quiet and attractive village boasting a wide, sheltered bay but also an unappealing mud beach.

Lying just offshore is the humpbacked **Holy Island** ⓘ *www.holyisland.org.* Owned by Buddhists since 1992 they have established a meditative retreat and since 2003 a Peace Centre (see Sleeping, page 144) on slopes grazed by feral goats and countless rabbits. A ferry runs to Holy Island (April to September several times daily, limited winter service, £9 return). For day visitors, there's just enough time to ascend **Mullach Mór** (1030 ft).

Renowned for its golf, the little fishing village of **Blackwaterfoot** is set round a bay with a tiny harbour. Two miles (45 minutes' walk) north along the coast are the **King's Caves**, where, according to legend, Robert the Bruce watched a spider try, try and try again and was thus inspired to secure his own and Scotland's destiny. The cathedral-like main cave has an unlocked iron gate to keep out sheep.

If you are a golfer then tee off at the Machrie golf course, for a memorable golfing experience.

In Brodick, seek out James's irresistible home-made chocolates. Two miles north you'll also find a tasty Arran Blonde at the Cladach Brewery.

Four miles north of Blackwaterfoot, off the main coast road, is **Machrie Moor,** site of the most impressive of Arran's Bronze Age **stone circles**. Park by the Historic Scotland sign and then walk for 1½ miles up the farm track to reach an area boasting no fewer than six mystical stone circles. Many of them are barely visible above the ground, but the tallest is over 18 ft high. A few miles further on, just south of the turn-off to Machrie village, is another Historic Scotland sign for **Moss Farm Road Stone Circle,** which lies about half a mile walk along the farm track.

North Arran

The northern half of Arran, with its wild, heather-strewn hillsides, brooding glens and dramatic mountains, contrasts sharply with the south. Sparsely populated, this remote, unspoiled region is paradise for the dedicated hillwalker. Six miles north of Brodick is the quaint village of **Corrie**. In addition to its craftshop, hotel and friendly pub, Corrie is also an alternative start-point to Brodick for the ascent of Goatfell. The main coastal road continues north from Corrie to **Sannox,** with its sandy beach and fine hotel before winding northwest into the heather-strewn glen and dropping into the beautiful setting of the former herring village of Lochranza.

Nestling under dramatic mountains and reached by road or the ferry from Claonaig, Arran's most northerly village of **Lochranza** is dominated by the ruins of 13th-century **Lochranza Castle** and the seal rich, U-shaped bay in which it stands. If the herds of deer grazing on the golf course contribute to Lochranza's air of serenity, the Highland atmosphere is accentuated by the presence of **Isle of Arran Distillery**

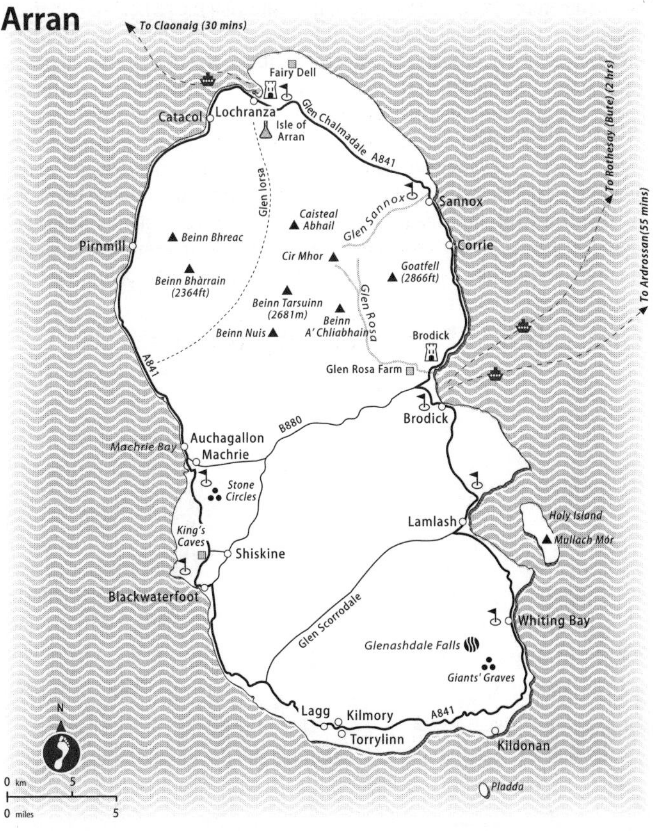

 ⓘ *T01770-830264, www.arranwhisky.com, Apr-end Oct daily 1000-1800 (call for winter opening hrs), £3.50, £2.50 concessions.* Opened in 1995, it's the island's first legal whisky distillery for over 180 years. Taste a dram here or off the malt menu at the nearby **Lochranza Hotel**. They also have a very good restaurant (see Eating, page 144, for details).

▲ Walks on Arran → *OS map No 69 covers these walks.*

Arran is paradise for the outdoor enthusiast, offering a variety of forest, hilltop and coastal walks. There's even a 60-mile circuitous island route called the **Arran Coast Way** ⓘ *www.coastalway.co.uk*. The north part of the island boasts ten peaks of over 2000 ft and several challenging ridge walks while the gentler south features less strenuous forest walks. Note all mountain routes should only be undertaken in good weather, whilst some – **A'Chir**, **Witches Step**, **Suidhe Fherghas** and **Cioch Na Oighe** – involve scrambling and can be very dangerous for the inexperienced and unprepared. In all cases, good OS maps (and ropes) are (available from the TIC office in Brodick) whilst local advice must be sought before venturing onto the hills during the deer-stalking season (late August to late October).

The **Glenashdale Falls and Giants' Graves walk** is one of the most popular in south. It's a steady, easy climb through woodland with the considerable incentive of a beautiful waterfall at the end of it. Both walks can be done together and should take around two to three hours in total, though you should allow some time to enjoy the falls. If you want to take a picnic, pop into the Village Shop which has a wide range of deli-type foods and local cheeses. The trail starts by the bridge over **Glenashdale Burn**. There's a map board here showing the route. Walk up the track alongside the burn till you see the sign for the path leading to the left up to the **Giants' Graves**. It's about 40 to 45 minutes up to the graves and back to this point, but it's a stiff climb up a steep staircase of 265 steps. At the top continue left along a path through the trees, which then curves right till you reach a clearing and the graves, which are chambered tombs, believed to be around 5000 years old. Depending on the light, this can be a very eerie, but almost magical place. Return back down the steps, and head left along the main path as it climbs steadily above the burn, past smaller falls, till you reach the main falls. The setting is stunning and the falls are spectacular as they plummet 140 ft into the pools below. You can rest

Ordnance Survey map no 69 covers these walks on Arran.

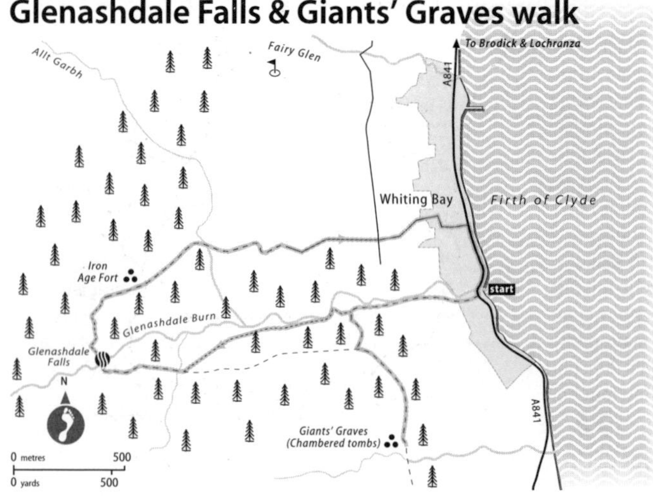

and have a picnic at the top of the falls, or follow the paths down to the pools below which you can swim. The path back down to **Whiting Bay** passes the scant remains of an Iron Age fort, then turns back uphill to reach a broad track. Turn right, cross a small burn by stepping stones, then follow the track downhill all the way to the main road, a short way along from the car park.

Arran's most popular peak, **Goatfell**, is also its highest, at 2866 ft. There's a path leading up from Corrie, but most people begin the walk from the car park at Cladach sawmill, near Brodick Castle. The path is well marked, easy to follow and, apart from the final section, relatively easy. It runs initially through the **Brodick Country Park**, then follows the Cnocan burn as it rises steadily through woodland before crossing the Mill burn. Beyond the burn is a deer fence above which the landscape changes to heather moorland and the path begins to climb the flanks of the mountain. The final 650 ft up to the top is steep and rocky though the path is clear even when undertaking a gentle scramble on loose scree. Hopefully, your climb will be rewarded with spectacular views down the Firth of Clyde, over Arran's ridges and westwards towards Islay and Jura. In total the walk should take about five hours. Despite the hordes of walkers, treat this ascent with the same caution and respect as on any Scottish mountain. Certainly, the adjacent ridges should only be attempted by experienced hill-goers. In all instances, you should be dressed and equipped appropriately and be prepared for any sudden change in the weather.

Many of the walks start from Glen Rosa Farm. One of these takes in the three Beinns; **Beinn Nuis, Beinn Tarsuinn** (2681 ft) and **Beinn A'Chliabhain.** Start at Glen Rosa Farm and go up the Wood Road to the High Deer Gate, then to Torr Breac and the 'Y' junction at the top of the Garbhalt and on to the path which runs round the Three Beinns. This is a full day's walk.

Another excellent walk is from Glen Rosa to the head of the Glen; then take the path up into the Coire Buidhe and on to the ridge between **Cir Mhor** (2617 ft) and **A'Chir** (known as the Ceems Ridge). Then follow the path around the west side of A'Chir. This is not easy to find, but takes you around the back of A'Chir to Bowman's Pass and the north end of Beinn Tarsuinn. From here take the path to Beinn A'Chliabhan and down to the foot of Garbhalt Ridge and back down to Glen Rosa.

Cir Mhor can also be climbed from Glen Rosa. Before going over into Glen Sannox take the steep path straight up. On the way back down, head into Coire Buidhe and back down the glen. You can also continue from the top of Cir Mhor and take the path around the west side of A'Chir to the north end of the Bowman's Pass up on to Beinn Tarsuinn and along the ridge to Beinn Nuis, then down the path to the Garbhalt Bridge.

Finally, in **Lochranza** there's an easy two-hour coastal walk from the youth hostel along the north shore of Lochranza Bay (Newton Shore) to the viewpoint at Kirn Point affording lovely views down the Kilbrannan Sound. A mile northwards, past the geological phenomenon known as Hutton's unconformity is the rustic cottage of 'Fairy Dell' above which a track briefly climbs and leads back to North Newton and past the creative croft at The Whins where artist Reg assembles and sells his delightfully quirky 'stone-men'.

There are also several walks in and around **Glen Sannox**. It's a pleasant walk just to make your way up the head of the Glen and return the same way. You can walk up the Glen to beyond the old mine then make your way up towards the Devil's Punchbowl until you reach the main path and follow that down into the Coire. Take the main path back down into Glen Sannox instead of trying to climb out of the Devil's Punchbowl. You can also walk from Glen Sannox to Glen Rosa, which takes around four hours.

Sleeping

Brodick *p140*

L **Kilmichael Country House Hotel,** T01770-302219, www.kilmichael.com. 7 rooms. Take the road north towards the castle, turn left at the golf course and follow the signs for about a mile. Enjoy refined elegance in the island's oldest house. Their award-winning restaurant (TTT) is arguably the best on the island. Booking is essential for non-residents. No children under 12, though; it's that sort of place.

L-A **Auchrannie Country House Hotel**, just beyond the turning to Kilmichael, T01770-302234, www.auchrannie.co.uk. 28 rooms. Lacks the charm of **Kilmichael** but makes up for it with a superb child-friendly facilities and leisure complex. Very popular, it also has a 36-bedroom spa resort. Their **Garden Restaurant** (TT) is highly rated and the **Brambles Bistro** offers reasonable bar meals (TT-T). Also self-catering.

A **Belvedere Guest House**, Brodick, T01770-302397. Take a holistic break in a friendly guesthouse combining dinner B&B with a complimentary reiki or aromatherapy session.

Camping

Glen Rosa, 2 miles from town on the road to Blackwaterfoot, T01770-302380. Apr-Oct.

South Arran *p140*

C-F **Holy Isle Peace Centre**, T01770-601100, www.holyisland.org. Year-round. Comfortable rooms and 3 vegetarian meals a day form part of relaxing experience on this Buddhist-run isle.

D **Eden Lodge Hotel**, Whiting Bay, T01770-700357, www.edenlodgehotelco.uk. Friendly family-run, 5-room hotel with views to Holy Isle. Tempts guests with home-cooking and beer garden.

North Arran *p141*

D **Castlekirk**, Lochranza, T01770-830202. Heavenly B&B stay in a converted church with outlook to castle.

F **Lochranza SYHA**, Lochranza, T0870-0041140. Mar-Oct. Friendly, well-equipped hostel with views over the bay.

Self-catering

Butt Lodge, Lochranza, T01770-302303. A secluded luxury Japanese-influenced house complete with huge, authentic Japanese hinoki hot-tub. (£700-£1500 per week).

Camping

Well-equipped campsite next to the golf course near the Isle of Arran Distillery, Lochranza. T01770-820273, Apr-Oct.

Eating

Brodick *p140*

TTT-TT **Creelers Seafood Restaurant**, at the Home Farm, a mile north of Brodick near the castle, T01770-302797. Over 16 years experience of serving excellent seafood, game and vegetarian dishes with a smile.

TT-T **Café Rosaburn**, by the Heritage Museum Delicious freshly made salads and home-cooking in a converted croft at northern edge of Brodick.

North Arran *p141*

TT **Isle of Arran Distillery**, Lochranza, T01770-830264. Apr-Oct daily 1000-1800 (call for winter/evening hours). Locally sourced produce cooked with not a little flair. Try the Sun roast.

TT **The Lighthouse**, Pirnmill, T01770-850240. Mar-Oct 1200-1500, 1700-2200. Tasty local beef, seafood, home-made puddings.

Activities and tours

Arran *p139*

Arran Adventure. on the seafront at Brodick, T01770-302244, www.arranadventure.com. Arran is a fantastic island fo cycling. Hire a bike here (from £12). They also offer sea kayaking, power-boating, climbing and canyoning.

Flying Fever, T01770-860526. You can quad-bike at Balmichael, and paraglide (see page 60 for full details).

North Sannox Pony Trekking Centre, T01770-810222. For horse riding.

Transport

Arran *p139*
Bus There's a bus connection to and from **Edinburgh**. Once on the island, there are regular daily buses from **Brodick** to **Blackwaterfoot** (30 mins) via 'The String'; to **Lamlash** (10 mins) and **Whiting Bay** (25 mins) and on to **Blackwaterfoot** (1 hr 10 mins); to **Corrie** (20 mins), **Sannox** (25 mins), **Lochranza** (45 mins), **Catacol** (50 mins), **Pirnmill** (1 hr), **Machrie** (1 hr 10 mins) and **Blackwaterfoot** (1 hr 20 mins). **Kildonan**, **Whiting Bay** and back to Brodick. Take the bus to **Lochranza** to connect with the **Claonaig ferry**.

Car By car, from the south the main route to Arran is from the M74 motorway, on to the A71 via Kilmarnock, to Irvine and Ardrossan.

Car hire: Whiting Bay Garage, T/F01770-700345.

Ferry The main ferry route is from **Ardrossan** to **Brodick**. CalMac car/passenger ferry makes the 55-min journey 5-6 times daily Mon-Sat, 4 times on Sun, 55 mins, £5 single per passenger, £36.50 one-way per car. There's a regular train connection between Ardrossan and **Glasgow Central**.

The other ferry route to Arran is from **Claonaig**, near **Skipness**, to **Lochranza** in the north of the island. The non-bookable car/passenger ferry makes the 30-min trip 7-9 times daily during the summer (Apr-Oct), less frequently in winter, £4.55 per passenger, £20.35 per car. For ferry times, T08705-650000, www.calmac. co.uk.

Directory

Brodick *p140*
Banks Brodick has banks with ATMs but these are the only ones on the island.
Post The post office is just off the seafront, opposite the petrol station and pharmacy.

Mull and Iona → *Colour map 3, B3-4, C3-4.*

Whether bathed in sunshine or shrouded in mist, each of Scotland's isles possess a magical quality. The Isle of Mull, a 50-minute sail from Oban and the third largest of the Hebridean islands, is no different. Teeming with wildlife and a gateway to the tiny and spiritual isle of Iona, Mull (derived from the Norse meaning 'high, bold headland') supports 2800 inhabitants and remains one of Scotland's most popular Hebridean isles. Indeed, Mull, just 26 miles east to west and 24 miles north to south, has enough going for it to appeal to most tastes: spectacular mountain scenery, 300 miles of wild coastline, castles, a narrow-gauge railway, fine cuisine and, in Tobermory, one of Scotland's prettiest coastal villages that also served as the main setting for the recently ended cult children's TV series, Balamory. ▸▸ *For Sleeping, Eating and other listings, see pages 154-157.*

Ins and outs

Getting there and around Mull is served by regular car/passenger ferry services, mostly from Oban but also from Kilchoan on the Ardnamurchan Peninsula and Lochaline on the Morvern Peninsula. Once on the island you can get to most places by bus. Services given in the Transport section are for April to October. Winter services are less frequent. There are regular five-minute sailings to and from Iona. ▸▸ *For further details, see Transport page 156.*

Tourist information **Craignure TIC** ⓘ *opposite the pier in the same building as the CalMac office, T01680-812377, daily, all year.* **Tobermory TIC** ⓘ *at the far end of Main St, T01688-302182, Apr-Sep,* is also in the same building as the CalMac office.

Mull » pp154-157. Colour map 3, B3-4, C3-4.

Craignure to Tobermory

The arrival point for visitors is the village of Craignure. One and a half miles south of here is **Torosay Castle** ⓘ *T01680-812421, Easter to mid-Oct daily 1030-1730, gardens open all year daily 1030-1700, £5.50*, more of a baronial family home than a full-blown castle. The best way to arrive is by the **Mull and West Highland Railway** ⓘ *T01680-812494, Easter to mid-Oct, £4 return*, affectionately known as the Balamory Express.

A couple of miles east of Torosay is **Duart Castle** ⓘ *T01680-812309, Apr Sun-Thu, May to mid-Oct daily 1030-1730, £4.50, concession £4*. The 13th-century ancestral seat of the Clan Maclean stands imperiously at the end of a promontory, commanding impressive views over Loch Linnhe and the Sound of Mull. Every five years (the next is in June 2007) the castle and Mull hosts the Clan Maclean Gathering. The castle's main feature is the tower house, built in the late 14th century when it became the main residence of the Macleans of Duart. Today it's a fascinating place to visit, with many relics and artefacts on display. The former byre is now a cosy tea-room serving home-made scones.

Midway between Craignure and Tobermory on the main A849 is the pretty village of **Salen**, where a fantastic culinary experience awaits at **Mediterranea** (see Eating, page 155). Salen, situated at the narrowest point on the island, has several sites of interest on its doorstep. Two miles south is Mull's tiny and only airfield adjacent to which is the excellent **Glenforsa Hotel** (see Sleeping, page 154) where majestic views down the Sound of Mull can also be enjoyed. One mile north of Salen, overlooking the bay, is the ruin of **Aros Castle**, built in the 14th century and one of the strongholds of the Lords of the Isles. Tradition holds that the treasure of the Spanish galleon sunk in Tobermory Bay in 1588, see page 147, was recovered by the Macleans and lies buried beneath Aros Castle.

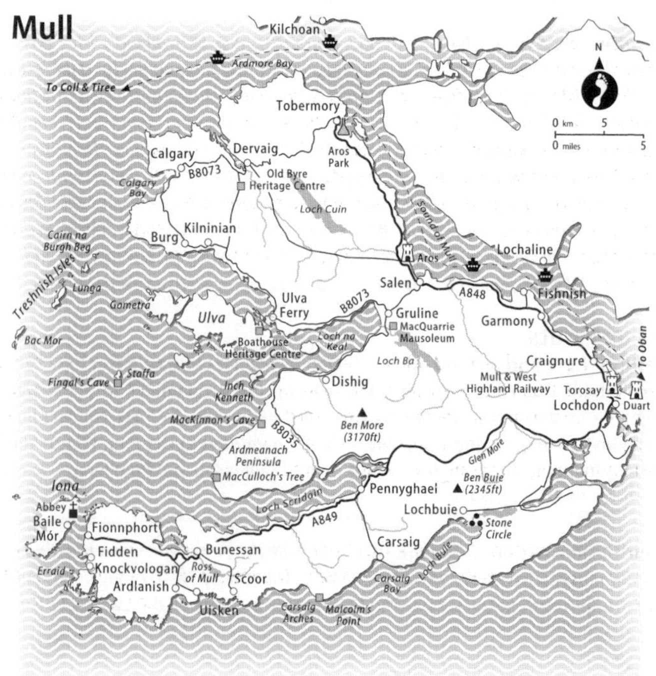

Shiver me timbers

The history of 16th-century Europe is littered with the remains of carefully forged and hastily broken political alliances between the various superpowers. One such deal between England and Spain was broken in 1588, prompting Philip II of Spain to send the Spanish Armada, a massive force of 130 ships, to take on the English navy. Originating in Cádiz, the Spanish force moved north and left Lisbon on 20 May. They met Queen Elizabeth's ships in the English Channel, where they were duly routed.

A number of Spanish ships fled up the east coast, chased by the English fleet as far as the Firth of Forth. Denied entry into the estuary by further English naval forces, the tattered remnants of these great Spanish galleons were no longer considered to pose a threat and were left to their own fate. Many continued up the east coast of Scotland, only to be wrecked in the perilous North Sea. Not all the crews drowned, however, and several integrated into local communites, where their descendants still live to this day. Most of their offspring were distinctively black haired and there is strong facial resemblance even today between some on the northeast coast of Scotland and the residents of Cádiz, from where the Armada originally sailed.

Some Spanish ships headed for the west coast, but were lost in a violent storm in the Hebrides. One galleon, the *Florida*, was lost in Tobermory harbour, reputedly carrying £300,000 worth of gold bullion. However, during recent dives all that was found on the seabed were rotted timbers, a sailor's bangle and a silver spoon.

Four miles southwest of Salen, near Gruline and Loch Ba, is the **MacQuarrie Mausoleum**, which houses the remains of Major-General Lachlan MacQuarrie (1761-1824). He took over as Governer-General of New South Wales from the unpopular William Bligh, formerly of the *Bounty*, and became known as the 'Father of Australia'. The mausoleum is maintained by the NTS, on behalf of the National Trust of Australia.

Tobermory

There is surely no prettier port in the west of Scotland than Tobermory, Mull's main village and setting for most of the popular children's TV series *Balamory*. Followers of the now-defunct series should ask for the Balamory leaflet at the TIC office which highlights the key filming locations. Tobermory got its name from a small settlement once situated northwest of the current village where there's a spring known in Gaelic as Tobar (well) Mhoire (Mary). The brightly painted houses that line Tobermory's harbour front date from the late 18th century when the British Fisheries Society built Tobermory as a planned herring port. During the Second World War, as a naval training base Tobermory was euphemistically called HMS Western Isles. Nowadays, only a few fishing boats, but dozens of yachts, bob at anchor in the protected waters of the natural harbour. Lying at the bottom of the harbour is a galleon of the Spanish Armada, which sank in mysterious circumstances, along with its treasure of gold doubloons, see box page 147. Remnants of a Spanish galleon can be seen on Main

For many years a skull rumoured to have come from the Spanish galleon in Tobermory bay and said to bring bad luck to anyone who touched it, lay displayed in a local hotel. Apparently, it caused such ill-fortune that in the 1990s a group of islanders made the decision to rebury the skull at sea.

 Street in the wonderful **Mull Museum** ⓘ *T01688-302493, Easter-end Oct Mon-Fri 1000-1600, Sat 1000-1300, £1*, housed in an old bakery. Raining or not it's worth visiting to gleen a fascinating insight of the island's history.

The harbour front – known as Main Street – is where you'll find most of what you want: the tourist office, tours, hotels, guesthouses, restaurants, pubs and the award-winning baker. Mercifully, though, it's free from the tartan tat that blights so many other tourist hot-spots. At the foot of the main road down to the harbour is the tiny **Tobermory Distillery** ⓘ *T01688-302645, www.burnstewartdistillers.com, year-round Mon-Fri 1000-1700, £2.50, concession £1, children free*, which offers a guided tour rounded off with a sampling of the island's single malt. At the top of Back Brae, on Argyll Terrace, is **An Tobar** ⓘ *T01688-302211, www.antobar.co.uk, all year Mon-Sat 1000-1700, Sun 1300-1600, free*, an excellent arts centre housed in the old school and featuring a varied programme of exhibitions, music and workshops. Or you can just have a coffee and admire the view.

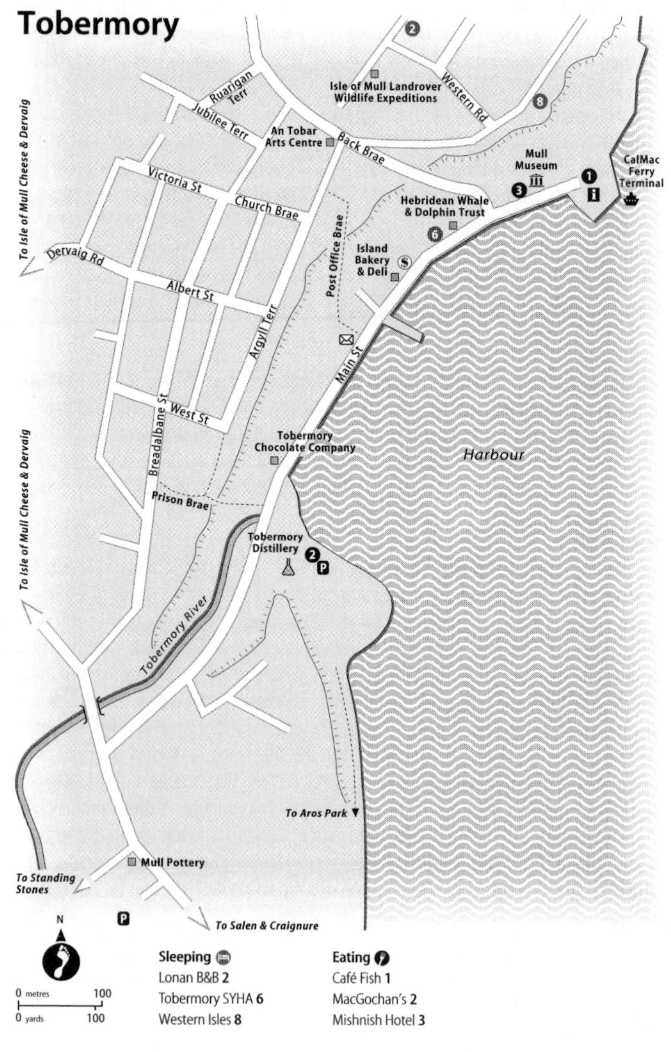

West coast Mull

Mull's west coast is where you'll find some of the island's most stunning scenery. The B8073 winds its way anti-clockwise from Tobermory in a series of twists and turns as it follows the contours of the coastline. The road climbs west from Tobermory then makes a dramatic descent, with hairpin bends, to Dervaig.

Dervaig is a lovely village of whitewashed cottages, beautifully situated at the head of Loch Cuin. Here sits **Kilmore Church**, with its unusual pencil-shaped spire. Until its closure in 2006, Dervaig was also the home of the smallest professional theatre in Britain. Whilst a fundraising campaign aims to establish a new theatre south of Tobermory by 2009, the famous **Mull Touring Theatre Company** ⓘ *T01688 302828*, will move into their new production facility in 2007. One mile beyond Dervaig take the turn-off to Torloisk to reach Glen Bellart and the highly informative **Old Byre Heritage Centre** ⓘ *T01688-400229, Easter-end Oct Wed-Sun 1030-1830, £4, concession £3, children £2*. Over 25 exhibits and several films (including one for toddlers!) highlight the history of Mull through the ages and its varied wildlife. Ask about the location of the nearby Neolithic standing stones. The tearooms delicious home-baking is an additional treat see Eating, page 155.

Five miles west of Dervaig is **Calgary Bay**, Mull's most beautiful beach ringed by steep wooded slopes with views across to Coll and Tiree. Calgary in Alberta, Canada, was named after the former township. Many emigrants were forcibly shipped to Canada from here during the Clearances. There are some wonderful paths through Calgary Wood, just past **Calgary Farmhouse Hotel**, including a half-hour circular walk.

Isle of Ulva

If you have the time and need to escape the hectic bustle of Mull, then take a day out on idyllic Ulva (meaning 'wolf island' in Norse), just off the west coast. You won't see any wolves around, but you're almost guaranteed to spot deer, golden eagles, buzzards and seals offshore. There are several woodland and coastal trails across the island, including one to the southwest where there are basalt columns similar to those on Staffa. Alternatively, you can follow the trail to the top of the hill for views across to the Cuillins on Skye (on a clear day), or else cross the causeway to Ulva's even smaller neighbour **Gometra**. For more information on the island walks and on its history, visit the **Boathouse Heritage Centre** ⓘ *close to the ferry slip, T01688-500241, Easter-Oct Mon-Fri 1000-1700 and Sun Jun-Aug only, entry is included in the ferry fare* *(see Transport, page 156)*. There's also a tearoom where you can try the local oysters with Guinness.

Staffa

The tiny uninhabited island of Staffa, 5 miles off the west coast of Mull, is one of the most spectacular sights not just in Scotland but anywhere in the world. It consists of immense hexagonal, basalt pillars which loom up out of the sea like a giant pipe organ. Staffa was formed 60 million years ago by the slow cooling of Tertiary basalt lavas. These have been carved by the pounding sea into huge cathedral-like caverns such as the mightily impressive **Fingal's Cave**. The sound of the sea crashing against the black crystalline columns made such an impression on Felix Mendelssohn in 1829 that he immortalized the island in his *Hebrides Overture*. The composer was obviously aware of its original name in Gaelic, which means 'The Melodious Cave'. You can land on the island – if the weather is good enough – and walk into the cave via the causeway; an experience not be missed. But even if the seas are too rough, it's worth making the 90-minute boat trip just to witness the columns and cave.

South Mull

From Ulva Ferry the B8073 heads east along the north shore of **Loch na Keal** then enters a wide flat valley, where the road forks east to Salen and west along the south shore of

Things to do on Mull when it's wet

It rains a lot on Mull, but luckily there's a fairly large number of indoor options to keep you nice and dry until the weather changes. If you've just arrived off the ferry from Oban and it's chucking it down, then head straight for **Torosay Castle**, just to the south of Craignure. And if the weather changes whilst exploring the interior, don't miss the gardens. Just beyond the castle is **Wings Over Mull**, a bird of prey conservation centre which offers indoor hawk-handling and a chance to learn about the island's incredible bird life. Nearby is Mull's greatest fortification, **Duart Castle**, which is also worth a peek. If all that history gets too much then you could do worse than hole up in the bar of the **Craignure Inn** and relax in front of their roaring log fire.

In the north of the island, the most appealing option by far is the **Old Byre Heritage Centre**, not far from the picturesque village of Dervaig. When in Tobermory do as the locals do, and get yourself down to the **bar of the Mish**, see Eating and Entertainment page 155, though you shouldn't really need the excuse of inclement weather. Meanwhile, over in Fionnphort, the departure point for the pilgrimage to Iona, you can seek spiritual assistance with a wee dram in the cosy **Keel Row Bar**.

Loch na Keal. This part of Mull is dominated by **Ben More** (3170 ft), the island's highest mountain. All around is a spectacular region of high jutting mountains and deep glens, extending west to the **Ardmeanach Peninsula**. The peninsula may look impenetrable, but with the proper walking gear can be explored on foot. On the north coast, about a mile from the road, is the massive entrance to **MacKinnon's Cave**, which runs for about 100 yards back under the cliffs. Make sure to visit only at low tide. The area around the headland, now owned by the National Trust for Scotland, is known as **The Wilderness**. Near the headland is **MacCulloch's Tree**, a remarkable fossilized tree 40 ft high and thought to be 50 million years old, which was discovered in 1819. The tree is only accessible by a 7-mile footpath which begins at Burg Farm. You should have a map of the area and also time your arrival with low tide.

Mull's southernmost peninsula stretches west for 20 miles from the head of Loch Scridain as far as Iona. Most visitors use it merely as a route to Iona but there are a couple of interesting little detours along the way. A twisting side road leads south from Pennyghael over the hills and down to **Carsaig Bay**, from where you can head east or west along the shore for some dramatic coastal scenery. Two roads lead south from Bunessan. One leads to **Scoor**, near where is a great beach at Kilveockan. The other road splits near the coast: the left branch leads to **Uisken Bay**; the right-hand branch leads to **Ardlanish Bay**, each with a good beach.

The road ends at **Fionnphort**, the departure point for the small passenger-only ferry to Iona, just a mile across the Sound of Iona. The village is little more than a car park, a row of houses, a pub and a shop, but there are several inexpensive B&Bs for those arriving too late to make the crossing. Even if you're not staying, it's worth stopping off in the village to visit the **Columba Centre** ⓘ *Apr-Sep daily 1100-1700, free*, where interpretive displays tell the story of St Columba.

A road runs south from Fionnphort to **Knockvologan**, opposite **Erraid Island**, which is accessible at low tide. The island has literary connections, for it was here that Robert Louis Stevenson is believed to have written *Kidnapped*. **Balfour Bay** on the south of the island is named after the novel's hero who was shipwrecked here.

Walks on Mull → *OS Landranger maps 47, 48 and 49 cover the entire island.*

Mull presents numerous walking opportunities, ranging from gentle forest trails to wild and dramatic coastal routes, or even a spot of Munro-bagging for the more intrepid. With the exception of the Cuillins on Skye, Mull's highest peak, Ben More (3170 ft) is the only Munro not on the mainland.

The trail starts at a lay-by on the B8035, at Dishig, and is fairly clear, though it can be tricky near the top. Return the same way, or more experienced climbers could continue down the narrow ridge to the eastern summit, **A'Chioch**, then descend the eastern face to the road that skirts **Loch Ba**. The views from the top are magnificent, across the other Hebridean islands and even as far as Ireland. If it's a cloudy day, it's worth postponing the ascent until there's clear weather. Allow around six hours for the round trip.

There are a couple of excellent coastal walks which start out from Carsaig Bay. A good path heads west along the shore to **Carsaig Arches** at Malcom's Point. The path runs below the cliffs out to the headland and then around it, and after about a mile reaches **Nun's Cave**, a wide and shallow cave where the nuns of Iona took refuge after being expelled during the Reformation. The path continues for another mile or so, but becomes a bit exposed in places and traverses a steep slope above a sheer drop into the sea. The famous arches are columnar basalts worn into fantastic shapes. One is a free-standing rock stack and another is a huge cave with two entrances. You'll need to allow about four hours in total plus some time at the arches.

Heading east from Carsaig Bay is a spectacular 4½-mile walk to **Lochbuie**, past **Adnunan stack**. It starts out through woodland, then follows the shore below the steep cliffs, with waterfalls plunging straight into the sea. It's easy at first but then gets very muddy in places and there's quite a bit of wading through boggy marsh, so make sure you've got good walking boots. Allow about five to six hours in total.

A shorter walk takes you to the Bronze Age **Lochbuie Stone Circle** at the foot of **Ben Buie**. Leave your car at the stone bridge before you reach the village. Look for the green sign on the gate to your left and follow the white marker stones across the field. The stone circle is hidden behind a wall of rhododendrons, so follow the marker stones across the plank bridge until you see it. It takes about 30 minutes.

There are several marked trails through Forestry Commission land on Mull. The first walk is to **Aros Park**, on the south side of Tobermory Bay. Start out from the car park near the distillery in Tobermory and follow the shoreline for about a mile to Lochan a'Ghurrabain, which is good for trout fishing. From here there is also a marked path around the loch (1 mile). A longer walk is to **Ardmore Bay**, 3 miles north of Tobermory. The trail/cycle path starts at the car park by the road that runs northwest from Tobermory. From here, it runs out almost to Ardmore point and back again, passing a couple of ruined villages on the way. There's a good chance of seeing seals and lots of sea birds in Ardmore Bay. The trail is 4 miles in total.

Four miles north of Craignure is the car park and picnic site at **Garmony Point**, where a 2-mile trail leads to the ferry terminal at **Fishnish**, hugging the shore all the way. Another trail (4 miles) runs out to Fishnish Point and back through the forest to the car park by the old harbour.

Iona

pp154-157. Colour map 3, C3.

→ *Phone code: 01681. Population: 130.*

Iona is a small island – barely 3 miles long and a little over a mile wide – but its importance to Christianity is out of all proportion to its size. Iona's place in religious history was guaranteed when St Columba arrived with his 12 disciples and founded a monastery there in AD 563. The Irish monk then set about converting a large part of pagan Scotland and much of northern England. Iona went on to become the most sacred religious site in Europe and has been a place of pilgrimage for several centuries. Today that pilgrimage has turned into more of an invasion, with day trippers making the five-minute ferry trip from Mull to visit the abbey. Few, however, venture beyond the main village, **Baile Mór**, and it's easy to find a quiet spot, particularly on the west coast with its sparkling silver beaches washed by turquoise sea. It's worth spending a day or two here to soak up the island's unique spiritual peace so well conveyed in the words of Dr Johnson: "that man is little to be envied whose...piety would not grow warmer among the ruins of Iona".

Background

Iona is known as the 'Cradle of Christianity in Scotland', and was once a centre of the arts. The monks produced elaborate carvings, manuscripts, ornate gravestones and Celtic crosses. Their greatest work was the beautiful *Book of Kells*, which dates from AD 800, and which is now on display in Dublin's Trinity College. This proved to be the high point of the church's history. Shortly after came the first of the Viking raids, in AD 806, when many monks were slaughtered at Martyrs' Bay, followed by another in AD 986 which destroyed the work of many years. The relentless pressure from the established church ended with the suppression of the Celtic Church by King David in 1144.

In 1203 Iona became part of the mainstream church with the establishment of a nunnery for the Order of the Black Nuns, as well as a Benedictine Abbey by Reginald of the MacDonalds of the Isles. Iona became overshadowed by the royal city of

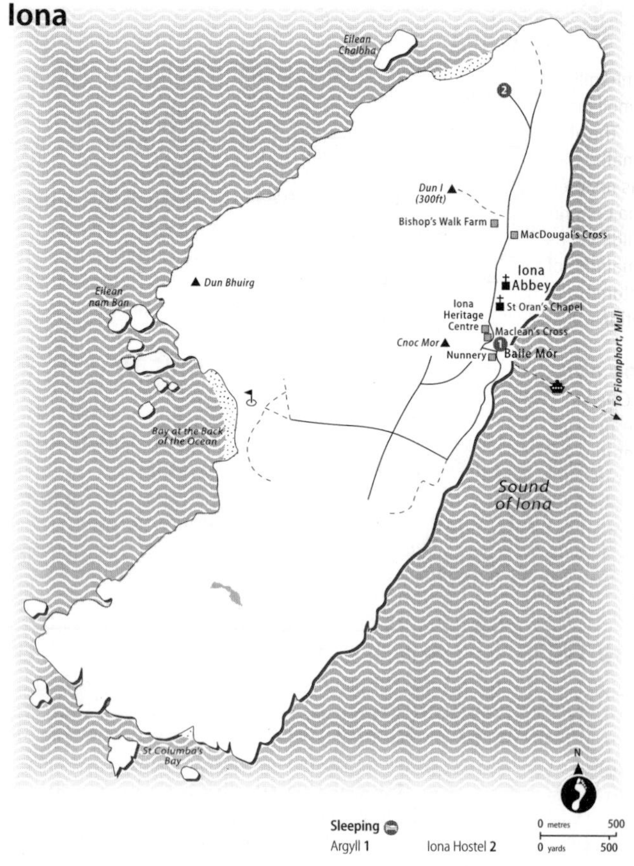

The story of St Columba

St Columba (*Colum Cille* in Gaelic), a prince of Ireland and grandson of the Irish King, Niall of the Nine Hostages, came to Scotland not as a missionary, but as an act of self-imposed penance for his actions. He stubbornly refused to hand over his copy of the Gospels, illegally copied from St Finian's original, which led to a bitter dispute with the king. This ended in a pitched battle in which Columba's supporters prevailed, but he was so overcome with remorse at the bloodshed he had caused that he fled Ireland, finally settling on Iona as it was the first place he found from where he couldn't see his homeland. Columba, however, was not retiring into obscurity. His missionary zeal drove him to begin building the abbey. He banished women and cows from the island, declaring that "where there is a cow there is a woman, and where there is a woman there is mischief". Workers at the abbey had to leave their womenfolk on nearby Eilean nam Ban (Women's Island). Not content with that, he also banished frogs and snakes from Iona, though there are plenty on Mull. He is even said to have pacified the Loch Ness Monster during a visit to Inverness. He went on to found the Celtic Church, or the Church of the Culdees, with centres through- out Scotland, which differed in many ways from the Church of Rome.

Dunfermline, and its final demise came with the Reformation when buildings were demolished and all but three of the 360 carved crosses destroyed.

The abbey lay in ruins until, in 1899, the island's owner, the eighth Duke of Argyll, donated the buildings to the Church of Scotland on condition that the abbey church was restored for worship. Then, in 1938, the Reverend George Macleod founded the Iona Community as an evangelical Church of Scotland 'brotherhood', with the abbey buildings as its headquarters, and by 1965 had succeeded in rebuilding the remainder of the monastic buildings. Now the abbey complex has been completely restored and the island of Iona, apart from the abbey buildings, is owned by the National Trust for Scotland.

The abbey

ⓘ *Open all year and at all times, free but a donation at the entrance is appreciated.*

The present abbey dates from around 1200, though it has been rebuilt over the centuries and was completely restored in the 20th century. The oldest part is the restored **St Oran's Chapel**, to the south of the abbey on the right, which is plain and unadorned save for its splendid 11th-century Norman doorway. It is said that Columba was prevented from completing the building of the original chapel until a living person had been buried in the foundations. His friend Oran volunteered and was duly buried. Columba later asked for the face to be uncovered so that he could bid a final farewell to his friend, but Oran was found to be alive and claimed he had seen Heaven and Hell, describing them in such blasphemous terms that Columba ordered he be covered up immediately!

You get a good view of the whole complex from the top of the small grassy knoll opposite the abbey entrance.

Surrounding the chapel is the **Reilig Odhrain**, the sacred burial ground, which is said to contain the graves of 48 Scottish kings, including Macbeth's victim, Duncan, as well as four Irish and eight Norwegian kings. The stones you see today are not the graves of kings but of various important people from around the West Highlands and Islands, including that of John Smith, leader of the British Labour Party from 1992 until his untimely death in 1994.

Beside the Road of the Dead, which leads from the abbey church to St Oran's Chapel, stands the eighth-century **St Martin's Cross**. This is the finest of Iona's Celtic high crosses and is remarkably complete, with the Pictish serpent-and-boss decoration on one side and holy figures on the other. Standing in front of the abbey entrance is a replica of **St John's Cross**, the other great eighth-century monument. The restored original is in the **Infirmary Museum**, at the rear of the abbey, along with a fine collection of medieval gravestones.

No part of St Columba's original buildings survives, but to the left of the main entrance is **St Columba's Shrine**, the small, steep-roofed chamber which almost certainly marks the site of the saint's tomb. This is **Torr an Aba**, where Columba's cell is said to have been. The **abbey** itself has been carefully restored to its original beautiful simplicity and inside, in a side chapel, are marble effigies of the eighth Duke of Argyll and his third wife, Duchess Ina.

Baile Mór

The passenger ferry from Fionnphort on Mull lands at Baile Mór, Iona's main village, which is little more than a row of cottages facing the sea. There are over a dozen places to stay but, as demand far exceeds supply during the busy summer season, it's best to book in advance at one of the tourist offices on Mull or in Oban. There's also a post office, a very good craft shop and general store in the village. Just outside the village, on the way to the abbey, are the ruins of the **Augustinian nunnery**. Just to the north, housed in the parish church manse, built by Thomas Telford, is the **Iona Heritage Centre** ⓘ *Apr-Oct Mon-Sat 1030-1630, £1.50*, which features displays on the island's social history. Nearby stands the intricately carved 15th-century **Maclean's Cross**.

Around the island

On the west coast are some lovely beaches of white sand and colourful pebbles. The best of the lot is the **Bay at the Back of the Ocean**, beside the golf course, and only a 1½-mile walk from the ferry. This was one of John Smith's favourite places and it's easy to see why. At the southern tip of the island is another sandy beach at **St Columba's Bay**, believed to be the spot where the saint first landed. Another good walk is to the top of **Dun I**, the only real hill, which rises to a height of 300 ft.To get there, continue on the road north from the abbey, past MacDougal's Cross, then go through a gate to the right of Bishop's Walk Farm and follow the fence up to where you join a footpath up to the top. It's only about half an hour up and down and there are great views from the top of the entire island and the coastline of Mull.

Sleeping

Craignure to Tobermory *p146*

C Glenforsa Hotel, 2 miles south of Salen, T01680-300377. Easter-Oct. Delightful hotel run by friendly hotelier and aviator above whose reception hangs a propeller off a WWI aircraft! Tastefully furnished rooms, beautiful views down the Sound of Mull; lovely restaurant serving seafood and game (ƚƚ) and real ales.

D Craignure Inn, Craignure, T01680-812305, www.craignure-inn.co.uk. 3 rooms. Open all year. 18th-century inn with a cosy bar serving real ales and reasonable food (ƚƚ-ƚ).

E Arle Lodge, Aros, T01680-300299/343, www.arlelodge.co.uk. Open all year. Friendly, independent hostel.

Camping

Balmeanach Park, Fishnish, T/F01680-300342. Well equipped, child-friendly caravan and campsite.

Tobermory *p146*

L-A Western Isles Hotel, Tobermory, T01688-302012. Open all year. 23 rooms in a large Victorian sandstone villa with views over Tobermory harbour. 2 reasonable restaurants including the conservatory bar.

E Lonan B&B, off Western Rd, T01688-302082. Easter-Oct. Welcoming, small B&B with lovely garden, terrific breakfasts and only 5 mins' walk from Main St.

F Tobermory SYHA, Main St, T0870-0041151. Terrific harbour front location. Always busy so book ahead.

West Coast Mull *p149*
C Druimard Country House Hotel, Dervaig, T01688-400345, www.druimard.co.uk. Open end Mar-Oct. 6 tastefully furnished rooms with views to Glen Bellart. Good breakfast and can arrange wildlife and island tours.
F Dervaig Bunkhouse, 6 miles from Tobermory, in tiny Dervaig, T01688-400249. A terrific budget accommodation option.

South Mull *p149*
C Pennyghael Hotel, in Pennyghael, overlooking the loch, T01681-704288, www.pennyghaelhotel.com. Serving local seafood/game in restaurant (ΨΨ) and with 2 self-catering cottages in grounds. Mixed reports on service.

Iona *p151*
B-D Argyll Hotel, T01681-700334, www.argyllhoteliona.co.uk. Open Apr-Oct. 17 rooms. This remains the better of the island's 2 upmarket hotels with a good restaurant and they organize tours.
E Iona Hostel, T01681-700781, www.ionahostel.co.uk. A fabulous hostel with views to the Treshnish Islands. 25-min walk north from the village and ferry. It's best to book ahead in summer.

Eating

Craignure to Tobermory *p146*
ΨΨΨ-ΨΨ Mediterranea, Salen, T01680-300200, www.mullonthemed.com. Apr-Jun and Oct Thu-Tue 1800-2000, Jul-Sep daily. An island gem serving Sicilian classics! Beyond the bright yellow door awaits mouth-watering seafood and pasta creations, delightful staff and a cosy ambience. Book ahead.

Tobermory *p146*
ΨΨΨ-Ψ Western Isles Hotel, Tobermory, see Sleeping, above. Good menu offers à la carte in the dining room or cheaper bar meals in the **Conservatory Bar**.
ΨΨ The Café Fish, right on the pier above the TIC, T01688-301253, www.thecafefish.com. Mon-Sat. Choose the cosy interior or al fresco for dining on the freshest seafood including squat lobster. A real delight.
ΨΨ-Ψ Mishnish Hotel, see Entertainment, below. Despite its makeover, 'the Mish' retains an element of charm and serves up hearty meals to accompany your real ale.
MacGochan's, on the harbour front. Similar good pub grub and live music.

The best value **fish n' chips** are sold nightly by the mobile vendor at the harbour front.

West Coast Mull *p149*
Ψ Old Byre Heritage Centre, Dervaig, see Sights, above. Apr-end Oct. Simple, home-made delights offered all day. Not a huge menu but a worthwhile lunch stop.

Entertainment

Mull *p146*
Mishnish Hotel, Main St, Tobermory. Despite the 'themed' old-world decor it wins over **MacGochan's** for its ambience. Both pubs run live music events and attract healthy numbers of revellers.

There are also music events at **An Tobar**, Tobermory, see Sights, page 147.

Festivals and events

Mull *p146*
Apr Mull Music Festival, known as the **Whisky Olympics**, is held on the last weekend of the month. It is a great time to be on Mull when you can enjoy a feast of Gaelic folk music and, of course, whisky. The focus of the festival is the bar of the **Mishnish Hotel**, Tobermory. For details T01688-302383.
Jul Mendelssohn on Mull Music Festival, held over 10 days in early Jul, is another great festival. It commemorates the famous composer's visit here in 1829. **Tobermory Highland Games**, is held annually on the 3rd Thu of the month.
Sep Mull and Iona Food Festival. This mid-Sep festival showcases the wealth of outstanding produce cultivated on the island.
Oct Tour of Mull Rally, held in early Oct for over 30 years, this should not be missed by rally enthusiasts.

Shopping

Mull *p146*
From the local butcher and baker to the chocolate-maker, Tobermory is foodie-heaven. It's also where to pick up fishing tackle, camping and bike spares. Thankfully, it continues to defy the scourge of tartan tack.
Island Bakery and deli, Main St, T01688-302225. Try their award-winning organic lemon melts and oat crumbles.
Isle of Mull Cheese, on the edge of town,. 500 yds off the Dervaig Rd, at Sgriob-Ruadh Farm, T01688-302235. Here you can savour their award-winning, traditionally made cheese and admire their wonderful glass barn. Open Apr-end Sep Mon-Fri 1000-1600.
Mull Pottery, southern edge of Tobermory en-route to Salen, T01688-302347. Tasteful pots in different shapes and sizes. Café-bistro upstairs.
Tobermory Chocolate Company, Main St, T01688-302526. Open all year Mon-Sat 0930-1700, Sun 1000-1600. Here you can try out their speciality – chocolate made with the local whisky and delicious Staffa Cake.

Activities and tours

Mull *p146*
Boat trips
Alternative Boat Hire, T01681-700537, www.boattripsiona.com. Trips around the coastline and handline fishing on a traditional wooden boat. You can hire by the hour or for an afternoon, May-Oct, from Fionnphort and Iona.
Turus Mara, www.turusmara.com. T01688-400297. Birdwatching and wildlife trips to Staffa, Iona and the Treshnish Isles costing from £20 (from Mull) and £40 (from Oban). Chance to spot seals, puffins and visit the classic Fingal's Cave on Staffa.

Fishing
Sea Angling Trips, Tackle and Books, Main St, Tobermory, T01688-302336. Fish for mackerel, pollock and dogfish aboard *Amidas*. Trips last approximately 3 hrs and include equipment. £20, children £15. Min 6 people. The shop also sells fishing permits (from £4) for inland lochs. Ask the shop for its small leaflet with destinations. Shop also well stocked with walking maps and equipment.
A Brown and Son Ironmonger, Main St, Tobermory, T01688-302020. In addition to trout-fishing permits, this is where to stock up on everything from camping gas to tent pegs and even get your watch battery changed! Bike hire from £15 per day.

Wildlife tours
Recent, acclaimed wildlife documentaries have further fuelled demand for wildlife tours on the island. Visit www.wildisles.co.uk, for a list of operators.

You can find out about the sea-life around Mull by visiting the **Hebridean Whale and Dolphin Trust**, 28 Main St, Tobermory, T01688-302620, www.hwdt.org, Apr-Oct daily 1000-1700, Nov-Mar Mon-Fri 1100-1700, a charity which aims to protect the marine environment through education.
Island Encounter Wildlife Safaris, Salen, T01680-300441, www.mullwildlife.co.uk. A full-day wildlife safari with local guide Richard Atkinson costs £32 including lunch. You'll see golden eagles, white-tailed sea eagles, hen harriers, divers, merlins, peregrine falcons, seals and porpoises, to name but a few.
Isle of Mull Landrover Wildlife Expeditions, Ulva Ferry, T01688-500121, www.scotland wildlife.com. David Woodhouse runs these excellent day-long tours with lunch £33.50, children £28.50 and the chance to spot golden eagles, otters, seals and porpoise.
Sea Life Surveys, T01688-302916, www.sealifesurveys.com. Everything from whale, dolphin and shark-watching trips to gentle Ecocruz's in sheltered waters to inter-island (Staffa, Eigg and Muck) voyages can be booked with this operator. Half-day prices from £35 per day. Their Tobermory operation is beside **McGochan's** pub.

Transport

Mull *p146*
Bus There's a bus from Tobermory post office to **Dervaig** and **Calgary**, 4 times a day Mon-Fri and twice on Sat (operated by RN Carmichael, T01688-302220). The **Craignure** to Tobermory via **Salen** service runs 6 times a day Mon-Fri, 4 times on Sat and 4 times on Sun (operated by Bowman's Coaches, T01680-812313. There's a Bowmans bus from **Craignure** to **Fionnphort** (for Iona) 4 times a

day Mon-Fri, 3 times on Sat and 1 on Sun. For bus times, contact the operators or ideally pick up the comprehensive *Mull Area Transport Guide* at the tourist office in Oban, Tobermory or Craignure. This also includes ferry times. There are daily buses from Craignure which coincide with ferry arrivals.

Car Tobermory is a 30- to 40-min drive (2-hr cycle) north from the ferry pier at **Craignure**.

Cycle There are several places to rent bikes. In Tobermory there's **Brown's Hardware** shop on Main St, T01688-302020, or try the **youth hostel** in Tobermory. In Salen there's **On Yer Bike**, T01680-300501, which also has a shop by the ferry terminal in Craignure, T01680-812580.

Ferry From **Oban** to **Craignure** (45 mins) 5-7 times daily Mon-Sat and 5 times daily on Sun, £4.05 one way per passenger, £36 per car, 5-day return £6.95 and £48.50. **CalMac** offices: Oban, T01631-566688, and Craignure, T01680-812343. **Lochaline** on the Morvern Peninsula (see page 218) to **Fishnish** (15 mins, £2.50 per passenger, £10.90 per car) every 45 mins 0700-1830 Mon-Sat and 9 times on Sun. There are also ferries from **Kilchoan** on the Ardnamurchan Peninsula (see page 218) to **Tobermory** 7 times daily Mon-Sat and 5 times daily on Sun (May-Aug).

A small bicycle/passenger-only ferry makes the 2-min crossing on demand from Ulva Ferry, all year for Mon-Fri sailings 0900-1700; Sun sailings Jun-Aug only. From Easter-Sep show signal at the pier to cross. Oct-Easter best to call the ferryman on T01688-400352 or via T01688-500241. Note that there's no bus to Ulva Ferry. Either cycle or take the bus to Salen and jump on a pre-booked bike (T01680-300501).

Iona *p151*
To Iona, a passenger-only ferry leaves from **Fionnphort** on Mull (5 mins) frequently Mon-Sat 0815-1815 and hourly 0900-1800 Sun, £3.75 per passenger, bicycles £2.

Directory

Mull *p146*
Banks Clydesdale Bank, Main St, Tobermory, is Mull's only permanent bank. There's also a mobile bank which tours the island.

Coll, Tiree and Colonsay

Just 13 miles long and 4 miles wide, the trickle of visitors who come to explore low-lying, windswept Coll step onto one of the best-kept secrets in Scotland. Here, tourism remains almost invisible, the 100 islanders enjoying a natural playground where families can picnic on deserted pearl-white beaches with views towards Mull and the Inner Hebrides. Idyllic neighbouring Tiree or Tir-Iodh (land of corn) also boasts stunning beaches caressed by the waters of the Gulf Stream. Statistically one of the sunniest and windiest locations in the UK, Tiree's billiard-flat hinterland teems with rare birdlife and excited wildlife enthusiasts whilst offshore, windsurfers, surfers and kite-surfers play in towering waves that since the 1980s have earned Tiree the nickname of 'mini-Hawaii'. Little wonder Tiree now offers a healthy numbers of B&Bs! Colonsay too is remote, tranquil and undemanding; an island brimming with wildlife, flowers and even a miniature mountain range. Like Tiree, Colonsay has also steadily embraced tourism and in particular self-catering accommodation. It may not be the easiest island to reach but clearly its magic has already been discovered. ▸▸ *For Sleeping, eating and other listings, see pages 160-161.*

Coll

▸▸ *pp160-161. Colour map 3, B3.*

→ *www.visitcoll.co.uk. Phone code: 01879.*

The best of Coll's 23 beaches are on the west coast, at **Killunaig, Hogh Bay** and **Feall Bay**. The latter is separated from the nearby **Crossapol Bay** by giant sand dunes managed by the RSPB to protect the resident corncrake population. The **CalMac** ferry from Oban calls in at Coll's only village, **Arinagour**, where half of the island's population live and where you'll find the post office (and bike hire opposite), petrol station, general store, and cosy **Island Café**. There's no public transport but a taxi is available. If it's not too windy, it's best to explore by bike. It's worth taking a walk up **Ben Hogh** (341 ft), the island's highest point, overlooking Hogh Bay on the west coast, to get a terrific view of the island. Tired of beaches? Try some fishing or the nine-hole golf course at Cliad 2 miles west of Arinagour.

Tiree » *pp160-161. Colour map 3, B2.*

→ *Phone code: 01879.*

Tiree is a low, flat island, only about 11 miles long and 6 miles across at its widest, and is also known by the nickname *Tir fo Thuinn*, or 'Land below the waves'. When seen from a distance most of it disappears below the horizon, save its two highest hills, **Ben Hynish** (462 ft) and **Beinn Hough** (390 ft), on the west coast. Though flat, remember that Tiree's fierce winds can make cycling hard work! Campervans laden with surf-gear are a reminder that this is a windsurfing paradise and each October Tiree hosts the spectacular, week-long **Tiree Wave Classic**. Scores of world-class windsurfers come to compete and party putting accommodation at a premium.

The ferry port is at **Scarinish**, at the western edge of the sweep of **Gott Bay**. The main village of Scarinish is also where to find the **Co-op** supermarket, the post office and bank (and there's a garage at the pier head). About 4 miles from Scarinish, is Vaul Bay, where aside from golf, there are the well-preserved remains of **Dun Mor**, a Pictish Broch built around the first century AD and standing on a rocky outcrop to the west of the bay.

The island's main road runs northwest from Scarinish, past the beautiful beach at **Balephetrish Bay** to **Balevullin**, where you can see some good examples of restored traditional thatched houses. Just to the south, at Sandaig, is the **Sandaig Museum** ⓘ *Jun-Sep Mon-Fri 1400-1600*, a thatched croft inside which displays tell of the island's fascinating social history.

In the southwestern corner of the island is the spectacular headland of **Ceann a'Mara**, or Kenavara. The massive cliffs are home to thousands of sea birds. East from here, across the golden sands of **Balephuil Bay**, is the island's highest hill, **Ben Hynish**, topped by a radar-tracking station resembling a giant golf ball. It's worth the climb to the top for the magnificent views over the island and to the distant Outer Hebrides. Below Ben Hynish, to the east, is the village of **Hynish**, where you'll find the **Signal Tower Museum**, which tells the fascinating story of the building of the **Skerryvore Lighthouse** (1840-1844) by Alan Stevenson, an uncle of Robert Louis Stevenson. This incredible feat of engineering was carried out from Hynish, where a dry dock/reservoir was built for shipping materials by boat to the Skerryvore reef, 11 miles to the southwest.

Tiree is one of the best places to surf in the British Isles.

Colonsay » *pp160-161. Colour map 3, C3.*

→ *Phone code: 01951.*

Colonsay's population of around 120 lives in the three small villages, the largest of which is **Scalasaig**, the ferry port. A few miles north of the ferry, in the middle of the island, is **Colonsay House**, dating from 1772. It was sold, along with the rest of the island, in 1904 to Lord Strathcona, who had made his fortune in Canada with the Hudson Bay Company and went on to found the Canadian Pacific Railway. The house is not open to the public but the lovely gardens and woods, full of rhododendrons, giant palms and exotic shrubs, are worth a stroll. The estate cottages are now self-catering holiday homes.

The end of innocence

On 26 October, 2006, the population of Colonsay was scandalized by an event that would shake the very foundations of island life: a hitherto unthinkable deed so heinous it would have everyone talking about it for many weeks and months to come, not to mention thrusting this quiet, unassuming Hebridean island onto the front pages of the national press. We are talking here about the theft of £60 from 75-year-old Davie Sutherland's money box. Perhaps not so exceptional in the grasping, corrupt and greedy 21st-century world of the Scottish mainland, but this is a place where the front door key is a redundant item. Islanders never lock their doors, and this was the first theft in living memory. Not since the Viking invasion had the residents seen the like. Only this time, the sneak thief was a visiting worker from Glasgow, not Norway, and arrived on a car ferry, not in a longboat. With no local bobby on the island (crime is non-exisitent), and the next ferry to the mainland not due to leave till the following day, the culprit had to spend an uncomfortable night under the suspicious eye of every islander, as word of his crime was passed from neighbour to neighbour. Indeed, he was fortunate that a number of community leaders were off the island. As one of them put it: "He was a lucky boy. If a few of the other lads were still on the island, they would have murdered him for picking on wee Davie". A few days later, the thief was fined £400 at Oban Sheriff Court and ordered to pay back Davie's £60. But despite the pensioner's unique place in the annals of true crime on Colonsay, Mr Sutherland has no intention of locking his door in future. "Nobody locks their door here and why should they?" he said defiantly.

There are several standing stones, the best of which are **Fingal's Limpet Hammers**, at Kilchattan, southwest of Colonsay House. There are also Iron Age forts, such as **Dun Eibhinn**, next to the hotel in Scalasaig (see below). Colonsay is also home to a wide variety of wildlife. You can see choughs, one of Britain's rarest birds, as well as corncrakes, buzzards, falcons, merlins and perhaps even the odd golden eagle or sea eagle. There are also otters, seals and wild goats (said to be descended from the survivors of the Spanish Armada ships wrecked in 1588). The jewel in the island's crown, though, lies 6 miles north of Scalasaig, past Colonsay House, at **Kiloran Bay**. The beach here is described as the finest in the Hebrides, and who could argue? Just a glimpse of this magnificent half mile of golden sands, backed by tiers of grassy dunes, with massive breakers rolling in off the Atlantic, is worth the two-hour ferry crossing alone.

Just off the southern tip of Colonsay is the island of Oronsay, 2 miles square with a population of six and one of the highlights of a visit to Colonsay. The name derives from the Norse for 'ebb-tide island', which is a fitting description as Oronsay can be reached on foot at low tide, across the mud flats known as 'The Strand'. It takes about an hour to walk from the south end of Colonsay to the ruins of a 14th-century **Augustinian Priory**. This was the home of some of the most highly skilled medieval craftsmen in the Western Highlands. A surviving example of their work is the impressive Oronsay Cross and the beautifully carved tombstones, on display in the **Prior's House**. Make sure you take wellies for the walk across the Strand and check on the tides. Tide tables are available at the hotel or shop. Spring tides (new and full moon) allow about three to four hours to walk across and back, which is just enough time to see the priory but little else. An alternative is to time one way to coincide with the postbus.

Sleeping

Coll *p157*
B-D Coll Hotel, Arinagour, T01879-230334. A comfortable 6-bedroom family hotel serving very good food (ΨΨ-Ψ).
D Caolas House, T01879-230438. A friendly, cosy farmhouse B&B south of Arinagour by the beach with terrific home-cooking. Bothy also available for let.

Tiree *p158*
D Glebe House, Scarinish, T01879-220758, www.glebehousetiree.co.uk. Comfortable accommodation with sea views across Gott Bay. Also dinners if requested.
F Tiree Mill House, Cornaig, T01879-220435. Fantastic bunkhouse accommodation close to Loch Bhasapol.

Colonsay *p158*
Accommodation on Colonsay is limited and must be booked well in advance. Even self-catering options are hard to come by, because the same families return year after year (and who can blame them?). For details on 20 self-catering options see **Colonsay Cottages**, T01951-200312, www.colonsay.org.uk/estate
B Isle of Colonsay Hotel, a few hundred yds from the ferry, T01951-200316. A cosy 18th-century inn with 11 rooms, a friendly bar and excellent food. They can also arrange trips on the island.
E The Hannahs, 4 Uragaig, T01950-200150, thehannahsbandb@aol.com. 2 rooms. Cosy and friendly, with a breakfast that will 'blow your socks off'. Be prepared!
F Colonsay Keeper's Lodge, T01951-200312, www.colonsay.org.uk. A comfortable back-packers' hostel, 2 km from the ferry, sleeps 16 and open all year, phone for lift from ferry.

Eating

Tiree *p158*
ΨΨ The Glassary Restaurant, Sandaig T01879-220684. Mon-Sat 1700-2100. Delicious dinners and Sun lunch.
Ψ The Cobbled Cow, by the airport. Terrific home-baking, good for a snack.

Activities and tours

Tiree *p158*
Sand-yachting, Gott Bay, T01879-220317.
Skipinnish Tours, www.skipinnish-sea-tours.co.uk, T01879-220009. From £10-35 per person for wildlife spotting and trips out to Skerryvore Lighhouse.
Suds, T07793-063849, www.surfschool scotland.co.uk. For fun surfing.
Tiree on Horseback, T01879-220881.
Wild Diamond Surf, based at the **Tiree Lodge Hotel** and Loch Bhasapol, T01879-220399. Fantastic kite-surfing and windsurfing lessons and hire.

Transport

Coll *p157*
Cycle Coll is best navigated on foot or by bike. Bike hire from **An Acarsaid**, T01879-230395.

Ferry CalMac car/passenger ferries leave from **Oban**, 2 hrs 40 mins, 1 daily (not Thu) £21.85 return and £127 per car.

Taxi T01879-230402.

Tiree *p158*
Air Tiree has an airport with 1 flight daily Mon-Sat (45 mins), all year round to **Glasgow**. The airport is at The Reef, T01879-220309.

Bus From 0700-1800 (Mon-Sat) the whole island is covered by a **Ring n' Ride** service, T01879-220419. A bus-taxi service operates with standard fares. It's ideal for exploring the island. Pick-up a copy of the *Area Transport Guide to Tiree and Coll* from Oban TIC.

Cycle Bicycle hire is available at the **Millhouse Hostel**, Cornaigmore, T01879-220435.

Ferry CalMac car/passenger ferries sail to the island from **Oban**, via **Coll** once daily (3 hrs 50 mins, £21.85 return passenger, £127 per car) once daily. From Coll to Tiree (50 mins) costs £3.30 single per passenger and £19.75 one-way per car. The ferry port is at Scarinish (T01879-220337).

Taxi For shared and private taxi hire call John Kennedy Taxis, T01879-220419.

Colonsay *p158*
Bus There's a limited bus and postbus service around the island Mon-Sat, for those without their own transport. For wildlife, archaeological and sightseeing tours by bus or foot T01951-200320. From £15. www.colonsay.org.uk.

Cycle As the island is only 8 miles long by 3 miles wide, you might consider hiring a bicycle. Bike hire from A McConnel, T01951-200355.

Ferry There are ferry sailings from **Oban** (2 hrs, £11.40 one way per passenger, £55 per car) once daily Mon, Wed, Thu, Fri and Sun, arriving at Scalasaig on the east coast. From **Kennacraig** there is 1 sailing (3 hrs 35 mins) on Wed. From **Port Askaig** there is 1 sailing (1¼ hrs, £4.30 per passenger, £22.30 per car) also on Wed. Ferries need to be booked well in advance during the summer months.

Islay and Jura

Islay (pronounced eye-la*), the most southerly of the Hebridean islands and one of the most populous, with around 4000 inhabitants, enjoys a rich farming and crofting heritage but it has one particular claim to fame – single malt whisky. Aside from whisky, people also come here to watch birds. The island is something of an ornithologists' wonderland, and from October to April plays host to migrating barnacle and white-fronted geese flying down from Greenland in their thousands for the winter. The short ferry crossing from Islay takes you to Jura, a primeval and uncompromising place; a lost world, pervaded by an almost haunting silence. The words 'wild' and 'remote' tend to get overused in describing the many Hebridean islands, but in the case of Jura they are, if anything, an understatement. Jura has one road, one hotel, six sporting estates and 5000 red deer, which outnumber the 160 people by 25:1, the human population having been cleared to turn the island into a huge deer forest. Rather appropriately, the name Jura derives from the Norse 'dyr-ey', meaning deer island.* ⏩ *For Sleeping, Eating and other listings, see page 167-168.*

Islay ⏩ *pp167-168. Colour map 5, A1.*

→ *Phone code: 01496.*

Islay offers the unique opportunity to visit several of Scotland's most impressive distilleries in one day. The island has eight working distilleries in total (see box page 163) and their distinctive peaty malts are considered to be among the finest. At the end of May each year, the island hosts the **Islay Whisky and Music Festival** for which the distillers produce their own special edition malts. Further details at www.feisile.org. **Islay's TIC** ⓘ *Bowmore, T01496-810254, Apr-Sep Mon-Sat 1000-1700, Sun 1400-1700, Oct-Mar Mon-Fri 1000-1600*, will find accommodation for you. ⏩ *For Transport details, see page 168.*

Port Ellen and around

Port Ellen is the largest place on Islay and the main ferry port, yet it still has the feel of a sleepy village. There are many day trips from Port Ellen. A road runs east out to **Ardtalla**, where it ends. Along the way, it passes three distilleries, first **Laphroaig**, then **Lagavulin** and lastly **Ardbeg**, all of which offer guided tours, see page 163. Between the Lagavulin and Ardbeg distilleries is the dramatically sited 16th-century ruin of **Dunyvaig Castle**, once the main naval base and fortress of the Lords of the Isles. Five miles further on is the impressive **Kildalton Cross**, standing in the graveyard of the ruined 13th-century

Weapons of mass drunkeness

The US Defence Threat Reduction Agency (DTRA), whose mission is "to safeguard the US and its allies from weapons of mass destruction" had been monitoring the Bruichladdich Distillery on Islay.

The distillery installed webcams to show the world that their whisky is made using traditional methods, but in September 2003 discovered that the DTRA was spying on them. According to the agency, it only takes a 'tweak' – their words – in the process of whisky making and Bruichladdich could be producing deadly chemical weapons, hence their interest. The DTRA had emailed the distillery to inform them that one of their webcams was faulty and when the distillery replied to thank them and inquire who they were, the agency went right ahead and revealed who they were and what they were doing.

Once they had been 'outed', the DTRA had to admit that the distillery posed no threat to world peace, though many would contest that excessive consumption of the amber liquid has been known to contribute to the occasional breach of local peace in the island's bars.

Mark Reynier, the managing director of the Port Charlotte distillery, took it all in good humour: "we're a sinister-looking bunch, so I can see how we might be mistaken for Al-Qaeda", he quipped.

As they say, only in America.

chapel. The eighth-century cross is well preserved and one of Scotland's most important Early Christian monuments, and the carvings depict biblical scenes.

Southwest of Port Ellen a road runs out to a small, rounded peninsula known as **The Oa**, an area of varied beauty, both wild and pastoral, and with a wonderful coastline. The road runs as far as **Upper Killeyan**, from where it's about a mile uphill to the spectacular headland at the **Mull of Oa**. Here you'll see the strange-looking **American monument**. The obelisk commemorates the shipwrecks offshore of two US ships, the *Tuscania* and the *Ontranto*, both of which sank in 1918 at the end of the First World War. There's a great walk north from the Mull of Oa up to Kintra, but it's best to start out from Kintra.

A turn-off from the road to The Oa leads north to **Kintra**, at the south end of **The Big Strand** at Laggan Bay, with 5 miles of sands and dunes. There's a restaurant and accommodation here, and it's a great place for camping. The restaurant is at the end of the road, with the beach on one side and, on the other, a wild and spectacular coastal walk incorporating caves and the impressive **Soldier's Rock** sea-stack. Ask at the TIC for the *Explore Islay* walking trail leaflet. Just to the north of Kintra is the **Machrie golf course**, a golfing experience that shouldn't be missed.

Bowmore and the Rinns of Islay

The A846 runs north from Port Ellen, straight as a pool cue, to Bowmore, the island's administrative capital and second largest village. Founded in 1768 by the Campbells, it retains a sleepy air. The village is laid out in a grid plan with the main street running straight up the hill from the pier to the unusual round church, designed to ward off evil spirits, who can hide only in corners. Thankfully, the good spirit stayed behind and can be found at the **Bowmore Distillery**, just to the west of Main Street. This is the oldest of the island's distilleries, founded in 1779.

North of Bowmore, **Bridgend**, is the site of the tiny **Islay Ales Brewery**. Here too the A846 joins the A847 which runs west to the hammerhead peninsula known as the **Rinns of Islay** (*rinns* is derived from the Gaelic for promontory). A few miles west of

Islay's malts distilled

Ardbeg, T01496-302244, www.ardbeg.com, tours all year Mon-Fri 1030, 1130, 1430 and 1530, Jun-Aug daily, £2. Describes itself as the peatiest malt whisky in the world. This may be a robust and powerful malt but in 1981 all operations were sadly mothballed. In 1997 it was bought by Glenmorangie and reopened to ensure the malt first distilled in 1815 continued to flow from within the whitewashed walls on Islay's rocky eastern shoreline.

Bowmore, T01496-558 9011, www.bowmore.com, tours Easter-end Jun, Mon-Sat 1000, 1100, 1400 and 1500, end June-end Sep, daily, 1000, 1100, 1400, 1500, mid-Sep to Easter, Mon-Fri 1000, 1100, 1400, 1500 and Sat 1000, £2. Established in 1779, Bowmore is the oldest distillery on Islay. Its flagship is the 12 year-old single malt. It opened a new visitor centre in September 2006 with additional information on the history of the distillery.

Bruichladdich, T01496-850191, www.bruichladdich.com, 45-min tours Easter-Nov, Mon-Fri 1030, 1130, 1430, Sat 1030 and 1430 only, £4 including dram. Produces a range of innovative malts including Mood Malts, Multi-Vintage and Single Vintage. Claims to produce different Bruichladdich's by drawing upon its maturing stocks that date back to 1964 (pronounced 'brook-laddie').

Bunnahabhain, T01496-840646, www.bunnahabhain.co.uk, Easter-Oct Mon-Fri 1030, 1245, 1400, 1515, by appointment only, you are strongly advised to call ahead to double check all tour times and distillery opening hours. Started in 1881 (and pronounced 'bun-a-havan'), this is known as the 'gentle giant' of Islay because it's the least peaty of the Islay malts. The distiller produces a 12, 18 and 25 year-old malt and also a 34 year-old malt.

Caol Ila, T01496-302760, www.discovering-distilleries.com, open only by appointment on selected days Apr-Oct, £4. Pronounced 'coal-eela', this distillery was founded in 1846 and lies close to Port Askaig, with great views across the Sound of Islay to Jura. Unlike most of its island peers, this single malt is best before dinner.

Kilchoman, Rockside Farm, Bruichladdich, T01496-850011, www.kilchomandistillery.com, café and shop with tours all year but request call for opening hours. Pronounced 'Kilhoman', Islay's first new distillery for 124 years is also officially Scotland's most westerly. It claims to be unique by overseeing the entire whisky process on-site; from growing and malting the barley on the farm, to its distillation, maturity and bottling. On 14 December 2005, the first cask of Kilchoman was filled. By 2008 the distillery expects to be producing 750 casks.

Lagavulin, T01496-302730, www.discovering-distilleries.com/lagavulin, tours Mon-Fri by appointment only 1000, 1130, 1430, £4, (pronounced 'laga-voolin') is a mile along the shore by the romantic ruin of Dunyvaig Castle. Their 16-year-old single malt is one of the classics and also makes the ideal after-dinner tipple. A very interesting tour.

Laphroaig, T01496-302418, www.laphroaig.com, tours all year by appointment only 1015 and 1415, free, (pronounced 'la-froyg'), is the closest to Port Ellen, and its wonderful setting is summed up by its name, meaning 'The beautiful hollow by the broad bay' in Gaelic. According to many this is the ultimate in malt whisky and is at its best after dinner.

Bridgend the B8017 turns north to the **RSPB Reserve** at **Loch Gruinart**. The mudflats and fields at the head of the loch provide winter grazing for huge flocks of barnacle and white-fronted geese from Greenland, arriving in late October. There's an excellent RSPB visitor centre at **Aoradh** (pronounced *oorig*) which houses an observation point with telescopes and CCTV, and there's a hide across the road. There are about 110 species of bird breeding on Islay, including the rare chough and corncrake.

The coastal scenery around the Rinns is very impressive, particularly at **Killinallan Point**, a beautiful and lonely headland at the far northeast of Loch Gruinart.

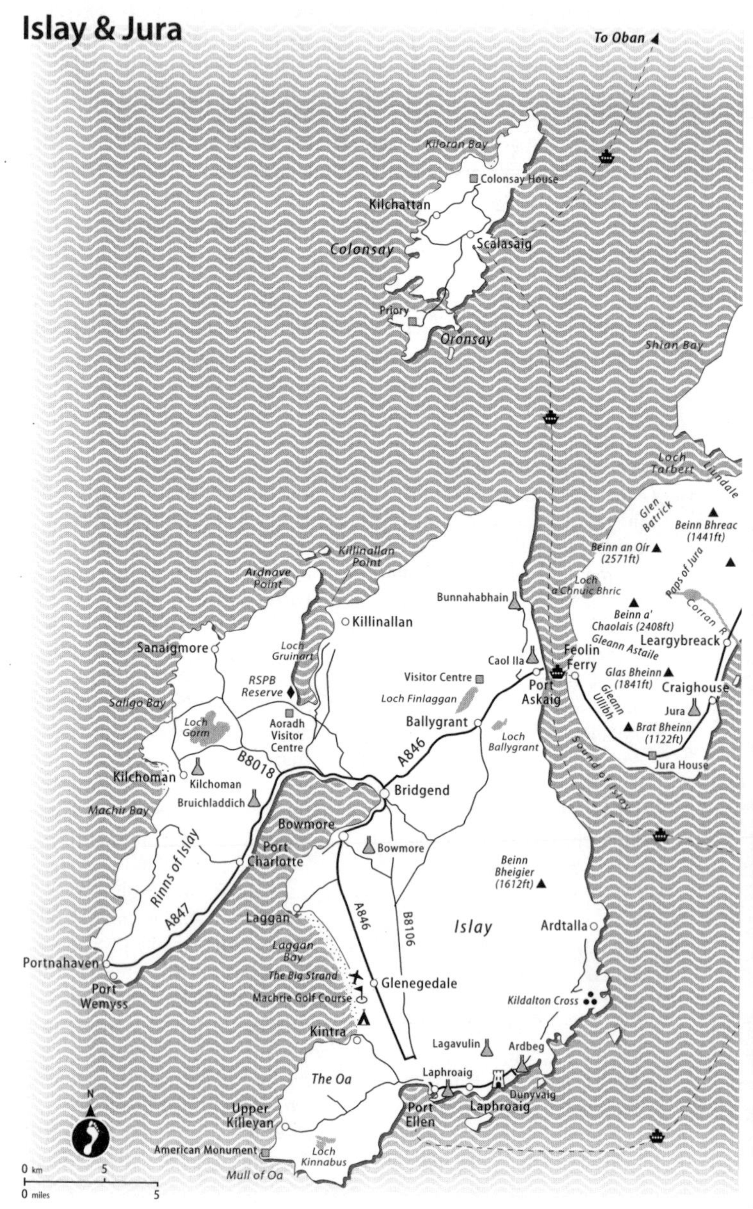

Also impressive is **Ardnave Point**, west of Loch Gruinart, and further west along the north coast, **Sanaigmore.** The best beaches are at **Saligo** and **Machir Bay** on the west coast, past Loch Gorm. Both are lovely, wide, golden beaches backed by high dunes but swimming is ill-advised due to dangerous undercurrents. Less than a mile behind Machir Bay you'll also find **Kilchoman Distillery and Visitor Centre** ⓘ *T01496-850011*, the isle's newest working distiller of the water of life.

Port Charlotte is without doubt the most charming of Islay's villages, with rows of well-kept, whitewashed cottages stretched along the wide bay. Here, below the comfortable youth hostel is the **Islay Natural History Trust** ⓘ *T01496-850288, Easter-Oct, Mon-Fri 1000-1500 (Jul-Aug 1000-1700) and Sun 1400-1700, £3, concession £2*. It's a must for anyone interested in flora and fauna with good displays on geology and natural history, a video room and reference library. Housed 300 yards away in a former Free Church, the compact **Museum of Islay Life** ⓘ *T01496-850358, Easter-Oct Mon-Sat 1000-1700, Sun (Jul-Aug only) 1400-1700, £3*, is especially worth a visit with photographs and over 1600 exhibits, including an illicit still found on the island, highlighting the rich past and culture of the native Ileach's (*ee-lach's*). At the southern end of the Rinns is the picturesque fishing and crofting village of Portnahaven, its Hebridean cottages rising steeply above the deeply indented harbour.

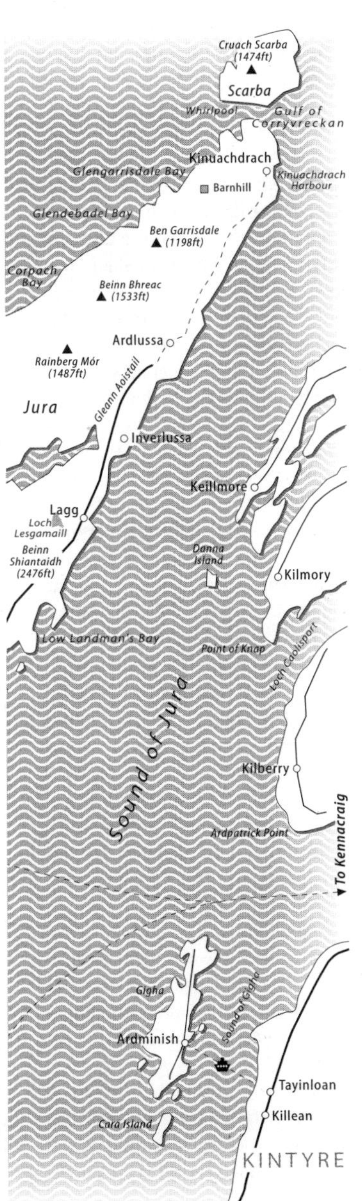

Port Askaig and around

Port Askaig is Islay's other ferry port, with connections to the mainland and to the islands of Jura and Colonsay. It's little more than a dock, a car park and a pub huddled at the foot of a steep, wooded hillside. A short walk north along the coast is the **Caol Ila distillery**, and a couple of miles further north, at the end of the road which branches left before you enter Port Askaig, is the beautifully situated **Bunnahabhain Distillery**.

The A846 runs east from Bridgend out to Port Askaig passing through **Ballygrant**, just to the south of **Loch Finlaggan**. Here, on two *crannogs* (artificial islands), were the headquarters of the Lords of the Isles, the ancestors of Clan Donald. The MacDonalds ruled from Islay for nearly 350 years, over a vast area covering all of the islands off the west coast and almost the whole of the western seaboard from Cape Wrath to the Mull of Kintyre. To the northeast of the loch, there's a **visitor centre** ⓘ *May-Sep Sun-Fri 1400-1700, Easter and Oct Tue, Thu and Sun 1400-1630, £2*, where you can see some of the archaeological remains. You can walk across the fen to **Eilean Mor**, where you'll find a medieval chapel and several ornately carved gravestones. On neighbouring, **Eilean na Comhairle** (The Council of the Isle) the Lords of the Isles decided policy.

Jura

» *pp167-168. Colour map A 1-2.*

→ *Phone code 01496.*

Three things bring people to sparsely populated Jura. First there's the scenery. This is one of the last, true wildernesses in the British Isles and perfect for some real off-the-beaten-track walking. The appealingly named **Paps of Jura**, are three breast-shaped peaks that dominate not only the island itself but also the view for miles around. From Kintyre, Mull, Coll and Tiree, and from the mountains of mainland Scotland from Skye to Arran, they can be seen on the horizon. The Paps provide some tough hillwalking and require good navigational skills, or a guide. It takes a good eight hours to cover all three peaks, though during the Paps of Jura fell race they are covered in just three hours. A good place to start is by the three-arch bridge over the Corran River, north of Leargybreack. The first pap you reach is **Beinn a'Chaolais** (2408 ft), next is the highest, **Beinn an Oír** (2571 ft) and the third is **Beinn Shiantaidh** (2476 ft). To find out about guides, ask at **Jura Hotel**, see Sleeping, page 167.

Next there's wildlife. Aside from the thousands of red deer, there are sea eagles and golden eagles in the skies above and the surrounding seas are full of seals, dolphins and porpoises, with the elusive otter making an occasional appearance. And finally, there's whisky. The island's only road leads from the ferry to the only village, Craighouse, 8 miles away on the southeast coast. Here you'll find the **Jura distillery** ⓘ *T01496-820240, www.isleofjura.com, all year round, tours by appointment only, free*, which produces 1½ million litres annually and offers a snifter of the stuff at the end of a friendly and informative tour.

Another of the island's draws is the **Corryvreckan whirlpool** at the very northern tip, between Jura and the uninhabited island of **Scarba**. The notorious whirlpool, the second largest in the world, is in fact a tidal race that creates an action like a gigantic washing machine. It is seen at its awesome best during spring tides, especially with a westerly gale, when this most treacherous stretch of water creates oar falls of 25 ft and the terrible roar can be heard for up to 10 miles away. A two-hour tidal difference between the sound on the east and the Atlantic flood tides combine with the gulf of Corryvreckan's steep sides and underwater pinnacle, the Hag, to create the vortex. The Royal Navy officially says it's unsailable, but that doesn't stop several local boat tours actually going over the top of it. It is named after a Viking, Bhreacan, who anchored his boat here for three days and nights with a rope woven from the hair of virgins. Unsurprisingly, the rope parted under the strain, casting doubt on the status of one of the contributors, and Bhreacan drowned. To get there, follow the rough track from **Ardlussa** to **Kinuachdrach**, or get someone to drive you, then it's a 2-mile walk. Before setting out, ask at the hotel for information and directions.

In 1947, the Corryvreckan nearly claimed the life of one Eric Arthur Blair – aka George Orwell – who had come to Jura to finish the novel that would later become *Nineteen Eighty-Four*. Despite being diagnosed with TB, Orwell went to live on Jura with his three-year-old adopted son, Richard, in spartan conditions at **Barnhill**, a cottage in the middle of nowhere and 25 miles from the nearest doctor. That summer he invited his niece and nephew to stay, and one day took them out into the Corryvrekcan in a tiny boat. When the outboard motor was ripped off by the force of the tide and the boat capsized, Orwell and the others only just escaped with their lives by clambering onto a small island; they were later rescued by a passing lobster boat. Today, Barnhill attracts many literary pilgrims and, though closed to the public, can be rented for a week's stay (see Sleeping, below).

Money to burn

In 2006, Conservative Party leader, David Cameron, sang Jura's praises on Radio 4' s *Desert Island Discs*, but Cameron was not the first media manipulator to lay claim to the place. Back in 1994, Scottish acid house band, the KLF – aka anarcho-situationists, Bill Drummond and Jimmy Cauty – came to Jura to burn one million pounds in cash, the total net profits from their brief but highly successful music career, and film themselves doing it. The reason they chose Jura was that Cauty had become friends with the son of the major landowner, Francis Riley Smith, in his late teens. They would travel to the island by helicopter from Glasgow to run riot in Jura House. The outrageous publicity stunt took place in an abandoned boat house at Ardfin, just below Jura House, on 23 August; a significant date (add up the numbers in 1994 – genius).

Exactly one year later Drummond and Cauty returned to the island to show the film – *Watch the K Foundation Burn a Million Quid* – to a less than enthusiastic audence. Many were upset by such a flagrant waste of money that could have better spent on 'good causes'. The subject still provokes an angry response.

The KLF's motivation was to destroy the money they'd made from an evil music industry they'd found it so easy to manipulate, with hits ranging from the excellent 'Justified and Ancient' (featuring Tammy Wynette) to the execrable 'Doctoring the Tardis' (which reached number one – go figure). Were they justified? Not to your average Hebridean.

Also on the island, 3 miles south of Craighouse village, at Ardfin, is the beautiful **walled garden at Jura House** ⓘ *daily 0900-1700, £2*, which is filled with wild flowers and Australasian plants and trees. There's also a tea tent open in summer and plenty of good walks through the surrounding woods or down to the nearby beaches. See Sleeping, below, for details of self-catering accommodation in Jura House.

Sleeping

Islay *p161*

A-B Harbour Inn, Main St, Bowmore, T01496-810330, www.harbour-inn.com. 4 rooms. Central location with a cosy bar and an acclaimed restaurant serving the freshest seafood (🍴).

A-B Kilmeny Farmhouse, Ballygrant, 4 miles from Port Askaig, T/F01496-840668, www.kilmeny.co.uk. A working beef farm with stylish, comfortable rooms, excellent food and a warm, friendly atmosphere. Dinner is a treat with Colonsay lamb, smoked venison, local scallops and more. Excellent.

B-C Port Charlotte Hotel, Port Charlotte, T01496-850360. 10 rooms. Restored Victorian inn with gardens and conservatory on seafront; tasty locally sourced seafood meat dishes. One of the best around.

C Glenmachrie, Machrie golf course. T01496-302560. 5 rooms. A genuine farm-house offering hospitality and a gargantuan breakfast that earned this wonderful B&B the accolade of 2006 Best Breakfast in Britain Award. Apart from a sideboard of fresh fruit salad and home-made muesli, guests receive porridge followed by either a traditional cooked breakfast, kippers or a cheese platter. I almost forgot the fresh scones and home-made preserves! Brilliant but book ahead.

C Sornbank, Bridgend, T01496-810544, www.sornbank.co.uk. Well-appointed B&B close to amenities with excellent breakfast. They also let 2 self-contained flats on a weekly/fortnightly basis.

F Port Charlotte Youth Hostel, Port Charlotte, T0870-0041128. Apr-Oct. This very comfortable, spacious hostel is close to the ales, malts and tasty meals served by the Port Charlotte Hotel (ŸŸ-Ÿ) and Lochindaal Hotels (ŸŸ-Ÿ).

Self-catering

Coillabus Cottage, near Port Ellen, T0131-5531911. From £380 per week. Sleeps 2-6 people on the Mull of Oa peninsula. Roaring fire and solitude.
Coull Farm Cottage, Bruichladdich, T01496-850317. From £190 per week. Sleeps 5 in a cosy cottage with panoramic views and excellent nearby walks.

Jura *p166*

B-C Jura Hotel, in the village of Craighouse, T01496-820243, www.jurahotel.co.uk. 20 rooms. Open all year. The island's one and only hotel, overlooking the Small Isles Bay. The hotel bar is the island's social hub and hosts Steve and Fiona Walton, who have been here for 25 years, can provide information on walks as well as arranging tours to the Corryvreckan and fishing trips. The restaurant serves good food, try the fresh langoustines or famed venison pie. Camping is also possible in the hotel grounds.

Self-catering

Barnhill, contact Mrs D Fletcher, T01786-850274, lennieston@aol.com, or book through www.roomfinderscotland.co.uk. From £500 per week. Sleeps 6-8 people. For more ascetic souls, and devotees of George Orwell.
Jura House, contact Mirjam Cool in Craighouse, T01496-820315, mirjam cool@aol.com. £900-1400 per week. Sleeps up to 15. At the top end of the comfort scale.
Jura Lodge, T01496-820240, www.isleof jura.com. From £1500 for the week. The most salubrious choice. Housed inside the distillery grounds, the refurbished lodge was reopened in 2006 and is available for private use at certain times of the year. It sleeps up to 8. They also run residential whisky appreciation courses.

Activities and tours

Jura *p166*

Mike Richardson, T07899-912116, guides hill walks and Orwell trails (Easter-Oct) from £25 per person (minimum charge of £75 if fewer than 3 people) and runs a landrover taxi service on Jura.

Transport

Islay *p161*

Air Islay can be reached by air from Glasgow (for details, see page 116). The airport is at Glenegedale, a few miles north of Port Ellen on the road to Bowmore.

Bus For those without their own transport, there's a regular bus service around Islay, with **Islay Coaches**, T01496-840273, and **post buses**, T08457-740740. There are buses from **Portnahaven** to **Port Ellen**, via **Port Charlotte**, **Bridgend**, **Bowmore** and the airport; from **Port Askaig** to **Port Ellen** via **Ballygrant**, **Bridgend**, **Bowmore** and the airport; from **Port Ellen** to **Ardbeg**, **Bowmore**, **Port Askaig** and **Portnahaven**, and also a postbus to **Bunnababhain**. Buses run regularly at least from Mon-Sat, but only once on Sun.

Ferry CalMac offices are in Kennacraig, T01880-730253; Port Ellen, T01496-302209. The ferry to Islay (and Jura) from **Kennacraig** to **Port Ellen** (2 hrs 10 mins, £8.10 one way per passenger, £58 per car) sails twice daily on Mon, Tue, Thu, Fri and Sat and once on Wed and Sun. A ferry also sails from **Kennacraig** to **Port Askaig** (2 hrs, same prices as above) once daily on Tue, Thu, Sat and Sun and twice daily on Wed and Fri and 3 times on Mon. The Wed ferry continues to **Colonsay**. The ferry from **Oban** to Port Askaig sails on Wed (4¼ hrs, £11.60 per passsenger, £56 per car).

Jura *p166*

Bus There is a bus service on Jura, which runs from **Feolin Ferry** to **Craighouse** several times a day, Mon-Sat. A few buses continue to **Lagg** and **Inverlussa** and return to Craighouse. Note that some journeys are by request only and must be booked the day before. Contact Alex Dunnichie, T01496- 820314.

Ferry A small car and passenger ferry makes the regular 5-min crossing daily to Jura, from **Port Askaig** on Islay to Feolin Ferry (£2.50 return per passenger, £12 per car). For times, contact **Argyll & Bute Council**, T01496-840681.

North & Northwest

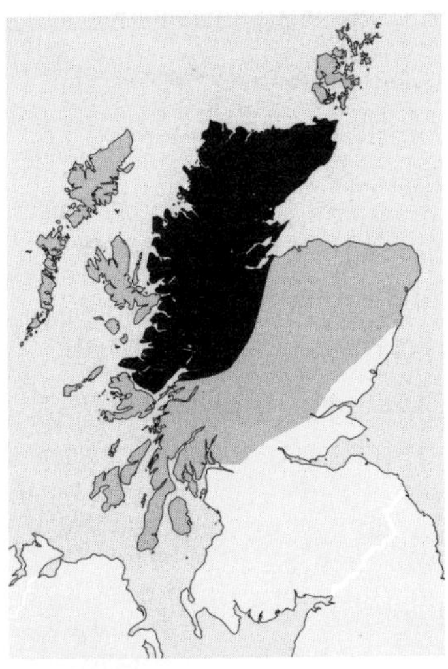

Footprint features

Introduction

The Northwest Highlands is the part of Scotland that best reflects the romantic image of the country. Wild, rugged, and sparsely populated after the infamous 17th- to 18th-century Highland Clearances, this is the Scotland of mist-shrouded glens, towering mountain peaks, windswept purple heather hillsides, brooding lochs, ghostly ancient castles and quaint coastal ports.

Inverness is the 'capital of the Highlands'. It lies at the northeastern end of the Great Glen, which cuts diagonally across the southern Highlands to Fort William like a surgical incision, linking deep and mysterious Loch Ness with the west coast and giving access to Lochaber, the self-proclaimed 'outdoor capital of the UK'. Still further south is Glencoe, another climber's paradise and one of the Highland's most evocative Highland glens. Inverness is also ideally situated for exploring the northeast coast, dotted with charming fishing ports and archaeological sites, while the storm-battered, remote northern coastline, running west from John O'Groats to Cape Wrath, attracts surfers and those probing the history of the Clearances.

The main town on the northwest coast is Fort William, which lies in the shadow of Britain's highest mountain, Ben Nevis. Northwest from here stretches a dramatic shoreline of deep sea lochs and sheltered coves of pure white sand backed by towering mountains and looking across to numerous Hebridean islands. West of Fort William, via the lyrical Road to the Isles, is work-a-day Mallaig, the main departure point for ferries to Skye. Further north is Ullapool, a key ferry port for the Outer Hebrides and the ideal base from which to explore Assynt and the wild and near-deserted far northwest.

★ Don't miss...

1 **Moray Firth** Cruise with the dolphins in the Moray Firth, page 183.

2 **West Highland Railway** Get on board the Jacobite Steam Train and ride the West Highland line, one of the world's great train journeys, page 209.

3 **Glen Coe** The most hauntingly beautiful of all the Highland glens and, incredibly, the most accessible, page 210.

4 **Glenelg** Drive from Shiel Bridge to this splendidly isolated village, home of Gavin Maxwell's famous otters, page 227.

5 **Applecross** Travel the vertigo-inducing route over the mountains to this village where you can enjoy a pint of fresh prawns washed down with Red Cuillin ale in the cosy Applecross Inn, page 237.

6 **Sandwood Bay** Go for a walk along the beach and watch the sun set with a bottle of single malt and a loved one, page 246.

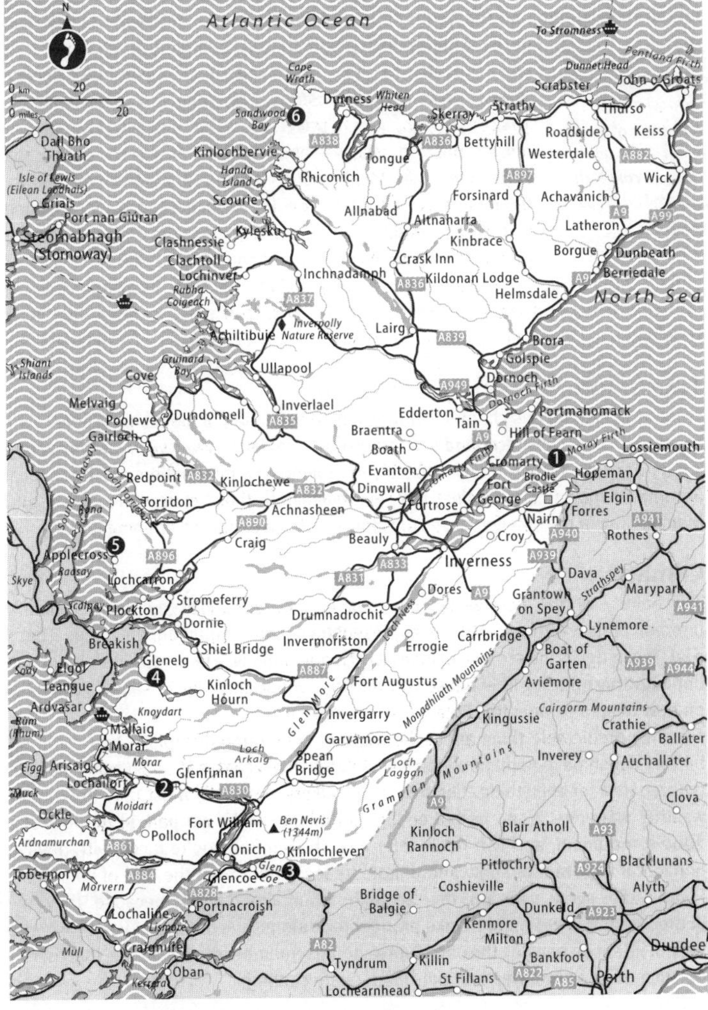

Ins and outs

Getting there

There are daily flights to Inverness airport from London, Edinburgh and Glasgow. Inverness is linked to the south by the notorious A9 from Edinburgh and Perth, to Aberdeen by the A96 and to Fort William by the A82, and is well served by buses. Wick, Thurso, Ullapool, Portree (Skye), Fort William and Aberdeen all enjoy regular bus connections with Inverness. Daily trains from Glasgow and Edinburgh run to Inverness with subsequent connections north to Wick and Thurso, west to Kyle of Lochalsh and east to Aberdeen. Fort William is easily reached from Glasgow by bus whilst the train (via Fort William) terminates at Mallaig for the ferry to Skye (Armadale).
▸▸ *For further details, see Transport, page 181.*

Getting around

To explore the northwest Highlands is undeniably easier with your own transport though the main tourist centres, including Ullapool and Wick, are easily accessed by bus or train. Getting off the beaten track requires patience but is worthwhile and easily achieved with a little forward planning. Much of the time you'll need to rely on the local **postbus service** ⓘ *www.royalmail.com/postbus, www.postbus.royalmail.com, T08457-740740,* which travel countless single-track roads to deliver post to villages and hamlets scattered across the highlands. Ask local tourist offices and post offices for timetables. An excellent on-line source of travel information including timetables and operators across the Highlands can be found at www.travelinescotland.com, T0870-6082608. Tourist offices throughout the Highlands also carry leaflets on their local and regional transport network. Details of ferries from the mainland ports to Skye, the Outer Hebrides and Orkney are given in the respective island chapters.

By far the most scenic route to the Highlands is the spectacular West Highland Railway, one of the world's great rail journeys, particularly the section from Fort William to Mallaig.

Tourist information

Roughly speaking, this chapter includes the northern half of mainland Scotland. It's covered by **Visitscotland**'s highland region ⓘ *www.visithighlands.com, T0845-2255121,* whose tourist offices can provide free information and book local accommodation (for a nominal fee). However, note that between November and March many of the smaller offices are closed or have restricted opening hours.

Climate

The beauty of the northwest Highlands is only enhanced by the notoriously unpredictable weather and that ever-present travelling companion, the midge. That's a lie. The midge is the scourge of many a Highland holiday: a ferocious, persistent and unbelievably irritating little beast who will drive you to the edge of sanity. For details on how best to combat this little terror, see page 62.

The only predictable thing about the weather is its unpredictability. You can have blazing sunshine in April, pouring rain in July and a blizzard in May. So, you'll need to be prepared for everything. Climbers and walkers especially must take heed of all weather warnings. It can be hot enough for bikinis in the car park at the foot of a 2000-ft mountain, and two hours later near the summit you're faced with driving, horizontal hail, rain or snow and unable to see further than the end of your nose. People die every year on the Scottish mountains simply because they are ill-prepared; it is essential to take proper precautions, see page 52. Even those who are not intent on bagging the odd Munro should remember the old adage, that there's no such thing as bad weather, only inadequate clothing.

Inverness

→ *Phone code: 01463. Colour map 2, C2. Population: 42,000.*

Inverness is the only city in the Highlands and the busy and prosperous hub of the region. All main routes through the Highlands pass through here at some point, so it's a hard place to avoid. The town's position at the head of the Great Glen and on the shores of the Moray Firth have made it a firm favourite with tourists, who flock here in their legions during the summer months to look for the evasive Loch Ness Monster. Although Inverness offers little in the way of major sights, it's a pleasant place to base yourself as you explore the other attractions in the surrounding area, including the possibility of spotting pods of dolphins in the Moray Firth. The city, however, is not without its own appeal, particularly the leafy banks of the River Ness, which runs through its heart, linking Loch Ness with the Moray Firth. »» *For Sleeping, Eating and other listings, see pages 176-182.*

Ins and outs

Getting there

There are daily flights to and from London Gatwick, Glasgow and Edinburgh with **British Airways**, and daily flights to and from London Gatwick, London Luton and Bristol with **EasyJet**. There are also flights (Sunday to Friday) to and from Birmingham, Leeds and Manchester; Newcastle (Monday to Friday) with **Eastern Airways**, and Stornoway (Monday to Saturday) with **British Airways Express**. The **airport** ⓘ *T01667-464000, www.hial.co.uk*, is 7 miles east of the town at Dalcross. There's a daily airport bus every 45 minutes to and from the town centre. It takes 20 minutes and costs £3.50. A taxi to/from the airport costs £12-14. The **bus station** ⓘ *just off Academy St, T01463-239292*, has left luggage costing a maximum of £5 per item per day (open Monday to Saturday 0830-1800, Sunday 1000-1800). The **train station** ⓘ *at the east end of Academy St, T01463-239026*, also has left-luggage lockers charging a maximum of £5 per 24 hours. »» *For further details, see Transport, page 181.*

Getting around

Inverness town centre is compact and easy to explore on foot, and most of the hotels and guesthouses are within a 15-minute walk of the TIC. Loch Ness is not within walkable distance, so you'll either need your own transport, or you'll have to book a tour (see pages 179 and 198).

Tourist information

The very busy **TIC** ⓘ *T0845-2255121, Easter-end Oct, Mon-Sat, 0900-1700, May-Aug daily 1000-1600*, is in an unattractive building at the foot of Castle Wynd, near Ness Bridge, a five-minute walk from the train station. It stocks a wide range of literature on the area, can book accommodation and transport and gives out free maps of the town and environs. Information (and possibly tickets) for the tours listed on the next few pages are available from the TIC. Also visit www.inverness-scotland.com.

History

One of the old town's first visitors was that much-travelled cleric, St Columba, who came in AD 565 to confront the Pictish King Brude, whose fortress was reputedly at Craig Phadraig, a few miles west of Inverness. Around the mid-12th century King David I built the original castle and made Inverness a royal burgh on the strength of its

Inverness

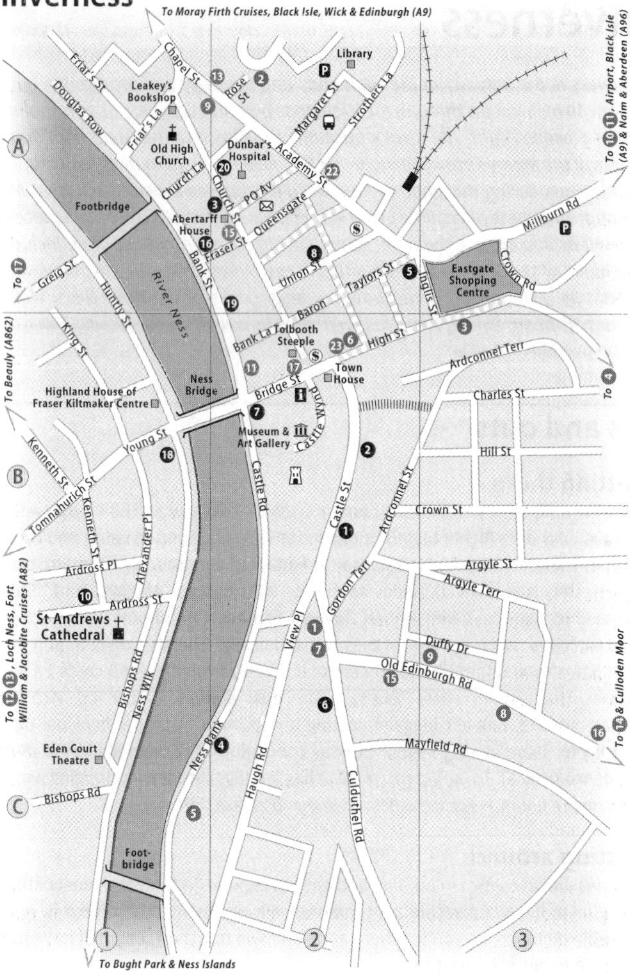

To Moray Firth Cruises, Black Isle, Wick & Edinburgh (A9)

To 10 11, Airport, Black Isle (A9) & Nairn & Aberdeen (A96)

To 4

To 14 & Culloden Moor

To Bught Park & Ness Islands

To 12 13, Loch Ness, Fort William & Jacobite Cruises (A82)

To Beauly (A862)

To 17

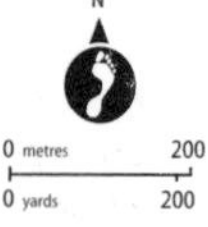

0 metres 200
0 yards 200

Sleeping

Bazpackers Hostel **1** *B2*
Culloden House **10** *A3*
Dionard Guest House **16** *C3*
Dunain Park **13** *C1*
Eastgate Backpackers Hostel **3** *B3*
Glenmoriston Town House & Abstract Restaurant **5** *C1*
Glenruidh House **14** *C3*
Ho Ho Hostel **6** *B2*
Inverness Marriot **4** *B3*
Inverness Student Hotel **7** *C2*
Inverness Tourist Hostel **2** *A2*
Ivybank Guesthouse **8** *C3*
Kinkell House **9** *C3*
Melness Guest House **15** *C2*
Moyness House **12** *C1*
SYHA Youth Hostel **11** *A3*
Trafford Bank **17** *A1*

Eating

Café No 1 **1** *B2*
Castle **2** *B2*
Chez Christophe **10** *B1*
Dickens **3** *A2*
Glen Mhor Hotel **4** *C2*
Jimmy Chung's Chinese Buffet **8** *A2*
Lemon Tree **5** *A2*
Mustard Seed **16** *A1*
Red Pepper **20** *A2*
Riva & Pazzo's Pizzeria **18** *B1*
River Café & Restaurant **19** *A2*
Rocpool Reserve **6** *C2*
Shapla **7** *B2*

Bars & clubs

Bakoo **23** *B2*
Blackfriars **9** *A1*
Gellions **17** *B2*
Hootananny **15** *A2*
Johnny Foxes **11** *B2*
Phoenix **13** *A2*
Pivo **22** *A2*

growing importance as a trading port. Furs, hides, wool and timber were all exported as far afield as the Mediterranean. The town's economic prosperity and status as the most important northern outpost, however, made it a prime target for marauding Highland clansmen, and during the Wars of Independence in the 13th century Inverness was also a regular target for both English and Scots armies.

The town's renaissance came with the completion of the Caledonian Canal and rail links with the south in the 19th century. These improved communications heralded something of a tourist boom amongst the wealthy and fashionable who came north to the Highlands to shoot anything that moved in the name of sport. In the mid-19th century Queen Victoria decided to embrace all things Scottish, which only boosted the town's popularity. Over recent decades Inverness has grown rapidly, not only as a prime base for visiting tourists, but also as the main administrative and commercial centre for the Highlands. Since being conferred city status in 2000, Inverness has continued to enjoy a boom period, though not always on the pitch of the beloved Inverness Caledonian Thistle FC. In 2006, the 750 seat **Ironworks** (see Entertainment, page 179) opened its doors, the Highland capitals first ever purpose-built live concert venue.

Sights

The city is dominated by its red sandstone **castle** ⓘ *Mon-Fri, 0900-1700, free.* Built in 1834, this Victorian edifice is very much the new kid on the block in terms of Scottish castles. The original castle dates from the 12th century and was built on a ridge to the east of the present structure. Nothing remains of the old castle, which is unsurprising given its bloody and eventful history. It was here that King Duncan of Scotland was slain by Macbeth, an event dramatically (and erroneously) portrayed in Shakespeare's eponymous work. The castle was occupied three times during the Wars of Independence in the 13th century, and when Robert the Bruce recaptured it in 1307 he destroyed it. In the mid-17th century Cromwell ordered his men to build a stone version on the same site. In 1715 James Francis Edward was proclaimed king there, but not long after it was destroyed by the Jacobites to prevent it from falling into enemy hands following the defeat of Bonnie Prince Charlie at Culloden, see page 194. The present castle houses the Sheriff Court which is currently the only part accessible to the public. On the castle terrace is a statue of Flora MacDonald, a poignant memorial to her role in helping the prince to escape, see box page 279.

Below the castle, on Castle Wynd by the TIC is **Inverness Museum and Art Gallery** ⓘ *Mon-Sat 0900-1700, free.* During the summer and autumn this wonderful museum, complete with café to rest tired feet, underwent a £1 million refurbishment. Scheduled to reopen in time for the year-long Highland 2007 celebrations, the museum provides an overview of the history of the town and the region, while the gallery hosts some special exhibitions that have included paintings by the Scottish colourist JD Fergusson. Just around the corner, on High Street, is the Gothic-style **Town House**, where Prime Minister Lloyd George held an emergency cabinet meeting in 1921, the first ever to be held outside London.

Opposite, on the corner of Bridge Street and Church Street, is the **Tolbooth Steeple** which dates from 1791 and which had to be repaired after an earth tremor in 1816. Among the cafés and bars to be found on historic Church Street – a fascinating part of the city local 'culture vultures' aim to steadily rejuvenate – is the town's oldest building, **Abertarff House**. Built around 1592, it is now a contemporary art and jewellery gallery. Almost opposite is the much-restored **Dunbar's Hospital**, built in 1688 as an almshouse for the town's poor. At the end of Church Street, where it meets Friar's Lane, is the **Old High Church** founded in the 12th century and rebuilt in 1772, though the 14th-century vaulted tower remains intact. In the adjoining atmospheric graveyard prisoners taken at Culloden were executed, and you can still see the bullet marks left by the firing squads on some of the gravestones. At the far end of Church Street you'll also find the fascinating **Leakey's Bookshop** (Monday-Saturday, 1000-1700) housed within a former church. Jam packed with second-hand books and with a delightful café upstairs, the owners estimate their towering shelves contain over 100,000 books.

The **Highland House of Fraser Kiltmaker Centre** ⓘ *4-9 Huntly St, T01463-240189, www.highlandhouseoffraser.com, May-Sep, daily 0900-2200, Oct-Apr Mon-Sat 0900-1730; factory Mon-Fri only, £2, £1 concessions or children*, still has a working kilt factory upstairs. In addition to watching kilts being made, two informative videos provide insights to the history of highland dress (including what Scotsmen wear under their kilts). In addition to mannequins dressed in period outfits, there are props used in the making of *Braveheart*. Nearby, directly opposite the castle, is the neo-Gothic **St Andrews Cathedral** which dates from 1869, and is worth a peek if you're passing by. Continuing south along Ness Bank, past the extensively refurbished **Eden Court Theatre** (see Entertainment, page 179) you reach **Bught Park** (see Sleeping page 177), which overlooks the Ness Islands, joined by footbridge to both banks. The islands are attractively laid out as a park and are a favourite with local anglers. This also happens to be a lovely place for a peaceful evening stroll.

Sleeping

Inverness *p173, map p174*
With an abundance of guesthouses and B&Bs and several good-quality hotels in and around Inverness, you shouldn't have much trouble finding somewhere to stay though it does become very busy in Jul and Aug. Ideally, reserve ahead or consider booking through the tourist office.

The best places to look are along both banks of the river south of the Ness Bridge, Old Edinburgh Rd and Ardconnel St (east of the castle) and around Bruce Gardens, Ardross St, Kenneth St and Fairfield Rd (the west bank). There are also several budget hostels in and around the centre, and a couple of campsites.

L Culloden House Hotel, Milton of Culloden, 3 miles east of town near the A9. T01463-790461, www.cullodenhouse.co.uk. Within this delightful Georgian mansion where Bonnie Prince Charlie prepared for battle at Culloden, you'll discover 1st-class accommodation and award-winning fine dining (TTT).

L-A Dunain Park Hotel, about 3 miles southwest of the town centre, just off the A82 Fort William Rd, T01463-230512, www.dunainparkhotel.co.uk. 11 rooms. An elegant Georgian mansion house within extensive gardens, Victorian 4-poster beds, luxurious marble bathrooms, and an excellent restaurant, see Eating, page 178. Arrange fishing, golf and riding.

L-A Glenmoriston Town House Hotel, 20 Ness Bank, T01463-223777. 30 rooms, many recently refurbished. Unquestionably, this classy establishment boasting an award-winning Abstract restaurant (TTT) and Contrast Brasserie (TT) is where to stay and dine in style, see Eating, page 178.

B Inverness Marriot, Culcabock Rd, 1 mile south of the city centre near A9, T01463-237166, www.marriott.com/property/propertypage/invkm. 82 rooms. Parts of hotel date back to 18th century. Comfortable rooms and superb leisure facilities.

B-C Trafford Bank, 96 Fairfield Rd, T01463-241441, www.traffordbankguesthouse.co.uk. 5 en suite rooms. Open all year. It's a guesthouse, Jim, but not as we know it. Lorraine Feel and Koshal Pun have raised the bar for highland accommodation so high it may require a stepladder for most others to see it, never mind reach it. This is, quite simply, one of the very finest guesthouses in the country, if not the best. The rooms are exquisitely furnished, all with DVD and CD players and free Wi-Fi. Breakfasts are delicious, bathrooms delightful and the owners de-lovely. We can't recommended this place highly enough.

C Glenruidh House Hotel, Old Edinburgh Rd South, 2 miles from the town centre and adjacent to Loch Ness Golf Course (phone for directions), T01463-226499, www.cozzeenessie-bed.co.uk. 5 rooms. Packed with history and character, this peaceful, friendly 'boutique' hotel serves organic, fresh produce in a secluded setting...and even welcomes the occasional badger!

C Melness Guest House, 8 Old Edinburgh Rd, T01463-220963, www.melnessie.co.uk. Rooms include en suite and family. Very clean and comfortable accommodation in an 18th-century building that long-ago was the 'Craigneish School for Young Ladies'!

C Moyness Guest House, 6 Bruce Gardens, T/F01463-233836, www.moyness.co.uk. Fine Victorian villa in a quiet area near the theatre, with 7 very comfortable en suite rooms and nice touches like Botanics products in the bathrooms. Big breakfasts including porridge and fruit compote.

C-D Highland Voyages, Eala Bhan tall ship, T01463-404441, www.highlandvoyages.co.uk. When moored at Seaport Marina has on board accommodation in 5 (bunk-bed) cabins. (Dinner), B&B format. Aboard this converted herring drifter, enjoy day sails on Loch Ness and the Moray Firth (£48) to week-end and 7-night sailing trips to the Hebrides. See also Activities and tours, page 179.

C-D Ivybank Guesthouse, 28 Old Edinburgh Rd, T/F01463-232796, www.ivybankguesthouse.com. 5 rooms, 3 with en suite bathroom. Delightful Georgian house with lots of character, nice garden and friendly welcome.

D Dionard Guest House, 39 Old Edinburgh Rd, T01463-233557, www.dionardguesthouse.co.uk. 4 rooms, friendly and very comfortable B&B a few mins' walk from |the centre of the city.

D Kinkell House, 11 Old Edinburgh Rd, T01463-235243, www.kinkellhouse.co.uk. Very clean, comfortable Victorian family home with spacious rooms close to all amenities.

F Bazpackers Hostel, 4 Culduthel Rd (at the top of Castle St), T01463-717663. Several doubles/twins and numerous comfy dorms, with good cooking facilities, garden for barbecues and a laundrette. Close to the city centre.

F Eastgate Backpackers Hostel, 38 Eastgate T/F01463-718756, www.hostelsaccommodation.com. 50 beds including 2 twins and 4 6-bed dorms. Free tea and coffee.

F Ho Ho Hostel, 23a High St, T01463-221225, www.scotland-hostels.com and 5 mins from the train and bus stations is a cheap option. Slightly run-down air.

F Inverness Student Hotel, 8 Culduthel Rd, next door to **Bazpackers**, T01463-236556. 9 dorms with 54 beds. Friendly and laid-back atmosphere. Packed with tour information and cosy social area. Laundry service (£2.50) and breakfast (£1.90). All great value but as a **MacBackpacker Tours** haunt can get very busy.

F Inverness Tourist Hostel, 24 Rose St T01463241962, www.hostelsaccommodation.com Don't let the dingy entrance fool you. This is the city's best backpacker accommodation by far. 62 dorm-style beds in 10 rooms, satellite TV, internet access, friendly staff, terrific cooking facilities, complimentary tea and coffee. The budget traveller's dream.

F SYHA Youth Hostel, Victoria Drive, off Millburn Rd, T0871-3308529. 166 beds. Huge hostel in former school hall of residence. Good amenities, quieter location that many hostels but further from city centre.

Self-catering

Easter Dalziel Farm Cottages, 6 miles east of Inverness, T01667-462213, www.easterdalzielfarm.co.uk. 3 comfortable, traditional cottages (sleep 4-6) on a 200 acre farm. A farmhouse B&B (**D**) is also available. From £160 per week.

Camping

Bught Caravan and Camping Site, Bught Park, on the west bank of the river near the sports centre, T01463-236920. The largest and most centrally located campsite, with good facilities, £5 per tent and £4 per head thereafter. £14.50 per caravan pitch with electricity.

Bunchrew Caravan and Camping Park T01463-237802. 3 miles west of Inverness. Excellent campsite with good hot showers and views across the Beauly Firth. 2 people can pitch a small tent for £10. Mar-end Nov.

For an explanation of sleeping and eating price codes used in this guide, see inside the front cover. Other relevant information is found in Essentials, see pages 40-47.

Eating

Inverness *p173, map p174*

As you'd expect in a major tourist centre, there's the usual plethora of pubs, cafés and restaurants serving cheap and basic food for the non-discerning palate, but those looking for a high standard of cuisine won't be disappointed either. Takeaways and chain restaurant options are plentiful particularly on Academy St, Eastgate, around the train station and on Young St, just across the Ness Bridge.

£££ **Abstract**, Glenmoriston Town House Hotel, 20 Ness Bank. The award-winning French-inspired cuisine comes at a price but for those who seek fine-dining in style, it's worth it. Tue-Sun 1900-2200. Book ahead. For those seeking a treat on a more modest budget, delicious fare can also be enjoyed in the hotels **Contrast Brasserie** (££) T01463-227889, daily 1200-1430,1700-2200.

£££ **Chez Christophe**, 16 Ardross St, T01463-717126. Enjoy a taste of France in the Highlands. Gourmets should indulge on the mouthwatering taster option (£36.95). Lovely ambience and good wines.

£££ **Dunain Park Hotel**, see Sleeping, above. Fine combination of elegance and Scottish cuisine including fresh Ness salmon and diver scallops, topped off with excellent wine and malt lists. Take a post-dinner stroll in the lovely gardens.

£££ **Riverview**, 9-12 Ness Bank, T01463-234308. The **Glen Mhor Hotel** restaurant boasts tasty fine dining on seafood, vegetarian and game (in season) whilst the adjoining **Nico's** bistro (££) is also worth a visit.

£££ **Rocpool Reserve**, Culduthel Rd T01463-240089. The decor oozes style and chic. Fortunately, the excellent lunch and dinner menu of tasty treats like pumpkin ravioli or seafood pie also hits the mark. Not the cheapest in town but delivers a delicious Inverness culinary experience.

£££-££ **The Mustard Seed**, 16 Fraser St, T01463-220220. Terrific restaurant that fuses delightful interior of cheery yellow walls and artwork with attentive staff and imaginative dishes. Weekly changing lunch and dinner menus based on local produce and international themes. Treats include fillets of Scrabster red fish, hot smoked salmon and polenta. Daily 1200-1500, 1800-2200.

££ **Café No 1**, 75 Castle St, T01463-226200. Questionable decor but reasonable selection of meat and vegetarian dishes. Friendly service. Mon-Sat 1200-1400 and 1800-2130.

££ **Dickens**, 77 Church St, T01463-713111. Offers a mix of oriental and international dishes with an emphasis on fish. Reasonable set lunches. Daily 1200-1400 and 1730-2300.

££ **Shapla**, 2 Castle Rd, T01463-241919. Good Indian restaurant with Tandoori and Balti menu and good views of the river in the upstairs lounge. Daily 1200-2330.

££-£ **Riva & Pazzo's Pizzeria**, 4-6 Ness Walk, T01463-237377. Riva is a bustling, stylish and reasonably priced Italian café/bistro offering the standard penne, gnocchi and antipasti fare. Good cakes and coffee. Pop directly next door for a satisfying pizza.

££-£ **The River Café and Restaurant**, 10 Bank St, T01463-714884. Popular for lunches and delicious high teas with home-baking. Mon 1000-2030, Tue-Sat 1000-2130, Sun 1200-2030.

£ **Castle Restaurant**, 41 Castle St. Clean, no-nonsense café serving huge portions of stodgy, filling grub at low prices, convenient for backpackers' hostels. Daily till 2100.

£ **Jimmy Chung's Chinese Buffet**, 28-36 Union St, T01463-237878. Cheap Chinese food served into late evening.

£ **The Lemon Tree**, 18 Inglis St. Located in the pedestrianized town centre, family-run café offering good home-baking and basic but filling meals. Popular with older visitors.

£ **The Red Pepper**, Bow Court, 74 Church St, T01463-237111. Bustling little café/takeaway offering fresh paninis, sandwiches, soups and salads. Mon-Sat 1930-1630. Great value.

Bakeries

For picnic supplies check out **Gourmet's Lair**, 8 Union St, a great deli with all sorts of goodies. **Ashers**, Church St, is a good bakery that prides itself on its famous whisky cakes.

Bars and clubs

Inverness *p173, map p174*

Bakoo, High St is where the young clubbers let their hair down. Also at **G's**, on Castle St.

Blackfriars, Academy St, a decent pub that runs ceilidhs and live music for the backpacker fraternity on most nights.

Gellions, Bridge St, is ok for a pint stop and has varied live music throughout the week.

Hootananny, 67 Church St. A great bet for all things Scottish, has live music including ceilidhs most nights. Don't be surprised if you find yourself dancing on the tables with the backpacker crowd. Arguably the best pub atmosphere in Inverness.
Johnny Foxes, 26 Bank St, has Irish folk music most nights in summer as well as boasting one of the most unusual pub menus around.
Phoenix, 108 Academy St. This is one of the older Inverness pub haunts. You'll be sure to bump into locals here.
Pivo, 38-40 Academy St is enjoyed by those in search of the real Czech brews and a trendier atmosphere.

Entertainment

Inverness *p173, map p174*
Cinema The cinema attached to Eden Court Theatre, see below, shows a programme of art house and newly released movies. Prices vary depending on the performance.
Warner Village, A96 Nairn Rd, 2 miles from town centre. 7 screens, tickets cost from £5.
The Ironworks, 122b Academy St, T08717-894173, www.ironworksvenue.com. Opened in 2006, this is the Highland capital's first purpose-built live music venue.
Theatre Eden Court Theatre, Bishops Rd, overlooking the River Ness, T01463-234234. This renowned theatre and cinema has been undergoing renovation for months but is expected to reopen in the spring of 2007 with its staple of theatre and art-house productions.

Festivals and events

Inverness *p173, map p174*
There are numerous events held in and around Inverness throughout the year. These range from a humble pub ceilidh and a food festival to a full-blown Highland Games and the Baxters Loch Ness Marathon (Sep). For details contact the TIC or log onto www.visitscotland.com.
Feb/Mar Inverness Music Festival, T01463-716616.
Mar/Apr Local **folk festivals** are held over the Easter weekend, T01738-623274.
Jun Highland Festival is an excellent music, dance, drama and arts extravaganza, www.highlandfestival.org.uk.
Jul The Inverness Highland Games is held in the 3rd week of the month.

Shopping

Inverness *p173, map p174*
Inverness is a good place to buy a kilt, or practically anything else in tartan. To find your own clan tartan, head for the Highland House of Fraser Kiltmaker Centre, see Sights, page 176.

Bookshops
Leakey's, Church St, is a brilliant second-hand bookshop which has about 100,000 books with a huge wood-burning stove in the middle of the shop and a café upstairs.
Waterstone's, 50-52 High St.

Highland dress and traditional gifts
Chisholm's Highland Dress, 47-51 Castle St, T01463-234599.
Highland House of Fraser , Bridge St, T01463-240189.
James Pringle Weavers of Inverness , 21 Bridge St, T01463-236517.

Mall
Eastgate Shopping Centre has all the usual high-street branches like Gap and Marks and Spencer.

Market
Victorian Market, accessed off Church St and Academy St and established in the 18th century, has a wide range of shops.

Activities and tours

Inverness *p173, map p174*
Boat tours
Fingal of Caledonia, T01397-772167, www.fingal-cruising.co.uk, run all-inclusive 4- and 6-day cruises in a converted Dutch 'spitz' barge that gently ploughs its way through the 60-mile waterway of the Great Glen. During this time guests can make use of mountain bikes, canoes, sailing dinghies and windsurfers lashed to the deck. Guides and instructors are included. Cruises operate Apr-Oct and cost from £262-£565 per person.
John O'Groat's Ferries, T01955-611353, www.jogferry.co.uk. For the ultimate day-trip Orkney Islands Day Tours leave from

Inverness every day throughout the summer, Jun-Sep (depart 0730, return 2100), £46, under 16 half price. Booking essential. Details from the tourist office. (For tours from John O'Groats, see page 255.)

Bus tours

Guide Friday run open-topped bus tours around the city. Tours leave from Bridge St outside the TIC at 1000 and then every 45 mins till 1600 May-end Sep. Tickets, valid for 24 hrs from the time of travel, can be bought online at www.guidefriday.com, or onboard the bus £6, concession £4.50, children £3.
Canny Tours, T01349-854411, www.cannytours.com, run good-value, day-long tours visiting Culloden, Loch Ness and Eilean Donan Castle for £25.
Jacobite Tours, T01463-233999, www.jacobite.co.uk, operate all kinds of informative tours that leave (1030) from outside the tourist information office. A 6½-hr packed day-long tour (£29.50, concession £27.50, child £19.50) will see you sail on the dark waters of **Loch Ness** (for 30 mins), popping into the Loch Ness Monster 2000 Exhibition and visiting atmospheric Urquhart Castle before venturing onto the infamous site of **Culloden battlefield**. They also operate daily (morning and afternoon) 2½-hr bus trips to Culloden and the ancient **Clava Cairns** standing stones.
Puffin Express, T01463-717181, www.puffinexpress.co.uk, are an excellent operator running day trips to **Loch Ness**, **Skye** (£29) and multi-day minibus tours as far afield as **Lewis** and **Orkney** (from £55).

Cycling

The recently opened **Great Glen Way** (see Walking, below) can be cycled. The stretch alongside the **Caledonian Canal** is flat and good for families. For a free leaflet, T01320-366322.

Cycle hire **Bikes of Inverness**, 39 Grant St, T01463-225965. Ideal for all repairs and spares. **Highland Cycles**, Telford St, T01463-234789. Mon-Sat 0900-1730 all year.

Ghost tours

Davey the Ghost, T07730-831069, leaves from outside the tourist office at 1900 nightly (£6) and tells the tale of the town's gory past, complete with ghosts and murders. Appropriately, the tour finishes in a reputedly haunted pub! During the summer months there are usually daily walking tours (about 60 mins) departing from outside the TIC (1100 and 1400), £4.50. Ask in the TIC or see the advertising boards directly outside.

Golf

The best golf course in the area is at Nairn (see page 184). There's an 18-hole public course at Torvean, 2 miles from town on the A82 to Fort William, T01463-711434.

Horse riding

Highland Riding Centre, Borlum Farm, Drumnadrochit, T01456-450892, www.borlum.com.

Loch Ness tours

Jacobite Cruises, T01463-233999, www.jacobite.co.uk, run a variety of coach tours, boat cruises and combined coach and cruise trips around the loch.
Discover Loch Ness, T0800-7315565 (freephone), www.discoverlochness.com, run highly rated cultural tours. A year-round operator, their Mar-Oct itinerary refreshingly provides more than simply a hyped-up account of Nessie on its 30-min cruise on Loch Ness and a visit to Urquhart Castle, £29, child £19.
George Edwards, contact Loch Ness Cruises, T01456-450395, www.lochness-cruises.com, or Original Loch Ness Monster Visitor Centre, see page 190. He takes would-be monster-spotters out on the loch in his boat, Nessie Hunter, which is based near Drumnadrochit. He not only once caught a glimpse of Nessie but also discovered the deepest part of the loch (812 ft), now known as Edward's Deep. Cruises run hourly Apr-Sep 0930-1800. They last 1 hr and cost £10 per adult and £6 per child.
Loch Ness Express, T0800-3286426, www.lochnessexpress.co.uk, offers a superb way to travel the whole length of Loch Ness. Hop aboard the free shuttle bus at Bridge St TIC (0900, 1315, 1540) to rendezvous at Dochgarroch with your high-speed boat down to Fort Augustus. One way from Inverness to Fort Augustus is £13 (£25 return) or take the afternoon-only trip to Urquhart Castle (£11.50).

Walking
For the GreaT Glen Way, see box, page 190

Other sports
Iceskating **Ice Centre**, Bught Park, T01463-235711, www.inverness-ice-centre.org.uk. Ice-skating from 1400-1630 and 1900-21.30, £4.30, child £3.50.
Swimming **Aquadome Leisure Centre**, Bught Park, T01463-667500, Mon-Fri 1000-2000, Sat-Sun 1000-1700 . Competition-sized pool, flumes, wave machine and kiddies' pool, also health suites, gym and other indoor sports facilities.
Tennis and squash **Inverness Tennis and Squash Club**, Bishop's Rd, T01463-230751.
Ten-pin bowling **Roller Bowl**, 167 Culduthel Rd, T01463-235100, Mon-Fri 1200 till late, Sat-Sun 1100 till late.

Transport

Inverness *p173, map p174*
Bus
Bus timetables and even operators on some routes change frequently. If in any doubt and for the very latest information call Traveline Scotland, T0870-6082608, www.travelinescotland.com.

There are regular daily buses to **Glasgow** and **Edinburgh** (via **Aviemore**), **Pitlochry** and **Perth** with Scottish Citylink, T08705-505050. Change at Perth for **Dundee**. There are regular daily Citylink buses to **Ullapool**, connecting with the ferry to **Stornoway**; also to **Fort William** and **Oban**. There are daily Citylink buses to **Kyle of Lochalsh**, **Portree** and **Uig** (connecting with ferries to **Tarbert** and **Lochmaddy**). There are regular Citylink buses to **Fort** Augustus via **Drumnadrochit** and **Urquhart Castle** (also with Rapsons, T01463-710555), and to **Scrabster**, for the ferry to **Stromness**, via **Wick** and **Thurso**; also with Morrison's Coaches, T01847-821241.

To **Ullapool** via **Gairloch** and **Aultbea**, there are buses (Mon-Sat) with Spa Coaches, T01997-421311, and Westerbus T01445-712255. To **Tain** there is a daily service with Citylink, but to reach **Lairg** there's an irregular service with MacLeods and Royal Mail, T08457-740740. To **Tain** and **Helsmdale**, via **Dornoch** there are regular daily buses with Citylink. To **Lochinver** from **Ullapool** there's a Mon-Sat service operated by KSM Coaches, T01571-844236, and Highland Country Buses, T01463-710555. To **Durness** via **Lairg** and **Tongue**, or via Ullapool (not in winter) there's a daily service with Tim Dearman Coaches, T01349-883585, and Royal Mail postbuses, T08457-740740. Dearman Coaches carry a bike trailer on this route. To **Grantown-on-Spey**, daily service with Highland Country Buses, T01463-710555. Stagecoach Inverness T01463-239292, run services to places around **Inverness**, including **Beauly**, **Muir of Ord** and **Dingwall**. To reach **Tomich** (and **Glen Affric**) via Beauly use the Ross Minibuses service, T01463- 761250. **Fort George and Cawdor Castle** are reached from Inverness with Highland Country Buses, T01463- 710555. Stagecoach runs daily services to **Aberdeen** via Nairn whilst the battle scene of Culloden is reached using Highland Country Buses that also offers a special daily RoverBus ticket on key historical routes (£9). It's worth noting that Rapsons, T01463-710555, www.rapsons.com, operate a 'Rack and Ride' scheme for some cyclists on certain routes including **Inverness** to **Aviemore**. Call for details.

Car hire
Avis is at the airport, T01667-462787; Budget is on Railway Terr behind the train station, T01463-713333; Europcar has an office at 16 Telford St, T01463-235337, and at the airport, 0870-8700120; Sharps Reliable Wrecks, Railway Station, Academy St, T01463-709517, www.sharpsreliablewrecks.co.uk, and at the airport. Thrifty is at 33 Harbour Rd, T01463-T224466. Expect to pay from around £30 per day.

Ferry
For details of connections to **Stornoway** (Lewis), or contact the CalMac office in Inverness, T01463-717681. For **Scrabster** to **Stromness**, run by Northlink Ferries, T01856-851144, www.northlinkferries.co.uk.

Taxi
Tartan Taxis, T01463-719719. Central Highland Taxis .T01463-222222.

Train
For more information, T0845- 7484950. There are direct trains to/from **Aberdeen**, **Edinburgh** (via **Aviemore**) and **Glasgow**. There are several daily services to/from **London King's Cross** (via **Perth**) and **Edinburgh**, and a Caledonian Sleeper service from **London Euston** to **Inverness** and **Fort William**, ScotRail, T08457 550033, www.firstscotrail.co.uk. There is also a regular service to **Wick** and **Thurso**, via **Tain**, **Lairg** and **Helmsdale**. The journey from Inverness to **Kyle of Lochalsh** (for Skye) is one of the most scenic in Britain. There are 2-3 trains daily (none on Sun).

Directory

Ilnverness *p173, map p174*
Banks Most of the major banks can be found in the town centre. The Royal Bank is on the High St; the Bank of Scotland is opposite the Town House on the High St; the Clydesdale is opposite the train station; and Lloyds TSB is on Church St. **Currency exchange**: Money can be changed at the TIC at 2.5% commission. Also Thomas Cook, 9-13 Inglis St, T01463-711921, Mon-Fri 0900-1700; and Alba Travel (American Express agents), 43 Church St, T01463-239188, Mon-Sat 0900-1700. **Internet** Available from the TIC, the Mail Box Etc, Station Sq and at the Inverness Library. Several of the backpacker hostels (see Sleeping, above) also provide internet access. **Library** Inverness library is opposite the bus station. It has an excellent genealogical research unit. Consultations with the resident genealogist cost around £12 per hr; T01463-236463. The library also houses the Highland archives, where you can research the history and culture of the region; Mon-Fri 1000-1300 and 1400-1700; Oct-May 1400-1700 only. **Medical services Hospitals**: Raigmore Hospital, on the southeastern outskirts of town near the A9, T01463-704000, for accidents and emergencies. **Pharmacies**: Boots, main branch is at 14-16 Queensgate, T01463-225167. Mon-Wed and Fri 0845-1800, Thu 0845-1900, Sat 0830-1800, Sun 1100-1700; also at Eastgate Shopping Centre, 0900-1730, Thu till 1900.

Around Inverness

→ *Colour map 2, C2.*

East of Inverness along the Moray Firth stretches a long coastline of clifftop walks, fine beaches, attractive old towns and many historic sites and castles. The Moray Firth is perhaps best known for its large resident population of dolphins. Scores of these beautiful and intelligent mammals live in the estuary, the most northerly breeding ground in Europe, and there's a very good chance of seeing them, particularly between June and August. The Moray Firth dolphins have become a major tourist attraction and several companies run dolphin-spotting boat trips. You can also see them from the shore. Two of the best places are on the southern shore of the Black Isle, see page 259, and Fort George, on the opposite shore, see below. The Kessock Bridge, which crosses the Moray Firth to the Black Isle, is another good dolphin-spotting location and also has a visitor centre, where you can listen in to their underwater conversations.

West of Inverness, the Moray Firth becomes the Beauly Firth, a relatively quiet little corner despite its proximity to Inverness, as most traffic heading north crosses the Kessock Bridge on the main A9. The A862 west to Beauly offers a more scenic alternative, and the chance to visit a 13th-century priory and a distillery. South of Beauly, the A831 leads to two of Scotland's most beautiful glens, Glen Strathfarrar and Glen Affric. ▸▸ *For Sleeping, Eating and other listings, see pages 187-189.*

The Moray Firth

» pp187-189. Colour map 2, C2.

Culloden

→ Colour map 2, C2.

ⓘ T01463-790607, www.culloden.org.uk; site open daily all year, visitor centre open daily Mar 1000-1600, Apr-May 0900-1730, Jun-Aug 0900-1800, Sep-Oct 0900-1730, Nov-Dec 1100-1600, Feb 1100-1600, (Jan closed), £5, concession £4; owned by the National Trust for Scotland, in the late summer of 2007, a new £8.5 million visitor and interpretive centre will open, complete with state-of-the-art audio visual, educational rooms, restaurant/café and shop.

The eerie and windswept Culloden Moor, 5 miles to the east of Inverness on the B9006, was the site of the last major battle fought on the British mainland. The Jacobite cause was finally lost here, on 16 April 1746, when the army of Prince Charles Edward Stuart was crushed by the superior Government forces, led by the Duke of Cumberland, whose savagery earned him the nickname 'Butcher'. Contrary to popular myth this was not a battle between the Scots and the English, more a civil war: there were actually English Jacobites while many Scots fought for the Government.

The battlefield has been restored to its original state (minus the dead bodies). The visitor centre is the obvious starting point and gives a graphic audio-visual description of the gruesome episode. From the visitor centre paths lead across the field to the clan graves, marked by simple headstones which bear the names of the clans who fought. Next to the visitor centre, the restored cottage of Old Leanach – which was used by the Jacobites as a headquarters, and where 30 Highlanders were burnt alive – is arranged as it would have been at the time of the battle. A memorial cairn, erected in 1881, is the scene each April of a commemorative service organized by the Gaelic Society of Inverness.

Clava Cairns

This impressive and important Bronze Age site lies only a mile southeast of Culloden and is well worth a short detour. The 5000-year-old site consists of three large burial cairns encircled by standing stones, set in a grove of trees. The less imaginative visitor may see it as merely a pile of stones but no one can fail to be affected by the spooky atmosphere of the place, especially if no one else is around. To get there, continue on the B9006 past Culloden Moor, then turn right at the **Culloden Moor Inn** and follow the signs for **Clava Lodge**. Look for the sign on the right of the road.

Fort George

→ Colour map 2, C2.

ⓘ T01667-460232, Apr-Sep daily 0930-1830, Oct-Mar daily 0930-1630, £6.50, concession £5, children £2.50; wheelchair access, café.

Standing proudly on a sandy spit that juts out into the Moray Firth is Fort George, Europe's finest surviving example of 18th-century military architecture. In today's money it's estimated the mightiest artillery fortification in Britain would cost over £1 billion to build. Begun in 1748, it was the last in a chain of three such fortifications built in the Highlands – the other two being Fort Augustus and Fort William – as a base for George II's army to prevent any potential threats to Hanoverian rule. It was completed in 1769, by which time the Highlands were more or less peaceful, but it was kept in use as a military barracks. Today it remains virtually unchanged, and there are even armed sentries at the main gate. You can walk along the ramparts to get an idea of the sheer scale of the place and also enjoy the sweeping views across the Moray Firth. You may even be lucky enough to see a school of dolphins. Within the fort are the barracks, a chapel, workshops and the Regimental Museum of the Queen's Own Highlanders, which features the fascinating Seafield Collection of arms and military equipment, most of which dates from the Napoleonic Wars.

Battle of Culloden

The second Jacobite rebellion of 1745 was ill-fated from the start. Bonnie Prince Charlie's expedition south lacked sufficient support and was turned back at Derby. After their long and dispiriting retreat north, the half-starved, under-strength army – exhausted after an abortive night attack on Hanoverian forces at Nairn – faced overwhelmingly superior forces under the command of the ambitious Duke of Cumberland at Culloden.

The open, flat ground of Culloden Moor was hopelessly unsuitable for the Highlanders' style of fighting, which relied on steep hills and plenty of cover to provide the element of surprise for their brave but undisciplined attacks. In only 40 minutes the Prince's army was blown away by the English artillery, and the Jacobite charge, when it finally came, was ragged and ineffective. Cumberland's troops then went on to commit the worst series of atrocities ever carried out by a British Army. Some 1200 men were slain, many as they lay wounded on the battlefield. Prince Charlie, meanwhile, fled west where loyal Highlanders protected him until he made his final escape to France.

But the real savagery was to come. Cumberland resolved to make an example of the Highlands. Not only were the clans disarmed and the wearing of Highland dress forbidden, but the Government troops began an orgy of brutal reprisals across the region. Within a century the clan system had ended and the Highland way of life changed forever. For further information, see page 395.

Cawdor Castle → *Colour map 2, C2.*

ⓘ *T01667-404401, May to early-Oct daily 1000-1700, £7, concessions £6, children £4.30.*

Though best known for its legendary association with Shakespeare's *Macbeth*, Cawdor Castle post-dates the grisly historical events on which the great Bard based his famous tragedy. The oldest part of the castle, the central tower, dates from 1372, and the rest of it is mostly 16th or 17th century. But despite the literary disappointment, the castle is still one of the most appealing in Scotland. It has been in the hands of the Cawdor family for over six centuries and each summer they clear off, leaving their romantic home and its glorious gardens and Big Wood of native trees species open for the enjoyment of ordinary folks like us. There's also a nine-hole golf course.

According to family legend, an early Thane of Cawdor, wanting a new castle, had a dream in which he was told to load a donkey with gold, let it wander around for a day and watch where it lay down, for this would be the best spot for his new castle. He duly followed these instructions and the donkey lay down under a thorn tree, the remains of which can still be seen in the middle of a vaulted chamber in the 14th-century tower.

Just to the west of Cawdor is **Kilravock Castle** ⓘ *T01667-493258, www.kilravockcastle.com*. This lovely 14th-century stately home (pronounced *Kilrawk*) is still the seat of the Rose family. In recent years Kilravock has opened its doors as a castle B&B and self-catering experience (see Sleeping, page 187). Guests can enjoy a guided tour of the castle at 1030 each morning whilst every Wednesday and Thursday (1430 and 1600) a public guided tour is offered for £7.50 (including afternoon tea) and £5 child. From April to September (1430-1600) there's delicious home-baking in the castle tea-room.

Nairn and around → *Phone code: 01667. Colour map 2, C2. Population: 11,190.*

With two championship golf courses, the seaside town of Nairn also claims to have the driest and sunniest climate in the whole of Scotland. This alone should be reason enough to pay a visit, but there are other attractions besides the sunshine for there are miles of sandy beach stretching east to the Culbin Forest and two of the best castles in the country await within easy reach – Cawdor Castle, see above, and Brodie Castle, see below.

Nairn Museum ⓘ *Viewfield House, Viewfield Drive, May-Sep Mon-Sat 1000-1630, £2.50*, gives an insight into the area's history whilst its **Fishertown Museum** provides an insight into the lives of families who depended on the herring industry.

About 2 miles east of Nairn, in the little village of **Auldearn**, is a 17th-century *doocot* (dovecote). Nearby the Boath Doocot information boards record the 1645 Battle of Aldearn in which the victorious troops of Charles I, led by the Marquess of Montrose, defeated and killed almost 2000 Covenanters.

Nairn is only 5 miles from the airport and makes a pleasant alternative to staying in Inverness.

Ten miles south of Nairn on the A939 to Grantown is **Dulsie Bridge**, a very popular local beauty spot which is a great place for a summer picnic or to swim in the River Findhorn. On the southern shores of the Moray Firth, just east of Nairn, is **Culbin Sands**, a stretch of sand home to a variety of birdlife and managed by the RSPB. The best time to visit is from autumn to spring when bar-tailed godwits, oystercatchers, knots, dunlins, ringed plovers, redshanks, curlews, shellducks, red-breasted mergansers, greylag geese and snow buntings, to name but a few, come here in their droves.

Brodie Castle → *Colour map 2, C3.*

ⓘ *T01309-641371, castle Apr-Oct daily 1100-1630, grounds open all year 0930-sunset, castle and grounds £10, concessions £7.*

Brodie Castle, 8 miles east of Nairn, just off the main A96 to Forres, is one of Scotland's finest castles. The oldest part of the castle, the Z-plan tower house, is 16th century, with additions dating from the 17th and 19th centuries, giving it the look of a Victorian country house. The interior of the house is the epitome of good taste, with fabulous ceilings, and you can look round several rooms, including the huge Victorian kitchen. The collections of French furniture and Chinese porcelain are wonderful but most notable are the outstanding paintings, which include Edwin Landseer and Scottish Colourists. The grounds, too, are a delight, especially in spring when the daffodils are in bloom. There's also a tearoom.

Highlights include the impressive paintings and tapestries, the fascinating kitchen and the genuinely witty captions that have visitors laughing all over the castle.

The Beauly Firth ›› pp187-189. Colour map 2, C1-2.

Beauly and around → *Phone code: 01463. Colour map 2, C1-2.*

The sleepy little market town of Beauly is 10 miles west of Inverness, where the Beauly river flows into the Firth. It's a lovely wee place – hence its name. According to local legend, when Mary, Queen of Scots stayed here, at the priory, in 1564, she was so taken with the place that she cried (in French, of course) "Ah, quel beau lieu!" (What a beautiful place!).

At the north end of the marketplace is the ruin of **Beauly Priory** ⓘ *daily 1000-1800, free*, founded in 1230 for the Valliscaulian order but, like so much else of Scotland's ecclesiastical heritage, it was destroyed during the Reformation. Close by, the **Beauly Centre** ⓘ *1000-1800, £2*, provides local clan history and tourist information.

Four miles east of Beauly, at Balchraggan just off the main Inverness road, is **Moniack Castle Winery** ⓘ *Mon-Sat 1000-1700 summer, 1100-1500 winter £2.50*, where you can try a whole range of wines, including elderflower and birch. Four miles to the north and just off the A832 is the **Glen Ord Distillery** ⓘ *T01463-872004, www.malts.com, daily 1000-1700; summer hours vary so call ahead to check; £4 (including a dram)*, which was established in 1838. The malt tour is enjoyable – particularly the dram! If travelling by bus take the No 19 **Stagecoach** service from Inverness.

Dolphin cruises

The waters in this area are renowned for their populations of that well-loved mammal, the dolphin. Buckie is the home of the **Moray Firth Wildlife Centre**, which houses a dolphin exhibition, where you can find out evrything you ever wanted to know about them., while Spey Bay (1 hour east of Inverness) is the home of the **Whale and Dolphin Conservation Society** (WDCS) T01343-820339. Its wildlife centre is packed with information about the dolphins and their latest sightings. There are various dolphin-spotting cruises around the Moray Firth, but there is a code of conduct for boat operators. Before you choose a cruise, make sure the company is part of the accreditation scheme.

Moray Firth Dolphin Cruises, Inverness, T01463-717900, www.inverness-dolphin-cruises.co.uk, March-Oct, daily, 1030-1800, £12.50, £10, £9 child, are accredited and offer trips Mar-Oct daily 1030-1800, for £12.50, concession £10, children £9. Boat departs from Shore Street Quay, Inverness harbour. Take the courtesy bus from the tourist office. Throughout the 90-minute tour, this professional operator pro- vides a chance to spot the bottlenose dolphins while also pointing out common and grey seals and abundant birdlife. Take warm clothes.

McAuley Charters, Harbour offices, Longman Drive, Inverness, T01463-717337, are also accredited and offer dolphin-spotting cruises which leave from Cromarty (see page 259) and Buckie.

Ecoventures, The Dolphin Centre, Cromarty, Black Isle, T01381-600323 www.ecoventures.co.uk. Leave daily subject to weather conditions, £20, £15. Just 40 minutes north of Inverness by car over the Kessock Bridge (A9) and A832, this experienced operator uses a high-speed RIB boat for a thrilling ride out to spot the bottlenose dolphins and possibly minke whale.

The River Beauly is one of Scotland's best salmon-fishing rivers, and 5 miles south of Beauly, at **Aigas**, is a **fish lift** ⓘ *Mon-Fri 1000-1500*, where you can watch salmon bypass the dam with the aid of technology.

Glen Strathfarrar → *Colour map 1, C6.*

Southwest of Beauly are glens Affric and Strathfarrar. Glen Strathfarrar, the lesser known of the two, is unspoiled and considered by some to be the more beautiful. To get there, take the A831 9 miles south from Beauly to Struy and follow the signs. Access to the glen is restricted by the estates in the area to 25 cars at a time. As a general rule there's gate access from Easter to late summer but it's best to call (T01463-761260) for advice. Once you're in there is a tremendous feeling of peace, and there's good climbing, fishing and walking. The little ungraded road runs for 14 miles all the way to the impressive **Monar Dam** at the head of the glen. Glen Strathfarrar can also be reached from Drumnadrochit, via Cannich (see below). Most of the walks and cycle routes here are covered by OS Landranger Nos 25 and 26.

Glen Affric → *Colour map 3, A6. OS Landranger Nos 25 and 26.*

The A831 continues south from Struy through Strathglass to the village of **Cannich**, gateway to glorious Glen Affric, a dramatic and beautiful gorge, with the River Affric

Mountain bike enthusiasts will love the 30 miles of new forest trail developed by Moray Monster Trails to the south of Forres. See www.forestry.gov.uk.

rushing through it, and surrounded by Caledonian pine and birch forest – in fact this is one of the few places where you can still see the native Scots pine. There are few, if any, more stunning sights in the Scottish Highlands and it's perfect for walking, or even just to drive through and stop for a picnic on a sunny day.

▲ Beyond Loch Affric the serious walking starts. From **Affric Lodge**, 9 miles west of Cannich, begins a 20-mile trail west to **Morvich**, near Shiel Bridge, on the west coast near Kyle of Lochalsh, see page 226. This strenuous walk is for experienced hikers only, and takes around 10 hours. You can stop off half way at one of the most remote youth hostels in Scotland, **Glen Affric Youth Hostel** at Allt Beithe, see Sleeping, below.

▲ There are also many shorter, easier walks around Glen Affric. There are some short, circular marked trails at the end of the road which runs west from Cannich almost to Loch Affric, and also from the car park at the impressive **Dog Falls**, 4½ miles from Cannich and a great place to stop for a picnic and swim. Cycling in the forests around Cannich is good too – you can hire bikes at the friendly **Cannich Caravan and Camping Park** (see Sleeping, below). The owner's a keen cyclist.

▲ Glen Affric can also be reached from **Drumnadrochit**, see page 189, by heading west on the A831 through Glen Urquhart to Cannich. Just before Cannich, on the road from Drumnadrochit, a single-track road leads left (south), past the Caravan and Camping Park, to the tiny village of **Tomich**. From here, it's a 3-mile hike up a woodland trail to a car park. A few hundred yards down through the trees takes you to the 70-ft plunging **Plodda Falls**. An old iron bridge affords a spectacular view of the waterfall.

Glen Affric reaches west into the very heart of the Highlands and is great for a spot of Munro-bagging, see further page 51.

Sleeping

Nairn and around *p184*

L The Boath House Hotel and Spa, Aldearn T01667-454896, www.boath-house.com. Apparently once described as the most beautiful regency house in Scotland, this stunning hotel with 6 tastefully appointed bedrooms combines award-winning dining with luxury spa treatments (see also Eating, below).

L The Swallow Golf View Hotel, Seabank Rd, next to the golf course, T01667-452301, www.swallowhotels.com. A haven for golfers with views of the course and the sea beyond. Luxurious with pool, sauna, spa, gym, tennis courts and fine restaurant (ΨΨΨ-ΨΨ).

B-E Kilravock Castle, T01667-493258, www.kilravockcastle.com. This atmospheric 14th-century castle lies 7 miles west of Nairn. Just like Mary Queen of Scots you can be a guest of what has been described as a historical gem housing artefacts from Culloden. Beautiful gardens...spooky dungeons!

D Bracadale House, Albert St, T01667-452 547, www.bracadalehouse.com. Very fine B&B.

Camping

Nairn Camping and Caravanning Club, Delnies Wood, Nairn, T01667-455281, Apr-Oct. Clean with good amenities in a secluded spot, but it's 3 miles to the pub!

Beauly and around *p185*

L The Priory Hotel, on the main street, T01463-782309, www.priory-hotel.com. Delightful but at a price.

B-C Lovat Arms Hotel, opposite end of the main street from **The Priory Hotel**, T01463-782313, lovat.arms@cali.co.uk. A wonderful 22-bedroom country house with a relaxed air and a tartan touch. Terrific Scottish game and seafood in the restaurant (ΨΨΨ-ΨΨ) or relax with a dram or cup of tea beside the log fire.

Glen Affric *p186*

B The Tomich Hotel, Tomich, T01456-415399, www.tomichhotel.co.uk. You'll find a friendly welcome and good food at this former Victorian hunting lodge that will appeal to the visitor in search of walking, stalking and fishing alike.

F Cougie Lodge, near Tomich, T01456-415459, www.cougie.com. Apr-Sep. It's a long walk from Tomich but call ahead and the owners of this delightful independent hostel will pick you up.

F Glen Affric Backpackers, Cannich, T/F01456-415263, open all year (closed Christmas and New Year). 70 beds with great open fire. Owner has extensive contacts for local activities and walks.
F Glen Affric Youth Hostel, Allt Beithe, T0870-1553255. Mid-Mar to end Oct.

Self-catering

Culligran Cottages, Glen Strathfarrar, T01463-761285. Enjoy your own cottage or chalet along 15 miles of private road in which to spot deer, fish or ride the hire bikes. A rural idyll.

Camping

F Cannich Camping and Caravan Park, Cannich, T01456-415364. Mid-Mar to end Oct. Just 5 mins' walk from the **Spar** shop. Handy campsite with caravans for rent. Very friendly and bike hire available.

Eating

Cawdor Castle *p184*

ŶŶ-Ŷ Cawdor Tavern, in the village of Cawdor, close by the castle, T/F01667-404777. A very popular, traditional country pub serving excellent food in a friendly atmosphere. Perfect for lunch or dinner after visiting the castle.

Nairn and around *p184*

ŶŶŶ-ŶŶ The Boath House Hotel and Spa, see Sleeping, above. Dripping with awards for their cuisine, this delightful rural retreat is well worth a visit.
Ŷ Asher's Tea-room, 2 Bridge St, Nairn. Recommended for a hot snack. Run by the same folk as the one in Inverness.
Ŷ The Classroom, High St, Nairn. Great for coffee, tasty home-baking and sandwiches.

Beauly and around *p185*

See also Dinwall and around, page 267.
ŶŶŶ-Ŷ Lovat Arms Hotel, see Sleeping, above. Serves up terrific food in the restaurant or relax in the bar with tasty snacks.
Ŷ Beauly Tandoori, The Square, T01463-782221. Good for a cheap curry.

Activities and tours

Nairn and around *p184*

Cycle hire

Bike and Buggy, Leopold St, Nairn, T01667-455416.
Rafford Cycles, Forres, T01309-672811.

Horse riding

Heatherfield Riding Centre, Lochloy Rd, Nairn, T01667-456682, offer pony trekking.

Mountain biking

Moray Monster Trails (south east of Nairn), **Urquhart Forest** (Cannich) and **Learnie Forest** (Black Isle) provide miles of forest/trail cycling for all standards on state-of-the-art tracks. See www.forestry.gov.uk for details.

Transport

Culloden *p183*

Bus Highland Country Bus (Rapsons) No 12 leaves from Queensgate in **Inverness** Mon-Sat (last bus back about 1928). It's a 10-min walk from the final drop-off point to the visitor centre. It's worth calling T01463-710555 to check if they can drop you closer to the site.

Fort George *p183*

Bus Highland Country Bus No 11 from the Post Office in **Inverness**, several daily except Sun, also buses from **Nairn**.

Cawdor Castle *p184*

Bus Highland Country Bus No 12 leaves from **Inverness** Queensgate and runs several times Mon-Sat as far as Cawdor Church. It's a 10-min walk from there to the castle. The last bus returns around 1822; also regular buses from **Nairn**.

Brodie Castle *p185*

Bus Bluebird/Stagecoach buses run to Brodie from **Inverness** via **Nairn**, 45 mins.

Nairn and around *p184*

Bus There are regular daily buses to Nairn from **Inverness** (30 mins) with **Highland Country Buses** and **Stagecoach/Bluebird**, see page 181.

Train Nairn is on the **Inverness–Aberdeen** rail line, and there are several trains daily from Inverness (20 mins).

Beauly and around *p185*

Bus There is an hourly No 19 **Stagecoach** bus, T01463-239292, to **Beauly** (Mon-Sat), and on to **Muir of Ord** and Dingwall from **Inverness**. There's also a **Ross's Minibus** service from Beauly 3 days a week, T01463-761250.

Train The train station at Beauly (with the shortest platform in the UK, so take care getting off) is now open; trains between **Inverness** and **Thurso** stop here.

Glen Affric *p186*

Bus Highland County Buses, T01463-710555 (No 17), **Ross's Minibus**, T01463-761250, and **Stagecoach** T01463-239292, all share the **Inverness** to **Cannich** and **Tomich** run (1 hr) via **Beauly**. Technically, they run at least once a day Mon-Sat but it's strongly advised that you double check times with operators. It's very difficult to reach Glen Affric from **Drumnadrochit**. On a Sun only (summer), **Ross's Minibus** runs from the Drumnadrochit TIC (1015) to Cannich. It makes the return trip from Cannich at 1600.

Loch Ness and around

One of Scotland's biggest attractions is the narrow gash of Loch Ness, Britain's deepest body of fresh water, stretching 23 miles from Fort Augustus in the south almost to Inverness in the north. The loch is scenic in its own right, with rugged hills rising steeply from its wooded shores, but visitors don't come here for the views. They come every year, in their hundreds of thousands, to stare across the dark, cold waters in search of its legendary inhabitant, the Loch Ness Monster. A huge tourist trade has grown up around 'Nessie', as the monster is affectionately known, and every summer the main A82, which runs along its western shore, is jam packed with bus-loads of eager monster-hunters, binoculars trained on the loch surface, desperate for one glimpse of the elusive beast. If you do see it, bear in mind your photograph could be worth a fortune! ▸▸ *For Sleeping, Eating and other listings, see pages 195-199.*

Ins and outs

The best way to see the loch is on a cruise from Inverness (see page 180) or jumping aboard the Loch Ness Express (see page 198). There are also boat trips from Drumnadrochit and Fort Augustus. Most of the tourist traffic uses the congested A82, which offers few decent views of the loch. By far the best views of are from the quiet and picturesque B862/852, which runs along the eastern shore from Fort Augustus up to Inverness. It's possible to make a complete circuit of the loch, which is best done in an anti-clockwise direction heading south from Inverness on the A82, but you'll need your own transport (or take a tour), as there are no buses between Fort Augustus and Foyers. There are regular daily bus services between Inverness and Fort William, with additional buses between Invergarry and Fort Augustus. ▸▸ *For further details, see Activities and tours, page 198 and Transport, page 199.*

Around the loch ▸▸ *pp195-199.*

Drumnadrochit → *Phone code: 01456. Colour map 2, C1.*

The Nessie tourist trade is centred on the village of Drumnadrochit, 15 miles south of Inverness, where the canny locals have cashed in on the enduring popularity of the monster myth. The monster hype is almost overpowering, with two rival Monster exhibitions and the inevitable souvenir shops selling all manner of awful tartan tack,

▲ The Great Glen Way

The Great Glen Way is a waymarked walking trail that runs for 73 miles between Inverness and Fort William. Panoramic views of Loch Ness can be seen at many of the sections between Fort Augustus and Inverness. Although a relatively easy walk, there are some fairly tough sections around Loch Ness and you'll need to be properly equipped and have a good map. OS Landranger Nos 26, 34 and 41 cover the entire route. It should take 4-5 days to complete, depending on your level of fitness. It is probably better to walk it in 'reverse', from Fort William to Inverness, as the easiest section is then at the start. The Great Glen Way also has its own website at www.greatglenway.fsnet.co.uk.

including those scary-looking tartan dolls with flickering eyelids, the 'See-You- Jimmy' tartan bonnet, complete with ginger 'hair', and not forgetting the Loch Ness Monster novelty hat. Fortunately, the very friendly **TIC** ⓘ *in the car park, T01456-459076, summer 0900-1700, winter Mon-Fri 1000-1330*, can offer alternative suggestions, such as exploring peaceful Glen Affric (see page 186).

One of the two Monster Exhibitions is the **'Original' Loch Ness Monster Visitor Centre and Lodge Hotel** ⓘ *T01456-450342, www.lochness-centre.com, daily Jul-Aug 0900-2100, rest of year 0900-1700, £5.50, students £3.50, children and concessions £3*, features a wide-screen cinema documenting the 'latest' facts and 'sightings' of Nessie. There's also a gift shop but the most authentic experience of all is the restaurant's tasty home-baking (🍴). **Loch Ness Cruises** operate from here, see page 198. The rival exhibition is **Loch Ness 2000 Exhibition** ⓘ *T01456-450573, Easter-end May 0930-1700, Jun and Sep 0900-1800, Jul-Aug 0900-2000, Oct 0930-1730, Nov-Mar 1000-1530, £5.95, concessions £5, children £4*. This Nessie exhibition also details eye-witness accounts of Nessie but more pertinently provides a more elaborate audio-visual experience which it plans to further upgrade in time for the 2007 season.

If it all gets too much, then fear not, for Drumnadrochit gives easy access to one of the most beautiful corners of Scotland. The A831 heads west from the village through Glen Urquhart to Cannich, about 12 miles away, at the head of Glen Affric, a great place for walking or enjoying a picnic.

Castle Urquhart

ⓘ *T01456-450551, Apr-Sep 0930-1830, Oct-Mar 0930-1630, £6.50, concession £5, children £2.50.*

A few miles south of Drumnadrochit are the ruins of Castle Urquhart. The castle bears the scars of centuries of fighting but its setting, perched on a rocky cliff on the loch's edge, is magnificent and, not surprisingly, one of the most photographed scenes in Scotland. Dating from the 14th century, the castle was a strategic base, guarding the Great Glen during the long Wars of Independence. It was taken by Edward I, held by Robert the Bruce against Edward II, and was then almost constantly under siege before being destroyed in 1692 to prevent it from falling into Jacobite hands. Most of the existing buildings date from the 16th century, including the five-storey tower, the best-preserved part of the complex, from where you get great views of the loch and surrounding hills. There's also a visitor centre with the obligatory café and shop.

Invermoriston → *Phone code: 01320. Colour map 4, A1.*

Between Drumnadrochit and Fort Augustus is the tiny village of Invermoriston, probably the most tranquil spot on the entire Inverness to Fort Augustus stretch of the A82. It's a beautiful little piece of Highland scenery, with a photogenic old stone

Great Monster Hunt

In a country full of myths and legends, the Loch Ness Monster is the greatest of them all. As elusive as a straight answer from a politician, Nessie has single-handedly sold more tins of tartan-wrapped shortbread to foreign visitors than Edinburgh Castle.

Tales of Nessie go way back to the sixth century, when St Columba is said to have calmed the beast after she had attacked one of his monks. But the monster craze only really took off with the completion of the A82 road along the loch's western shore in 1933. Since then there have been numerous sightings, some backed up with photographic evidence, though the most impressive of these – the famous black-and-white movie footage of Nessie's humps moving through the water, and the classic photograph of her head and neck – have been exposed as fakes.

In recent decades determined monster hunters have enlisted the help of new technology, such as sonar surveys but have failed to come up with conclusive evidence. Enter Cyber Nessie, the latest attempt to end the years of rumours, hoaxes and speculation. Nessie's very own website – www.lochness.co.uk – is a 24-hour real-time video watch of Loch Ness, and has already produced a couple of claimed sightings.

bridge over foaming river rapids. There are marked woodland trails leading off into the hills past some lovely waterfalls and it's worth popping into the **Glenmoriston Arms** for a pint or food.

At Invermoriston the A887 heads west through **Glen Moriston** to meet the A87, which runs from Invergarry (see page 192) all the way through the rugged and dramatic Glen Shiel and under the shadow of the Five Sisters of Kintail en route to Kyle of Lochalsh and Skye.

Fort Augustus → *Phone code: 01320. Colour map 4, A1.*

At the more scenic southern end of Loch Ness stands the village of Fort Augustus, originally set up as a garrison after the Jacobite rebellion of 1715, and headquarters of General Wade's campaign to pacify the Highlands. Today, Fort Augustus, where the **Loch Ness Express** docks from Inverness, is a very busy little place, full of monster-hunting tourists and boats using the flight of five locks to enter or leave Loch Ness on their journey along the Caledonian Canal. The **TIC** ⓘ *T01320-366779, Apr-Oct*, is in the car park next to the petrol station and cashpoint.

Fort Augustus Abbey, a Benedictine Monastery, once stood on the shores of Loch Ness. Founded in 1876 on the site of the original fort, it is now the site of luxury flats; your time is better spent admiring the first of the canal locks or popping into **The Clansman Centre** ⓘ *T01320-366444, Easter-Oct daily 1000-1800, £3.50, concession £3*, where young guides in traditional dress provide a lively and entertaining presentation of 17th-century Highland family life in an old turf house. There are also displays of weaponry whilst the craftshop sells the more tasteful kind of souvenirs. If you've time, pop into the **Caledonian Canal Heritage Centre** ⓘ *Jun-Sep daily, free*, with its history of the impressive canal system.

Fort Augustus to Dores → *Colour map 4, A1-2.*

A very worthwhile detour from Fort Augustus is to take the B862/852 up the east shore of Loch Nesson, a mostly single-track road that skirts the loch for much of its length to the village of Dores. It's a much quieter and more scenic route than the busy

A82 and follows General Wade's original (and very straight) military road which linked Fort Augustus with Fort George. Though it makes a more interesting alternative to the more popular A82 route from Inverness to Fort Augustus, it's best done from south to north, if you have the time.

The road winds its way up into rugged hills passing the excellent real ale house of the historic Whitebridge Hotel and the nearby 1732 White Bridge. The road then drops back to the lochside at **Foyers**. It's worth stopping here to see the impressive waterfall where the River Foyers plunges into Loch Ness or to enjoy an overnight stay at Foyers House (see Sleeping). To get there, follow the steep (and slippery) track down from opposite the shops. Three miles further north, at **Inverfarigaig**, is **Boleskine House**, once home of Alastair Crowley, who is said to have practised devil worship here. In the 1970s the house was bought by Jimmy Page of Led Zeppelin, but sold some years later after the tragic death of his daughter. Those of a nervous disposition may wish to pass on quickly and continue to the little village of **Dores**, at the northeastern end of the loch, where you can enjoy some fine forest walks or reasonable pub grub at the **Dores Inn**.

You can then continue to Inverness, or return via the beautiful hill road that leads up to **Loch Mhorand** back to Fort Augustus via the **Stratherrick Valley**. From **Errogie**, at the northern end of Loch Mhor, there's a dramatic section of road that winds down to the loch through a series of tight, twisting bends, reminiscent of an Alpine pass, and great for cyclists. There are also interesting marked woodland trails around Errogie.

Fort Augustus to Fort William » *pp195-199.*

South of Fort Augustus, the A82 leaves behind Loch Ness and runs along the west shore of Loch Oich and then the east shore of Loch Lochy, till it reaches Spean Bridge. Here the A82 continues south to Fort William, while the A86 branches east through Glen Spean to join the A9 Perth to Inverness road finally at Kingussie. All along this route are many opportunities to get off the beaten track and explore huge chunks of real wilderness, deserted since the Clearances and soaked in the blood of history.

Invergarry and around → *Phone code: 01809. Colour map 4, A1.*

The old village of Invergarry stands where the A82 turns west to meet the A87. There's not much to see or do in the village, but the surrounding area merits some exploring, particularly the route west through Glen Garry, and there are several places to stay.

Inside the entrance to the **Glengarry Castle Hotel**, on the shores of Loch Oich (see Sleeping, page 195) stand the ruins of **Invergarry Castle**, once the stronghold of Clan Ranald of Glengarry and later destroyed by the Duke of Cumberland as he wreaked revenge on the Highlands in the aftermath of Culloden (see page 40). The hotel was later built as the main house of the Ellice family, who made their fortune from the Hudson Bay Company in Canada and who were the main driving force behind the creation of the Victorian planned village.

A mile or so south of the village, at **North Laggan**, is a monument by the side of the road standing over **The Well of the Seven Heads**. This tells the grisly story of the **Keppoch Murders**, one of the most infamous clan murders which took place at **Roy Bridge** (see page 194) in the 17th century. It all began when the chief of the clan MacDonnell died, leaving two young sons, who were sent away to complete their education before returning to Roy Bridge to celebrate the elder brother's accession to chieftainship. Another branch of the clan present at the celebrations started a fight in which both brothers were killed. Believing they had been murdered, one of their cousins persuaded a fellow clan member to raise 50 men and march on the murderers' house at nearby Inverlair. The accused murderers – a father and his six sons – were duly slaughtered and their heads cut off, to be displayed before the local laird at Glengarry. On the way to his lodge, the heads were washed here in this well.

Old as the hills

The Great Glen, which splits the Scottish mainland from Fort William in the south to Inverness in the north, is one of the world's major geological fault lines. The Glen was formed millions of years ago when the northern part of the Caledonian mountains 'slid' more than 60 miles south, leaving behind a massive glen with four freshwater lochs – Loch Linnhe, Loch Lochy, Loch Oich and Loch Ness.

The most famous of these is Loch Ness, which attracts hordes of visitors eager to catch a glimpse of its elusive monster.The renowned engineer, Thomas Telford, succeeded in connecting all these lochs when he built the impressive Caledonian Canal. The canal took 22 years to complete, and when it was opened in 1822 was the first in Britain to take ships from one coast to the other. It remains the only canal in the country capable of carrying ships of up to 500 tons. The best way to appreciate the glen is by boat, through the 38 miles of natural lochs and rivers and the 22 miles of canal, and every summer pleasure craft of all shapes and sizes ply its length. The main A82 runs from Inverness south to Fort William. The southern section, from Fort Augustus, follows the original line of the road constructed in 1727 by General Wade to link the military garrisons at Fort William and Fort Augustus (hence their names).

Another way to travel through the Great Glen is along the excellent cycle route, which follows the canal towpaths, forest trails and quiet minor roads to avoid the busy main road. The route is outlined in the Forestry Commission leaflet, available from most TICs.

A few miles further south, at **Laggan**, where the A82 crosses to the east bank of Loch Lochy, is the site of the **Battle of the Shirts**, see box. The A87 leads west from Invergarry through Glen Shiel to Shiel Bridge, on the way to Kyle of Lochalsh on the west coast, see page 226. About 7 miles along the A87, past the turning for Kinloch Hourn (see below), is the **Glen Garry viewpoint**, from where you get one of the most stunning, and famous, of all Highland views. From this angle Loch Garry looks uncannily like a map of Scotland, so get out the camera for that classic holiday snap.

Glen Garry to Kinloch Hourn → *Colour map 3, A5-6.*

A mile or so before the Glen Garry viewpoint, where the A87 begins to leave the shores of Loch Garry, is the turning left for the road through Glen Garry, described as the longest and most beautiful cul-de-sac in Britain. The little single-track road turns and twists for 22 glorious miles along the shores of Loch Garry and Loch Quoich all the way to Kinloch Hourn at the head of Loch Hourn. Known as 'the loch of the devil' this sea loch forms part of the wonderful wilderness area of Knoydart.

Glen Garry is now virtually deserted but was once home to some 5000 people who were driven out during the infamous Highland Clearances in the 19th century. The road passes the tiny hamlet of **Tomdoun**, once the junction of the main road to Skye, until the massive post-Second World War hydroelectric schemes changed the landscape. Experienced hillwalkers can still follow the old route to Skye, through Glen Kingie, along Loch Hourn and then across the wild Knoydart Peninsula till they reach the tiny but welcoming settlement of **Inverie**. From here a little ferry runs twice a day (Monday Friday) to Mallaig, see page 221.

Beyond Tomdoun the road passes a huge dam, built in the 1950s, which raised the waters of **Loch Quoich** by over 100 ft, flooding many of the old settlements. Also flooded was **Glen Quoich Lodge**, which can count Edward VII and Sir Edward

 Landseer among its notable guests. It was reputedly Glen Garry that gave Landseer the inspiration for his famous painting *The Monarch of the Glen*. The road then reaches its highest point, at 1200 ft, before descending to **Kinloch Hourn**, once a thriving crofting and fishing village. See Sleeping, page 195.

Spean Bridge → *Phone code: 01397. Colour map 3, B6.*

The main A82 runs down the east shore of Loch Lochy to the village of Spean Bridge, at the head of Glen Spean, beneath the towering Lochaber Mountains. The village gets its name from Thomas Telford's bridge across the River Spean. Two miles west are the remains of the old 'Highbridge', built in 1736 by General Wade, and the site of the first clash between Government troops and the Jacobites, three days before Prince Charles raised his standard at Glenfinnan.

Spean Bridge is only 8 miles north of Fort William so gets busy in the summer, but it still makes a more peaceful and attractive alternative base for exploring this astoundingly beautiful part of the Highlands. There's a **TIC** ⓘ *T01397-712576, Easter-Oct*, just off the main road behind the **Spean Bridge Hotel**. This hotel, complete with its **Shinty Bar** watering hole, also houses the excellent **Commando Exhibition** ⓘ *free*. The area is also the starting point for the excellent **Grey Corries ridge walk** (OS Landranger Map No 41).

Loch Arkaig and around → *Phone code: 01397. Colour map 3, A5-6.*

A mile north of Spean Bridge on the A82 is the **Commando Memorial**, which commemorates the men who trained here during the Second World War. It's worth lingering for a few moments to appreciate the fantastic views all around. From here the B8004 branches west to **Gairlochy**, crossing the Caledonian Canal, then the B8005 heads north to Loch Arkaig, a long, deep and mysterious loch stretching west through the mountains. Bonnie Prince Charlie passed this way, before and after Culloden, through an area which has, for centuries, been the seat of the Camerons of Lochiel. The Camerons were fervent supporters of the Jacobite cause and when Prince Charles landed at Loch nan Uamh, on the road from Fort William to Mallaig, he called on Cameron of Lochiel to join him at Glenfinnan.

In the tiny township of **Achnacarry**, nestled between the shores of Loch Lochy and Loch Arkaig, you can find out about the Camerons and their involvement in the Jacobite rebellion of 1745 at the **Clan Cameron Museum** ⓘ *T01397-712480, Easter to mid-Oct daily 1330-1730, Jul-Aug 1100-1730, £3, concessions £1.50, children free.* This museum is housed in an old cottage, rebuilt after being burned by government troops in 1746.

Beyond the turn-off to Achnacarry, the single-track road runs through the Clunes Forest and The Dark Mile, a long line of beech trees which completely cuts out daylight. At the east end of Loch Arkaig, a stone bridge crosses the Caig Burn. Beside the bridge is a car park, from where a path leads up to the spectacular **Cia-Aig Falls** which tumble into a deep, dark pool known as **The Witch's Cauldron**. It was here that an old hag was accused of casting her evil eye over Lochiel's cattle, causing them to fall ill and die. But when she fell into the pool and drowned, the cattle miraculously began to recover from their illness. The road runs along the north shore of Loch Arkaig all the way to the head of the loch, from where experienced and well-equipped hill walkers can hike through the glens to Loch Nevis, 'the loch of heaven', and Knoydart.

Glen Roy and Loch Laggan → *Phone code: 01397. Colour map 4, A-B1.*

From Spean Bridge the A86 runs east through Glen Spean to meet the A9 Perth to Inverness road which leads to Aviemore, see page 104. The road passes through **Roy Bridge**, which is the turn-off for Glen Roy, noted for its amazing 'parallel roads'. These are not in fact roads, but three gravel ledges etched on to the mountains at different heights. The 'roads' marked the shorelines of a glacial lake formed during the last Ice Age. Roy Bridge was also the site of the infamous Keppoch Murders, see page 192.

Getting shirty

One the bloodiest battles in Scottish clan history was the Battle of the Shirts, fought in 1544. It was so named because it was fought on a hot day and the combatants took off their shirts before proceeding to butcher each other. One side – the Frasers – were almost wiped out and their opponents – a combined force of MacDonalds, MacDonnells and Camerons – suffered less heavy losses and claimed victory. Over 1000 were killed and a plaque beside the canal locks describes the terrible events.

The road continues east towards Loch Laggan. After a couple of miles it passes **Cille Choirille**, an ancient church built by a 15th-century Cameron chief as penance for a life of violence. The church fell into disrepair but was restored and reopened in 1932 and now attracts people of all creeds as it's said to inspire peace and spiritual healing. Further east, at the eastern end of Loch Laggan, is the massive **Laggan Dam**, built in 1933 to provide water for the aluminium smelter at Fort William. The water is piped through tunnels up to 15 ft in diameter carved through the core of Ben Nevis. The road runs along the north shore of the loch, past the **Creag Meagaidh National Nature Reserve**, where you can see herds of red deer right by the reserve car park. A track leads from here up to **Lochan a' Choire** (about four hours).

Sleeping

Drumnadrochit *p189*

B Polmaily House Hotel, 3 miles from Drumnadrochit on the A831 to Cannich, in Glen Urquhart, T01456-450343, polmaily.co.uk. 14 rooms. This is a delightful rural escape for families and couples alike. Aside from the opportunity to relax in over 20 acres of grounds, at least 1 room boasts a 4-poster bed. There's a reasonable restaurant (🍴🍴🍴-🍴🍴) and the conservatory bar is just the place to unwind with a malt after a dip in the heated swimming pool. Oh yes, there are also tennis courts, whilst fishing, horse riding and walking are all easily arranged.

C Gillyflowers, T/F01456-450641, gillyflowers@cali.co.uk. Good-value guesthouse in converted croft.

D The Benleva Hotel, T01456-450080. A former manse, this small, atmospheric hotel and 2005 Highland Pub of the Year prides itself on a fine range of real ales and its use of freshly prepared local produce. Recommended. Each Sep, it helps host the **Loch Ness Beer Festival** so book ahead. Scared of ghosts? The 400 year-old chestnut tree outside the front door was the former hanging tree!

D Kerrow House, Cannich by Beauly. T01456-415243. A fantastic B&B and self-catering (Fisherman's Cottage) hideaway (from £207-£721 per week) on a 12-acre woodland estate. Well worth the trip.

D-E Loch Ness Backpackers Lodge, Coiltie Farmhouse, Lewiston, T01456-450807, www.lochness-backpackers.com. A terrific, low-budget option run by friendly, helpful owners who can arrange boat trips and walks in the area. Recommended.

Invermoriston *p190*

L-A Glenmoriston Arms Hotel, T01320-351206. Formerly a 17th-century drovers inn, this very comfortable hotel on the route of the Great Glen Way which boasts a tasty (🍴🍴🍴-🍴🍴) dinner menu and over 100 malt whiskies behind the bar.

F SYHA Loch Ness Youth Hostel, a few miles north, on the main A82. T0871-3308537. Mid-Apr to end Oct. Fantastic views across Loch Ness.

Self-catering

Invermoriston Chalets, Invermoriston, T01320-351254, www.invermoriston-holidays.com. Various chalets and cottages located by River Moriston Falls. Sleep 2-6 people. From £215-£525.

Camping

Loch Ness Caravan & Camping Park, 1½ miles south of Invermoriston, and 6 miles north of Fort Augustus, T01320-351207. Right on the shores of the loch with great views and excellent facilities (Mar-Jan).

Fort Augustus *p191*

D Lovat Arms Hotel, T0845-450110, www.lovatarms-hotel.com. 25 rooms. Beautiful, family-run mansion house standing above the village combines a warm welcome with excellent service and a mouth-watering menu (ΨΨΨ-ΨΨ). Little wonder it's popular. Family also run the luxurious **Loch Torridon Hotel**.

D Sonas, on the Inverness Rd, T01320-366291. Run by Mrs Service who certainly lives up to her name.

E-F Stravaigers Lodge, Glendoe Rd, T01320- 366257. Open all year. Another good backpacker place.

F Morag's Lodge, Bunoich Brae, T01320-366289. www.moragslodge.com. Open all year. Friendly and good value.

Fort Augustus to Dores *p191*

C Evergreen Guest House, Inverfarigaig T01456-486717, www.evergreenlochness.co.uk. Open all year. The very friendly owners of this east-shore guesthouse also offer dinner B&B (£60) and innovative car and walking tours around the Loch Ness area (see Activities and tours, below).

C-D Whitebridge Hotel, 3 miles south of Foyers, T01456-486226. Comfortable accommodation and also serves terrific real ales and bar food.

D Foyers House, Foyers, T01456-486405. Small guesthouse that prides itself on its view of Loch Ness from the decking and tasty evening treats such as game pie (ΨΨ).

Invergarry and around *p192*

L-B Glengarry Castle Hotel, T01809-501207, www.glengarry.net. Mar-Nov. 26 tastefully appointed bedrooms set in 60 acres of woodland running down to Loch Oich. The hotel prides itself on its traditional Highland hospitality with the daily changing dinner menu (ΨΨΨ) serving up the best of local Scottish produce.

D Forest Lodge, South Laggan, south of Invergarry, T01809-501219, www.flgh.co.uk. 24 miles north of Fort William. A welcoming and comfortable B&B that can also rustle-up a 4-course Scottish dinner whilst you enjoy the spectacular scenery.

F Invergarry Lodge, Mandally Rd, Invergarry, T01809-501412, www.invergarrylodge.co.uk. Independent hostel sleeping up to 26 in 4-6 bed rooms. Open all year. Fully equipped kitchen and safe cycle shed.

F SYHA Loch Lochy Youth Hostel, 11 miles north of Spean Bridge, T0870-0041135. 58 beds. Good stop for walkers and cyclists.

Self-catering

Faichmard Farm Chalets, Invergarry, T01809-501314, www.glengarryselfcatering.co.uk. Rustic, secluded, cosy and peaceful. Sleeps 3 at a modest price: £200-£310 per week.

Camping

Faichem Park, Ardgarry Farm, 15 mins' walk from the village, T01809-501226, www.ardgarryfarm.co.uk. A very good and well-maintained camping and caravan site with spectacular views of the surrounding mountains. Ardgarry Farm also offers self-catering in Highgarry Cottage (from £220 per week).

Glen Garry to Kinloch Hourn *p193*

The **Cluanie Inn** (see page 228 for details), sits in an isolated spot before the road presses further westward into Glen Shiel under the mighty Sisters of Kintail. 30 mins further west is the turn-off towards Loch Hourn and the remote, roadless wilds of the beautiful Knoydart Peninsula. With the lodge at Skiary now closed, call the Knoydart Foundation rangers office at Inverie (T01687-462242) for details of accommodation options near Loch Hourn and around the peninsula.

Spean Bridge *p194*

There's no shortage of accommodation in Spean Bridge. There are lots more guesthouses and B&Bs than are listed here.

L Corriegour Lodge Hotel, 9 miles north of Spean Bridge on the A82, T01397-712685, www.courriegour-lodge-hotel.com. 9 rooms. Feb-Dec. Lovely Victorian hunting lodge on the shores of Loch Lochy, with fine views and an excellent restaurant. £46.60 for a 5-course candlelit dinner, 𝕿𝕿𝕿).

L Old Pines Restaurant with Rooms, just past the Commando Memorial on the B8004, T01397-712324, www.oldpines.co.uk. This delightful boutique hotel is where discerning guests will experience a true personal touch. Each of the 8 rooms is individually appointed to a very high standard. The warm scones and tea on arrival are just a hint of the treat in store at dinner where venison, local lamb, prime beef and shellfish feature. It's not inexpensive but for a touch of class in an unpretentious manner this could be a fine choice for a stay and/or dinner (TTT).

D Corriechoille Lodge, 2 miles north of Spean Bridge, T/F01397-712002, www.corrichoille.com. Apr-Oct. This secluded former fishing lodge offers a very comfortable stop for the night and a roaring open fire.

D Invergloy House, T01397-712681. 2 en suite rooms. A friendly, comfortable former coach house converted into a B&B, set in 50 acres of gardens.

E Smiddy House, in Spean Bridge village, T01397-712335, F01397-712043. A comfortable guesthouse with a small restaurant (TT). Self- catering also available in the adjacent **Old Smiddy**.

Camping

Stronaba Caravan & Camping, north of the village, T01397- 712259. Apr-Oct.

Gairlochy Holiday Park, west towards Gairlochy, T01397-712711, F01397-712712, Apr-Oct. Camping and self-catering chalets from £250-550 per week.

Glen Roy and Loch Laggan *p194*

F Aite Cruinnichidh Achluachrach, 1½ miles from the village, T01397-712315, This comfy bunkhouse even has a sauna!

F Grey Corrie Lodge, T01397-712236. Very handy for the nearby pub grub, transport and local shop.

F Station Lodge, 5 miles east at Tulloch train station, T/F01397-732333. Ideal if arriving by train or planning to hike in the hills. The friendly owners will even cook very early breakfasts to accommodate walkers and climbers. The train stop is practically at the door!

Eating

Drumnadrochit *p189*

The hotels all tend to serve decent bar food and some B&Bs offer evening meals.

TT Fiddler's Bistro, T01456-450678. Has expanded in recent years and continues to serve up generous portions. Open for lunch and dinner, last orders 2100.

TT-T Karasia, T01456-450002. Scotland's love-affair with curry has recently even reached the shores of Loch Ness. Great food.

Fort Augustus *p191*

TT-T Bothy Bite, down by the canal bridge, T01320-366263. A cosy choice serving simple but tasty bistro-style meals.

T Lock Inn, by the canal, or nearby **Poachers** are both good for a drink and pub grub.

Spean Bridge *p194*

TT-T Old Station Restaurant, T01397-712535. As long ago as 1894 trains on the West Highland Railway Line puffed up to its door. Now a converted railway station its fascinating interior serves snacks Tue-Sat 1000-1600 and delicious evening meals 1830-2100 (bar food 1830-1930). There are current plans to create accommodation – possibly in a railway carriage.

TT-T Spean Bridge Hotel, T01397-712250. Aside from its **Commando Museum** and reasonable food in the restaurant (TT) it's worth popping into the hotels **Shinty** bar to share a real ale or pub grub (T) with the locals whilst admiring the local shinty team's silverware.

Glen Roy and Loch Laggan *p194*

TTT-TT Best Western Glenspean Lodge Hotel, T01397-712223. 1½ miles east of Roy Bridge, for those in search of sustenance this 1880s hunting lodge still rustles up a tasty lunch (TT-T) and dinner.

TT-T Stronlossit Inn, T01397-712253, www.stronlossit.co.uk. Serves good meals. Also has rooms (**C**)

For an explanation of sleeping and eating price codes used in this guide, see inside the front cover. Other relevant information is found in Essentials, see pages 40-47.

Festivals and events

Fort Augustus *p191*
Jun-Sep Late Jun and Jul, mid-Aug and early Sep is the period when Fort Augustus hosts **Highland Gatherings**, featuring traditional dancing and piping competitions, tossing the caber and sheep dog trials.

Activities and tours

Loch Ness and around *p189*

Climbing
Nevis Guides, Bohuntin, Roy Bridge, T01397-712356.

Cycling
If you have a mountainbike, bring it to Lochaber and Glen Affric. **Glen Urquhart Forest** has fantastic trails outside Cannich (hire at the caravan park and see www.forestry.gov.uk) whilst **Laggan Wolftrax Mountain Bike Centre**, T01528-544786, www.laggan.com, 20 miles west of Roy Bridge, has miles of purpose-built trail in **Strathmashie Forest**, bike hire (from £15) and an excellent cafe. You can also hire bikes (and boats) at **Monster Activities**, 25 miles north of Fort William at the southern edge of Loch Oich, T01809-501340.

Fishing
Fishing Scotland, T/F01397-712812, www.fishing-scotland.co.uk. Jimmy Coutts runs professional fly-fishing courses for trout and salmon across Lochaber. Loch Arkaig in particular is renowned for its trout fishing.
Fishing with a ghillie, T01456-450279. Bruce is the guy to contact for a less formal but equally fun time on the water of Loch Ness. For around £20 per head (Easter-end Sep) he'll take a group of 4 (max) out on a 2-hr fishing trip from Drumnadrochit. He can't promise you'll catch anything but then again, you could hook Nessie!

Horse riding
The Pier House Guest House, Fort Augustus, T01320-366418, offers guests 2-hrs' horse riding for £25.
Highland Riding Centre, T01456-450358, Borlum Farm, Drumnadrochit.

Quad-biking
Quad Bike Tours, Inverlair, Tulloch near Roy Bridge, T01397-732371, offer the chance to explore the countryside on a powerful quad-bike (£25) or test your skills at 4WD technical driving (£35).

Tour operators
There are various monster-spotting tours of Loch Ness which leave from the tourist office in Drumnadrochit or Fort Augustus.
Cruise Loch Ness, Fort Augustus, T01320-366277, www.cruiselochness.com, on board the *Royal Scot*. Cruises set off from the canal in the centre of Fort Augustus, Mar-Nov hourly from 1000. The trip lasts 1 hr and costs £8 per adult.
Evergreen B&B and Car Tours, T01456-486717, www.evergreenlochness.co.uk. Whilst their comfortable B&B (**C**) is nestled on the east shore of Loch Ness at Inverfarigaig, Fiona and Graeme Ambrose also run fabulous car tours to some of the Highlands' most beautiful locations. Even if not staying at their guesthouse, you can arranged to be picked up at Fort Augustus. Depending on the season and conditions, trips explore around Loch Ness, as far south as Fort William and Glencoe and even northwest to romantic Plockton and Loch Carron. Trips cost from £65 per car (not person) so squeeze up for a tour of the countryside with your own driver and guide.
Jacobite Cruises, T01463-233999, www.jacobite.co.uk, run a courtesy bus from Inverness TIC to connect with their Loch Ness cruises that incorporate Castle Urquhart, the Caledonian Canal and a visit to the Loch Ness Monster 2000 Exhibition. Whilst this 6½-hr odyssey costs £29 there are various shorter tours including a 60-min Loch Ness cruise (daily 1000-1600) £9, children £6.50, which leaves from the **Clansman Hotel** about 10 miles north of Drumnadrochit. In all cases, it's recommended that you contact the operator for specific pick-up/drop-off points.
Loch Ness Express, T0800-3286426, www.lochnessexpress.co.uk, is ideal if you wish to make the single (£13) or return trip (twice daily) from Fort Augustus up Loch Ness to the head of the loch where a shuttle bus will whisk you into Inverness city centre. The boat also pops into Dores on the east

side and runs separate (£11) trips to Urquhart Castle.

Watersports

Monster Activities at Great Glen Water Park, east shore of Loch Oich, near South Laggan, T01809-501340. An outdoor activities centre with hostel accommodation (£10 per person) nearby offering adventure sports including whitewater rafting, canoeing, mountain biking, rock climbing, sailing, windsurfing, hill walking and water skiing. Self-catering lodges for rent too.

Transport

Drumnadrochit *p189*

Bus **Citylink** buses between **Inverness** and **Fort William** stop at here several times daily in either direction. Additional services run between **Inverness** and **Urquhart Castle** during the summer months. There are also buses from **Inverness** to **Cannich** and **Tomich**, via Drumnadrochit (see page 189). **Citylink** buses between **Inverness** and **Kyle of Lochalsh** stop at Urquhart Castle, Loch Ness Youth Hostel, Invergarry and Invermoriston.

Fort Augustus *p191*

Bus Fort Augustus is a convenient stopover between **Fort William** and **Inverness**, and there are several buses daily (No 919) in either direction making the 1-hr journey. There is an additional service between **Fort Augustus** and **Invergarry** (see below) once a day Mon-Fri.

Fort Augustus to Dores *p191*

Bus This route is only possible if you have your own transport. There are buses south from **Inverness**, but they only run as far as **Foyers**. En route, the bus stops at **Inverfarigaig** and **Dores Inn** (2 daily Mon-Sat). If you're feeling very fit, it can be done by bike, as a tough trip from Fort Augustus or from Inverness, possibly using the **Loch Ness Express** (see page 198) for the return leg.

Invergarry and around *p192*

Bus Invergarry is on the **Fort William** to **Inverness** bus route (see Fort Augustus above). It is also on the main **Fort William** to **Kyle of Lochalsh** (and Skye) **Citylink** route (Nos 915, 916) and a couple of buses pass through daily in both directions. For times T08705-505050.

Glen Garry to Kinoch Hourn *p193*

Bus There's a post bus from **Invergarry** on Mon, Wed and Fri, which runs halfway to Kinloch Hourn. A 4-seater post car runs all the way to Kinloch Hourn from **Invergarry** on Tue, Wed, Thu and Sat. It is strongly recommended that you check with Royal Mail (T0845-7740740) on postbus times before travelling. Otherwise, it's a very long walk!

Bus A more scenic return would be to take the passenger ferry from Kinloch Hourn to **Arnisdale** (year-round; daily by arrangement, T01599-522774) and either use the local postbus (Mon-Fri) or Skyeways Bus (T01599-555477) to **Glenelg** (see page 227), from where you can take a ferry across to **Kylerhea** on Skye. Note: if planning to explore the Knoydart Peninsula it's advisable to call **Knoydart Foundation**, T01687- 462242, for travel and accommodation advice, including information on stalking activity.

Spean Bridge *p194*

Bus There are regular buses to and from **Fort William** and **Inverness**. Spean Bridge is also on the **Fort William–Glasgow** railline.

Loch Arkaig and around *p194*

Bus There's no public transport beyond Achnacarry village, though at least 1 bus per day (Mon-Sat) travels the route from **Fort William** via **Banavie** and **Gairlochy**. T01397-702373, for details.

Glen Roy and Loch Laggan *p194*

There is a No 40 bus from **Fort William** to **Roy Bridge**, 3 times daily Mon-Fri, 1 on Sat. **Roy Bridge** is also on the **Fort William–Glasgow** rail line.

Fort William and around

Fort William, the self-proclaimed Outdoor Capital of the UK, is also the gateway to the Western Highlands and one of the country's main tourist centres. It stands at the head of Loch Linnhe, with the snow-topped mass of Ben Nevis towering behind. You could be forgiven for assuming that it's quite an attractive place, but you'd be wrong. Despite its magnificent setting, Fort William has all the charm of a motorway service station. After passing a string of B&Bs on the southern outskirts the visitor finds a dual carriageway running along the lochside past uninspiring 1960s- to 1970s-era concrete boxes masquerading as hotels. Unsurprisingly, the majority of Fort William's attractions are out of town. The surrounding mountains and glens are amongst the most stunning in the Highlands and attract hikers and climbers in their droves: Ben Nevis – Britain's highest peak at 4406 ft – and also the very beautiful Glen Nevis, which you may recognize from movies such as Braveheart *and* Rob Roy. *There are also snowsports on the slopes of nearby Aonach Mor, one of Scotland's top ski areas. Here, in and above, Leanachan Forest, you'll find world-class cross-country and downhill mountain biking. Since 2002, Fort William has hosted the annual Mountain Bike World Cup and in 2007 will stage the prestigious World Mountain Bike Championships (www.ridefortwilliam.co.uk).* ▸▸ *For Sleeping, Eating and other listings, see pages 204-210.*

Ins and outs

Getting there

Fort William is easily reached by bus, from Inverness, Glasgow and Oban, and by train, direct from Glasgow via the wonderful West Highland Railway, see page 209. The train and bus stations are at the north end of the High Street, next to the supermarket. If you're driving, parking can be a problem. There's a big car park beside the loch at the south end of town, and another behind the tourist office. You can also walk to Fort William, if you have a week to spare, from just north of Glasgow, along the 95-mile-long West Highland Way, see page 54.

Getting around

The town is strung out for several miles along the banks of Loch Linnhe though the centre is compact and easy to get around on foot. Many of the B&Bs and several backpacker hostels and camping options are within Glen Nevis or around Corpach, 1½ miles to the north. Both areas are serviced by frequent buses from the town centre. ▸▸ *For further details, see Transport page 208.*

Tourist information

The very busy **TIC** ⓘ *Cameron Sq, just off the High St, T01397-703781, open year round Apr-Sep Mon-Sat 0900-1700, Sun 1000-1600; Oct Mon-Fri 1000-1700, Sat 1000-1600, Sun 1000-1400, Nov-Mar, Mon-Fri 1000-1700, Sat 1000-1600*, stocks a good range of books, maps and leaflets covering local walks. Staff will also help arrange transport to more remote Highland parts.

Fort William ▸▸ *pp204-210. Colour map 3, B6.*

→ *Phone code: 01397. Population: 10,774.*

Though it's not a pretty sight, Fort William is the largest town hereabouts and has all the services and facilities you'd expect. There are banks with ATMs on the pedestrianized High Street, as well as a large supermarket, a bike shop and a couple of well-stocked outdoor-equipment outlets.

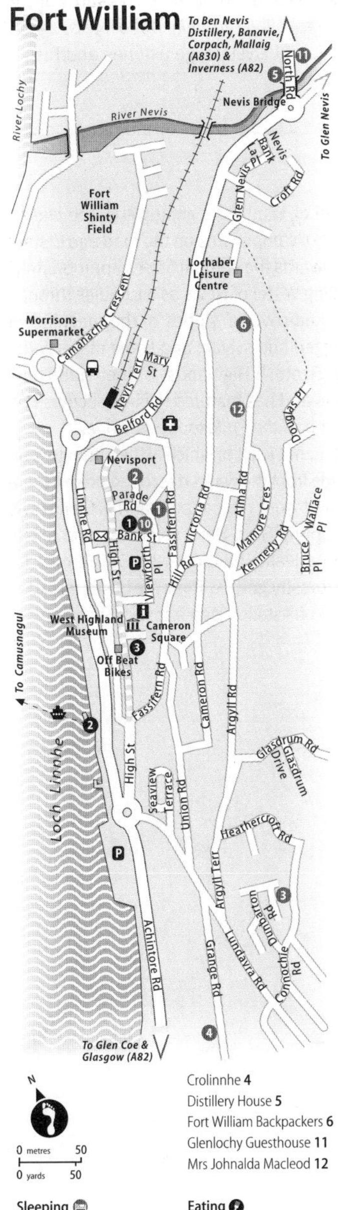

Sleeping
6 Caberfeidh **1**
Alexandra **2**
Bank Street Lodge **10**
Calluna **3**
Crolinnhe **4**
Distillery House **5**
Fort William Backpackers **6**
Glenlochy Guesthouse **11**
Mrs Johnalda Macleod **12**

Eating
Café Chardon **1**
Crannog Seafood **2**
Grog & Gruel **3**

Sights

There's little of real interest in the town, though the **West Highland Museum** ⓘ *Cameron Sq by the TIC, T01397-702169, Jun-Sep Mon-Sat 1000-1700, Oct-May 1000-1600, Jul-Aug daily 1400-1700, £3, concessions £2, children £0.50, under 12s free*, is a worthwhile exception. It contains excellent exhibits of Jacobite memorabilia, including a 'secret' portrait of Bonnie Prince Charlie which is revealed only when reflected in a cylindrical mirror. There are also fine displays of Highland clans and tartans, wildlife and local history. The fort from which the town gets its name was built in 1690 by order of William III to keep the rebellious Scottish clans in order. The garrison fought off attacks by Jacobites during the rebellions of 1715 and 1745 but was then demolished to make way for the railway line. Remnants of the forts outer walls are all that remain and can be seen by the lochshore near the train station.

Ben Nevis Distillery ⓘ *T01397-700200, www.bennevisdistillery.com, Mon-Fri 0900-1700, Easter-Sep Mon-Sat 1000-1600, Jul-Aug Mon-Fri 0900-1800, Sat 1000-1600, Sun 1200-1600, tours £4,* is at Lochy Bridge, at the junction of the A82 to Inverness and the A830 to Mallaig, about a mile north of the town centre. It's a bit too polished for some though the imaginative audio-visual display that features the mythical giant Hector McDram provides some light amusement. There's also a pleasant café and restaurant. Just before the distillery, on the left, are the 13th-century ruins of **Inverlochy Castle**.

Three miles from the town centre along the A830 to Mallaig, in the suburb of Banavie, is **Neptune's Staircase**, a series of eight linked locks on the Caledonian Canal. The locks lower the canal by 90 ft in less than 2 miles between Loch Lochy and Loch Eil and comprise the last section of the canal which links the North Sea with the Irish Sea. It's a pretty dramatic sight, with equally dramatic views of Ben Nevis and its neighbours behind Fort William. In fine weather, the **Moorings Hotel** (see page 205) by the canal is great for watching boats come and go as you enjoy a pint or mid-day bite. You can also walk or cycle along the canal towpath from here. For details on the new Great Glen Way ⓘ *www.greatglenway.fsnet.co.uk*, which links Fort William with Inverness, see page 207.

Further along the A830 to Mallaig, in the village of Corpach, is **Treasures of the Earth** ⓘ *T01397-772283, all year, daily 1000-1700; Jul-Sep daily 0930-1900, £3.95, concessions £3.25, children £2.50*, an exhibition of crystals, gemstones and fossils displayed in a huge simulated cave.

Glen Nevis

» *pp204-210. Colour map 3, B6.*

Only 10 minutes' drive from Fort William is one of Scotland's great glens, the classic Glen Nevis. If you can forget the sight of streams of campervans on the road and distant figures threading their way up the steep track towards the summit (dress appropriately) you could almost be mesmerized by the sparkling Water of Nevis as it tumbles through a wooded gorge, closed in by the steep, bracken-covered slopes of the magnificent hulk of Ben Nevis. The whole scene is both rugged and sylvan, and some may say the nearest you'll get to a Himalayan valley in the Scottish Highlands. It's not surprising, then, that this is a favourite with movie directors and has featured in films such as *Rob Roy*, *Braveheart*, *Highlander III* and *Harry Potter and the Philosopher's Stone*.

There are many walks in and around the glen, not least of which is the return trek up to the summit of Britain's highest mountain. Aside from the walks described below, there are several easy, marked forest walks which start from the car park at the **Glen Nevis Visitor Centre** ⓘ *open daily*, about half a mile up the Glen. Here, you'll also find toilets and an interesting interpretive display. Pick up a leaflet here or at the TIC (£0.50) for scenic walks around the area or check out www.forestry.gov.uk. There are buses into Glen Nevis, as far as the youth hostel, from Fort William bus station, see Transport, page 208.

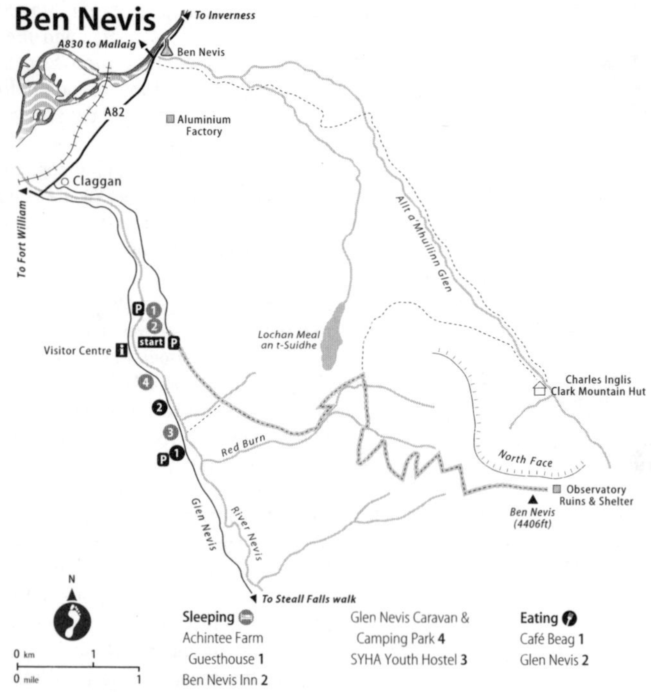

Ben Nevis → *OS Landranger No 41.*

Every year many thousands of people make the relatively straightforward ascent of Ben Nevis, and every year a frighteningly high percentage end up injured, or lost, or dead. Don't let the infamous ascent by a Ford Model T car in 1911 fool you. It's reported an average of four people perish on the mountain every year. Whatever the figure, it's vital that anyone venturing up the Ben is appropriately dressed and equipped for the hike. It should be remembered that the weather in Scotland's mountains can change at an alarming speed. Though it may be 20°C in the Glen Nevis car park when you set off, even far from the summit you may quickly find yourself in a disorientating blizzard or hill fog. It goes without saying that you need to be well prepared. You will need a good, strong pair of boots, warm clothing, waterproofs, food and drink. You should also take a map and a compass. Allow six to eight hours for the return trip. In the winter months the top part of the mountain is covered in snow. You should not attempt the walk unless you are an experienced hill climber.

The main tourist path, built as a pony track to service the long-gone observatory on the summit, starts from the car park at Achintee Farm, on the north side of the river, reached by the road through Claggan. It climbs gradually at first across the flank of Meal an t-Suidhe, before joining the alternative path from the youth hostel. This latter route is shorter but much steeper.

The trail continues to climb steadily as it begins to follow the Red Burn, until it reaches a junction, with Lochan Meal an t-Suidhe down to the left. Here, an alternative route down from the summit heads left under the north face of the mountain (see below). This is the halfway point of the main route. The path crosses the Red Burn and then climbs by a series of long and seemingly never-ending zigzags up to a plateau. If you're tired, consider that the record for the annual 10-mile run from Fort William to the summit and back is one hour 25 minutes! The path splits in two, but both paths take you up to the summit, marked by a cairn and emergency shelter, on the ruins of the old observatory. Note that on the upper sloping plateau the path can 'disappear' in mist and snow, and some cairns and beacons have been removed by vandals masquerading as purists. If conditions deteriorate, a compass is a life-saver. There is a form of shelter on the summit but ensure you're carrying extra clothes.

To return simply retrace your steps all the way. If the weather is settled enough and you have time, you can follow the alternative route below the north face. This leads right round the mountain to the Charles Inglis Clark mountain hut, then heads down into the Allt a' Mhuilinnglen which leads all the way down to the distillery on the A82, a mile north of the town centre. Note that this route adds an extra 3 or 4 miles to the descent and should only be attempted by fit and experienced hillwalkers.

Steall Falls → *OS Landranger No 41.*

A fairly easy low-level walk is to the spectacular 300 ft-high Steall Falls at the head of the glen. It's a popular walk, especially in the summer but this doesn't detract from its stunning natural beauty.

The path starts at the end of the road, at the second car park. Before setting off you might like to note the sign by the steep waterfall that cascades down to the edge of the car park. It reads 'Warning! This is not the path to Ben Nevis'. If you need to be warned against attempting to climb up Ben Nevis through a waterfall, you probably shouldn't be left alone in possession of this book, never mind let loose on the Scottish mountains. Once you've shaken your head in disbelief at the apparent mind-numbing stupidity of some of your fellow travellers, follow the track alongside the Water of Nevis. The path climbs steadily through the woods and becomes rocky, with the river thundering below through the steep gorge. It runs close to the river before emerging from the gorge and opening up into a wide, flower-filled meadow, with a high waterfall at the far end. It's a beautiful, tranquil place and ideal for a picnic. Follow the path across the valley floor till it crosses the river via a precarious bridge that consists of three ropes of thick wire in a V-shape. The path then leads to the bottom of the falls. You can also head left at the bridge and continue up the valley to some ruins. From here the path leads to Corrour station, 14 miles away. However, it's for fit, well prepared and experienced hillwalkers only. You can then catch a train back to Fort William. It's a very popular route, and there's even accommodation at the end of it, near the train station.

Nevis Range

ⓘ *T01397-705825, www.nevis-range.co.uk, the gondola is open all year (except Nov to the week before Christmas) 1000-1700, Jul-Aug 0930-1800. The resort runs four 'Music Up the Mountain' evenings in the summer (£9.50 lift ticket includes gondola ride but not the food!); gondola prices: £8.25 return, concessions £7.50, children (5-17, under 5s free) £5; day ticket £10, child £6.50; there is wheelchair access and guide dogs ride free.*

Nevis Range, 3 miles north of Fort William at Torlundy, just off the A82 to Inverness, is situated on the mountain of **Aonach Mhor** (4006 ft) and is Scotland's highest skiing and snowboarding resort. In a good season, enthusiasts the extensive lift system permits skiing between Christmas and May. The ski area is reached by Scotland's only gondola lift system. The 1½-mile (15-minute) ride is a popular attraction not only with wintersport enthusiasts but also with summer hillwalkers keen to gain easy access to the mountains. A couple of easy walks lead from the gondola station to Sgurr Finnisgaig (40 minutes) and Meal Beag (one hour), both of which offer stunning views from the top. Beside the top gondola station there's a small shop and a large self-serving **Snowgoose** restaurant (ŦŦ-Ŧ) providing fantastic vistas across Lochaber. Mountain bikers also come for some truly world-class riding (see page 208).

Sleeping

Fort William *p200, map p201*

Fort William has an abundance of accommodation, ranging from large luxury hotels to modest guesthouses and B&Bs. You'll find B&Bs and hostels on the road north towards Corpach and Banavie whilst the southern entrance to Fort William on **Achintore Rd** is truly packed with B&Bs and hotels. Running parallel is **Grange Rd**, which is also lined with B&B accommodation. Nearer to the town

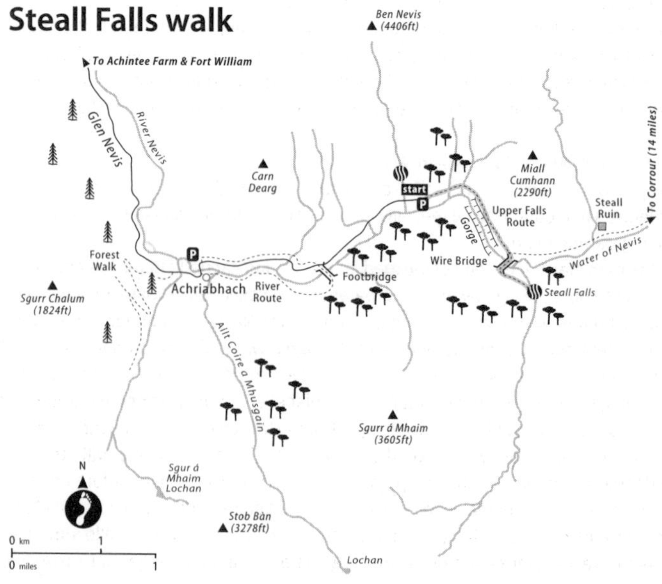

centre, **Fassifern Rd** and **Alma Rd** are also a hive of hostel and B&B activity. Wherever you search for a pillow, remember that as a tourist hub Fort William gets extremely busy in the high season and during key events such as the mountain bike World Cup, Highland Games and Ben Nevis Race. Ideally, book ahead or through the tourist office for a small fee. The TIC carries copies of the *Fort William and Lochaber Accommodation Guide*.

South of Fort William, on the A82, the villages of Onich and North Ballachulish, make an attractive alternative to staying in Fort William.

L Inverlochy Castle Hotel, 3 miles north of town on the A82 to Inverness, T01397-702177, www.inverlochy.co.uk. This is your castle in the Highlands. A luxurious stay is assured; unsurpassed elegance, impeccable service and superb food (see Eating page 206), all set in 500 acres of beautiful grounds.

B The Moorings Hotel, 3 miles out of town in Banavie, on road to Corpach and Mallaig, T01397-772797, www.moorings-fortwilliam.co.uk. Recently upgraded, overlooks Neptune's Staircase; well situated and comfortable with an excellent Jacobean restaurant (ΨΨΨ-ΨΨ).

B-C Crolinnhe, Grange Rd, T01397-702709. Mar-Nov. 10 mins' walk from town, this grand Victorian villa is a luxurious B&B. The welcome is friendly and the food delicious but don't dare take those muddy boots into the hall! If you opt for the luxury double your room includes a jacuzzi.

C Alexandra Hotel, The Parade, T01397-702241. 97 rooms. Large sandstone hotel that provides a reasonable standard of accommodation and food (ΨΨ). Very handy for the town centre.

C Distillery House, Nevis bridge, T01397-700103, www.visit-fortwilliam.co.uk/distillery-house. Situated between the Glen Nevis and Achintee turn-offs, this smart, comfortable guesthouse will appeal to those who seek a touch of class close to the town centre. 6 rooms. Also offer self-catering in nearby cottages; £200-£490 per week.

D 6 Caberfeidh, Fassifern Rd, T01397-703756. A friendly B&B that will prepare packed lunches after you've slept in your 4-poster bed.

D Glenlochy Guesthouse, Nevis Bridge, North Rd, T01397-702909. Almost directly opposite Distillery House. This substantial villa with 10 (including family) rooms is another smart choice for those in search of a friendly welcome, good food and relaxation.

D Glenloy Lodge Guest House, about 6 miles from town on the B8004 north from Banavie, T01397-712700. It's not the easiest guesthouse to find but good breakfasts and a welcome awaits.

D Mrs Johnalda Macleod, 25 Alma Rd, T01397-703735. Open all year. Unpretentious and comfortable.

D Rhiw Goch, Banavie, T01397-772373. Unbeatable views of Ben Nevis (when not shrouded in mist) and overlooking the Caledonian Canal. Owners are welcoming and serve terrific breakfast in this small B&B about 500 yds north of the **Moorings Hotel**. Also hire kayaks (see Activities and tours, page 207).

E-F Bank Street Lodge, Bank St, T01397-700070, www.bankstreetlodge.co.uk. 43 beds. Open all year. Independent, centrally located backpackers' hostel with family/double rooms and en-suite.

F Fort William Backpackers, Alma Rd, 500 yds from the train station, T01397-700711, www.scotlandstophostels.com. Packed with information and young backpackers.

F The Smiddy Bunkhouse & Snowgoose Apartments, next to the Corpach train station, 4 miles west of Fort William on A8309 to Mallaig, T01397-772467, www.highland-mountain-guides.co.uk. Alpine-style bunkhouse accommodation for up to 12 plus hostel for 14, fully self-catered. This recommended escape also runs the **Snowgoose Mountain Centre** which offers lessons and/or hire in mountaineering, canoeing, kayaking, skiing and mountain biking.

Self-catering

Birchbrae Luxury Scandinavian Lodges, 8 miles south of Fort William. T01855-821261. Sleeps 6. From £490 per week.

Calluna, T01397-700451, www.fortwilliamholiday.co.uk, is at Heathercroft, about a 15-min walk from the tourist office (see map, page 201). 2 modern-semi detached apartments have been configured to suit groups or families whilst the ground-floor will suit a wheelchair-bound visitor and carer. Run by experienced mountain guide, Alan Kimber, 22 beds, open all year. 6-bed apartment from

£340 per week. 8-bed apartment from £440 per week. Recommended.

The Old School Chalet, Duisky by Fort William. T01397-722227. Perfect peace and quiet assured in this basic (centrally heated) log cabin by the sea loch of Loch Eil. Forget shops. Think nature! Sleeps 6. From £195-£265 per week.

Glen Nevis *p202*

Glen Nevis is excellent for camping whilst Achintee at the start of the Ben walk has several excellent budget and guesthouse accommodation options.

E Achintee Farm Guesthouse, by the start of the path to Ben Nevis, T01397-702240, achinteefarm.com. Lovely setting and terrific welcome. Recommended. For details of how to get there, see Transport, page 208.

F Ben Nevis Inn, above Achintee Farm; across the river and up the steep steps from the visitor centre, T01397-701227, www.ben-nevis-inn.co.uk. An independent hostel where you'll find walkers and climbers enjoying banter, a real ale and hearty food (ŸŸ-Ÿ) beside a roaring fire in this rustic 17th-century inn. Best atmosphere in Fort William. Worth the walk.

F Farr Cottage Lodge and Activity Centre, Corpach, T01397-772315, www.farrcottage.com. This lively set-up can accommodate individuals or groups in bunkhouse or self-catering style. Terrific facilities including internet and laundry and cheap snacks (Ÿ). Can organize everything from hillwalking and mountain biking trips to sea-fishing, kayaking, go-karting and canyoning.

F SYHA Youth Hostel, 3 miles out of town in Glen Nevis, near the start of the path up Ben Nevis, T0870-0041120, www.syha.org.uk. Though remote, this is an excellent choice if you plan to hike on the Ben.

Camping

Glen Nevis Caravan & Camping Park, 2 miles up the Glen Nevis Rd, T01397-702191, www.glennevisholidays .co.uk. Mid-Mar to late Oct. Excellent facilities.

Eating

Fort William *p200, map p201*

With notable exceptions, Fort William isn't the culinary capital of the Highlands. Fortunately, there are some gems amidst those still earning a crust off run-of-the-mill bar lunches and uninspiring dinners. Note that many stop serving after 2200 – in which case it's a chippie dinner!

ŸŸŸ Crannog Seafood Restaurant, Town Pier, T01397-705589, www.crannog.net. Revamped after a horrendous flood in 2004, this restaurant (lunch £15-£20; dinner £20+) in an old smokehouse boasts the best seafood and ambience in town. It's unpretentious, the service is fair and there's a good wine list to help wash down that delicious lobster or salmon. Definitely book ahead.

ŸŸŸ Inverlochy Castle, see Sleeping, above. At over £300 per night to stay, think luxury. Here too, you'll experience exquisite fine dining – at a price. Will it be the black pudding with white truffles and scrambled eggs? Perhaps the saddle of rabbit or poached loin of venison? The food and wine list is first class – and so is the view out the window!

ŸŸŸ-ŸŸ The Moorings Hotel, 3 miles out of town in Banavie, on road to Corpach and Mallaig, T01397-772797, www.moorings-fortwilliam.co.uk. Good- value bar meals whilst the more formal Jacobean restaurant serves up some delicious evening treats.

ŸŸ An Crann, Seangan Bridge, at very northern edge of Banavie on the B8004, T01397-773114. This converted barn serves delicious Scottish, freshly prepared cuisine in a relaxed, informal atmosphere. Vegetarian options and mouth-watering venison, lamb and scallops. Popular so book ahead. Open 1700-2100. Recommended.

ŸŸ The Eagle Inn, Laggan Locks, at the northern end of Loch Lochy, T07789-858567. The owner of this lovingly restored Dutch barge will tell you the menu is whatever has been caught. Whatever his clean, cosy galley concocts, the ambience and real ale are terrific.

ŸŸ The Grog & Gruel, 66 High St, T01397-705078. This pub-cum-restaurant offers standard pizza and pasta but a good range of superb cask ales. Open until 2400. Also Ben Nevis Bar across the road.

Ÿ Café Chardon, just off High St. The best freshly prepared sandwiches in town.

Glen Nevis *p202*

ŸŸ-Ÿ The Ben Nevis Inn, Achintee, Glen Nevis, T01397-701227, www.ben-nevis-inn.co.uk. Yes, it's a long walk into the glen but many of the lunch (¥) and dinner (¥¥) treats are filling and freshly prepared whilst there's often live music and a generally great atmosphere. Best in the area.

¥¥-¥ **Glen Nevis Restaurant**, near the SYHA hostel, T01397-705459. Serves a standard 2-course lunch, 3-course dinner. Apr-Oct daily 1200-2200.

¥ **Café Beag**, T01397-703601. A cosy place with log fire. At time of writing may not open for 2007.

Festivals and events

Fort William and around *p200*

May The **UCI Mountain Bike World Cup** is held annually in late May at Nevis Range when the riders and over 20,000 spectators produce an electrifying highland air.

Jul The **Lochaber Highland Games** take place in Fort William with tossing the caber and Highland dancing.

Sep The **Ben Nevis Race**, www.bennevisrace.co.uk, with 500 runners undertaking the gruelling 10-mile run from Fort William to the summit of Ben Nevis and back. Staged for over a 100 years, the record stands at 1 hr 25 mins!

Activities and tours

Fort William *p200, map p201*

Boat trips

Crannog Cruises, T01397-700714, www.crannog.net, runs trips of 1½ hrs from Mar-Oct, £7.50, children £4.00. Board the *Souter's Lass* at Fort William's Town Pier (daily 1000, 1200, 1400, 1600) for a chance to spot local marine wildlife including seals, otters and seabirds.

Sea Ventures, T01397-701687, www.seaventures-scotland.com. Thrilling fast-boat trips from 60 mins to 1 week in search of dolphins, whales, seals and birdlife or simply to explore the Isles of Staffa and Mull. Cruises start from £15 for the Loch Linnhe experience and they'll be happy to arrange a customized itinerary subject to sea conditions.

Canoeing and kayaking

There are several good whitewater rivers around Fort William ranging in difficulty from Grade I to VI, or you can paddle the Caledonian Canal.

The Smiddy Bunkhouse and Snowgoose Mountain Centre, see Sleeping, above, run canoe courses.

Rhiw Goch, Top Locks, Banavie, T01397-772 373, www.rhiwgoch.co.uk. Close to Neptune's Staircase, hires out canoes and sea kayaks from around £25 per day.

Canyoning, fun-yakking and whitewater rafting

Vertical Descents, Inchree, 8 miles south of Fort William, T01855-821593, www.verticaldescents.com. There are many excellent outdoor adventure operators in Scotland – this is one of them.

Fishing

Torlundy Trout Fishery, Torlundy Farm in Tomacharich, 3 miles north off the A82, T01397-703015, has 3 lakes filled with rainbow trout and hires out rods. 3 hrs fly-fishing £15. Instruction available from £5.

Hiking and climbing

Fort William is a mecca for hikers and climbers and boasts one of the highest concentrations of guides and instructors in the land! For information on the climb up Ben Nevis and walks around Glen Nevis, see page 203. Nevis Range offers some of the most accessible winter climbs in the country for experienced climbers. For details of the gondola ride, see page 204. If you want to hire a guide, note that the information board/staff in **Nevisport** (see below) can provide useful advice. **Abacus Mountaineering**, www.abacusmountaineering.com, T01397- 701624; **Alan Kimber at West Coast Mountain Guides** , T01397-700451; **Alba Walking Holidays**, T01397-704964; **Snowgoose Mountain Centre** (see above); and **Mountain Motion**, T01397-701731.

Fort William has 2 good outdoor activity equipment shops: **Nevisport**, T013967-704921, is on the High St, and has a huge selection of books, maps and guides, a bureau de change and good café-bar. At the other end of the High St is **West Coast Outdoor Sports**, T01397-705777. There's an indoor climbing wall at the **Lochaber Leisure Centre** (below) but for true indoor adventure see also page 216 for **Ice Factor** in Kinlochleven.

Mountain biking

Fort William has hosted the World Cup since 2002. In 2007 it will also proudly host the World Mountain Bike Championships. Here, it's easy to see why Scotland is now regarded as one of the world's top mountain biking destinations. The Leanachan Forest, below Aonach Mhor, 3 miles north of town, covers a huge area with over 25 miles of mountain bike trails, ranging from easy to demanding and including the (world-class) **Witch's Trail**. These are free cross-country routes run by the Forestry Commission (www.forestry.gov.uk/ www.ridefortwilliam.co.uk).

Nevis Range is also home to the bone-jarring 2-mile-long World Cup downhill mountain bike course. Not for the faint- heated or inexperienced, bikers (over 12s) and their bikes, reach the top of this steep descent using the resort's gondola system (see page 204). Adult single £10, multi-trip £18.50, single youth £7.25, multi-trip £13.90. The track is open May-Sep daily 1100-1500 (subject to weather).

A more gentle alternative is the new **Great Glen Cycle Route**, mainly off-road, running from Fort William to Inverness. See page 190. For bike hire, sale, repair and advice visit **Off Beat Bikes**, 117 High St, T01397-704 008, www.off beatbikes.co.uk, or at the base station in Jul-Aug. Bikes from £18 per day. Specialist bikes, helmets and armour also available.

Skiing

Nevis Range ski centre, see page 204. Nevis Range hires all the snowboard and ski equipment required. You can also try **Nevisport**, see Hiking and climbing, above.

Steam train

Jacobite Steam Train, contact **West Coast Railway Company**, T01524-737751/53, www.steamtrain.info, runs from Fort William to Mallaig Jun to mid-Oct Mon-Fri (Jul and Aug daily) departing Fort William at 1020, arriving in Mallaig at 1225, departing Mallaig at 1410 and arriving back in Fort William at 1600. Day return £27, children £15.50; 1st-class return £40/£20 (see box, page 209).

Swimming

There's an indoor pool at **Lochaber Leisure Centre**, off Belford Rd, T01397-704359. Mon-Fri 1000-2100, Sat and Sun 1000-1800.

Transport

Fort William *p200, map p201*

Bus For the Fort William area contact **Highland Country Buses**, T01397-702373, www.rapsons. co.uk. There are buses every 10-20 mins to and from **Caol** and **Corpach**, and every hr on Sun and in the evening. Mon-Sat 0655-2205 there is a 60- to 90-min service (No 42) to **Glen Nevis Youth Hostel**, Jun-Sep only (fewer on Sun). 6 buses (Nos 41/42) daily to **Nevis Range** during the summer. During the ski season there are at least 3 daily buses (from 0745) to Nevis Range with the last return journey at 1630.

Long-distance services include several daily **Citylink** buses to **Inverness** (1 hr, £8.80); to **Oban** (1¾ hrs, £8.20) via **Ballachulish** (30 mins); and to **Uig** (3½ hrs), via **Portree** and **Kyle of Lochalsh** (1 hr 50 mins, £18.10). **City- link** buses go several times daily to **Glasgow** via **Glencoe** and **Tyndrum** (3¼ hrs, £14.00) and to **Edinburgh** (4 hrs, £19.90), via **Stirling** (3 hrs). There is a bus to **Mallaig** (1½ hrs, £4) Mon- Sat with **Shiel Buses**, T01967- 431272. **High- land Country Buses** run several times a day to **Kinlochleven** (50 mins) via **Glencoe**. There's a **postbus** service (Mon-Sat) to **Glen Etive**.

Car hire **Easydrive**, Lochy Bridge, T01397-701616 (from £32 per day); **Volkswagen Rental**, Nevis Garage, Argour Rd, Caol, T01397- 702432 (£36 inclusive); **Practical Car & Van Hire**, Slipway Autos, Corpach, T01397- 772404. Prices start from around £35 per day.

Ferry There is a passenger-only ferry service to **Camusnagaul**, on the opposite bank of Loch Linnhe, from the Town Pier. It sails Mon-Sat 0900-1740 and takes 10 mins, £1.20, £0.50 child. The **Corran Ferry** (T01855-841243) to **Ardgour** (see page 218) is 8 miles south of Fort William, just off the A82. Throughout the year the ferry makes the 5-min crossing every 20-30 mins from 0710 and every hr thereafter till 2100 (Fri-Sat 2130). Single £5.20, pedal bikes go free. Slight timetable variation in winter. For further details contact Corran Ferry T01855-841243, ask at the TIC or log onto www.lochabertransport.org.uk.

Riding the rails

Running from Glasgow to Mallaig via Fort William, the **West Highland Railway** is only 164 miles long but is widely acknowledged as one of the most scenic railway journeys in the world. The great thing about this journey is its variety, taking you from the distinctive red tenements of Glasgow and the former ship-building areas of the River Clyde, to the windy wilderness of Rannoch Moor and the chilly splendour of the hills. It's about an hour after leaving Glasgow that you get your first taste of Highland scenery when the train hugs the eastern bank of sinewy Loch Long. Then it's on past the 'bonnie banks' of Loch Lomond, Britain's largest body of inland water. It's impossible not to pass this serene loch without thinking of the famous ballad about two Jacobite soldiers captured after the '45 rebellion. The soldier taking 'the low road' is due to be executed, his companion taking the 'high road' is due to be released.

After Ardlui, at the top of Loch Lomond, the countryside gets more rugged. Wherever you look you see something of interest: a waterfall gushing down a hillside, a buzzard surfing on the breeze, perhaps a herd of Highland cattle wallowing in a river.

The **West Highland Way**, the long-distance footpath from Glasgow to Fort William, is close to the line now and at stations such as Crianlarich, Upper Tyndrum and Bridge of Orchy you can often spot footsore walkers with muddy boots – who get on the train looking slightly guilty and collapse on their seats with sighs of relief.

The landscape gets wilder and bleaker as the railway crosses the lonely, peaty wastes of Rannoch Moor and on to Corrour, which featured in the film version of Irvine Welsh's cult book *Trainspotting*. Then you descend to the lusher country around Tulloch, before pulling in to Fort William. This is a popular visitor centre as it's close to Ben Nevis, Britain's highest mountain, and beautiful Glen Nevis, which has featured in films such as *Braveheart* and *Rob Roy*. Now comes the most spectacular part of the journey. Leaving Fort William, the train crosses Thomas Telford's Caledonian Canal – where you can see an impressive series of eight locks known as 'Neptune's Staircase' – hugs the shore of Loch Eil, then crosses the magnificent Glen- finnan Viaduct, a masterpiece in concrete. You soon get superb views of the evocative Glen-finnan Monument that commemorates the start of the 1745 rebellion, before pulling in to Glenfinnan Station. The train now takes you through a landscape of craggy hills and glacial lochs etched with birch and pine trees. You pass Loch nan Uamh, from where Bonnie Prince Charlie fled for France after his defeat at Culloden, then draw in to Arisaig, the birthplace of the man who inspired RL Stevenson's Long John Silver. Next is beautiful Loch Morar, Britain's deepest inland loch and home – so legend has it – to a mysterious monster. Soon you get great views across the water to the craggy islands of Eigg and Rùm, before finally pulling in to the port of Mallaig.

Taxi You can call a taxi on T01397-706070, T01397-703334 or T01397-701122.

Train There are 2-3 trains daily from **Glasgow** to **Fort William** (3¾ hrs) via **Crianlarich**. These continue to **Mallaig** (1 hr 20 mins) where they connect with ferries to **Armadale** on Skye(see page 274). There are no direct trains to Oban; change at Crianlarich. There is a sleeper service from **London Euston** (see page 30), but you'll miss the views.

Directory

Fort William *p200, map p201*
Banks Plenty with ATMs on the High St. Note that if you planning to travel into remoter areas such as Ardnamurchan or Knoydart banks are few and far between.
Internet The library on the High St.

Glen Coe

Phone code: 01855. Colour map 3, B6.

There are many spectacular places in the Scottish Highlands, but few, if any, can compare to the truly awesome scenery of Glen Coe. No-one could fail to be moved by its haunting beauty, with imposing mountains, their tops often wreathed in cloud, rising steeply on either side from the valley floor. The brooding atmosphere of the landscape is only enhanced by the glen's tragic history. Once you've heard of the Glen Coe Massacre it sends a shiver down the spine every time you pass this way. Scotland's most famous glen is also one of its most accessible, with the A82 Glasgow to Fort William road running through it. Much of the area is owned by the National Trust for Scotland and is virtually uninhabited, leaving huge tracts of glen and mountain which provide outstanding climbing and walking. There's also skiing at the Glencoe Mountain Resort and canoeing on the rivers Coe and Etive. » *For Sleeping, Eating and other listings, see pages 214-217.*

Onich, North Ballachulish and Kinlochleven

The A82 south from Fort William passes through tiny Onich and the car ferry for Ardnamurchan at Corran before the B863 turns east at North Ballachulish and heads to Kinlochleven, at the head of Loch Leven. It can also be reached on the same road from Glencoe village, 7 miles west. Until the late 1990s a huge, unsightly aluminium factory dominated and was the lifeblood of the community. Fortunately, the entrepreneurial ingenuity of a Lochaber climber has since transformed the defunct factory into **Ice Factor**, the world's largest indoor ice-climbing facility (see Activities and tours, page 216). There's even the **Atlas** microbrewery next door! Industrialists can find out all about the history of aluminium-working in Kinlochleven at **The Aluminium Story** ⓘ *Linnhe Rd, T01855-831663, Apr-Sep Mon-Fri 1000-1300 and 1400-1700, free.*

The **West Highland Way** passes through the village and many walkers spend the night here before setting out on the last stretch before Fort William. There are also good walks in the surrounding hills and glens of the Mamores, a few of which are described below.

Walks near North Ballachulish

Five miles north of the village of North Ballachulish and having turned off the road for Inchree and **Vertical Descents** (see Activities and tours, page 216) a moderate one-hour circular walk up to **Inchree Waterfall** begins at the car park just 100 yards past the Vertical Descents bothy. A clearly marked trail, the huge waterfall is very dramatic to the eye, particularly when it's in spate. So too are the views back towards Loch Linnhe. The path continues up past the waterfall to the forest road which leads back downhill to the car park.

Walks around Kinlochleven

OS landranger No 41.

There are some relatively easy short walks from Kinlochleven up the glen of the River Leven, including the one to the impressive **Grey Mare's Tail waterfall**. It's a short walk of under an hour, signposted from the village.

The Devil's Staircase was named by the 400 soldiers who had to endure severe hardship while building it in the 17th century.

A stab in the back

Glen Coe is probably best known as the scene of one of the most shameful and notorious incidents in Scottish history.

Following his succession to the throne, William III wanted all the clans to swear an oath of allegiance by 1 January 1692. After much hesitation, the Jacobite clans of the West Highlands agreed to do so. However, Maclain of Glencoe, chief of a small branch of the MacDonalds, was not only late in setting off on the journey, but mistakenly went to Fort William to sign, instead of Inveraray. By the time he reached Inveraray it was 6 January and the deadline had passed.

The government decided that the rebellious clan be punished, in order to set an example to other clans, some of whom had not taken the oath. A company of 120 soldiers, under the command of Campbell of Glenlyon, were sent to Glen Coe and, since their leader was related by marriage to Maclain, the troops were billeted in MacDonald homes, in keeping with the long-standing Highland tradition of hospitality.

There they stayed for almost two weeks, until the cold-blooded order came through to "... put all to the sword under seventy". And so, on a cold winter's night, in the early hours of 13 February 1692, the Campbells ruthlessly slaughtered their hosts. Maclain and 37 men, women and children were slain in their beds, while many others fled into the hills, only to die of hunger and exposure. It was a bloody incident which had deep repercussions and proved to be the beginning of the end of the Highland way of life. For further information, see page 395.

There's a monument to the fallen MacDonalds in the village of Glencoe, where members of the clan still gather on 13 February each year. For a powerful and evocative account of the Massacre, read *Glencoe* by John Prebble (Penguin, first published 1966).

Dressed for the outdoors, a rewarding half-day walk is to follow the **West Highland Way** south from the village to the top of the **Devil's Staircase**, where it meets the A82 at the eastern end of Glen Coe. The well-signposted route begins at the wooden bridge north of Ice Factor and climbs gradually on a dirt jeep-track up to **Penstock House**, at 1000 ft. At the top, near the house, the track forks to the right and continues on a rough footpath to the Devil's Staircase. The path is marked with the West Highland Way thistle sign, so it's easy to follow uphill to the top of the pass (1804 ft), from where you get great views of Loch Eilde Mór and the Mamores to the north. The path then descends down the staircase to Glen Coe, with breathtaking Buachaille Etive Mór in front of you all the way. You'll have to return to Kinlochleven by the same route, or you could carry on to the **Kingshouse Hotel** (see Sleeping, page 215). The return trip from Kinlochleven should take four or five hours, or you can start out from Glencoe (see below). Before leaving, ensure you are properly equipped. This section of the West Highland Way was once part of the old military road which ran from Fort William to Stirling.

Another good hike, though more strenuous, is to **Beinn na Callich** (2507 ft). You'll need to be fairly fit as it's a steep climb; allow around six to seven hours for the return trip. The route is well marked and starts from the West Highland Way footpath opposite the school, which is on the road heading northwest out of the village towards Fort William. The path climbs steeply at first, crosses the tarmac road to **Mamore Lodge**, then continues till it joins General Wade's old military road, which takes the West Highland Way on its final 11 miles to Fort William. From here, you'll see the path zigzagging up the mountain. Continue along the old military road for about 400 yards until you cross a wooden bridge. Then follow a path down to another wooden bridge, where the ground is quite boggy. Cross the bridge and the path begins to zigzag uphill till it levels out on to a plateau, before continuing relentlessly upwards through a long series of zigzags to the summit, marked by a couple of cairns and a commemorative plaque. The views from the top make the tiring climb worthwhile. You can see down on to Loch Leven, over to Glen Coe and across the magnificent Mamores.

Fit and experienced hillwalkers can access the **Mamores** from the **Mamore Lodge** road. Once you're up there you have the opportunity to bag several Munros, via a series of excellent ridge walks connecting **Am Bodach** (3386 ft) with **Stob Coire a' Chairn** (3219 ft), **Na Gruagaichean** (3461 ft), **An Gearanach** (3222 ft), **Sgor An Iubhair** (3285 ft), **Sgurr a'Mhaim** (3606 ft) and **Stob Ban** (3278 ft). These peaks and ridges can also be reached from Glen Nevis, see page 202. As well as a good pair of lungs and the proper equipment, take a map and a compass.

Ballachulish

On the southern shore of Loch Leven, a mile or so west of Glencoe village on the A82, is the old slate quarrying village of Ballachulish. There are a few B&Bs and a couple of hotels close by. In the car park just off the main road is the **TIC** ⓘ *T01855-811866, daily 0900-1700*, with a good coffee-shop. Here, you can also find out all about the quarries.

Glencoe village

At the western entrance to the glen, on the shores of Loch Leven, is Glencoe village, 16 miles south of Fort William just off the A82. There are several places to stay in and

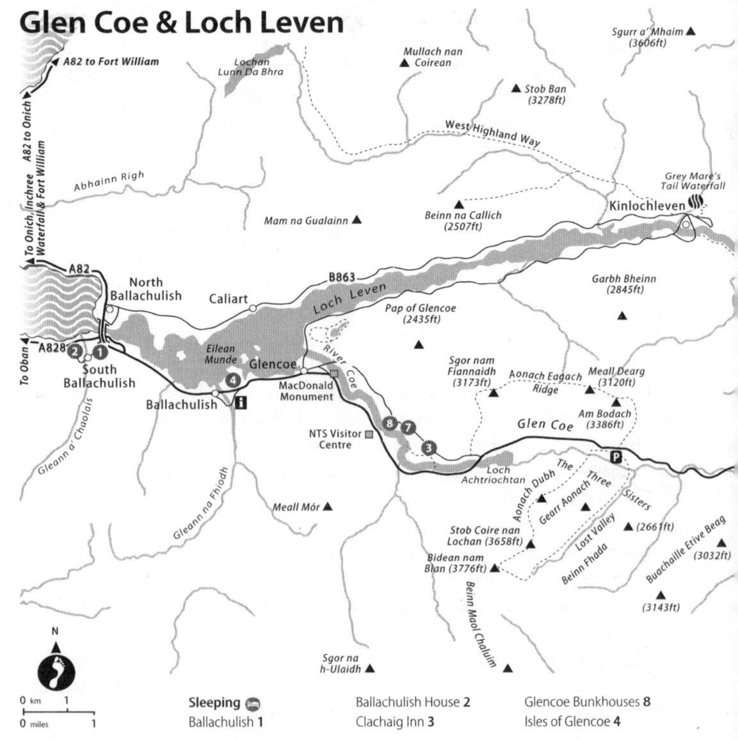

around the village, as well as a general store, post office and the fascinating thatched **Glencoe Folk Museum** ⓘ *late May-Sep 1000-1730, £2.20*, which has collections of 17th- to 18th-century costumes, military memorabilia and, according to the owner a chair that once belonged to none other than the Young Pretender. The most significant development in recent years has been the revamped and impressive **National Trust for Scotland Visitor Centre** ⓘ *1 mile south of Glencoe village, T01855-811307, Mar daily 1000-1600, Apr-end Aug 0930-1730, Sep-Oct daily 1000-1700, Nov-end Feb Thu-Sun 1000-1600, £5, concession £4*. There are interesting interpretive displays, information about the area's history (including the massacre), geology, fauna and flora. During the summer, the ranger service organizes guided walks. This eco-friendly building also boasts a lovely café.

Climbing and hiking in Glen Coe → *OS Landranger No 41.*

www.glencoemountain.com.

Glen Coe offers some of Britain's most challenging climbing and hiking, with some notoriously treacherous routes and unpredictable weather conditions that claim lives every year. The routes described below are some of the least strenuous, but you'll still need a map, good boots, warm clothing, food and water, and you should take the usual precautions, including checking on the weather forecast, see page 51.

One of the most popular walks is the relatively straightforward hike up to the **Lost Valley**, a secret glen where the ill-fated MacDonalds hid the cattle they'd stolen. Allow around four hours for the return trip. Start from the car park by the large boulder (see map), opposite the distinctive **Three Sisters**. Head down to the valley floor and follow the gravel path which leads down to a wooden bridge across the River Coe. Cross the bridge and follow the path up and over the stile. From here there's a choice of two routes. The less obvious route heads right and offers an easier climb into the valley. This eventually meets the lower, well-worn track, which involves a bit of scrambling but is more exciting as it follows the rushing waters of the **Allt Coire Gabhail**. The upper and lower paths meet a few miles further up and here you cross the river by some stepping stones. Proceed up the steep scree slope till you reach the rim of the **Lost Valley**, where many of the MacDonalds fled on the night of the infamous massacre. Once in the valley there are great views of Glencoe's highest peak, Bidean nam Bian ('pinnacle of the mountains') at 3776 ft, Gearr Aonach and Beinn Fhada and you can continue for a further 50 minutes to the head of the valley. From here it's possible to climb **Bidean**, but you'll need to be fit, experienced and well equipped.

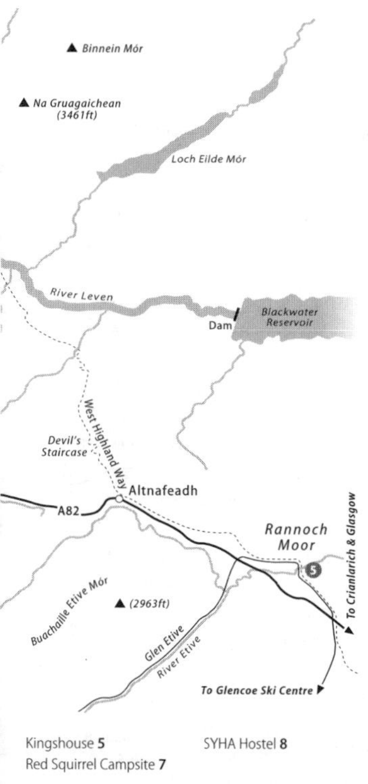

Glen Coe also offers one of Scotland's classic ridge walks, the **Aonach Eagach**. With potentially fatal drops it's not for the inexperienced or faint-hearted as there are some very exposed pinnacles you must climb around. The exposed ridge runs almost the entire length of the glen, starting at **Am Bodach** and ending at **Sgor nam Fiannaidh**. Don't make the mistake of descending from the last summit straight down to the **Clachaig Inn**. Instead, take the safer marked route.

Another difficult route is to the summit of **Buachaille Etive Mór**, one of the most photographed mountains in Scotland and one you'll probably recognize immediately the first time you see it from the A82, especially on the road north up to Glencoe. The mountain is best viewed from the **Kingshouse Hotel** and the route starts from Altnafeadh, a couple of miles west of the hotel. This is also the start or finish point for the fairly easy half-day walk over the **Devil's Staircase**, which is part of the West Highland Way. For a description of the route, see page 211. **Glen Etive** runs southwest from the hotel. It's a very beautiful and little-visited place, and great for wild camping. There's a postbus service once a day from Fort William.

Finally, there are some short, pleasant walks around **Glencoe Lochan**, an artificial loch created in the mid-19th century by Lord Strathcona for his homesick Canadian wife. Take the left turning off the minor road to the youth hostel just beyond the bridge over the River Coe. There's a choice of three walks of between 40 minutes and an hour, all detailed at the car park (or see www.forestry.gov.uk).

Glencoe Mountain Resort

ⓘ *T01855-851226, www.glencoemountain.com, chair lift operates Dec-Oct daily 0930-1700, £6.50; during the winter ski season an adult day pass £24, £16 junior.*

The **Glencoe Ski Centre** is just over a mile from the **Kingshouse Hotel**, on the other side of the A82, on **Meall A'Bhuiridh** (3636 ft). Established in 1956, it is Scotland's oldest ski centre and remains one of the best. The aptly titled *Flypaper* is the steepest 'black' marked piste in Scotland. The base station café sells terrific (¥) bacon 'butties'.

Sleeping

Onich, North Ballachulish and Kinlochleven *p210, map p212*

There's a wide selection of places to stay in the villages of Onich and North Ballachulish, mostly with good views of the loch. They make an attractive alternative to Fort William.

L Allt-nan-Ros Hotel, Onich, T01855-821210, www.allt-nan-ros.co.uk. Price includes dinner. James and Fiona Macleod's Victorian country house overlooks Loch Linnhe with views across to Appin and the hills of Ardgour and Morvern. There are pretty gardens, great food (¥¥¥-¥¥), and even a 10% discount on the new 'Dragon's Tooth' Ballachulish 9-hole golf course.

L The Lodge on the Loch Hotel, Onich, T01855-821237, www.lodgeontheloch.com Recently extensively upgraded to attract a discerning clientele, guests can expect luxurious bedrooms and, for dinner, a fusion of Scottish and European cuisine (¥¥¥-¥¥).

B Cuilcheanna House, Onich, T01855-821226. Easter-Oct. A comfortable guest-house just off the main road with lovely food.

B Onich Hotel, Onich, T01855-821214. Loch views and good meals (¥¥) in its busy bar.

C MacDonald Hotel, Fort William Rd, Kinlochleven, T01855-831539. Year-round. A welcoming hotel with a cosy bar and reasonable food (¥¥). Round the back of the hotel the owners have added several modern but small bunk-bed-based cabins (from £21 per person) and space for 11 camp pitches. In the morning, walk inside for a full Scottish breakfast (£6).

D The Inn at Ardgour, Ardgour, T01855-841225. This historic '2000 and 2004 Inn of the Year' is just 300 yds across the water from the Corran Ferry.

E Tigh-na-Cheo Guest House, Garbhein Rd, Kinlochleven, T01855-831434. 9 en-suite bedrooms. Friendly with superb outlook over Loch Leven and the Mamores. Very close to Ice Factor and the West Highland Way.

F Blackwater Hostel, Lab Rd, Kinlochleven, T01855-831253, www.blackwaterhostel.co.uk. Based in a row of old stone cottages, this is a friendly, well-run backpackers' hostel. Also 30 camping pitches outside the door with Ice Factor only 200 yds away and the West Highland Way at your feet.

F Inchree Hostel, at Inchree, on the A82 to Fort William, T01855-821287, T0800-3101536, www.inchreecentre.co.uk. Buses stop 100 yds from the hostel. Accommodation dorms and twin and double rooms. Good facilities and on-site bistro and bar (₸₸-₸). Vertical Descents just up the road.

Ballachulish *p212, map p212*

As well as one of the most historic hotels in Scotland, there's a wide selection of cheaper B&Bs and guesthouses in the village.

L Ballachulish House, T01855-81126, www.ballachulishhouse.com. Mar-Sun. 8 rooms. Some 200 yds beyond the **Ballachulish Hotel** on the A828 to Oban. This is a beautiful hotel, oozing style and an eclectic history, including an alleged role in inspiring RL Stevenson's *Kidnapped* classic and possibly once host to the treacherous officers who slaughtered the MacDonald's in Glencoe. Today, the fine bedroom decor is complemented by personal touches such as the home-made shortbread and **Arran Aromatics** toiletries. The recent recipient of a Michelin star, this retreat's style and taste extends seamlessly to the restaurant (₸₸₸).

L-C Ballachulish Hotel, South Ballachulish by the bridge, T01855-831500, www.ballachulishhotel.com. 54 rooms. With a touch of tartan the rooms are tasteful with some affording stunning loch views. However, it's the **Bulas Bar & Bistro** (₸₸₸-₸₸) that attracts many for its daily *bulas* (Gaelic pot) creations drawing on fresh, locally sourced produce.

A-C The Isles of Glencoe Hotel, T01855-831800, www.islesofglencoe.com. 39 rooms. A modern hotel and leisure complex adjacent to **Lochaber Watersports** on the shores of the loch. Lovely sea views from the 'top-deck' bedrooms whilst families will enjoy the excellent facilities including heated pool and sauna. The restaurant serves a 3-course lunch (₸₸) and 3-course dinner (₸₸₸).

E Fern Villa, T01855-811393. A good-value guesthouse.

Glencoe village *p212, map p212*

There are several B&Bs and guesthouses in the village and quite a few options around.

C Clachaig Inn, about 3 miles south just off the A82 on the old 'B' road that winds back to the village, T01855-811252, www.clachaig.com. If driving south from Glencoe village, this is a favourite haunt of climbers and walkers (despite the 'highland theme' make-over). 19 rooms. There's good-value accommodation and self-catering in chalets (from £545 per week) but it's the real ales, live music, hearty pub grub (₸₸-₸) that attract locals and visitors in droves.

D Kingshouse Hotel, east end of the glen, almost opposite the turn-off to the Glencoe Ski Centre, T01855-851259. 22 rooms. This is Scotland's oldest established inn and, judging by the decor it feels like it! However, thanks to the congenial, cosy **Climber's Bar** (₸) and the West Highland Way which passes its door, it's little wonder this historic hotel is popular with the many who camp across the old stone bridge. The sign on 'The Kingy' hotel door is telling: it advises non patrons there's a toilet in the village (10 miles away!)

E The Glencoe Guesthouse, T01855-811244. On the outskirts of the village, at Upper Carnoch.

E Scorrybreac Guesthouse, T/F01855-811354, www.scorrybreac.co.uk. Dec-Oct. This is a pleasant guesthouse but it's over a mile from the village itself.

F Glencoe Bunkhouses, near the **SYHA Youth Hostel**, T01855-811256, www.glencoehostel.co.uk. This is a basic but friendly bunkhouse (and cottage – £13 per person) alternative to the SYHA. There's no food or services and it's a 10- to 15-min walk for a pint at the **Clachaig Inn**.

F SYHA Youth Hostel, on the same road as **Clachaig Inn**, about 2 miles from the village, T01855-811219. An excellent hostel, open all year and very popular with climbers, so you should book ahead.

Camping

Red Squirrel Campsite, T01855-811256. Year-round. If walking south from Glencoe village on the 'B' road you'll reach this modest campsite before the hostels further along the road.

Eating

Onich, North Ballachulish and Kinlochleven *p210, map p212*

₸₸₸ **Ballachulish House**, some 200 yds beyond the **Ballachulish Hotel** just off the A828 to Oban, T01855-811266, www.ballachulishhouse.com. Mar-Oct.

8 rooms. Steeped in history, delicious game and seafood are just some of the tempting dishes served in style. Book ahead.

Ⱦ **Inchree Bistro and Bar**, Inchree, T01855-821393. A friendly and informal place that produces good food and attracts a fun-loving outdoor crowd. Open daily.

ⱦ-Ⱦ **Ice Factor**, Kinlochleven, T01855-831100. Mon-Thu 1400-2400, Fri 1400-0100, Sat 1100-0100, Sun 1230-1145. Opened in 2005, **Chillers Bar and Bistro** is a hip post-climb gathering place within **Ice Factor**. In addition to the delicious restaurant menu including venison and Loch Leven shellfish there are tasty bar snacks (pizza after 2100) whilst the refreshing real ales from Kinlochleven's own **Atlas** microbrewery are here on tap; Blizzard, Sisters and Latitude. I almost forgot the wonderful wood-burning stove, the chance to watch fellow climbers on the walls and enjoy the view of Loch Leven and the Mamores.

Ⱦ **Fishnet fish and chip shop**, Kinlochleven, opposite the **Tail Race Inn**. All year. Proudly proclaims to be the West Highland Way's only chip-shop. Great portions.

Glencoe village *p212, map p212*
Se also Sleeping, above,

ⱦ-Ⱦ **The Glencoe Hotel**, in the village, T01855-811245. Serves decent bar food.

Bars and clubs

Onich, North Ballachulish and Kinlochleven *p210, map p212*
Chillers Bar in Ice Factor in Kinlochleven and the **Tail Race Inn** (the local worthies' haunt) both serve beer from the local **Atlas** microbrewery. It's also worth popping into the cosy bar in the **MacDonald Hotel** along the road.

Activities and tours

Glen Coe and Kinlochleven *p210*

Brewery Tour

Atlas Brewery, Kinlochleven, T01855-831111, www.atlasbrewery.com. Easter-end Sep. Free tour of the microbrewery at 1730. Formerly the carbon bunker for the massive aluminium smelter, **Atlas** microbrewery produced its first beers in February 2002.

Climbing

Ice Factor, Kinlochleven, T01855-831100, www.ice-factor.co.uk. Tue-Thu 0900-2200, Fri-Mon 0900-1900. Housed in a former aluminium smelter, the world's largest indoor ice-climbing facility is truly spectacular. A giant refrigerated toy-box for anyone in search of vertical fun, over 500 tonnes of snow are packed onto the 15-m-high vertical walls. Novice (under instruction) or expert, the ice wall simulates as closely as possible outdoor conditions. There are also 15-m-high rock-climbing walls, a bouldering area, a well-stocked equipment shop and even a sauna and steam room, before you reflect on your day in the **Chillers Bar and Bistro** upstairs. Annual membership £10 adults and £5 (14-17 year olds). Daily rates vary according to the activity, with beginners only permitted to climb under instruction or expert supervision. Call for rates and times. If you don't want to participate, enjoy a coffee or sandwich whilst you watch. A competent climber can enjoy all-day rock climbing for £6.50 or 2 hrs ice climbing for £17.50, £11.50 junior. Rock+ice+ steam room package £23 and £18 junior.

Guides Ice Factor's professional climbing staff also run outdoor mountaineering and climbing courses.

Alan Kimber at West Coast Mountain Guides, T01397-700451, www.westcoast-mountainguides.co.uk, and **Mike Pescod** at Abacus, www.abacusmountainguides.com, are both recommended professional climbing guides in the Lochaber area.

For additional advice contact the Mountaineering Council of Scotland (MCofS) on T01738-493942, www.mountaineering-scotland.org.uk.

Glencoe Guides and Gear, in Glencoe village (north towards the bridge), T01855-811402. Daily 0930-1730. Sells great outdoor gear and hires out winter climbing gear including boots, crampons and ice-axes. Pop into **Crafts and Things** next door for a browse and tasty home-baking over a coffee.

Cycling

Glencoe Guides and Gear (see above), hire out mountain bikes at £12 for a half day, £20 per day and £30 for 2 days. The nearest bike shop, **Off Beat Bikes** T01397-704008, is in

Fort William. However, **Vertical Descents**, T01855-821593, www.verticaldescents.com, in Inchree (see Watersports, below) also hire out mountain bikes (£10 half-day/£15 per day).

Snowsports

Glencoe Ski Centre, the oldest resort in Scotland, has pistes suitable for beginners and experts. The *Flypaper* is reportedly the steepest black-marked run in Scotland. Definitely for experts only, it affords stunning views southwards over Glencoe – assuming you have time to look up! There is also a small café (winter only) above the first chairlift.

Watersports and other activities

Lochaber Watersports, West Harbour, West Laroch, Ballachulish, T07831-846025, www.lochaberwatersports.co.uk. Sailing courses (£325 for 5 days), kayaking (£25 for 3 hrs), 2-person dinghy (£30 for 3hrs), fast (RIB) powerboat with driver (£12 per person per hr). In addition, it's possible to undertake an exhilarating half-day fast powerboat (RIB) cruise to Tobermory at the northern end of Mull (min 3 people, £35 per person).
Vertical Descents, Inchree Falls, Onich, T01855-821593, www.verticaldescents.com. Yes, it can rain in Scotland but who cares if you've a wetsuit on and are having fun experiencing the thrills and spills of fun-yakking (£40, a mix of rafting and kayaking) or the adrenaline-pumping activity of canyoning (from £40). After a day climbing (or jumping off) waterfalls or blasting through the water in a kayak you're certain to come back refreshed.

Golf

Ballachulish House, T01855-811695. This challenging and scenic 9-hole golf course (from £13 per round) is open to the general public.

Transport

Onich, North Ballachulish and Kinlochleven *p210, map p212*
Bus Highland Country Buses, T01397-702373, run Mon-Sat 6 times a day, Sun 3 times, between **Fort William** and **Kinlochleven** (50 mins). En route these (No 44) buses stop at Onich and Corran Ferry. They also stop at Glencoe Junction (the southern edge of the village).

Glencoe village *p212, map p212*
Bus There are daily **Citylink** buses to **Glasgow** (2½ hrs) and **Fort William**. To reach the **Kingshouse** from Glencoe village you'll need to walk 15-20 mins to the road entrance of the White Corries (Glencoe) ski area where **Citylink** buses pull over.

West of Fort William

West of Fort William lie some of the Britain's most extravagantly scenic landscapes and some of the its most remote places. From southernmost Morvern, through the ruggedly handsome Ardnamurchan Peninsula, across the evocatively named 'Road to the Isles', through the haunting and tragic 'Rough Bounds' and on to the hopelessly isolated and utterly wild lands of Knoydart, this is serious wilderness, with little pockets of accessible and user-friendly Highlands thrown in for good measure. ▸▸ *For Sleeping, Eating and other listings, see pages 222-226.*

Ardgour, Ardnamurchan and Morvern

▸▸ *pp222-226. Colour map 3, B4-5.*

This lonely, southwestern corner features a dramatic landscape of rugged mountains, desolate moorland and near-deserted glens, fringed by a coastline of sparkling white beaches and clear turquoise seas with wonderful views across to the isles of Mull and Skye. This is one of the least-populated areas in Britain, mainly due to the legacy of the Highland Clearances in the mid-19th century, when whole communities were evicted by landlords in favour of more profitable sheep. With so few people around, this is an area noted for its wildlife, with a huge variety of birds and animals, such as deer, pine martens, wildcats and eagles. If you have both the time and the energy, it's worth exploring on foot. There's a series of footpaths throughout the area, particularly around Ardnamurchan.

Ins and outs

Getting around Once you leave the A830 Fort William to Mallaig road, buses are few and far between, so it's not easy to get around quickly without your own transport. You'll need your own transport to reach Ardnamurchan Point and Sanna Bay as there are no buses beyond Kilchoan. It's an area of few roads. » *For further details, see Transport page 217.*

Tourist information The website www.ardnamurchan.com, has lots of information on walks, as well as local events and attractions. Some 40 walks in the area are listed in a local guidebook, *Great Walks* (£3.75), available at tourist offices. OS Explorer Maps 383, 390 and 391 cover the entire region. See also Activities and tours, page 225.

Ardgour → *Phone code: 01967. Colour map 3, B5.*

The name Ardgour means 'height of the goats', and you can still see feral goats in this huge, sparsely populated wilderness bordered by Loch Shiel, Loch Eil, Loch Linnhe and Loch Sunart. Access is via the A861 south from Kinlocheil, or on the Corran Ferry to the tiny lochside villages of **Corran** and **Clovulin**.

The attractive little village of **Strontian** on the shores of Loch Sunart gave its name to the element strontium, which was first discovered in the nearby lead mines in 1790. These now-abandoned mines also produced most of the lead shot used in the Napoleonic wars. Strontian is the largest settlement in these parts and has a couple of shops, a post office and a **TIC** ① *T01967-402131, Apr-Oct Mon-Fri 0900-1700, Sat 1000-1600, Sun 1000-1400*. About 2 miles north of the village is the **Ariundle Nature Reserve**, which offers a pleasant two-hour nature trail through the glen and a 40-minute forest walk.

Morvern → *Phone code: 01967. Colour map 3, B6.*

Just east of Strontian the A884 leads south through the bleak, desolate landscape of Morvern to the tiny remote community of **Lochaline** on the Sound of Mull, departure point for the **CalMac** ferry to Fishnish. About 3 miles before Lochaline is the turning left for the track which leads down the side of Loch Aline to the 14th-century ruins of **Ardtornish Castle**. First you'll come to **Kinlochaline Castle** (keys available at the cottage) and **Ardtornish House**. This house stands on the site of the original house, which was visited on several occasions by Florence Nightingale, who was a family member of the original owners. The author John Buchan spent many summers here in the 1930s. There's a path which leads from the estate office uphill across open moorland for an hour till it reaches **Loch Tearnait**. In the centre of the loch is a 1500-year-old crannog, an artificial island built for defensive purposes. This walk is detailed in the tourist board's leaflet, along with the Ariundle Nature Trail (see above).

Ardnamurchan Peninsula and Moidart → *Phone code: 01972 & 01967. Colour map 3, B4.*

The main places of interest in this area are to be found on the rugged Ardnamurchan Peninsula (from the Gaelic *Aird nam Murchan*, meaning 'Point of the High Seas'), the end of which is the most westerly point on the British mainland. The winding A861 runs west from Strontian along the north shore of Loch Sunart to **Salen**, where the single-track B8007 branches west and runs all the way out to the tip of the peninsula. The A861 meanwhile turns north to Acharacle.

The first settlement you reach heading west out to Ardnamurchan Point is **Glenborrodale**. Before you reach the tiny hamlet look out on the left for the castellated late-Victorian towers of **Glenborrodale Castle**, once the property of a certain Jesse Boot, who founded a chain of chemist shops which you may have heard of. Just west of Glenborrodale is the excellent **Glenmore Natural History Centre** ⓘ *T01967-500254, Apr-Oct 1030-1730 (Sun 1200-1730), £2.50, concession £2, children £1.50*, local photographer Michael McGregor's interactive exhibition which features some of his most stunning photographs of local wildlife. The centre is designed to interact with the environment and there's live video action of the surrounding wildlife, including pine martens, birds and even fish in the nearby river. It's a good place for kids, and a life-saver when the weather is just too bad to venture outside. There's a good little café serving snacks and light lunches, and a decent gift shop. A mile to the east is the **RSPB Reserve** where you can see golden eagles, otters and seals. You can take a two-hour wildlife trip to the seal colonies – or further afield to Tobermory on Mull or Staffa and the Treshnish Islands, see Activities and tours, page 225. A few miles west of the centre, the B8007 turns away from the coast. Here you'll see the beautiful bay of **Camas nan Geall** (Bay of the stranger or pledge, the precise meaning is unclear). It's worth stopping at the car park to admire the fantastic views, or take the path down to the beach. Between Glenborrodale and Kilchoan, a road runs to the north coast of the peninsula and the beautiful beaches at **Fascadale**, **Kilmory** and **Ockle**.

During the stalking season (1 July-20 October) check at the estate office before setting out on the walk to Loch Tearnait.

The straggling crofting village of **Kilchoan** is the main settlement on Ardnamurchan. Shortly after passing the sign for the village, you can turn left to the scenic ruin of **Mingary Castle**, built around the 13th century. There's a **TIC** ⓘ *T01972-510222, Easter-Oct daily*, which provides information on local scenic walks and will help with accommodation. Beyond Kilchoan the road leads to the lighthouse at mainland Britain's most westerly point, with stunning views (on a clear day) across to the small isles of Rùm, Eigg, Muck and Canna, with the Cuillins of Skye rising behind Rùm. The former lighthouse was designed by Alan Stevenson, father of Robert Louis, and built in 1849. The buildings have been converted into the **Ardnamurchan Visitor Centre** ⓘ *T01972-510210, www.ardnamurchan.u-net.com, Apr-Sep daily 1000-1800, Oct 1000-1700, £2.50, concession/children £1.50*, where you can learn about the history and workings of lighthouses. There's also self-catering accommodation, a café and gift shop.

A mile northwest of Kilchoan a road branches to the right to the beautiful long, white beach at **Sanna Bay**. It's worth making the trip here just to walk on the beach, but this is also a good place to spot whales and dolphins. On the road to Sanna Bay is the tiny settlement of **Achnaha**, which is famed for its rare 'ring-dyke' system, a huge, natural rock formation which is the crater of an extinct volcano.

North of Salen on the A861 is the scattered crofting township of **Acharacle**, at the western end of Loch Shiel surrounded by rolling hills. The village has several shops, a post office, garage and plenty of places to stay. A couple of miles to the west a road leads to beautiful **Kentra Bay**. Cross the wooden bridge, follow the footpath round the side of Kentra Bay and then follow the signs for Gortenfearn, where you'll find the famous 'singing sands'. Not only is the beach music to the ears as you walk its length, but the view across to Skye and the small isles is a feast for the eyes.

Three miles north of Acharacle is **Loch Moidart**. Here, perched on a rocky promontory in the middle of the loch, is the 13th-century ruin of **Castle Tioram** (pronounced 'Cheerum'), one of Scotland's best-loved castle ruins. This was the seat of the MacDonalds of Clanranald, until it was destroyed by their chief in 1715 to prevent it from falling into Hanoverian hands while he was away fighting for the Jacobites. There are plans to restore the castle, but you can visit it (free) via the sandy causeway that connects it to the mainland at low tide. The A861 follows the shores of Loch Moidart, into the region of the same name, before joining the A830 Fort William to Mallaig road at Lochailort.

The Road to the Isles » pp222-226. Colour map 3, A4-B6.

The Road to the Isles, the 46-mile stretch of the A830 from Fort William to Mallaig, runs through a series of magnificent glens before emerging on a coastline of vanilla-coloured beaches and sinuous bays backed by machair and washed by turquoise seas, with views across to Rùm, Eigg and the Cuillins of Skye. This is also the route followed by the West Highland Railway (see page 209), frequently hailed as one of the great railway journeys in the world. Either way – by road or rail – this is a beautiful journey, through a landscape that resonates with historical significance. For this is Bonnie Prince Charlie country, where the ill-fated Jacobite Rising began, and ended, with the Prince's flight to France.

Glenfinnan → *Phone code: 01397. Colour map 3, B5.*

Some 17 miles west of Fort William, at the head of Loch Shiel, is Glenfinnan, a kind of single-malt distillation of Highland beauty. A grand monument marks the spot where Bonnie Prince Charlie raised the Jacobite standard in 1745. It was erected in 1815 by Alexander MacDonald of Glenaladale in memory of the clansmen who fought and died for the Prince. You can climb to the top (mind your head, though) for even better views down the loch. There's a powerful sense of history here and as you gaze across eerie Loch Shiel stretching into the distance, veiled by steep mountains, you can almost hear the wail of the bagpipes in the distance, through the mist. On the other side of the road is the **National Trust for Scotland Visitor Centre** ⓘ *T01397-722250, Apr-Oct daily 1000-1700, Jul-Aug 0930-1730, Nov weekends only 1000-1600, £3, concession £2, café*, which has displays and an audio programme of the Prince's campaign, from Glenfinnan to its grim conclusion at Culloden. The **Glenfinnan Games** are held here in mid-August.

A mile away, in Glenfinnan village, is the **Station Museum** ⓘ *T01397-722295, Jun-Oct daily 0930-1630, other times by appointement, £0.50*, which is housed in the railway station on the magnificent Fort William to Mallaig railway line. It has displays of memorabilia from the line's 100-year history. You can also sleep and eat here (see below). The 1000-ft span of the **Glenfinnan Viaduct**, between the visitor centre and the village, is one of the most spectacular sections of the famous West Highland Railway, see page 209.

About 10 miles west of Glenfinnan the road passes through the village of **Lochailort**, where the A861 branches south to the remote Ardnamurchan Peninsula, see above. A couple of miles further on, is **Loch nan Uamh**, where Prince Charles first landed on the Scottish mainland and from where, a year later, he fled for France following the disastrous defeat at Culloden, see page 184. A path leads down from the car park to the Prince's Cairn, which marks the beginning and the end of the Jacobite cause.

Arisaig and Morar → *Phone code: 01687. Colour map 3, A4.*

At the western end of the Morar Peninsula is the little village of Arisaig, scattered around the head of a sheltered bay with An Sgurr's knobbly peak peering above the narrow mouth. The village has sleeping and eating options, as well as a post office, general store (with ATM) and doctor's surgery and is a useful service centre for the many self-catering cottages and caravans that line this stretch of coastline. There are some nice beaches around, and the road west from the village out to the **Rhue Peninsula** is great for seal spotting. You can also take a cruise from Arisaig to the islands of Rùm, Eigg and Muck, see Transport, page 225.

Arisaig was the birthplace of Long John Silver, who worked on the construction of the nearby lighthouse at Barrahead, one of many designed by the father of Robert Louis Stevenson who met Silver and was so impressed that he immortalized him in his classic Treasure Island.

The main A830 bypasses Arisaig on its way to Mallaig, while a wiggly single-track road hugs the coast and heads north, past the golf course and on past beautiful Camusdarach beach (which featured in the film *Local Hero*) before joining the main road by the tiny village of Morar. A single-track road leads up behind the village of Morar to dark, mysterious **Loch Morar**, the deepest inland loch in the country and home of Morag, Scotland's other, lesser-known, but more attractive (according to the locals) monster. Two locals reported seeing her in August 1969 and a scientific investigation two years later uncovered a remarkable number of eye-witness accounts. You could always try to elicit further information from the locals over a wee dram in the bar of the **Morar Hotel**. The road runs along the north shore of the loch for 3 miles till it reaches the pretty little hamlets of **Bracora** and **Bracorina**. Here the road stops, but a footpath continues all the way to **Tarbet** on the shores of Loch Nevis, from where it's possible to catch a boat back to Mallaig, see Transport, page 225. It takes about three hours to walk to Tarbet – where there's now a bothy – and you'll need to get there by 1530 for the boat.

Mallaig ➔ *Phone code: 01687. Colour map 3, A4.*

The end of the road – and railway line – is Mallaig, a busy fishing port and main departure point for ferries to Skye. It's a no-nonsense, workmanlike place, with little in the way of worthwhile diversions, but there are decent facilities and at least the train and bus stations and **CalMac** ferry office are all within a few yards of each other. Also close by are banks with ATMs and the post office. The **TIC** ⓘ *by the harbour, T01687-462170, Apr-Oct daily, Nov-Mar Mon, Tue, Fri*, has a café and internet terminal but staff are not well informed.

If you have some time to kill, or if it's bucketing down, you could visit the rather optimistically titled **Mallaig Marine World** ⓘ *T01687-462292, Jun-Sep Mon-Sat 0900-2100, Sun 1000-1800, Oct-May Mon-Sat 1200-1730, £2.75, children £1.35*, an aquarium with indigenous marine creatures plus a few tired-looking displays on the history of the local fishing industry. Beside the train station is the **Mallaig Heritage Centre** ⓘ *T01687-462085, Apr, May, Jun and Oct Mon-Sat 1100-1600, Jul-Sep Mon-Sat 0930-1630, Sun 1230-1630, Nov-Mar Wed, Thu, Fri and Sat 1200-1700, £1.80, children £1*, with interesting descriptions of the local Clearances, the railway line and the fishing industry.

Leaving on the morning boat from Mallaig to Inverie and returning in the afternoon allows time for lunch at the Old Forge.

Knoydart Peninsula ⏩ *pp222-226. Colour map 3, A5.*

➔ *Phone code: 01867.*

The Knoydart Peninsula, the most remote and unspoilt region in Britain and one of Europe's last great wildernesses, literally lies between Heaven and Hell, for it is bordered to the north by Loch Hourn (Loch of Hell) and to the south by Loch Nevis (Loch of Heaven). Knoydart is not for wimps. It can only be reached on foot, or by boat from Mallaig, and consequently attracts walkers, who can wander for days around a network of trails without seeing another soul.

A two-day hiking route starts from Kinloch Hourn, reached by bus from Invergarry, see page 192. The trail winds its way around the coast to Barrisdale and on to Inverie. Another route into Knoydart starts from the west end of Loch Arkaig, see page 194, and runs through Glen Dessarry. Both are tough hikes and only for fit, experienced and well-equipped hillwalkers. An easier way in is by boat, see Transport, page 225.

The peninsula's only settlement of any size is tiny **Inverie**, with just 60 inhabitants, one of only a few villages in Scotland which can't be reached by road, but still has a post office, a shop, a few places to stay and Britain's most remote pub. Much of the peninsula

Raising standards

It all started on 19 August 1745 at Glenfinnan, 19 miles west of Fort William at the head of Loch Shiel. Less than a month earlier, Prince Charles Edward Stuart had landed on the Scottish mainland for the first time, on the shores of Loch nan Uamh, between Lochailort and Arisaig (see below). He had come to claim the British throne for his father, James, son of the exiled King James VII of Scotland and II of England.

The clan chiefs had expected French support, but when the Prince arrived with only a handful of men they were reluctant to join the cause. Undeterred, the prince raised his standard and his faith was soon rewarded when he heard the sound of the pipes and Cameron of Lochiel, along with 800 men, came marching down the valley to join them. It must have been an incredible moment.

is mountain, with four peaks over 3000 ft. Its 85 square miles is a mix of private sporting estate, conservation trust and community partnership. Five years ago one chunk of the peninsula, the 17,000-acre **Knoydart Estate**, was rescued from a succession of indifferent landlords by a community buy-out, funded by public money and individual donations. The **Knoydart Foundation**'s trustees include the conservationist Chris Brasher and impresario Cameron Mackintosh, and if you sit outside the **Old Forge** long enough, one of them might pass by, or stop for a chat. Equally possible is the sighting of otters in the Sound of Sleat or golden eagles soaring overhead.

Sleeping

Ardgour *p218*

L-A Kilcamb Lodge Hotel, Strontian, T01967-402257, www.kilcamblodge.com. Mid-Feb to end Dec. This luxurious Victorian country house standing in its own grounds on the shores of Loch Sunart has its own private beach. The perfect bolthole, with only the occasional otter or eagle to disturb the peace, also serves superb food.

B-C The Inn at Ardgour, Ardgour, next to Corran Ferry, 9 miles from Fort William, T01855-841225, www.ardgour.biz. Open all year. 10 en suite rooms. Small hotel dating originally from 1746 but recently modernized. All facilities, cosy bar with a fine selection of malts and its own library. Good choice for walkers.

E Craigowan, Strontian, 15 miles from Corran Ferry, T01967-402253, peternliz@craigowancroft.freeserve.co.uk. Open all year. 2 en suite rooms. Set on 15-acre working croft with livestock and domestic animals. Families and pets welcome. Discount for children. Storage for bikes. Meals arranged Oct-Mar. Owners also have self-catering crofthouse from £180-450 per week.

E Heatherbank, Upper Scotstown, Strontian, T01967-402201, www.heatherbankbb.co.uk. Open Easter-Oct. 3 en suite rooms. Modern house with great views to the Ardgour hills. Spacious guest lounge with log fire. Non smoking. Discounts for longer stays.

Ardnamurchan Peninsula and Moidart *p218*

A Feorag House, Glenborrodale, T01972-500248, admin@feorag.co.uk. Superb guesthouse set in 13 acres of grounds. Great views out to sea and top-class cuisine. Price includes dinner. Highly recommended.

A-B Meall Mo Chridhe, Kilchoan, T/F01972-510328. Apr-Oct. A beautiful 18th-century converted manse with great sea views and fine cooking. Full board also available. Dinner available for non-residents (TTT), but booking essential.

B Far View Cottage, Kilchoan, T01972-510357, www.ardamurchan.com/farview. Mar-Nov. Superior and friendly B&B with great views and excellent food (ΨΨ, also for non-residents, but booking is essential).

B Water's Edge, Kilchoan, T01972-510261, www.ardnamurchan.com/watersedge. As intimate and private as it gets, accommodation for 2 in an open-plan suite only yards from the water's edge. TV/video/CD and excellent home-cooking (bring your own wines). Price includes dinner. Non smoking.

B-F Glen Uig Inn, Glen Uig, by loch Ailort, T01687-470219, www.glenuig.com. 18th-century inn offering bunkhouse accommodation for £7 per person in adjoining chalet. Also has en suite accommodation for families or groups. Local fare served in the inn's restaurant and a good night's entertainment in the lively bar.

C Loch Shiel House Hotel, Acharacle, T01967-431224. 8 en suite rooms. Comfortable hotel and decent bar meals (ΨΨ-Ψ). Contact them for details of cruises on Loch Shiel.

D Kilchoan House Hotel, Kilchoan, T01972-510200, www.kilchoanhotel.co.uk. 7 en suite rooms. Comfortable option with views of Mull from most of the rooms. Also good meals served 1200-1400 and 1800-2030, in the bar (Ψ) and dining room (ΨΨ).

D Sonachan Hotel, a few miles beyond Kilchoan, on the road to Ardnamurchan Point, T/F01972-510211, www.sonachan.u-net.com. Open all year. The most westerly hotel on the UK mainland, close to the lighthouse and beaches and surrounded by 1000 acres of grounds with walking and fishing opportunities. Good food available and children welcome. Also has a 4-bedroom self-catering house and 2 rooms.

D-E Cala Darach, Glenmore by Glenborrodale, T01972-500204. Mar-Oct. 3 en suite rooms. Lovely country house with views across Loch Sunart.

D-E Salen Inn, Salen, T01972-431661, www.thesalen-ardnamurchan.co.uk. Open all year. Decent hotel accommodation and food (ΨΨ), cosy bar and information on local walks.

Self-catering and camping

Glenmore House and Cottage, Port An Aiseig, Glenborrodale, T01972-500263, www.michael-macgregor.co.uk. Luxury self-catering cottage and lodge on shores of Loch Sunart, facilities include whirlpool baths and sauna. Available all year, £275-775 per week.

Glenbay Cottages, Glenborrodale, T01972-500201, ll@nacyp.org.uk. 2 well-equipped self-catering cottages, with games room and boats for hire. £250-690 per week. Also available is a round tower for 2.

Resipole Farm Caravan Park, a mile or so east of Salen, Resipole, T01967-431235, www.resipole.co.uk. Self-catering chalets, caravan and tent pitches and caravans for rent, also a restaurant and bar on site.

Glenfinnan *p220*

A The Prince's House, main road, ½ mile past monument on the right, heading west, T01397-722246, www.glen finnan.co.uk. Mar-Nov. 9 en suite rooms. Comfortable old coaching inn which offers good food (ΨΨ).

B-C Glenfinnan House Hotel, off the main road, T/F01397-722235, www.glenfinnan house.com. Mar-Oct. 17 en suite rooms. Historic house with lots of charm and a variety of rooms, from standard doubles to family room and suites with jacuzzi, all very stylishly furnished and decorated. A la carte dinner (ΨΨΨ) or cheaper meals in bar. You can also walk in the vast grounds or fish on the loch. Great value. Recommended.

F Glenfinnan Sleeping Car, at the train station, T01397-722400. Bunkhouse accommodation for 10 people, also mountain bike hire. You can eat here, too, in the **Glenfinnan Dining Car** (ΨΨ-Ψ).

Arisaig and Morar *p220*

B Arisaig Hotel, Arisaig, T01687-450210, www.arisaighotel.co.uk. Open all year. 18th-century former coaching inn with 10 en suite rooms and good sea views. Meals (ΨΨ) served in the restaurant, 1200-1400 and 1800-2100, and bar (Ψ). Child-friendly, with separate playroom. Bike hire also available for £10/day.

B The Old Library Lodge, Arisaig, T01687-450651. Apr-Oct. 6 en suite rooms. Highly acclaimed restaurant (ΨΨΨ) with well-furnished rooms. The owner is like a Highland version of Basil Fawlty and very entertaining with it. Recommended.

Mallaig *p221*

C Marine Hotel, next to the train station, T01687-462217, www.marinehotel-mallaig.co.uk. Much nicer inside than it appears. The restaurant also serves the best food in town (ΨΨ).

D-E Glencairn House, East Bay, T01687-462412, www.glencairn-house.co.uk. Apr-Sep. 2 en suite rooms. Comfortable rooms with TV and DVD.

E-F Western Isles Guesthouse, follow the road round the harbour to East Bay, T/F01687-462320. Jan-Nov. Excellent-value guesthouse which serves dinner to guests.

F Sheena's Backapackers' Lodge, T01687-462764. The cheapest place to stay is this friendly, easy-going independent hostel, with dorm beds, double rooms and kitchen facilities.

Knoydart Peninsula *p221*

B Doune Stone Lodge, 3-4 miles up the peninsula's only road, standing in splendid isolation, T01687-462667, www.doune-marine.co.uk. 3 en suite rooms, all with bunk beds for 2 children. Minimum stay 3 nights. Price includes breakfast, packed lunch and dinner. The food is superb and cannot be praised highly enough. Guests are picked up by boat from Mallaig, where you can leave your car. The owners also run the nearby **Doune Bay Lodge**, with shared facilities, for parties of up to 14. Can be self-catered, fully catered, or somewhere in between. £40 per person for fully catered. Highly recommended.

C Pier House, Inverie, T01687-462347, www.thepierhouseknoydart. 4 rooms, 2 en suite, 2 with extra beds for children. Price includes dinner. Good, old-fashioned hospitality and wonderful local seafood (**ΨΨ**). Recommended.

F Knoydart Hostel, near Inverie House, T01687-462242. This is the only alternative hostel to **Torrie Shieling**. Much cheaper, but less appealing.

F Torrie Shieling, Inverie, T01687-462669. It's a bit more expensive than most other hostels, but is very comfortable, and popular with hikers. They also have their own transport for trips around the peninsula and will collect guests from Mallaig by arrangement.

Eating

Ardgour *p218*

ΨΨ Ariundel Centre, Strontian, T01967-402279, www.ariundle.co.uk. 0900-1730. Licensed tearoom/restaurant serving soups, salads and snacks. Also does candelit suppers during the summer; phone for details.

ΨΨ The Inn at Ardgour, Corran, T01855-841225, www.ardgour.biz. Family-run inn serving bar meals, full à la carte and take-away snacks. Dogs and children welcome.

Morvern *p218*

ΨΨ Lochaline Hotel, Lochaline, T01967-421657. Hotel serving decent bar meals.

ΨΨ Whitehouse, Lochaline, T01967-421777. Open for lunch and dinner till 2100 Mon-Sat. Local organic produce cooked well. We need more of this kind of place.

Ardnamurchan Peninsula and Moidart *p218*

All the hotels in Sleeping serve good food.

ΨΨ-Ψ Clanranald Hotel, at Mingarry, T01967-431202. Food is also available here.

Arisaig and Morar *p220*

Very good meals can be had at the Arisaig Hotel and Old Library Lodge and Restaurant, see Sleeping, above.

Ψ Rhu Café, Arisaig, next door to the Spar store, T01687-450707. Open daily 1000-1800. Snacks, soups, filled rolls and burgers, also takeaway, internet terminal £1/hr. Friendly and good with kids.

Mallaig *p221*

ΨΨ Cabin Seafood Restaurant, by the harbour, serves decent meals and a great value 'teatime special'.

Ψ Tea Room, below **Sheena's Backpackers** (see Sleeping, above). Decent meals and snacks at reasonable prices.

Andy Race, by the harbour, T01687-462626, www.andyrace.co.uk. If you're heading across to Skye you could buy some delicious peat-smoked salmon and eat it on the ferry with some brown bread. Alternatively, arrange to have some sent home. You won't be sorry.

Knoydart Peninsula *p221*

ΨΨ The Old Forge, Inverie, T01687-462267. The most remote pub on mainland Britain, where you can enjoy some tasty local seafood and a pint of real ale in front of an open fire. There's even the occasional impromptu ceilidh. Dress code is 'wellies, waterproofs and midge cream'.

Activities and tours

West of Fort William *p217*

Boat trips and wildlife cruises

Ardnamurchan Charters, T01972-500208, offers a 2-hr wildlife trip to the seal colonies – or further afield to Tobermory on Mull or Staffa and the Treshnish Islands.

Arisaig Marine, see Transport, below.

The Brightwater Experience, T07747-034767, www.seaotter.co.uk. This fast RIB (rigid inflatable boat) cruises to Eigg (£25, under 8s £20), Skye (£25/£20), Tobermory (£50/£40) and Eilean Donan (£25/£20) at breakneck speeds, slowing down to check out the local marine life.

Loch Shiel Cruises, T/F01687-470322, www.highlandcruises.co.uk, run a variety of cruises down Loch Shiel, from Glenfinnan to Acharacle. Sailings most days from Apr-Oct. Parking available at the **Glenfinnan House Hotel**, see Sleeping, page 222. Prices from £10 for a 2-hr cruise up to £13 for 3½ hrs.

MV Grimsay Isle, T01687-482652, www.lochaber.com/grimsayisle. Available for fishing charters and ferry service.

Outdoor activities

The Achnanellan Centre, cross from Dalilea Pier, T02967-431265, is an outdoor activities centre on the south shore of Loch Shiel at the foot of Beinn Resipol (2772 ft). They hire out mountain bikes, canoes, sail boats and camping equipment, as well as providing cheap, basic bunkhouse accommodation (**F**). It was from Dalilea Pier that Bonnie Prince Charlie left to sail up Loch Shiel to raise his standard at Glenfinnan, see page 222.

Swimming

Indoor pool in Mallaig, next to the school on Frank Brae, £2 per session.

Transport

Ardgour, Ardnamurchan and Morvern *p217*

Bus Shiel Buses, T01967-431272, run most of the bus services. There's a bus once a day on Tue, Thu and Sat from **Fort William** to **Lochaline** (2 hrs), via the **Corran Ferry**. There's a bus once a day (Mon-Sat) from **Fort William** to **Acharacle** (1½ hrs), via Lochailort. There's also a bus (Mon-Fri) to **Acharacle** from **Mallaig** (1½ hrs). There's a bus once a day (Mon-Sat) from **Fort William** to **Kilchoan** (2 hrs 25 mins), via **Strontian** (1 hr), **Salen** and **Glenborrodale**.

Car If you're travelling by car, access is via the A861, leaving the A830 before Glenfinnan or at Lochailort. You can also make the 5-min ferry crossing to Ardgour from the Corran Ferry, about 8 miles south of Fort William on the A82, see page 208.

Ferry For details of the ferry from Lochaline to Fishnish on Mull and from Kilchoan to Tobermory, see page 156.

Arisaig and Morar *p220*

Ferry Arisaig Marine, T01687-450224, www.arisaig.co.uk, sail from Arisaig pier to **Rùm**, **Eigg** and **Muck** daily Mon-Fri all year and also Sat-Sun Apr-Sep. The islands are visited on different days, though there is a boat to Eigg every day except Thu in summer. You can visit all 3 islands in a day, allowing between 2 and 5 hrs ashore. Fares range from £16 return to Eigg, £17 to Muck and £22 return to Rùm (children 2 and under free to all islands, 3-10 years £8, 11-16 years £11). See also page 298. These trips cater for the island's residents as much as tourists, so don't expect a running commentary, though hot and cold drinks are served on board.

Mallaig *p221*

Bus Shiel Buses, T01967-431272, run 2 buses daily Mon-Sat from **Mallaig** to **Fort William** (1½ hrs, £4.50) from Jul-Sep, and on Mon, Thu and Fri the rest of the year. **Oban Minibus Services**, T01852-314247, run a new direct service from **Oban** to Mallaig daily leaving Oban at 0945, arriving in Mallaig at 1215 for the 1300 sailing to **Skye** and returning at 1810, arriving in Oban at 2040; £15 single, £25 return, bikes £3/5. It's possible to get off and on at **Onich**, **Fort William** and **Glenfinnan** but book in advance.

Ferry CalMac, T01687-462403, ferries run throughout the year to **Armadale** on Skye (see page 274), to **Lochboisdale** and **Castlebay** (see page 329), and to the **Small Isles** (see page 293).

Train The best way to arrive in **Mallaig** is by train. There are several services daily (1 on Sun) to and from **Fort William**, with connections to **Glasgow**. There's also a steam train which runs in the summer months (see page 209).

Knoydart Peninsula *p221*
Ferry Bruce Watt Sea Cruises, T01687-462320, www.knoydart-ferry.co.uk, have trips to the remote village of **Inverie** (45 mins), on the Knoydart Peninsula, and **Tarbet** on Loch Nevis. They sail on Mon, Wed and Fri all year and Mon-Fri in summer (May-Sep), departing Mallaig at 1015 (to Inverie only) and returning to Mallaig at 1200 and also leaving at 1415 (to Inverie and Tarbet), and returning to Mallaig 1745. Though billed as a wildlife cruise, this is essentially a working ferry. Fares are £9 return and £14 for the afternoon sailing. There's also a ferry service from **Arnisdale**, on the north shore of Loch Hourn, to **Barrisdale**. To arrange a crossing, contact **Len Morrison**, Croftfoot, Arnisdale, T01599-522352. It's a small open boat which takes 5 passengers, and all sailings are subject to weather.

Great Glen to Kyle of Lochalsh

The A87 is one of the main Highland tourist routes, connecting the Great Glen with the west coast and the Isle of Skye. It runs west from Invergarry between Fort Augustus and Fort William, through Glen Moriston and Glen Shiel to Shiel Bridge, at the head of Loch Duich, and on to Kyle. At Shiel Bridge a road branches off to Glenelg, from where you can sail across to Skye. It's a beautiful journey and by far the best way to reach the island. ›› *For Sleeping, Eating and other listings, see pages 228-230.*

Glen Shiel → *Colour map 3, A5. OS Landranger No33.*

The journey from Invergarry to Shiel Bridge is worth it for the views alone. Glen Shiel is a sight to make the heart soar as high as the 3000-ft peaks that tower overhead on either side. This is one of the most popular hiking areas in Scotland, with the magnificent and much-photographed **Five Sisters of Kintail** on the north side of the glen, and the equally beautiful South Glen Shiel Ridge on the other.

There are several excellent hiking routes in Glen Shiel, but these mountains are to be treated with great respect. They require fitness, experience and proper equipment and planning. None of the routes should be attempted without a map, compass and detailed route instructions. You should be aware of the notoriously unpredictable weather conditions and also check locally about deer stalking. The season runs from August to October, but for more details contact the local stalkers (T01599-511282). A good trekking guide is the *SMC's Hill Walks in Northwest Scotland*.

The **Five Sisters Traverse** is a classic ridge route. It starts at the first fire break on the left as you head southeast down the glen from Shiel Bridge and finishes at Morvich, on the other side of the ridge. Allow a full day (eight to 10 hours). You can also hike from Morvich to **Glen Affric Youth Hostel** at Cannich. It's a strenuous 20-mile walk, but you can stop off midway at the remote **Allt Beithe Youth Hostel**. For details, see Glen Affric, page 187.

The magnificent **South Glen Shiel Ridge** is one of the world's great hikes. It starts from above the **Cluanie Inn**, see Sleeping, page 228. From here, follow the old public road to Tomdoun; it then meets up with a good stalking path which climbs to the summit of the first Munro, Creag a' Mhaim (3108 ft). The ridge then runs west for almost 9 miles and gives you the chance to pick off no fewer than seven Munros. Allow a full day for the walk (nine to 10 hours), and you'll need to set off early.

Glenelg and around → *Phone code: 01599. Colour map 3, A5.*

One of the most beautiful journeys in Scotland is the road from Shiel Bridge to the sublime little outpost that is Glenelg; a tiny village on the shores of the Sound of Sleat, only a short distance opposite Kylerhea on Skye (for transport details see page 230). The unclassified single-track road turns off the A87 and climbs steeply and dramatically through a series of sharp switchbacks to the top of the **Mam Ratagan Pass** (1115 ft). From here the view back across Loch Duich to the Five Sisters of Kintail is simply amazing, and the all-time classic calendar shot.

The road then drops down through Glen More to Glenelg, the main settlement on the peninsula, which lies on the old drovers' route that ran from Skye to the cattle markets in the south. This little-known corner of the Western Highlands is Gavin Maxwell country and was featured in *Ring of Bright Water*, his much-loved novel about otters. He disguised the identity of this beautiful, unspoiled stretch of coastline, calling it Camusfearna, and today it remains a quiet backwater.

You can see the famous otters at **Sandaig**, on the road running from Glenelg, where Gavin Maxwell lived. The site of his cottage is now marked with a cairn. As well as otters, you can see numerous seabirds, seals and porpoises in the Sound of Sleat, and around the peninsula you may be lucky enough to catch a glimpse of wildcats, pine martens, golden eagles and the recently reintroduced sea eagles. The village itself consists of a row of whitewashed cottages surrounded by trees and overlooked by the ruins of the 18th-century **Bernera Barracks**. Just before the village the road forks. The right turning leads to the Glenelg-Kylerhea ferry, which makes the 10-minute crossing to Skye, see page 230.

A road runs south from Glenelg to Arnisdale. About 1½ miles along this road, a branch left leads to the **Glenelg Brochs** – Dun Telve and Dun Dun Troddan – two of the best-preserved Iron Age buildings in the country. Dun Telve stands to a height of over 30 ft and the internal passages are almost intact. The road south from Glenelg continues past Sandaig Bay and runs along the north shore of unearthly Loch Hourn, with great views across the mountains of Knoydart. The road ends at the impossibly cute little fishing hamlet of **Arnsidale**, from where you can take a boat across the loch to Barrisdale on the Knoydart Peninsula. For details, see page 221. A bit further along the coast, the road ends at the even tinier hamlet of **Corran**.

Eilean Donan Castle → *Phone code: 01599. Colour map 3, A5.*

ⓘ T01599-555202, wwweileandonancastle.com, Apr-Oct 0900-1730, £4.95, concession £3.95, group rates £3.80.

Some 10 miles west of Shiel Bridge on the A87 is the little village of Dornie, home to the one of Scotland's most-photographed sights, the stunningly located Eilean Donan Castle. It stands on a tiny islet at the confluence of Loch Duich and Loch Alsh, joined to the shore by a narrow stone bridge and backed by high mountains. This great calendar favourite has also featured in several movies, including *Highlander*, which starred Sean Connery.

The original castle dates from 1230 when Alexander III had it built to protect the area from marauding Vikings. It was destroyed by King George in 1719 during its occupation by Spanish Jacobite forces sent to help the 'Old Pretender', James Stuart. It then lay in ruins, until one of the Macraes had it rebuilt between 1912 and 1932. Inside, the Banqueting Hall with its Pipers' Gallery is most impressive, and there's an exhibition of military regalia and interesting displays of the castle's history. The views from the battlements are also worthwhile.

Kyle of Lochalsh → *Phone code: 01599. Colour map 3, A5.*

Before the coming of the controversial Skye Bridge a mile to the north, see page 274, the little town of Kyle, as it is known, was the main ferry crossing to Skye and consequently a place which attracted a busy tourist trade. Now though, the tourist traffic bypasses Kyle, which is probably the most sensible thing to do as it's not the most attractive of places. There are a couple of banks with ATMs, two small supermarkets and a post office in the village. The **TIC** ⓘ *T01599-534276, Apr-late Oct,* is at the main seafront car park.

Plockton → *Phone code: 01599. Colour map 3, A5.*

If there were a poll taken of visitors' favourite Highland villages, then you can bet your sporran that Plockton would come top with most folk. If you look for a definition of picturesque in your dictionary, it'll say 'see Plockton'. Well, maybe not – but it should.

Plockton's neat little painted cottages are ranged around the curve of a wooded bay, with flowering gardens and palm trees. Yachts bob up and down in the harbour and there are views across the island-studded waters of Loch Carron to the hills beyond. Even on the telly Plockton's charms proved irresistible, and millions of viewers tuned in each week to watch the TV series *Hamish Macbeth*, which featured Robert Carlyle as the local bobby. Plockton's a popular place with artists who are drawn by the village's setting and the wonderful light. A good place to find some of their work, as well as other souvenirs, is **The Studio Craft Shop**, on the corner of the seafront and the road leading out of town.

There are lots of good walks around the village. One of the best ways to appreciate it is to head up to **Frithard Hill**, from where there are great views of the bay. Another good walk is along the beach, starting from the High School playing fields at the top of the village.

Sleeping

Glen Shiel *p226*

B-C Cluanie Inn, Glenmoriston, some 9 miles east of Shiel Bridge, T01320-340238, www.cluanieinn.com. Open all year. 10 en suite rooms. This is one of the Highlands' classic hotels. It's a firm favourite with hikers and climbers and it's easy to see why. After a hard day's ridge walking, what could be better than jumping into the jacuzzi, then having a hot dinner and a good pint beside a log fire. Recommended.

B-D Kintail Lodge Hotel, T01599-511275, www.kintaillodgehotel.co.uk. 12 rooms. Open all year. Small, cosy hotel beautifully located by theshores of Loch Duich, dinner also available. **Bunkhouse** attached with 12 beds. You can also camp nearby.

C-D Grants at Craigiellachie, Ratagan, T01599-511331, www.housebytheloch.co.uk. 2 en suite rooms. Open all year. About 1 mile along the road to Glenelg/Kylrerhea ferry is the turn-off to tiny Ratagan and this genuine hidden gem of a place. Hosts Tony and Liz Taylor have created a little haven of peace, comfort and fine cuisine. It's a restaurant with rooms and the rave reviews for the former (ΨΨΨ) are matched by the style and comfort – and superb views – of the latter. There's also cheaper bunkhouse accommodation for the hiking fraternity plus a family-friendly chalet for rent. Highly recommended.

D Glomach House, Aullt-Na-Chruinn, Glen Shiel, T01599-511222, www.glomach.co.uk. 3 en suite rooms. Open all year. Tidy and comfortable B&B on the shores of Loch Duich at Shiel Bridge.

F Ratagan Youth Hostel, T01599-511243, just outside Shiel Bridge. Open all year except Jan. One of the great hikers' hostels.

Camping

Morvich Caravan Club Site, 1½ miles past Shiel Bridge in driection of Kyle, T01599-511354. Open late Mar to late Oct. Large site with full facilities.

Shiel Shop and campsite, Shiel Bridge, T01599-511211. Recently upgraded and closer to pub and shops.

Glenelg and around *p227*

D Glenelg Inn, T01599-522273, www.glenelg-inn.com. Open all year. It's worth stopping in Glenelg, if you've got the time, to experience a night in this wonder-fully cosy place. Even if you can't spend the night, at least spend an hour or two enjoying the atmosphere, good ale and superb food, either in the dining room (ΨΨΨ) or the flagstone-floored bar (ŸŸ), and the peerless hospitality of owner, Chris Main, who may even take you for a spin in his RIB if you ask nicely. If you're really lucky, you may even chance upon an impromptu folk jam. Rooms are spacious and inviting. Warmly recommended.

E Mrs Chisholm, T01599-522287. Open all year. Cheaper B&B option in Glenelg village. Will cook dinner on request.

Eilean Donan Castle *p227*

There are several places to stay in the nearby village of Dornie.

B Conchra House Hotel, Ardelve, T01599-555233, www.conchrahouse.co.uk. 5 en suite rooms. Open all year. This historic 18th-century hunting lodge is peaceful, has lovely views and a reputation for good food. To get there, cross the bridge in Dornie and turn right for Killilan, a tiny hamlet at the head of Loch Long, the hotel is ¾ mile up this road.

C-D Loch Duich Hotel, across the bridge from **Dornie Hotel**, T01599-555213. 12 en suitw rooms. Open all year. Offers comfortable accommodation, meals and live music in the bar on a Sun evening.

D Dornie Hotel, Dornie, T01599-555205, www.dornie-hotel.co.uk. 8 en suite rooms. Open all year. A good option and serves very good food (ŸŸ).

E Caberfeidh House, Ardelve, by Dornie, T01599-555293, www.caberfeidh.plus.com. 6 rooms. Open all year. Friendly and comfortable guesthouse. Very good value.

F Silver Fir Bunkhouse, Carndubh, T01599-555264, 6-bed bunkhouse, and

F Tigh Iseabeal, near **Cochra House Hotel**, at Camasluinie, T01599-588205, a 6-bed independent hostel.

Kyle of Lochalsh *p227*

It's a good idea to get the TIC to book a room for you, as there's not much choice in Kyle.

B Kyle Hotel, Main St, T01599-534204, www.kylehotel.co.uk. 31 en suite rooms. Open all year. The more luxurious of the of couple of hotels here. Great views across to Skye and good food.

D Old Schoolhouse, Erbusaig, a mile north of Kyle, off the road to Plockton (look for signs on right heading north), T01599-534369, www.oldschoolhouse87.co.uk. 3 en suite rooms. Open all year. A very comfortable option offering dinner for guests (24 hrs notice required).

D Tingle Creek Hotel, Erbusaig, T01599-534430. Open all year. Small hotel with a big friendly welcome. Lovely setting and great views. Good food in restaurant and guests can enjoy a drink in the **Galleon** bar before dinner.

F Cuchulainn's, Station Rd, T01599-534492. Cheap hostel accommodation.

Camping

Reraig Caravan Site, T01599-566215, 4 miles east of Kyle, at Balmacara.

Plockton *p228*

B The Haven Hotel, Innes St, T01599- 544223, www.havenhotel plockton.co.uk. 15 en suite rooms. Open all year. Under new management and the jury's still out; rooms were in need of upgarding at time of writing. Still serves very good food in the restaurant (ŸŸŸ).

C Plockton Gallery @ the Manse, Innes St, T01599-544442. 2 en suite rooms. Open all year. Part gallery, part guesthouse, this place offers something different. A bit more expensive than the average but worth it for the quality and service. Veggie options available with a bit of notice, disabled access and parking. Recommended.

C Plockton Inn, Innes St, T01599-544222, www.plocktoninn.co.uk. 14 rooms. Open all year. Recently refurbished small hotel with 7 bedrooms added in annexe across the road. Very good seafood in restaurant or in lively bar where you can also hear live folk music twice a week.

D Plockton Hotel, T01599-544274, www.plocktonhotel.co.uk. 11 en suite rooms. Open all year. Comfortable and tastefully furnished rooms above a perenially busy wee bar. All have views across the bay. There are quite a few places along the waterfront and this may be the best. Restaurant serves superb local produce (ŸŸŸ-ŸŸ) and there's also a great little beer garden at the front where you can sit and enjoy a drink on a balmy summer evening. Highly recommended.

D-E Heron's Flight, Cooper St, T01599-544220, www.heronsflight.org. 3 rooms. Open all year. Friendly and welcoming B&B run by Ann Mackenzie and her dog, Yarrow. Veggie and continental options for breakfast, no cards accepted. Recommended.

E Craig Highland Farm, on the road to Achmore, T01599-544205. Farm offering B&B accommodation and self-catering cottages. The farm is also a conservation centre, where you can see and feed rare and ancient breeds of domestic animals.
E Shieling, Harbour St, T01599-544282. At the far end of the harbour. There are lots of B&Bs to choose from on the seafront and this is one of the nicest.
F Nessun Dorma, Burnside, T01599-544235. Bunkhouse a few miles out of Plockton at the old railway station, run by Mick and Gill Coe. Cheapest option. Packed lunches available on request.

Eating

Eilean Donan Castle *p227*

Aside from the hotels listed above, there are a couple of places in Dornie serving decent food, best of which is probably the **Clachan Pub** where you can enjoy a good-value 3-course evening meal (ƚƚ).

Kyle of Lochalsh *p227*

ƚƚƚ-ƚƚ The Seafood Restaurant, at the railway station, T01599-534813, has a good reputation for seafood. Open Easter-Oct 1000-1500 and 1830-2100.
ƚƚƚ-ƚƚ Seagreen Restaurant & Bookshop, T01599-534388. Just outside the village, on the road to Plockton is this bistro-cum-bookshop and gallery serving wholefood and local seafood throughout the day.

Plockton *p228*

ƚƚ Off the Rails, at the railway station, T01599-544423. Open from 0830 for breakfast, snacks, lunch and evening meals. Apart from the hotels listed above, this is the best place to eat in Plockton.

Activities and tours

Kyle of Lochalsh *p227*

Boat trips There are a couple of interesting boat trips from Kyle. One is on board the *Seaprobe Atlantis*, which is fitted with underwater windows. Check sailing times at the pier. If you prefer, you could take a seafood cruise – a 2½-hr wildlife-spotting and seafood-eating boat trip. Contact **Neil MacRae**, T01599-577230.

Plockton *p228*

Boat trips Leisure Marine, T01599-544306, runs 1-hr seal- and otter-watching cruises in the summer.They also hire boats.
Sea Trek Marine, T01599-544346. Similar trips are run by this outfit.

Transport

Glen Shiel *p226*

Bus Citylink buses between **Fort William**, **Inverness** and **Skye** pass through Glen Shiel several times daily in each direction. There's a **postbus** service between **Kyle** and **Glenelg** (see below) and **Highland Country Buses** run from Ratagan Youth Hostel to **Kyle** (30 mins) and on to **Plockton** (50 mins), on schooldays only, departing at 0755 and returning at 1640.

Glenelg and around *p227*

Bus There's a **postbus** service from **Kyle of Lochalsh** to **Arnisdale** and **Corran** via Glenelg at 0945 Mon-Sat. It takes 3¾ hrs. The return bus from **Corran** departs at 0725. The Glenelg-Kylerhea ferry provides the most scenic connection to Skye. 10-min crossing Oct to mid-May Mon-Sat 0900-1800; mid-May to end-Aug Mon-Sat 0900-2000, Sun 1000-1800; end-Aug to end-Oct Mon-Sat 0900-1800, Sun 1000-1800. Per car with up to 4 passengers, £6; day return £10, T01599-511302.

Eilean Donan Castle *p227*

Citylink buses between **Fort William** and **Inverness** and **Skye** stop by the castle.

Kyle of Lochalsh *p227*

Bus Scottish **Citylink** buses, T0990-505050, run to Kyle from **Inverness** (3 daily, 2 hrs); **Glasgow** via **Fort William** (4 daily, 5 hrs); and **Edinburgh** via **Fort William** (1 daily, 6½ hrs). These buses continue to **Portree** (1 hr) and **Uig** (1½ hrs), for ferries to **Tarbert** on Harris and Lochmaddy on North Uist. There's also a regular shuttle service across the bridge to **Kyleakin** (every 30 mins).

Train The train journey from **Inverness** to Kyle, though not as spectacular as the West Highland line, is very scenic. It runs 3-4 times Mon-Sat (2½ hrs) and once or twice on Sun from May to Sep. There's also an observation car and dining car in the summer.

Wester Ross

From Loch Carron north to Ullapool, is the region of Wester Ross, an area of dramatic mountain massifs, fjord-like sea lochs and remote coastal villages. Here lies some of Europe's most spectacular scenery, from the isolated peninsula of Applecross to Tolkien-esque peaks of Torridon, which offer some of Scotland's best climbing and hillwalking. There are also gentler attractions such as the vast, sprawling gardens at Inverewe and the beguiling pink sands of Gruinard Bay. » *For Sleeping, Eating and other listings, see pages 236-240.*

Loch Carron and around » *pp236-240.*

Along Loch Carron

East of Plockton, just before the road meets the A890 at **Achmore** is the **West Highland Dairy**, where you can pick up some good local cheese for a picnic – weather permitting of course. The road passes the turn-off for Stromeferry and continues along the east shore of Loch Carron to **Strathcarron** at its northeastern end, on the Inverness to Kyle of Lochalsh rail line.

Lochcarron village → *Phone code: 01520. Colour map 1, C4. Population: 870.*

Lochcarron village consists of little more than a main street along the shore of the loch, but it has more facilities and services than most other places in these parts. Here you should take the opportunity to withdraw cash at the Bank of Scotland ATM, fill up with petrol and buy some supplies at the small self-service store. The **TIC** ⓘ *T01520-722357, Apr-Oct*, has details of some excellent walks in the surrounding hills.

Two miles south of the village on the road to the 15th-century ruins of **Strome Castle** is **Lochcarron Weavers**, where you can see tartan being made and also buy from a vast range of woven goods.

Loch Kishorn to Applecross → *Colour map 1, C4.*

There are many scenic routes in the Highlands but the road from Kishorn, west of Lochcarron to Applecross beats them all. The **Bealach na Ba** ('Pass of the Cattle') is the highest road in Scotland and is often closed during the winter snows. It climbs relentlessly and dramatically through a series of tortuous switchbacks – both spectacular and terrifying in equal measure. The high plateau, at 2053 ft, is cold and desolate, but from here you have the most amazing views: from Ardnamurchan Peninsula to Loch Torridon, taking in Eigg, Rùm, the Cuillins of Skye, the Old Man of Storr and the Quirang.

The narrow, single-track road then begins its gradual descent to the isolated little village of **Applecross**, site of one Scotland's first Christian monasteries, founded in AD 673. The village consists of a row of whitewashed fishermen's cottages looking across to the island of Raasay and backed by wooded slopes. It's a beautifully tranquil place where you can explore beaches and rock pools or enjoy a stroll along sylvan lanes – and then of course there's the very wonderful **Applecross Inn**, see Sleeping, page 237.

Torridon and around » *pp236-240.* *Colour map 1, C4.*

→ *Phone code: 01445.*

Torridon is perhaps the most striking skyline in the Scottish Highlands. The multi-peaked mountains of **Beinn Alligin**, **Liathach** (pronounced *Lee-ahakh*) and

 Beinn Eighe (*Ben-eay*) form a massive fortress of turrets, spires and pinnacles that provides an awesome backdrop to Loch Torridon, as well as the most exhilarating walking and climbing on the Scottish mainland. The straggly little village of Torridon makes the ideal base from which to tackle these mountains.

Ins and outs

Torridon may offer some of the best walking on the Scottish mainland but it also presents some of the most serious challenges. You need to be fit, experienced and well prepared and also be aware of the notoriously unpredictable weather. You should have a compass and the relevant map. OS Outdoor Leisure series No 8 covers the area. For recommended mountain guides, see page 240.

Around Loch Torridon

The coast road from Applecross meets the A896 from Lochcarron at the lovely little village of **Shieldaig** on the southern shore of Loch Torridon. There's a shop, a post office, a campsite and a couple of B&Bs. Several miles east, a side road turns off the A896 by **Torridon village** and winds its way along the northern shore of the loch, then climbs through dramatic scenery before dropping to the beautiful little village of **Diabaig** (pronounced *Jee-a-beg*), 10 miles from Torridon village. It's a worthwhile side trip, as the views across to the Applecross peninsula and Raasay are fantastic. There's also a great 7-mile coastal walk from Diabaig to Redpoint (see below).

Much of the Torridon massif is in the care of the National Trust for Scotland, and just before Torridon village is the **NTS countryside centre** ⓘ *T01445-791221*, where you can get information and advice on walks in the area, as well as books and maps. About 400 yards past the centre is the **Deer Museum**, which has a small display describing the management of red deer in the Highlands as well as some live specimens outside.

▲ Beinn Alligin

Beinn Alligin (3232 ft) is the most westerly of the Torridon peaks and probably the least demanding. The **Allt a'Bhealaich Walk** is a steep but short walk of about two hours. It starts from the car park just beyond the stone bridge that crosses the Abhainn Coire Mhic Nobuil. Follow the path that runs beside the river gorge until you reach the first bridge, cross it and follow the east bank of the Allt a' Bhealaich burn. Higher up, cross the second bridge and continue to follow the track up to the 380-m contour line, then turn back retracing your steps. This walk doesn't include the ascent of the peak but the views are magnificent. Those who wish to climb the three **Horns of Beinn Alligin** can continue from the 380-m contour line above the second bridge. The track that follows their ridge is exposed and requires rock scrambling experience.

▲ Liathach

Seven-peaked Liathach (3460 ft) stretches over 5 miles, and the magnificent ridge walk is considered by many to be the most impressive in Britain. This walk requires a high level of stamina and will take at least seven to eight hours. It also helps if you have a car waiting at the end.

A good place to start this long and strenuous challenge is about half a mile or so east of Glen Cottage, which is just over 2 miles east of the Countryside Centre. A steep climb takes you to a point just west of **Stuc a'Choire Dhuibh Bhig** (3000 ft). Then retrace your route to climb the twin tops of **Bidein Toll a'Mhuic** (3200 ft), linked by a narrow ridge. The path from here descends to the head of a deep ravine and keeps to the crest of the ridge around the rim of **Coireag Dubh Beag** which plunges steeply to the north. The ridge then rises across a field of huge and unstable boulders to the highest peak – **Spidean a'Choire Leith**. The view from this point is stunning, with Coire na Caime before you, surrounded by 2000-ft sheer cliffs. From here, the path follows a narrow exposed ridge for over a mile towards **Mullach an Rathain** (3358 ft).

Unless you are an experienced scrambler with a good head for heights, the best way from here is to take the path to the south, below the sharp pinnacles. Beyond the pinnacles the climb to Mullach an Rathain is straightforward. The track from here to **Sgorr a'Chadail** is a long but fairly easy walk and ends on the path in Coire Mhic Nobuil, see Beinn Alligin, above.

Coire Walk

A less difficult walk, but still requiring a fair degree of fitness and taking most of the day, is the Coire Walk. It follows the River Coire Mhic Nobuil to its watershed and down again by the **Allt a'Choire Dhuibh Mhoir** to the main road in Glen Torridon. Again, two cars will shorten the distance considerably.

The walk starts at the same point as the Beinn Alligin walk (see above). It follows the path up to the first bridge then branches east and continues on the path that runs north of the river, all the way to its source in the pass between Liathach and Beinn Dearg. Here the ground is boggy between the string of pools and lochans and the path is less distinct, but it becomes clear again in the upper reaches of the Coire Dubh Mor, a huge gully that separates Liathach from Beinn Eighe. A little further on, the track joins a stalkers' path which curves round Sail Mhor to the famous **Coire Mhic Fhearchair**, considered to be the most spectacular corrie in Scotland (see Beinn Eighe, below). The Coire path leads to a ford, which is crossed by stepping stones, then descends following the west side of the burn down to the car park on the Torridon road, from where it's about 4½ miles to Torridon village.

Diabaig to Red Point Walk → *OS Landranger No 19.*

An excellent low-level coastal walk is from Diabaig to Red Point. It is far less strenuous or daunting than the others described above and there is a clear path. It starts at the wooden gate to the right of the post office in Diabaig and ends at Red Point Farm, 7 miles away.

After 4 miles the coastal path reaches the derelict croft houses in the Craig Valley. One of these has been converted into a **SYHA Hostel**. There are two possible routes from here. You can follow the footpath above the coastline, or leave the footpath after crossing the wooden bridge over the Craig river and climb through an area of woodland. Take a reference from your OS map and you'll reach the highest point, **Meall na h-Uamha**, from where there are superb views. You can then descend to rejoin the coastal path and continue till you reach the glorious golden sands of Red Point, with wonderful views across to Skye and Raasay. Keep to the path through the farm till you reach the car park. Unless you've arranged your own transport here, you'll have to walk back the way you came, or catch the schoolbus to Gairloch, see page 240.

Beinn Eighe National Nature Reserve

While most of the Torridon massif is managed by the National Trust of Scotland, Beinn Eighe (which means 'File Peak' in Gaelic) is under the control of Scottish Natural Heritage. It is Britain's oldest National Nature Reserve, set up in 1951 to protect the ancient Caledonian pine forest west of Kinlochewe. It has since been designated an International Biosphere Reserve and extended to cover 30 square miles. The reserve is the home of a great variety of rare Highland wildlife, including pine martens, wildcats, buzzards, Scottish crossbills and golden eagles. There's also a wide range of flora which can best be appreciated on the excellent mountain trail described below which climbs from the ancient pine woods through alpine vegetation to the tundra-like upper slopes.

About half a mile northwest of Kinlochewe on the A832, is the Beinn Eighe Visitor Centre, which has information on the flora and fauna in the reserve and sells pamphlets on the trails described below.

Beinn Eighe (3309 ft) has nine peaks and is the largest of the Torridon Mountains. To traverse its ridge is a mighty undertaking and can take two days. A much shorter and easier walk around the base of the mountain is described here. The mountain and woodland trails both start and end in the car park at the side of Loch Maree, about 2 miles beyond the visitor centre. The woodland trail heads west along the lochside then crosses the road and climbs for about a mile up to the Conservation cabin before descending back to the starting point. It should take about an hour and is easy to follow, though quite steep in parts, and you'll need a good pair of walking boots. The mountain trail is 4 miles long and rough and steep in parts. You should be well equipped with good walking boots, waterproofs, food and warm clothing. It should take three to four hours. The route is well marked with cairns and you should not stray from the path. The trail heads south from the car park and begins a gentle ascent through woodland to a boggy area and then begins to zigzag up a very steep and rugged section, climbing to over 1000 ft in less than half a mile. This is the steepest section of the trail, but the views back across Loch Maree to Slioch are fabulous. The summit of the mountain trail is **Conservation cairn** (1800 ft) from where you can see the tops of 31 Munros on a clear day and enjoy a close-up view of the impressive Beinn Eighe ridge a few miles to the south. The trail now begins to descend as it heads northwest towards **An t-Allt** (1000 ft), turns northwards down to a small enclosure, then heads east to the deep Allt na h-Airidhe gorge. From here the trail continues down to the treeline and runs through woodland to join up with the top of the Woodland Trail. Follow the path to the right to get back to the car park.

Kinlochewe and Loch Maree → *Phone code: 01445. Colour map 1, C5.*

On the north side of the Torridon Mountains is the sprawling village of Kinlochewe, at the southeastern end of beautiful Loch Maree. It's a good base for walking in and around Loch Maree, and has a post office, shop and garage. The loch is dotted with islands and bordered by the mass of Slioch (3215 ft) to the north and ancient Caledonian pine forest to the south. Running along its northern shore, from **Slioch** almost as far as **Poolewe**, is the remote **Letterewe Estate**, one of Scotland's great deer forests. The A832 skirts the south shore of the loch, running northwest from Kinlochewe, and passes the **Victoria Falls**, a mile or so beyond Talladale. The falls commemorate Queen Victoria's visit in 1877. To find them, look for the Hydro Power signs.

Gairloch and around » *pp236-240. Colour map 1, C4.*

→ *Phone code: 01445.*

Gairloch consists of a string of tiny crofting townships scattered around the northeastern shore of the loch of the same name. It's a beautiful place, attracting a large number of visitors who come for the many sandy beaches, excellent walks, golf and fishing, and the chance of seeing seals, porpoises, dolphins and whales in the surrounding waters.

Ins and outs

Getting there and around There are buses to and from Inverness three times a week, also buses to Kinlochewe and a local postbus service. A passenger ferry service now operates from Gairloch to Portree on Skye. » *For further details, see Transport page 240.*

Tourist information **TIC** ⓘ *T01445-712130, year round, Apr-Oct daily,* at the car park in Auchtercairn, where the road branches to Strath. They book accommodation and sell books and maps. There are shops and takeaways in Strath and Auchtercairn, a petrol station in Auchtercairn, and a bank near the harbour at Charleston.

Gairloch Heritage Museum

ⓘ *T01445-712287, Apr-Sep Mon-Sat 1000-1700, Oct 1000-1330, £2.50, concession £2, children £0.50.*

If you are interested in local history, or the weather is bad – not unknown – then this museum may entertain for a hour or so. Included are archaeological finds, a mock-up of a crofthouse room, schoolroom and shop, the interior of the local lighthouse and an archive of old photographs. It is found beside the tourist office on the A832 to Poolewe, a few yards beyond the turn-off to Strath.

Big Sand, Melvaig and Midtown

The beach by the golf course at Gairloch is nice, but the beach at Big Sand, a few miles northwest of Strath, is better, and quieter. Further north is Melvaig, from where you can walk to **Rubha Reidh Lighthouse**, see Sleeping, page 236. Around the headland from the lighthouse is the beautiful, secluded beach at **Camas Mor**. This is a good place for spotting sea birds, and there's a great walk from here on a marked footpath to Midtown, 4 miles northwest of Poolewe. You'll have to walk or hitch from here as there's no public transport to Poolewe.

The waters around Gairloch are home to a wide variety of **marine mammals** such as seals, otters, porpoises, dolphins, minke whales and even killer whales. For details of wildlife cruises, see page 240.

Destitution Road

Many of the roads in the area were built during the Potato Famine of 1840 in order to give men work, with funds supplied by Dowager Lady Mackenzie of Gairloch. These became know as the 'Destitution Roads', and one of these is the narrow B8056 which runs west for 9 miles to Red Point from the junction 3 miles south of Gairloch, at Kerrysdale. This is a lovely little side trip and well worth it, especially on a clear evening to enjoy the magnificent sunsets at **Red Point beach**. The beach itself is extremely seductive, backed by steep dunes and looking across to the Trotternish Peninsula on Skye. So romantic is this spot that some people (naming no names) have been known to plight their troth here. Red Point is also the start or finish point for the excellent coastal walk to or from Diabaig, see page 233. On the road to Red Point is the picturesque little hamlet of **Badachro**, tucked away in a wooded, sheltered bay with fishing boats moored in its natural harbour. It's worth stopping off here on the way back from Red Point for a wee dram at the **Badachro Inn**.

There are many other good walks in the area, including to **Flowerdale Falls**, the **Fairy Lochs** and the **USAAF Liberator**. The TIC has a selection of walking guides and OS maps.

Poolewe → *Phone code: 01445. Colour map 1, B4.*

Five miles east of Gairloch on the other side of the peninsula is the neat little village of Poolewe, straddling the mouth of the River Ewe, where it cascades into sheltered Loch Ewe. There are some good walks around Poolewe, including the one around Loch Kernsary described below. There's also a nice little drive up the side road running along the west shore of Loch Ewe to Cove. You can walk from Midtown, midway along the road, to Rubha Reidh, north of Gairloch (see above).

Loch Kernsary → *OS Landranger Map No 19.*

This straightforward but rewarding walk covers 6 miles and should take around 2½ to three hours. The track is very boggy underfoot in places, especially after rain, so you'll need good boots.

Start in Poolewe, from the car park by the school near the bridge over the Ewe. Head up the single-track road with the river on your right. Go through the gate, then the track heads away from the river and up into woodland. At the Letterewe Estate gate cross the stile and continue to the next fork. Turn left here to Kernsary Estate, with views of Loch Maree and Beinn Eighe to the south. Follow the track to the next gate, go through and cross the wooden bridge. Continue along the track and you'll see Loch Kernsary on your left. At the next fork, turn left over the bridge and pass Kernsary Cottage on the right. Beyond the cottage, go through the gate and immediately head left down towards the burn, where the ground may be boggy. There's no path here, but cross the wooden footbridge and continue straight on, past the piles of stones on your left. Cross the stile, and the path follows the length of Loch Kernsary. At the head of the loch, the path climbs to give you views down to Poolewe. Follow the path down till it eventually takes you to the main road. Turn left and follow the road back to the car park.

Inverewe Garden

ⓘ *T01445-781200. Garden Jan-Mar daily 0930-1600, Apr-Oct 0930-2100; free guided garden walks mid-May to early Sep Mon-Fri at 1330; visitor centre and shop Apr-Sep daily 0930-1700, Oct 0930-1600. £8, concession £5, family £20.*

The reason most people come this way is to visit Inverewe Garden where you'll find an astonishing collection of exotic subtropical plants growing on the same latitude as Siberia, thanks to the mild climate created by the North Atlantic Drift. This wonderful 50-acre oasis of colour is a mecca for garden lovers, but even those who flinch at the mere sight of a lawn-mower will be bowled over by the sheer scale and diversity of plants and flowers on view. The garden was created from a treeless wilderness by Osgood Mackenzie, starting in 1862. By the time of his death in 1922 he had produced an internationally renowned walled and woodland garden. His work was continued by his daughter, who then gave the garden to the National Trust for Scotland in 1952. Since then, the plant collection has diversified even more and an intricate maze of paths leads you through ever-changing displays of Himalayan rhododendrons, Tasmanian eucalyptus, many Chilean and South African species, together with a large collection of New Zealand plants.

The garden is well worth visiting in any weather and at any time of the year, but especially from the end of April through the summer when the rhododendrons are in bloom. You should allow at least a couple of hours to do it justice. The garden is about a mile north of Poolewe on the main A832. There's a visitor centre and gift shop and a good restaurant, which serves snacks and hot meals.

Gruinard Bay → *Phone code: 01445. Colour map 1, B5.*

North of Poolewe the A832 passes Aultbea on its way to Laide, where it then skirts the shores of Gruinard Bay, with its lovely coves of pink sand. From Laide Post Office a side road branches north to **Mellon Udrigle** and **Opinan**, both with great beaches. Between Laide and Mellon Udrigle, at **Achgarve**, a road branches left for about mile. From the end of this road you can walk all the way to **Slaggan**, a ruined village on the other side of the peninsula. It's a nice spot for a picnic but don't be tempted to swim in the sea as the tidal race makes it dangerous.

Gruinard Bay is a very beautiful part of the northwest coast but will always be synonymous with **Gruinard Island**, standing ominously in the middle of the bay. The island was used as a testing ground for biological warfare during the Second World War and was contaminated with anthrax spores. The Ministry of Defence finally agreed to decontaminate it in 1990 and it has now been declared 'safe'.

Sleeping

Loch Carron and around *p231*

There's a wide range of accommodation and several places to eat.

C Shore House, Ardarroch, Kishorn, a few miles west of Lochcarron on the A896, T01520-733333, www.shorehouse.co.uk.

3 rooms. Comfortable with traditional Celtic character and superb food also on offer. Best of the bunch.

C-D Applecross Inn, Applecross, T01520-744262. 7 rooms. Open all year. There are, sadly, too few authentic Highland hostelries where you could quite happily while away a few hours, or even days, but if you have to be holed up somewhere to escape the rotten weather, then this place is as good as any and better than most. The welcome is warm, the atmosphere is friendly and the seafood is so fresh you can almost see it swimming past as you order (try the local prawns for £6.95 or the sublime haddock and chips for £7.95). Bar food served 1200-2100, children welcome till 2030, ceilidhs on Fri evening. Sit outside in the beer garden on a summer's eve. The rooms upstairs have recently been refurbished to a high standard and all have sea views. No smoking throughout. Excellent value and highly recommended.

D Rockvilla Hotel, Main St, Lochcarron, T01520-722379, www.rockvilla-hotel.co.uk. 4 rooms. Open all year. Small, family-run hotel offering very good food (🍴🍴).

D-E Clisham Guest House, Main St, Lochcarron, T01520-722995, www.clishamguesthouse.co.uk. 3 en suite rooms. Open all year. Friendly and comfortable accommodation, tea room out front serves home-baked cakes and scones. Also self-catering chalet for rent.

D-E Little Hill of my Heart, Applecross, T01520-744432. 3 rooms. Open all year. Lovely wee B&B overlooking Camursterrach Bay. Rooms tastefully furnished and breakfasts are a bit out of the ordinary with kedgeree, smoked haddock and salmon fishcakes alongside more familiar staples.

D-E The Old Manse, Lochcarron, on the outskirts of the village, T01520-722208, www.theoldmanselochcarron.com. 5 en suite rooms. Open all year. This recently refurbished vicarage offers comfortable B&B accommodation.

Self-catering

Jam Factory, 15 mins' walk from Applecross village, contact **Cottages and Castles**, T01463-226990, www.cottages-and-castles.co.uk. This 18th-century building once used for jam making is an excellent option. It sleeps 2 and costs from £220-380 per week.

Camping

Applecross Campsite, 1 mile from the village, T01520-744268. Open Mar-Oct. Decent facilities, upgraded in 2006. Family friendly and lots to do, with its own café on site (see **Flower Tunnel** under Eating, below).

Torridon and around *p231*

L Loch Torridon Hotel, 1 mile south of the turn-off to Torridon village, T01445-791242, www.lochtorridonhotel.com. 19 en suite rooms. Open all year. This fairytale Gothic pile sits on the lochside surrounded by mountains and offers the ultimate in style and comfort. Rooms are sumptuous, with enormous beds and romantic bathrooms. Breakfast is positively Olympian in proportion and the restaurant is one of the finest in the area (🍴🍴🍴). The views cap it all, though.

A The Old Mill Highland Lodge, on Loch Maree at Talladale, halfway between Kinlochewe and Gairloch, T01445-760271, www.theoldmillhighlandlodge.co.uk. 6 rooms. Open Mar-Oct. The best accommodation around here, this converted mill is set in its own gardens. It's friendly and comfortable, offers great food (price includes dinner), seclusion and great views.

B Loch Maree Hotel, on Loch Maree, T01445-760288, www.lochmareehotel.co.uk. This beautifully located hotel is being returned to its former glory. Queen Victoria was here! It also offers superb cuisine (**A** including dinner).

B Tigh-an-Eilean Hotel, Shieldaig, Loch Torridon, T01520-755251. 11 rooms. End Mar-Nov. Great wee hotel overlooking loch, so views are wonderful. Good food in restaurant or bar and also occasional impromptu busrts of folk music. Recommended.

C-D Ben Damph Lodge, by Achnasheen, T01445-791242, www.bendamph.lochtorridonhotel.com. 12 en suite rooms. Open Mar-Oct. Set in the grounds of the more palatial **Loch Torridon Hotel** (see above), this may look downmarket by comparison but offers very good value, motel-style accommodation. Up to 6 in some rooms for a small supplement. Bar meals all day.

D Ferroch, Achnasheen, T01445-791451. 3 en suite rooms. Open all year. Superior B&B in former crofthouse in beautiful location. (**B** including dinner).

D Hillhaven B&B, Hillhaven, Kinlochewe, T01445-760204, www.kinlochewe.info. 3 en suite rooms. Open all year. Good-value B&B catering for walkers and cyclists.

D Kinlochewe Hotel, T01445-760253, www.kinlochewehotel.co.uk. 9 rooms. Open all year. Offers B&B as well as cheaper bunkhouse beds and cheap bar meals.

D-E The Shieling, Laide, by Achnasheen, T01445-731487, www.theshielingholidays.com. 2 en suite rooms. Open Jan-Nov. Very comfortable B&B in modern bungalow.

F SYHA hostels, T01445-791284. There are 2 of these. One is in Torridon village, open 29 Jan-31 Oct, with an adjacent campsite. The other is much smaller and more basic, 4 miles north of Diabaig on the trail to Redpoint, at the disused crofting township of Craig (no phone; open 14 May-3 Oct).

Camping

There is a basic campsite at **Taangan Farm**, at the head of Loch Maree.

Gairloch and around *p234*

There are numerous B&Bs scattered throughout the area. Most of the owners will provide maps and information on local walks.

L Pool House Hotel, Poolewe, T01445-781272, www.poolhousehotel.com. 7 en suite rooms. Open all year. On the Cove road by the lochside, this former home of Osgood Mackenzie (who designed the nearby gardens) has been transformed into one of the very best hotels in the country (witness the numerous awards and accolades on their website). A stay here does not come cheap but if you've got the money then look no further, for there is, quite simply, no better place to stay in this category. The dishes created by chef John Moir on the **North by Northwest** dining room are worthy of such luxurious surroundings (ΨΨΨ). Very highly recommended.

B-C Myrtle Bank Hotel, Gairloch, T01445-712004, MyrtleBank@email.msn.com. 12 rooms. Modern hotel in the centre of Gairloch overlooking the loch, very good food and service in the restaurant (ΨΨΨ-ΨΨ).

C The Creel Restaurant & Charleston House, Gairloch, T01445-712497, www.charlestonhouse .co.uk. 4 en suite rooms. Open Mar-Dec. Guesthouse/ restaurant with a reputation for high-quality food (ΨΨ), especially the local seafood. Also delicious home-made bread and ice cream. No smoking (**A-B** including dinner).

C The Old Inn, Gairloch, T01445-712006, www.theoldinn.co.uk. 14 rooms. Open all year. This venerable old pub/restaurant with rooms is constantly winning awards for its fine ales and superb seafood (ΨΨ). Located by the harbour, it makes an excellent base for exploring the area and staying here gives the advantage of not having to move far after enjoying the best pint of real ale for miles around. Recommended for those who don't turn in too early.

C-D Old Smiddy Guest House, in Laide, near Gruinard Bay, T01445-731425, www.old smiddy.co.uk. 3 rooms. Mar-Oct. Superior guesthouse in great location, lavish breakfasts and its excellent restaurant (ΨΨΨ for 4-course diiner) is open to non-residents, but it's best to book well in advance (and BYOB). Highly recommended.

C-D Rubha Reidh Lighthouse, 3 miles north of Gairloch, at the end of the road, T/F01445-771263, ruareidh@netcomuk.co.uk. Open all year. This comfortable B&B and hostel has 5 double, twin or family rooms (4 are en suite) and 2 4-6 bed dorms (**F** per person). Rooms are fairly plain but it's the wonderful setting you're paying for, and the history (it was built in 1910 by RL Stevenson's cousin). Breakfast is £5.50 extra and dinner is £13.50. It's essential to book well ahead in the high season. They also have a tearoom serving home-baking, snacks and light lunches, open Easter-Oct on Sun, Tue and Thu 1100-1700. The whole lighthouse can also be rented on a self-catering basis for parties of 20+ (£993 for 3 nights in high season). To get here without your own transport take a bus from Gairloch as far as Melvaig (see below), then it's a 3-mile hike along the road.

D Dry Island, Badachro, T01445-741263. Open all year. 1 en suite room. Here's a chance to stay in a B&B on a private island, accessed from the mainland by a floating bridge or on foot at low tide. Beautiful surroundings and all the peace and tranquility you can handle. Also nice touches such as dressing gowns and slippers.

D Kerrysdale House, Gairloch, T01445-712292, www.kerrysdalehouse.co.uk. 3 rooms. Open all year. Charming B&B with the added benefit of a lovely garden to enjoy in summer.

E Duisary, Gairloch, T01445-712252, www.duisary.freeserve.co.uk. 3 rooms. Apr-Oct. Cosy B&B run by Isabel Mackenzie. This modernized crofthouse is on the road that turns off to the right by the **Millcroft Hotel**, beyond the fire station.

E Mrs A MacDonald, Tregurnow, 57 Strath, T01445-712116. 3 rooms. Jun-Sep. Good-value B&B..

E Mrs A MacIver, Charleston, by the harbour, T01445-712388. 3 en suite rooms. Mar-Nov. Friendly, comfortable B&B.

F Auchtercairn Hostel, T01445-712131. Open Mar-Nov. At Gairloch Sands Apartments, just before the turn-off to Strath.

F Badachro Bunkhouse, Badachro, T07760-344008. Cheap bunkhouse accommodation.

F Carn Dearg Youth Hostel, 3 miles beyond Gairloch, on the road to Melvaig, T01445-712219. Open 15 May-3 Oct.

F Sail Mhor Croft Independent Hostel, south of Ullapool in Camusnagaul, T01854-633224, sailmhor@btinternet.com. Call before arriving.

Camping

Badrallach Bothy & Camp Site, near Gruinard Bay, T01445-633281. This campsite is situated in the tiny, remote hamlet of Badrallach. A few miles east of Dundonnell, take a side road which branches left and runs for 7 miles.

Camping and Caravan Club Site, between Poolewe village and Inverewe Garden, T01445-781249. An excellent site.

Gairloch Caravan & Camping Park, Strath, T01445-712373. With full facilities and close to all amenities.

Gruinard Bay Caravan Park, in Laide near Gruinard Bay, T01445-731225. Open Apr-Oct.

Sands Holiday Centre, Big Sand, about a mile beyond Strath, T01445-712152. Open Easter-Oct.

Eating

Loch Carron and around *p231*

ƚƚ Carron Restaurant, about 5 mins' drive from the village, across the loch on the A890, T01520-722488. An excellent option. Open Apr-Nov Mon-Sat 1030-2100.

ƚƚ-ƚ Kishorn Seafood Bar, on the road to Lochcarron from Applecross, after the Bealach na Ba Pass, T01520-733240. Open Apr-Oct. This oasis of culinary excellence must not be missed. Fish and seafood is superfresh and at £3.75 for half a dozen queen scallops (you read that correctly) is there anywhere in the UK offering such amazing value? We think not. More standard fare also on offer for those unfortunate souls who can't eat seafood. Highly recommended.

ƚ Flower Tunnel, at Applecross campsite (see Sleeping, above). Mar-Nov daily from 0900, meals from 1200. Serves pizza, steak pie, fish and chips, etc, in large flow-filled plastic tunnel.

Gairloch and around *p234*

Hotels are often the best options for eating out. See Sleeping, above. Of particular note are the **Old Inn**, the **Creel Restaurant** and the **Myrtle Bank Hotel**.

ƚƚ Mustn't Grumble, Melvich, on road north of Gairloch towards lighthouse, T01445-771212. Open all year 1100-2300. This café-bar/restaurant leans heavily towards meat and chicken though there's also local fish and seafood. All mains are under a tenner, so very good value. Views from beer garden will blow you away – quite literally.

ƚƚ-ƚ Badachro Inn, Badachro, T01445-741319, www.badachroinn.com. Good food in this handily placed hotel on the road to Red Point. Try the local fish and seafood. Nice views from the dining room.

ƚƚ-ƚ Blueprint Café, on main road through Gairloch, opposite **Mountain Restaurant** (see below), T01445-712397. Open Mar-Nov till 1600 for lunch and snacks and till 2100 for dinner. Food is fairly standard but good value nonetheless.

ƚƚ-ƚ Inverewe Garden, see Sights. Daily 1000-1700. The best place to eat cheaply around Poolewe is probably the licensed restaurant here.

ƚƚ-ƚ Mountain Restaurant, Strath Sq, Gairloch, T01445-712316. Open till 1800 Mar-Nov, later in Jul-Aug. Good veggie options in this very friendly restaurant with outside terrace overlooking Gair Loch and mountains beyond. It is run by mountaineers and also has an adjacent bookshop.

Activities and tours

Wester Ross *p231*

Climbing and hillwalking

For those who are not experienced hillwalkers, there's a Ranger Service for visitors. During Jul and Aug the ranger, **Seamus McNally**, takes guided walks up into the mountains 3 times a week. For more details call, T01445-791221. A recommended local mountain guide is **Steve Chadwick**, T01445-712455. For guided walks around Lochcarron, contact **Island Horizons**, Kirkton Rd, T01520-722238.

Fishing

For information on sea-angling trips, contact the chandlery shop at the harbour, T01445-712458.

Quad biking

If you prefer dry land, try a quad bike tour of the Flowerdale Deer Forest with **Highland Trails**. Book at The Anchorage post office/craft shop at the harbour or at Flowerdale Estate office, T01445-712378.

Wildlife cruises

You can take a wildlife-spotting cruise with **Sail Gairloch**, T01445-712636. The cruise lasts 2 hrs and leaves daily from Gairloch Pier (subject to weather conditions). It can be booked at the **Gairloch Marine Life Centre** by the pier.

Transport

Loch Carron and around *p231*

Bus There's a postbus service from **Strathcarron** to **Shieldaig** and **Torridon** twice a day Mon-Sat. It's possible to reach **Applecross** by public transport, but only just. A postbus service leaves **Strathcarron** train station daily (except Sun) at 0955, arriving in **Shieldaig** at 1040. Another postbus then leaves **Shieldaig** at 1130 and arrives in Applecross at 1300, via the beautiful and winding coast road. No buses run over the Bealach na Ba. A postbus leaves **Applecross** at 0915 and arrives in **Shieldaig** at 1010. It continues to **Torridon** (see below) and arrives at 1030. Another postbus leaves **Shieldaig** at 1045 and arrives at **Strath carron** train station at 1130. There are train connections from **Strathcarron** to **Inverness** and **Kyle** (for times T08457-484950).

Torridon and around *p231*

Bus The postbus from **Applecross** to **Shieldaig** continues to **Torridon village** (see above). There's a postbus from **Strathcarron** station at 0955 which arrives in **Shieldaig** at 1040. **Duncan Maclennan** buses, T01520-755239, have a service which leaves **Strathcarron** at 1230 and arrives in **Torridon** at 1330 (daily except Sun). There's also a postbus service (Mon-Sat) from **Diabaig** to **Kinlochewe** and **Achnasheen**, via **Torridon**, at 0955. **Duncan Maclennan** buses also run between **Torridon** and **Shieldaig** and **Strathcarron**. For **Loch Maree**, **Kinlochewe** is 9 miles west of **Achnasheen** rail station which is on the Inverness-Kyle line. There's a daily (except Sun) postbus service. There's also a postbus (Mon-Sat) from **Kinlochewe** to **Torridon** and **Diabaig**, and a bus to **Torridon** and **Shieldaig**, T01520-755239. Buses between **Gairloch** and **Inverness** (see below) stop in **Kinlochewe**.

Gairloch and around *p234*

Bus There's a bus from **Inverness** to **Gairloch** 3 times a week (Mon, Wed and Sat) at 1705 with **Westerbus**, T01445-712255. The return bus is at 0805. **Westerbus** also have services to **Kinlochewe** (Mon-Sat, 0730) and to **Mellon Charles/Laide**, via **Poolewe** (Mon-Sat). There's a **Melvaig- Gairloch-Red Point** postbus service Mon-Sat which leaves Gairloch at 0820 heading north to **Melvaig** and leaves Gairloch heading south to **Red Point** at 1035. On Fri only there's a taxi service between **Gairloch** and **Melvaig** 1030-1230 (to book T01445-712559).

For **Gruinard Bay**, daily buses go to **Laide** from **Gairloch** with Westerbus, T01445-712255. Some continue to **Mellon Udrigle**. Buses between **Laide** and **Inverness** 3 times a week (Tue, Thu and Fri), leaving at 0805 and returning at 1705. There are also buses on other days between **Gairloch** and **Inverness** which stop at **Laide** (see above).

Ferry West Highland Seaways, T01445-712777, www.overtheseatoskye.com, have withdrawn their passenger ferry between **Gairloch** and **Portree** (Skye) but should be starting again in spring 2007. Check the website for latest information.

Ullapool and around

The attractive little fishing port of Ullapool, on the shores of Loch Broom, is the largest settlement in Wester Ross. The grid-pattern village, created in 1788 at the height of the herring boom by the British Fisheries Society, is still an important fishing centre as well as being the major tourist centre in the northwest of Scotland and one of the main ferry terminals for the Outer Hebrides. At the height of the busy summer season the town is swamped by visitors passing through on their way to or from Stornoway on Lewis, heading north into the wilds, or south to Inverness. It has excellent tourist amenities and services and relatively good transport links, making it the ideal base for those exploring the northwest coast and a good place to be if the weather is bad.

North of Ullapool you enter a different world. The landscape becomes ever more dramatic and unreal – a huge emptiness of bleak moorland punctuated by isolated peaks and shimmering lochs. A narrow and tortuously twisting road winds its way up the coast, past deserted beaches of sparkling white sand washed by turquoise seas. There's not much tourist traffic this far north and once you get off the main A835 and on to the backroads, you can enjoy the wonderful sensation of having all this astonishingly beautiful scenery to yourself. » *For Sleeping, Eating and other listings, see pages 247-251.*

Ins and outs

Getting there and around Ullapool is the mainland terminal for ferries to Stornoway (Lewis). **Scottish Citylink** buses, T08705-505050, to and from Inverness (twice daily Monday to Saturday, just under 1½ hours; £13.10 return) connect with the ferry to and from Stornoway. The local **CalMac** office on Shore Street, opposite the pier, T01854-612358, also has details. There are also buses to places further north, and south along the coast. Buses stop at the pier near the ferry dock. » *For further details, see Transport page 251.*

Tourist information The **TIC** ⓘ *6 Argyle St, T01854-612135, Easter-Oct daily, Nov-Easter Mon-Fri 1300-1630*, is well run and provides an accommodation booking service as well as information on local walks and trips, and has a good stock of books and maps. To find out what's on locally, tune in to Loch Broom FM (102.2 and 96.8) or pick up a copy of the *Ullapool News* on Fridays.

Ullapool » *pp247-251. Colour map 1, B5.*

→ *Phone code: 01854. Population: 1800.*

Ullapool's attractions are very much of the outdoor variety and include the Falls of Measach, Achiltibuie and Stac Pollaidh. However, whist in town it's worth taking a stroll around the harbour to watch the comings and goings of the fishing fleet and you might even see the occasional seal or otter swimming close to the shore. The only real 'sight' as such is the **Ullapool Museum and Visitor Centre** ⓘ *T01854-612987, www.ullapoolmuseum.co.uk. Apr-Oct Mon-Sat 1000-1700, Nov-Mar by prior arrangement only, £3, concession £2, children £0.50*, in a converted church in West Argyle Street. It has some interesting displays on local history, including the story of those who set sail from here in 1773 on board *The Hector*, the first ship to carry emigrants from the Highlands to Nova Scotia in Canada.

Walks → *All routes are covered by OS Maps Nos 15, 19 and 20.*

There are several good walking trails which start in Ullapool. One of these is to the top of **Ullapool Hill**, or **Meall Mhor** (886 ft). Starting from the tourist office, head to the end of Argyle Street, turn left on to North Road and then cross the road at the **Far Isles Restaurant**. Walk down the lane between Broom Court and the Hydro sub-station and then follow the path which zigzags up the hillside. There's a good cairned path up to the top of the hill. The views from the top over Glen Achall, and on a clear day, the mountains of Sutherland, are superb. You can return by traversing the hillside to the top of the Braes, or take a track leading to Loch Achall and follow the Ullapool river through the quarry road back to the village. The return trip takes one to two hours.

A relatively easy, but much longer walk, of five to six hours, is to **Rhidorroch Estate**. Take the A835 north out of Ullapool. Opposite the petrol station and before the bridge, take the road on the right signed 'Quarry'. Go through the quarry keeping to the left, and follow the Ullapool river till you see Loch Achall. Continue along the north bank of the loch for another 6 miles. East Rhidorroch Lodge is on the right; cross the bridge to get there, then skirt the lodge fences and cross to the track which leads up the southwestern hill. This brings you out to Leckmelm, about 4 miles south of Ullapool on the A835. This last section offers wonderful views across Loch Broom to An Teallach. From Leckmelm you can also climb Beinn Eilideach (1837 ft).

A good coastal walk is to **Rhue Lighthouse** and back. From the north end of Quay Street go down the steps to the river. Cross the bridges and head left by the football field. Follow the path to the left by the duck pond and cross in front of the bungalow. Then follow the shoreline north for about 2 miles, climbing up the hillside when the

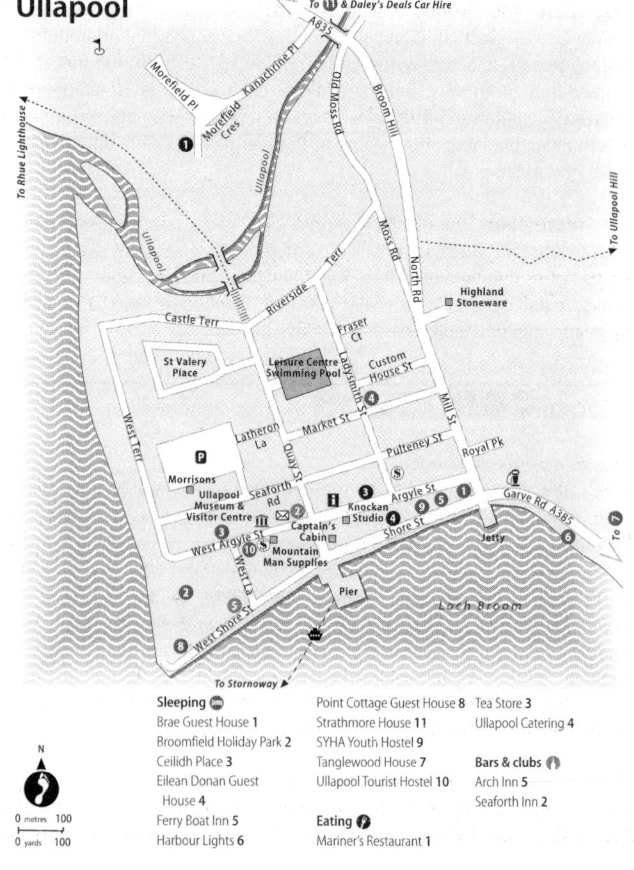

Sleeping
Brae Guest House **1**
Broomfield Holiday Park **2**
Ceilidh Place **3**
Eilean Donan Guest House **4**
Ferry Boat Inn **5**
Harbour Lights **6**
Point Cottage Guest House **8**
Strathmore House **11**
SYHA Youth Hostel **9**
Tanglewood House **7**
Ullapool Tourist Hostel **10**

Eating
Mariner's Restaurant **1**
Tea Store **3**
Ullapool Catering **4**

Bars & clubs
Arch Inn **5**
Seaforth Inn **2**

tide is high. Follow the path till you reach the little white lighthouse at Rhue Point. To return, take the single-track road out of Rhue back to the main road and up over the hill to Ullapool. It's about 6 miles in total.

There are many more strenuous hiking routes around Ullapool. The A835 south of town gives access to **Beinn Dearg** (3556 ft) and the **Fannichs**, a range of hills on the southern side of Dirrie More. There's also **An Teallach**, a favourite with Scottish climbers, see page 243. North of Ullapool are the mountains within the Inverpolly National Nature Reserve (see below).

All routes require hillwalking experience and you should be well prepared for the unpredictable weather conditions. A good guidebook is *The Northern Highlands, SMC District Guide*, by Tom Strang. ▸▸ *For details of a tour operator offering trips, see page 250.*

South of Ullapool

▸▸ *pp247-251. Colour map 1, B5.*

On the southern shore of Little Loch Broom is the village of **Dundonnell**, from where there are spectacular views of awesome An Teallach (3483 ft), a mountain of almost mythical status amongst Scottish climbers and spoken of in hushed, reverential tones. The path to the highest of its summits is clear and begins southeast of the **Dundonell Hotel**. It will take a full day and you'll need to be well prepared (OS map No 19) and heed the usual advice.

The A832 coastal road meets the A835 Ullapool-Inverness main road at Braemore junction, 12 miles south of Ullapool. Before heading on to Ullapool it's worth stopping at the very impressive **Falls of Measach**, just by the junction. The falls plunge 150 ft into the spectacular **Corrieshalloch Gorge** (or 'ugly/fearsome gorge' in Gaelic) and can be crossed by a distinctly wobbly suspension bridge (not for vertigo sufferers). The falls can be reached from the A835, but the most dramatic approach is from the A832 Gairloch road.

North of Ullapool

▸▸ *pp247-251. Colour map 1, A5/B5-6.*

The region immediately north of Ullapool is called Assynt, and is heaven for serious hillwalkers and climbers. Though most are not Munros, and not particularly difficult by Scottish standards, they can attract some of the worst weather imaginable, even in the height of summer. Amongst the most spectacular of Assynt's distinctive 'island peaks' are **Suilven** (2398 ft), **Ben More Assynt** (3275 ft), **Quinag** (2650 ft) and **Canisp** (2775 ft). Much of this region is protected in the Inverpolly and Inchnadamph National Nature Reserves, home to an extremely rich and diverse wildlife.

Inverpolly National Nature Reserve

→ *Phone code: 01854. OS Landranger No 15.*

About 12 miles north of Ullapool on the main A835 is the exceptional **SNH Visitor Centre** ⓘ *T01854-666234, open all year round 24 hrs a day*, at Knockan Crag. It's an interactive display of the geology, flora and fauna of the area. From the visitor centre there's a marked trail which leads up to the **Crag**, and the views from the clifftop are excellent, across to Inverpolly's 'island' peaks of Cul Mór, Cul Beag and Stac Pollaidh.

A few miles north of here is the village of **Knockan**. Nearby, at **Elphin**, is the **Highland and Rare Breeds Farm** ⓘ *mid-May to end of Sep, 1000-1700*. Beyond Elphin is **Ledmore**, where the A837 branches east towards Lairg and Bonar Bridge. There's a good craft shop at Ledmore where you can buy hand-knitted sweaters.

Between Ullapool and Knockan Crag is the turn-off west (left) to the distinctive craggy peak of **Stac Pollaidh**. A path has been established by the John Muir Trust, which takes you on a circular walk around the peak from the car park. Take the right-hand path and go round at the same level, or climb up the rear to the top, go around the summit and descend by the same path. You'll need a head for heights to reach the summit as much of the route is exposed, but the stunning views are worth it. Be careful not to stray from the path; it's been put there because of the damage inflicted by tens of thousands of pairs of boots each year, resulting in serious erosion on the south face. It's a fairly easy 2½-hour walk.

Achiltibuie → *Phone code: 01854.*

The unclassified single-track road winds its way west past Stac Pollaidh to the turn-off for Achiltibuie. This old crofting village, with whitewashed cottages set back from the sea with views across to the beautiful Summer Isles, is home to one of the northwest's main tourist attractions, **Hydroponicum** ⓘ *T01854-622202, www.thehydroponicum.com, Apr-Sep daily 1000-1800, guided tours every hour on the hour, Oct Mon-Fri 1130-1530, £5.50, concession £4.50, children £3.50.* This 'Garden of the Future' is a gigantic greenhouse which is pioneering the system of hydroponics to grow plants from all over the world. Hydroponics uses water instead of soil to carry nutrients to the plants and can be carried out anywhere. Here you can see an incredible variety of subtropical trees, orchids, flowers, vegetables, herbs and fruits. A guided tour takes you through the different climatic zones, and you can taste their produce, including the famous strawberries, in the **Lilypond Café**, which serves meals and snacks (also serves dinner end May to end August, Friday-Sunday).

Another worthwhile attraction is the **Achiltibuie Smokehouse** ⓘ *T01854-622353, May-Sep Mon-Sat 0930-1700, free*, at Altandhu, 5 miles north. Here you can watch the salmon, herring, trout and other fish being cured before buying some afterwards.

Lochinver and around → *Phone code: 01571.*

The road from Achiltibuie north to Lochinver is known locally as the 'wee mad road', and you'd be mad to miss this thrilling route which twists and winds its way through some the northwest's most stunning scenery. The village of Lochinver is a working fishing port and the last sizeable village before Thurso. It has a good tourist office, lots of accommodation, a bank with ATM, post office and petrol station.

The best place to start is the **Assynt Visitor Centre** ⓘ *T01854-844330, Apr-Oct Mon-Fri 1000-1700, Sun 1000-1600*, which houses the TIC. It has displays on the local geology, history and wildlife and there's also a ranger service with guided walks throughout the summer. Those looking for local souvenirs should head for **Highland Stoneware**, see page 250.

▲ A few miles south of Lochinver, beyond Inverkirkaig, is the trail along the river to the **Kirkaig Falls**. The path starts near the **Achins Bookshop**, which has a good stock of Scottish titles and a café. Follow the path for about 2 miles till it branches right to the falls in the gorge below. Continue along the main path for about another ¾ mile till you reach Fionn Loch, with superb views of mighty Suilven. The walk up to the falls and back should take around 1½ hours. This is one of the main approaches to the foot of the mountain.

Loch Assynt and Inchnadamph → *Phone code: 01571.*

The area east of Lochinver is a remote wilderness of mountains and moorland dotted with lochs and lochans. As well as being a favourite haunt of hardy climbers and walkers, Assynt is a paradise for anglers. Most of the lochs are teeming with brown trout, and fishing permits are readily available throughout the area from the TIC in Lochinver or at local hotels, guesthouses and B&Bs. There's also salmon fishing on the River Kirkaig, available through the **Inver Lodge Hotel** and on Loch Assynt through the **Inchnadamph Hotel**, see Sleeping, page 247.

The A837 Lochinver-Lairg road meets the A894 to Durness 10 miles east of Lochinver at Skiag Bridge by Loch Assynt. Half a mile south of here, by the loch, are the ruins of **Ardvreck Castle**. The castle dates from 1597 and was the stronghold of the Macleods of Assynt until a siege of the castle in 1691, when it was taken by the

Seaforth Mackenzies. Before that, the Marquess of Montrose had been imprisoned here following his defeat at Carbisdale in 1650. Access to the castle is free, but the ruins are in a dangerous state and should be approached with care.

To the east of the road lies the **Inchnadamph National Nature Reserve**, dominated by the massive peaks of Ben More Assynt and Conival, which should only be attempted by experienced hillwalkers. A few miles south of the village of Inchnadamph, at the fish farm, is a steep, but well-marked footpath up to the **Bone Caves.** This is one of Scotland's oldest historical sites, where the bones of humans and animals such as lynx and bear were found together with sawn-off deer antlers dating from over 8000 years ago.

Lochinver to Kylesku → *Phone code: 01571.*

The quickest way north from Lochinver is the A837 east to the junction with the A894 which heads to Kylesku. But by far the most scenic route is the B869 coast road that passes moorland, lochs and beautiful sandy bays. It's best travelled from north to south, giving you the most fantastic views of the whale-backed hump of **Suilven,** rocky talisman of the great poet, Norman MacCaig. Untypically, most of the land in this part of Assynt is owned by local crofters who, under the aegis of the **Assynt Crofters' Trust**, bought 21,000 acres of the North Assynt Estate, thus setting a precedent for change in the history of land ownership in the Highlands.

The trust now owns the fishing rights to the area and sells permits through local post offices and the tourist office in Lochinver. It has also undertaken a number of conservation projects, including one at **Achmelvich**, a few miles north of Lochinver, at the end of a side road which branches off the coast road. It's worth a detour to see one of the loveliest beaches on the west coast, with sparkling white sand and clear turquoise waters straight out of a Caribbean tourist brochure.

From the beach car park below the hostel a path leads northwest along the coast. Bear left off the sandy path shortly after the white cottage on the hill ahead comes into view, and follow the footpath until the road is reached at Alltan na Bradhan, where there are the remains of an old meal mill. Continue north from here along the coast for about a mile till you reach a small bay just before Clachtoll, the **Split Rock**. Close by are the remains of an Iron Age broch, but don't cause further damage by clambering over the ruins. Return to the beach by the same path. The walk there and back should take about 1½ hours.

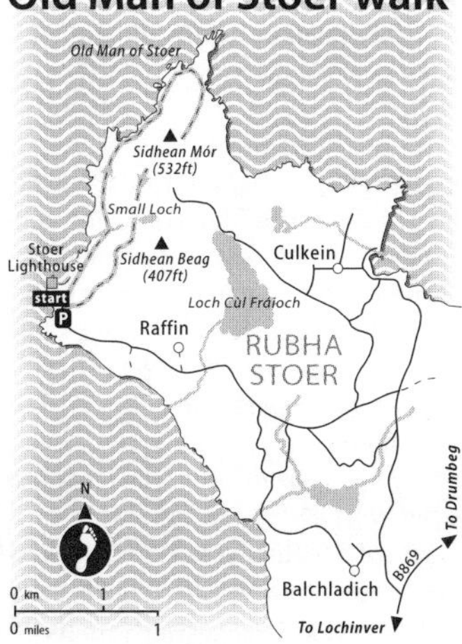

Old Man of Stoer

A side road turns left off the B869 north of Stoer and runs out to **Stoer lighthouse**. From here you can walk across the Stoer Peninsula to the **Old Man of Stoer**, a dramatic rock pillar standing offshore, surrounded by sheer cliffs. Allow about three hours for the circular walk which starts and ends in the lighthouse car park. There is no public transport to the lighthouse, but the Lochinver-Drumbeg postbus runs to Raffin, 1 mile away. A clear path runs from the car park to the cliffs then follows the line of the cliffs northwards. The path heads inland for a short distance as it bypasses a deep gully

Remember to check access locally during the deer-stalking season which runs from mid-August to mid-October.

 then meets the clifftop again, and after a mile or so you can see the Old Man tucked away in a shallow bay, battered by huge waves. Beyond the Old Man the path continues to the headland, the **Point of Stoer**, from where it turns back on itself and climbs **Sidhean Mór** (532 ft). The views from here are fantastic, across to Harris and Lewis and south to the mountains of Assynt. From here, follow the faint path south, back towards the lighthouse, passing a small loch below Sidhean Beag on your left and an obvious cairn on your right. Then you pass a radio mast and follow the clear track back to the lighthouse car park. OS Landranger Map No 15 covers the route. Nine miles further on, in beautiful **Eddrachillis Bay**, is **Drumbeg**, a popular place for anglers who come to fish in the many lochs of North Assynt.

Kylesku → *Phone code: 01971. Colour map 1, B5.*

The road runs east from Drumbeg, under the shadow of towering Quinag (2654 ft), to meet the A894 heading north to Kylesku, site of the sweeping modern road bridge over Loch a'Cháirn Bháin. From Kylesku you can visit Britain's highest waterfall, the 650-ft high **Eas a'Chùal Aluinn**, near the head of Loch Glencoul. Cruises leave from the old ferry jetty below the **Kylesku Hotel** to the falls, see Activities and tours, page 250.

▲There's also a trail to the top of the falls. It starts at the south end of Loch na Gainmhich, about 3 miles north of Skiag Bridge. Skirting the loch, follow the track in a southeasterly direction up to the head of the Bealach a Bhuirich (the Roaring Pass). Continue until you meet a stream, with several small lochans on your right. Follow this stream until it plunges over the Cliffs of Dubh (the Dark Cliffs). You can get a better view of the falls by walking to the right about 100 yards and descending a heather slope for a short distance. Allow about three to four hours for the round trip.

Scourie and Handa Island → *Phone code: 01971. Colour map 1, A5.*

Ten miles north of Kylesku is the little crofting community of Scourie, sitting above a sandy bay. Anyone remotely interested in wildlife is strongly advised to make a stop here to visit Handa Island, a sea bird reserve run by the Scottish Wildlife Trust, and one of the best places in the country for bird life. The island is now deserted, except for the warden, but once supported a thriving community of crofters, until the potato famine of 1846 forced them to leave, most emigrating to Canada's Cape Breton. Now it's home to huge colonies of shags, fulmars, razorbills, guillemots and puffins, in season. The best time to visit is during the summer breeding season, from late May to August. There's a footpath right round the island, which is detailed in the free SWT leaflet available at the warden's office when you arrive. You should allow three to four hours. There's a ferry service to the island, see Transport, page 251.

Another excellent wildlife boat trip leaves from **Fanagmore**, a mile from Tarbet on the other side of the peninsula, see Activities and tours, page 250.

Kinlochbervie and around → *Phone code: 01971. Colour map 1, A5.*

The road north from Scourie passes Laxford Bridge, where it meets the A838 running southeast to Lairg, see page 263. The A838 also runs north to Durness, on the north coast (see page 252). At Rhiconich, the B801 branches northwest to Kinlochbervie, a small village with a very big fish market. This is one of the west coast's major fishing ports, and huge container lorries thunder along the narrow single-track roads carrying frozen fish and seafood to all corners of Europe. It's worth heading down to the fish market in the evenings to see the day's catch being landed and sold.

A few miles beyond Kinlochbervie is **Oldshoremore**, a tiny crofters' village scattered around a stunning white beach, and a great place to swim. The less hardy can instead explore the hidden rocky coves nearby.

At the end of the road is **Blairmore**, from where a footpath leads to **Sandwood Bay**, the most wonderful beach on the entire west coast. It's a long walk, but because of its isolation you'll probably have this glorious mile-long stretch of white sand all to yourself. At one end is a spectacular rock pinnacle and it is said to be haunted by the ghost of an ancient shipwrecked mariner. Allow three hours for the walk there and back, plus time at the beach. Romantic souls may wish to take a tent and watch the sunset with a loved one and a bottle of their favourite single malt. Sandwood Bay can also be reached from Cape Wrath, a day's hike to the north, see page 253.

Sleeping

Ullapool *p241, map p242*

There is no shortage of places to stay in Ullapool ranging from one of the very finest hotels in the UK to numerous guesthouses and B&Bs, a couple of good youth hostels and a campsite. Garve Rd, heading south out of town, has several guesthouses, and there are lots of B&Bs along Seaforth Rd and Pulteney St. Unfortunately the famous **Altnaharrie Inn** has closed, though the ferry from Ullapool to the other side of Loch Broom is running; for details T01854-612656.

A Tanglewood House, T01854-612059, www.tanglewoodhouse.co.uk. 3 en suite rooms. Open all year. Chalet-style house in stunning location overlooking Loch Broom, with its own private beach. Part of the **Wolsey Lodge** scheme so you dine with the hostess, Anne Holloway, who offers superb cooking in a civilized atmosphere. All rooms have their own balcony and wonderful views across the loch. Highly recommended.

B The Ceilidh Place, 14 West Argyle Pl, T01854-612103, www.theceilidhplace.com. 23 rooms. This former boat-shed has grown over the years to become one of the most refreshingly different hotels in the country, with comfortable bedrooms, cosy lounge, bookshop, restaurant, bar and café. They also host a varied programme of arts events such as live music, plays, poetry readings, exhibitions and ceilidhs (see below); a great place to relax and soak up some local culture. Across the road is their clubhouse, with basic but comfortable dorms (**E-F**). Highly recommended.

C-D Harbour Lights Hotel, Garve Rd (on the left, heading into Ullapool on the A835), T01854-612222, www.harbour-lights.co.uk. 22 rooms. Open Mar-Oct. Modern hotel offering good service and very good food available all day (**TT**).

D Braemore Square Country House, Braemore, T01845-655357, www.braemoresquare.com. 3 rooms. Open all year. 11 miles south of Ullapool and set in 46 acres of grounds is the former estate house of Victorian engineer Sir John Fowler, who designed the Forth Rail Bridge. B&B in comfortable and tastefully furnished rooms, all in splendid isolation. Guests have use of kitchen. Self-catering also available. Recommended.

D Ferry Boat Inn, Shore St, T01854-612366, www.ferryboat-inn.com. On the lochside, decent accommodation and food and the best pub in town.

D Point Cottage Guest House, 22 WestShore St, T01854-612494, www.pointcottage.co.uk. 3 en suite rooms. Open Feb-Nov. Lovely old fishing cottage at the quieter end of the loch-front.

E Brae Guest House, Shore St, T01854-612421. 8 rooms. Open May-Oct. Comfortable guesthouse on the loch-front.

E Eilean Donan Guest House & Restaurant, 14 Market St, T01854-612524. 5 rooms. Open all year. Friendly and central (**C** including dinner).

E Strathmore House, Strathmore, Morefield, 1 mile north of town, T01854-612423, murdo@strathmore.fsnet.co.uk. Open Apr-Oct. Friendly, comfortable and good value.

F SYHA youth hostel, Shore St, T01854-612254. Mar-Dec. A very good hostel. You can pick up some information on local walks, also bike hire, internet and laundry facilities.

F Ullapool Tourist Hostel, West House, West Argyle St, T01854-613126, open all year. This independent hostel has the full range of facilities, including free internet for guests, hires mountain bikes and runs local bus tours.

Camping

Broomfield Holiday Park, Shore St, T01854-6120020. Open Easter-Sep. At the west end of the village, this campsite has great views across to the Summer Isles and a laundrette on site. It's open Easter-Sep.

South of Ullapool *p243*

B-C Dundonnell Hotel, in Dundonnell, south of Ullapool, T01854-633204, www.dundonnellhotel.com. Open Feb-Dec.

Good value hotel and good food (₸₸₸-₸₸) in their **Claymore Restaurant**.

Achiltibuie *p244*

L **Summer Isles Hotel**, near the Hydroponicum, T01854-622282, www.summerisles hotel.com. 3 en suite rooms, 2 suites and 1 cottage. Open Easter to mid-Oct. This relaxing, civilized hotel enjoys magnificent views across to the Summer Isles. Mark and Geraldine Irvine also boast a Michelin-starred restaurant serving some of the best seafood on the planet. The sublime 5-course set dinner (served at 2000) will set you back around £50 a head but you can enjoy delicious bar lunches for a fraction of the price. Even if you're not staying or eating here, it's worth stopping to have a drink on the terrace and watch the sun set over the islands. Very highly recommended.

F **SYHA Youth Hostel**, a few miles south at Achininver, T01854-622254. Mid-May to early Oct. Basic and very cheap.

Lochinver and around *p244*

L **The Albannach Hotel**, Baddidaroch, T01571-844407, www.thealbannach.co.uk. 6 en suite rooms. Open Mar-Nov. This wonderful 18th-century house overlooking Loch Inver is one of the very best places to stay in the northwest and everything a romantic highland hotel should be. Rooms are tall, dark and handsome and the food in the award-winning restaurant is imaginative and generous, featuring only the freshest of local fish, fowl and game. The price includes dinner. Non-residents are also welcome but booking is essential. Highly recommended.

L **Inver Lodge Hotel**, Iolaire Rd, T01571-844496, stay@inverlodge.com. 20 en suite rooms. Open Apr-Oct. A modern luxury hotel standing above the village with great views across the bay. Hospitality, service and the food served in the restaurant (₸₸₸-₸₸) are all faultless. Recommended.

D-E **Veyatie Lochinver**, 66 Baddidarroch, T01571-844424, www.veyatie-scotland.co.uk. 3 rooms. Open all year. Superior B&B, wlecomes pets and hill walkers.

E **Ardglas Guest House**, T01571-844257, www.ardglass.co.uk. 8 rooms. Open all year. Comfortable and very good-value accommodation.

E **Polcraig**, T01571-844429, cathelmac@aol.com. 5 en suite rooms. Open all year. Large modern house offering a friendly welcome and good value B&B..

Loch Assynt and Inchnadamph *p244*

C **Inchnadamph Hotel**, T01571-822202, www.inchnadamphhotel. co.uk. An old-fashioned Highland hotel on the shores of Loch Assynt, catering for the hunting and fishing fraternity, see page 244.

F **Inchnadamph Lodge**, Assynt Field Centre, T01571-822218, assynt@presence.co.uk. Basic hostel accommodation in bunk rooms, as well as twin, double and family rooms. Continental breakfast is included. It's open all year, but phone ahead Nov-Mar. It's ideally situated for climbing Ben More Assynt and guides are available.

Lochinver to Kylesku *p245*

There's not much accommodation around here other than self-catering cottages.

Camping

Clachtoll Beach Campsite, 6 miles north of Lochinver, T01571-855377. May-Sep. Good facilities, friendly owners and superb location. Recommended.

Kylesku *p246*

A **Kylesku Hotel**, T01971-502231, www.kyles kuhotel.co.uk. 9 rooms. Mar-Oct. Comfortable rooms and renowned for its delicious and great-value pub seafood. There's also a more formal and expensive restaurant next door.

B-C **Newton Lodge**, T/F01971-502070, www.newtonlodge.co.uk. 7 en suite rooms. mid-Mar to mid-Oct. Non-smoking hotel with great views.

F **Kylesku Lodges**, T01971-502003. Easter-Oct. A small hostel.

Scourie and Handa Island *p246*

There are lots of options in this area.

C **Eddrachilles Hotel**, Badcall Bay, T01971-502080, www.eddrachilles.com. 12 en suite rooms. Mar-Oct. This is one of the most magnificently situated hotels in the country. The 200 year-old building stands in 300 acres of grounds overlooking the bay, the food on offer is superb, though the atmosphere is a little stuffy (their Eddrachilles heel, you might say).

B **Scourie Hotel**, T01971-502396, www.scourie-hotel.co.uk. 20 rooms. Apr-Oct. 17th-century former coaching inn popular with anglers. Also an excellent place to eat (lunch TT, dinner TTT).

C **Scourie Lodge**, T01971-502248. 3 rooms. Open Mar-Oct. There are several B&Bs in the village, but none better than this welcoming lodge. Also does good evening meals.

Camping

There's a campsite on Harbour Rd, T01971-502060.

Kinlochbervie and around *p246*

C **Rhiconich Hotel**, Rhiconich, T01971-521224, www.rhiconichhotel.co.uk. 10 en suite rooms. Open all year. Modern functional hotel with good facilities and surrounded by superb scenery. (**B** including dinner.)

D **Old School Hotel**, halfway between Kinlochbervie and the A838 at Rhiconich, T/F01971-521383, www.oldschoolhotel.co.uk. 4 en suite rooms. Open all year. This is the best place to stay here. It used to be a school, as the name implies, and this only adds to the charm. They also serve great food (see Eating, below). Recommended.

E **Benview**, T01971-521242. Apr-Sep. A friendly B&B.

Camping

There's a good campsite at Oldshoremore, T01971-521281.

Eating

Ullapool *p241, map p242*

TT **The Ceilidh Place**, see Sleeping, above. One of those places that tourists seem to hang around for hours or even days. It exudes a laid-back, cultured ambience. The self-service coffee shop does cheap whole-food all day during the summer, while the restaurant serves more expensive full meals, with an emphasis on vegetarian and seafood at night. There's even outdoor seating. Open 1100-2300. Also live music and various other events, see Bars and clubs, below.

TT **Mariner's Restaurant**, Morefield Hotel, North Rd, T01854-612161. May-Oct. On the edge of town heading north, in the middle of a housing estate. The setting may be a little incongruous but the seafood is sensational, which is why people travel from miles around and it's always busy. Excellent value.

TT-T **Seaforth**, Quay St, T01854-612122. Popular pub with bistro upstairs serving decent fish and seafood and other staples. Bar meals downstair are good value. Their **chippie** next door is very good indeed and was voted the UK's best takaway a few years back by the those good people at Radio 4.

T **Tea Store**, 27 Argyll St, T01845-612995. Daily 0800-2000. No-nonsense café serving all day breakfasts, etc, and home- baked goodies.

T **Ullapool Catering**, The Frigate, Shore St, T01854-612969. Great picnics made up from local organic produce at good-value prices.

Lochinver and around *p244*

TT **Riverside Bistro**, on the way into town on the A837. Main St, T01571-844356. Apart from the hotels listed above, the best food is here. Try their famous pies which use the best in local venison, beef, poultry and seafood, there are also vegetarian and sweet options. Eat in or take away.

T **Caberfeidh**, T01571-844321. Near to the bistro, this is the cheap and cheerful option.

Scourie and Handa Island *p246*

TT **Seafood Restaurant**, just above the jetty at Tarbet. Run by Julian Pearce, who also runs **Laxford Cruise**, see Activities and tours, below. If you're up this way, don't miss a visit to this restaurant which serves seafood caught by Julian during his boat trips. It's a great place and you can stay here, in the self-catering caravan next door, which sleeps up to 6.

Kinlochbervie and around *p246*

TT **Old School Hotel & Restaurant**, Inshegra, halfway between Kinlochbervie and the A838 at Rhiconich, T/F01971-521383, www.oldschoolhotel.co.uk. See also Sleeping, above. Daily 1200-1400 and 1800-2000. Serve really good, home-cooked food to grateful souls who have ventured this far north. Best for miles around.

Bars and clubs

Ullapool *p241, map p242*

Arch Inn, 11 West Shore St, T01854-612454. Another local fave, this place is compact and bijou so gets rammed at weekends. Don't even try to get on the pool table.

The Ceilidh Place, see Sleeping. For something a wee bit more sedate and civilized than the other choices, head here where you can enjoy a quiet drink in the cosy **Parlour Bar** or take advantage of their varied programme of events. There's live music nightly (except Sun) throughout the summer and on a Mon in winter, also ceilidhs and poetry readings. The clubhouse opposite stages plays.

Ferry Boat Inn (or 'FBI' as it's known locally), on Shore St. Ullapool's favourite pub. It has a Thu night live music session year round and during the summer you can sit outside on the sea wall and watch the sun go down as you drain your pint of superb real ale.

Seaforth, see Eating, above. Gets pretty rowdy at weekends but a good place to hear live music.

Shopping

Ullapool *p241, map p242*

The town is well supplied with shops.

The Captain's Cabin, on the corner of Quay St and Shore St, also sells books, as well as crafts and souvenirs.

The Ceilidh Place, see Sleeping, above, has the best bookshop in the northwest.

Highland Stoneware, T01854-612980, on Mill St, heading north towards Morefield. Look no further than here for pottery. You can wander round the studios before browsing in their gift shop, which is pricey but you may have luck in their bargain baskets. They also have a factory in Lochinver, T01854-844376, www.highland trail.co.uk/stoneware, Mon-Fri 0900-1800 (Easter-Oct also Sat 0900-1700), a local pottery factory just outside the village of Lochinver. See page 244.

Knockan Studio, opposite the TIC on Argyle St, T01854-613365, open Mar-Oct, Mon-Sat 0900-1800, is an excellent jewellers.

Mountain Man Supplies, opposite the museum on West Argyle St, is a good outdoor equipment shop.

Festivals and events

Ullapool *p241, map p242*

Sep Loopallu Festival, www.loopallu.co.uk. Big music festival held over a weekend in late Sep. Only started in 2005 but 2006 line-up included likes of The Stranglers and Alabama 3. Gigs in various venues around town. Tickets £40.

Activities and tours

Ullapool *p241, map p242*

Boat tours

During the summer the *MV Summer Queen*, T01854-612472, www.summerqueen.co.uk, runs 4-hr cruises to the Summer Isles, with a 45-min landing on Tanera Mór. These leave Mon-Sat at 1000 from the pier and cost £14 per person. There are also 2-hr wildlife cruises around Loch Broom, Annat Bay and Isle Martin, which leave daily at 1415 and also on Sun at 1100, and cost £8 per person. Cruises can be booked at the booth by the pier or by calling the number above.

Walking tours

Walking tours around Ullapool and throughout the Northwest Highlands can be arranged daily with **Northwest Frontiers**, NWF@compuserve.com, ourworld.compuserve.com/homepages/NWF, T01854-612628, with the very experienced Andy Cunningham, and **Celtic Horizons**, T01854-612429.

Achiltibuie *p244*

I Macleod, Achiltibuie Post Office, T01854-622200, or at home, T018754-622315, for cruises to the Summer Isles from Achiltibuie pier on board the *Hectoria*. Cruises leave Mon-Sat at 1030 and 1415 and last 3½ hrs, with 1 hr ashore on the islands. They cost £12 per person (half price for children). There are also deep-sea angling trips (1800-2100).

Kylesku *p246*

On board the *MV Statesman*, T01571-844446, cruises go to Eas a'Chùal Aluinn waterfall leaving from the old ferry jetty below the **Kylesku Hotel**. You can also see porpoises, seals and minke whales en route. The 2-hr round trip runs Apr-Sep daily at 1100 and 1400 (Jul and Aug also at 1600), and costs £9, children £3. You may be able to get closer to the falls by getting off the boat and walking to the bottom, then getting on the next boat.

Scourie and Handa Island *p246*

Laxford Cruises, T01971-502251, sail around beautiful Loch Laxford, where you can see lots of birds from nearby Handa Island, as well as seals, porpoises and otters. Trips leave Easter till the end of Sep daily except Sun at 1000, 1200 and 1400 (also at 1600 in Jul and Aug). The trips last 1¾ hrs and cost £10 for adults, £5 for children. For bookings contact Julian Pearce, who also runs the wonderful **Seafood Restaurant**, see Eating, above, just above the jetty at Tarbet.

Transport

Ullapool *p241, map p242*

Bus Scottish Citylink buses run 2-3 times daily (except Sun) between Ullapool and **Inverness**, connecting with the ferry to **Stornoway**. There are also buses Mon-Sat to and from **Inverness** with Rapson's Coaches, T01463-710555, and Spa Coaches, T01997-421311. There's a service to **Lochinver** (1-2 times daily Mon-Sat, 1 hr) with Spa Coaches and Rapson's of Brora, T01408-621245, and to **Achilitibuie** (2 daily Mon-Thu, 1 on Sat, 1 hr) with Spa Coaches. There's also a daily bus to and from **Gairloch**, which continues to **Inverness**, during the summer only.

Car hire Daley's Deals, Morefield Industrial Estate, T01854-612848.

Cycle hire At hostels (see page 247).

Achiltibuie *p244*

Bus There are 2 buses daily (Mon-Thu) to **Ullapool** with Spa Coaches, T01997-421311, leaving Achiltibuie Post Office at 0800 and 1300. The early bus starts in **Reiff** (at 0740); the other leaves from **Badenscallie**. The journey takes 1 hr. There's also a bus on Sat, at 0750.

Lochinver and around *p244*

Bus There's a postbus service from **Lochinver** to and from **Drumbeg**, via the coast road, which continues to **Lairg**. It runs once a day, Mon-Sat. There are also buses to and from **Drumbeg** and on to **Ullapool**, once or twice a day Mon-Sat, with Rapsons of Brora, T01408-621245, and Spa Coaches, T01997-421311.

Scourie and Handa Island *p246*

Bus There's a postbus service to Scourie from **Durness** and **Lairg** once a day, Mon-Sat. It leaves Durness at 0820 and arrives at 0935 and continues to Lairg. It returns at 1245 and arrives at 1420. There's also a postbus service between Scourie and **Elphin**, with connections to **Lochinver**. There's a ferry service to Handa Island from **Tarbet Beach**, 3 miles northwest off the A894, about 3 miles north of Scourie. It sails continuously, depending on demand, Apr-Sep Mon-Sat 0930-1700. The 15-min crossing costs £7.50 return, T01971-502077.

Kinlochbervie and around *p246*

Bus A postbus leaves Kinlochbervie harbour at 0900 and goes to **Scourie** (35 mins) and on to Lairg (1 hr 50 mins) from where there are connections to **Inverness**. The same postbus returns from **Lairg** at 1245, arrives in Kinlochbervie at 1448, then continues to **Durness** (35 mins).

Directory

Ullapool *p241, map p242*

Bank Royal Bank of Scotland on Ladysmith St, and Bank of Scotland with ATM, on West Argyle St.

North coast

Scotland's rugged north coast is not for the faint hearted: over 100 miles of storm-lashed cliffs, sheer rocky headlands and deserted sandy coves backed by a desolate and eerily silent wilderness of mountain, bog and hill loch; the only place on mainland Britain where arctic flora and fauna come down to sea level. This is Britain's most spectacular and undisturbed coastline, a great place for birdwatching, with vast colonies of seabirds, and there's also a good chance of seeing seals, porpoises and minke whales in the more sheltered estuaries. ▸▸ *For Sleeping, Eating and other listings, see pages 255-258.*

Ins and outs

Getting there and around

Getting around the far north without your own transport can be a slow process. Getting to Thurso, the main town, by bus or train is easy, but beyond that things get more difficult. » *For further details, see Transport page 257.*

Tourist information

Durness TIC ⓘ *T01971-511259, Apr-Oct Mon-Sat, Jul and Aug daily*, arranges guided walks and has a small visitor centre with displays on local history, flora and fauna and geology. The **Thurso TIC** ⓘ *Riverside Rd, T01847-892371, Apr-Oct Mon-Sat 0900-1800, Jul and Aug also Sun 1000-1800*, has a leaflet on local surfing beaches.

Durness and around

» *pp255-258. Colour map 1, A6.*

→ *Phone code: 01971.*

Durness is not only the most northwesterly village on the British mainland, but also one of the most attractively located, surrounded by sheltered coves of sparkling white sand and machair-covered limestone cliffs. It's worth stopping here for a few days to explore the surrounding area. One of the village's most famous visitors was John Lennon, who used to spend childhood summers here with his Aunt Elizabeth, a local resident. This unlikely relationship was marked in 2002 with the creation of the **John Lennon Memorial Garden**. Beatles fans can now visit this lovely spot which features sculptures by local artists Lotte Glob, as well as standing stones bearing the lyrics to the fab four's classic *In my Life*.

Smoo Cave

A mile east of the village is the vast 200-ft-long Smoo Cave. A path from near the youth hostel leads down to the cave entrance which is hidden away at the end of a steep, narrow inlet. Plunging through the roof of the cathedral-like cavern is an 80-ft waterfall which can be seen from the entrance, but the more adventurous can take a boat trip into the floodlit interior.

A few miles east of the Smoo Cave are a couple of excellent beaches, at **Sangobeg** and **Rispond**, where the road leaves the coast and heads south along the west shore of stunning **Loch Eriboll**.

Balnakeil

About a mile northwest of Durness is the tiny hamlet of Balnakeil, overlooked by a ruined 17th-century church. In the south wall is a graveslab with carved skull-and-crossbones marking the grave of the notorious highwayman Donald MacMurchow. If you're looking for souvenirs, or an escape from the rat race, then head for the **Balnakeil Craft Village** ⓘ *Apr-Oct daily 1000-1800*, an alternative artists' community set up in the 1960s in a former RAF radar station. Here you can buy weavings, pottery, paintings, leatherwork and woodwork in the little prefab huts. There's also a café. Balnakeil has also become well known in golfing circles. The nine-hole **golf course** ⓘ *T01971-511364*, is the most northerly in mainland Britain, and its famous ninth hole involves a drive over the Atlantic Ocean. The beach here is glorious, especially in fine weather when the sea turns a brilliant shade of turquoise. Even better, walk north along the bay to **Faraid Head**, where you can see puffin colonies in early summer. The views across to Cape Wrath in the west and Loch Eriboll in the east, are stupendous.

Cape Wrath

There are several excellent trips around Durness, but the most spectacular is to Cape Wrath, Britain's most northwesterly point. It's a wild place and the name seems entirely appropriate, though it actually derives from the Norse word *hwarf*, meaning 'turning place'. Viking ships used it as a navigation point during their raids on the Scottish west coast. Now a lighthouse stands on the cape, above the 1000 ft-high Clo Mor Cliffs, the highest on the mainland, and breeding ground for huge colonies of seabirds.

You can walk south from here to **Sandwood Bay**, see page 246. It's an exhilarating but long coastal walk, and will take around eight hours. It's safer doing this walk from north to south as the area around the headland is a military firing range and access may be restricted, which could leave you stranded.

Tongue to Thurso → *Colour map 2, A1-2.*

The road east from Durness runs around **Loch Eriboll** on its way to the lovely little village of **Tongue**. A causeway crosses the beautiful Kyle of Tongue, but a much more scenic route is the single-track road around its southern side, with great views of Ben Hope (3041 ft) looming to the southwest. The village of Tongue is overlooked by the 14th-century ruins of **Varick Castle**, and there's a great beach at **Coldbackie**, 2 miles northeast.

The A836 runs south from Tongue through Altnaharra to Lairg, see page 263. It also continues east to the crofting community of **Bettyhill**, named after the Countess of Sutherland who ruthlessly evicted her tenants from their homes in Strathnaver to make way for more profitable sheep. The whole sorry saga is told in the interesting **Strathnaver Museum** ⓘ *T01641-521418, Apr-Oct Mon-Sat 1000-1300 and 1400-1700, £2, concession £1.50, children £0.50*, housed in an old church in the village. There are also Pictish stones in the churchyard behind the museum.

The museum sells a leaflet detailing the many prehistoric sites in the Strathnaver Valley which runs due south from Bettyhill. There are a couple of great beaches around Bettyhill, at **Farr Bay** and at **Torrisdale Bay**, which is the more impressive of the two and forms part of the **Invernaver Nature Reserve**. There's a small **TIC** ⓘ *T01641-521342, Easter-Sep Mon-Sat*, in Bettyhill.

East from Bettyhill the hills of Sutherland begin to give way to the fields of Caithness. The road passes the turn-off to Strathy Point before reaching **Melvich**, another wee crofting settlement overlooking a lovely sandy bay.

South from Melvich the A897 heads to Helmsdale, see page 265, through the **Flow Country**, a vast expanse of bleak bog of major ecological importance. About 15 miles south of Melvich at Forsinard is an **RSPB Visitor Centre** ⓘ *T01641-571225, Easter-Oct daily 0900-1800*; guided walks through the nature reserve leave from here. These peatlands are a breeding ground for black- and red-throated divers, golden plovers and merlins as well as other species. Otters and roe deer can also be spotted.

Thurso and around » *pp255-258.*

Thurso is the most northerly town on the British mainland and by far the largest settlement on the north coast. In medieval times it was Scotland's chief port for trade with Scandinavia, though most of the town dates from the late 18th century when Sir John Sinclair built the 'new' extension to the old fishing port. The town increased in size to accommodate the workforce of the new nuclear power plant at nearby Dounreay, but the plant's demise has threatened the local economy. Today Thurso is a fairly nondescript place, mostly visited by people catching the ferry to Stromness in Orkney, or the occasional hardcore surfer.

Loch Eriboll, Britain's deepest sea loch, was used by the Royal Navy during the Second World War as a base for protecting Russian convoys.

Thurso → *Phone code: 01847. Colour map 2, A3. Population: 9000.*

There's little of real interest in the town centre. Near the harbour are the 17th-century ruins of **Old St Peter's Church**, which stand on the site of the original 13th-century church founded by the Bishop of Caithness. In the town hall on the High Street is the **Heritage Museum** ⓘ *T01847-892459, Jun-Sep Mon-Sat 1000-1300 and 1400-1700, £0.50*, which features some Pictish carved stones. There may be little in the way of activity in the town, but 10 miles west of Thurso there's plenty of radioactivity at the **Dounreay Nuclear Power Station**. Though its fast breeder reactors were decommissioned in 1994, the plant is still a major local employer and now reprocesses spent nuclear fuel. There's a permanent exhibition at the **visitor centre** ⓘ *T01847-802572, Easter-Sep daily 1000-1700, free*, where you learn all about the 'benefits' of nuclear power.

▲ Strathmore to Braemore → *OS sheet No 11 covers the route.*

This walk gives a flavour of the bleak but beautiful landscape of the Caithness hinterland. The 16-mile linear route starts from **Strathmore Lodge.** To get there, head south from Thurso on the B874. After a short distance turn on to the B870 and follow it for 10 miles to the little hamlet of Westerdale, which stands on the River Thurso. Turn right here on to an unnumbered road and follow this road for about 5 miles. Just past the white Strathmore Lodge the road splits. Follow the right-hand track which runs through commercial forestry, before emerging on to open moor with Loch More on the left.

Where the forestry begins again on the right, the track swings left across an arm of the loch and heads southwards. At the southern end of the loch a track runs left to **Dalnaha**, but keep going straight ahead, along the valley of the River Thurso. You then reach a cluster of buildings at **Dalnawillan Lodge**. Ignore the track which heads off to the right and carry straight on, past the house at **Dalganachan**, over Rumsdale Water and on to the junction before **The Glutt**, which is a series of buildings. Turn left here and follow the track for a further 4 miles till you reach the junction beside Lochan nan Bò Riabach. Continue down the valley of Berriedale Water to Braemore. There is no public transport from here, so you'll have to arrange your own transport if you don't want to retrace your steps.

Dunnet Head → *Phone code: 01847. Colour map 2, A3.*

About 10 miles northeast of Thurso is the most northerly point on the British mainland. No, not John O'Groats, but Dunnet Head. It's reached by turning off the Thurso–John O'Groats road at Dunnett, at the east end of Dunnett Bay, a 3-mile-long sandy beach that's popular with surfers who come to tackle the gigantic waves of the **Pentland Firth**, the wild and treacherous strait between the mainland and Orkney. Dunnet Bay has an excellent reef break and there's another good reef break at Brims Ness to the west. Further west still, at Strathy Bay, you'll find rollers that can match anything in Hawaii (though the water's obviously a lot colder). Dunnett Head is a much nicer place than John O'Groats, with marvellous views across to Orkney and along the entire north coast (on a clear day). There's a Victorian lighthouse out at the

point, and the dramatic seacliffs are teeming with seabirds. There's also a great little café, see Eating page 257.

Some 15 miles east of Thurso are the **Castle and Gardens of Mey** ⓘ *T01847-851473, www.castleofmey.org.uk, mid-May to end Jul and early Aug to end Sep, Sat-Thu 1030-1600, £7, concessions £6, children under 16 free*. Built by the 4th Earl of Caithness, the castle's future was under threat until the intervention of the late Queen Mother who bought it in 1952 and who holidayed here every year. The castle still welcomes royal visitors in the shape of Prince Charles who holidays here each summer.

John O'Groats → *Phone code: 01955. Colour map 2, A4.*

If you really must visit this dreary tourist trap, then that's your prerogative, but don't say we didn't warn you. It's the kind of boring, miserable place that any self-respecting traveller should avoid like the plague. It gets its name from the Dutchman Jan de Groot, who was commissioned by King James IV to run a ferry service to Orkney in 1496. Ferries still operate from here to Burwick in Orkney, see Transport, page 257. There's a **TIC** ⓘ *T01955-611373, Apr-Oct Mon-Sat*, as well as a post office, craft shops and a chippie.

Two miles east of John O'Groats is **Duncansby Head**, which is far more rewarding. South of the headland a path leads to the spectacular **Duncansby Stacks**, a series of dramatic rock formations. The 200-ft cliffs are home to countless seabirds and you can see the narrow, sheer-sided inlets known locally as *geos*.

Sleeping

Durness and around *p252*

B-C Mackays Rooms & Restaurant, Durness, T01971-511202, www.visitmackays.com. Easter-Nov. 7 en suite rooms. Modern, uninpiring exterior hides one of the best hotel experiences in the north of Scotland. Rooms are spacious and tastefully furnished with not a hint of tartan cheesiness on display. Staff are efficient and food in the restaurant a revelation. Excellent value. Highly recommended.

B-C Tongue Hotel, Tongue, T01847-611206. Open Apr-Oct. 19 en suite rooms. This former hunting lodge of the infamous Duke of Sutherland has great views across the Kyle of Tongue and the staff are extremely accommodating. Catering mostly for anglers it can arrange impromptu fishing trips and the restaurant does good food.

C-D Ben Loyal Hotel, Tongue, T01847-611216, www.benloyal.co.uk. Open all year. 11 en suite rooms. Friendly, hospitable small hotel and a good choice for the area. Food is recommended and the bar is a good place to while away an evening or two.

D Bighouse Lodge, Melvich, T01641- 531207, www.bighouseestate.com. 7 rooms. May-Oct. 18th-century mansion converted into small hotel at the mouth of the Halladale river in 4 acres of its own grounds. Mainly aimed at the huntin' shootin' an' fishin' brigade.

D Shieling Guest House, Melvich, T/F01641-531256, www.theshieling.co.uk. 3 en suite rooms. Open Apr-Oct. Top-class B&B in lovely location with great views. Excellent breakfasts. Highly recommended.

E Cloisters, Talmine, T01847-601286, www.cloisteral.demon.co.uk. 3 en suite rooms. Open all year. B&B in Beautiful 19th-century converted church.

E Farr Bay Inn, Bettyhill, T01641-521230, www.bettyhill.com. Good rooms and decent bar food too.

E Port-Na-Con Guest House, on the west shore of Loch Eriboll, 7 miles from Durness, T01971-511367, portnacon70@hotmail.com. 3 rooms. Open all year. This has to be the best value around Durness. It's popular with anglers and divers so you'll need to book ahead to take advantage of such comfort amidst all this great scenery. The food in the adjoining restaurant is superb and also great value, especially the seafood. Non-residents are welcome but should book. Recommended.

E Puffin Cottage, Durness, T01971-511208, www.puffincottage.com. 2 rooms. Apr-Sep. Best of the B&Bs in Durness.

E Rhian Cottage, Tongue, T01847-611257, rhiancottage.co.uk. 5 rooms. Open all year. Good value B&B.

F Bruachmor, Bettyhill, T01641-521265. Apr-Oct. Good value B&B.

F SYHA Youth Hostel, Smoo, to the east of the village, T01971-511244. Mid-Mar to early Oct. Basic.

F SYHA Youth Hostel, Tongue, T01847-611301. Mid-Mar to late Oct. Beautifully situated at the east end of the causeway.

Camping

Kincraig Camping and Caravan Site, Tongue, T01847-611218, just to the south of the village.

Salgo Sands Caravan Park, T01971-511222, caravans and camping.

Talmine, T01847-601225, 5 miles north of Tongue by the beach.

Thurso and around *p253, map p256*

Thurso has a wide variety of accommodation, most of it fairly average.

A Forss Country House Hotel, 4 miles out of Thurso at Bridge of Forss, T01847-861201, www.forsshousehotel.co.uk. 13 en suite rooms. Price includes dinner. The nicest place to stay by far around Thurso, if not the entire north coast. This small family-run hotel is set in 20 acres of lovely woodland and has an excellent restaurant, open to non-residents (TTT). Rooms are spacious (the en suite bathrooms are bigger than many other hotel rooms), the attention to detail is impressive and the service is spot on. Nothing is too much trouble for the staff here. Highly recommended.

A-B Station Hotel, 54 Princes St, Thurso, T01847-892003, www.stationthurso.co.uk. Open all year. 21 en suite rooms. Central, well-appoined rooms, friendly and welcoming, decent food, good value.

B Borgie Lodge Hotel, Skerray, by Thurso, T01641-521332, www.borgielodgehotel.

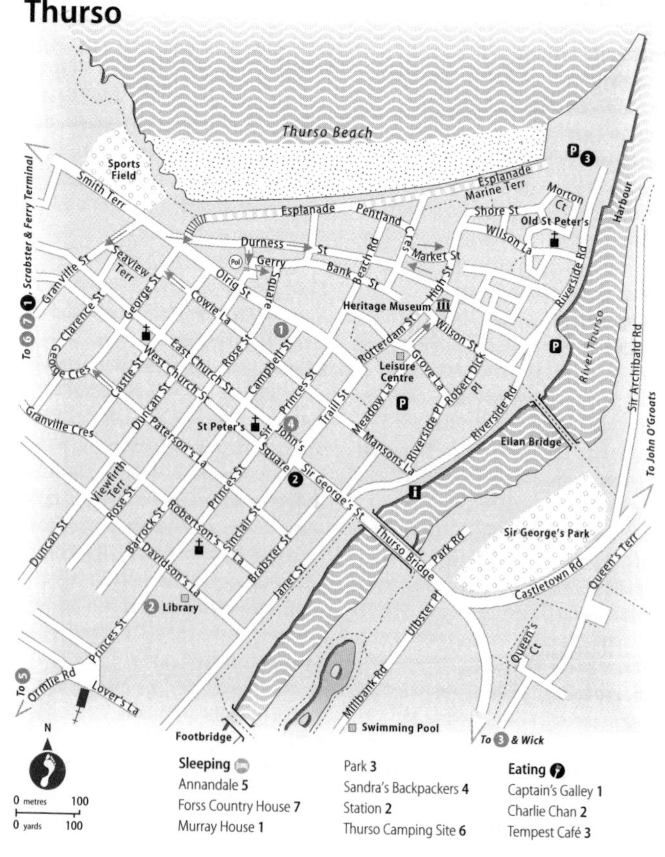

co.uk. 8 en suite rooms. Open all year. Fine small country hotel with appeal for gun sports and fishing types but also very fine food.

C-D Park Hotel, Oldfield, at the south end of town, 10 mins' walk from train station, T01847-893251, www.parkhotelthurso.co.uk. Open all year. 21 en suite rooms. Modern and rather functional building but clean, comfortable and extremely hospitable with good food at reasonable prices. Rooms at front have best views.

D Sharvedda, Strathy Point, by Thurso, T01641-541311, www.sharvedda.co.uk. 3 rooms. Open all year. Good quality B&B also offering evening meals (**B** with dinner).

D-E Murray House, 1 Campbell St, Thurso, T01847-895759, www.murrayhousebb.com. 5 en suite rooms. Open all year. Friendly and welcoming B&B, dinner also available (**C** with dinner). Good value.

E Annandale, 2 Rendel Govan Rd, Thurso, T01847-893942, thomson@annandale2.freeserve.co.uk. 3 rooms. Open all year. Very good-value B&B.

E Bencorragh House, Upper Gills in Canisbay, a few miles west of John O'Groats, T01955-611449, www.bencorraghhouse.com. Mar-Oct. A very decent B&B.

F Sandra's Backpackers, 24-26 Princes St, Thurso, T01847-894575, www.sandras-backpackers.ukf.net. Probably the best option at the very cheapest end of the scale.

Camping

Thurso Camping Site, T01847-607771, north of town on the road to Scrabster is the nearest to Thurso. There are a couple of campsites at **John O'Groats** and further west by the beach at **Huna**. Ask at the TIC.

Eating

Thurso and around *p253, map p256*

The **Forss Country House Hotel** (see Sleeping, above), is the best place to eat in the area; the other hotels listed are good options in town for a decent meal.

TTT **The Bower Inn**, between Thurso and Wick, turn off the coast road at Castletown and follow the B876 till you see the sign for Gillock, T01955-661292. A close second to the **Forss** for upmarket places to eat in the area.

TT **The Captain's Galley**, Scrabster, T01847-894999. Top-notch seafood restaurant in unpretentious surroundings, just the freshest of food brought to you within mins of being landed (or so it seems). Best choice hereabouts.

TT **Charlie Chan**, 2 Sinclair St, T01847-890888. Best of the ubiquitous Chinese restaurants in town.

T **Dunnett Head Tearoom**, Dunnett Head, a few miles from the lighthouse, T01847-851774. Apr-Oct daily 1500- 2000. Serves snacks and meals to hardy surfers.

T **Tempest Café**, by the harbour next to the surf shop of the same name (see Activities and tours, below). Tue-Sun 1000-1800. Good, chilled vibe, menu features typical surfer-type fare (ie loads of carbs).

Entertainment

Thurso and around *p253, map p256*

Viking Bowl, Ormlie Rd, T01847-895050. Compex with **bowling** and **cinema**.

Activities and tours

Thurso and around *p253, map p256*

Boat trips

John O'Groats Ferries, Ferry Office, John O'Groats, T01955-611353, www.jogferry.co.uk, operate **Orkney Islands Day Tours**, which leave daily 1 May-30 Sep at 0900, and return at 1945 (£35, children £17.50, under 5 free). A shorter day tour goes daily from 1 Jun-2 Sep 1030, and returns at 1800 (£32, children £16). There's also a wildlife cruise 20 Jun-31 Aug, which departs at 1430, £14, children £7.

Surfing

The best break in the region, indeed, one of the best breaks in the world, is Thurso East. For a detailed description of the wave and how to access it, see Footprint's *Surfing Britain*, which describes all the breaks along this coast. A good surf shop is **Tempest Surf**, by the harbour in Thurso, T01847-892500, www.tempest-surf.co.uk. Daily 1030-1800.

Transport

Durness and around *p252*

Bus A daily bus runs to and from **Thurso**, via **Tongue** and **Bettyhill** (Jun-Aug, Mon-Sat) with **Highland Country Buses**, T01847-893123, leaving Thurso at 1130 and

Durness at 1500. There's also a daily bus service (May to early Oct) to and from **Inverness** via **Ullapool** and **Lochinver**, with Bluebird/Inverness Traction, T01463-239292. There's a postbus service to **Lairg** via **Tongue** and **Altnaharra**, Mon-Sat at 1115; also via **Kinlochbervie** and **Scourie** Mon-Sat at 0820.

To get to **Cape Wrath**, first take the passenger ferry across the Kyle of Durness from Keoldale, 3 miles south of Durness, T01971-511376. It runs May-Sep hourly 0930-1630. The ferry connects with a minibus, T01971-511287, for the 11 miles to the cape (40 mins).

Thurso and around *p253, map p256*
Bus Citylink buses run to/from **Inverness** (3½ hrs) 4 times daily, T0870-5505050, continuing to **Scrabster** to connect with ferries to/from **Stromness** in **Orkney**. Citylink buses to **Inverness** connect with buses to **Edinburgh**. Highland Country Buses, T01847-893123, run local services to **Bettyhill** (3 times daily Mon-Thu, twice on Sat; 1 hr 10 mins) and to **Reay** (4 times daily Mon-Thu, 3 times on Sat). There are regular daily buses to and from **Wick** via **Halkirk** or **Castletown**. Highland Country Buses also run the service between Thurso train station and **Scrabster** ferry pier (5-10 mins). Harrold Coaches, T01955-631295, run a service to/from **John O'Groats** (4 times daily Mon-Thu, twice on Sat; 1 hr). Also from **Wick** (5 daily Mon-Fri, 4 on Sat) with **Highland Country Buses**. A **postbus** service runs to Wick airport, leaving Riverside Rd at 0920 and arriving at 1000. Buses arrive at Sir George's St Port Office and depart from Sir George's St Church.

Car hire William Dunnett & Co, T01847-893101.

Cycle hire The Bike & Camping Shop, the Arcade, 34 High St, T01847-896124, rents mountain bikes for £8 per day.

Ferry Northlink Ferries, www.northlinkferries.co.uk, to **Stromness** in **Orkney** leave from **Scrabster**, 2 miles north of Thurso. For details, see page 364). John O'Groats Ferries (see above for details) sail to **Burwick** (Orkney) twice daily from Jun to Sep (45 mins, £16 one way). A connecting bus takes passengers on to **Kirkwall** (40 mins, price incl in ferry ticket).

Train 3 trains leave daily from **Inverness** (3½ hrs), 2 of them connecting with the ferries from **Scrabster** to **Stromness** in **Orkney**. Trains continue to **Wick** (30 mins) and return trains to **Inverness** leave from **Wick**. The train station is at the south end of Princes St.

East coast

The east coast of the Highlands, from Inverness north to Wick, doesn't have the same draw as the west coast and attracts far fewer visitors, but it has its own, gentler appeal, and there are many lovely little seaside towns to explore, especially the singular former sea port of Cromarty. The main attraction in these parts, though, is undoubtedly the resident pod of bottlenose dolphins, which can be seen along the Moray coast between May and September. ▸▸ *For Sleeping, Eating and other listings, see pages 267-270.*

The Black Isle ▸▸ *pp267-270. Colour map 2, C2.*

→ *Phone code: 01381.*

Across the Kessock Bridge from Inverness is the Black Isle, which is neither an island nor black. It enjoys long hours of sunshine and low rainfall, and is an attractive landscape of rolling acres of barley and stately woods of oak and beech dropping down to the Moray coast. It also has a compelling atmosphere – a combination perhaps of its soft microclimate, lush vegetation and attractive architecture. Its main attractions are the picturesque town of Cromarty and Chanonry Point, on the southern side near Rosemarkie, which is one of the best dolphin-spotting sites in Europe.

North Kessock to Tore

On the north side of the Kessock Bridge, just north of the village, is the **North Kessock TIC** ⓘ *T01463-731505, Easter-Oct daily*. Next door is the Dolphin and Seal Visitor Centre, which gives details of accredited dolphin cruises. You can see dolphins from the village of North Kessock just to the south.

One of the many sacred wells (and caves) in the area is the unmissable **Clootie Well**, on the verge of the main road between Tore and Munlochy Bay Nature Reserve. It was once blessed by St Curitan (see below under Rosemarkie) and is thought to cure sick children. Thousands of rags still flutter from the surrounding trees, though well-worshippers are in danger of being mown down by traffic. Despite the presence of traffic, it's an eerie place. Go at night – if you dare.

Fortrose and Chanonry Point

Further east on this road, beyond Munlochy and Avoch (pronounced *Och*) is the village of Fortrose, on the east shore. The magnificent cathedral at Fortrose is now largely a ruin; rainwashed carved faces of rose-coloured sandstone peer down from roof bosses, and snapped-off stumps of window tracery are a reminder of Reformation vandalism. On the golf course at **Chanonry Point**, see box, page 260, overlooking the Moray Firth, a plaque marks the spot where the Brahan Seer was boiled in a barrel of tar (see box, page 260). Chanonry Point is also a great place for seeing dolphins. They come close to shore at high tide and there's a good chance of seeing them leaping above the waves.

Rosemarkie

A few miles from Fortrose on the north side of Chanonry Point is the tiny village of Rosemarkie. Celtic saints Curitan and Boniface selected this sheltered spot on the southern shore for their Christian mission in the seventh century. St Boniface is remembered at nearby St Bennet's Well. **Groam House Museum** ⓘ *T01381-620961, Easter-Sep Mon-Sat 1000-1700, Sun 1400-1630, Oct-Apr Sat and Sun 1400-1600, free*, houses a huge collection of Pictish sculptured stones found locally, imaginatively displayed alongside contemporary artwork inspired by them. A year-round programme of events and lectures is devoted to the study of Pictish culture. A lovely marked trail leads into Fairy Glen, now a nature reserve, from the top end of the High Street, through a wooded gorge where you may spot woodpeckers and treecreepers. The name obviously derives from the fairies that live here, though the last sighting was in the 1970s.

Cromarty → *Phone code: 01381.*

On the northeastern tip of the Black Isle Peninsula, at the mouth of the Cromarty Firth, is the gorgeous wee town of Cromarty, one of the east coast's major attractions. Its neat white-harled houses interspersed with gracious merchants' residences are almost unchanged since the 18th century when it was a sea port thriving on trade as far afield as Russia and the Baltic. Many emigrants bound for the New World embarked here. The town's prosperity, based on textiles and fishing, turned to decline and dereliction. Although restored and fully populated, Cromarty now has the atmosphere of a backwater, though a very attractive one at that, where you feel as if you're stepping back in time, in stark contrast to the numerous oil rigs moored on the opposite shore in Nigg Bay.

For a fascinating insight into the history of the area, visit the 18th-century **Cromarty Courthouse** ⓘ *Church St, T01381-600418, Apr-Oct daily 1000-1700, £4.50, concession/children £3.50, includes loan of headset for recorded tour of the town's other historic buildings*, which houses the town's museum. Next to the courthouse is the thatch-roofed **Hugh Miller's Cottage** ⓘ *T01381-600245, 31 Mar-30 Sep daily 1230-1630, Oct Sun-Wed 1230-1630, £5, concession £4, family £14*, birthplace of the eminent local geologist and author. Also worth seeing is the elegant 17th-century **East Church**.

A seerious crime

The Brahan Seer was boiled in a barrel of tar in 1660 but not before he had foretold the building of the Caledonian Canal and Kessock Bridge, the Highland Clearances and the Second World War. He also predicted the demise of the local lairds and the Seaforths. It was Lady Seaforth who ordered his execution, after the seer had a vision of her husband in the arms of another woman. Apparently the precise spot where he met his end is now the 13th hole of the golf course at Chanonry Point, which just goes to prove that it is indeed unlucky for some.

There's a good walk along a coastal path from the east end of the village through woodland to the top of the South Sutor headland, one of the two steep headlands guarding the narrow entrance to the Cromarty Firth. There are excellent views from here across the Moray Firth. Leaflets describing this and other local walks are available at the Cromarty Courthouse.

One of Cromarty's main attractions is its **dolphins**. They can be seen from the shore, or with a boat trip, see Activities and tours, page 270. To the west, the mudflats of **Udale Bay** are an RSPB reserve and a haven for wading birds and wintering duck and geese, which can be viewed from a hide. In the winter other birds such as pinkfooted geese and whooper swans use the bay as a roost.

Poyntzfield Herb Garden is an organic plant nursery specializing in rare and native medicinal herbs. Worth visiting if only for a glimpse of the house, and the view from the car park over the Cromarty Firth through massive beech trees.

The Cromarty Firth

» *pp267-270. Colour map 2, C1-2.*

Dingwall and around → *Phone code: 01349.*

Dingwall, at the head of the Cromarty Firth, has two major claims to fame. Not only is it believed to be the birthplace of Macbeth, it was also the home for many years of Neil Gunn (1891-1973), perhaps the Highlands' greatest literary figure, see also page 405. It's a fairly dull, though functional town, with good shops and banks lining its long main street. **Dingwall Museum** ⓘ *T01349-865366, May-Sep Mon-Sat 1000-1700, £1.50, concessions £1, children £0.50*, tells the history of this Royal Burgh.

East of Dingwall, before Evanton, is **Storehouse of Fowlis** ⓘ *T01349-830033, www.clanland.co, open all year Mon-Sat 0930-1800, Sun 1000-1700, free*, which has history and wildlife exhibitions and offers the chance to see the local seal population. Standing on a hill above **Evanton** is the **Fyrish Monument**, a replica of the Gate of Negapatam in India, built by local men and funded by local military hero, Sir Hector Munro, to commemorate his capture of the Indian town, in 1781. To get there, turn off the B9176 towards Boath. It's a stiff two-hour climb up to the top.

The Cromarty Firth is a centre for repairing North Sea oil rigs, and many of the villages along its north shore have benefited from the oil industry. One of these is **Invergordon**, just west of Nigg Bay, which has suffered in recent years due to the closure of the local aluminium factory. Beyond Invergordon, a road branches south to Nigg Ferry. The ferry from Cromarty to **Nigg** was once a major thoroughfare, and now a tiny two-car ferry makes the 20-minute crossing in the summer months, see Transport, page 270. From the ferry you get a good view of **Nigg Bay**, a vast natural harbour used in both world wars by the Royal Navy. Its entry is guarded by the dramatic headlands of the Sutors, identified in folklore as friendly giants. Also gigantic are the oil rigs ranged along the firth and the oil terminal at Nigg, a dramatic and not unpleasant contrast with Lilliputian Cromarty.

Strathpeffer and around → *Phone code: 01997.*

Just along from the Cromarty Firth is Strathpeffer, which gets busy in the summer with coach parties, but it's a pleasant place and there are some excellent walks in the surrounding hills. The little village gained recognition in 1819 when Doctor Morrison, a physician from Aberdeen, bathed in its sulphur springs and cured himself of rheumatoid arthritis. He quickly spread the word and Strathpeffer became a fashionable spa resort attracting thousands of visitors. Two world wars intervened and the town's popularity declined. Today the only reminder of its past is the **Water Sampling Pavilion** in the square where you can test the waters. There's a seasonal **TIC** ⓘ *main square, T01997-421415, Easter-Nov Mon-Sat 1000-1700.*

Just outside Strathpeffer on the road to Dingwall is the **Highland Museum of Childhood** ⓘ *T01997-421031, Mar-Oct Mon-Sat 1000-1700, Sun 1400-1700, Jul and Aug Mon-Thu 1000-1700 and 1900-2100, Sat 1000-1700, Sun 1400-1700, £1.50, concession £1*, which has many historical displays on childhood in the Highlands, as well as collections of dolls, toys and games.

A fine walk is to **Knock Farrel** and the **Touchstone Maze**, site of an Iron Age vitrified fort which lies at the north end of a ridge known locally as the **Cat's Back**. A marked trail starts from Blackmuir Wood car park. Head up the hill from town, turn left up a road immediately before the youth hostel, and the car park is on the left. The walk is 6 miles in total and takes about three hours. Aside from OS Landranger sheet 26, the route is also described in a Forestry Commission leaflet *Forests of Easter Ross*, available from tourist offices.

Another excellent side trip is to **Rogie Falls**, near Contin, which is 3 miles southwest of Strathpeffer on the main A835 Inverness–Ullapool road. The short walk up to the falls starts from the car park 3 miles north of Contin on the A835. There are also some pleasant woodland walks around here. Experienced hikers can tackle magnificent **Ben Wyvis** (3432 ft). The route to the summit starts 4 miles north of Garve, 7 miles northwest of Contin.

Tain and around » *pp267-270. Colour map 2, B2-C2.*

Squeezed between the Cromarty Firth to the south and the Dornoch Firth to the north is the Tain Peninsula, whose largest town is Tain, a place with a 1950s time-warp feel. It has an impressive historical portfolio: its backstreets are an intriguing jigsaw of imposing merchants' houses, steep vennels, secret gardens and dormer windows. The town serves a vast hinterland. Among the hills are little-visited backwoods and farm towns, narrow valleys lined with crofts where cattle graze in boggy haughs and, to the west, glens and moorland. Along the seaboard are the windswept fields of the Tarbat Peninsula. Good sea angling is to be had from the harbours of the otherwise dull coastal villages such as Balintore, and at Shandwick is a massive Pictish stone. It is said that unbaptized children were buried near the stone which is now in the Museum of Scotland in Edinburgh.

Tain

The **Collegiate church**, see box, page 262, is on Castle Brae, just off the High Street, and inside is a 17th-century panel painted with the badges of the trade guilds, a reminder of the town's busy international trade. Another reminder is the imposing 16th-century **Tolbooth** in the High Street. Next to the church is **Tain through Time** ⓘ *T01862-894089, Apr-Oct Mon-Sat 1000-1700, £3.50, concession £2.50*, a museum housed in the Pilgrimage which charts the town's medieval history. One of Tain's main attractions, just off the A9 to the north of town, is the very fine **Glenmorangie whisky distillery** ⓘ *T01862-892477, www.glenmorangie.com, all year Mon-Fri 0900-1700, Jun-Aug Mon-Sat 1000-1600, Sun 1200-1600, tours (45 mins) from 1030-1530, £2.50,*

Saintly beginnings

Tain was the birthplace of the 11th-century missionary St Duthac. Pilgrims flocked here in the Middle Ages to his shrine, and a ruin near the links is thought to be the original chapel. His head and heart, encapsulated in gold and silver reliquaries, were later kept in the still extant medieval Collegiate church until their disappearance during the Reformation. The shrine was much favoured by the Stewart kings, notably James IV who on one of his frequent pilgrimages reputedly approached walking penitentially barefoot along the King's Causeway. Tain's status as a place of sanctuary probably explains why Bruce's family fled here during the Wars of Independence.

where you can see how the world-famous whisky is made and try a sample. Famous for its various wood finishes, Glenmorangie remains Scotland's best-selling single malt whisky. You can now stay here, in some considerable style and comfort, at **Glenmorangie House** (see Sleeping, page 268).

Just to the south of town, off the A9, is the **Aldie Water Mill**, a restored 16th-century mill in working order, with various high-quality craft shops attached. Nearby is the **Tain Pottery** ⓘ *T01862-893786, 1000-1700*, which you can also visit.

Portnahomack

The seaside village of Portnahomack, or 'port of Colman', is named after the missionary who was keen as mustard to found a religious settlement here. Archaeological work is revealing the importance of this area in Pictish times. The **Tarbat Discovery Centre** ⓘ *T01862-871790*, in Tarbat Old Church, displays recently discovered Pictish stonecarving. From the harbour, with its 18th-century girnals (grain warehouses) and sheltered sandy beach, you can see a huge stretch of the Sutherland coast, and the great sandbanks – the 'gizzen brigs' – at the mouth of the Dornoch Firth. Boat trips are available from the harbour for sea angling. A worthwhile trip is out to Tarbat Ness lighthouse, about 3 miles north.

Hill of Fearn

South from Portnahomack, just west of the junction of the B9165 and the B9166, is Hill of Fearn. Fearn Abbey was moved here around 1250 from its original site near Edderton, where it was too vulnerable to sea raiders. It later became the parish church, but one Sunday in 1742 lightning struck the roof which fell in, killing 38 worshippers. This tragedy was preceded by a fairy harbinger sighted at nearby Loch Eye. In Hill of Fearn is the excellent **Anta Factory Shop** ⓘ *Mon-Sat 1000-1700, Jun-Sep also Sun 1000-1600*, one of the very best places in the country for classy tartan furnishing fabrics, as well as tartan rugs and throws, and pottery.

The Dornoch Firth

» *pp267-270. Colour map 2, C2.*

Fairies were said to cross the Dornoch Firth on cockle shells and were once seen building a bridge of fairy gold, perhaps a forerunner of the Dornoch Bridge which carries the A9 across the firth just north of Tain. A more pleasant and interesting route is to follow the A836 along the south shore. From The Struie, reached by the B9176 which branches south at Easter Fearn, there's a panoramic view over the Dornoch Firth and the Sutherland hills.

Edderton to the Kyle of Sutherland

In the churches of Edderton and Kincardine are Pictish stones. Another stands in a field northwest of Edderton (but don't disturb the crops or livestock). A quartz boulder at **Ardgay**, the 'Clach Eiteag', commemorates the cattle tryst and fair which once took place locally.

Ten miles from Ardgay, at the end of lovely Strathcarron, is the isolated **Croick church**, one of the most poignant reminders of the infamous Clearances. Here, in 1845, 90 local folk took refuge in the churchyard after they had been evicted from their homes in Glencalvie by the despicable Duke of Sutherland to make way for his sheep flocks. A reporter from *The Times* was there to describe this "wretched spectacle", as men, women and children were carted off, many never to return. His report is there to read, but far more evocative and harrowing are the names and messages the people scratched in spidery copperplate in the window panes.

North of Ardgay is the **Kyle of Sutherland**, where several rivers converge to flood into the sea through lush water meadows. Montrose was defeated here, at Carbisdale, in 1651. Overlooking the Kyle, at **Culrain**, is the 19th-century **Carbisdale Castle**, once home of the exiled King of Norway. It now houses a youth hostel, see Sleeping, page 267. After the Dornoch Ferry disaster of 1809, a bridge was built over the Kyle at **Bonar Bridge**, from where the A949 runs eastwards to join the main A9 just before Dornoch, while the A836 continues north to Lairg (see below). A few miles north of Invershin are the **Falls of Shin**, an excellent place to watch salmon battling upstream on their way to their spawning grounds (best seen June to September). The visitor centre has information about six easy walks in the immediate area; all are under an hour long. It also boasts an excellent café/shop (see Eating, page 269) and a shop described as 'Harrods of the north' (Mohammed Al Fayed's estate is close by, which explains the goods on offer.

Lairg → *Phone code: 01549.*

Eleven miles north of Bonar Bridge is the uninspiring village of Lairg, the region's main transport hub. Lairg is best known for its annual lamb sale, when young sheep from all over the north of Scotland are bought and sold. It is said that all roads meet at Lairg, and it's certainly a hard place to avoid. From here, the A839 heads east to meet the A9 between Dornoch and Golspie, and west to meet the A837 which runs out to Lochinver. The A836 heads north to Tongue, and south to Bonar Bridge. The A838 meanwhile heads northwest to Laxford Bridge and on to Durness, near Cape Wrath. There's a **TIC** ⓘ *T01549-402160, Apr-Oct daily.*

There are several interesting walks around the village, some of which lead to prehistoric sites, such as the Neolithic hut circles at nearby **Ord Hill**. These walks, and many others in the region, are described with maps in the Forestry Commission's leaflet *Forests of the Far North*, which is available at the Ferrycroft Countryside Centre and the TIC.

Dornoch and around → *Phone code: 01862. Colour map 2, B2.*

Dornoch is another architectural delight, with its deep, golden sandstone houses and leafy cathedral square. Bishop Gilbert of Moravia (Moray) built the cathedral circa 1245. His family's success in gaining a foothold in northeast Scotland against the Norsemen was rewarded with the Earldom of Sutherland. It was trouble with the Jarls which prompted Gilbert to move his power base here from Caithness, mindful that his predecessor had been boiled in butter by the locals (proof that too much of the stuff can kill you). The **TIC** ⓘ *T01862-810400, Apr-Oct Mon-Sat*, is on the main square.

The 13th-century **cathedral** ⓘ *Mon-Fri 0730-2000, you can climb the cathedral tower during Jul and Aug*, was badly damaged in 1570, then subjected to an ill-conceived 'restoration' by the Countess of Sutherland in 1835. Among the few surviving features is a series of gargoyles, including a green man, and the effigy of an unknown knight. Opposite the cathedral is the 16th-century Bishop's Palace, now a hotel, see Sleeping, page 267.

Nowadays Dornoch is famous for its links golf course, one of the world's finest and relatively easy to get on. It overlooks miles of dunes and a pristine sandy beach. A stone near the links marks the spot where the last witch in Scotland was burned, in 1722. Folklore recounts a bloody battle against raiding Vikings in 1259 on the beach at Embo, just to the north, in which Sir Richard Murray was killed. The battle is commemorated at the Earl's Cross. Trout fishing is available on Dornoch Lochans; enquire locally.

Straggling crofting townships such as **Rogart** are scattered through the glens and around the coast, all occupied and worked vigorously. The coastal population was swollen in the 19th century by tenants evicted from the inland glens; they were resettled here and encouraged to try fishing at such villages as Embo. Others joined the eager flood of emigrants to the New World already under way. Crofting tenancies still exist, but crofters now enjoy more protection, see page 307.

North of Dornoch is **Loch Fleet**, a river estuary with a ferocious tidal race at its mouth and an SNH reserve protecting rare birds and plants. The rotting skeletons of the fishing fleet abandoned in the First World War lie in the sand on the south shore west of the car park. Nearby is **Skibo Castle**, where Mr and Mrs Madonna tied the knot, in relative secrecy. It is home to the very, very exclusive Carnegie Club (www.carnegieclub.co.uk, for envious voyeurs or those with too much money). There are several walks in the forestry plantations in the area.

Far northeast coast » pp267-270.

North of Dornoch, the A9 follows the coast of Sutherland into the neighbouring county of Caithness through a series of straggling villages, still haunted by the memories of the Duke of Sutherland, one of Scotland's most odious landowners. The chief town in these parts is Wick, once the busiest herring port in Europe.

Golspie → *Phone code: 01408. Colour map 2, B2. Population: 1650.*

There is little to recommend the little town of Golspie, though it does have a couple of banks and supermarkets. There's an 18-hole golf course, and the **Orcadian Stone Company** has a large display of fossils and geological specimens from the Highlands and beyond. The town lives in the dark shadow of the Sutherlands: on **Beinn a'Bhraggaidh** (1293 ft), to the southwest, is a huge, 100 ft-high monument to the Duke of Sutherland. Those who make it up to the monument and who know something of the Duke's many despicable acts may find the inscription risible, as it describes him as "a judicious, kind and liberal landlord". There's no reference to the fact that he forcibly evicted 15,000 tenants from his estate. Not surprisingly, locals would like to see this eyesore removed from the landscape, broken into tiny pieces and then scattered far and wide. Unfortunately, and most surprisingly, they have thus far been unsuccessful.

A mile north of the village is the grotesque form of **Dunrobin Castle** ⓘ *T01408-633177, Apr-May and 1-15 Oct Mon-Sat 1030-1630, Sun 1200-1630, Jun-Sep Mon-Sat 1030-1730, Sun 1200-1730, £6.50, concession £5.50, children £4.50*. This is the ancient seat of the Dukes of Sutherland, who once owned more land than anyone else in the British Empire. Much enlarged and aggrandized in the 19th century, with fairytale turrets, the enormous 189-room castle, the largest house in the Highlands, is stuffed full of fine furniture, paintings, tapestries and objets d'art. The whole unedifying spectacle is a legacy to obscene wealth and unimaginable greed, on a par with Nicolae Ceausescu's palace in Bucharest. The hideous confection overlooks admittedly beautiful gardens laid out with box hedges, ornamental trees

The light fantastic

A feature of visiting the far north of Scotland in winter is the chance of seeing the *Aurora Borealis*, or Northern Lights, which decorate the night skies like a gigantic laser show. The best time to see them is between October and March – especially during December and January. Try to get as far north as you can, though there are no guarantees of a sighting as cloud cover can obscure visibility. Any of the north-facing coastal villages are a good bet.

and fountains. The museum is an animal-lover's nightmare and almost a caricature of the aristocracy, with a spectacular Victorian taxidermy collection. There are also local antiquities, some from ancient brochs, and Pictish stonecarvings.

Brora → *Phone code: 01408. Colour map 2, B2. Population: 1860.*

Brora sits at the mouth of the River Brora which, as everywhere on this coast, is the site of a once-lucrative salmon netting industry. At the harbour, the ice house is a relic of the herring boom. Coal mines, opened in the 16th century, salt pans and a brickworks are all defunct. Still very much alive, however, is **Hunter's**, the local weavers of heavyweight traditional tweeds, and a good place to invest in some natty headwear. A mile or so north of town is the interesting **Clynelish distillery** ⓘ *T01408-623003, www.malts.com, Easter-Sep Mon-Fri 1000-1700, Oct 1100-1600, Nov-Easter by appointment, £4*. Something of a cult amongst whisky lovers, this malt is distinctive for its briny falvour. **Castle Cole** in lovely Strath Brora, 8 miles northwest, is one of several ruined brochs. Another, **Carn Liath** (signposted), is by the main road, 3 miles south of Brora.

Helmsdale → *Phone code: 01431. Colour map 2, B3.*

North of Brora is the former herring port of Helmsdale, which gets busy in the summer. The village is most notable for its excellent **Timespan Heritage Centre** ⓘ *T01431-821327, Easter-Oct Mon-Sat 1000-1700, Sun 1400-1700, £4, concession £2, children £1.75*, which brings the history of the Highlands to life through a series of high-tech displays, sound effects and an audio-visual programme. There's also a café and shop on site. The **TIC** ⓘ *T01431-821640, Apr-Sep Mon-Sat 1000-1700*, is on the south side of the village, by the A9.

North from Helmsdale the A9 climbs spectacularly up the **Ord of Caithness** and over the pass enters a desolate, treeless landscape; an area devastated during the Clearances. To get some idea of the hardships people had to endure, stop at the ruined crofting village of **Badbea**, just beyond Ousdale. At **Berriedale**, a farm track leads west to the Wag, from where you can climb **Morven** (2313 ft), the highest hill in Caithness, with amazing views across the whole county.

Dunbeath → *Phone code: 01593. Colour map 2, B3.*

The A9 coast road then drops down into Dunbeath, a pleasant little village at the mouth of a small *strath* (or glen). This was the birthplace of one of Scotland's foremost writers, Neil Gunn (1891-1973). His finest works, such as *The Silver Darlings* and *Highland River*, reflect his experiences of growing up in the northeast and are fascinating accounts of life here during the days of the herring boom, though the sleepy harbour of today is barely recognizable as the erstwhile bustling fishing port. The villages of Dunbeath, and Latherton to the north, are included on the **Neil Gunn Trail**, as is the beautiful walk up the glen, described in the leaflet available at the **Dunbeath Heritage Centre** ⓘ *T01593-731233, www.dunbeath-heritage.org.uk,*

After the goldrush

A short drive from Helmsdale, up the Strath of Kildonan (or Strath Ullie), is Baile an Or (Gaelic for 'goldfield'), site of the great Sutherland Gold Rush of 1869. It all started after local man Robert Gilchrist returned home from the Australian gold fields only to discover gold here, on his doorstep. His success brought others rushing to Kildonan, and soon a shanty town had sprung up to accommodate them.

Within a year the gold rush was over, but small amounts are still found today. Anyone who fancies their luck can try a bit of gold panning in the Kildonan Burn at Baile an Or, about a mile from Kildonan train station. You can rent out gold panning kits at Strath Ullie Crafts & Fishing Tackle, opposite the Timespan Heritage Centre in Helmsdale, for £2.50 per day, and licences are free.

Easter-Oct daily 1000-1700, £2, concession £1, children free. Here, in Neil Gunn's former school, you can learn all about the life and works of the famous novelist as well as the history of Caithness. Just outside the village is the **Laidhay Croft Museum** ⓘ *T01593-731370, Easter-Oct daily 1000-1700, £1, children £0.50*, a restored traditional longhouse with stable, house and byre all under the same roof.

Wick and around → *Phone code: 01955. Colour map 2, A4.*

A century ago Wick was Europe's busiest herring port, its harbour jam-packed with fishing boats and larger ships exporting tons of salted fish to Russia, Scandinavia and the West Indian slave plantations. The fishing industry has long since gone, and the demise of the nearby nuclear power station at Douneray has only added to the tangible sense of ennui. There are, however, some interesting archaeological sites in Caithness, as well as the dramatic landscapes, and Wick makes a useful base for exploring the area. There is a **TIC** ⓘ *Whitechapel Rd (just off the High St), T01955-602596, all year Mon-Fri 0900-1700, Sun 0900-1300.*

Wick is actually two towns. On one side of the river is Wick proper and on the other is Pulteneytown, the model town planned by Thomas Telford for the British Fisheries Society in 1806 to house evicted crofters who came to work here. Now it's one great living museum of fishermen's cottages and derelict sheds and stores around the near-deserted quays. It gives a good idea of the scale of the herring trade during its heyday in the mid-19th century, when over 1000 boats set sail to catch the 'silver darlings'. Here, on Bank Row, is the superb **Wick Heritage Centre** ⓘ *T01955-605393, www.wickheritage.org/, Easter-Oct Mon-Sat 1000-1545, £2, children £0.50.* The highlight of the centre is its massive photographic collection dating from the late 19th century.

Whether you're staying or just passing through, don't miss Capaldi's, on the High Street, for exquisite home-made Italian ice cream.

Three miles north of Wick are the impressive 15th-century clifftop ruins of **Sinclair and Girnigoe Castle**. On the A99 heading north out of town is the **Caithness Glass Visitors Centre** ⓘ *T01955-602286, Mon-Thu 0900-1630*, where you can watch the famous glass being blown. There is a good walk along the rocky shore east of town to The Trinkie, a natural rock pool fed by the sea, and about a mile further on to the Brig o' Trams. Ask for details at the TIC. Before Wick, at Ulbster, is another archaeological site, the **Cairn o' Get**. Opposite the sign are the precipitous **Whaligoe Steps**, which lead to a tiny, picturesque harbour.

Archaeological sites around Caithness

Caithness may lack the impressive henges of other parts of the UK but it does boast a number of stone rows: areas covered by large numbers of small stones arranged in geometric patterns. These are thought to date from circa 2000 BC. The best and most easily accessible is the **Hill o' Many Stanes**. To get there, drive 9 miles south of Wick. On the A9 and turn right onto a minor road where you see the signpost. A short way up this road is a signposted gate into the field, on the left-hand side. A path leads to the curious fan-shaped configuration of Bronze Age standing stones; 200 of them in 22 rows. No one yet knows their precise purpose but studies have shown that there were once 600 stones here.

There are also a couple of Pictish Brochs in Caithness. These were almost entirely unique to the north and northwest of Scotland and were windowless, dry-stone towers, between 10 and 45 ft in height, with a circular ground plan. The walls were hollow in places to allow staircases and small chambers. These were built between 2000 BC and AD 200, though they continued in use after that time, and were used for both domestic and defensive purposes. There are remains of a broch at **Nybster,** 7 miles south of John o' Groats on the A9. Look out for the sign for the harbour and broch on the right heading north. Turn onto the minor road which leads down to a small car park. Follow the path along the clifftop to the broch, which stands on a headland surrounded by steep cliffs on three sides. Just to the south of here, at Keiss, are the remains of another broch.

One of the most fascinating archaeological sites in the north are the well- preserved **Grey Cairns of Camster**. These chambered cairns, dating from the third and fourth millenia BC, are burial mounds of stone raised around carefully structured circular chambers with narrow entrance passages. To get there, head a mile east of Lybster on the A9, then turn left on to the minor road leading north to Watten. The cairns are 5 miles along this road, on the left-hand side. They comprise two enormous prehistoric burial chambers dating from 2500 BC. They are amazingly complete, with corbelled ceilings, and can be entered on hands and knees through narrow passageways.

Sleeping

Cromarty *p259*

For such an appealing place, there's precious little accommodation, so it's advisable to book ahead during the summer months.

B-C Braelangwell House, Balblair, T01381-610353, www.braelangwellhouse.co.uk. 3 rooms. Mar-Dec. Superior standard of B&B in elegant Georgian house. Recommended.

C Royal Hotel, Marine Terr, T01381-600217, www.royalcromartyhotel.co.uk. 10 rooms. Open all year. The best place to stay, with a good restaurant (**ΨΨΨ**), and cheaper meals are available in the bar.

Dingwall and around *p260*

A The Dower House, 2 miles north of Muir of Ord on A862 to Dingwall, T01463-870090, www.thedowerhouse.co.uk. 3 en suite rooms. Open all year. Very comfortable small hotel set in 5 acres of woodland and gardens, excellent food (dinner **ΨΨΨ**) and also self-catering cottage available. Worth the money. Recommended.

B Kinkell House Hotel, Easter Kinkell, Conan Bridge, by Dingwall, T01349-861270, www.kinkellhousehotel.com. 9 en suite rooms. Lovely country hotel in farmland, style and comfort and attention to detail, also superb cooking (**L-A** including dinner).

B Tulloch Castle Hotel, T01349-861325, www.tullochcastle.co.uk. 19 en suite rooms. Open all year. This 12th-century castle is the smartest place around, 4-poster bed costs a bit more.

D Fairfield House, Craig Rd, Dingwall, T01349-864754, www.fairjell.com. 4 en suite rooms. Open all year. Better-than-average B&B.

Strathpeffer and around *p261*

A-B Coull House Hotel, Contin, 3 miles southwest of Strathpeffer, T01997-421487, www.coulhousehotel.com. 21 rooms. Open all year. Top of the list is this elegant 19th-century country house offering fine food. Excellent choice.

B-C Brunstane Lodge Hotel, Golf Course Rd, Strathpeffer, T01997-421261, www.brunstanelodge.com. 6 en suite rooms. Open all year. Good little hotel serving decent cheap bar meals.

D Craigvar, on the Square, Strathpeffer, T01997-421622, www.craigvar.com. 3 en suite rooms. Open all year. Elegant Georgian house offering considerable style and comfort at this price, one of the best B&Bs in the region. Recommended.

D Dunraven Lodge, Golf Course Rd, Strathpeffer, T01997-421210, www.dunravenlodge.co.uk. 3 en suite rooms. Open all year. Good value B&B.

D-E White Lodge, The Square, Strathpeffer, T01997-421730, www.the-white-lodge.co.uk. 3 en suite rooms. Open all year. Another very good B&B.

Tain *p261*

L Glenmorangie House at Cadboll, Fearn, by Tain, T01862-871671, www.thegelnmorangiehouse.com. 6 en suite rooms. Owned by the whisky people, this place simply oozes style from every pore. Accommodation in the main house is supplemented by 3 cottages which sleep a total of 6. Price includes a lavish 5-course dinner and also afternoon tea as well as breakfast. Recommended.

L-A Mansfield House Hotel, Scotsburn Rd, T01862-892052, www.mansfield-house.co.uk. 19th-century baronial splendour and superb cuisine. Restaurant also open to non-residents (TTT). Highly recommended.

B Morangie House Hotel, Morangie Rd, T01862-892281, www.morangiehotel.com. 26 rooms. Open all year. Now part of the Swallow chain, this Victorian hotel still serves excellent food (dinner TTT, lunch TT) in its restaurant. Very good value.

E Golf View House, 13 Knockbreck Rd, T01862-892856, www.golf-view.co.uk. 3 en suite rooms. Feb-Nov. Sunstantial house offering very fine B&B.

Lairg *p263*

D The Nip Inn, Main St, T01549-402243, www.nipinn.co.uk. 6 en suite rooms. Open all year. Decent value, also does bar meals.

D-E Highland House, 88 Lower Torroble, T01549-402414. 3 en suite rooms. Open all year. Good quality B&B, also dies evening meals (**C** including dinner).

F Sleeperzzz.com, T01408-641343, www.sleeperzzz.com. There are several B&Bs and a campsites, but the most interesting place to stay is 9 miles east at Rogart train station, where you can get cheap hostel accommodation at the 2 old rail carriages that have been converted to sleep 16 people. There's a 10% discount for bike or train users.

Dornoch and around *p263*

There are also lots of good B&Bs and a campsite, in addition to these options.

L The Royal Golf Hotel, T/F01862-810283, www.swallowhotels.com. 25 en suite rooms. Open all year. Next to the 1st tee, this plush chain hotel obviously caters to golfers, but also has a very good restaurant (TTT-TT).

B 2 Quail Restaurant and Rooms, Castle St, T01862-811811, www.2quail.com. 3 rooms above one of the very best (and smallest) restaurants in the region, run by Michael and Kerensa Carr. Rooms not huge but the magnificent set 4-course menu (TTT) more than compensates. Open Apr-Oct Tue-Sat for dinner, winter Fri and Sat only. Highly recommended.

B-D Dornoch Castle Hotel, T01862-810216, www.dornochcastle.com. Apr-Oct. Formerly the Bishop's Palace, this 16th-century building is full of character and boasts excellent food (TTT).

E Auchlea Guest House, T01862-811524. 3 en suite rooms. Open all year. Notable for its very good food (dinner TT).

F Carbisdale Castle Youth Hostel, T01549-421232. End Feb-end Oct (except the first 2 weeks in May). The largest and most sumptuous hostel in Scotland, and possibly anywhere else, is ½ mile up a steep hill from the station. Staying here is a truly amazing experience and will charm any frustrated would-be aristocrat.

Brora *p265*

A Royal Marine Hotel, Golf Rd, T01408-621252, www.highlandescapehotels.com. 22 rooms. Open all year. Early 20th-century country house designed by Robert Lorimer, this fine golf hotel boasts an indoor pool, spa and gym as well as a café-bar, bistro and more formal dining room, and an excellent reputation for its food.

D Glenaveron, Golf Rd, T/F01408-621601, www.glenaveron.com. 3 en suite rooms.

Opan all year. Among the many B&Bs here this is an excellent choice and good value.

Helmsdale *p265*

B-C Navidale House Hotel, T01431-821258. Feb-Nov. Most upmarket choice, also a good place to eat.

E Broomhill House, T01431-821259. 2 en suite rooms. Open all year. Good-value B&B run by Sylvia Blance, with a distinctive turret.

E Torbuie, Navidale, T01431-821424. 2 en suite rooms. Apr-Oct. Good-value B&B.

F SYHA Youth Hostel, T01431-821577. Mid-May to early Oct.

Wick and around *p266*

A-B Portland Arms Hotel, 15 miles south, in Lybster, T01593-721208, www.portland arms.co.uk. 22 rooms. Open all year. Best around, a 19th-century coaching inn, full of character serving great food (ΨΨΨ).

E The Clachan, 13 Randolph Place, South Rd, TT01955-605384. 3 en suite rooms. Open all year. Best B&B in town in our opinion.

E Wellington Guest House, 41-43 High St, T01955-603287. Open Mar-Oct. Worthwhile choice is above is full.

Eating

Cromarty *p259*

ΨΨΨ Sutors Creek, 21 Bank St, T01381-600855. Wed-Sun till 2100. Cooperative café/restaurant that's famous for its superb wood-fired pizzas, but also other dishes using local ingredients in season. Recommended.

ΨΨ Cromarty Arms, opposite the Cromarty Courthouse. Cheap bar food. Also has live music some nights.

ΨΨ Thistle's Restaurant, Church St, T01381-600471. Has an imaginative menu, including interesting vegetarian dishes.

Ψ Binnie's Tearoom, Church St. A great place for tea and scones.

Portnahomack *p262*

ΨΨ The Oyster Catcher, T01862-871560. A great place to eat out here is this small café-restaurant serving snacks and lunches, and dinner from 1930 (if booked). Crêpes are a speciality, but it also does pasta, seafood and fish.

Edderton to the Kyle of Sutherland *p263*

ΨΨ-Ψ Falls of Shin Restaurant, Achany Glen, by Lairg, T01549-402231. Mar-Sep 0930-1730, Oct-Mar 1000-1700. A gastronomic oasis housed in the most unlikely of places. Plain and simple food cooked to perfection, probably better than your mum makes. Excellent value.

Brora *p265*

ΨΨ The Quiet Piggy, Station Sq, T01408-622011. Tue-Sun for lunch and dinner. Very good food cooked with flair and imagination.

Helmsdale *p265*

ΨΨ La Mirage, opposite the TIC. Daily 1200-2045 (Dec-Apr till 1900). Famous tearoom whose erstwhile proprietress, the inimitable Nancy Sinclair, modelled herself, and her tearoom, on Barbara Cartland, queen of romantic novels. The whole effect is pure kitsch. Good food though, especially the fish and chips.

Wick and around *p266*

The best places to eat are out of town at the Portland Arms Hotel (see above) and the Bower Inn, see page 257.

ΨΨ Bord de L'Eau, Market St, T01955-604400. Tue-Sat for lunch and dinner. French bistro-style cooking. Very popular with locals.

ΨΨ Queen's Hotel, Francis St, T01955-602992. Probably the next best place in town, varied menu.

Ψ Cabrelli's, 134 High St. Great caff serving large portions of carbs to locals.

Shopping

Tain *p261*

Bannerman's, Knockbreck Av. A fish and seafood wholesalers, sells local mussels.

Brown's Gallery, Castle Brae. Showcases work by Highland artists.

Dornoch and around *p263*

The Dornoch Bookshop, High St, T01862-810165, is the only bookshop in the area and stocks local books.

Activities and tours

Cromarty *p259*
Dolphin-spotting boat trips leave from Cromarty, but make sure you go with an accredited operator.
Dolphin Ecosse, T01381-600323. Half- and full-day trips leave from the harbour to see porpoises, seals, dolphins, and perhaps even killer whales further out. Accredited operator.

Transport

Cromarty *p259*
Bus Highland Bus & Coach, T01463-233371, runs a service from **Inverness** to **Fortrose** and **Cromarty** (4-7 times daily Mon-Sat). There is also a Wed and Thu service to/from **Dingwall**.

Ferry A 2-car ferry crosses to **Nigg** every ½ hr from Apr to Oct, 0900-1800.

Dingwall and around *p260*
Bus There are hourly buses between **Inverness** and **Invergordon**, via Dingwall. There are also hourly buses between **Inverness** and Dingwall via **Muir of Ord**. There are buses between Dingwall and **Rosemarkie** (twice a day Mon-Thu), and between Dingwall and **Cromarty** (Wed and Thu).

Train Dingwall is on the rail line between **Inverness** and **Kyle of Lochalsh** and **Thurso**. There are several trains daily in each direction (30 mins to Inverness).

Strathpeffer and around *p261*
Bus There are regular buses between Strathpeffer and **Dingwall** (see above).

Tain *p261*
Bus Citylink buses between **Inverness** and **Thurso** pass through Tain 4 times a day. There are also buses to **Portmahomack** (4 times daily Mon-Thu), **Balintore** (5-6 times daily Mon-Sat), **Lairg** via **Bonar Bridge** (3 times daily Mon-Sat) and **Dornoch** via **Bonar Bridge** (once a day Mon-Thu) with **Inverness Traction**, T01463-239292, and **Rapson's of Brora**, T01408-621245.

Train Tain is on the **Inverness-Thurso** rail line and there are 3 trains daily in each direction.

Lairg *p263*
Bus Inverness Traction buses, T01463-239292, run from here to **Ullapool**, with connections to **Lochinver** and **Durness**, from May to early Oct (Mon-Sat). Lairg is also the central point for several **postbus** routes, T01463-256228.

Train Trains between **Inverness** and **Thurso** stop at Lairg and Rogart stations 3 times daily.

Dornoch and around *p263*
Bus Hourly Mon-Sat (5 times on Sun) between **Inverness** and **Lairg** stop in **Ardgay** and **Bonar Bridge**. **Citylink** buses between Inverness and Thurso also stop in Dornoch 4 daily.

Train Services between **Inverness** and **Thurso** stop at **Ardgay** and **Culrain**.

Helmsdale *p265*
Buses and trains are the same as for Wick (see below). Helmsdale is on the **Inverness–Wick/Thurso** rail line.

Wick and around *p266*
Air A few miles north of town, is Wick airport, T01955-602215. Daily direct flights to and from **Kirkwall** (Orkney), **Sumburgh** (Shetland), **Aberdeen** and **Edinburgh** with and **British Airways Express**, T08457-733377. Also direct flights to/from **Newcastle** with **Eastern Airways**, T01955-603914. There's a **postbus** service to Wick airport Mon-Sat at 1015.

Bus Scottish Citylink, T08705-505050, buses between **Inverness** and **Thurso** stop en route in **Wick** (3 daily). There are also regular local buses to **Thurso**, via **Halkirk** or **Castletown**, and buses to **Helmsdale** (2-6 times daily Mon-Sat, 1-4 on Sun) and **John O'Groats** (5 daily Mon-Sat, 4 on Sun).
The train and bus stations are next to each other behind the hospital.

Car/bike hire **Richard's Garage**, Francis St, T01955-604123.

Train Trains leave for **Inverness** (3 daily Mon-Sat, 2 on Sun; 3¾ hrs) via **Thurso**, **Helmsdale**, **Golspie**, **Lairg** and **Dingwall**. The train station is behind the hospital.

Skye & the Small Isles

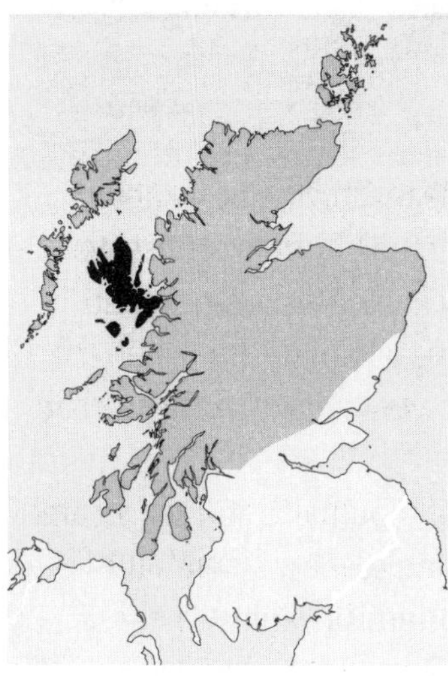

Footprint features

Introduction

The Isle of Skye (An t-Eilean Sgitheanach), the best known of all the Scottish islands, gets its name from the Norse word for cloud (skuy) and is commonly known as Eilean a Cheo (the Misty Isle), so it obviously rains a lot here. But when the rain stops and the mist clears, the views make the heart soar.

Skye's spectacular combination of mountains and sea creates some of Britiain's most breathtaking scenery. There's the surreal rock formations of the Trotternish Peninsula, the hummocky strangeness of Fairy Glen and the gentler pleasures of Sleat in the south. And then there's the Cuillins. Standing in the centre of the island, these proud, implacable mountains are the greatest concentration of peaks in Britain. This is one of the best places in Scotland for outdoor types: it offers air, sea, land and light in their purest form and any visitor will return home physically refreshed and spiritually uplifted.

The Small Isles is the collective name given to the four islands of Eigg, Muck, Rùm and Canna, lying south of Skye. Seen from the mainland, they look a very tempting prospect, especially the jagged outline of Rùm and curiously shaped Eigg. Visiting the islands is not easy; ferry transport is designed purely for the inhabitants and not geared towards the convenience of island-hopping tourists, and accommodation and facilities are limited. However, the determined traveller, with time on their hands, will be well rewarded, particularly on mountainous Rùm, with its superb walking and abundant wildlife.

★ Don't miss...

1 **Trotternish Peninsula** Walk the mighty Quiraing and then tackle the Old Man of Storr, page 276.

2 **Duirinish Peninsula** Walk out to the lighthouse at Neist Point, page 278.

3 **Loch Coruisk** Take a boat trip into the gaping mouth of this loch, page 283.

4 **Raasay** Sail to this island, only a few miles off Skye's east coast yet well off the beaten track, and climb to the top of Dun Caan, page 284.

5 **Three Chimneys** Sample some of the finest food in the country, page 290.

6 **Eigg** Walk across the 'Singing Sands' on this tiny island, page 294.

7 **Rùm** Brave the wilds of this island, home to the rare white-tailed sea eagle, and explore the bizarre and extravagant interior of Kinloch Castle, page 294.

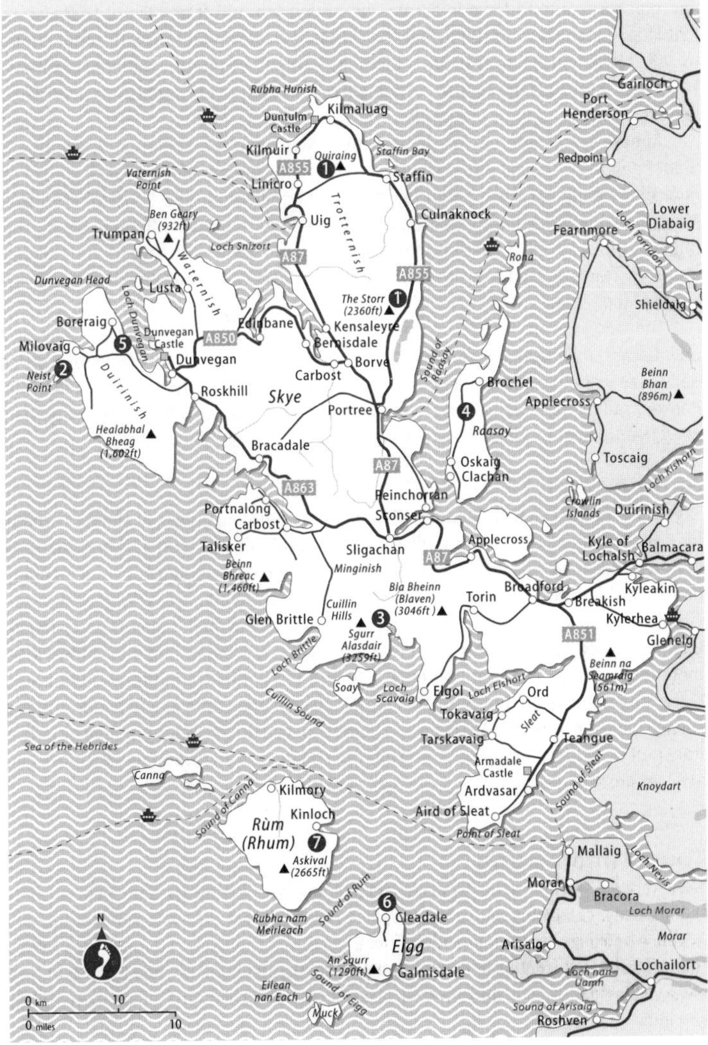

Isle of Skye

Aside from swooning at the island's natural beauty, the most popular destination is Dunvegan Castle, stronghold of the Macleod clan, while their old enemies, the MacDonalds hail from the Sleat Peninsula in the south of the island. The most famous Macdonald, Flora, who helped Bonnie Prince Charles flee to France, hailed from the northern tip of the island and is buried there. ▸▸ *For Sleeping, Eating and other listings, see pages 287-293.*

Ins and outs

Getting there

The quickest route to Skye is across the bridge (no toll) from Kyle of Lochalsh to Kyleakin. Coach services run to Skye from Glasgow and Inverness, with connections to all main cities in the UK (**Citylink**, T08705-5505050; **National Express**, T08705-808080). There is also a train service from Kyle of Lochalsh to Inverness, see page 230.

A more scenic approach is by ferry from Mallaig to Armadale, on the southern Sleat Peninsula. The car and passenger ferry makes the 20-minute crossing eight to nine times daily each way (Monday to Saturday only from mid September to mid May). Booking is recommended during the summer months, T08705-650000. The one-way trip costs £3.30 per passenger and £18 per car. Five-day saver return is £5.65 and £31. Trains to and from Fort William and Glasgow Queen Street connect with some of the ferries.

The best way to Skye is from Glenelg to Kylerhea, south of Kyleakin. The tiny private car ferry makes the 10-minute crossing when required from Easter to October daily, see page 230 for details. There is also a passenger ferry from Gairloch to Portree, sailing twice daily, see page 240. For more details and ticket bookings, visit www.overtheseatoskye.com. ▸▸ *For further details, see Transport page 292.*

Getting around

Skye is the second largest Hebridean island (after Harris and Lewis), at almost 50 miles long and between seven and 25 miles wide. It is possible to run up a hefty mileage as the extensive road system penetrates to all but the most remote corners of its many peninsulas. It is possible to get around by public transport midweek, with post buses supplementing the normal services, but, as everywhere in the Highlands and Islands, buses are few and far between at weekends, especially Sunday, and during the winter months. Buses run between Portree, Broadford, Uig (for ferries to the Western Isles), Kyleakin, Armadale (for ferries to Mallaig), Dunvegan and Carbost, and a more limited service runs from Broadford to Elgol and Portree to Glen Brittle. Getting around by public transport is virtually impossible in winter (October to March) as bus and post bus services are severely limited. ▸▸ *For further details, see Activities and tours page 291 and Transport page 292.*

Tourist information

Skye is well served by all types of accommodation: B&Bs, guesthouses, hostels, bunkhouses, campsites and some very fine hotels. During the peak summer months advance bookings are recommended. These can be made directly or through the island's tourist information centres in Portree (open all year), Broadford, Uig and Dunvegan. See www.visithighlands.com, and www.isleofskye.com. For local tourist information centres see individual sections.

Portree

» pp287-293. Colour map 1, C3.

→ *Phone code: 01478.*

Portree is Skye's capital and, as such, is a functional kind of place with all the attendant facilties and services you'd expect to find in the island's main settlement. That said, it's fairly attractive; a busy fishing port built around a natural harbour, with a row of brightly painted houses along the shorefront and the rest of the town rising steeply up to the central Somerled Square, which becomes clogged with tour coaches in the height of summer.

Ins and outs

Getting there and around Portree is ideally placed for trips to all parts of the island. Buses leave from the bus station in Somerled Square to Dunvegan, Uig, Broadford, Kyleakin, Armadale, the Talisker Distillery and Glenbrittle. There are also services to the mainland. The **CalMac ferry office** ⓘ *T01478-612075*, is on Park Road, just off Somerled Square. The town is compact enough to get around easily on foot, though there is a regular town bus service for those needing to get into the centre from the outskirts.

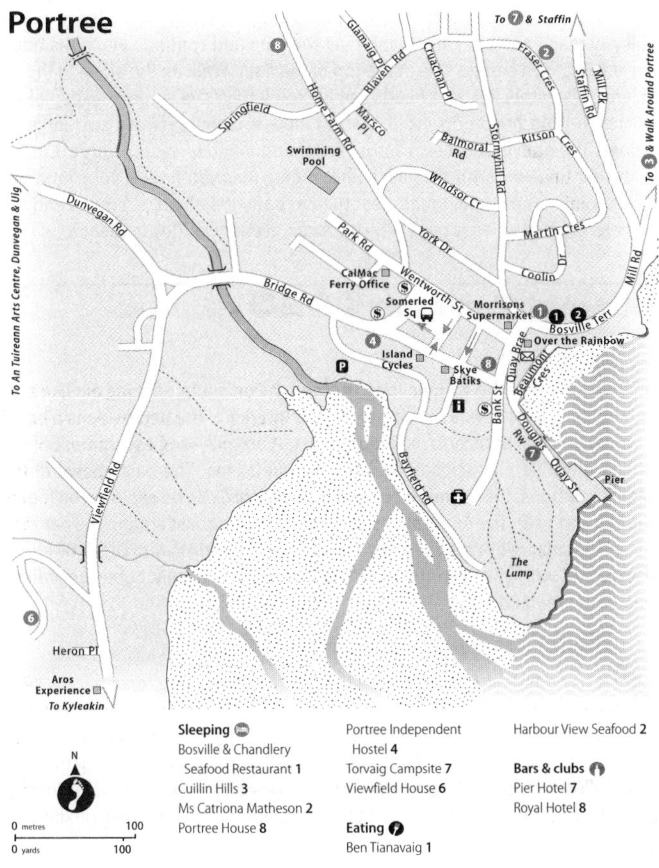

Sleeping
Bosville & Chandlery Seafood Restaurant **1**
Cuillin Hills **3**
Ms Catriona Matheson **2**
Portree House **8**
Portree Independent Hostel **4**
Torvaig Campsite **7**
Viewfield House **6**

Eating
Ben Tianavaig **1**
Harbour View Seafood **2**

Bars & clubs
Pier Hotel **7**
Royal Hotel **8**

 Tourist information The **TIC** ⓘ *Bayfield Rd, T01478-612137, mid-May to mid-Aug daily, mid-Aug to mid-May Mon-Sat*, has bus timetables and a good selection of books and maps.

Sights

Aros Experience ⓘ *Viewfield Rd, ½ mile from the town centre on the road to Broadford, T01478-613649, www.aros.com, daily 0900-2100 (off season 0900-1800), £4, concession £3, children £2, under 12 free*, is an exhibition and audio-visual display of the island's history and cultural heritage. The island's only theatre is housed here and features a varied programme of events, including drama, traditional music and movies; see Entertainment page 291. There's also a restaurant with good-value snacks and meals, a shop and a network of forest trails to explore.

An Tuireann Arts Centre ⓘ *Struan Rd, T01478-613306, www.antuireann.org.uk, Mar-Oct Mon-Sat 1000-1700, Nov-Feb Tue-Sat 1000-1700, free*, hosts exhibitions of contemporary visual arts and crafts. It has a fine café; see Eating, page 290.

▲ A nice, gentle introduction to walking in the area, and an opportunity to stretch your legs before tackling more strenuous routes such as the Old Man of Storr or the Quiraing, starts out from Bosville Terrace. Follow the street as it curves round, then take the right fork at the first junction, down towards the shore. Just after the car park to the right the road splits: follow the path to the right along the northern shore of the bay. The path follows the shore and passes a viewpoint and flagpole. It then becomes rougher as it swings round the headland and reaches a gate in a dyke. Go through the gate and cross the muddy field, then follow the fence up to the left till you reach another gate. Climb over the gate and continue along the edge of the next field, then cross a stile at the top of the field. Walk up the slope to the clear track and follow this left as it heads uphill. You'll then see some houses; take the track beyond the house on the left and follow it down between two large farm buildings. The path heads down across rough moorland towards Portree. Cross the stile and continue downhill through some woods; then you'll see a hotel on your left before rejoining the original road near the car park. It's about 2½ miles and takes about 1½ hours at an easy pace. The path can get very muddy in places.

Trotternish Peninsula

▸▸ pp287-293. Colour map 1, C3.

→ *Phone code: 01470.*

North from Portree is the 30-mile-long Trotternish Peninsula, sticking out like a giant thumb hitching a lift from a passing ferry. The interior of the peninsula is a basaltic lava wilderness full of bizarre rock formations. A 20-mile-long escarpment of sheer cliffs and towering pinnacles dominates the landscape. The best known of these strange formations, the **Quiraing** and **Old Man of Storr**, can be explored on foot (see pages 277 and 278). The A855 and A87 roads follow the coast around the peninsula, and a spectacular minor road bisects the ridge from Staffin Bay to Uig. Trotternish is best explored with your own transport, but there a few daily buses covering the circular route from Portree.

Uig

The A87 runs northwest from Portree to the tiny ferry port of Uig, dramatically set in a horseshoe bay and the departure point for ferries to **Tarbert** (Harris) and **Lochmaddy** (North Uist). Everything in the village revolves around the ferry timetables, and the regular bus service to and from Portree coincides with the arrival and departure of the ferries. The **TIC** ⓘ *T01470-542404, 1 Apr-31 Oct Mon-Sat, also Sun Jul-Sep*, is inside the CalMac office at the ferry pier, and will book accommodation anywhere on the island.

“” It’s almost inconceivable that these are natural formations and the inevitable mist only adds to the spooky strangeness of the place...

Just outside the village is the magical **Fairy Glen**. Turn right just before the **Uig Hotel** coming down the hill from the Portree direction. About a mile up the single track road you enter an eerie, mysterious world of perfect conical hills, some up to 60-ft high. It’s almost inconceivable that these are natural formations and the inevitable mist only adds to the spooky strangeness of the place.

Uig to Duntulm

At **Kilmuir** is the **Skye Museum of Island Life** ⓘ *Easter-Oct Mon-Sat 0930-1700, £1.75, children £1*. The group of thatched houses give a fascinating insight into the way of life of a crofting community at the end of the 19th century, and is the most authentic of several such museums on Skye. Behind the museum, at the end of the road, is **Flora MacDonald’s Monument**, which marks the grave of Skye’s most famous daughter, with her husband buried alongside. The rather austere memorial is inscribed with Dr Johnson’s poignant tribute, see box, page 279.

At the northwest tip of the peninsula, 15 minutes’ drive from Uig, is **Duntulm Castle**, a dramatic ruin perched atop a steep cliff, haunted by keening winds and the ghosts of its tragic past: according to local legend, the castle was abandoned around 1732 when a nursemaid accidentally let the baby heir fall from a window onto the cliffs below. The 15th-century structure, built on the site of an ancient Norse stronghold, became the chief Skye residence of the powerful MacDonalds and was the most imposing castle in the Hebrides.

▲ The Quiraing

Beyond Duntulm the A855 heads across the tip of the peninsula to the east coast, where the famous bizarre rock scenery is found. At the north end of **Staffin Bay**, a minor road cuts across the peninsula to Uig. This road is the access point for the Quiraing, the famous jumble of strangely shaped hills and rocks that is one of the island’s classic walks. This 4-mile walk is quite demanding, but the dramatic scenery more than compensates. To get to the starting point, drive 19 miles north from Portree on the A855. At Brogaig, just north of Staffin, take the single-track road to Uig. Follow it and, just after the road has zigzagged its way up the face of the ridge, park in the car park to the left. Cross the road and follow the well-defined path along the base of the cliffs, with a steep grassy slope down to the right. After about 1 mile you’ll start to see some of the well-known rocky features on the far side of a rough valley. The most imposing of these is **The Prison**, a huge, tilted square block. On the left, among the towering cliffs, is **The Needle**, a shaft of rock about 120-ft high. Scramble up the narrow gully to the left of The Needle to reach **The Table**, an area of flat grassland surrounded by high cliffs (local shinty teams used to play here!). From The Table continue along the path at the foot of the cliffs, past a small lochan on the right and through a stone dyke, until you reach the lowest point of the ridge on your left. Scramble up on to the ridge and make your way back along the tops of the cliffs (take care at this point). There’s a hard climb up the slopes of Meall na Suirmamach, but the views from the top are spectacular. Continue along the top of the cliffs for just over a mile and you’ll see the car park.

Even if you don’t attempt the walk, the road over the back of the Trotternish ridge from Uig makes a worthwhile detour.

Take no prisoners

Violent conflict between neighbouring clan chiefs was so commonplace on Skye and in the rest of the Western Highlands that it was almost accepted as part of the very fabric of society. One particularly gruesome example took place on Eigg in 1577. The Macleods had taken refuge in a cave but their presence was discovered by the MacDonalds, who piled brushwood at the entrance and set fire to it, burning alive the 395 people sheltering inside, almost the entire population of the island. Revenge came the following year, at Trumpan church in Ardmore Bay on Skye. The Macleods landed under cover of the early morning fog and set light to the church, burning the congregation inside.

Kilt Rock

A few miles south of Staffin Bay is Kilt Rock, an impressive 60-m sea cliff which gets its name from the vertical columnar basalt strata overlying horizontal ones beneath. A rather tenuous comparison perhaps, but the cliffs south of Staffin are particularly spectacular, as are the **Lealt Falls**, a torrent of mountain water at the head of a gorge, a few miles south of Kilt Rock. The falls are signposted by the road, so all you have to do is park the car and peer over. Just before the turn for Kilt Rock is a wee museum sporting such finds as a dinosaur bone and Bronze Age artefacts (open May to October).

Old Man of Storr

A few miles further south, and 7 miles north of Portree, is a car park which is the starting point for another of Skye's famous walks: up to the Old Man of Storr, the distinctive pinnacle which has detached itself from the cliffs of the Storr behind. This basalt finger of rock, 165 ft high, stands beneath the steep cliffs of The Storr (2360 ft) and is visible from the A855. The starting point for the 3½-mile walk up and back (1½ hours) is the car park on the left, just over 6 miles north of Portree, near the northern end of Loch Leathan, which can be reached by bus from Portree. Cross the stile over the wall by the Forestry Commission sign and follow the clear track up through the conifer plantation. The track is a gradual uphill climb until you come out into open grassland. Go through the gate in the fence and then it's a steep climb up the grassy slope with the massive pinnacle towering overhead. Once at the top you enter an area of weird and impressive rock formations. You can follow any of the dozens of paths that lead between the rocks, or just enjoy the fantastic views across to Raasay and the mainland beyond. You can follow the same path back down to the car park.

Waternish, Dunvegan and Duirinish

▸▸ *pp287-293. Colour map 1, C2-3.*

→ *Phone code: 01470.*

In the northwest of Skye the peninsulas of Waternish (or Vaternish) and Duirinish point out into the Minch towards the Western Isles. The larger Duirinish Peninsula holds more interest for the visitor, featuring the beautiful green valley of **Glendale**, an area brimming with history, the dramatic walk to **Neist Point** and **Dunvegan Castle**, Skye's most famous landmark.

Faithful Flora

In Kilmuir graveyard is the memorial which marks the grave of Flora MacDonald, one of the most famous characters in Skye's long history. The memorial bears Dr Johnson's fitting epitaph: *A name that will be mentioned in history, and if courage and fidelity be virtues, mentioned with honour.*

It was Flora MacDonald who helped Bonnie Prince Charlie to escape capture following the Jacobite defeat at Culloden in 1746. Pursued by government troops, the prince fled from South Uist 'over the sea to Skye' aboard Flora's boat, disguised as an Irish servant girl by the name of Betty Burke. He then made his way to Portree, where he bade farewell to the young woman who had risked her own life to protect his.

When Flora's part in the prince's escape became known, she was immediately arrested and sent to the Tower of London. She was released a year later, married a Skye man and then emigrated to North Carolina where she spent the next 12 years of her life. They returned to her husband's house in Kingsburgh in 1786. Flora died in Skye in 1790, and it is said that her funeral was the largest ever witnessed in the Highlands.

Edinbane

The turn-off to this much-visited part of the island is 4 miles northwest of Portree. The A850 swings west towards Dunvegan, by-passing the tiny village of Edinbane, where there's a campsite, two hotels, several B&Bs, a petrol station and the renowned **Edinbane Pottery** ⓘ *T01470-582234, Easter-Oct 0900-1800 workshop and showroom*, which is a must for souvenir hunters.

Waternish Peninsula

The A850 continues west. Those with their own transport and time on their hands might wish to make an interesting little detour at the **Fairy Bridge**, where the B886 runs north to **Trumpan**, near the tip of the Waternish Peninsula. If the weather's good (and it is, occasionally), this is the best place to watch the sun set in a blaze of red over the Outer Hebrides. If there's no sunset, then you could always visit **Skyeskins** ⓘ *T01470-592237, www.skyeskins.co.uk, daily 1000-18000*, in Loch Bay, the country's only traditional exhibition tannery. While here, you could also pop into the island's oldest pub at **Stein** (see Sleeping, page 288).

The ruined church at Trumpan, at the end of the road, has some grisly skeletons in its cupboard (see box, above). In the graveyard is the 'trial stone'. A hole in the stone was used to test whether or not an accused person was telling the truth. If they could quickly find the hole and stick their arm through it while blindfolded, they were found innocent, but if not, they were guilty. The church is also the starting point for the strenuous 8-mile walk out to **Waternish point** and back.

Dunvegan

A few miles further on from the turn-off to Waternish is the little village of Dunvegan. Just to the north of the village is proud **Dunvegan Castle** ⓘ *01470-521206, www.dunvegancastle.com, mid-Mar to Nov daily 1000-1730, rest of the year 1100-1600, castle £7, £6 concession, £4 children, gardens only £5/3.50/3*, the island's most important tourist attraction. This is the home of the chiefs of the Clan Macleod who have lived here for over seven centuries, making it the oldest inhabited castle in Britain. The present structure dates from the 15th and 16th centuries and,

Things to do on Skye when it's raining

Just in case you didn't know, it can rain quite often on Skye and, unless you're one of those hardy souls who's prepared to brave the elements, you'll need to know about the island's main indoor attractions. There are numerous opportunities to shelter from the rain, but most of them cost money and many will leave you regretting it, so here's our list of the top 10 things to do. Details of opening times and admission prices are given under each relevant destination.

Beginning in Portree, there's the **Aros Experience**, which gives a good introduction to the island's history. North of Uig, at Kilmuir on the Trotternish Peninsula, is the **Skye Museum of Island Life**, which pretty much does what it says on the sign. Northwest from Portree is **Dunvegan Castle**, home of the Clan Macleod and top of most visitors' itineraries. On the road to Dunvegan is **Edinbane Pottery**, where you can buy pots of every shape and size and watch them being made.

Travelling south from Dunvegan, you'll reach the turn-off to the **Talisker Distillery**, the island's only whisky distillery, where you can sample the distinctive peaty taste. While you're there you can visit nearby **Carbostcraft Pottery**, in the village of Carbost, and indulge in some more gift buying. If you're in need of some refreshment after all that culture and shopping, you could do a lot worse than the bar at the **Sligachan Hotel**, which boasts an impressive array of whiskies and climbers' beards. In the southern peninsula of Sleat, near the Armadale ferry terminal, is **Armadale Castle**, with a visitor centre that is actually worth visiting. Nearby is one of the branches of **Skye Batiks**, with a huge selection of these 'new age' style fabrics in a range of original Celtic designs (the other branch is in Portree). And for that final drink before boarding the ferry to Mallaig, why not pop into the cosy bar of the **Hotel Eilean Iarmain**, which also happens to serve wonderful food.

though the Victorian restoration has left it looking more like a baronial house, a look inside reveals its true age. Among the few genuinely interesting relics on display is Rory Mor's horn, a huge drinking vessel which the chief's heir must drain 'without setting down or falling down', when filled with claret (about 1½ bottles). There's also a lock of Bonnie Prince Charlie's hair, clipped from his head by Flora MacDonald as a keepsake, but pride of place goes to the Fairy Flag. The flag has been dated to between the fourth and seventh centuries and is made of Middle Eastern silk. It is said to have been given to the clan chief by a fairy, and has the power to ensure victory in battle for the clan on three occasions. It has been used twice so far. The lovely castle gardens lead down to the lochside jetty, from where you can take a seal-spotting cruise or a boat trip around the loch. There's also a busy restaurant and gift shop by the castle gates.

In the village of Dunvegan is **Giant Angus MacAskill Museum** ⓘ *T01470-521296, Mar-Oct daily 0930-1830, £1.50, concession £1, children free*, housed in a thatched, whitewashed cottage, which relates the life story of the tallest ever Scotsman, Angus MacAskill, who grew to 7 ft 9 ins tall. He emigrated to Novia Scotia and toured the United States with the midget General Tom Thumb, who is said to have danced on his outstretched hand. More interesting than the museum, though, are the stories of its owner, Peter MacAskill, in particular the one about the replica coffin, which is worth the admission fee alone. Peter is a descendent of Angus and also runs the museum at Colbost (see below).

Duirinish Peninsula

West of Dunvegan is the Duirinish Peninsula. The northern half is populated along the western shores of **Loch Dunvegan** and in the beautiful and green **Glendale**, an area brimming with history but with hardly an island family left. Glendale is now dubbed 'Little England', owing to the large number of incoming settlers from the south. The area is famed throughout the Highlands and Islands, for it was here in 1882 that local crofters, spurred on by the **Battle of the Braes**, see page 284, resisted the cruel and petty tyranny of their estate manager. The authorities sent a gunboat to deal with the uprising and arrested the ringleaders, some of whom were imprisoned in Edinburgh and became known as the 'Glendale Martyrs'. This episode sparked a radical movement throughout the Highlands and led to the Crofter's Holdings Act of 1886, which gave the crofters a more secure tenure and fair rent, see page 307. The uninhabited southern half of the peninsula is dominated by Healabhal Bheag (1601 ft) and Healabhal Mhor (1538 ft), a pair of decapitated hills known as **Macleod's Tables**.

The **Glendale Visitor Route** is signposted from just before Dunvegan village and leads westwards along the shores of the loch and across the peninsula. There are several interesting little sights along the way. Those interested in finding out more about the region's history, and crofting on the island, should head for the fascinating **Colbost Folk Museum** ⓘ *T01470-521296, Easter-Oct daily 0900-1800, £2, concession £1.50, children free*, housed in a restored blackhouse, with a peat fire burning and an illicit still out the back. The museum is 4 miles from Dunvegan on the B884 to Glendale. A little further on is **Skye Silver** ⓘ *www.skyesilver.com, daily 1000-1800*, where you can buy silver jewellery in traditional Celtic designs. Further north is the **Borreraig Park Exhibition Croft** ⓘ *daily 0900-1800, £1.50*, which features a huge display of farm equipment from days gone by.

Borreraig was home to the famous MacCrimmons, hereditary pipers to the Macleod chiefs and the first composers, players and teachers of *piobaireachd* (pibroch), which can be heard at an annual recital at Dunvegan Castle in early August. The ruins of the ancient piping college can still be seen. Moving from the sublime to the ridiculous, in the village of **Glendale** is a **Toy Museum** ⓘ *T01470-511240, all year Mon-Sat 1000-1800, £3, children £1*, which should appeal to kids of all ages.

▲ The B884 continues west, then a road turns off left for Waterstein. At the end of this road (just over 2 miles) is a car park which is the starting point for the walk out to the lighthouse at **Neist Point**, the most westerly point on Skye and one of the most pleasant walks on the island. It's about 1½ miles there and back and well worth the effort. The path is easy to follow and the views of the sea cliffs are wonderful. There are lots of nesting seabirds around and you might even spot whales offshore. The **lighthouse**, built in 1909, is now unmanned, and you can stay in one of the self-catering cottages ⓘ *T/F01470-511200*.

The Cuillins and Minginish

▸▸ *pp287-293. Colour map 3, A3. OS Landranger No 32 & OS Outdoor Leisure No 8.*

The district of Minginish is the wildest and least-populated part of the island, but for many it is the greatest attraction, for this is where the Cuillins are to be found. This hugely impressive mountain range, often shrouded in rain or cloud, is the spiritual heartland of the island and, when it's clear their heart-aching grandeur can be appreciated from every other peninsula on Skye. Though officially called the Cuillin 'Hills', these are the most untamed mountains in Britain. The magnificent scenery and vast range of walks and scrambles have attracted climbers and walkers for centuries,

Macleod's Tables are so named because legend has it that the clan chief held a huge open-air feast for King James V on one of the hilltops.

Law of the land

One of the most significant incidents in the island's history took place in April 1882, when a group of around 100 local crofters and their families fought a pitched battle against a force of 60 police sent by the government from Glasgow. The 'Battle of the Braes', as it became known, was caused, like many other such uprisings throughout the Highlands and Islands, by threatened evictions. The local crofters were so incensed by the injustice of the eviction notices served on them that they destroyed the offending documents, leading the government to dispatch its police force. The defeat of the government forces of law and order by a bunch of men, women and children with sticks and stones is often described as the last battle fought on British soil, and led eventually to the establishment of a Royal Commission to look into the crofters' grievances.

but have also claimed many lives. It cannot be stressed too strongly that the Cuillins are the most dangerous mountains in Britain and only for experienced climbers, see further information, page 52.

The Cuillins

There are three routes into the Cuillins: from the Sligachan Hotel, from Glen Brittle, and from Elgol. The eastern part of the range is known as the **Red Cuillins**. Their smoother, conical granite peaks contrast sharply with the older, darker gabbro of the jagged-edged **Black Cuillins** to the west. The latter are particularly suitable for rock climbing and best approached from Glen Brittle, while the former are accessed from the Sligachan Hotel. There are 20 'Munros' (mountains over 3000 ft in height) in the Cuillins, with the highest being Sgurr Alasdair, at 3251 ft. Though the sheer majesty of the mountains can only be appreciated at close quarters by the climber, there are impressive views from Elgol, from the road into Glen Brittle and, more distantly, from the west coast of Sleat. **Glen Sligachan** is one of the most popular routes into the Cuillin range and the main access point for the more forgiving Red Cuillins, the walk to **Loch Coruisk**, or the ascent of **Marsco**.

Glen Brittle → *Phone code: 01478.*

Six miles along the A863 to Dunvegan from Sligachan is a turning left to Portnalong, Carbost and the Talisker Distillery (B8009; see below), which soon leads to the entrance to Glen Brittle. The road down Glen Brittle affords great views of the western side of the imposing Black Cuillins, until it ends at the campsite and shore at the foot of the glen. From Glen Brittle there are numerous paths leading up to the corries of the Black Cuillins. There are many alternative options for those wishing to continue up to the upper corries or to the main ridge. One of the finest of the Cuillin corries is **Coire Lagan**. This walk starts from the beach at Glen Brittle village and takes you up to the lochan in the upper coire, with Sgurr Alasdair, the most difficult of the Munros, towering overhead. A fine Cuillin sampler is the short walk to the spectacular **Eas Mor** waterfall.

Talisker → *Phone code: 01478.*

A recommended trip for whisky drinkers, or if it's raining, is to the excellent **Talisker Distillery** ① *T01478-614308, www.malts.com, Easter-Oct Mon-Sat 0930-1700, Nov-Easter Mon-Fri 1400-1700, tours every 15-20 mins, £5*, at **Carbost** on the shores of Loch Harport, on the B8009 (not in the village of Talisker itself, which is on the west coast). This

Every year there's a hill race up Glamaig, near Glen Sligachan. In 1899, it was climbed in 55 minutes (up and down) by a Gurkha soldier – in bare feet!

is Skye's only whisky distillery and produces a very smoky, peaty single malt, with a distinctive hot, peppery palate, particularly the 20- and 25-year-old expressions. The entry fee includes a voucher for a £3 discount on any whisky sold in the shop.

Near the distillery is **Carbostcraft Pottery** ⓘ *T01478-640259, Feb-Dec Mon-Sat 0900-1700, daily in summer*, which produces a wide range of traditional and original pottery, including the famous 'torn pots'. They also have a shop in Portree.

Elgol → *Phone code: 01471.*

One of the most rewarding drives on Skye is the 14-mile single-track road from Broadford to Elgol (Ealaghol), a tiny settlement near the tip of the Strathaird Peninsula, from where you can enjoy the classic view of the Cuillins from across Loch Scavaig and also see the islands of Soay, Rùm and Canna. It was from here, on 4 July 1746, that the Young Pretender finally left the Hebrides. Before leaving, he was given a farewell banquet by the MacKinnons in what is now called **Prince Charlie's Cave**. There's also the added attraction of a dramatic boat trip, see page 292, to the mouth of **Loch Coruisk**, in the heart of the Black Cuillin. The glacial sea loch, romanticized by Walter Scott and painted by Turner, is over 2 miles long but only a few hundred yards wide, closed in by the sheer cliffs on either side and overshadowed by the towering mountains of black basalt and gabbro. The road to Elgol also gives great views of Bla Bheinn (pronounced Blaven), best seen from Torrin, at the head of Loch Slapin.

Elgol to Camasunary Bay

Elgol is the starting point for the walk to Camasunary Bay. This 9-mile coastal walk is quite demanding, but on a clear day the views of the Cuillins make it well worth the effort. It starts from the car park in Elgol. From here, walk back up the road for a short distance, then turn left along a track behind some houses, signposted for 'Garsbheinn'. Beside the last of these houses is a sign for the path to Coruisk. Follow this path along a steep grassy slope. The views across Loch Scavaig to the island of Soay and the Cuillins behind are marvellous. The slope gets even steeper beneath Ben Cleat, and you'll need a good head for heights to continue across the foot of Glen Scaladal, crossing a burn in the process (which can be tricky if it's in spate). Then it's on along the path beyond Beinn Leacach to Camasunary Bay, with its backdrop of mighty Sgurr na Stri and Bla Bheinn. The shortest way back is to retrace your steps but, as an alternative, follow the clear track from Camasunary up the right side of Abhainn nan Lean over the hills to the east until it joins the B8083 from Broadford. From here it's about 3½ miles back along the road to Elgol.

Broadford and the east coast

▸▸ pp287-293. Colour map 3, A4-5.

Broadford (An t-Ath Leathann), Skye's second-largest village, basically consists of a mile-long main street strung out along a wide bay. The village may be low on charm but it's high on tourist facilities and makes a good base for exploring the south and east of the island. The road north from Broadford to Portree passes through Sconser, departure point for the short ferry ride to the little-visited island of Raasay.

Broadford

Broadford has plenty of accommodation and places to eat. Next to the Esso station is a Co-op, there's a laundrette in the petrol station shop (open 24 hours) and a bank with ATM. There is no tourist office as such, just an information point housed in the **Otter Shop** in the main car park (with erratic opening hours). Broadford is also home to one of the most incongruous attractions on the island, or elsewhere in the Highlands, the **Skye Serpentarium** ⓘ *The Old Mill, Harrapool, T01471-822209,* *www.skyeserpentarium.org.uk, Apr-Oct Mon-Sat 1000-1700 (also Sun in Jul/Aug), £2.50, children £1.50*, a rescue centre for all kinds of snakes, lizards and other reptiles, which you can look at or touch: a welcome retreat, if it's raining. When the weather's clear you can take a trip on a glass-bottomed boat from the pier; see Activities and tours, page 291.

Kyleakin

The opening of the Skye Bridge, linking the island with the Kyle of Lochalsh, see page 227, has turned the former ferry terminal of Kyleakin (Caol Acain) into something of a backwater, as well as infuriating the locals with its hefty toll. The absence of road traffic, though, makes it a quiet place to stay, and it's now a favourite with backpackers, judging by the number of hostels. The bridge is supported in the middle on the small islet of **Eilean Ban**, erstwhile home of author and naturalist, Gavin Maxwell, and now home to an otter sanctuary. It can be visited as part of tour from the **Bright Water Visitor Centre** ⓘ *Kyleakin, T01599-530040, www.eileanban.org, Apr-Oct Mon-Fri 1000-1700, free (donations welcome), tour costs £6, children £4*. The centre is worth a visit, especially if you have kids. Maxwell's former home can also be rented; for details visit www.cottageguide.co.uk. There's precious little else to do here, other than look at the small ruin of **Castle Moil**.

Kylerhea

About 4 miles out of Kyleakin a road turns left off the A87 and heads southeast to Kylerhea (pronounced Kile-ray). The bridge may be the most convenient route to Skye, but the best way to cross is on the small car and passenger ferry that makes the 10-minute crossing to Kylerhea from Glenelg. For full details of times and prices, see page 274. Near Kylerhea is the Forestry Commission **Otter Haven** ⓘ *T01320-366322, daily 0900 till 1 hr before dusk, free*. An hour-long nature trail takes you to an observation hide where you can look out for these elusive creatures.

Broadford to Portree

The road north to Portree runs between the fringes of the Red Cuillins and the coast, giving good views across to the **Isle of Scalpay**. The road then turns west along the shores of Loch Ainort to the turn-off for the **Luib Folk Museum** ⓘ *0900-1800, £1*, another of Peter MacAskill's island museums. The restored croft house has a smoky atmosphere and has old newspaper cuttings telling of the 'Battle of the Braes' and the 'Glendale Martyrs'.

The road runs north to **Sconser**, departure point for the ferry to Raasay, then runs around Loch Sligachan and heads north to Portree. On the opposite side of the loch from Sconser are the crofting communities known as **The Braes**, who successfully opposed their landlords' eviction notices and brought the crofters' cause to the public's attention.

Isle of Raasay → *OS Landranger No 24.*

The lush and beautiful island of Raasay lies only a few miles off the east coast of Skye yet remains completely off the tourist trail. The island is a nature conservancy, where you may see seals, eagles and otters. Its hilly terrain and superb cliff scenery also offer numerous walking opportunities, the best of which is to the distinctive flat-topped summit of **Dun Caan**, the island's highest point at 1456 ft. The views from the top are amongst the finest in Scotland. Raasay falls away to the sea, with the Cuillins on one side and the peaks of Torridon and Kintail on the other, shouldering past one another, their great blunt heads bumping the clouds. The walk to the top of the extinct volcano, via an old iron mine, is relatively straightforward and one of the most rewarding anywhere in the islands. So much so, in fact, that Boswell was inspired to dance a Highland jig on reaching the top in 1773, during his grand tour with Dr Johnson. Another excellent walk starts from North Fearns, at the end of a road running east from

Gaelic spread

Outside the Outer Hebrides, Skye is the most important centre of Gaelic culture, with a large proportion of the island's population speaking the Gaelic language in everyday life. This in itself is remarkable given the significant drop in population during the Clearances and the continued undermining of the Gaelic culture ever since, especially through the State education system.

Today, as in other parts of the Hebrides, the native culture is again under threat, this time from the huge influx of 'white settlers' from the south, but there is also a new-found pride and interest in the Gaelic language. This has been helped by the existence of the Gaelic college on Sleat, through Gaelic writers such as the late Sorley Maclean, a radical local newspaper (*The West Highland Free Press*), economic support from Highlands and Islands Enterprise, and spiritual underpinning from the Sabbatarian Free Church. Gaelic is being taught again in schools and can be heard on television. The ancient heritage of the Highlands and Islands is fighting back and reasserting itself as a major European culture.

Inverarish, to the deserted township of **Hallaig**, down the side of Beinn na Leac and back to North Fearns. The circular route is 5 miles long.

Raasay was for much of its history the property of the Macleods of Lewis, whose chief residence was the ruined **Brochel Castle**, before moving to **Clachan**, where **Raasay House** is now located. The original Raasay House was torched by government troops after Culloden, along with all the island's houses and its boats, as punishment for the Macleods giving refuge to Bonnie Prince Charlie. After the Macleods sold the island in 1843, the Clearances began in earnest and Raasay suffered a long period of emigration, depopulation and poverty. It is not surprising, then, that the island's most famous son, the great poet **Sorley Maclean**, wrote so passionately about this lost society. Born in Oskaig in 1911, he wrote in his native Gaelic as well as in English, and is highly regarded internationally. He died in 1996. Raasay's population now numbers around 150 and the island is a bastion of the Free Church, whose strict Sabbatarian beliefs should be respected by visitors.

Those who make it to the north of the island may wish to note that the 2 miles of road linking **Brochel** to **Arnish** were the work of one man, Calum Macleod. He decided to build the road himself after the council turned down his requests for proper access to his home. He spent between 10 and 15 years building it with the aid of a pick, a shovel, a wheelbarrow and a road-making manual which cost him three shillings. He died in 1988, soon after its completion, and it continues to be known as 'Calum's Road'.

Sleat Peninsula

» *pp287-293. Colour map 3, A4.*

→ *Phone code: 01471.*

East of Broadford is the turn-off to the peninsula of Sleat (pronouned 'slate'), a part of the island so uncharacteristically green and fertile that it's known as 'The Garden of Skye'. Sleat is another entry point to the island. Ferries cross from Mallaig on the mainland to Armadale on the southeastern shore of the peninsula. While the rest of the island is the preserve of the Macleods, Sleat is MacDonald country. The MacDonalds of Sleat are one of the major surviving branches of Clan Donald, and have the right to use the title Lord MacDonald (but not Lord of the Isles, which is now used by the heir to the throne). » *For Sleeping, Eating and other listings, see pages 287-293.*

Isle Ornsay

South of Duisdale is the signed turning for Isle Ornsay, or Eilean Iarmain (pronounced *eelan yarman*) in Gaelic, a very beautiful place in a small rocky bay overlooking the tidal Isle of Ornsay with the mountains of Knoydart in the background. This was once Skye's main fishing port, and the neat whitewashed cottages and tiny harbour are still there. It is also largely Gaelic-speaking, thanks mainly to the efforts of its landlord, Sir Iain Noble, who owns the hotel and his own local Gaelic whisky company as well as the northern half of the peninsula, which is known as Fearan Eilean Iarmain. ▸▸ *See Sleeping, page 289.*

A few miles further on is a turn-off to the left to the villages of **Ord, Tokavaig** and **Tarskavaig**, on the west coast of the peninsula, from where, on a clear day, there are views across to the Cuillins. Near Tokavaig is the ruin of **Dunsgaith Castle**, home of the MacDonalds of Sleat until the 17th century. Tarskavaig is a typical crofting township. In the early 19th century the MacDonalds claimed the more fertile glens inland for their sheep farms and evicted the people to coastal townships like Tarskavaig. Just beyond the turn-off to Ord are the remains of **Knock Castle**, yet another MacDonald stronghold.

Ostaig

At Ostaig is the Gaelic College, **Sabhal Mor Ostaig** ⓘ *T01471-844373*, where all subjects are taught in Gaelic, including full-time courses in business studies and media, as well as short courses in Gaelic music and culture during the summer months. The bookshop has a good selection of books and tapes for those wishing to learn the language. The college was founded by Sir Iain Noble. Ostaig is also the beginning or end (depending on which direction you're heading) of the detour to Tarskavaig, Tokavaig and Ord.

Armadale to the Point of Sleat

Just before the ferry pier at Armadale is **Armadale Castle** ⓘ *T01471-844305, www.clandonald.com, Apr-Oct daily 0930-1730, £4.90, concession £3.80*, which was built in 1815 as the main residence of the MacDonalds of Sleat. Most of the castle is now a roofless ruin but the servants' quarters contain an excellent exhibition and accompanying video explaining the history of the Lordship of the Isles. The Clan Donald Lords of the Isles took over from their Norse predecessors in ruling the Hebrides until their power was broken in 1493. The former stables at the entrance comprise offices, a restaurant and bookshop, while the estate manager's house has been converted to accommodate an extensive library and archives. The castle is surrounded by 40 acres of handsome gardens and woodland, and there are ranger-led walks along nature trails with fine views across to the mainland.

Just beyond Armadale Castle is the tiny village of **Armadale**, which is strung out along the wooded shoreline and merges into the neighbouring village of **Ardvasar** (pronounced Ard-vaa-sar), which has a post office and general store. Armadale's raison d'être is the ferry pier and there's not a huge amount to keep you occupied except for a couple of good handicraft shops. At the turn-off to the pier is **Skye Batiks** ⓘ *T01471-844396*, which also has a shop in Portree, see page 291. Here you'll find the colourful cotton garments which make a unique souvenir of the island. They also now have B&B accommodation. On the ferry pier is **Ragamuffin** ⓘ *T01471-844217, daily 0900-1800*, which sells a wide range of knitwear. About 4 or 5 miles past the ferry port, at the end of the road, is **Aird of Sleat**, a crofting township, from where you walk out to the lighthouse at the **Point of Sleat**. It's a 5-mile walk on a clear path across moorland with fine coastal scenery.

Sleeping

Accommodation can be hard to find in the busy summer season. The local TICs have lists of available accommodation and for a small fee will book it for you. A couple of good websites are www.isleof skye.com and www.isleofskyescotland.com.

Portree *p275, map p275*

There are several guesthouses on Bosville Terr and many B&Bs on Stormyhill Rd and the streets running off it. Prices tend to be slightly higher in Portree than the rest of the island, though B&Bs on the outskirts of town are usually cheaper.

L-A Cuillin Hills Hotel, off road north to Staffin, on edge of town, T01478-612003, www.cuillinhills-hotel-skye-co.uk. 28 rooms. Open all year. Set in 15 acres of gardens overlooking the bay with everything you'd expect at these prices. Variety of rooms at different rates but all have great views. Also has a very good restaurant.

A-B Bosville Hotel, Bosville Terr, T01478-612846, www.macleodhotels.co.uk/bosville. 18 rooms. Comfortable and stylish accommodation with friendly service. Boasts 2 award-winning restaurants (see Eating, page 290).

B Viewfield House Hotel, on the road into Portree from the south, T01478-612217, www.viewfieldhouse.com. 12 rooms. Open mid-Apr to mid-Oct. 200-year-old country house full of antiques, set in 20 acres of woodland garden. Good food and hospitality and the log fire adds to the welcoming atmosphere. **L-A** with 5-course dinner included. Recommended.

D Portree House Hotel, Home Farm Rd, T01478-611711,www.portreehouse.co.uk. Open all year. 6 rooms. Comfortable accommodation in early 19th-century house, with good food in restaurant and bar. Good for families with children's play area and lovely gardens to explore.

D-E Ms Catriona Matheson, Drumorell, 15 Fraser Cres, T01478-613058, www.visithighlands.com. 2 en suite rooms. Open all year. One of the best B&Bs in the town. Good value.

F Portree Independent Hostel, Old Post Office, The Green, T01478-613737. 60 beds. Right in the centre of town, with laundrette (£3 per wash) and email facilities (£3 per hr).

Camping

There's a campsite at Torvaig, just outside the town, T01478-612209, open Apr-Oct.

Trotternish Peninsula *p276*

A Flodigarry Country House Hotel, a few miles north of Staffin and 20 miles north of Portree, T01470-552203, F552301. Beautifully located at the foot of the mighty Quiraing and with stunning views across Staffin Bay, this is one of the great country house hotels, with a relaxing old-world atmosphere and excellent restaurant. Flora MacDonald's actual cottage is in the grounds and has been tastefully refurbished, giving the chance to stay in a place steeped in the island's history. The lively bar is a good place to enjoy a laugh and a jig.

A Uig Hotel, on the right of the road into the village from Portree, beside a white church and opposite Frazer's Folly, Uig, T01470-542205, www.uighotel.com. 16 en suite rooms. Open all year. Classy accommodation with great views across the bay, good food and a friendly island welcome. Offers clay pigeon shooting and fly fishing.

C Duntulm Castle Hotel, near Duntulm Castle, T01470-552213, www.duntulm castle.co.uk. Open Mar-Nov. Friendly and homely with great views across the Minch to the Outer Hebrides. Idyllic and good value. Restaurant is open to non-residents.

C Glenview Hotel, at Culnacnock, just north of the Lealt Falls, T01470-562248, www.glenviewskye.co.uk. 5 rooms. Cosy and relaxed accommodation with a very fine restaurant.

D The Ferry Inn, Uig, T01470-542242, www.ferryinn.co.uk. 6 rooms. Open all year. Close to the ferry pier, also serves decent and affordable bar meals.

D-E Cuill Lodhe Guest House, Cuill, Uig, T01470-542216, www.isleofskye scotland.com. 3 en suite rooms. Open all year. Cosy B&B set on shore of Uig Bay, all rooms with sea views.

F Dun Flodigarry Backpackers Hostel, T/F01470-552212. 66 beds. Open Mar-Oct. Only 100 yds from the bar of the **Flodigarry Country House Hotel**. Those who can't afford the luxury of the **Flodigarry House**

 Hotel can always opt for this more modest alternative. Laundry facilities, breakfast.
F SYHA Youth Hostel, Uig, T01470-542211, is high above the port on the south side of the village and is open mid-Mar to Oct.

Camping

There's a campsite south of Staffin Bay, T01470-562213, open mid-Apr to end Sep.

Waternish, Dunvegan and Duirinish *p278*

There are numerous places to stay in and around Dunvegan, and the TIC in the village will arrange accommodation for you, T01470-521581.
L-A Skeabost Country House Hotel, at Skeabost Bridge, 6 miles north of Portree on A850 to Dunvegan, T01470-532202, www.skeabostcountryhouse.com. 30 rooms. Open all year. This former Victorian hunting lodge on the shores of Loch Snizort has been transformed into a sumptuous and stylish retreat with snooker room, beautiful guest lounges, a 9-hole golf course and salmon fishing on nearby River Snizort, also has an excellent restaurant. Worth splashing out on.
A The House Over-By, a few yards away from the very wonderful **Three Chimneys**, see Eating, on Duirnish Peninsula, and run by the same folk. 6 sumptuous rooms, all with sea views.
A-B Greshornish House Hotel, Edinbane, T01470-582266, www.greshornish house.com. 9 rooms. Open all year. Set in 10 acres of land at the end of a single-track road by the shores of the eponymous loch. If you're after peace and tranquility then look no further, Neil and his wife are the perfect hosts and a fund of local knowledge. Superb food in the dining room (**L-A** including dinner), also billiard room, tennis court and croquet lawn for those clement days.
B Harlosh House Hotel, just beyond Roskhill is a turning south off the A863, T/F01470-521367, harlosh.house@virgin.net. 6 rooms. Easter to mid-Oct. Cosy, comfortable, great views and a reputation for superb food (evenings only).
C Lyndale House, Edinbane, T01470-582329, www.lyndale.net. 2 rooms. Quiet, delightful retreat hidden down a private drive off the A850 to Dunvegan. 300-year-old house with lovely views and sunsets from the sitting room. Nice touches, such as fresh flowers and bathrobes, and organic produce for breakfast.
D The Lodge at Edinbane, Edinbane, T01470-582217, www.the-lodge-at-edinbane.co.uk. Open all year. 6 en suite rooms. If it's old-world character you're after, this place has it in spades; there's even a ghost of two. A 16th-century former hunting lodge by the shores of Loch Greshornish owned by Peter, who is very knowledgeable about the island, and Hazel, who is a great cook. Pub next door has a fine selection of ales. Recommended.
D Roskhill House, 3 miles south of Dunvegan Castle on the A863, T01470-521317, stay@roskhill.demon.co.uk. 5 cosy rooms, peaceful setting, great food. Recommended.
D Stein Inn, Waternish, T01470-592362, www.stein-inn.co.uk. 4 en suite rooms. This 18th-century inn is the oldest such place on the island. Great location on the shores of Loch Bay and all rooms benefit from this. Dinner served in restaurant (🍴🍴🍴) or cheaper meals on offer in the very wonderful bar (see Bars and pubs, page 291). There's also a 1-bedroom apartment for rent (£245-295 per week). Families welcome. No smoking. Recommended.
E Drynoch Farmhouse, Carbost, T01478-640441, www.isleofskye.net. 2 en suite rooms. Open all year. Working farmhouse on the shore of Loch Harport. Good views, cosy guest lounge with coal fire, huge breakfast. Good value.

The Cuillins and Minginish *p281*

C Sligachan Hotel, 7 miles south of Portree, where the A87 Kyleakin–Portree road meets the A863 to Dunvegan, T01471-8650204, F650207. The legendary rallying point for climbers who come to Skye for the Cuillins. The hotel's **Seamus** bar stocks an impressive selection of malts and also serves the island's real ales as well as meals.
D Coruisk House, on the right-hand side just after the Elgol village sign on the road from Broadford, T01471-866330, www.seafood-skye.co.uk. Open Apr-Sep. Restaurant with rooms. No smoking, all rooms en suite. Worth coming here for the freshest of seafood (lunch 🍴🍴, dinner 🍴🍴🍴), which can be enjoyed al fresco (they have a

Midge Master!). Also have a self-catering cottage and traditional crofthouse for rent.
D **Rowan Cottage**, a mile east at Glasnakille, T01471-866287, www.rowancottage-skye.co.uk. Open mid-Mar to end Nov. Attractive B&B offering the best of home cooking (lunch ŸŸ, dinner ŸŸŸ, restaurant closed Tue).
F **Croft Bunkhouse & Bothies**, north of Carbost, near Portnalong, T/F01471-640254, pete@skyehostel.free-online.co.uk. Sleeps 26. Also room for camping, transport from Sligachan or Portree, rents mountain bikes, pub and shop nearby.
F **Skyewalker Independent Hostel**, T01471-640250, skyewalker@easynet.co.uk. In a converted school beyond Portnalong on the road to Fiscavaig. 32 beds.
F **SYHA Hostel**, Glen Brittle, T01471-640278, in the village. It's open mid-Mar to end of Oct and has 39 beds.

Camping

The campsite opposite **Sligachan Hotel** is the most popular place to stay in the area. There's also a campsite by the shore in Glen Brittle, T01471-640404.

Broadford and the east coast *p283*

D **Lime Stone Cottage**, 4 Lime Park (behind the Serpentarium), Broadford, T01471-822142, kathielimepark@btinternet.com. One of the best places to stay around here, full of rustic charm.
D **White Heather Hotel**, Kyleakin, T01599-534577, www.whiteheatherhotel.co.uk. Open mid-Mar to end Oct. 9 en suite rooms. No smoking. Friendly and welcoming small hotel overlooking the harbour. Hosts Gilllian and Craig are super-helpful and breakfasts are excellent with views of the harbour thrown in for good measure. Recommended.
D-E **Tir Alainn**, 8 Upper Breakish, T01471-822366. Open all year. 3 rooms, 2 en suite. Just outside Broadford on road to Kyleakin. Pam and Ron are extremely welcoming and run a cosy B&B, offering great food, great views too and a comfy guest lounge.
F **Dun Caan Hostel**, near the old ferry quay, Kyleakin, T01599-534087, www.skyerover.co.uk. Open all year. Of all the hostels around this part of the island, this one stands out for the personal service. Also hires bikes.
F **Fossil Bothy**, a mile or so south of Broadford, at Lower Breakish off the A87 to Kyleakin, T01471-822297. Has 8 beds and is open Easter-Oct, book in advance.
F **Skye Backpackers Hostel**, Kyleakin, T/F01599-534510, skye@scotlands-top-hostels.co.uk. A more relaxed option. Open all year, breakfast £1.50.
F **SYHA Hostel**, Kyleakin, T01599-534585. Large, modern building a few hundred yards from the pier. Open all year.

Isle of Raasay *p284*

E **Churchton House**, Isle of Raasay, T01478-660260; and **Isle of Raasay Hotel**, on the Isle of Raasay nearby to the Outdoor Centre, T/F01478-660222. Open all year.
E **Mrs Mackay**, at Oskaig on the Isle of Raasay, T01478-660207. A good B&B, price includes dinner.
E **Raasay Outdoor Centre**, T01478-660266, the main settlement on the island is Inverarish, a 15-min walk from the ferry dock. Half a mile further is this centre housed in the huge Georgian mansion that was Raasay House, which runs many and various adventure courses, from climbing to windsurfing, as well as offering basic accommodation from Mar to mid-Oct, and a campsite.
F **SYHA Hostel**, T01478-660240, open mid-Mar to end-Oct. Reached via a rough track leading up a steep hill from tiny Oskaig.

Sleat Peninsula *p285*

L **Hotel Eilean Iarmain**, at Isle Ornsay, T01471-833332, www.eileanarmain.co.uk. 12 rooms. Award-winning Victorian hotel full of charm and old-world character, with wonderful views. It is utterly lovely and romantic and an absolute must if you're in the area and can afford it. Award-winning restaurant features local shellfish landed only yards away (open to non-residents). A cheaper option is to eat in the cosy bar next door, which serves pub grub of an impossibly high standard in a more informal atmosphere. The hotel also offers winter

For an explanation of sleeping and eating price codes used in this guide, see inside the front cover. Other relevant information is found in Essentials, see pages 40-47.

shooting on the local estate, and you can enjoy a tasting of the local whisky.

L Kinloch Lodge, at the head of Loch na Dal, T01471-833214, www.kinloch-lodge.com. Open Mar-Nov. 10 en suite rooms. Lord and Lady MacDonald's family home is also an award-winning restaurant, offering the rare chance to enjoy superb food in the grandest of settings. The track that leads to the 19th-century **Sporting Lodge** turns off the A851 about 8 miles south of Broadford. Lady Claire MacDonald is one of the best-known cooks in Scotland and author of several cookbooks, and if you do decide to treat yourself make sure you leave enough room for their exquisite puddings. The 5-course fixed menu is in our expensive range, but well worth it.

A-B Toravaig House Hotel, Knock Bay, Teangue, T01471-820200, www.skyehotel.co.uk. Open all year. 9 en suite rooms. Scottish Island Hotel of the Year in 2005, and it's easy to see why. Perfect for those seeking peace and quiet, though it may be a tad isolated for those who like a pub within walking distance. Good food in their **Iona Restaurant**.

B Duisdale Hotel, Duisdale, T01471-833202, www.duisdale.com. 19 rooms (2 with 4-poster beds). Country house hotel set in lovely grounds with great views across the Sound of Sleat. The restaurant serves good traditional Scottish cooking; a 5-course meal is in the expensive range.

B-C Ardvasar Hotel, in Ardvasar, near the ferry terminal, T01471-844223, www.ardvasar. com. Traditional whitewashed coaching inn with 9 rooms, an excellent restaurant and the liveliest pub in the vicinity.

F Flora MacDonald Hostel, at Kilmore, between the turning for Isle Ornsay and Armadale, T01471-844440, www.isle-of-skye-tour-guide.co.uk. Newly refurbished with all facilities, 32 beds, open all year, and free transport to and from Armadale Pier.

F SYHA Hostel, just before the turn-off to the ferry pier, T01471-844260. 42 beds. Open mid-Mar to end Oct, rents bikes.

Eating

With the notable exception of the magnificent **Three Chimneys** restaurant, the best food on Skye is normally served in hotel dining rooms, so also check the Sleeping section for places to eat. Many B&Bs also provide evening meals on request.

Portree *p275, map p275*

TTT Chandlery Seafood Restaurant, next door to the **Bosville Hotel**, see Sleeping. Best in town. Superb French/Scottish cuisine using local produce. Cheaper lunch options in hotel bistro.

TTT-TT Harbour View Seafood Restaurant, 7 Bosville Terr, T01478-612069. Apr-Oct 1200-2200. Freshest of seafood in cosy surroundings. Good 2nd choice after **Chandlery**. Lunch in the **Seafood Winebar** is excellent value at around £5-7 for a main course.

TT Ben Tianavaig, 5 Bosville Terr, T01478-612152. Excellent vegetarian bistro. Seating is limited so you'll need to book. Open for lunch at weekends, and Tue-Sun 1800-2130.

T Tuireann Café, part of the arts centre, see Sights, page 275. Natural wholefoods and organic produce, home-made bread, cakes and pastries. Excellent quality and value. Mar-Oct Mon-Sat 1000-1800, Nov-Feb Tue-Sat 1000-1630.

Trotternish Peninsula *p276*

TT Oystercatcher Restaurant, in the village of Staffin, T01470-562384, closed Sun. A good place for food.

T Pub on the Pier, Uig, has cheap bar meals, and the famous Cuillin ales are brewed at the nearby Skye Brewery.You can also change foreign currency here. Open till 2300.

Waternish, Dunvegan and Duirinish *p278*

TTT The Three Chimneys, Duirnish Peninsula, T01470-511258, www.three chimneys.co.uk. Considered by many to be the best restaurant in the north of Scotland and, judging by the numerous awards they've won, that judgement can't be far wrong. Local seafood, meat, veg and dairy produce and a great wine list. Open daily 1230-1400 (except Sun) and 1830-2130.

TT Lochbay Seafood, Waternish Peninsula, T01470-592235. You should finish off the day with a meal at the this wonderful restaurant where you can almost see your dinner being landed. Open Apr-Oct for lunch and till 2030 (closed Sat).

Broadford and the east coast *p283*
¥¥¥ **Rendezvous**, at Breakish, south of Broadford on the main road to Kyleakin, T01471-822001. Expensive place to eat but excellent food.
¥¥ **The Crofter's Kitchen**, outside Kyleakin on the road to Broadford, T01599-534134. Good food, from snacks to 3-course meals. Mon-Sat 1000-2100, Sun 1230-2100.
¥¥-¥ **Claymore Bar-Restaurant**, at the south end of the Broadford, T01471-822333. Decent bar meals.

Sleat Peninsula *p283*
¥¥ **Pasta Shed**, by the ferry pier in Armadale. Pizza and pasta but also very good seafood. Open daily 0900-1930 (-ish) in high season.

Bars and pubs

Portree *p275, map p275*
The town's nightlife is mainly confined to eating and drinking: **Pier Hotel**, Quay St, T01478-612094, by the harbour, is a real fishermen's drinking den; and the **Royal Hotel**, Bank St, T01478-612525, is also popular.

Waternish, Dunvegan and Duirinish *p278*
Stein Inn, see Sleeping above. There are few pleasures in life equal to sitting outside this venerable old pub with a pint of ale from the local Isle of Skye brewery while watching a Hebridean sunset. Actually, we can't even think of one. On less clement evenings the old peat-burning fire inside provides an alternative feelgood factor.

Entertainment

Portree *p275, map p275*
Aros Experience, see Sights page 275, has a theatre which shows drama, movies and live music. Call the box office for details of their monthly programme, T01478-613750.
Portree Community Centre, Camanahd Sq, Park Rd, T01478-613736. This is the place to come if you fancy a wild Fri night ceilidh.

Festivals and events

Portree *p275, map p275*
Early Aug Highland Games are a 1-day event held in Portree.

Broadford and the east coast *p283*
Jun Isle of Skye Music Festival, www.skyemusicfestivals.co.uk. Held over a weekend in mid-Jun at Ashaig Airstrip, near Broadford, this has grown over the years to become one of Scotland's best music festivals, featuring the likes of KT Tunstall. Expect local boy Mylo to make an appearance. Tickets £75.

Shopping

Portree *p275, map p275*
Carbostcraft Pottery, Bayfield Rd, sells pottery with a huge variety of designs. They also have a shop near the Talisker Distillery, see page 283.
Jackson's Wholefoods, at Park Pl, opposite the council offices, a wholefood store.
Supermarket, diagonally opposite the Bosville Hotel.
Outdoor Sports, Bridge Rd, next to **Skye Batiks**, Portree. Good for mountain gear.
Over the Rainbow, at the top of Quay Brae, T01478-612555. Open 0900-2200 in the high season. A good place to buy woollens.
Skye Batiks, The Green, near the TIC, T01478-613331. Sells handmade 'batiks' (colourful cotton fabrics), which are pricey but unique souvenirs of Skye, see also page 286.
Skye Woollen Mill, Dunvegan Rd, T01478-612889. Knitwear and tartan souvenirs can be found here.

The Cuillins and Minginish *p281*
Cioch Direct, 4 Ullinish, Struan, T01470-572307. For mountain gear.

Activities and tours

Portree *p275, map p275*
If the weather's good, Portree offers opportunities for a wide variety of outdoor activities.
Boat trips, T01478-613718, or ask for Peter Urquhart at the pier, can be made to the island of Rona, north of Raasay, with the *MV Brigadoon*. Trips leave from the pier

(Apr- Sep) and cost from £10 per person. Full-day charters are also available for £75-150 (12 passengers).

Island Cycles, on The Green, T01478-613121, Mon-Sat 1000- 1700, hire mountain bikes.

Portree Riding and Trekking Stables, a couple of miles from the town centre; follow the Struan Rd (B885) for 2 miles, then bear right at the fork towards Peiness, T01478-582419. Horse riding.

Skye Riding Centre, 2 miles north of Portree, at Borve on the road to Uig, T01470-532439. Horse riding.

Swimming pool, Camanahd Sq, T01478-612655.

Trotternish Peninsula *p276*

Whitewave Activities, a few miles north of Uig, on the A855 at Linicrowhere, T01471-542414, info@white-wave.co.uk. Here you can try windsurfing and sea kayaking. There's also a café specializing in vegetarian, seafood and Celtic music, and a B&B.

The Cuillins and Minginish *p281*

Boat trips

The Bella Jane, T0800-7313089 (freephone 0730-2200), www.bellajane.co.uk, makes the spectacular trip from Elgol into the gaping maw of Loch Coruisk, one of the highlights of any trip to Skye. It lasts 3 hrs, including about 1½ hrs ashore, and cost £15, £7.50 children. You should be able to see seals and porpoises en route. There's also a one-way trip for experienced walkers/climbers who wish to make the return journey on foot or to explore the Cuillins. There are also trips on the *AquaXplore* to Rùm or Canna.

Climbing

The following guides have all been recommended: **Colin Threlfall**, Outdoor Sports, Bridge Rd, next to Skye Batiks, Portree; **Cuillin Guides**, Gerry Achroyd, Stac Lee, Glen Brittle, T01478-640289; **Hugh Evans**, 4d Wentworth St, Portree, T01478-612682. **Richard MacGuire**, 4 Matheson Place, Portree, T01478-613180. **Skye Highs**, Mike Lates, 3 Luib, Broadford, T01471-822116.

Broadford and the east coast *p283*

Wildlife cruises, T0800-7832175, www.glassbottomboat.co.uk, run from Broadford pier. You can choose the glass-bottomed *Family's Pride II*, or the much faster *SkyeJet*, a rigid inflatable boat (RIB) which has the advantage of taking you further afield.

Kyleakin Private Hire, T01599-534452, run a taxi service and guided tours of the island.

Transport

Portree *p275, map p275*

Bus There are 4 buses daily (Mar-Oct) Mon-Fri (2 on Sat) around the Trotternish Peninsula, in each direction, via **Uig**. There are daily buses (4 Mon-Sat, 3 on Sun) to **Kyleakin**, and 3 buses daily Mon-Sat to **Armadale** via **Broadford**. There are 2 daily buses to **Carbost** (for the **Talisker Distillery**) and Mon-Fri (1 on Sat), and 2 daily buses to **Glenbrittle** (in the summer only). There are 3 buses daily Mon-Fri to **Glendale** via **Dunvegan** (1 on Sat), and 3 buses to **Waternish** via **Dunvegan** (Mon-Sat). For taxis call **Ace Taxis**, T01478-613600 or **A2B Taxis**, T01478-613456.

There's a **Scottish Citylink** service from **Inverness** (3 Mon-Sat, 2 on Sun, 3 hrs) and also from **Glasgow** via **Fort William** to **Kyleakin**, **Portree** and **Uig** 3-4 times daily (3 hrs from Fort William to Portree). Winter services are severely limited with only a few buses in each direction each day.

Trotternish Peninsula *p276*

Bus Scottish Citylink runs a service to/from **Inverness**, **Fort William** and **Glasgow**. **Ferries** leave from **Uig** to **Lochmaddy** on **North Uist** (1¾ hrs) and to **Tarbert** on **Harris** (1¾ hrs). For details see page 273, or contact Uig, T01470-542219.

Waternish, Dunvegan and Duirinish *p278*

Bus There are 3 buses daily (Mar-Oct, Mon-Fri) from **Glendale** to and from **Portree** via **Dunvegan**. The bus leaves Portree at 1000, arrives at the castle at 1048 and returns at 1252 (Mar-Oct only). There is 1 bus on Sat and a daily bus from Dunvegan to Glendale (not Sun).

The Cuillins and Minginish *p281*
Bus There are 2 daily buses from **Portree** to **Glen Brittle** Mon-Sat during the summer only. Otherwise, take the **Portree-Carbost-Fiscavaig** bus, which leaves twice Mon-Fri and once on Sat, and get off at the turn-off, then walk the remaining 7 miles, or hitch, though it can be slow. The only public transport to **Elgol** is the **postbus** from **Broadford**, which runs twice Mon-Sat and once on Sun, and takes 2 hrs. There's a regular bus service (weekdays only) from **Portree** and **Sligachan** to **Portnalong**, T01470-532240.

Broadford and the east coast *p283*
Bus Daily **Citylink** buses run from **Broadford** to and from **Portree**, **Inverness** and **Fort William**. **Waterloo** buses run daily to and from **Kyleakin**, **Portree** (£6 return) and **Armadale/Ardvasar**. There are buses from **Kyleakin** to **Portree** via **Broadford** (4 daily), to **Armadale** and **Ardvasar** via Broadford (3 daily Mon-Sat) and ½ hourly to **Kyle of Lochalsh**, see page 227, via the Skye Bridge.

Car hire Sutherlands at the Esso Garage, Broadford, T01471-822225, from £30 per day.

Cycle hire Fairwinds Bicycle Hire, just past Broadford Hotel, T01471-822270, Mar-Oct.

Ferry CalMac car and passenger ferry runs from **Sconser to Raasay** daily Mon-Sat every hr. It takes 15 mins and costs £4.75 per person return, plus £18.70 per car and £1 per bicycle.

Sleat Peninsula *p285*
Bus There are 3 buses daily, except Sun, from **Armadale Pier** to **Portree** (1 hr 20 mins) and **Kyleakin** (1 hr) via **Broadford** (40 mins). The first bus leaves at 0935.

Ferry For full details of ferry crossings to Mallaig, see page 274.

Directory

Portree *p275, map p275*
Banks Bank of Scotland and Clydesdale Bank, both on Somerled Sq; **Royal Bank of Scotland**, Bank St. All have ATMs.
Internet Portree Independent Hostel, see Sleeping page 287, at the post office and at Portree Backpacker's Hostel, Dunvegan Rd.
Laundry Portree Independent Hostel.
Post At the top of Quay Brae.

Broadford and the east coast *p283*
Banks Bank of Scotland, by the shops opposite the road to the new pier in Broadford.

The Small Isles

These four tenacious little siblings are a world away from the Scottish mainland and not for the faint or fickle traveller. It takes longer to reach them from London than it does to fly to Australia, so you have to be pretty determined. Those who do make it this far are rewarded with perfect peace and an almost primeval silence and solitude. This is nature in the glorious, unabashed raw; a slow-moving, sepia-tinged counterpoint to the frenetic pace and special effects of 21st-century life. ▸▸ *For Sleeping, Eating and other listings, see pages 297-298.*

Ins and outs

Getting there A **CalMac** passenger-only ferry sails from Mallaig to all four islands once daily Monday to Thursday and twice on Friday and Saturday, returning on the same days. For more details contact the CalMac office in Mallaig, T01687-462403. At Muck passengers are transferred to small boats as there are no suitable piers. There aren't any transport connections with Skye.

From April to September the **CalMac** ferries from Mallaig are supplemented by cruises from Arisaig with **Arisaig Marine** ⓣ *T01687-450224, www.airsaig.co.uk.* There's a good chance of seeing dolphins, porpoises and even whales during the bumpy ride. ▸▸ *For further details, see page 225 and Transport page 298.*

Eigg

pp297-298. Colour map 3, A3-B3.

→ *Phone code: 01687.*

Little Eigg (pronounced *egg*), only 5 miles long by 3 miles wide, has had something of a chequered past. In 1577 it was the scene of one of the bloodiest episodes in the history of clan warfare (see box, page 278). More recently it has been at the heart of a bitter land ownership debate. Having endured a succession of absentee landlords, ranging from the merely eccentric to the criminally negligent, the 70 remaining islanders seized the moment in 1997 and bought the island themselves, in conjunction with the Scottish Wildlife Trust. Now everyone can enjoy the island's wildlife, which includes otters, seals, eagles and many other birds, such as the Manx shearwater, guillemots and black-throated divers. It's worth tagging along on one of the regular walks organized by the **Scottish Wildlife Trust** warden, John Chester.

The island is dominated by **An Sgurr**, a distinctive 1289-ft flat-topped basalt peak with three vertical sides. It can be climbed fairly easily by its western ridge, though the last few hundred feet are precipitous, and there are superb views of the Inner Hebrides and mountains of Knoydart from the summit. Sitting in the shadow of the Sgurr, at the southeastern corner, is the main settlement, **Galmisdale**. This is where the ferries drop anchor (passengers are transferred to a smaller boat), and there's a post office, shop and tearoom, all by the pier. At the northern end is the small township of **Cleadale**, on the Bay of Laig. Just to the north are the **'Singing Sands'**, a beach that makes a strange sound as you walk across it. At the end of the island's only road you'll find its most famous property, **Howlin' House**, which apparently once belonged to JRR Tolkien. More details on the island are available at www.isleofeigg.org.

Muck

pp297-298. Colour map 3, B3.

→ *Phone code: 01687.*

Tiny Muck, just 2 miles long by 1 mile wide, is the smallest of the four islands and is flat and fertile, with a beautiful shell beach. It has been owned by the MacEwan family since 1879. The island gets its unfortunate name (*muc* is Gaelic for pig) from the porpoises, or 'sea pigs', that swim round its shores. The ferry drops anchor near **Port Mór**, where there's accommodation. The tearoom here does snacks and sells fresh bread. Visit the island's website, www.islemuck.com.

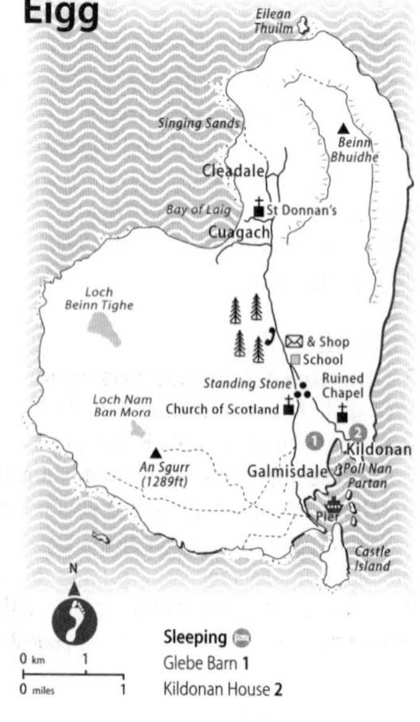

Rùm

pp297-298. Colour map 3, A3.

→ *Phone code: 01687.*

Diamond-shaped Rùm, known as the Forbidden Island, is the largest of the group and the most wild, beautiful and mountainous. The island is owned and run by Scottish Natural Heritage as an enormous outdoor laboratory and research station, and most of the 30 or so inhabitants are employed by them. Studies of the red deer population are among the most important areas of their work, and access to parts of the island is restricted. This is not prohibitive, though, and there are many marked nature trails, walks and birdwatching spots. The island is a haven for wildlife and perhaps its most notable resident is the magnificent white-tailed sea eagle, successfully re-introduced on to Rùm in the 1980s and now spreading beyond the island. Rùm is also home to golden eagles, Manx shearwaters and, less appealingly, millions of midges. The island is the wettest of the Small Isles and a haven for the little buggers.

Ins and outs

Ferries are anchored at the new pier, at the mouth of Loch Scresort, from where it's a 15-minute walk to Kinloch Castle. The castle stands at the head of narrow Loch Scresort by the little hamlet of **Kinloch**, where you'll find the one-and-only shop and the community hall which sometimes operates as a café.

Kinloch Castle

ⓘ *By guided tour only; Mon at 1330, Tue-Thu and Sat/Sun at 1400 and Fri at 1200, £2, children free.*

Though it looks like a wilderness, Rùm once supported a population of 300. Most of them were shipped off to Canada in the mid-19th century, leaving behind an uninhabited deer forest for sporting millionaires. One of these, John Bullough, a cotton millionaire from Accrington, bought it in 1888 and passed it on to his son, Sir George Bullough, who built the extravagant and extraordinary Kinloch Castle. No expense was spared on this massive late-Victorian mansion, built in 1900 at a cost of £250,000 (which equates to £15 mn today). It took 300 men nearly three years to build Bullough's dream, using red Annan sandstone from Dumfriesshire shipped by

The end of an era

George Bullough and his wife, Lady Monica, brought a slice of Belgravia to the tiny Hebridean island of Rùm. Every autumn the family showed up to stalk deer and throw lavish parties for the glitterati and aristocracy of the day. Guests would be met at the pier by chauffeur-driven Albion cars while those arriving by ferry would step into a horse-drawn carriage, or be given a piggy-back by the castle staff when the tide was out. The outrageously wealthy Bulloughs guarded their privacy with a level of ruthlessness that would make even today's pop and film stars blush. Guns were routinely fired at passing boats to warn off any unwanted commoners and discourage the curious.

All this frivolous excess ended suddenly with the outbreak of war in 1914. George Bullough was appointed to a military post, the island's able-bodied staff were sent to the trenches to die for their country and the family's 220-ft steam-yacht, *Rhouma*, became a minesweeper. After the war, the Bulloughs visited less and less often and the castle began to show signs of neglect. Even the poor hummingbirds died when the heating failed. Sir George himself died in 1939 and Lady Monica abandoned the place in 1954 – literally – leaving musical instruments on the stands in the ballroom and wine in the cellar. In 1957 the Bullough family sold Rùm to the Nature Conservancy for £23,000.

puffer from the mainland. For the gardens, 250,000 tons of soil were shipped from Ayrshire and used for planting exotic specimens collected from around the world. A nine-hole golf course and bowling green were laid out, along with a Japanese-style garden and huge walled garden. Hothouses were built to grow tropical fruits and palm houses were home to hummingbirds, turtles and even alligators. One of these creatures escaped, only to be shot by Bullough to prevent them 'interfering with the comfort of the guests'. As well as the elaborate carvings, wood panelling, furniture and flooring, the castle also incorporarated many state-of-the-art features such as an electricity generator, central heating, air conditioning and an internal telephone system (the first private residence in Scotland to do so). Pride of place, however, went to the magnificent Orchestrion, a fantastical mechanical contraption that simulated a 40-piece orchestra and belted out military marches, polkas, operatic excerpts and popular tunes of the day from its position under the main staircase. It is still in working order and visitors today will be treated to a gloriously surreal rendition of *The*

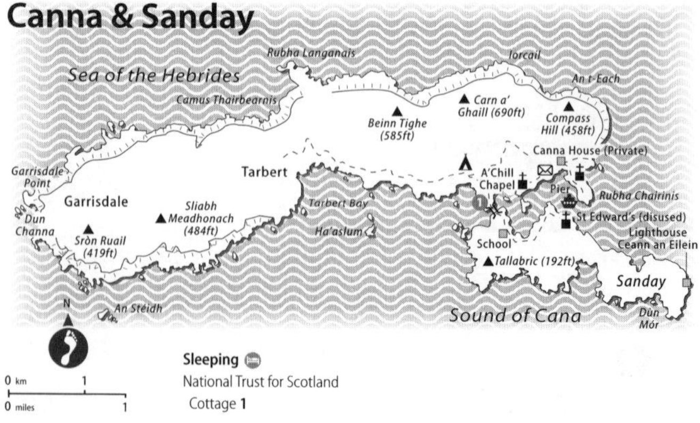

Liberty Bell March (the Monty Python theme tune to you and me). Michael Palin would heartily approve.

Kinloch Castle was a finalist in the BBC's first *Restoration* series and is currently undergoing a major refurbishment. Visitors must take off their shoes as they are escorted round the lavish rooms, many of them fading, peeling or leaking. The castle is a genuinely fascinating testament to Edwardian wealth and extravagance and the tour is worth the boat trip alone. You can even stay at the castle; in the hostel which occupies the former servants' quarters (what else did you expect?).

Island walks

Rùm's other great attraction is its mountain range, which offers some of the best island mountain treks outside the Cuillins of Skye. The highest point is **Askival** (2664 ft), which can be reached by the main ridge from **Hallival**, though the route involves some rock scrambling and is only advised for fit and experienced walkers. Before setting out, ask permission from the manager of the reserve office at the **White House** ⓘ *T01687-462026, Mon-Fri 0900-1230.*

The Bullough family mausoleum, built in the style of a Greek Doric temple, stands incongruously on the west coast at **Harris Bay**. It's an interesting 7½-mile walk across to the mausoleum from Kinloch. A less strenuous alternative is the **Kinloch Glen Trail** which is signposted by the stone bridge as you head from the castle to the farmstead. The circular route is 4 km and takes a leisurely 1½ hrs.

Canna

» *pp297-298. Colour map 3, A3.*

Canna is the most westerly of the Small Isles and is owned by the National Trust for Scotland. It's a small island, 5 miles long by 1 mile wide, bounded by cliffs and with a rugged interior, fringed by fertile patches. It's attached to its smaller neighbour, **Sanday**, by a narrow isthmus which is covered, except at low tide. There's now also a bridge linking them.The main attraction for visitors is some fine walking. It's about a mile from the ferry jetty up to the top of **Compass Hill** (458 ft), so called because its high metallic content distorts compasses. The highest point on the island is **Carn a' Ghaill** (690 ft). During the summer, a day trip from Mallaig allows you over nine hours in which to explore Canna and enjoy the fantastic views across to Rùm and Skye.

The population of 20 mostly work on the island's farm. Canna was gifted to the National Trust by its benevolent owner, the late Dr John Lorne Campbell, a notable Gaelic scholar. The island continues to be run as a single working farm and, since it was sold in 1938, has been an unofficial bird sanctuary with 157 recorded bird species, including Manx shearwater and puffins.

Sleeping

Eigg *p294*

D **Kildonan House**, T01687-482446. The island's only guesthouse, price includes dinner and the food is superb.

F **The Glebe Barn**, T01687-482417, www.glebebarn.co.uk. 24-bed independent hostel and outdoor centre. Open Apr-Oct (all year for groups). Comfortable accommodation in twin, family and bunk rooms. Sitting room with log stove. Residencial courses and retreats, self-catering or fully catered options for groups and exclusive lets.

Self-catering cottages are also available, for details visit www.isleofeigg.org.

Muck *p294*

D **Port Mór House**, T01678-462365. The price includes dinner which is also available to non-residents. Alternatively, you can ask permission to camp at the tearoom.

Rùm *p294*

E Bay View, T01687-462023. The only B&B. Book well in advance.

E-F Kinloch Castle, T01687-462037, castleman ager@rumcastle.free_/online.co.uk. Open Mar to end-Oct. 42-bed hostel in the old servants' quarters, with twin, 4-bed and 6-bed dorms, also 3 double rooms and 1 family room (**D**) available for B&B. Also has café selling snacks and meals to guests only.

Camping

F Bothies, and camping is allowed at Kinloch. Contact the reserve manager at the White House, T01687-462026.

Canna *p297*

Those wishing to stay can camp rough, with permission from the **National Trust for Scotland**, or rent out their self-catering cottage, T0131-226 5922, www.nts.org.uk.

Eating

The Small Isles *p293*

There is a tearoom and shop on each island with the exception of Canna, where there are no shops so you'll need to bring your own supplies. Most of the B&Bs and guesthouses serve food. The well-stocked shop on Eigg is at the jetty, T01687-482432, open Mon-Sat. The café/tearoom on Rùm is housed in the village hall, it serves hot drinks, cakes, soup and other home-made food and is open several afternoons a week during summer. The shop has limited opening hours, depending on the requirements of island life, but is always open after 1700. Call the Reserve Office, T01687-462026, to check in advance. The village hall is always open as an escape from the rain or midges.

Activities and tours

The Small Isles *p293*

Guided walks are organized on Eigg (Sat and Sun) and Muck (Wed), ranging in length and difficulty, for groups of 4-10. All cost £4.50. Book through **Arisaig Marine**, T01687-450224, www.arisaig.co.uk, 0900-1730.

Transport

The Small Isles *p293*

Bus For a bus/taxi service on Eigg, call Davie Robertson, T01687-482494.

Cycle hire from Eigg Bikes, call Stuart Thomson, T01687-482469.

Ferry CalMac operates the passenger-only ferry from **Mallaig** to all 4 islands once daily Mon-Thu and twice on Fri and Sat, returning on the same days. There's also a **non-landing cruise** around all the islands which costs £13.75 but you can sail to all 4 islands if you catch the 0620 ferry on Sat. A second ferry leaves on Sat, making it possible to spend time on one of the islands. Bicycles cost £2 for any trip.

To **Eigg** 1 hr 10 mins direct, £5.50 one way) on Mon, Tue (via **Muck**), Thu, Fri and Sat. To **Muck** (1½ hrs direct, £8.35 one way) on Tue, Thu (via Eigg), Fri and Sat (via Eigg). To **Rùm** (1 hr 10 mins direct, £8.15 one way) on Mon (via Eigg), Wed, Fri and Sat. To **Canna** (2 hrs direct, £10.35 one way) on Mon (via **Eigg** and **Rùm**), Wed (via **Rùm**), Fri (via Rùm) and Sat.

Arisaig Marine, T01687-450224, www.arisaig.co.uk, sail from Eigg to **Muck** (£10 return) and **Rùm** (£16 return).

Outer Hebrides

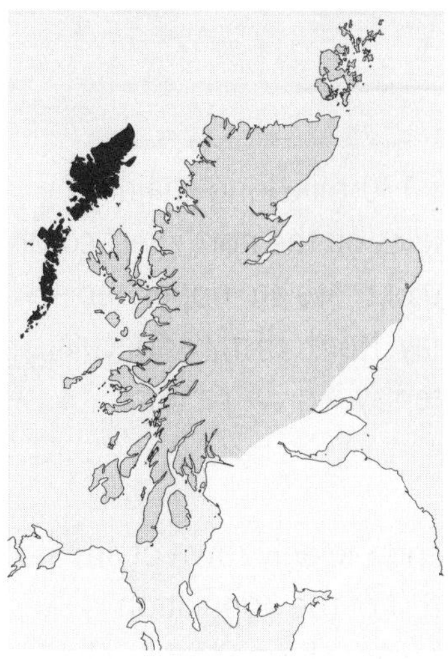

Footprint features

Introduction

The Outer Hebrides are a narrow, 130-mile long chain of more than 200 islands lying 40 miles off the northwest coast of the Scottish mainland. Only 10 of these are populated – Lewis and Harris, Scalpay, Berneray, North Uist, Benbecula, South Uist, Eriskay, Barra and Vatersay – giving a total population of just under 30,000.

The main administrative centre and the only town of any size is Stornoway on Lewis. The rest of the population is scattered throughout the islands in much smaller villages, mostly strung out along the coast. Despite the frequency of transport connections with the mainland, the Outer Hebrides remain remote in every sense. Unlike Skye and the Inner Hebrides, tourism is of far less importance to the local economy. In many ways, the islands are the last bastion of the old Highland life. Though newer industries such as fish farming have been introduced, the traditional occupations of crofting, fishing and weaving still dominate and, outside Stornoway, life is very much a traditional one, revolving around the seasons and the tides.

Relentlessly battered by fierce Atlantic winds, the islands can seem a hostile environment and an unappealing proposition. Much of the interior is bleak peat bog, rocks and endless tiny lochs, and the long, straggling crofting communities only add to the feeling of desolation. But anyone who has stood on a clifftop and felt a thrill at the power and potential of all that water should come here. Nowhere else in Britain is there such a sense of emptiness and of the sheer forces of nature. These are islands at the very edge of our imagination.

★ Don't miss...

1 **Calanais** Visit the standing stones here, preferably at night when there's a spooky atmosphere, page 310.
2 **Uig sands** Take a stroll along these wonderful sands, the loveliest beach on Lewis page 312.
3 **Bays** Hire a car and drive through the weird lunar landscape at Bays, on the east coast of Harris, page 320.
4 **Barra** Fly to this island, where the planes land on the beach, page 329.
5 **St Kilda** Take a trip here, home to some of the largest seabird colonies in Europe, page 335.

Outer Hebrides

Ins and outs

Getting there

British Airways/Loganair fly from Glasgow to Stornoway on Lewis, Barra and Benbecula on North Uist. There are also flights from Edinburgh to Stornoway, Inverness to Stornoway, and from Benbecula to Barra and Stornoway. **CalMac** car and passenger ferries sail to and from Stornoway (Lewis), Tarbert (Harris), Lochmaddy (North Uist), Lochboisdale (South Uist) and Castlebay (Barra). Ferry details are given under each respective destination, but note that times change according to the day of the week and time of the year. For full details of ferry timetables contact **CalMac**, T08705-650000, www.calmac.co.uk. Car space is limited during the summer months, so it's advisable to book ahead. (For details of bus connections on Skye and on the mainland, contact **Scottish Citylink**, T0990-505050.) A much cheaper way to get around the islands with a car is with one of **CalMac**'s Island Hopscotch Tickets. There are various route options, and tickets give you 30 days unlimited travel on each route. For example, a ticket for the Oban–Lochboisdale–Berneray–Leverburgh–Stornoway–Ullapool route allows you to visit South and North Uist, Harris and Lewis and costs £37.50 per passenger and £157 per car. See the **CalMac** guide or call the numbers above for full details of the Island Hopscotch Tickets, and the Island Rover Ticket, which gives unlimited travel on most **CalMac** routes for eight or 15 days and costs £49.50/72 per passenger and £238/357 per car. ➡ *For further details, see Transport pages 315, 322 and 334.*

❢ Weather conditions are so changeable that flights are prone to delay and can be very bumpy. Flights to Barra have an added complication. They land on the beach, meaning that the runway disappears twice a day under the incoming tide.

Getting around

You should allow plenty of time to explore the islands fully. With your own transport and travelling from top to bottom, a week would be enough time for a whistle-stop tour but not enough to explore in any depth or scratch beneath the surface. You will need to allow for the lack of public transport on Sundays on most islands (taxi is the only way around), and for the fact that weather conditions frequently affect ferry and flight timetables.

Air **British Airways/Loganair** fly between Barra, Benbecula and Stornoway daily.

Ferry A ferry sails to Berneray from Leverburgh (Harris) three or four times daily. Several ferries sail daily from Barra to the island of Eriskay. There's also a regular passenger ferry from Ludag in South Uist to Eoligarry on Barra.

Bus Bus services have improved and now run regularly to most main towns and villages on the islands.

Car Most of the islands' roads are single track but in good condition and, unlike other parts of the Highlands and Islands, not too busy. On Sunday you'll barely meet another soul. Petrol stations are few and far between, expensive and closed on Sundays. The normal rules for single track roads apply and, as elsewhere in the Highlands, you need to look out for wandering sheep. Distances are greater than most people imagine. For example, the distance from Nis (Ness) at the northern tip of Lewis to Leverburgh in the south of Harris is 85 miles. From Stornoway to Tarbert is 37 miles. And the distance from Otternish in the north of North Uist to Lochboisdale, the main ferry port on South Uist, is 50 miles. Several local car hire agencies offer reasonable rental deals. Expect to pay around £20-25 per day, depending on the size of engine and age of the car. You cannot take a rented car off the islands.

Cycle Cycling is a great way to explore the islands. You can fully appreciate the amazing scenery around, and it only costs a few pounds to transport a bike by ferry. There is, of course, the major problem of strong winds, which can leave you frustrated and exhausted, especially when cycling into the prevailing easterly wind. ➡ *For further details, see Transport pages 315, 322 and 334.*

Tourist information

There are tourist information centres in Stornoway and Tarbert, which are open all year round, and also in Lochmaddy, Lochboisdale and Castlebay, which are open early April to mid October. Full details are given under each destination. **Visit Hebrides** ⓘ *www.visithebrides.com*, produces an accommodation brochure as well as the essential *Western Isles Official Tourist Map* (Estate Publications; £3.95), which gives place names in English and Gaelic. Its website also provides lots of information on the islands, including accommodation and up-and-coming events. You should also invest in a copy of the *Highlands & Islands Travel Guide*, which is available from the local TICs. Accommodation on the islands is generally not difficult to find, except perhaps at the height of the summer when you should book in advance, either directly or through the local tourist office. It's also a good idea to book ahead if you're staying on a Sunday and, if you're staying in the countryside, you should check if there's a convenient pub or hotel to eat in, and if not, make arrangements to eat at your B&B. There are many self-catering options on the islands and this is a most cost-effective way to get to know one particular island. Check out the **Visit Hebrides** website listed above.

Activities

Those intent on walking in the islands visit the excellent website www.walkhebrides.com, which has details of over 30 walks, or pick up a copy of *Walks in the Western Isles* by Mary Welsh (Clan Walk Guides, £5.99). Several operators offer guided walking holidays, see Essentials chapter, page 54. A great way to experience the islands is to get out onto the water. Sea kayaking is available on North Uist (see page 333) and Barra (see page 333). If surfing's your thing then you're in the right place. The northwest coast of Lewis, especially the stretch between Dal More Bay and the beach at Barabhas, has some of the best surfing in Britain (see page 306).

Leodhas (Lewis)

→ *Phone code: 01851. Colour map 1.*

Lewis constitutes the northern two thirds of the most northerly island in the Outer Hebrides. It is by far the most populous of the Outer Hebridean islands and, with over 20,000 inhabitants, makes up two thirds of the total population. Just over 8000 people live in Stornoway, the largest town in the Hebrides and the administrative capital of the Western Isles. The majority of the rest of the population live in the long line of crofting townships strung out along the west coast between Port Nis (Ness) and Càrlabhagh (Carloway). The west coast is also where you'll find the island's most interesting sight: the prehistoric remains of Dùn Chàrlabhaigh (Carloway) Broch, the impressive Calanais (Callanish) Standing Stones, the restored blackhouse village of Garenin and the Arnol Blackhouse. These can all be visited as a day trip from Stornoway, either on an organized tour or on the 'West Side Circular' bus service. The interior of the northern half is flat peat bog, hence the island's name which means 'marshy' in Gaelic. Further south, where Lewis becomes Harris, the scenery is more dramatic as the relentlessly flat landscape gives way to rocky hills, providing the backdrop to the sea-lochs that cut deep into the coast and the beautiful beaches around Uig. ▸▸ *For Sleeping, Eating and other listings, see pages 313-315.*

Never on a Sunday

The islands are the *Gaidhealtachd*, the land of the Gael. Gaelic culture has remained more prominent here than in any other part of Scotland, and the way of life and philosophy of the islanders will seem totally alien and fascinating to many visitors. Gaelic is the first language for the majority of the islanders – and the only one for the older generation – but the all-pervading influence of the English media has taken its toll and the language is under threat. Though Gaelic is still taught in schools, the younger generation tends to speak to each other in English. Visitors will not have any language problems, as the Gaelic-speaking inhabitants are so polite they will always change to English when visitors are present (though place names and signposts are in Gaelic).

The church is also an important factor in preserving the language, and services are usually held in Gaelic. In fact, religion is one of the most pervasive influences on Hebridean life, and the islanders' faith is as strong as the winds that pound their shores. The islands are split between the Presbyterian Lewis, Harris and North Uist, and the predominantly Roman Catholic South Uist and Barra. Benbecula, meanwhile, has a foot in both camps. On Lewis and Harris the Free Church is immensely powerful and the Sabbath is strictly observed. Don't expect to travel anywhere by public transport; shops and petrol stations will be closed, and you'll be hard pressed to find a place to eat. Even the swings in the playgrounds are padlocked! Things are changing, however, and October 2002 saw the revolutionary move to allow Loganair to fly to Stornoway on a Sunday. Despite a tsunami-like wave of protest from the church, who described the idea as "a breach of God's moral law", Loganair's tourist-friendly flights went ahead.

Background

Lewis was controlled by the Vikings and the Norse influence can be seen in many of the place names, such as Uig (which is Norse for 'a bay'). After the end of Norwegian sovereignty in 1266, the island was ruled by the Macleods, said to be descendants of early settlers from Iceland. Control of the island was wrested from them by the Mackenzies, who then proceeded to sell it, in 1844, to Sir James Matheson. The new owner built Lews Castle in Stornoway and began to develop the infrastructure of the island, as well as investing in new industries. Though many crofts were cleared and families sent to Canada, the people of Lewis fared well and certainly much better than their counterparts in the Southern Isles.

The next proprietor was Lord Leverhulme, founder of Lever Brothers, who bought the island (along with Harris) in 1918. He planned to turn Lewis into a major fishing centre and ploughed money into developing the infrastructure. He was forced to abandon his plans, however, partly because of the decline of the fishing industry, and partly owing to the growing conflict between him and the islanders returning from the war who wanted land of their own to farm. As a final benevolent gesture, Lord Leverhulme offered Lewis to the islanders, but only Stornoway Council accepted. The island was then divided into estates and sold, and hundreds of people emigrated.

Today the economy of Lewis is still based on the traditional industries of crofting, fishing and weaving, though there are other economic activities such as fish farming, which is now a major employer, service industries, tourism, construction and the onshore oil yard at Stornoway.

Steòrnabhagh (Stornoway) » pp 313-315.

Colour map 1, B3.

→ *Population: 8132.*

The fishing port of Stornoway, the only town in the Outer Hebrides, is the islands' commercial capital and, as such, boasts more services and facilities than you might expect in any town of comparable size. It's not a pretty place, dominated as it is by the oil industry, but has the full range of banks, shops, hotels, guesthouses, pubs and restaurants, garages, car hire firms, sports facilities, an airport and ferry terminal, and, for the visiting tourist, it presents a rare opportunity to stock up on supplies.

Stornoway is also the administrative capital and home to the Comhairle nan Eilean (Western Isles Council), which has done much to broaden the local economy and to promote and protect Gaelic language and culture, but is probably best known

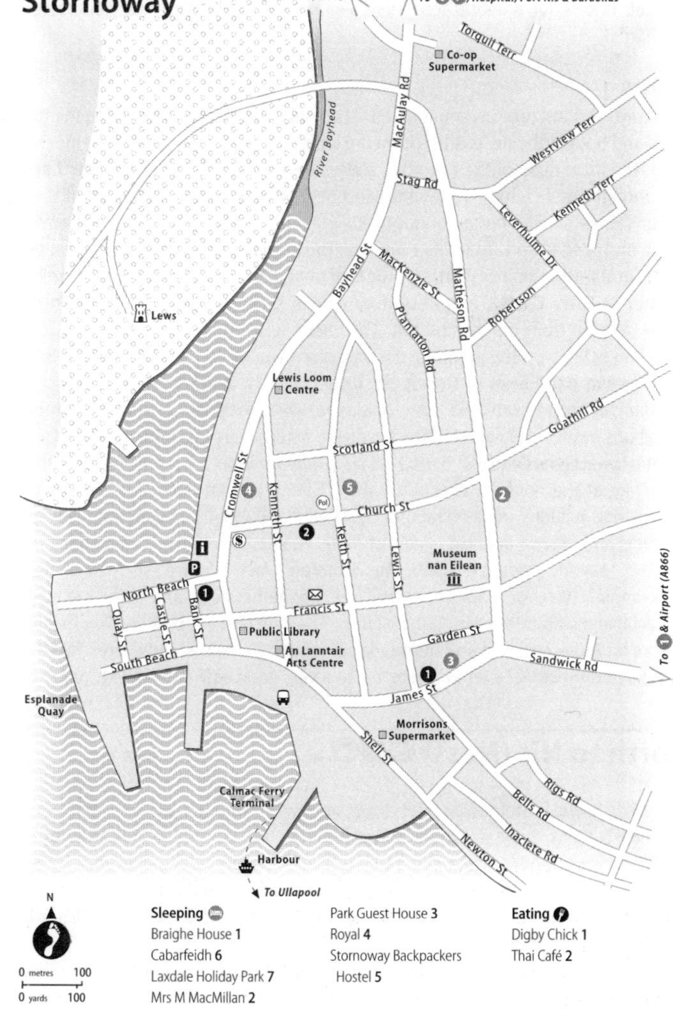

 for its disastrous financial dealings with the Bank of Credit and Commerce International (BCCI), which collapsed in 1991, losing the islands a cool £23 million.

Ins and outs

Getting there and around Stornoway is the island's transport hub. The airport is 4 miles east of the town centre, a £5 taxi ride away. The **CalMac** ferry terminal is just beyond the bus station, which is on South Beach, a short walk from the town centre. Buses leave from Stornoway to all parts of the island and also to Tarbert and Leverburgh on Harris. Bus timetables are available from the tourist office. The town is compact and most of what you need is within easy walking distance of the tourist office. Some of the B&Bs in the residential areas are quite a distance from the centre, but there's an hourly town bus service, or hire a taxi. ›› *For further details, see Transport page 315.*

Tourist information The TIC ⓘ *26 Cromwell St, T01851-703088, Apr-May and Sep-Oct Mon-Fri 0900-1800, Sat 0900-1700, Jun-Aug Mon-Fri 0900-2000, Oct-Mar Mon-Fri 0900-1700*, stocks maps, bus timetables and various books and brochures, and sell tickets for minibus tours to Calanais and for wildlife trips around Lewis and Harris.

Sights

Stornoway is short on conventional tourist sights and once you've been to the tourist office and bought the necessities from the local supermarkets, there's not much else to do. The focal point of the town has always been its sheltered deep-water **harbour** and, though the fishing industry has declined since its peak at the end of the last century, there's still a fair amount of activity, especially at the fish market on North Beach on Tuesday and Thursday evenings. The harbour is usually full of seals, giving the town its nickname of Portrona (port of seals). There's a good view across the harbour to **Lews Castle**, a 19th-century edifice built by Sir James Matheson with money earned from opium and tea. The castle now houses a college and its real attraction is the wooded grounds, the only place you'll see trees on the islands.

Museum nan Eilean ⓘ *Francis St, T01851-703773, Apr-Sep Mon-Sat 1000-1730, Oct-Mar Tue 1000-1700 and Sat 1000-1300, free*, features a range of temporary exhibitions on island life and history. Anyone remotely interested in Harris Tweed should visit the **Lewis Loom Centre** ⓘ *T01851-703117, Mon-Sat 1000-1700, £2*, housed in the Old Grainstore at the northern end of Cromwell Street, just off Bayhead. The 40-minute guided tour includes demonstrations of traditional methods of warping, dyeing and spinning, and offers a detailed history of Harris Tweed. There's also a craft shop.

The eagerly awaited new **An Lanntair Arts Centre** ⓘ *T01851-703307, www.lanntair.com, Mon-Sat 1000-late, free*, opened in 2005 and is the main venue for social and cultural events on the islands. The light and airy building has exhibition spaces for local, national and international artists, a cinema, and stages for various musical and theatrical events. There's also a very good café (see Eating, page 314).

North to Nis (Ness) ›› *pp 313-315. Colour map 1, A3.*

The A857 leaves Stornoway and runs northwest through barren, treeless and relentlessly bleak moorland to **Barabhas (Barvas)**. The landscape is scarred by deep gashes caused by peat digging, and the unfamiliar smell you detect in your nostrils is peat burning – a strange mixture of burning grass, whisky and coffee. Peat is the main source of domestic fuel used on the islands, and outside most houses you'll see large stacks of peat, or *cruachs*.

The road from Barabhas northeast to Nis runs through a series of forlorn-looking, scrawny settlements that all seem identical and merge into one. They consist of

Croft conversion

The word 'croft' is derived from the Gaelic *croit*, meaning a small area of land. Crofting has been the traditional way of life in the Scottish Highlands for many centuries. Its emotive hold on the psyche of the Highlander comes from the long, hard struggle for security of tenure, see page 395.

A croft is aptly described as a parcel of land entirely surrounded by regulations. Most crofts consist of a few acres of arable land with a proportion of grazing land shared with other crofts. Each crofter is, in effect, a kind of small tenant-farmer, the distinction being that he has almost absolute security of tenure and has the right to assign the croft to a member of his family whether the landlord agrees or not. In fact, over the years, the crofter has managed to acquire most of the rights of ownership with few of the disadvantages.

The croft is the area of land involved and not the house which is called the 'croft house'. Crofts can vary in size, from a quarter of an acre upwards. Those on Lewis are small and relatively unproductive, with an average size of only about 5 acres, while on the Uists, where the land is more fertile, crofts are up to 50 acres or more.

As well as having the sole tenancy of the croft, the crofter usually also has a share in a huge area of 'common grazing' along with the other members of the crofting community – commonly called a township. They also work together in such activities as fencing, sheep dipping or cutting peat.

In reality, crofting does not provide a viable means of living. Very few crofters rely solely on their smallholding for an income and most need to have several occupations (including running a B&B) to make ends meet. But without the family croft, whole communities would just pack up and leave, so crofting functions as a means of preventing the depopulation of remote rural areas.

The crofter's lot may change for the better, however, thanks to the Scottish Parliament's new Land Reform Bill, which includes a special right to buy for the crofting communities.

modern, characterless grey pebble-dash cottages with the ubiquitous piles of peat in the gardens; the abandoned cars and vans scattered around everywhere only adds to the ugly and depressing scene.

Just beyond Barabhas a sign points left to the **Morvern Art Gallery**, which has a café, making it a welcome refuge in bad weather. A few miles further on is a turning right to **Baile an Trùiseil (Ballantrushel)**, site of the huge **Clach an Trùiseil**, a 20-ft monolith (the largest in Europe), which was the scene of the last major battle on the island, fought between the Morrisons of Nis and the MacAuleys of Uig. This is the first of a number of prehistoric sights between here and **Siadar (Shader)** which may be of interest to the keen archaeologist. Otherwise there's little of note on the road north to Nis as it passes through the typical crofting townships of **Coig Peighinnean Buirgh** (Five Penny Borve), **Gàbhsann bho Dheas** (South Galson), **Dail** (Dell), **Suainebost** (Swainbost), **Tàbost** (Habost) and **Lìonal** (Lionel). In saying that, those who are keen to buy souvenirs should look in at the **Borgh Pottery** ⓘ *T01856-850345, Mon-Sat 0930-1800*, by the bridge at Coig Peighinnean. Here you'll find a wide range of beautiful and original domestic and decorative ware.

The road continues north, passing through a number of villages that collectively make up **Nis (Ness)**, until it ends at the fishing village of **Port Nis (Port of Ness)**. It's a lovely spot, with a picturesque little harbour and golden sweep of

Gatliff Trust

The Gatliff Hebridean Hostels Trust (GHHT) is a non-profit-making charitable organization run entirely by volunteers, working with the island community to establish, maintain and develop a chain of 'value-for-money' hostels offering clean, cheap, simple, safe, welcoming and traditional croft-style accommodation in dramatic and beautiful locations for visitors to the Outer Hebrides.

The GHHT is independent of the SYHA but has adopted status. Visitors do not have to be members of either organization to use and stay in the hostels. First established in 1961 by Herbert Gatliff, the Trust was originally intended to provide young persons of limited means with the opportunity to meet local people and enjoy the unique natural environment and cultural heritage of the islands. However, in recent years, visitors of all incomes, ages, nationalities and interests have been encouraged to use the facilities.

The Trust is currently involved in the operation of four hostels situated at **Garenin** (Isle of Lewis), **Rhenigidale** (Isle of Harris), **Berneray** (North Uist) and **Howmore** (South Uist). Further hostels may be opened on other islands in the future.

The hostels are open all year and looked after by non-resident wardens who live and practise crofting nearby. No advance bookings are accepted but it is very unlikely that visitors will find themselves turned away and without a bed for the night. There is also limited space for camping at the hostels. Hostels provide bunk/camp beds, cooking facilities and cutlery, piped water, toilets and coal/wood fires, but visitors should bring their own food and a sleeping bag is recommended.

Current charges are: £8 per night, under 18s £5.50, camping £4.50, day visitors £1. Annual membership £10, under 18s £7.50. Further information, including membership and contact details, hostel locations and photographs, a reading list and places of interest to visit in the surrounding area, can be found at the GHHT website: www.gatliff.org.uk.

beach enclosed by steep cliffs. Each September the locals head out to the island of **Sula Sgeir**, 30 miles to the north, for the annual cull of young gannets (or *gugas*), which are considered something of a delicacy by the people of Lewis (but be warned: they're an acquired taste).

Just before Port Nis, is Lìonal, where the B8015 turns off right and leads to the start of the 10-mile coastal trail to **Tòlstadh (Tolsta North)** and the beautiful beaches of Traigh Mhor and Garry. Numerous shielings (basic stone huts where farming communities lived during summer grazings in high pasture) pepper the landscape from an earlier era when local crofters drove their cattle to the summer pastures in the island's interior. The beaches can be reached much more easily by road north from Stornoway. For details of the coastal walk, ask at the tourist information centre in Stornoway.

Another minor road heads northwest to the tiny hamlet of **Eòropaidh (Eoropie)** (pronounced 'Yor-erpee'). By the road junction that leads to Rubha Robhanais is the ancient **Teampull Mholuaidh (St Moluag's Church)**, thought to date from the 12th century and restored to its present state in 1912. It is now used on certain Sundays by Stornoway's Episcopal Church. From Eòropaidh a narrow road runs to the lighthouse at **Rubha Robhanais (Butt of Lewis)**, the most northerly tip of the the island. It's a great place for spotting seabirds or whales and dolphins, but also very wild and windy (just don't tell any visiting Americans where you've been). Half a mile back down the road a path leads to the tiny beach of **Port Sto**, which is more sheltered.

West coast of Lewis

» pp 313-315. Colour map 1, A2-3/B2.

Arnol

At the end of the village of Arnol is the **Blackhouse Museum** ⓘ *(HS) T01851-710395, Apr-Sep Mon-Sat 0930-1830, Oct-Mar Mon-Sat 0930-1630, £4.50, concessions £3.50, children £2*, one of the best surviving examples of an original blackhouse in Scotland and well worth visiting. These traditional thatched houses were once common throughout the Highlands and Islands, and were inhabited until the 1960s. They were built in the tradition of 'longhouses', which can be traced back 1000 years to the time of the Viking invaders. The name 'blackhouse' dates back to the 1850s when modern buildings were introduced. These were known as 'white houses' so the older-style houses were called 'blackhouses'. The blackhouses were well adapted to the harsh local climate. They had no windows or chimney and were built with local materials – stone, turf and thatch of oat, barley or marram grass – with a peat fire burning continually in the central hearth. Attached to the living quarters was the cattle byre. This particular blackhouse was built in 1885 and inhabited until 1964. **Hebridean Replicas**, T01851-710562, in the village, offers quality handmade Lewis chess sets from local stone, and provides a welcome alternative to much of the tacky tourist paraphernalia to be found in Stornoway.

The west coast of Lewis contains most of what you'll want to see and can be covered in a day trip from Stornoway, either with your own transport, by public bus or as part of a minibus tour.

Siabost and around

Two miles south of the Arnol turn-off, at **Bragar**, look out for an archway, formed from the jawbone of a blue whale that was washed up on the coast nearby in 1920. A few miles further on is the township of Siabost (Shawbost), where the charmingly ramshackle **folk museum** ⓘ *Mon-Sat 0900-1800, free*, which was started as a project by local schoolchildren, now contains an interesting collection of Hebridean artefacts.

Just south of Siabost, beside a small loch, is the sign for the recently restored **Norse Mill and Kiln**, which are a half-mile walk over the hill from the car park. There's not much to see as yet, but it's worth getting out of the car if you want to stretch your legs. A little further on is the turning for **Dail Beag (Dalbeg)**, a lovely secluded beach.

Gearrannan (Garenin)

The landscape gradually becomes more undulating and scenically interesting as the road then passes through the village of **Càrlabhagh (Carloway)**, Lord Leverhume's proposed fishing port. Here, a branch road leads to the ruined and deserted blackhouse village of Gearrannan (Garenin). The old village has been extensively renovated, with the aid of EU funding, and several derelict crofts have been painstakingly restored to their original style of stone walls and thatched roofs. One of these is now a **museum** ⓘ *T01851-643416, Apr-Sep Mon-Sat 0930-1730, £2.20, concession £1.70*. There's also a **Gatliff Trust** hostel (see Sleeping, page 313), a café serving snacks and light lunches, and four self-catering cottages. An old cart track leads down to the bay, from where the sight of the sun setting out at sea really is something to behold. Above the village, a footpath can be followed through the lazy beds (see page 320) and above the sea cliffs to reveal a stunning view of beautiful **Dal More Bay**. The Atlantic waves seem to break relentlessly on golden sands and the beach is, not surprisingly, a favourite haunt of surfers from Stornoway and further afield. Swimmers and bathers should be careful, however, because, as with many of the west coast beaches, there can be a fierce rip-current carrying the unwary into deeper water out at sea.

Dùn Chàrlabhaigh (Doune Carloway) Broch

A little further on, standing a few hundred yards from the main road, is the Dùn Chàrlabhaigh Broch, the best-preserved building of its type in the Outer Hebrides. The impressive 2000-year-old drystone habitation is beautifully situated on a rocky outcrop, commanding great views across Loch Carloway to the sea beyond. The remaining outer wall is 30-ft high and slopes inwards, with an inner wall which rises vertically, leaving chambers between the walls. Parts of the inner wall have collapsed, revealing the interior stairs and galleries. Also here is also the **Doune Broch Visitor Centre** ⓘ *T01851-643338, Apr-Oct Mon-Sat 1000-1800, free*, which tastefully complements the architectural style of the site, and which gives a good audio-visual description of how life must have been in one of these structures around 50 BC.

Calanais (Callanish)

ⓘ *(HS) T01851-621422. Site: Apr-Sep daily 1000-1900, Oct-Mar daily 1000-1600, free. Visitor centre: Apr-Sep Mon-Sat 1000-1800, Oct-Mar 1000-1630, £1.85, concession £1.35, child £0.85.*

Five miles south of Dun Chàrlabhaigh is the jewel in the islands' prehistoric crown, and one of the most atmospheric and evocative places in Scotland, if not the UK. The **Calanais Standing Stones** are the equal of Stonehenge in historical value but what sets them apart is their imposing physical presence, which can be appreciated at close quarters, and their spectacularly beautiful setting. The stones are aligned in the form of a Celtic cross and, in the centre, is a main circle of 13 stones, with a central monolith over 12-ft tall, and a chambered burial cairn. The oldest part of this great ceremonial site – probably the stone circle – dates from around 3000 BC (older than Stonehenge) and continued in use until about 800 BC. The full significance of the site is not yet known, though it is thought to be a lunar calendar, built to track the path of the lunar cycle. Every 18.6 years the moon returns to the same point and the stones at Calanais plot its slow progress over the intervening years until the moon 'sets' inside the stone circle. This astounding event – known as a lunar standstill – last occurred in 2006. There are also a number of smaller and more isolated stone circles a few miles south of Calanais on the road to Gearraidh na h-Aibhne (Garynahine). Next to the stones is the **Calanais Visitor Centre**, which features 'The Story of the Stones' exhibition, a very good restaurant (see Eating, page 314) and shop. Margaret Curtis, who has been studying and excavating the site for over 30 years, offers a guided archaeological tour (see Activities and tours, page 314).

The Uig Peninsula

» *pp 313-315. Colour map 1, B2.*

From Gearraidh na h-Aibhne the main A858 runs back to Stornoway, while the B8011 forks west to the remote Uig Peninsula in the southwest of the island. Here are some of the Outer Hebrides' finest beaches and most dramatic coastal scenery, and you'll barely see another soul.

Bearnaraigh (Great Bernera) to Cnip

Four miles down this road is a turning to the right onto the B8059, which leads to the island of Bearnaraigh, now connected to the mainland of Lewis by a single-track road bridge. The main settlement on the island is **Breacleit** (**Breaclete**), where you can find out about the island's history in the **Bernera Museum** ⓘ *Jun-Sep Mon-Sat 1100-1800, £1.50*. The rest of the island is fairly interesting with tiny fishing villages, one or two brochs and some standing stones. The nicest part, though, is on the north coast, near the tiny hamlet of **Bostadh** (**Bosta**), where a lovely little sandy bay looks out to the nearby island of **Bearnaraigh Beag** (**Little Bernera**).

Music to your ears

As the heartland of Gaelic culture, the Outer Hebrides are host to many music events throughout the year ranging from a spontaneous ceilidh to one of the three local mods. Mods usually consist of three days of competition in piping, singing, instrumental music, drama and poetry, and are an opportunity to see the best of the local talent. More information can be obtained from An Comunn Gaidhealach, T01851-703487.

Also listed below are the various Highland Games and agricultural shows, where you can also see piping competitions and Highland dancing.

Late March Feis nan Coisir, Stornoway, Lewis.
First Friday in April Donald Macleod Memorial Piping Competition, Stornoway, Lewis.
May-June Highland Festival, held in various locations.
Early June Harris Mod, Tarbert, on Harris.
Second week in June Lewis Mod, Stornoway, Lewis.
Mid June Uist Mod, lochdar, on South Uist.
May-June Lochmaddy Boat Festival, Lochmaddy, North Uist.
Mid July Berneray Week, Bearnaraigh (Berneray), North Uist.
July Ceolas Music School, South Uist.
Early July Barra Festival for 2 weeks.
Early/mid July Feis Tir an Eorna, Paibeil, North Uist; Barra Highland Games, Borgh (Borve), Barra, lasting for a week.
11-14 July Hebridean Celtic Music Festival, Stornoway, Lewis.
Mid July North Uist Highland Games, Hosta, North Uist.
Mid/late July Harris Gala; South Uist Highland Games, Aisgeirnis (Askernish), South Uist; Lewis Highland Games, Tong, Lewis.
Mid July Barra Highland Games.
Third week of July Harris Festival
Late July Barra Live, Barra; West Side Agricultural Show, Barabhas (Barvas), Lewis; South Uist Agricultural Show, lochdar, South Uist; South Harris Agricultural Show, Leverburgh,.
July Feis Eilean an Fhraoich, Stornoway, Lewis.
Late July/early August North Uist Agricultural Show, Hosta, North Uist.
Early August Carloway Agricultural Show, Càrlabhagh (Carloway), Lewis; Fies Tir a Mhurain, Lionacleit, Benbecula; Lewis Carnival, Stornoway; Fish Festival, Stornoway; Twin Peaks Hill Race, North Uist.
Second week August Harris Arts Festival, Tarbert.

The B8011 continues across bleak moorland, then cuts north to **West Loch Roag**, which is fringed by some fine sandy beaches and backed by a much hillier landscape. Just beyond **Miabhag** (**Miavaig**) is the turn-off right to **Cliobh** (**Cliff**), with its picturesque beach which is unsafe for swimming. A mile further on is the little village of **Cnip** (**Kneep**), to the east of which is the beautiful **Traigh na Berie**, a long sandy beach backed by flat machair which is ideal for camping.

Gallan Head

Beyond Miabhag, the eerie peninsula of Gallan Head provides a setting befitting of a science fiction drama or Cold War Orwellian novel, with empty, decaying Ministry of Defence buildings battered by the Atlantic storms. Wandering around the abandoned site, it is easy to form ideas of bizarre, top-secret government experiments and early-warning missile tracking in this seemingly edge-of-the-world place, far removed from the unwanted, prying eyes of everyday society.

Ratpacker hostel

Lying about 5 miles off the east coast of Lewis, due east of Scalpay, are the Shiant (pronounced *shant*) islands, a group of three small, uninhabited, wild and rugged islands comprising **Garbh Eilean (Rough Island), Eilean an Tighe (House Island)** and **Eilean Mhuire (Mary Island)**. Though unknown to most, they do have one rather dubious claim to fame: they boast the largest black rat population in the British Isles. The islands are currently owned by writer, Adam Nicolson, who inherited them from his father, renowned novelist Nigel Nicolson, who bought them for £1400 after his mother, Vita Sackville-West, saw them advertised for sale in the *Daily Telegraph*. The owner has written eloquently and informatively about his beloved islands in *Sea Room* (Harper Collins, 2001) and at the end of the book he actually invites readers to go and visit. All they have to do is email him at adam@shiant isles.net and he'll send the keys. The sole accommodation on the islands is described by Nicolson as "extremely basic, rarely clean and at times rat-ridden", but the bonus is that there's no charge for staying there. It's recommended you sleep in tents and use the house as kitchen-cum-sitting room. The catch is (aside from the rats) that there's only one boat licensed to take passengers to the Shiants, from Stornoway. The price is negotiable but expect to pay around £500 return – although up to 10 people can travel for that price. For details, T01895-540250, woodfootloose@sol.com.

Mangersta and the Flannan Islands

Beyond Ardroil the road continues to Mangersta where, at Aird Fenish, is some of the most spectacular and photogenic coastal scenery in the Outer Hebrides. The cliffs plunge dramatically beyond the road to the inaccessible beach below, with a series of crumbling sea stacks battered by the fearsome waves, and seabirds riding the updraughts adding to the sense of natural beauty, energy and sheer power. Further south at **Brenish**, about a 10-minute walk from the road, is a menacing blowhole connected to the sea by an underground passage.

Far out into the Atlantic are the haunting Flannan Islands, scene of an unsolved mystery in 1900 following the disappearance of three lighthouse keepers. Various explanations have been put forward over the years, ranging from a freak wave in stormy weather to a monster sea serpent or even a dispute and fight between the men; whatever the real reason, the legend continues. See page 314 for boat trips.

Timsgearraidh (Timsgarry)

At Timsgearraidh (Timsgarry) are the **Traigh Chapadail (Uig sands)** at the village of **Eadar Dha Fhadhail (Adroil)**. This is the loveliest of all the beaches on Lewis, with miles of sand dunes and machair, but it is famous for an entirely different reason. It was here in 1831 that a crofter dug up the 'Lewis Chessmen', 78 pieces carved from walrus ivory and belonging to at least eight incomplete chess sets from 12th-century Scandinavia. Some are now in the Museum of Scotland in Edinburgh, but most can be found outside their country of origin, in the British Museum in London (where you'll also find the Elgin Marbles).

Sleeping

Stornoway *p305, map p305*
As the largest settlement on the islands, Stornoway has a good selection of accommodation from which to choose, though you should book in advance in the peak summer season. The TIC will do this for you, for a small fee.
L-B Cabarfeidh Hotel, Perceval Rd South, T01851-702604, www.cabarfeidh-hotel.co.uk. 46 rooms. Modern building on the outskirts of town and not as convenient as the **Royal** but is more upmarket with full range of facilities and a decent restaurant.
B Royal Hotel, Cromwell St, T01851-702109, www.calahotels.com. 24 rooms. Best of several centrally located hotels. Good value, and good food in its restaurant and bistro (see Eating, below).
C-D Braighe House, 20 Braighe Rd, T01851-705287, www.braighehouse.co.uk. 4 en suite rooms. Open all year. Very comfortable accommodation in modern house with sea views. Good food and friendly welcome. A good alternative to the more expensive hotels in town. Recommended.
C-D Park Guest House, 30 James St, T01851-702485, F703482. 10 rooms. This Victorian townhouse is comfortable, only 500 yds from the ferry terminal, and is the best of the guesthouses. It also has an excellent restaurant. **B** with dinner, **D** room only.

There are many B&Bs in and around the town centre, most of which offer a 'room only' rate for those requiring an early start to catch the first ferry. There are several along Matheson Rd, which is close to the town centre and the ferry terminal, including:
D-E Mrs M MacMillan, 'Fernlea', 9 Matheson Rd, T01851-702125, maureenmacmillan@amserve.com. 3 en suite rooms. Open Feb-Dec. **F** room only. Victorian listed building with original features. Off-street parking.
F Laxdale Holiday Park, Laxdale La, about a mile out of town on the road to Barabhas, T01851-703234. This bunkhouse has 16 beds, basic facilities and is open all year.
F Stornoway Backpackers Hostel, 47 Keith St, T01851-703628. Includes breakfast, open all year. Basic.

North to Nis *p306*
C Galson Farm Guest House, Gàbhsann bho Deas (South Galson), halfway between Barabhas and Port Nis, T01851-850492, www.galsonfarm.freeserve.com. 4 en suite rooms. Open all year. Friendly and beautifully restored 18th-century house with sea views. Dinner available (ΨΨΨ-ΨΨ). Owners also have Galson Farm Bunkhouse (**F**), which is obviously more basic accommodation.
D Mrs Catriona Thomson, 40 Cross Skigersta Rd, Nis, T01851-810661, norman.n.thomson@btinternet.com. 2 en suite rooms. Open all year. Modern B&B offering comfortable accommodation.

West coast of Lewis *p309*
If you want to stay near the stones and visit them at dusk or sunrise, there are several inexpensive B&Bs in the village of Calanais.
E Eshcol Guest House, 21 Breasclete, T01851-621357, www.eshcol.com. 3 rooms. Open Mar-Oct. High-quality accommodation in modern house overlooking Loch Roag.
E Debbie Nash, a few miles north of the stones, at 19 Tolsta Chaolais, T01851-621321. Recommended vegetarian B&B.
E-F Mrs Catherine Morrison, 27 Callanish, T01851-621392. 2 rooms. Open Mar-Sep. Friendly, good views over Loch Roag and only 200 yds from the stones.
F Garenin Hostel, one of 4 Gatliff Trust hostels in the Outer Hebrides (see box, page 308). This one is a renovated blackhouse, situated by a gorgeous beach and with the added benefit of a ground-source heat pump, making it awfully cosy in cold weather. Recommended.

Self-catering
Gearrannan Blackhouse Village, Carloway, T01851-643416, www.gearrannan.com. Open all year. 4 blackhouses have been restored and refurbished as self-catering thatched cottages in a fantastic location. 1 of the cottages sleeps up to 16. Prices from £75 per night.

The Uig Peninsula *p310*
C-E Baile Na Cille Guest House, Timsgarry, T01851-672242, randjgollin@compuserve.com. 7 en suite rooms. Easter-Oct.

One of the best places to stay around Uig bay, this restored 18th-century manse is beautifully located overlooking a 2-mile stretch of sand. Superb home cooking and one of the warmest welcomes in the islands. **B-C** including dinner.

E Bonaventure, at Aird, north of Timsgarry, T01851-672474, www.bonaventure lewis.co.uk. 5 rooms. Open all year (limited in Dec). Gallic flair allied to Highland hospitality makes this B&B-cum-restaurant a superb place to stay, and eat. Don't be put off by the grim-looking disused military buildings, accommodation here is very comfortable. And the food, c'est magnifique. Best on the island? Quite possibly. Highly recommended.

There are a couple of B&Bs on the island of **Great Bernera** which serve evening meals:

E Mrs Macauley, in Circebost (Kirkibost), on the east coast, T01851-612341.

E Mrs MacDonald, in Tobson, on the west coast, T01851-612347.

Eating

Stornoway *p305, map p305*

The pubs and hotels serve the usual range of bar meals. Note that pubs are closed on Sun and hotels cater only for residents. The only option then is to stock up on picnic food on Sat or try the local curry house, the **Stornoway Balti House**, near the bus station on South Beach.

TTT The Boatshed, in the **Royal Hotel**, see Sleeping, above. Recommended as best of the hotel options. Open daily. Less upmarket and cheaper is their **Barnacle Bistro**.

TT Digby Chick, 11 James St, T01851-700026. This contemporary restaurant is a popular local choice and one of the best places in town for seafood. Open Mon-Sat for lunch and dinner (closes 2100).

TT-T Thai Café, 27 Church St, T01851-701811. Few would expect such authentically good Thai cuisine so far north, but it's true. Come and be amazed. BYOB policy also helps keep prices down. Open Mon-Sat till 2300.

T Ann Lanntair Arts Centre, see Sights, page 305. Good for snacks and light lunches in pleasing, airy surroundings.

North to Nis *p306*

T Harbour View Gallery & Café, Port Nis, T01851-810735. Not much choice hereabouts but this place is OK. Also offers B&B.

West coast of Lewis *p309*

TT Tigh Mealros, a few miles south of the stones, Gearraidh na h-Aibhne, T01851-621333. They serve good local grub in a cosy, relaxed atmosphere, with scallops a speciality (closes at 2100).

T Calanais Visitor Centre Café, see Sights, page 310. This is the best place to eat near the stones. Clean and unassuming and a good place for lunch: soups, salads, home-baking – that kind of thing.

The Uig Peninsula *p310*

TTT-TT Bonaventure, north of Timsgarry, at Aird Uig, T01851-672474. Restaurant and B&B (see Sleeping, above) serving lunches and dinners of a French/Scottish style. Good, if rather expensive, wine list.

Shopping

Stornoway *p305, map p305*

There's a supermarket beside the ferry terminal and another (**Co-op**) by the first roundabout on the road out to Barabhas. There's also a smaller supermarket opposite the TIC.

Activities and tours

Stornoway *p305, map p305*

Elena C, 5a Knock, Point, T01851-870537, F706384. Wildlife trips that leave from Stornoway harbour.

Galson Motors, T01851-840269, leaving from Stornoway bus station, run day trips to Calanais.

Hebridean Exploration, 19 Westview Terr, T01851-705655, T0374-292746 (mob). Sea kayak tours.

Island Cruising, Uig, T01851-672381. For boat trips to the Flannan Islands.

MacDonald's Coaches, at the ferry terminal, T01851-706267. Coach tours.

W MacDonald, T01851-706267. Day trips to Calanais leaving from the pier.

West coast of Lewis *p309*

Margaret Curtis, Olcote, New Park, Calanais, T01851-621277, www.geo.org/callan/htm. The 1-hr tour of the site gives an insight into the history and purpose of the stones.

Transport

Lewis *p303*
Air British Airways/Loganair, T08708-509850, www.ba.com, flies from **Glasgow** to Stornoway (Mon-Sat 2 daily, 1 hr). There is a also a daily flight from **Edinburgh** to Stornoway (1 hr), and flights from **Inverness** to Stornoway (Mon-Sat 4 daily, 40 mins).

Bus Buses leave from Stornoway to all parts of the island. Note that buses do not run on Sun. To **Port Niss** (**Ness**) via **Barabhas** (**Barvas**) 4-6 times per day; to **Arnol**, **Siabost** (**Shawbost**), **Càrlabhagh** (**Carloway**), **Calanais** (**Callanish**), and back to Stornoway ('West Side Circular') 4-6 times per day; to **Bearnaraigh** (**Great Bernera**) via **Gearraidh na h-Aibhne** (**Garynahine**) 4 per day; to **Uig District** 3-4 per day; to **Ranais** (**Ranish**) 6-8 times per day. Contact the tourist office in Stornoway, or the bus station, T01851-704327, for further details. There are also buses from Stornoway to **Tarbert** and on to **Leverburgh** (for the ferry to North Uist) 4-5 times per day, T01859-502441.

Ferry CalMac ferry runs a service from **Ullapool** to Stornoway (2 hrs 40 mins) 2-3 daily Mon-Sat in the summer (Jun-Sep) and 2 daily Mon-Sat in the winter. One-way ticket costs £14.65 per passenger and £72 per car. A 5-day saver return costs £25.50 per passenger and £122 per car. Contact **CalMac** offices Ullapool, T01854-612358, and Stornoway, T01851-702361, for further details.

Car Car and bike rental is available at good rates from **Lewis Car Rentals**, 52 Bayhead St, T01851-703760, F705860. Also **Arnol Motors**, in Arnol (see page 309), T01851-710548, T0831-823318 (mob).

Cycle hire You can rent bikes at **Alex Dan's Cycle Centre**, 67 Kenneth St, T01851-704025, F701712.

Taxi Central Cabs, T01851-706900.

Directory

Stornoway *p305, map p305*
Banks Bank of Scotland is directly opposite the tourist office and has an ATM. The other major banks are also in the centre of town and also have ATMs. **Internet** Captions, 27 Church St, T01851-702238, www.captions.co.uk. Mon-Sat till late in the summer months. Internet facilities also available at the public library on Cromwell St. **Post** Main post office is on Francis St.

Na Hearadh (Harris)

→ *Phone code: 01859. Colour map1.*

Harris is not an island but, together with Lewis, forms the largest of the Outer Hebrides, with Harris taking up the southern third. The two parts are divided by the long sea lochs of Loch Seaforth in the east and Loch Resort in the west, though this division is rarely shown on maps. Though joined, the two are very different in terms of geography. Harris is largely mountain and rock, whereas Lewis is flat moorland. The largest town and site of the ferry terminal is An Tairbeart (Tarbert). To the north are the highest peaks in the Outer Hebrides, surrounded by some of the finest unspoilt wilderness in the whole country. To the south are miles of wonderful beaches; beaches like you've never seen before. It's not just the flawless white sand but the gin-clear water that breaks over them. When the sun comes out, it's as if someone had been fiddling with the colour control: cool greens mutate to psychedelic shades of turquoise and blue. The east coast is not so much a contrast as a shock to the system; a preternaturally strange lunar landscape straight out of a science fiction film. With your own transport you could 'do' Harris in a day quite comfortably, but, if the weather's good enough, you'll want to spend more time here and appreciate its precious natural beauty. ▸▸ *For Sleeping, Eating and other listings, see pages 321-323.*

Background

The separation of Harris and Lewis dates back to Norse times, when the island was divided between the two sons of Leod, progenitor of the Macleods. Harris remained in Macleod hands until 1834. The recent history of Harris is closely bound up with that of Lewis. Both were bought by the soap magnate, Lord Leverhulme, see page 304, whose grandiose schemes for Lewis came to nothing. Leverhulme then turned his attentions to Harris, where the peaceful little village of An t-Ob (Obbe) was renamed Leverburgh and transformed into a bustling port with all manner of public works programmes under development. His death in 1925 brought an end to all his plans for Harris and, instead of becoming a town with a projected population of 10,000, Leverburgh reverted to being a sleepy village, with only the harbour, the roads and the change of name to show for it all.

Since the Leverhulme era there has been no main source of employment for the population of 2400 on Harris, though a successful fishing industry continues on Scalpaigh (Scalpay). There is still some crofting supplemented by the Harris Tweed industry, though most production is now in Lewis, and whatever employment can be found: road-works, crafts and tourism. The proposal to create one of Europe's largest superquarries, which would have involved destroying an area of outstanding natural beauty for the sake of perhaps only a few dozen jobs, has finally been withdrawn. For the full story, see box on page 320.

Ceann a Tuath na Hearadh (North Harris)

›› *pp321-323. Colour map 1, B2.*

→ *Phone code: 01859.*

North Harris is the most mountainous part of the Outer Hebrides and its wild, rugged peaks are ideal for hillwalking. The A859 south from Lewis gets progressively more scenic as it skirts **Loch Siophort (Seaforth)** and the mountains rise before you like a giant barrier. The road then climbs past **Bogha Glas (Bowglass)** and **Aird a Mhulaidh (Ardvourlie)** with **Clisham** (2619 ft), the highest peak in the Outer Hebrides, and **Sgaoth Aird** (1829 ft) towering overhead on either side. Clisham in particular, though not a Munro, is a very staisfying peak to bag: steep, spectacularly craggy and the views from the top will break your heart.

Just off the A859 near Ardvourlie is **Ardvourlie Castle Guest House**, see Sleeping, page 321. If you can't afford such luxury but still crave the isolation, then carry on south until you reach the turn-off to **Reinigeadal (Rhenigidale)**, which was the most remote community on Harris and accessible only by sea or by a rough hill track until the access road was built. Here you'll find a **Gatliff Trust Youth Hostel**, see Sleeping, page 321. From Reinigeadal an ascent of shapely **Toddun** (528 m) provides exhilarating exercise rewarded with fine views east across the Minch to the mainland and, in the other direction, to the mountain wilderness of North Harris.

The A859 continues west across the crest of the craggy hills then drops down to the turn-off for the single-track B887, which winds its way all the way out to Huisinis (Hushinish) between the impressive mountains of the Forest of Harris on one side and the northern shore of West Loch Tarbert on the other, with views across to the Sound of Taransay and the beaches of South Harris. Immediately beyond the turn-off, you pass through **Bun Abhainn Eadarra (Bunavoneadar)**, which was a thriving whaling station until 1930 and one of Lord Leverhulme's many schemes for the island. The old whaling station is worth a visit even though the site has not been developed as a tourist attraction.

Right to buy

The Forest of Harris is a vast mountain wilderness extending north from West Loch Tarbert to Loch Resort and forming the de facto boundary with Lewis. It is one of the most isolated and unspoilt upland landscapes in Scotland and, because of its remoteness, receives very few visitors. For experienced hillwalkers, however, it is a paradise, offering rugged mountains, dramatic escarpments, airy ridges and desolate glens. There are endless walking possibilities, including a horseshoe walk around Clisham and a long walk through Glen Ulladale to Kinlochresort, a former crofting community now abandoned, but once described as the remotest habitation in Britain. Known as the North Harris Estate, this 22,000-acre tract of land was owned and managed by the family of the Bulmer cider empire – until 2003. In a move that had Scottish lairds incandescent with rage, the 800 residents of the estate were granted the right to take over the land on which they live, for more than £2 million, and finally throw off the shackles of feudal rule. Now that they have become masters of their own destiny, the community can relish the thought of a prosperous future, with energy development plans, sporting rights and tourism top of the agenda.

Just before the village of **Miabhag (Meavaig)**, a defined footpath heads north into the hills up Glen Meavaig to Loch Voshimid. Further on, though, is a better opportunity for walking. Just before the gates of **Amhuinnsuidhe Castle** (pronounced 'Avan-soo-ee') is a signpost for Chliostair Power Station. From here you can walk two miles up to the dam, then follow the right-hand track round the reservoir and the left-hand track round the upper loch, before you arrive in a wild and remote glen.

Just beyond the castle gates you'll see a beautiful waterfall spilling straight into the sea. The road then runs right past the front door of the castle, built in 1868 by the Earl of Dunmore, and still a private residence, before passing through an archway and continuing to the tiny crofting township of **Huisinis (Hushinish)**, beautifully situated in a sandy bay. This is where the road ends; next stop the USA. Follow the track to the right across the machair, where a footpath above the jetty and rocky beach can be followed to the old fishing lodge at **Cravadale** and Loch Cravadale beyond. Make a detour to the golden sands and turquoise waters of **Traigh Mheilein**, overlooking Scarp. From the coast, strong walkers can follow Glen Cravadale inland, eventually rejoining the main road near Amhuinnsuidhe Castle.

The rocky island of **Scarp** supported a population of more than 100 as late as the 1940s but was abandoned in 1971, and now the crofters' cottages are used as holiday homes. The island was the scene of a bizarre experiment in 1934, when a German rocket scientist, Gerhard Zucher, tried to prove that rockets could be used to transport mail and medical supplies to remote communities. His theory went up in smoke, however, when the rocket exploded before it even got off the ground, with 30,000 letters on board. Makes the Royal Mail look positively efficient.

An Tairbeart (Tarbert) and around

» *pp321-323. Colour map 1, B2.*

→ *Phone code: 01859. Population: 500.*

Tarbert, the largest settlement on Harris, lies in a sheltered bay on the narrow isthmus that joins North and South Harris. It's a tiny place and there's not much to do but, as it's

Tweed the world

Few visitors to Harris will not have heard of its most famous export. Harris Tweed was originally made by fishermen's wives to clothe their own families until the Countess of Dunmore, who owned a large part of Harris in the mid-19th century, took great interest and introduced many of her aristocratic friends to the local cloth. Very soon, much of the surplus was being sold and becoming quite a fashion statement in high places. Since its heyday as a de rigeur item of clothing for any self-respecting aristocrat, however, the future of Harris Tweed has largely been determined by the vagaries of the world's top fashion designers. The industry can produce around 5,000,000 yards of tweed annually, depending on demand, but that demand had been low, until the intervention of Nike, the US plimsoll manufacturer, in 2004 with a new range of retro trainers incorporating a swatch of Harris Tweed in the design, and so introducing the durable yet stylish material to a whole new generation of younger wardrobes. The trainers not only carried the Nike logo but also the famous Harris Tweed orb, thus carrying the name around the world (again). So successful was the launch that Nike are planning to extend their tweed-related range to include – wait for it – hooded tops. Can we expect to see gangs of teenagers loitering on grouse moors instead of their customary shopping malls?

the main ferry port for Harris, it has more facilities than anywhere else, with shops, a bank and post office. Tarbert's relatively wide range of accommodation and location makes it the ideal base from which to explore the island. The **TIC** ⓘ *T01859-502011, Apr-Oct Mon-Sat 0900-1700, also in winter (check times)*, is close to the ferry terminal.

An interesting little excursion from Tarbert is the 10-mile return route that runs east through the tiny villages of **Urgha** and **Caolas Scalpaigh** to **Carnach** at the end of the road. Just beyond Urgha, on the north side of the road, is a path which leads across the hills to **Reinigeadal**. It was originally used by the community in Reinigeadal; children would make the daily journey across the hills to Tarbert before the village was connected to the A859 by the new road. The wonderfully engineered zigzag path passes through enchanting scenery above **Loch Trollamarig** in a setting more reminiscent of Scandinavia's fjordland. A visit can easily be made to the deserted village of **Molinginish** nestled snugly in a small valley above the loch.

The island of **Scalpaigh** (**Scalpay**), now connected to Harris by a road bridge opened by Prime Minister Tony Blair in 1998, is a thriving fishing community with a population of over 400. It's a pleasant 3-mile walk across the island to **Eilean Glas Lighthouse**, built by the Stevensons and the first ever on the Outer Hebrides. There are diving trips here, see page 322.

Ceann a Deas na Hearadh (South Harris)

» *pp321-323. Colour map 1, B2.*

An absolute must while you're in the Outer Hebrides is the 45-mile circular route around South Harris. If you only do one thing while you're here, then make sure this is it, for the change in scenery from the west coast to the east is utterly astounding. One thing you're sure to puzzle over as you travel round is the fact that most people live on the harsh and inhospitable east coast, known as Na Baigh (Bays), while the beautiful west coast with its miles of glorious golden sands is scarcely populated. This is not through choice. The fertile west coast housed most of the population until the end of the 18th century when they were cleared to make way for sheep farms. Some emigrated to Cape Breton, while others chose instead to stay in Harris and moved to the east side.

West coast of Harris

The main road from Tarbert runs south, skirting East Loch Tarbert, then cuts inland and heads west through a dramatic lunar landscape of rocks dotted with tiny lochans. It then begins to descend towards the sea and you can see the vast expanse of **Losgaintir (Luskentyre)** beach directly ahead. A single-track road turns off to the right and runs out to the tiny settlement of Losgaintir. The road cuts through the rich machair as it follows the magnificent stretch of bleached white sand that fills the entire bay, washed by turquoise sea and backed by steep dunes. All this set against the backdrop of the mountains to the north. This is paradise refrigerated.

A short distance offshore is the island of **Tarasaigh (Taransay)**, which was well populated at the beginning of the 1900s but was recently abandoned. The island gained national prominence in 2000 as the setting for the popular BBC television series *Castaway*, in which an assortment of supposedly normal people from a variety of backgrounds were challenged to pit their wits against the elements and each other for a period of a full year.

The road follows the coast, passing through the tiny settlements of **Seilebost**, **Horgabost** and **Burgh (Borve)**. There's B&B accommodation at Seilebost and Horgabost, while, a few miles further on, is another beautiful stretch of white sands at **Sgarasta Bheag (Scaristabeg)**, and a couple of stunning places to stay (see Sleeping, page 321).

Beyond Sgarasta Bheag, the village of **Taobh Tuath (Northton)** provides access to the scenic promontory of **Toe Head**, almost cut off from the rest of Harris by the huge expanse of the golden sands at Sgarasta. At the **MacGillivary Machair Centre** you can learn about the ecology of the local machair, which forms such a distinctive and attractive element of the landscape of the west coast of the Hebrides. A ruined chapel of 16th-century origin is situated on the machair below **Chaipaval** (365 m), whose heathery slopes can be climbed for one of the best views out to sea towards St Kilda, some 40 miles distant.

Ant-Ob (Leverburgh)

The road then runs along the south shore till it reaches An t-Ob (Leverburgh), site of Lord Leverhulme's ambitious plan to turn a sleepy crofting township into a major fishing port, see page 316. The present village consists of little more than a row of incongruous Scandinavian-style wooden houses. A few of the original buildings can be seen near the pier, which is the departure point for **CalMac**'s car ferry to Berneray.

▸▸ *For further details, see Transport page 322.*

Ròghadal (Rodel)

Three miles east of Leverburgh, at the southeastern tip of Harris, is Ròghadal (Rodel), dominated by the beautiful 12th-century **St Clement's Church**, something of an unusual sight in such a remote spot and one of the most impressive religious building in the Hebrides. (Only the Benedictine abbey on Iona is larger.) The church stands on a site that dates back 1500 years and was built by Alastair Crotach (Hunchback) Macleod of Harris in the 1520s. Though impressive from the outside, particularly the huge tower, the real interest lies inside, with a collection of remarkable carved wall tombs. There are three tombs, the most notable of which is that of the founder, Alastair Crotach. The one in the south wall of the choir is also worth a close look.

Rumour has it that during the Castaway *television series, the bar in the Harris Hotel in Tarbert had never seen such good business, suggesting that some participants were less committed than others.*

Rock 'n' roll suicide

Like Newbury Bypass before it, the proposed Lingarabay superquarry represented a cause célèbre in the classic debate between the clashing interests of environment and development. Redland Aggregates originally proposed to develop the east face of Roineabhal (460 m) as a huge quarry providing a vast source of aggregate material for the construction industry in an economically impoverished part of Scotland perceived to be far removed from the mass tourism market.

The proposal provoked a local, national and international outcry as environmental groups objected to the likely visual, landscape and ecological impacts in a unique and essentially unspoilt mountain environment designated a National Scenic Area and representative of some of the oldest rock in the world. A Public Enquiry followed in 1994-1995 at which Redland presented the case for long-term local employment and the preference of one large quarry in a remote area rather than many smaller projects on the highly populated mainland. Objectors set out the concerns for the damage to a resource of national importance and the precedent it would set for environmental protection both within and outwith the industry in the future if planning legislation were to be overcome. Following a lengthy follow up the Secretary of State rejected the proposal in 2000.

Redland Aggregates, who by now had been taken over by French company, Lafarge, appealed against the decision, forcing the Scottish government to withdraw their rejection of the proposal. This was the worst possible outcome for the people of Harris, throwing their future into confusion and effectively precluding any planning and potential investment in the economic development of the area. Then, in a remarkable volte-face, Lafarge announced that they were withdrawing from the project. It was a victory for the island's precious environment and it was proof that sometimes, just sometimes, big business can act out of sense of responsibility to the environment and not just its shareholders.

Na Baigh (Bays)

Running north from Ròghadal up the east coast of South Harris is the **Golden Road**, so named by the locals because the of the huge cost of building it. This twisting, tortuous single-track road runs through a bizarre and striking moonscape, and driving through it is a unique experience (but keep your eyes on the road or you'll end up in one of the many narrow sea lochs). It seems inconceivable that anyone could survive in such an environment, but the road passes through a string of townships created in the 19th century by the people evicted from the west coast, see page 318. People here have spent years eking a meagre living from the thin soil by building 'lazy beds' (thin strips of piled-up earth between the rocks) for planting potatoes. Weaving and fishing also provide much-needed income.

At **Lingreabhagh (Lingarabay)** the road skirts the foot of **Roinebhal**, which was, until recently, the proposed site of one of the largest superquarries in Europe. This would have demolished virtually the entire mountain over many decades. Local people and environmentalists fought a successful campaign to prevent the proposal going ahead, thus protecting a precious natural asset. For a more detailed account of the campaign, see box, above. The road passes through a succession of tiny settlements before joining the A859 just south of Tarbert.

Sleeping

North Harris *p316*

B **Ardhasaig House**, Aird Asaig, 4 miles northwest of Tarbert off A859, T01859-502066, www.ardhasaig.co.uk. 6 en suite rooms. Open all year. Small hotel with a big reputation, especially for its wonderful cooking (dinner is £30 a head). Lovely location and also good disabled facilities. Recommended.

B **Ardvourlie Castle Guest House**, just off the A859 near Ardvourlie, T01859-502307, F502348. 4 rooms. Open Apr-Oct. This lovingly restored Victorian hunting lodge on the shores of Loch Seaforth just oozes charm and elegance and can't be recommended highly enough. As if that weren't enough, it also happens to serve excellent food. There can be no better end to a day spent walking in the surrounding mountains.

F **Gatliff Trust Youth Hostel**, Reinigeadal (Rhenigidale). Here you'll find a converted croft house (no phone) which sleeps 11 and is open all year (for details on how to get there on foot, see page 316).

Tarbert and around *p317*

Many hotels and B&Bs offer a room-only rate for those catching the 0730 ferry back to Skye on Mon, Wed and Fri.

C **Harris Hotel**, on the main road from Stornoway on the left, before the turning for the ferry, Tarbert, T01859-502154, F502281. An old established favourite, but more importantly the only place serving food on a Sun, see Eating. The bar next door also serves meals and is the social hub of the village.

C **Leachin House**, 1 mile out of Tarbert on the Stornoway road, T/F01859-502157. Luxurious Victorian home with great views and superb home-cooking (for residents only). **B** including dinner. Only 2 rooms, so book ahead.

D **Allan Cottage Guest House**, on the left after the turning into Tarbert, T01859-502146. Open Apr-Sep. Close to the ferry, very comfortable rooms and exceptional food. **B** including dinner. Book ahead.

D **Macleod Motel**, right beside the ferry pier, T01859-502364. 14 rooms, 4 en suite. Open May-Sep. Very handy for the early-morning ferry; **D** room-only.

E **Avalon Guesthouse**, 12 West Side, Tarbert, T01859-502334, www.avalonguesthouse.org. 3 rooms. Open all year. Comfortable B&B on family croft, ¾ mile before Tarbert on left-hand side of road coming from Stornoway direction. Wonderful views over Loch West Tarbert. Dinner also available for £15 a head.

E **Hirta House**, Scalpay, T01859-540394, m.mackenzie@tisacli.co.uk. 3 en suite rooms. Open all year. Lovely location, spacious rooms and guest lounge and library. Good value.

E **Mrs Annie Mackinnon**, 1 Scott Rd, Tarbert, T01859-502095. 2 rooms. Open Apr-Oct. Very friendly and welcoming B&B within 5 mins' walk of the ferry pier.

E **Seafield**, Scalpay, T01859-540250, seafieldscalpay@hotmail.com. 3 rooms. Open Feb-Nov. Comfortable, good sea views, fishing trips available.

E-F **Mrs Flora Morrison**, Tigh na Mara, Tarbert, T01859-502270. A B&B within 5 mins' walk of the ferry pier, very friendly.

F **Rockview Bunkhouse**, on the main street, Tarbert, T/F01859-5022211. Open all year.

South Harris *p318*

There is a wide range of accommodation in Leverburgh but on the east coast it is limited.

L-A **Scarista House**, Scaristabeg, T01859-550238, www.scaristahouse.com. 5 rooms, open all year. Overlooking the beach in a wonderful setting, To add to the peace and quiet, there's no TV, only an extensive library and drawing room with open fires. The food on offer is amongst the best on the islands, particularly the seafood. Even if you're not staying, you should treat yourself to dinner here (TTT). Breakfast is a majesterial feast of kippers, kedgeree, Stornoway black pudding and Ayrshire bacon. Expensive but well worth it. There are also self-catering cottages in the grounds. The golf course over the road is so scenic the views may put you off your swing.

For an explanation of sleeping and eating price codes used in this guide, see inside the front cover. Other relevant information is found in Essentials, see pages 40-47.

B Rodel Hotel, Rodel, T01859-520210, www.rodelhotel.co.uk. 4 en suite rooms. Closed Jan to mid-Feb. Overlooking a tiny harbour at the southern tip of the island. Recent makeover has brightened the place up and it now offers a more contemporary and comfortable stay. Restaurant (**ΨΨ**) sometimes flatters to deceive.

E Mrs Catherine Mackenzie, Ferry Rd, Leverburgh, T01859-520246. B&B just a few mins from the ferry terminal.

E Shieldaig House, Leverburgh, T01859-520378, kwhettall@aol.com. More secluded and with free cycle hire.

E Mrs Paula Williams, Sorrel Cottage, 2 Glen, Leverburgh, T01859-520319, www.sorrelcottage.co.uk. 3 rooms, open all year. Relaxing place to stay with meals available, including vegetarian (**C** with dinner), and cycle hire. **F** for room only.

E-F Caberfeidh House, Leverburgh, T01859-520276. Close to the ferry and also offers room only (**F**). One of the best B&Bs.

E-F Hillhead, T01859-511226, at Scada-bhagh (Scadabay), Bays, between Stocinis and Drinisiadar. Good-value B&B option.

F Am Bothan Bunkhouse, Leverburgh, T01859-520251, close to the ferry, has full facilities, space for tents and is open all year.

F Drinishader Bunkhouse, at Drinisiader (Drinishader), 3 miles south of Tarbert, Bays, T01859-511255. Open all year.

Camping

In Luskentyre, you can camp on the machair, but ask for permission at the first house.

Self-catering

Blue Reef Cottages, overlooking Scarista beach, T01505-352883, www.bluereef cottages.co.uk. Turf-roofed circular stone walled luxury retreat sunk like a modern day Scara Brae into the hillside with a panorama over pearl white sands and distant isles. Complete privacy (2 cottages) on a westerly facing outcrop and a wonderful sauna and jacuzzi to enjoy after some exhilarating beach combing or a visit to **Scarista House**'s wonderful dining room (see above) which is a 5-min walk away. This has to be the ultimate romantic self-catering option but not cheap at £1200 per week.

Eating

Options on places to eat are limited. Most guesthouses and B&Bs provide dinner on request, check if they do so on a Sun.

Tarbert and around *p317*

ΨΨ First Fruits Tearoom, Tarbert, T01859-502349. Aside from the guesthouses, this is probably the best food here, a cosy joint by the ferry pier. Apr, May and Sep Mon-Sat 1030-1630, Jun, Jul and Aug 1030-1830 .

ΨΨ Harris Hotel, see Sleeping, serves food every day till around 2030. They do a 3-course fixed menu or basic and cheap bar meals, as does the bar next door Mon-Sat.

Ψ Fish and chip shop next door to the **Rockview Bunkhouse**. The only other option in Tarbert, open for lunch and in the evening.

South Harris *p318*

Ψ An Clachan, Leverburgh, T01859-520370. Café/restaurant and shop, not far from the bunkhouse.

Ψ Skoon Art Café, T01859-530268. Bays, 12 km south of Tarbert. Serves soups and snacks all day, also good home baking.

Activities and tours

Tarbert and around *p317*

Scalpay Diving Services, T01859-540328, for diving.

Transport

Harris *p315*

Bus There's a regular bus service between **Tarbert** and **Stornoway** (1¼ hrs, which continues to **Leverburgh** (for the ferry to North Uist) via the west coast of South Harris. There's a also bus service 3-4 times per day from **Tarbert** to **Leverburgh** via the east coast (45 mins), along the so-called 'Golden Road'. There are also services to **Huisinis** (2-4 per day on school days, 45 mins), to **Reinigeadal** (2 per day on school days) and to **Scalpaigh** (2-5 per day, 10 mins). Bus timetables are available at the TIC.

Ferry Ferries sail from **Uig** (Skye) to **Tarbert** (1 hr 35 mins) 1-2 daily Mon-Sat. One-way ticket £9.60 per passenger, £46

A prickly issue

In a classic David and Goliath struggle, the hedgehogs of the Uists and Benbecula took on the might of the Scottish Executive, and lived to tell the tale – or so we think. The decision of the SNH to cull the islands' hedgehogs was made in order to protect the dwindling numbers of wading birds.

Hedgehogs, you see, just love eating their eggs for breakfast. So, while hedgehog numbers have soared to around 5000 since first being introduced by a South Uist man as a means of slug control, numbers of birds, such as ringed plover and red shank, have plummeted by up to 60%. SNH scientists believe it to be more humane to exterminate the spiky little imposters using gas and lethal injection rather than let them starve on the mainland, and so began the controversial cull, with the backing of the RSPB. But by the middle of 2003 only 66 had been killed and, only six weeks later, a further 60 baby hedgehogs had been born to take their place. At a total cull cost of £26,000, the cost per animal was nearly £4500. Meanwhile, animal welfare groups, including Mrs Tiggywinkle's Hedgehog Refuge, organized a massive rescue operation which resulted in 150 of the little blighters being relocated to southern Scotland and 50 to Bristol University; not to enrol on a media studies degree course, but to be electonically tagged to find out if they can survive the trauma of relocation and adapt to their new habitat. The world waits for the answer with bated breath.

per car (£16.40 and £79 for 5-day saver return). Contact Uig, T01470- 542219, or Tarbert, T01859-502444. A ferry sails from **Leverburgh** to **Berneray** 3 or 4 times daily. The trip takes 1 hr 10 mins and a one-way ticket costs £5.45 per passenger, £24.80 per car (£9.25 and £42.50 for 5-day saver return).

The Uists, Benbecula and Barra

South from Harris lies the southern 'half' of the Outer Herbides. The Uists, north and south, and Benbecula are all connected by a series of causeways; you can drive their length, past a never-ending series of fish-filled lochs and windswept beaches, tiny, straggling crofting communities and the bizarre giant 'golf balls' of Space City, on South Uist. The road ends at the southerly tip of South Uist, where you'll have to board a ferry to cross to the more relaxed island of Barra, or, better still, fly there from Glasgow, landing on the famous cockle strand – at low tide, of course! » *For Sleeping, Eating and other listings, see pages 331-334.*

Uibhist a Tuath (North Uist) » *pp331-334. Colour map 1, C1.*

→ *Phone code: 01876. Population. 1815.*

North Uist is the largest island in the southern chain of the Outer Hebrides, about 13 miles from north to south and 18 miles east to west at its widest point. At first sight it comes as something of a disappointment after the dramatic landscapes of Harris. In fact, it's barely a landscape at all, as over a third of the island's surface is covered by water. The east coast around Lochmaddy, the main settlement, is so peppered with lochs it resembles a giant sieve. But, heading west from Lochmaddy, the island's attractions become apparent, particularly the magnificent beaches on the north and west coasts. Also on the west coast, the Balranald Nature Reserve is the ideal place for bird watching. You're also likely to see otters. There are numerous prehistoric sites scattered across the island and, with all that water around, there's obviously plenty of good fishing to be had.

Ins and outs

Getting there There are two car ferry services to North Uist. One is to Berneray from Leverburgh on South Harris, the other to Lochmaddy from Uig on Skye. North Uist is joined to the islands of Benbecula and South Uist to the south by causeway and bridge. There are several buses daily (Monday to Saturday) from Otternish to Lochmaddy and on to Lochboisdale on South Uist. » *For further details, see Transport pages 300 and 334.*

Getting around There are four to six buses per day (except Sunday) from Berneray to Lochmaddy. These buses continue to Baile a Mhanaich (Balivanich) on Benbecula, where there is an airport, see page 326, and Lochboisdale and Ludag on South Uist, see page 327. There are four to seven buses per day from Lochmaddy to the island of Bearnaraigh (Berneray) just off the north coast in the sound of Harris. There are three buses per day from Lochmaddy to Clachan na Luib (Clachan-a-Luib) which run in an anti-clockwise direction around the north and west coasts. Two buses per day connect Clachan-a-Luib with Baile Sear (Baleshare) and also with Saighdinis (Sidinish). There are also postbuses linking the main settlements. Bus timetables are available at the tourist office in Lochmaddy.

Loch nam Madadh (Lochmaddy)

Lochmaddy, the island's main village and ferry port, is a tiny place; so small you're almost through it before you realize. Though it's on the east coast and not close to the beaches, it is the best base for exploring the island as it boasts most facilities. It has a bank (next to the tourist office), a hotel and pub, a tourist office, a few shops, post office, hospital and petrol station.

If you have time, the **Taigh Chearsabhagh Museum and Arts Centre** ⓘ *T/F01876-500293, www.taigh-chearsabhagh.com*, is worth visiting and has a café. The **TIC** ⓘ *near the ferry pier, T01876-500321, mid-Apr to mid-Oct Mon-Sat 0900-1700, and for the arrival of the evening ferry*, will provide transport timetables.

Around the island

There are a number of interesting archaeological sites of different periods dotted around the island. The most notable is **Barpa Langass**, 7 miles southwest of Lochmaddy on the slope of Ben Langass, just off the A867, which cuts across the bleak peaty hinterland of North Uist. This is a huge chambered burial cairn dating from around 3000 BC. Unfortunately, it is now too dangerous to enter. About a mile away, on the southern side of Ben Langass, is the small stone circle known as **Pobull Fhinn**, standing on the edge of Loch Langass. Three miles northwest of Lochmaddy on the A865 are three Bronze Age standing stones called **Na Fir Bhreige** (The False Men), said to be the graves of three spies who were buried alive.

The real charms of North Uist, though, are the fabulous beaches on its north and west coasts. Heading anti-clockwise from Lochmaddy, the A865 runs northwest, passing the turning for Otternish and Bearnaraigh (see below), which is now connected to North Uist by a causeway. It continues west through the township of **Sollas (Solas)**, where there are a couple of B&Bs, and then passes the beautiful sands of **Bhalaigh (Vallay) Strand**. Near the northwestern tip of the island, standing on an islet in Loch Scolpaig, is **Scolpaig Tower**, a 'folly' built to provide employment and income for local men in the 19th century.

Three miles south of here is the turning to **Balranald RSPB Reserve**, an area of rocky coast, sandy beaches and dunes, machair and lochs. The reserve is ideal for bird watching, especially waders. A two-hour guided walk along the headland allows you to see Manx shearwaters, gannets, skuas and storm petrels, and, during the summer, you can listen out for the distinctive rasping call of the corncrake, one of the rarest birds in Britain. There's a basic visitor centre (open April to September).

In Ceann a Bhaigh is the **Uist Animal Visitors Centre** ⓘ *Mon-Sat 1000-2200, £2*, where you can see Highland cattle and other rare native breeds, as well exotic species such as llamas. The road continues south to **Clachan na Luib**, at the crossroads of the A865 and A867, which heads east back to Lochmaddy. Offshore is the tidal island of **Baile Sear (Baleshare)**, now connected by a causeway to North Uist, with its 3-mile-long beach on the west coast. A further 5 miles west are the **Monach Isles** (also known by their old Norse name of *Heisker*), which were connected to North Uist at low tide until the 16th century, when a huge tidal wave swept away the sand bridge, thus isolating them. Even so, the islands were inhabitted until as recently as the 1930s. Now they are populated by the largest breeding colony of grey seals in Europe.

South of Clachan, the road runs past **Cairinis (Carinish)** over a series of causeways to the little-visited lobster-fishing island of **Griomasaigh (Grimsay)**, before heading across another causeway to Benbecula. Near Cairinis is **Feith na Fala** (Field of Blood), site of the last battle fought in Scotland solely with swords and bows and arrows, in 1601, between the MacDonalds of Sleat and Macleods of Harris. The bloodshed was provoked by one of the MacDonalds divorcing his Macleod wife. When 60 Skye Macleods set off to North Uist to wreak revenge, they were met by 16 MacDonalds who literally chopped them to pieces, proving that divorce was a messy business even back then.

Bearnaraigh (Berneray)

» *pp331-334. Colour map 1, B1.*

→ *Phone code: 01876.*

Ferries from Leverburgh on Harris arrive at the low-lying island of Bearnaraigh, now connected by a causeway to North Uist. The island is famous as the place where Prince Charles spent a holiday helping out on a croft. It's also the birthplace of the giant Angus MacAskill, see page 280. Its real attraction, though, apart from the splendid isolation, is the 3-mile-long sandy beach along its north and west coast.

▲ A booklet for Bearnaraigh, *Western Isles Walks*, available from Lochmaddy TIC, describes an enjoyable 8-mile walk around the island visiting all the main places of interest, including the 16th-century gunnery at **Baile**, the beaches and machair of the north and west coasts, and archaeological sites dating from the Viking period near **Borgh**.

Beinn na Faoghla (Benbecula)

» *pp331-334. Colour map 1, C1.*

→ *Phone code: 01870. Population: 1803.*

Tiny Benbecula may be suffering from delusions of stature. Its Gaelic name means 'mountain of the fords', but the highest point is a mere 407 ft, with the rest of the island as flat as a pancake. It lies between Protestant North Uist and Catholic South Uist, and most visitors use it solely as a means of getting from one to the other via the A865 which cuts straight through the middle.

Tight little island

Between Eriskay and South Uist is the wreck of the famous *SS Politician*, the island's other claim to fame. In 1941 the 12,000 ton ship went aground just off the island of Calvey and sank with its cargo, which included 20,000 cases of whisky. This not only provided many islanders with a supply of whisky for many years, but also provided the plot for Compton Mackenzie's book *Whisky Galore!*, which was later made into the famous Ealing comedy of the same name (it was called *Tight Little Island* in the US) and filmed on Barra. Part of the wreck can be seen at low tide, and there's more information on the famous incident on display in the appropriately named Am Politician pub (open 1230-1430), in the main settlement of Baile (Balla).

Ins and outs

Benbecula's airport is at Balivanich and there are direct flights to Glasgow, Barra and Stornoway. The island is connected by causeways to North and South Uist, and buses travelling to and from Lochmaddy and Lochboisdale pass through the villages of Balivanich, Lionacleit (Liniclate) and Creag Ghoraidh (Creagorry). There are also regular island buses which run between these settlements. » *For further details, see Transport, page 334.*

Sights

Like North Uist, the east of the island is so pitted with lochs that most people live on the west coast. A large percentage of the population are Royal Artillery personnel and their families stationed at **Baile a Mhanaich (Balivanich)**, a sprawling army base of utilitarian buildings in the northwest of the island. The influx of so many English-speakers has had a less than positive impact on Gaelic culture, and the military facilities have blighted much of the island's natural beauty, but Benbecula has benefited economically from the army's presence. Not only is there an airport here, but also a relatively large number of shops and amenities, including the only NAAFI (military) supermarket in the UK that's open to the public, a Bank of Scotland (with ATM) and A post office. There are worries, however, that the base may be scaled down or closed, which would have a devastating effect on the local economy.

South of Balivanich the B892 runs around the west coast before joining the main A865 at the southern end of the island. It runs past **Culla Bay**, overlooked by **Baille nan Cailleach (Nunton)**. It was from here in 1746 that Bonnie Prince Charlie set off with Flora MacDonald over the sea to Skye, disguised as her maid, see page 279. To the south is **Poll-na-Crann**, better known as 'stinky bay' because of the piles of seaweed deposited there by fierce Atlantic storms. From the mid-18th century this kelp was used to provide soda ash for making glass, and provided a source of income for many communities. By 1820 the so-called kelp boom was over, but it is still gathered today and used for fertilizer.

The B892 ends at **Lionacleit (Liniclate)**, where the new community school serves the Uists and Benbecula. It has extensive facilities, including internet, a swimming pool, library, theatre and even a small local history **museum** ⓘ *Mon, Tue and Thu 0900-1600, Wed 0900-1230 and 1330-1600, Fri 0900-2000, Sat 1100-1300 and 1400-1600, free.*

Uibhist a Deas (South Uist)

» pp331-334. Colour map 3, A1.

→ *Phone code: 01870. Population: 2285.*

South Uist is the largest of the southern chain of Outer Hebridean islands and the most scenically attractive. Like its southern neighbour, Barra, South Uist is Roman Catholic and generally more relaxed about Sunday openings. Its 20 miles of west coast is one long sandy beach, backed by dunes with a mile or two of beautiful, flowering machair behind. To the east of the main A865 which runs the length of the island, rises a central mountainous spine of rock and peat dotted with numerous lochs. Its two highest peaks, **Beinn Mhor** (2034 ft) and **Hecla** (1988 ft), tower over the rocky cliffs of an inaccessible eastern coastline indented by sea lochs.

Ins and outs

Getting there The island's main ferry port is Lochboisdale, which is reached from Oban four times a week (arriving at night) and twice a week from Castelbay on Barra. There's even a sailing on Sunday (in summer) from Oban, via Castlebay, but there are no boats leaving South Uist on Sunday. A private passenger-only ferry sails from Barra to Ludag, at the southern tip of South Uist, also on Sunday. There are no bus services on Sundays. » *For further details, see Transport page 334.*

Getting around A causeway connects South Uist to Benbecula by road and regular buses (four to six per day Monday to Saturday) run between Lochboisdale and Lochmaddy on North Uist, stopping en route at Dalabrog (Daliburgh), Tobha Mòr (Howmore) and Lionacleit and Balinavich on Benbecula. There is also a regular bus service between Lochboisdale and Ludag (for ferries to Barra). A new causeway links Eriskay to South Uist. There are ferries to Eriskay from Barra, see page 334.

History

The dominant family in South Uist was Clanranald, who also owned Benbecula. They were descendants of the first Lord of the Isles, who was a MacDonald. The island's connections with Clanranald came to a sorry end, however, in 1837, when it was sold, along with Benbecula, to pay off bad debts, and became the property of the infamous Lieutenant-Colonel John Gordon of Cluny. Though all the southern isles suffered during the brutal Clearances of the 19th century, the experiences of people on South Uist were particularly cruel and inhumane. Between 1849 and 1851 over 2000 were forcibly shipped to Quebec in Canada. Those who refused to board the transport ships were hunted down by dogs and bound, before being thrown on board and shipped to Canada, where they were left to starve.

Loch Baghasdail (Lochboisdale)

→ *Phone code: 01878. Colour map 3, A1.*

South Uists's largest settlement is set on a rocky promontory in a beautiful island-dotted sea loch. The imposing entrance is guarded by Calvay Island with its 13th-century castle ruin. Lochboisdale is a tiny place, with little in the way of tourist sights, though it does have a hotel, bank, post office and **TIC** ⓘ *Pier Rd, T01878-700286, early Apr to mid-Oct.*

About 10 miles south of Lochboisdale, on the southern coast of the island, is **Ludag jetty**, the departure point for the small private passenger ferry to **Eòlaigearraidh (Eoligarry)** on Barra. At **Cille Bhrìghde (West Kilbride)** nearby is **Hebridean Croft Originals** ⓘ *open daily*, which has a wide range of local crafts on show, as well as a photographic display of local history and a tearoom.

Around the island

At the north of the island a causeway leads across **Loch Bi** (pronounced 'Bee') to the distinctive modern statue of Our Lady of the Isles, standing by the main road on the lower slopes of **Rueval Hill**. Further up the hill is the Royal Artillery control centre, known by the locals as 'Space City', due to its forest of aerials and 'golf balls', which tracks the missiles fired from a range on the northwestern corner of the island out into the Atlantic.

Just to the south of here is **Loch Druidibeag Nature Reserve,** on the site of the large freshwater loch, one of the largest breeding grounds in the British Isles for greylag geese and also a favourite haunt of mute swans (there's a warden nearby at Groigearraidh Lodge). From here the main road runs down the spine of the island; all along the way little tracks branch off to the west, leading down to lovely beaches.

Not far south of Loch Druidibeag is the turning to the tiny village of **Tobha Mòr** (**Howmore**), where you can see a collection of old traditional thatched blackhouses beside the seemingly endless stretch of golden sand. One of the houses has been converted into a **Gatliff Trust Youth Hostel**, see Sleeping, page 331. From the hostel it's a five-minute walk across the machair to the sandy beach which stretches almost the entire length of South Uist.

From Tobha Mòr, there are superb walks through the lonely hills of **Beinn Mhor** (620 m), **Beinn Corodale** (527 m) and **Hecla** (606 m) to the picturesque and dramatic valleys of Glen Hellisdale, Glen Corodale and Glen Usinish on the east coast. In 1746 that ubiquitous troglodyte, Bonnie Prince Charlie is reputed to have taken refuge in a cave above **Corodale Bay** for three weeks after his defeat and escape from Culloden.

Near **Bornais** (**Bornish**) another minor road can be followed east of the A865 to **Loch Eynort**, which penetrates far inland from the Minch. An old stalkers' path can be followed along the north shore of the loch towards the sea, with views of numerous seals, the occasional otter and the steep upper slopes of Beinn Mhor towering above to the north.

A few miles south, at **Gearraidh Bhailteas** (**Milton**), a cairn marks the birthplace of that famous Hebridean lass, Flora MacDonald, see page 279. Nearby is the **Kildonan Museum**, which has a tearoom. The A865 continues south for a few miles to the village of Dalabrog (Daliburgh), then heads east to the island's main ferry port, **Lochboisdale**.

Eirisgeidh (Eriskay) » *pp331-334. Colour map 3, A1.*

→ *Phone code: 01878.*

The tiny island of Eriskay, with a population of less than 200, gives its name to the native breed of pony, said to have been ridden by King Robert the Bruce at the Battle of Bannockburn in 1314. In the late 1970s the ponies nearly became extinct, but one surviving stallion saved the breed and numbers are growing. A series of paths take you around the island in about three hours. For more details, see the 'Cuairt Eirisgeidh' leaflet published by the Western Isles Tourist Board and available at the Lochboisdale TIC.

Most people come to Eriskay to pay a visit to **Coilleag a' Phrionnsa** (**Prince's beach**), the sandy beach on the west coast. This is where Bonnie Prince Charlie first stepped on to Scottish soil on 23 July 1745, at the start of the ill-fated Jacobite Rebellion. The rare pink convolvulus which grows there today is said to have been planted by the Prince himself from seeds brought from France. A small memorial cairn in the dunes behind the beach was erected by the local school to commemorate the occasion.

As well as the wreck of the *SS Politician*, see box page 326, another sight worth seeing is **St Michael's**, the Roman Catholic church built in 1903 and funded by the local fishing fleet.

Bharraigh (Barra)

» pp331-334. Colour map 3, A1.

→ *Phone code: 01871. Population: 1316.*

It may be tempting to overlook the little island of Barra, only about 8 miles long by 5 miles wide, but that would be a mistake, as it's one of the most beautiful of all the islands in the Outer Hebrides – 'Barradise' indeed. Here you'll find the best of the islands in miniature – beaches, machair, peat-covered hills, tiny crofting communities and Neolithic remains – and a couple of days spent on Barra gives a real taster of Hebridean life. Gaelic culture is also strong here but, with its Catholic tradition, Barra is more laid-back than many of the other islands in the Outer Hebrides and doesn't follow the others' strict Sabbatarianism.

Ins and outs

Getting there The best way to arrive is by air at Tràigh Mhòr ('Cockle Strand'), the famous airstrip on the beach at the north end of the island. This is the only airport in the UK where flight schedules are shown as 'subject to tides'. Barra is reached by car ferry from Oban on the mainland, by car ferry from Lochboisdale on South Uist, and from Tiree. A private passenger-only ferry sails from Ludag on South Uist.

Getting around There is a regular bus/postbus service (five to eight times per day Monday to Saturday) that runs from Castlebay to the ferry port of Eòlaigearraidh, via the airport. There are also buses (three to four per day Monday-Saturday) from Castlebay to Bhatarsaigh (Vatersay). You can also hire a car or a bicycle to tour the island at your leisure. » *For further details, see Transport page 334.*

Bàgh a' Chaisteil (Castlebay)

The main settlement is Castlebay, on the southern side of the island, situated in a wide sheltered bay and overlooked by **Sheabhal** (383 m), on top of which is a marble statue of the Blessed Virgin and Child. It's a short but steep walk up to the top from the town, and the views are well worth it. The once-thriving herring port is also overlooked by the large Roman Catholic church, **Our Lady, Star of the Sea**.

As the main ferry port, Castlebay provides the full range of services: hotels, B&Bs, shops, a bank (with ATM) and post office. The **TIC** ⓘ *T01871-810223, Apr to mid-Oct Mon-Sat 0900-1700, also open for the arrival of the evening ferry*, is on the main street near the ferry terminal. It has information on local walks and will book accommodation.

Castlebay's most notable feature is the impressive 15th-century **Kisimul Castle** ⓘ *T01871-810313, Apr-Sep daily 0930-1830, £4, concession £3, children £1.60, includes boat trip*, reached by boat from Castlebay pier (five minutes), weather permitting, built on an island in the middle of the harbour. This was the ancient home of the Chief of the MacNeils, one of the oldest Scottish clans, who owned the island from 1427 till 1838. It was then sold to the notorious Colonel Gordon of Cluny, along with neighbouring South Uist and Benbecula, see page 327, and the poor people of Barra suffered the same cruel fate, 600 of them being shipped to Canada to starve. One hundred years later the castle and much of the island was bought back for the MacNeils by an American architect, Robert Lister MacNeil, who became the 45th Clan Chief and restored the castle to its present state before his death in 1970. His son, Ian Roderick MacNeil, used it as his residence when visiting the island, before handing it over to Historic Scotland in 2000 on a 1000-year lease, in exchange for a rent of £1 and a bottle of whisky.

If you're interested in finding out about the island's history, you should visit the Barra Heritage Centre, known as **Dualchas** ⓘ *T01871-810403, Apr-Sep Mon-Fri 1100-1700, £1.*

Net profit

Rather than watch their island be destroyed by the elements, the redoubtable inhabitants of tiny Vatersay have taken matters into their own hands. The northern and southern ends of the island are linked by a narrow, 600-yard-long isthmus and, in recent years, raging Atlantic storms have washed away parts of the isthmus. Fearing that their island might be split in two, crofters have fixed some old salmon nets from fish farms onto the beach, secured with wires and old wooden pallets, to prevent the sand being scattered by the gales. Over time, the build up of sand trapped in the netting can link up with the machair, thus allowing grass and flowers to grow. Hopefully, over time, successive layers of sand and earth will be built up to protect the coastline. About 100 yards of beach have so far been protected using this rudimentary method, and the island's local authority is donating £3000 so that the whole 600-yard stretch linking the two ends of Vatersay can be saved. News of the crofters' ingenuity and resourcefulness has spread and the plan is being adopted on nearby Barra, where erosion is also a serious problem.

Around the island

The A888 follows a circular route of 14 miles around the island, making an ideal day's bike tour from Castlebay. Heading west, it passes the turning for the causeway to **Vatersay** (see page 331), then runs northwest between two hills (Sheabhal to the east and Beinn Tangabhal to the west) to the west coast, where you'll find the nicest beaches. One of these is at **Halaman Bay**, near the village of **Tangasdal** (**Tangasdale**), overlooked by the **Isle of Barra Hotel**, see Sleeping, page 331. At the turning for **Borgh** (**Borve**) there are standing stones. Next is the turning for the small settlement of **Baile Na Creige** (**Craigston**), where you'll find the **Thatched Cottage Museum** ⓘ *Easter-Oct Mon-Fri 1100-1700, £1*, an original blackhouse and the chambered burial cairn of **Dun Bharpa**. From Dun Bharpa there are pleasant walks into the surrounding hills, with the summit of **Sheabhal** offering tremendous views from the highest point on the island.

North of the turning, near **Allathsdal** (**Allasdale**), is another lovely beach, and just beyond are the remains of **Dun Cuier**, an Iron Age fort. Make a short detour at Greian, and follow the headland to the rugged cliffs at **Greian Head**.

The A888 then heads east to **Bagh a Tuath** (**Northbay**), where a branch left leads to the village of **Eòlaigearraidh (Eoligarry)**, near the northern tip, surrounded by sandy bays washed by Atlantic rollers. A private passenger ferry leaves from here to Ludag on South Uist.

The road to Eoligarry passes the island's airport at **Tràigh Mhòr**, the 'Cockle Strand', which once provided 100 to 200 cartloads of delicious cockles each day. Now the cockleshells are gathered and used for harling, the roughcast wall covering used on many Scottish houses. By the beach is the house that was once the home of Compton MacKenzie, author of *Whisky Galore!*, see page 328. He lies buried at **Cille Bhara**, to the west of the village of Eòlaigearraidh, along with members of the MacNeil clan. This was one of the most important religious complexes in the Outer Hebrides, built in the 12th century, and consists of a church and two chapels. One of these, St Mary's, has been re-roofed and houses several carved medieval tombstones and a copy of a runic stone. The original stone is in the Museum of Scotland in Edinburgh.

Bhatarsaigh (Vatersay) and Mingulay » pp331-334.

A worthwhile trip from Castlebay is to the island of Vatersay, now linked to Barra by a causeway built in an effort to stabilize the island community (the present population is around 70). The island boasts two shell-sand beaches backed by machair, only a few hundred yards apart on either side of the narrow isthmus that leads to the main settlement of Vatersay. On the west beach, Bagh Siar, is the **Annie Jane Monument**, commemorating the terrible tragedy in 1853, when the emigrant ship *Annie Jane* was wrecked off the coast of Vatersay, with the loss of 333 lives, many of them islanders.

On a clear day from Vatersay you can enjoy the view of the smaller islands to the south – Sandray, Pabbay and Mingulay. The latter was inhabited until 1912 and can still be visited from Barra. It has recently been acquired by the National Trust for Scotland. » *For details of tours, see Activities and tours page 333.*

Sleeping

North Uist *p323*

B Langass Lodge, near Pobhull Fhinn, T01876-580285, www.langasslodge.co.uk. 6 en suite rooms. Open all year. Stylish and comfortable accommodation in a variety of rooms. Friendly and very good value, also welcomes children. The restaurant specializes in local seafood, game and homegrown veg (dinner ϒϒϒ). Recommended.

B Tigh Dearg Hotel, Lochmaddy, T01876-500700, www.tigh-dearg-hotel.co.uk. 8 en suite rooms. Open all year. This relative newcomer has raised the bar significantly for Hebridean hotel standards. Stylish and contemporary, from the bright red exterior (the name means 'Red House') to the designer rooms, it offers DVD/CD players, a highly rated restaurant and a leisure club with fully equipped gym, sauna and steam room. By the way, it's pronounced 'tie-jerack'. Recommended.

C Lochmaddy Hotel, Lochmaddy, T01876-500332, www.lochmaddyhotel.co.uk. 15 en suite rooms. Open all year. Right by the ferry terminal. The restaurant serves great seafood and the lively bar serves snacks. This is also the place to ask about fishing, as they rent out boats and sell permits for trout and salmon fishing.

D The Old Courthouse, Lochmaddy, T01876-500358, oldcourthouse@tiscali.co.uk. 4 en suite rooms. Open all year. Listed Georgian house offering good value B&B. **E** room only.

D-E Redburn House, Lochmaddy, T01876-500301, www.redburnhouse.com. 4 en suite rooms. Open all year. Fully refurbished B&B with wheelchair access and also several self-catering options (from £300/week for 2 up to £550 for 5-10). Handy for ferry and village facilities.

E Mrs Morag Nicholson, in Ceann a Bhaigh (Bayhead), T01876-510395. 2 en suite rooms. Open all year. Friendly and comfortable B&B. **F** room only.

E Mrs Kathy Simpson, near Balranald, in Hogha Gearraidh (Houghgarry), T01876-510312, sgeirruadh@aol.com. 3 en suite rooms. Open all year. Good-value B&B overlooking a beautiful beach.

F Taigh Mo Sheannair, a few miles south of Clachan, at Cladach a Bhaile Shear (Claddachbaleshare), T01876-580246, carnach@amserve.net. 2 en suite rooms with bunks for 4. Open all year. Renovated croft-house on a working farm which offers good hostel accommodation all year round, rents out bicycles and has space for those who want to camp. Gaelic spoken. No smoking.

Uist Outdoor Centre, ½ mile from the ferry pier, Lochmaddy, T01876-500480, www.uistoutdoorcentre.co.uk. Open all year. Independent hostel with room for up to 20 in 4-person bunk rooms, full range of facilities, outdoor activities and course (see Activities and tours, page 333) on full board or self-catering basis. Prices available on application.

For an explanation of sleeping and eating price codes used in this guide, see inside the front cover. Other relevant information is found in Essentials, see pages 40-47.

Berneray *p325*

E Burnside Croft, T01876-540235, www.burnsidecroft.biz. Here you can share Prince Charles' (not the Bonnie one) crofting experience with Don Alick (Splash) MacKillop and his Australian wife Gloria who cooks up a storm in the kitchen. Guests can place a stone on the 'mosaic of friendship', a drystone dyke that attests to the welcoming atmosphere here. The hosts also offer fishing and boat trips to uninhabited islands and Don Alick is a storyteller in the great Hebridean tradition for evenings round the fire.
F Gatliff Trust Hostel, in 2 restored blackhouses overlooking a lovely sandy beach and old Viking pier about a mile up the east coast from the old ferry pier. 12 beds, no phone, open all year.

Benbecula *p325*

C Isle of Benbecula House Hotel, Creag Ghoraidh, T01870-602024, www.isleshotelgroup.co.uk. 20 en suite rooms. Open all year. Fully refurbished and with sea views. No-smoking rooms available. Meals served in conservatory dining room (à la carte dinner TTT-TT).
D Inchyra Guest House, Lionacleit, T01870-602176. Reliable and much cheaper alternative to the hotel.
F Tigh-na-Cille Bunkhouse, Balivanich, T01870-602522, open all year and sleeps 10 in 2 dorms and 2 twin rooms.

Camping

Shellbay Caravan and Camping Park, Lionacleit, T01870-602447, open Apr-Oct.

South Uist *p327*

You should book accommodation in advance, as the ferry arrives in Lochboisdale late in the evening.
C Lochboisdale Hotel, Lochboisdale, T01878-700332, www.lochboisdalehotel.com. 15 en suite rooms. Open all year. So close to the ferry terminal you can virtually step off the peer and through the front door. Best place to stay on the island and also one of the best places to eat and have a drink. Music sessions every fortnight but frequent spontaneous outbreaks of fiddling while the real fire burns.
C Orosay Inn, T01878-610298, www.orosayinn.com. 10 en suite rooms. Open all year. Small, modern hotel at Loch a' Chairnain (Lochcarnan). Fairly basic rooms but the restaurant serves up fine food, especially superb is the seafood (TT).
C Polochar Inn, a few miles to the west of Ludag, at Pol a' Charra (Pollachar), T01878-700215, polocharinn@aol.com. 11 en suite rooms. Open all year. Charming place with great views across the Sound of Barra and its own beach close by. Also bar meals and à la carte in dining room (TT-T).
D Brae Lea Guest House, about a mile from the terminal, Lochboisdale, T/F01878-700497, braelea@supanet.com. 6 en suite rooms. Open all year. Comfortable guesthouse, also serves dinner (TT) and will collect you from the ferry.
E Mrs Angela MacDonald, 247/8 Garryhallie, T01878-700263, www.uistonline.com/clanranald.htm. 3 en suite rooms. Open Apr-Nov. 3½ miles from Lochboisdale on the main A865. Good- quality B&B accommodation. Dinner available (TT) and room-only rate is slightly cheaper.
F Gatliff Trust Youth Hostel, at Tobha Mòr (Howmore). Converted blackhouse which overlooks the ruins of an ancient church and graveyard, beside the seemingly endless stretch of golden sand. 13 beds, open all year, no phone. The warden lives at Ben More House, at the junction with the main road.

Eriskay *p328*

There is a **B&B**, T01870-720232, and a **self-catering flat**, T01870-720274, or you can wild camp – though there are few amenities, other than a shop, pub and post office.

Barra *p329*

It's a good idea to book in advance if arriving on the evening ferry from Oban. There are neither independent hostels nor a Gatliff Trust Hostel on Barra.
B Craigard Hotel, in Castlebay, T01871-810200, wwwisleofbarra.com/craigard.html. 7 en suite rooms. Open all year. A family-run hotel with hearty home cooking.
B Isle of Barra Hotel a few miles west of Castlebay, T01871-810383, www.isleofbarra.com/iob.html. 38 en suite rooms. Open Easter-Oct. Modern, purpose-built hotel overlooking a lovely beach with fantastic sea views.

B-C Castlebay Hotel, by the ferry terminal in Castlebay, T01871-810223, www.castlebay-hotel.co.uk. 10 en suite rooms. Open all year. **A-B** including dinner. The best place to stay on the island. Friendly, good food, good value and a great bar which is the hub of the island's social scene.

D Northbay House, Morghan, Bagh a Tuath (Northbay), T01871-890255, www.barra holidays.co.uk. 2 en suite rooms. Apr-Oct. 5 miles from Castlebay, this former school-house is now an excellent B&B with self-catering also available and disabled access.

D-E Tigh-Na-Mara, Castlebay, T01871- 810304, www.witb.co.uk/links/tighnamara.htm. 5 rooms. Open all year. Comfortable guesthouse only a few mins' walk from the ferry terminal. **E** for room only.

E Terra Nova, Nask, T01871-810458. 3 en suite rooms. Comfortable and friendly B&B, 10-min walk from the ferry.

Self-catering

There are many options on Barra. As well as the **Visit Hebrides** website (see page 300) also check out www.isleofbarra.com.

Camping

Although there are also no official campsites on Barra, there are endless opportunities for wild camping across the island, with the most popular spots to be found on the machair at Traigh Mhor (north Barra), Borve Point (west Barra) and Ledaig (Castlebay). Generally no permission is required from the landowner, but ensure all waste and litter is removed when you leave the site. For campers, there are 2 or 3 well-stocked mini-supermarkets in Castlebay.

Vatersay

Those who find Barra too busy can escape to the extreme isolation of neighbouring Vatersay. There is self-catering accommodation in a converted schoolhouse overlooking a glorious south-facing beach. Contact **Mrs Patricia Barron**, T/F01871-810283, www.vatersayschool.co.uk.
It sleeps 6 and costs £430-725 per week.

Eating

See Sleeping for further options.

Benbecula *p325*

TTT-TT Stepping Stone Restaurant, Balivanich, T01870-603377. By far the best place to eat on the island. Good wholesome Scottish food every day 1000-2100. Snacks, sandwiches, takeaways and home baking are all available, as well as 3- or 5-course meals.

Barra *p329*

TT Castelbay Hotel and **Isle of Barra Hotel**, both offer excellent local fish and seafood.

T Kismul Galley, on the main street in Castlebay, T01871-810645, offers all-day breakfasts, snacks and home baking, and is open Mon-Sat 0900-2100, Sun 1000-1800.

There's also a tearoom (T) at the airport.

Activities and tours

North Uist *p323*

Uist Outdoor Centre, is based in Lochmaddy, T01876-500480, www.uistoutdoorcentre.co.uk. Runs week-long kayaking courses as well as weekend beginners' trips, also scuba diving, rock climbing and abseiling from sea cliffs, survival courses and powerboat courses. For those wishing for even more solitude there are overnight expeditions to Pabbay and Boreray, where you can see dolphins, porpoises, minke whales, grey seals and basking sharks. You can also charter an RIB for a trip to St Kilda, the Shiants, Monach and Flannan Islands. The centre also provides accommodation (see Sleeping, page 331).

Barra *p329*

Boat trips

Mr John Allan MacNeil in Castlebay, T01871-810449, can arrange boat trips to Mingulay. He sails to the island in settled weather when sufficient people can be found to fill the boat. It is one of the most rewarding excursions in the Outer Hebrides, particularly during the puffin season from Jun to early Aug. The trip normally includes a 2-hr sail from Barra past the neighbouring islands of Sandray and Pabbay, a circumnavigation of Mingulay to view the spectacularly high western sea cliffs, and a landing on the east coast for a 3-hr exploration of the beautiful beach of Mingulay Bay, the deserted village and surrounding hills and coast. There are also fine views to the lighthouse on Barra Head, the most southerly outpost of the Outer Hebrides island chain.

Mr George McLeod, at the **Castlebay Hotel**, T01871-810223, can arrange a similar tour to that outlined above, or ask at the tourist office in Castlebay.

Kayaking

Clearwater paddling, Castlebay, T01871-810443, www.clearwaterpaddling.com. 6-night sea kayaking trips from £435 per person full board.

Taxi tours

Hatcher's Taxis, T01871-810486; and **Nellie's** Taxi, T01871-810302, conduct island tours.

Transport

North Uist *p323*

Ferry From **Uig** to **Lochmaddy** (1 hr 40 mins) 1-2 daily. One-way ticket £9.60 per passenger, £46 per car, 5-day saver return £16.40 and £79. Contact **Lochmaddy**, T01876-5000337.

Benbecula *p323*

Air British Airways/Loganair, T08708-509850, www.ba.com, flies from **Glasgow** to **Benbecula**, Mon-Sat 1 daily, 1 hr. There are also flights from **Benbecula** to **Barra**, Mon-Fri 1 daily, 20 mins.

Car hire Maclennan Self Drive, Balivanich, T01870-602191, also Ask Car Hire, Lionacleit, T01870-602818.

South Uist *p323*

Car hire Laing Motors, Lochboisdale, T01870-700267.

Cycle hire Rothan Cycles, Lochboisdale, T01870-620283.

Ferry **Oban** to **Lochboisdale** 1 direct sailing on Tue, Thu and Sat (5 hrs 20 mins); via Castlebay (Barra) on Sun (6 hrs 30 mins). There are also early morning departures (0700) from **Castlebay** on Wed and Fri. **Oban** to **Lochboisdale**, one-way ticket £21.10 per passenger, £77 per car, 5-day saver return £36 and £131. **Castlebay** to **Lochboisdale**, one way £6 per passenger, £35 per car, 5-day saver return £10.20 and £59.

Barra *p323*

Air British Airways/Loganair, T08708-509850, www.ba.com, flies from **Glasgow** to **Barra**, Mon-Sat 1 daily, 1 hr 5 mins. There are also flights from **Benbecula** to **Barra**, Mon-Fri 1 daily, 20 mins.

Car hire **Barra Car Hire**, T01871-810243.

Ferry **Oban** to **Castlebay**: 1 direct sailing daily except Tue and Thu (4 hrs 50 mins). Also sailings to Castlebay via **Lochboisdale** on Tue and Thu (7 hrs 20 mins); one way per passenger £21.10, £77 per car, 5-day saver return £36 and £131. There is also a sailing from Oban via **Coll** and **Tiree** on Thu (6 hrs 45 mins), £26.50 per passenger, £153 per car. From Tiree to Castlebay only is £10 per passenger and £44 per car. There is a ferry to **Castlebay** from **Lochboisdale**, on Tue and Thu at 2050, arriving at 2250; £6 per passenger, £35 per car, 5-day saver return £10.20 and £59.

There's also a regular passenger ferry from **Ludag** in **South Uist** to **Eoligarry** on **Barra**, T01878-720238. Ferries sail from **Barra** to **Eriskay** 5 times daily (4 on Sun). A one-way ticket costs £5.90 per passenger and £17.50 per car. 5-day return £10 and £30. Bikes £1.

St Kilda

More than 40 miles west of the Outer Hebrides lie the spectacular and isolated islands of St Kilda, Scotland's first UNESCO World Heritage site. St Kilda consists of several islands and manages to capture the imagination of most visitors to the Outer Hebrides, whether they actually get there or just dream about romantic voyages to mysterious lands across perilous seas. Owned by the National Trust for Scotland, St Kilda is a National Nature reserve. Each year, during the brief summer months when travel to the islands is possible, teams of volunteers work on Hirta, maintaining what remains of the abandoned houses, studying the wildlife and glorying in the peace and isolation of the place.

Ins and outs

The biggest problem apart from accessibility is cost, although it is definitely possible if you're prepared to break the bank. **Island Cruising** ⓘ *in Uig, on Lewis, T01851-672381, www.island-cruising.com*, arranges boat trips to St Kilda from April to October starting from about £300 (four-day all-inclusive). The tour comprises the journey to and from St Kilda and a landing on Hirta with a visit to the museum, the old village and a wider exploration of the island, including a climb up to the highest sea cliffs in the British Isles at Conachair (430 m). They also run a six-day cruise allowing an extra day or tweo on St Kilda. A 70-ft converted lifeboat also makes the trip, operated by **Northern Light Charters** ⓘ *Oban, T01680-740595, www.northern-light.co.uk*. A seven-day expedition costs £650 per person. For more details of tours, ask at one of the main tourist information centres in the Outer Hebrides.

National Trust for Scotland also organizes two-week long voluntary work parties throughout the summer every year to undertake restoration, maintenance and archaeology projects around the old village on Hirta. The groups are very popular and each volunteer must complete an application form, so apply early. The fortnight costs between £450 and £500 and this covers transport from Oban to St Kilda and all food and lodging costs while on the island. For details contact **National Trust for Scotland** ⓘ *Oban, T01631-570000, stkilda@nts.org.uk*. For more information, contact **Scottish Natural Heritage** ⓘ *135 Stilligarry, South Uist, HS8 5RS, T01870-620238.*

Sights

In 1957 the islands become the property of the National Trust for Scotland, who in turn leased them to the Nature Conservancy (the forerunner of Scottish Natural Heritage) as a National Nature Reserve. St Kilda is the most important seabird breeding station in northwest Europe. The islands are home to the largest colony of gannets in the world, the largest colony of fulmars in Britain and one the largest colonies of puffins in Scotland. These huge numbers of seabirds were vital to the islanders' survival. Their eggs provided food in the summer, and gannets and fulmers were caught each season to be plucked, dried and stored for the winter. Their feathers and oil were kept for export to generate income, whilst their bones were shaped into useful tools and their skins into shoes.

The largest of the islands, **Hirta**, was the remotest community in Britain, if not Europe, until 1930, when the remaining 36 Gaelic-speaking inhabitants were evacuated at their own request, in one of the most poignant episodes of Scottish history (see box, page 336). Today Hirta is partly occupied by the army as a radar-tracking station for the rocket range on South Uist and managed by Scottish Natural Heritage. Across a narrow channel lies **Dun**. Nearby **Boreray** is home to the world's largest colony of gannets, and **Soay** completes the group. There are several dramatic 'stacs' rising sheer from the Atlantic Ocean. At 430 m, the sea cliffs at Conachair are the highest in the British Isles.

How St Kilda was killed off

Friday 29 August 1930 was the end of life as it had been for centuries on St Kilda. For a least 1000 years the inhabitants of this remote group of islands had been tenants of the Macleods of Dunvegan on Skye. In earlier days the trip from Skye, undertaken in longboats, would require 16 hours of rigorous rowing and sailing. Even now, the trip to St Kilda is no easy matter.

Until 1930 the islanders had been supported from the mainland by the provision of a nurse and a post office. But the Scottish Office decided that their subsidy of the islands was no longer economic. This meant that life for the residents without those facilities would be untenable.

In 1930, to the younger of the 36 residents, including a man with nine children, evacuation was an attractive prospect. There would be better schooling for the children, and better health care. Although many had never seen a tree, a new life in forestry appealed. The more elderly residents, most of whom had never left the island and who could not speak English, must have viewed the drastic change with alarm but the younger majority view prevailed and evacuation was planned.

There were 500 Soay sheep to be moved first. Their coats of fine wool were not sheared but plucked by the inhabitants using only a penknife. The resultant locally woven tweed, either shipped ashore or sold to rare visitors, had provided the inhabitants' only contact with actual money. No taxes on income or on anything else were paid. Their internal economy took the form of barter. The plentiful supply of gannets, when dried, provided winter food. No inhabitant had ever fought in any war. Their distance and isolation earned them no consideration by the rest of Scotland.

Despite protestations by the Canine Defence League, all dogs were destroyed. Just two were put down by injections of hydrocyanic acid. The rest, at the islanders' insistence, had stones tied around their necks and were hurled from the jetty. Small boats were used to ferry only a dozen or so sheep out to the *SS Dunara Castle*. Ten cows with four calves were also evacuated. Then *HMS Harebell*, of the Fishery Protection Service, came on the final day to take the islanders to the mainland. The Under Secretary of State for Scotland imposed a ban on photography, thus ensuring the people of St Kilda privacy during the evacuation. It was not possible to house all of the inhabitants in Argyll, as had been hoped, so the community was split, their communal lives coming to an end.

The history of the island has been documented in a number of scholarly works, including *The Life and Death of St Kilda* by Tom Steel, and *Island on the Edge of the World*

Orkney & Shetland

Footprint features

Introduction

To some, these two archipelagos will never be anything other than distant and overlooked specks of land peppering the wild north Atlantic, above an already distant north coast of mainland Scotland. They certainly are remote and they have maintained a social and political, as well as geographical, distance from the rest of Scotland, which goes a long way to explaining the relatively few visitors each year. Both were under Norse rule until the mid-15th century and, somehow, seeing them as a part of Scotland can be very misleading. Each must be seen within the context of its own unique cultural background and unusual geography.

Shetland's northern islands, on the same latitude as Alaska, are as strange and different as Britain gets, while beguiling Orkney just smiles serenely as the rest of world races headlong into the future at alarming speed. It is these qualities that make the islands worth visiting and the ones that the tourist boards are keen to plug. Both Orkney and Shetland are littered with outstanding archaeological evidence, not just of six centuries of Norse occupation, such as at Jarlshof at the very southern tip of Shetland, but also of life back in 3000 BC at Skara Brae and the Knap of Howar in the Orkneys. They are also the best places in Britain to see wildlife as yet untamed by the 21st century. Here you can sail alongside porpoises and seals, and watch a million migratory seabirds nest and raise their young during the summer months. And, thanks to fast and frequent transport links, it doesn't take an Arctic expedition to get here.

★ Don't miss...

1 **Stromness** Explore the winding streets of one of the most fascinating fishing villages in Scotland, page 345.
2 **Skara Brae and Maes Howe** Discover these amazing archaeological wonders, pages 347 and 348.
3 **Island of Lamb Holm** Visit the incredible little Italian Chapel, page 351.
4 **Old Man of Hoy** Take the spectacular clifftop walk to meet the Old Man of Hoy, page 353.
5 **Westray to Papa Westray** Fly to one island from the other; it takes all of two minutes, page 357.
6 **Isle of Mousa** Visit the best-preserved broch in Scotland, page 373.
7 **Fair Isle** Brave the white-knuckle boat trip to one of the best places on earth for birdwatching, page 374.
8 **Hermaness National Nature Reserve** Explore the dramatic coastal scenery of this nature reserve, page 378.

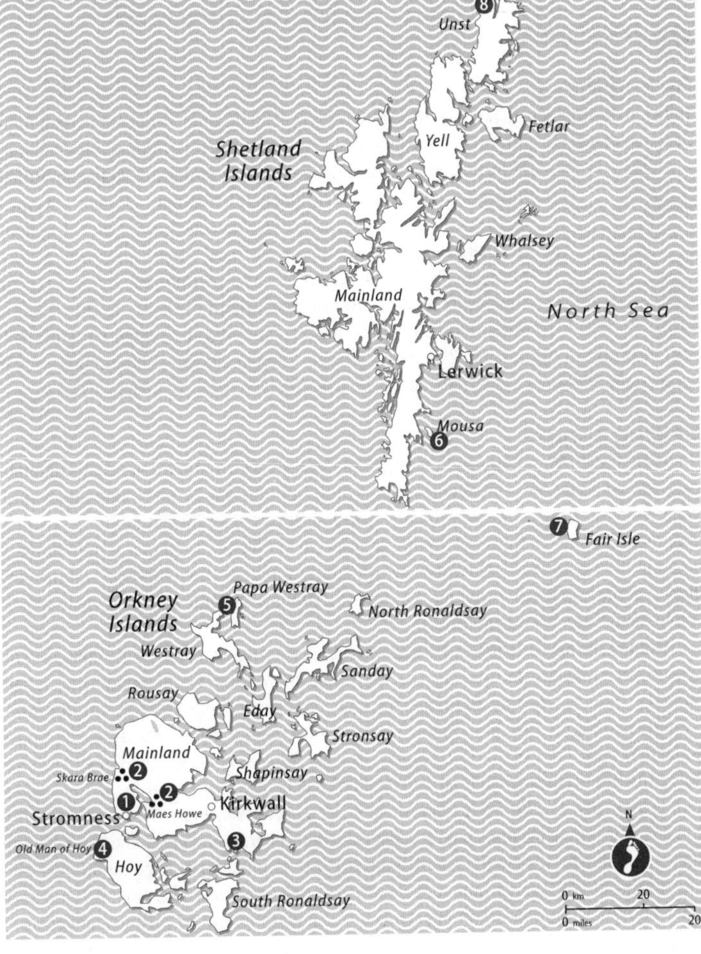

Orkney

Orkney may be separated from the north coast of Scotland by a mere 6 miles of the stroppy Pentland Firth, but to the fiercely independent Orcadians, 'Mainland' means the largest of the Orkney islands and not the Scottish mainland. Mainland is also the site of the two main towns and ferry terminals: the capital Kirkwall and the beautiful old fishing port of Stromness. Orkney has the densest concentration of prehistoric monuments in Britain and Mainland is where you'll find many of these archaeological relics: the Stones of Stenness, Maes Howe, the Broch of Gurness and the remarkable Neolithic village of Skara Brae, all of which give Orkney a rare continuity of past and present. Aside from Mainland, there are a dozen smaller islands to explore, including Hoy, with its wild, spectacular coastal scenery. The even more remote northerly islands offer miles of deserted beaches and nothing but the calls of birds to shatter the peace and quiet. Quiet also describes the taciturn locals. They aren't unfriendly – quite the opposite, in fact – but it's said that Orcadians will rarely use one word where none will do. ›› *For Sleeping, Eating and other listings, see pages 358-366.*

Ins and outs

Getting there

There are direct flights to Kirkwall airport daily except Sunday from Aberdeen, Edinburgh, Glasgow, Inverness and Shetland, with connections to London Heathrow, Birmingham, Manchester and Belfast. These are operated by **Loganair/British Airways** and can be booked through **British Airways** ⓘ *T08708-509850, www.britishairways.com*, or **Loganair** ⓘ *T01856-872494, www.loganair.co.uk*. There are several ferry routes to Orkney: Aberdeen–Kirkwall (7½ hours); Scrabster, near Thurso, to Stroness (90 minutes); John o' Groats to Burwick, on South Ronaldsay (40 minutes, from May to September) and Gill's Bay, near John o' Groats, to St Margaret's Hope. There's also an 'Orkney Bus', which leaves daily from Inverness, direct to Kirkwall. ›› *For further details, see Transport, page 364.*

The best way to travel to Orkney is by ferry from Scrabster to Stromness; 90 minutes of sheer spectacle, as the boat sails close to the Old Man of Hoy.

Getting around

There are flights from Kirkwall to many of the islands which are operated by **Loganair** (see above). They are very reasonable, costing £15 one way to North Ronaldsay and Papa Westray and £31 one way to Eday, Sanday, Stronsay and Westray. There are also inter-island flights costing £16 return, and excursion flights (requiring a minimum of one night's stay at the destination), which cost £12 return. There are also sightseeing flights in July and August costing £31, and the **Orkney Adventure** ticket, which allows you to fly to three islands for £68.

Orkney Ferries ⓘ *T01856-872044, www.orkneyferries.co.uk*, operates daily car and passenger ferries to Rousay, Egilsay and Wyre from Tingwall; to Shapinsay, Eday, Stronsay, Sanday, Westray and Papa Westray from Kirkwall; to Graemsay and Hoy from Stromness; and to Hoy and Flotta from Houton. There's a ferry on Friday to North Ronaldsay from Kirkwall. Fares to Rousay, Egilsay, Wyre, Shapinsay, Hoy, Graemsay and Flotta (the South Isles) cost £6.40/3.20 (adult/child or concession) return per passenger and £19.20 per car. To Eday, Stronsay, Sanday, Westray, Papa Westray and North Ronaldsay (North Isles) fares cost £12.80/6.40 return per passenger £28.60 per car. An inter-island fare for the North Islands is £3.20/1.60 return per passenger and £9.60 per car; for the South Islands fares are £6.40/3.20 per passenger and £14.30 per car. If travelling by car, book ferry journeys in advance. Single fares are 50% of the return price.

Learning the lingo

Despite the disappearance of the Norse language, many of the Viking place names have survived. Here are some of the most common Old Norse elements which will help explain the meaning of many place names:

a(y)	island	*holm*	small island
a, o	stream	*howe*	mound
aith	isthmus	*kirk*	church
ayre	beach	*lax*	salmon
bard	headland	*ler*	mud, clay
bister	farm	*lyng*	heather
brae, brei	broad	*minn*	mouth
fell, field	hill	*mool, noup*	headland
fors	waterfall	*setter*	farm
garth	farm	*thing*	parliament
geo	creek	*toft*	house site
grind	gate	*voe*	sea inlet
ham(n)	anchorage	*wick, vik*	bay

Only the main population centres on Mainland are served by public transport, and having a car is essential to visit many of the most interesting sights. Bringing a car to Orkney is expensive, but there are several car hire firms on the Mainland and on the other islands. An alternative could be taking to a bike. Orkney is relatively flat and most of its roads are quiet, which makes it ideal for touring on two wheels, though the wind can make it difficult if it's blowing in the wrong direction. Bicycles can be hired in Kirkwall, Stromness and on many of the other islands. Those with limited time may prefer to book a tour of the islands. » *For further details, see Activities and tours, page 363, and Transport, page 364.*

Tourist information

Orkney Tourist Board ⓘ *www.visitorkney.com*, has tourist offices in Kirkwall and Stromness. They will book accommodation for you, or provide a list of what's available, though many B&Bs are not included in the tourist board scheme. They can also provide information on various sights, walks and the islands' wildlife. Those wishing to leave Mainland and visit the smaller islands should pick up a free copy of the tourist board's excellent information and travel guide, *The Islands of Orkney*.

Many of Orkney's monuments are managed by **Historic Scotland**. They include the Bishop and Earl's Palaces, Broch of Gurness, Maes Howe, Skara Brae and Skaill House, Brough of Birsay and Hackness Martello Tower. If you plan to visit all or most of these sights, it may be cheaper to buy a **Historic Scotland Explorer Pass**. There are various types: three days out of five costs £18 (concession £13.50, family £36); seven days out of 14 costs £25.50 (concession £19.50, family £51; and 10 days out of 30 costs £30 (concession £22.50, family £60). Contact www.historicscotland.gov.uk.

Kirkwall » *pp358-366. See map, page 342.*

→ *Phone code: 01856. Population: 7000.*

Orkney's rugged, Nordic-feeling capital is built around a wide sheltered bay and is the main departure point for ferries to the northern islands. First impressions are a little misleading, as the harbour area has been blighted by modern development.

Orkney

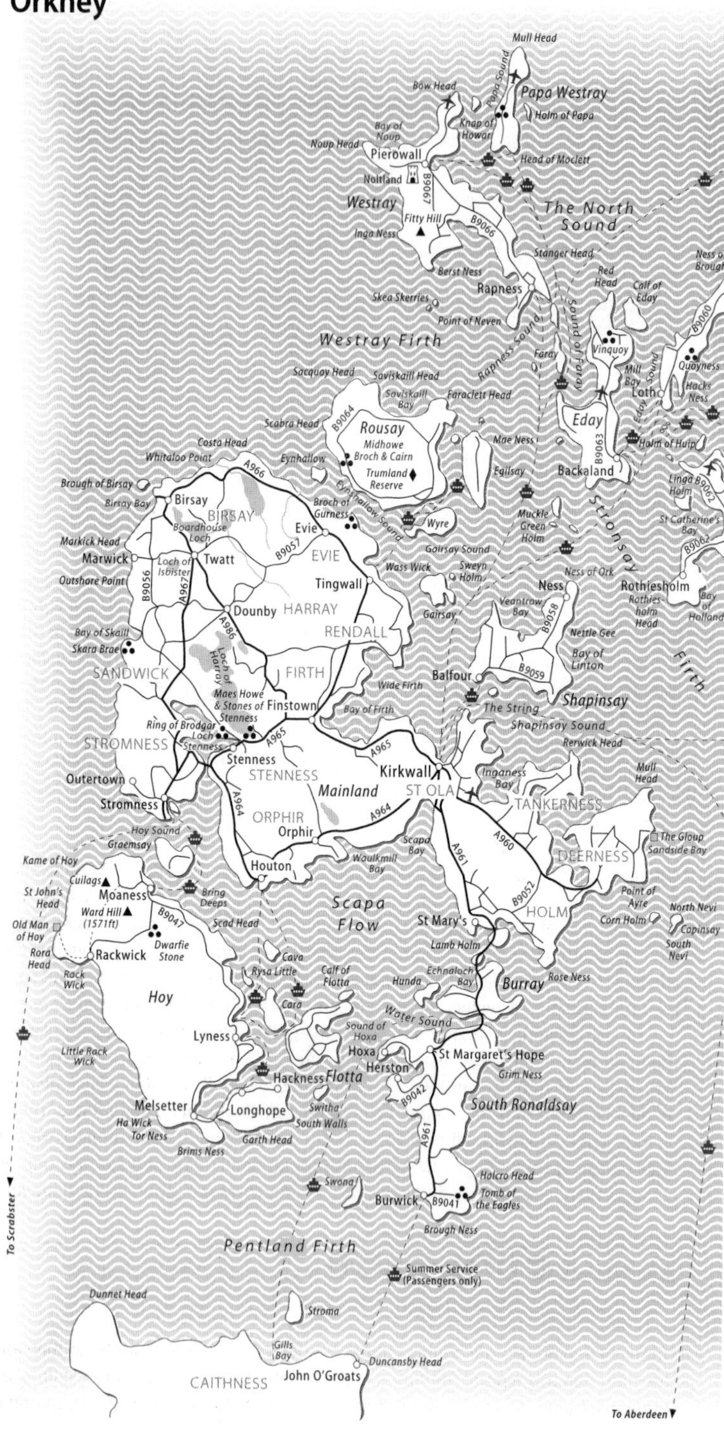
Mull Head
Papa Sound
Bow Head
Papa Westray
Holm of Papa
Knap of Howar
Bay of Noup
Noup Head
Pierowall
Head of Moclett
Noltland
B9067
Westray
Fitty Hill
B9066
The North Sound
Inga Ness
Stanger Head
Ness of Brough
Berst Ness
Red Head
Calf of Eday
Rapness
Skea Skerries
Point of Neven
B9060
Sound of Faray
Westray Firth
Rapness Sound
Vinquoy
Faray
Quoyness
Sacquoy Head
Saviskaill Head
Mill Bay
Eday Sound
Saviskaill Bay
Faraclett Head
Loth
Hacks Ness
Rousay
Eday
Scabra Head
B9064
Midhowe Broch & Cairn
Mae Ness
Costa Head
Holm of Huip
Whitaloo Point
Eynhallow
B9063
Trumland Reserve
Egilsay
Backaland
A966
Linga Holm
B9062
Brough of Birsay
Birsay Bay
Birsay
BIRSAY
Broch of Gurness
Eynhallow Sound
Wyre
Muckle Green Holm
Stronsay
St Catherine's Bay
Boardhouse Loch
Evie
Markick Head
B9057
Gairsay Sound
Marwick
Loch of Isbister
Twatt
EVIE
Wass Wick
Sweyn Holm
Ness of Ork
B9062
Outshore Point
B9056
A967
Tingwall
Ness
Rothiesholm
Veantrow Bay
Bay of Holland
Dounby
HARRAY
Gairsay
B9058
Rothiesholm Head
A986
RENDALL
Bay of Skaill
Nettle Gee
Skara Brae
Loch of Harray
Bay of Linton
SANDWICK
FIRTH
B9059
Firth
Balfour
Maes Howe & Stones of Stenness
Finstown
Wide Firth
Shapinsay
Bay of Firth
The String
Ring of Brodgar
Loch Stenness
A965
Shapinsay Sound
STROMNESS
Rerwick Head
Stenness
A965
Mull Head
Kirkwall
STENNESS
Inganess Bay
Outertown
Mainland
ST OLA
TANKERNESS
Stromness
A964
A964
ORPHIR
Hoy Sound
Orphir
A960
The Gloup
Sandside Bay
Graemsay
Scapa Bay
A961
DEERNESS
Kame of Hoy
Houton
Waulkmill Bay
Cuilags
B9052
Point of Ayre
St John's Head
Moaness
Bring Deeps
Scapa Flow
North Nevi
Ward Hill (1571ft)
B9047
Scad Head
St Mary's
HOLM
Corn Holm
Copinsay
Old Man of Hoy
Dwarfie Stone
Lamb Holm
South Nevi
Rora Head
Rackwick
Cava
Rack Wick
Rysa Little
Calf of Flotta
Hunda
Echnaloch Bay
Burray
Rose Ness
Hoy
Cara
Water Sound
Sound of Hoxa
Lyness
Hoxa
St Margaret's Hope
Little Rack Wick
Herston
Grim Ness
Hackness
Flotta
B9042
Melsetter
Longhope
Switha
South Ronaldsay
Ha Wick
Tor Ness
South Walls
Garth Head
Brims Ness
A961
Halcro Head
Swona
Burwick
B9041
Tomb of the Eagles
To Scrabster
Brough Ness
Pentland Firth
Summer Service (Passengers only)
Dunnet Head
Stroma
Gills Bay
Duncansby Head
CAITHNESS
John O'Groats
To Aberdeen

More appealing, however, are the narrow winding streets and lanes of the old town, which has not changed much over the centuries. There are many houses dating from the 16th, 17th and 18th centuries, as well as Kirkwall's greatest attraction, its magnificent cathedral, the finest medieval building in northern Scotland.

Ins and outs

Getting there and around The **airport** ⓘ *T01856-872421*, is 3 miles southeast of Kirkwall on the A960. There are no buses to and from town. A taxi will cost around £6. The bus station is five minutes' walk west of the town centre. The town is compact and it's easy to get around on foot. The main street changes its name from Bridge Street to Albert Street, then to Broad Street and Victoria Street as it twists its way south from the busy harbour. The cathedral is on Broad Street, and most of the shops and banks are on Broad Street and Albert Street. ▸▸ *For further details, see Transport, page 364.*

Tourist information On Broad Street, near the cathedral, is the very helpful **TIC** ⓘ *T01856-872856, www.visitorkney.com, Apr-Sep 0830-2000, Oct-Mar Mon-Sat 0930-1700.* Services they provide include booking accommodation and changing money; they also have various useful free leaflets including *The Islands of Orkney and the Kirkwall Heritage Guide*, stock a wide range of guidebooks and maps, and have details of forthcoming events. Another good source is the weekly newspaper *The Orcadian*.

Sights

The town's outstanding sight is the huge and impressive red sandstone **St Magnus Cathedral** ⓘ *Apr-Sep Mon-Sat 0900-1800, Sun 1400-1800, Oct-Mar Mon-Sat 0900-1300 and 1400-1700, Sun service at 1115*, built by masons who had worked on Durham Cathedral in the north of England. It was founded in 1137 by Rognvald Kolson, Earl of Orkney, in memory of his uncle, Magnus Erlendson, who was slain by his cousin, Haakon Paulson, on Egilsay in 1115. Magnus was buried at Birsay and it is said that heavenly light was seen over his grave. It soon became a shrine, attracting pilgrims from as far afield as Norway. Magnus was canonized in 1133, and four years later his nephew commissioned construction of the cathedral. The building wasn't completed until the 14th century. Major additions have been made over the centuries, the most recent of which was a new west window for the nave, to celebrate the cathedral's 850th anniversary in 1987. The bones of St Magnus now lie in the north choir pillar, while those of St Rognvald lie in the south one. There's also a memorial to John Rae, the 19th-century Arctic explorer who is buried in the graveyard, as well as a monument to the 833 men of the *HMS Royal Oak* who died when it was torpedoed in Scapa Flow in 1939.

Looming impressively nearby are the ruins of the **Bishop's Palace** ⓘ *entry by combined ticket with Earl's Palace*, built in the 12th century as the first Kirkwall residence of the Bishop of Orkney. Here King Haakon of Norway died in 1263 after his

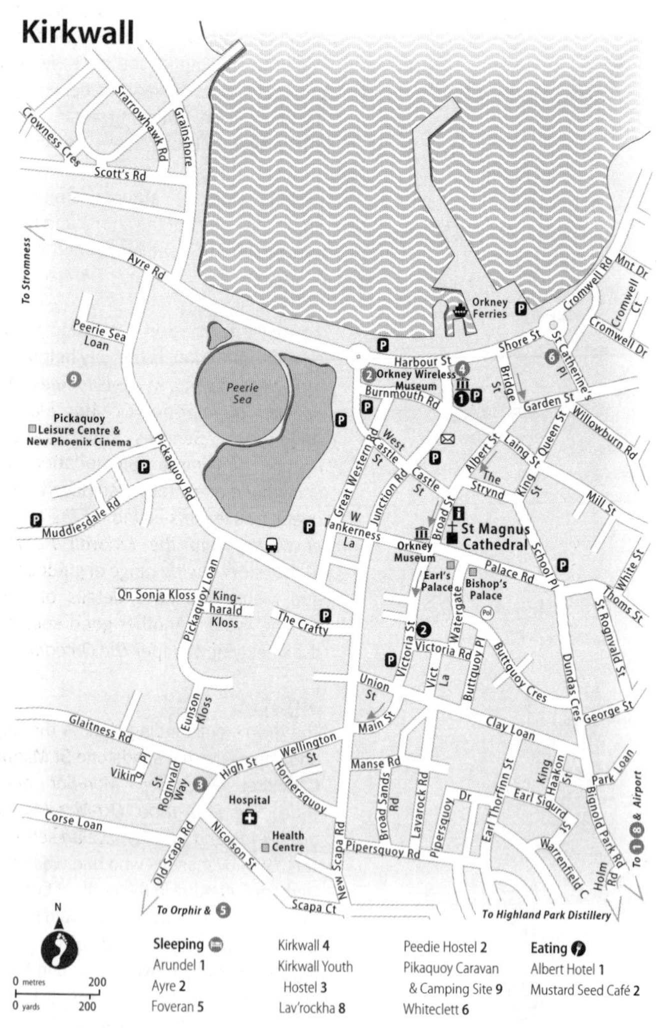

defeat at the Battle of Largs. The palace was repaired and extended in the mid-16th century by Bishop Reid, and most of what you see dates from that period. There's a good view of the town from the top of the 'Moosie Too'r'.

The adjacent **Earl's Palace** ⓘ *T01856-871918, Apr-Sep daily 0930-1830, £3, concession £2.30, children £1.30*, was built around 1600 by the notorious Patrick Stewart, Earl of Orkney, using forced labour. Still very much intact, it is one of Scotland's most elegant Renaissance buildings and was occupied by the tyrannical Stewart only for a very short time, until he was imprisoned and later executed. Wandering around both these spectacularly impressive and solid palaces is a very good way to get a feel for a period of Orkney's history that is very often ignored.

Opposite St Magnus Cathedral is **Tankerness House and Gardens**, a 16th-century former manse which has been restored and now houses the **Orkney Museum** ⓘ *T01856-873191, Oct-Mar Mon-Sat 1030-1230, 1330-1700, Apr-Sep 1030-1700, May-Sep daily 1400-1700, free*, which features various archaeological artefacts from Neolithic times to the Vikings. If you are spending any time in Kirkwall at the beginning of your stay, then this is an exceedingly worthwhile exhibition. It is a great way to whet your appetite for the archaeological treats that are lying in wait for you all over the islands, and it also puts them into a useful chronological context.

Old radio buffs should not miss the **Orkney Wireless Museum** ⓘ *Kiln Corner, at the harbour end of Junction Rd, Apr-Sep Mon-Sat 1000-1630, Sun 1400-1630, £2, children £1*, which houses a jumble of domestic and wartime communications equipment from the 1930s onwards.

A mile south of the town centre on the road to South Ronaldsay is the 200-year-old **Highland Park Distillery** ⓘ *T01856-874619, www.highlandpark.co.uk, tours every half hour Apr, Sep and Oct Mon-Fri 1000-1700, May-Aug Mon-Sat 1000-1700, Sun 1200-1700, Nov-Mar Mon-Fri at 1400 only, £4*. This is the most northerly of Scotland's whisky distilleries and one of the very best. It's one of the few that still has its own floor maltings – as well as its own mouser cat – and there's a dram of this particularly fine single malt at the end. Don't leave without buying a bottle, for this is one of the great all-round whiskies, with a distinctive smoky flavour. It rivals those from more fashionable Islay, especially the very wonderful 25-year-olds.

Stromness and West Mainland

▸▸ *pp358-366. See map, page 342.*

→ *Phone code: 01856.*

Ferries from Scrabster arrive in Stromness, and newcomers are greeted by rows of stone-built houses hugging the shore, each with its own jetty. Stromness is a much more attractive town than Kirkwall, and its narrow, winding main street, its *wynds* and *closes*, its fascinating shops, and its unique atmosphere make it the ideal base for exploring the West Mainland, the name given to everything west of Kirkwall. It's an area of rich farmland, rolling hills and moorland, fringed by spectacular cliffs along the Atlantic coastline and with the greatest concentration of prehistoric monuments in Britain. Here you'll find, amongst many others, the well-preserved Neolithic village of **Skara Brae**, silent monuments to human endeavour in the form of the **Standing Stones of Stenness** and the **Ring of Brodgar**, and the chambered tomb of **Maes Howe**, with its many still-unresolved mysteries.

Ins and outs

Stromness TIC ⓘ *T01856-850716, Apr-Oct Mon-Sat 0800-1800, Sun 0900-1600, Nov-Mar Mon-Fri 0900-1700*, is at the new ferry terminal. Its exhibition, *This Place Called Orkney*, is a useful introduction to the islands, and its free *Stromness Heritage Guide* takes you round all the town's buildings. ▸▸ *For details of Transport, see page 364.*

Scandanavian settlements

The history of Orkney and Shetland is bound up with the history of the Vikings, who first came to the islands in the latter half of the ninth century and stayed for about 650 years. This was part of a great Viking expansion westwards, and in less than a century emigrants from Norway and Denmark settled in Orkney, Shetland, Iceland, Greenland, Caithness, the Western Isles, Isle of Man and parts of Ireland and the northern half of England.

In 872 the King of Norway set up a Norse earldom in Orkney, from which the Vikings ruled Orkney, Shetland and the Western Isles and took part in raids around Britain and Europe, creating the popular image of Vikings as aggressive, bloodthirsty invaders. At home, however, they lived a peaceful life, adhering to the laws of their parliament, the 'thing', and many converted to Christianity.

In the late 14th century Norway, Denmark and Sweden were united under a Danish king. In 1469 the Royal estates and prerogatives in Orkney and Shetland were pledged to Scotland as part of the marriage dowry of Margaret, daughter of the King of Denmark, on her marriage to Prince James of Scotland, later to become King James III. Orkney and Shetland were to revert to rule by the kings of Norway when the debt was paid, but the pledge was never redeemed and the islands remained under Scottish control.

Soon after assuming control, the Scots began to change the old Norse laws which they had agreed to maintain, and Scottish influence grew. In 1564 Mary, Queen of Scots granted the control and revenues from Orkney and Shetland to her half-brother, Robert Stewart. His prime motivation, however, was to extract as much money as possible through taxes. He was succeeded by his son, the infamous Patrick Stewart, who demanded even more rents, dues and fines. Earl Patrick eventually got his come-uppance when he was executed in Edinburgh for treason, but the changes he had made continued and Scots and English gradually began to usurp Old Norse as the native language of the islands.

Stromness

Stromness is a classic Scottish fishing town and a perfect introduction to Orkney. Though referred to in the Viking Saga as *Hamnavoe*, the town dates from the 17th century. Its importance as a trading port grew in the 18th century when wars and privateers made the English Channel too dangerous and ships used the northern route across the Atlantic, calling in at Stromness for food and water and to hire a crew. Until the late 19th century, ships of the Hudson Bay Company made Stromness their main base for supplies. Whaling ships bound for Greenland also hired local labour. By the late 19th century the herring boom had reached Stromness and there were 400 boats using its harbour, but within two decades the boom was over due to over-fishing. Today Stromness remains a fishing port, as well as Orkney's main ferry terminal and the headquarters of the Northern Lighthouse Board.

Stromness consists largely of one narrow, winding main street, paved with flagstones, which hugs the shoreline. Running off the street are numerous little lanes and alleyways, many with fascinating names such as **Khyber Pass**, and full of interesting buildings that reflect the town's proud maritime heritage. The houses on the seaward side of the street are gable end to the waterfront and each has its own jetty. The town is not designed for the car, so you'll have to park by the harbour and explore its delights on foot. The main street changes its name from Victoria Street to Graham Place, Dundas Street, Alfred Street and South End as it runs south from the harbour.

Stromness Museum ⓘ *52 Albert St, T01856-850025, May-Sep daily 1000-1700, Oct-Apr Mon-Sat 1030-1230 and 1330-1700, £2.50, children £0.50*, has exhibitions on natural and maritime history, and contains artefacts from Scapa Flow and the days of the Hudson Bay company. Opposite the museum is the house where **George Mackay Brown** (1921-1996), Orkney's most famous poet and story-writer, spent the last two decades of his life, see also page 405. On a jetty to the south of the new harbour is the excellent **Pier Arts Centre** ⓘ *Tue-Sat 1030-1230 and 1330-1700, Jul and Aug also Sun 1400-1700, free*, housing a permanent collection of works of the St Ives school, including Barbara Hepworth, Ben Nicholson and Patrick Heron, amongst others, in a lovely gallery.

Skara Brae and Skaill House

ⓘ *T01956-841815. Apr-Sep (joint ticket) daily 0930-1830. £6.50, concession £5, children £2.50. Oct-Mar (Skara Brae only) Mon-Sat 0930-1630 and Sun 1400-1630, £5.50, concessions £4.50, children £2.*

Eight miles north of Stromness, in the magnificent setting of the dazzling white sands of the Bay of Skaill, is Skara Brae, the best-preserved Stone Age village in northern Europe. First revealed in 1850 after a violent storm blew away the dunes, the site dates from around 5000 years ago and was occupied for about 600 years.

The houses contain stone furniture, fireplaces, drains, beds, dressers and even have damp-proof coursing in the foundations. The whole complex presents a unique picture of the lifestyle of its inhabitants, and there's also a replica 'house' that you can wander around in the gloom, empathizing with that 3000 BC lifestyle.

The swish, modern visitor centre has a useful introductory video and exhibition which is definitely worth seeing before you look round the site (and it's also worth buying their guidebook). After leaving the visitor centre, you walk down a 'path of time', which takes you back through landmark achievements of the last seven millennia, gradually building up the suspense and putting the achievements of Skara Brae in perspective – they may only be rudimentary buildings that once had turf for their rooves, but they were built 2000 years before the pyramids of Egypt, and in one of the world's most northerly outposts.

During the summer a ticket to Skara Brae includes admission to nearby **Skaill House**, an early 17th-century mansion which contains a few old artefacts, including Captain Cook's dinner service from the *Resolution*, but it comes as a bit of a let-down after what you will have just witnessed, not 300 yards away, at Skara Brae.

Sandwick and Yesnaby

A short distance inland from here, at Sandwick, is Orkney's only brewery, housed in the old Quoyloo School. It brews the island's **Raven Ale** and various bottled beers, including **Skull-splitter**, named after the Viking earl, Thorfinn Skull-splitter.

South of the Bay of Skaill is Yesnaby, one of the most spectacular places on the islands, where the cliffs have been eroded into a series of stacks and geos by the fierce Atlantic seas. An exhilarating, and precarious, half-mile walk south from the car park and old Second World War lookout post brings you to **Yesnaby Castle**, a huge sea stack similar to the Old Man of Hoy. It's a dramatic sight, especially in a full force gale.

Standing Stones of Stenness and Ring of Brodgar

Northeast of Stromness on the road to Kirkwall is the tiny village of **Stenness**, near some of Orkney's most interesting prehistoric sites. The Standing Stones of Stenness comprise the four remaining stones from an original circle of 12 stones, dating from 3000 BC. The largest of the stones stands over 15 ft high. A path leads from the stones to the nearby **Barnhouse Settlement**, a recently excavated Neolithic village.

About a mile northwest of Stenness is another stone circle, the **Ring of Brodgar**. This is a particularly impressive henge monument. It is over 100 yards in diameter and

27 of the original 60 stones are still standing, some of them up to 15 ft high. Given the importance of these sites, it is particularly refreshing to realize when you get there that you can walk amongst the stones in the calm of a summer evening, with only a few oystercatchers for company, but both get busy with coach parties during the day.

Maes Howe

ⓘ *T01856-761606. Apr-Sep daily 0930-1830, Oct-Mar Mon-Sat 0930-1630 and Sun 1400-1630. £4.50, concession £3.50, children £2; tickets bought from Tormiston Mill, on the other side of the road, where there's an exhibition, introductory video and café.* Less than a mile northeast of the Stones of Stenness is Maes Howe, the finest Neolithic burial chamber in Europe. It was built around 2750 BC, making it contemporary with the Standing Stones and Skara Brae, and is amazingly well preserved. A huge mound covers a stone-built entrance passage which leads into a central chamber – over 12 ft square and the same in height – with three smaller cells built into the walls of the tomb.

When it was opened in 1861, no human remains or artefacts were found, giving no clues as to its usage. However, in the 12th century Vikings returning from the Crusades broke into the tomb searching for treasure. They found nothing but left behind one of the largest collections of runic graffiti anywhere in the world, as well as carvings of a dragon, serpent and walrus. Many of the inscriptions are pretty basic, along the lines of 'Thorfinn wrote these runes', but some are more intriguing, such as 'Many a woman has come stooping in here no matter how pompous a person she was'.

A guide gives you an excellent overview of the chamber's mysterious architectural attributes, but the fact remains that the history of this extraordinary place is still largely unsolved – something that obviously adds to the site's attraction. Unfortunately, you do not get the chance to spend very much time in the chamber, so you are unlikely to uncover any great secrets.

Orphir

On the southern shores of West Mainland, overlooking Scapa Flow, is the scattered community of Orphir, which has a few sights worth visiting, especially if you're heading across to Hoy from the ferry terminal at **Houton**, a little further west. The main point of interest in Orphir is the **Orkneyinga Saga Centre** ⓘ *all year daily 0900-1700, free*, where a small exhibition and video introduces the saga, written circa 1200, possibly by an Icelander, which tells the history of the Viking Earls of Orkney from around AD 900 to 1200, when the islands became a part of Scotland rather than Norway. As you would expect, there's plenty of gore and Machiavellian goings-on, including an assassination attempt that went disastrously wrong, when a poisoned shirt meant for Earl Harold was unwittingly and fatally worn by his brother Paul instead.

For details of ferries to Hoy and Flotta, see page 353. For details of buses to Houton, see page 364.

Behind the centre is **The Earl's Bu**, looking out across Orphir Bay south to Cava Island. These are the 12th-century foundations of the home of the Norse Earls of Orkney written about in the saga. Inside the cemetery gates is a section of the circular church built by Haakon and modelled on the rotunda of the Church of the Holy Sepulchre in Jerusalem.

Markwick Head

At the southern end of Birsay Bay are the wild and spectacular 300-ft-high cliffs of Marwick Head, topped by the distinctive **Kitchener Memorial**, erected after the First World War to commemorate Lord Kitchener and the crew of the *HMS Hampshire*,

A fascinating feature of Maes Howe is that the winter solstice sun sets directly over the Barnhouse Stone, half a mile away, and shines down the entrance passage of Maes Howe and on to the back wall of one of the cells.

Sitting pretty

One of Scotland's most distinctive pieces of furniture is the Orkney chair. Starting as a 'needs must' object, the chairs were originally made of driftwood and backed with oat straw. Their half-moon shape ingenuously gave protection from the many draughts in a house. Very often the back was extended upwards into a cowl, so that the chair looked rather like an upended cradle. This gave added protection. It has often been said that what an Orkney man could not make from straw was not worth having. The straw, which came from black oats, was particularly important as trees are not plentiful on Orkney. Even today bringing timber from across the Pentland Firth is an expensive business. Heavy storms still yield windfall wood but not such a variety as in the days of wooden ships which too often perished in these waters.

which was sunk by a German mine off the coast in 1916 with the loss of all but 12 of her crew. Marwick Head is also an **RSPB Reserve**, and during the nesting season in early summer is home to many thousands of guillemots, razorbills, kittiwakes and fulmars, as well as a few puffins.

A mile inland, by the Loch of Isibister, is another RSPB reserve, **The Loons**, an area of marshland where you can see breeding and migrating wildfowl and waders. Further east, between Boarhouse Loch and Hundland Loch, is the **Kirbuster Farm Museum** ⓘ *Mar-Oct Mon-Sat 1030-1300 and 1400-1700, Sun 1400-1900, free*, the last surviving Orkney blackhouse which was inhabited till the 1960s and gives an insight into 19th-century rural life on the islands.

Birsay

At the far northwestern corner of the Mainland is the parish of Birsay, which was a favourite residence of the Earls of Orkney in Viking times as well as the first seat of the Bishop, before the building of St Magnus Cathedral in Kirkwall. Earl Thorfinn the Mighty lived here (1014-1064) and built Orkney's first cathedral, **Christchurch**, for the new Bishop.

In the centre of the village are the ruins of the **Earl's Palace** ⓘ *T01856-721205, open at all times, free*, built by the infamous Earl Robert Stewart in the late 16th century, and once described as "a sumptuous and stately dwelling". Not much remains today, but enough to give some idea of the sheer scale of the place. Close by is **St Magnus church**, built in 1760 on the site of an earlier church, which in turn was built on the foundations of what is believed to be the original Christchurch. Also in Birsay, just south of the A966 and A967 junction, is **Barony Mills** ⓘ *Apr-Sep daily 1000-1300 and 1400-1700, £1.50*, the last working water-powered mill in Orkney.

Lying half a mile off the coast near the village is the **Brough of Birsay** ⓘ *open (when tides permit) mid-Jun to 30 Sep daily 0930-1830, £2.50, concession £2, children £1, phone the Earl's Palace (see above)*. The tidal island, managed by **Historic Scotland**, juts out into the north Atlantic and is visible from several other points all the way down the west coast of the Mainland. It is only accessible for a couple of hours at low tide (times available from Kirkwall and Stromness tourist offices) but, if possible, it is best seen at the end of the day, as the sun sets – you'll probably have the whole island to yourself. Pick your way over the causeway and wander at your leisure (but don't forget the tide!) amongst the remnants of a Pictish, and then Viking, community. The island was an important Pictish settlement from around the sixth century, and many artefacts have been found here. Some of these can be seen at the small ticket office at the entrance to the island. The Brough was also the site of an important Viking settlement, and there are extensive remains, including the 12th-century **St Peter's church** where St Magnus was buried after his murder on Egilsay. You can also walk out to the island's lighthouse along the top of the cliffs and see puffins – amongst other migrating seabirds – and possibly minke whales, pilot whales and killer whales.

Evie and the Broch of Gurness

Nine miles northwest of Kirkwall is the tiny village of Evie. A track leads from the village towards the coast, past a sandy beach, to the **Broch of Gurness** ⓘ *T01856-751414, Apr-Sep daily 0930-1830, £3, concession £2.30, children £1.* Standing on a lonely, exposed headland on the north coast, with warm, gentle views across towards the island of Rousay, this is the best-preserved broch on Orkney, thought to date from around 100 BC. It is surrounded by an Iron Age village whose houses are also remarkably well preserved, with the original hearths, beds, cupboards and even a toilet still in evidence. The broch and village were occupied by the Picts right up until Viking times, around AD 900. Many Pictish artefacts have been found on the site, and the grave of a ninth-century Norse woman was also discovered.

To the southwest of Evie is the **Birsay Moors RSPB Reserve**, and at **Lowrie's Water** on Burgar Hill there's a bird-hide from where you can watch breeding red-throated divers. Also on Burgar Hill you'll see several huge aerogenerators built to take advantage of Orkney's fierce winds.

East Mainland and South Ronaldsay

▸▸ *pp358-366. See map, page 342.*

→ *Phone code: 01856.*

The East Mainland is mainly agricultural land and though it contains little of the amazing archaeological wealth of its western counterpart, there are some attractive fishing villages, fine coastal walks and many poignant reminders of Orkney's important wartime role. Linked to East Mainland by a series of causeways, South Ronaldsay is the southernmost of the Orkney islands, only 6 miles from the Scottish mainland across the stormy Pentland Firth, the most dangerous stretch of water in the British Isles. A small passenger ferry crosses to Burwick on the southern tip of the island from John O' Groats.

Deerness

There is not much to see inland on the road running southeast from Kirkwall past the airport, but head on towards the Deerness Peninsula and you will be richly rewarded by a truly serene, gentle beauty. There are sandy bays, which make for very pleasant short walks and picnics (if you can find a sheltered spot), jutting cliffs and a great variety of birdlife. The peninsula makes the West Mainland seem positively crowded by comparison, and is one of the best places on the Mainland to 'get away from it all'.

▲ When the weather's good, the view southwest from Sandside Bay to the Isle of **Copinsay** (an RSPB reserve) is glorious, and is a perfect example of the whale-like properties that have been attributed to the Orkneys by the islands' most famous poet George Mackay Brown. There is a footpath following the coast from Sandside Bay to Mull Head (a nature reserve) and round the tip of the peninsula to the **Covenanters Memorial** (1679), a 5-mile circular walk.

▲ If you continue along the B9050, the road ends at The Gloup car park at Skaill Bay, from where it's a 200-yard walk to **The Gloup**, a dramatic collapsed sea cave, separated from the sea by a land bridge about 80 yards wide. The word comes from the Old Norse 'gluppa', meaning chasm, the local name for a blow-hole. A network of signposted footpaths covers the northeastern part of the peninsula and there are circular walks of between 2 and 5 miles which start from The Gloup car park. At the northeastern tip is **Mull Head**, a clifftop nature reserve which is home to guillemots, shags, fulmars, razorbills, terns and skuas.

On the south coast of East Mainland, near the northern end of the Churchill Barriers, is the old fishing village of **St Mary's**, once a busy little place but largely forgotten since the building of the causeways. To the east of the village is the **Norwood Museum** ⓘ *T01856-781217, May-Sep Tue-Thu and Sun 1400-1700 and 1800-2000, £3, children £1*, which features the large and eclectic antique collection of local stonemason Norris Wood.

The Churchill Barriers

East Mainland is linked to a string of islands to the south by four causeways, known as the Churchill Barriers, built on the orders of Prime Minister Winston Churchill during the Second World War as anti-submarine barriers to protect the British Navy which was based in Scapa Flow at the time. Churchill's decision was prompted by the sinking of the battleship *HMS Royal Oak* in October 1939 by a German U-boat which had slipped between the old blockships, deliberately sunk during the First World War to protect Scapa Flow, and the shore. After the war, a road was built on top of the causeways, linking the islands of Lamb Holm, Glimps Holm, Burray and South Ronaldsay to Mainland.

On the island of **Lamb Holm** camps were built to accommodate the men working on the construction of the barriers, many of whom were Italian Prisoners of War. The camps have long since gone, but the Italians left behind the remarkable **Italian Chapel** ⓘ *open all year during daylight hours, free*, fittingly known as 'The Miracle of Camp 60'. It is difficult to believe that such a beautiful building could have been made using two Nissen huts, concrete and bits of scrap metal, and the chapel's enduring popularity with visitors is a tribute to the considerable artistic skill of the men involved. One of them, Domenico Chiochetti, returned in 1960 to restore the interior paintwork.

Burray

On the island of Burray the road passes the **Orkney Fossil and Vintage Centre** ⓘ *Apr-Sep daily 1000-1800, Oct Wed-Sun 1030-1800, £2*, which houses a bizarre collection of old furniture, various relics and 350 million-year-old fish fossils found locally. There's also an archive room where you can browse through old books and photographs, and a coffee shop. Not really something to go out of your way for, but worth a look if it's raining.

South Ronaldsay

The main settlement is the picturesque little village of **St Margaret's Hope** on the north coast. It is said to be named after Margaret, Maid of Norway, who died near here in 1290 at the age of seven while on her way to marry Prince Edward, later Edward II of England. She had already been proclaimed Queen of Scotland, and her premature death was a major factor in the long Wars of Independence with England. The word 'hope' comes from the Old Norse word *hjop* meaning bay.

The village smithy has been turned into the **Smiddy Museum** ⓘ *May and Sep daily 1400-1600, Jun-Aug 1200-1600, Oct Sun 1400-1600, free*, with lots of old blacksmith's tools to try out. The museum also features a small exhibition on the annual **Boys' Ploughing Match**, a hugely popular event first held circa 1860. Each year in August, boys from the village (and now girls as well) dress up as horses and parade in the village square (prizes are given for the best costume). Afterwards the boys and their fathers, or grandfathers, head for the **Sand of Wright**, a few miles west, and have a ploughing match with miniature ploughs, which are usually family heirlooms. The categories are: best ploughed ring, best feering or guiding furrow, neatest ends and best-kept plough. This sheltered beach is well worth a visit anyway, ploughing or no ploughing. The views stretch in a spectacular 180° panorama, south

The graveyard of Scapa Flow

The huge natural harbour of Scapa Flow has been used since Viking times, and in the years leading up to the First World War the Royal Navy held exercises there, sometimes involving up to 100 ships. But Scapa was vulnerable to attack, and over the course of the war defences were improved with 21 blockships sunk at the eastern approaches. Scapa Flow continued to be used as the main naval base in the Second World War, but the blockships were not enough to prevent a German U-boat from torpedoing *HMS Royal Oak*, and the huge task of building the Churchill Barriers began, see page 351.

Scapa Flow's most famous incident happened at the end of the First World War, when, under the terms of the Armistice, Germany agreed to surrender most of her navy. Seventy-four German ships were interred in Scapa Flow, awaiting the final decision, but as the deadline approached the German commander, Admiral Von Reuter, gave the order for all the ships to be scuttled, and every ship was beached or sunk.

The scuttled German fleet, however, proved a hazard for fishing and a massive salvage operation began. Today seven German ships remain at the bottom of Scapa Flow – three battleships and four light cruisers – along with four destroyers and a U-boat and the Royal Navy battleships *HMS Royal Oak* and *HMS Vanguard*, which blew up in 1917.

across the Pentland Firth to Caithness on mainland Scotland, west to South Walls and Cantick Head on Hoy, and northwest to Flotta and the west Mainland. It is yet another good place to spot snipe, lapwing, curlew and redshank. Arctic terns nest nearby and you can spot them diving dramatically as they fish in the bay.

To the north of the beach is the **Howe of Hoxa**, a ruined broch where Earl Thorfinn Skull-Splitter was buried in AD 963, according to the Orkneyinga saga. South Ronaldsay is a good place to buy local arts and crafts, and there are several workshops dotted around the island. One of these is the **Hoxa Tapestry Gallery** ① *T/F01856-831395, Apr-Sep Mon-Fri 1000-1730, Sat and Sun 1400-1800, £2, concession £1.50, children under 12 free*, 3 miles west of the village on the way to Hoxa Head. Local artist Leila Thompson's huge tapestries are well worth a visit; you may not like the style, but you cannot help but marvel at the extraordinary amount of work and dedication involved in their creation; many of them take years to finish.

At the southeastern corner of South Ronaldsay is the **Tomb of the Eagles** ① *Apr-Oct daily 1000-2000, Nov-Mar 1000-1200, £3.50*, one of the most interesting archaeological sights on Orkney. The 5000-year-old chambered cairn was discovered by local farmer and amateur archaeologist, Ronald Simison, whose family now runs the privately owned site and museum. The contents of the tomb were practically intact and there were up to 340 people buried here, along with carcasses and talons of sea eagles, hence the name. Various objects were also found outside the tomb, including stone tools and polished stone axes.

Before visiting the tomb you can handle the skulls and other artefacts at the small 'museum' in the family home, which actually means their front porch! Then you walk for about five or 10 minutes through a field to visit a **burnt mound**, a kind of Bronze Age kitchen, where Ronald Simison will regail you with all manner of fascinating insider information about the excavation process, before walking out along the cliff edge to the spectacularly sited tomb which you must enter by lying on a trolley and pulling yourself in using an overhead rope. It is particularly eerie being here because there is generally no-one else around, and as you haul yourself into the tomb, with the sound of the North Sea crashing into the cliffs nearby, you wonder to yourself how those buried here met their fate. There is also a lovely, but generally wild and windy, walk back along the cliffs, via a different route, to the car park.

Hoy

» pp358-366. See map, page 342.

→ *Phone code: 01856.*

To the southwest of the Mainland is Hoy, the second largest of the Orkney islands. The name is derived from the Norse *Ha-ey*, meaning High Island, which is appropriate as much of the island is more reminiscent of the Scottish Highlands than Orkney, with only the southern end being typically low and fertile.

Ins and outs

There are two ferry services to Hoy, both run by Orkney Ferries, T01856-850624. Transport on Hoy is limited to a minibus between Moaness Pier and Rackwick. There are shops/petrol stations in Lyness and Longhope. » *For further details, see Transport, page 364.*

Sights

Orkney's highest point, **Ward Hill** (1571 ft) is in the north of the island, and the north and west coasts are bounded by spectacular cliffs. At **St John's Head**, the sheer cliffs rise out of the sea to a height of 1150 ft, the highest vertical cliffs in Britain. The island is most famous for its **Old Man of Hoy**, a great rock stack rising to 450 ft. This northern part of Hoy forms the **North Hoy RSPB Reserve** which has a variety of habitats ranging from woodland to tundra-like hilltops and sea cliffs. The reserve is home to a huge variety of birds including great skuas and Arctic skuas, Manx shearwaters and puffins. On the hills there are red grouse, curlews, golden plovers and dunlins, peregrine falcons, merlins, kestrels and even golden eagles. Mountain hares are quite common and, if you are lucky, you can also see otters along the Scapa Flow coastline.

On the southeast coast of the island is **Lyness**, site of a large naval base during both world wars when the British fleet was based in Scapa Flow. Many of the old dilapidated buildings have gone, but the harbour area is still scarred with the scattered remains of concrete structures, and there's also the unattractive sight of the huge oil terminal on **Flotta**. Lyness has a large **Naval Cemetery**, last resting place of those who died at Jutland, of Germans killed during the scuttle and of the crew of *HMS Royal Oak*. The old pump house opposite the new ferry terminal is now the **Scapa Flow Visitor Centre** ⓘ *T01856-791300, Mon-Fri 0900-1630, Sat and Sun 0930-1630, free*, a fascinating naval museum with old photographs, various wartime artefacts, a section devoted to the scuttling of the German fleet, and an audio-visual feature on the history of Scapa Flow. It's well worth a visit. At South Walls, overlooking Longhope Bay, is **Hackness Martello Tower and Battery** ⓘ *T01856-811397, Apr-Sep daily 0930-1830, £3.50, concessions £2.50, children £1.50*, which, along with another tower on the north side at Crockness, was built in 1815 to protect British ships in Longhope Bay against attack by American and French privateers while they waited for a Royal Navy escort on their journey to Baltic ports.

▲ Hoy's great attraction is its many excellent walking opportunities. A minibus runs between **Moaness Pier**, where the ferry from Stromness docks (see Transport, page 364), and **Rackwick**, on the opposite side of the island, but it's a lovely two-hour walk by road through beautiful **Rackwick Glen**, once populated by crofters and fishermen, but now quiet and isolated. On the way you'll pass the **Dwarfie Stone**, a huge, lonely block of sandstone which is the only rock-cut tomb in Britain, dating from around 3000 BC. Be careful, though, because, according to Sir Walter Scott, this is the residence of the Trolld, a dwarf from Norse legend. On your return you can take a different route through a narrow valley between the **Cuilags** (1421 ft) and **Ward Hill** and **Berriedale Wood**, the most northerly woodland in Britain. The most popular walk on Hoy is the spectacular three-hour hike from Rackwick to the cliffs facing the **Old Man of Hoy**. The path climbs steeply westwards from the old crofting township, then turns northwards before gradually descending to the cliff edge.

Rousay, Egilsay and Wyre » *pp358-366.*

See map, page 342.

These three islands lie a short distance off the northeast coast of Mainland and, together with Shapinsay to the southeast, are the closest of Orkney's North Isles to Kirkwall.

Rousay

Rousay is a hilly island about 5 miles in diameter and is known as the 'Egypt of the North' due to the large number of archaeological sites. It also has the important **Trumland RSPB Reserve**, home to merlins, hen harriers, peregrine falcons, short-eared owls and red-throated divers, and its three lochs offer good trout fishing.

A road runs right around the island, and makes a pleasant 13-mile bike run, but most of the sights are within walking distance of the ferry pier on the southeast side of the island, where most of the 200 inhabitants live. A short distance west of the pier by the road is **Tavershoe Tuick**, an unusual two-storey burial cairn, which was discovered in the late 19th century by Mrs Burroughs, wife of General Traill Burroughs who lived at nearby Trumland House. A mile further west, to the north of the road, is **Blackhammer**, a stalled Neolithic burial cairn. Further west still, and a steep climb up from the road, is **Knowe of Yarso**, another stalled cairn, which contained the remains of at least 21 people. The tomb dates from around 2900 BC.

Most of the island's archaeological sights are to be found along the **Westness Walk**, a mile-long walk which starts from Westness Farm, about 4 miles west of the ferry pier, and ends at the remarkable Midhowe Cairn. The walk is described in detail in a leaflet available from the tourist offices on Mainland. **Midhowe Cairn** is the largest and longest cairn – over 100 ft long and 40 ft wide – excavated on Orkney thus far and, like the others, dates from around 3000 BC. Housed in a large building to protect it, the 'Great Ship of Death', as it is known, contained the remains of 25 people in crouched position on or under the eastern shelves of the chamber, which is divided into 12 sections. Standing nearby, with fine views across to Eynehallow island, is **Midhowe Broch**, one of the best-preserved brochs on Orkney, occupied from around 200 BC to AD 200. The outer walls are about 60 ft in diameter and up to 14 ft high in places.

Another fine walk on the island is around the **RSPB Reserve**. A footpath leads from beside Trumland House and heads up towards the island's highest point, **Blotchnie Fiold** (821 ft). A leaflet describing the walk is available from the tourist offices on Mainland or the **Trumland Orientation Centre** by the pier.

Egilsay and Wyre

These two small islands lie to the east of Rousay and have a couple of interesting sights of their own. Egilsay's claim to fame is the murder here of St Magnus in 1115, and a **cenotaph** marks the spot where he was slain. The island is dominated by the 12th-century **St Magnus church**, built on the site of an earlier church, possibly as a shrine to St Magnus. It is the only surviving example on Orkney of a round-towered Viking church. Much of Egilsay has been bought by the RSPB as a reserve to preserve the habitat of the very rare **corncrake**, whose distinctive rasping call may be heard.

Tiny Wyre features strongly in the Viking saga as the domain of Kolbein Hruga, and the remains of his 12th-century stronghold, **Cubbie Roo's Castle**, and nearby **St Mary's chapel** can be still be seen. Kolbein's home, or Bu, was on the site of the nearby Bu Farm, where the poet Edwin Muir (1887-1959) spent part of his childhood. The far westerly point of the island, known as **the Taing**, is a favourite haunt of seals, and a great place to enjoy a summer sunset.

Shapinsay » pp358-366. See map, page 342.

→ *Phone code: 01856.*

Less than 30 minutes by ferry from Kirkwall is the fertile, low-lying island of Shapinsay, home to **Balfour Castle**, an imposing baronial pile which is in fact a Victorian extension to a much older house called 'Cliffdale'. The house, and the rest of the island, was bought by successive generations of the Balfour family who had made their fortune in India. Today the castle is the home of the Zawadski family and is run by them as a hotel (see Sleeping, page 360). The castle can also be visited as part of an inclusive half-day tour, which leaves from Kirkwall on Wednesday and Sunday at 1415, from mid-May to mid-September. Arrange in advance at the tourist office in Kirkwall. The ticket includes a guided tour of the castle and gardens (at 1500) and complimentary tea and cakes in the servants' quarters. You can also take an earlier ferry if you wish to explore the island.

In the village, built by the Balfours to house their estate workers, is the **Shapinsay Heritage Centre** ⓘ *T01856-711258, Mon, Tue and Thu-Sat 1200-1630, Wed and Sun 1200-1730, free*, in the old Smithy. It has displays on the island's history and a tearoom upstairs. There's a pub in the village, in the old gatehouse. Also a couple of shops and a post office.

A mile north of the village is the **Mill Dam RSPB Reserve**, where there's a hide overlooking a loch from which you can see many species of wildfowl and waders. Four miles from the pier, at the far northeast corner of the island, is the well-preserved **Burroughston Broch**, with good views of seals sunning themselves on the nearby rocks. West of here, at **Quholme**, is the original birthplace of the father of Washington Irving, author of *Rip Van Winkle*.

Eday » pp358-366. See map, page 342.

→ *Phone code: 01857.*

The long, thin and sparsely populated island of Eday lies at the centre of the North Isles group. It is less fertile than the other islands, but its heather-covered hills in the centre have provided peat for the other peatless Orkney islands. Eday's sandstone has also been quarried, and was used in the building of St Magnus Cathedral in Kirkwall.

Ins and outs

There are flights from Kirkwall to Eday airport, called London Airport. There are also ferries from Kirkwall. The ferry pier is at Backaland, on the southeast of the island, a long way from the main sights. **Orkney Ferries** ⓘ *T01856-872044*, also run the Eday Heritage Tour. » *For further details, see Transport, page 364.*

Sights

The island has numerous chambered cairns and these, along with the other attractions, are concentrated in the northern part. They are all covered in the signposted 5-mile **Eday Heritage Walk**, which starts from the Community Enterprises Shop and leads up to the Cliffs of Red Head at the northern tip. The walk takes about three hours to complete, and it's worth picking up the *Eday Heritage Walk* leaflet.

The walk starts at Mill Bay and heads past **Mill Loch**, where an RSPB hide allows you to watch rare red-throated divers breeding in spring and summer. Further north is the huge, 15-ft tall **Stone of Setter**, the largest standing stone in Orkney and visible from most of the chambered cairns. Close by are the **Fold of Setter**, a circular enclosure dating back to 2000 BC, and the **Braeside** and **Huntersquoy** chambered cairns. Further north along the path is **Vinquoy Chambered Cairn**, one of the finest in Orkney and similar to the better-known tomb at Maes Howe, dating from around the same time. An acrylic dome provides light to the main chamber, which can be entered by a narrow underground passage.

The path continues to the summit of **Vinquoy Hill**, which commands excellent views of the surrounding islands of Westray and Sanday. From here you can continue north to the spectacular red sandstone cliffs at **Red Head**, home to nesting guillemots, razorbills and puffins in summer, or head southeast along the coast to **Carrick House** ⓘ *T01856-622260, guided tour Mid-Jun to mid-Sep on Sun from 1400, £2.50, children £1*. Built for Lord Kinclaven, Earl of Carrick, in 1633, the house is best known for its associations with the pirate, John Gow, whose ship ran aground during a failed attack on the house. He was captured and taken to London for trial and hanged. Sir Walter Scott's novel, *The Pirate*, is based on this story.

Sanday

» *pp358-366. See map, page 342.*

→ *Phone code: 01857.*

Sanday is the largest of the North Isles, 12 miles long and flat as a pancake except for the cliffs at Spurness. It is well-named, as its most notable feature is its sweeping bays of sparkling white sand backed by machair, and turquoise seas.

There are numerous burial mounds all over the island, the most impressive being **Quoyness Chambered Cairn**, a 5000 year-old tomb similar to Maes Howe. The 13 ft-high structure contains a large main chamber with six smaller cells opening through low entrances. Most of the burial tombs remain unexcavated, such as those at **Tofts Ness** at the far northeastern tip, where there are over 500 cairns, making it potentially one of the most important prehistoric sites in Britain. At **Scar**, in Burness, a spectacular Viking find was made, and at **Pool** a major excavation has uncovered the remains of at least 14 Stone-Age houses.

Sanday is known for its **knitwear**, though the factory unfortunately closed down. You can still visit the **Orkney Angora craft shop**, in Upper Breckan, near the northern tip of the island.

Stronsay

» *pp358-366. See map, page 342.*

→ *Phone code: 01857.*

The peaceful, low-lying island of Stronsay has some fine sandy beaches and cliffs which attract large colonies of grey seals and nesting seabirds. There are few real sights on this largely agricultural island, but the coastline has some pleasant walks. One of the best is to the **Vat of Kirbister** in the southeast, a spectacular 'gloup' or blow-hole spanned by the finest natural arch in Orkney. To the south of here, at **Burgh Head**, you'll find nesting puffins and the remains of a ruined broch, and at the southeastern tip, at **Lamb Head**, is a large colony of grey seals, lots of seabirds and several archaeological sites.

The main settlement is the quiet village of **Whitehall**, on the northeast coast where the ferry arrives. It's hard to believe it now, but this was one of the largest

Prior to the herring boom, Stronsay's economic mainstay was the kelp industry. By the end of the 18th century 3000 people were employed in the collection of seaweed and the production of kelp for export, to be used in making iodine, soap and glass.

herring ports in Europe. During the boom years of the early 20th century 300 steam drifters were working out of Whitehall and nearly 4000 fishing crew and shore workers were employed. In the peak year of 1924 over 12,000 tons of herring were landed here, to be cured (salted) and exported to Russia and Eastern Europe. Whitehall developed considerably and the **Stronsay Hotel** was said to have the longest bar in Scotland. On Sundays during July and August there were so many boats tied up that it was possible to walk across them to the little island of Papa Stronsay. By the 1930s, however, herring stocks were severely depleted and the industry was in decline. The old Fish Mart by the pier houses a **heritage centre** ⓘ *T01856-616360, May-Sep 1100-1700, free*, with photos and artefacts from the herring boom days. It also has a café and hostel.

Westray

» *pp358-366. See map, page 342.*

→ *Phone code: 01857.*

Westray is the second largest of the North Isles, with a varied landscape of farmland, hilly moorland, sandy beaches and dramatic cliffs. It is also the most prosperous of the North Isles, producing beef, fish and seafood, and supports a population of 700.

The main settlement is **Pierowall**, in the north of the island, but, though it has one of the best harbours in Orkney, the main ferry terminal is at Rapness, on the south coast. Pierowall is a relatively large village for the North Isles and there are shops, a post office, a hotel and the **Westray Heritage Centre** ⓘ *early May to late Sep Tue-Sat 0930-1230 and 1400-1700, £2*, with displays on local and natural history, and a tearoom. Also in the village is the ruined 17th-century **St Mary's church**. About a mile west of the village is Westray's most notable ruin, **Noltland Castle**, a fine example of a 16th-century fortified Z-plan tower-house. To explore inside, pick up the key from the back door of the nearby farm.

There are guided minibus tours of Westray which connect with the ferry at Rapness. See page 363.

There are some great coastal walks on the island, particularly to the spectacular sea cliffs at **Noup Head**, at the far northwestern tip, which are an **RSPB Reserve** and second only to St Kilda in terms of breeding seabirds, with huge colonies of guillemots, razorbills, kittiwakes and fulmars, as well as puffins. The cliffs on the west coast of Westray are 5 miles long and there's an excellent walk down the coast from Noup Head, past **Gentleman's Cave**, used as a hiding place by four Jacobite lairds in 1746. Near the southern end of the walk is **Fitty Hill** (554 ft), the highest point on the island, which you can climb for great views, and the walk ends at **Inga Ness**, where you can also see puffins. The best place to see them is at **Castle o' Burrian**, a sea stack on **Stanger Head**, on the southeastern coast near the Rapness ferry terminal.

Papa Westray

» *pp358-366. See map, page 342.*

→ *Phone code: 01857.*

Tiny Papa Westray, known locally as 'Papay', is best known as being the destination for the world's shortest scheduled flight, from Westray; all of two minutes, or less with a good following wind, and there's no shortage of that.

But there are other reasons to visit this little island, one of the most remote of the Orkney group. Papay is home to Europe's oldest house, the **Knap of Howar** ⓘ *open at all times, free*, which was built around 5500 years ago and is still standing (they knew how to build 'em in those days). It's on the west coast, just south of the airport. Half a mile north is **St Boniface Kirk**, one of the oldest Christian sites in the north of Scotland, founded in the eighth century, though most of the recently restored building dates from the 12th century. Inland from the Knap of Howar is **Holland Farm**, former home of the lairds of the island, where you can rummage around the farm buildings and museum.

Papay is famous for its birds, and **North Hill**, on the north of the island, is an important RSPB Reserve. The cliffs are home to many thousands of breeding seabirds, and at **Fowl Craig** on the east coast you can see nesting puffins. The interior is home to the largest arctic tern colony in Europe, as well as many arctic skuas. If you wish to explore you have to contact the warden at **Rose Cottage** ⓘ *T01857-644240*, who runs regular guided walks.

It's worth taking a boat trip to the even tinier, deserted **Holm of Papay**, off the east coast. This is the site of several Neolithic burial cairns, including one of the largest **chambered cairns** on Orkney. You enter the tomb down a ladder into the main chamber which is nearly 70 ft long, with a dozen side-cells. Contact Jim Davidson, T01856-644259, for boat trips between May and September.

North Ronaldsay

» *pp358-366. See map, page 342.*

Remote and storm-battered, North Ronaldsay is the most northerly of the Orkney islands and a place where old Orcadian traditions remain. It seems remarkable that anyone should live here at all in these extreme conditions, but 'North Ron' – as it is known locally – has been inhabited for many centuries and continues to be heavily farmed. The island's sheep are a hardy lot and live exclusively off the seaweed on a narrow strip of beach, outside a 13-mile stone dyke which surrounds the island. This gives their meat a unique, 'gamey' flavour.

This small, flat island, only 3 miles long, has few real attractions, except to keen ornithologists who flock here to catch a glimpse of its rare migrants. From late March to early June and mid-August to early November there are huge numbers of migratory birds. The **Bird Observatory**, in the southwest corner of the island by the ferry pier, gives information on which species have been sighted, as well as providing accommodation. There are also colonies of grey seals and cormorants at **Seal Skerry**, on the northeast tip of the island.

Sleeping

Kirkwall *p341, map p344*
There are plenty of cheap B&Bs, though most rooms are small without en suite.

A-C Kirkwall Hotel, Harbour St, T01856-872232, www.kirkwallhotel.co.uk. 35 en suite rooms. Open all year. Large imposing building overlooking the harbour. Rooms are reasonably comfortable, service is friendly and efficient and the restaurant serves very good food.

B Ayre Hotel, Ayre Rd, T01856-873001, www.ayrehotel.co.uk. 33 en suite rooms. Open all year. Kirkwall's most upmarket hotel sits right on the harbour front. Very comfortable with a good restaurant and bar to boot.

B-C Foveran Hotel, 2 miles from town on the A964 Orphir road at St Ola, T01856-872389, www.foveranhotel.com. 8 en suite rooms. Open all year. Modern, chalet-style hotel overlooking Scapa Flow. It's friendly and comfortable, and also offers very good food, including a wide range of vegetarian dishes. Probably the pick of the bunch.

D Lav'rockha, Inganess Rd, T01856-876103, www.lavrockha.co.uk. 5 rooms. Open all year. Superior B&B in modern bungalow. Their breakfasts are superb and they also provide a 3-course dinner (TT). Great value. Recommended.

E Whiteclett, St Catherine's Pl, T01856-874193. This B&B is a 200-year-old listed house near the harbour.

E-F Arundel, Inganess Rd, T01856-873148. A modern bungalow offering B&B on a quiet road about a mile from the town centre.

F Kirkwall Youth Hostel, Old Scapa Rd, T01856-872243, www.syha.co.uk. 90 beds. Apr-end Oct. Large SYHA youth hostel about 15 mins' walk from the town centre.

F Peedie Hostel, Ayre Rd, T01856-875477, kirkwallpeediehostel@talk21.com. 8 beds. Smaller and more intimate alternative.

Camping

Pickaquoy Caravan & Camping Site, on the western outskirts of Kirkwall, off the A965, T01856-873535. May-Sep.

Stromness and West Mainland *p345*

B Merkister Hotel, on the shores of Loch Harray, Stenness, T01856-771366, www.merkister.com. 16 rooms. Open all year. A favourite with anglers, but also handy for archaeological sites, this place has a great location, an excellent restaurant and a popular bar. Great deals out of season. One of the best in Orkney. Recommended.
B Stromness Hotel, Pier Head, Stromness, T01856-850298, www.stromnesshotel.com. 42 en suite rooms. Open all year. The best hotel in town is this imposing old building overlooking the harbour. Refurbished a few years back and also offers good-value meals.
C Woodwick House, Evie, T01856-751330, www.woodwickhouse.co.uk. 7 rooms. Lovely old country house in beautiful surrounds. Perfect peace and walks through woods and down bay with views across to the islands. Very good food too (3-course dinner ΨΨΨ). Warmly recommended.
C-D Barony Hotel, Marwick Head, Birsay, T01856- 721327, www.baronyhotel.com. 10 rooms. May-Sep. Standing on the north shore of Boardhouse Loch, is this small hotel specializing in fishing holidays. It's about the only place offering food round here.
D Mill of Eyreland, Stenness, 3 miles from Stromness, T01856- 850136, www.millofeyreland.co.uk. 5 rooms. A lovely converted mill.
D-E Orca Hotel, on Victoria St near the harbour, Stromness, T01856-850447, www.orcahotel.co.uk. 6 en suite rooms. Open all year. Clean and tidy rooms in this small hotel/guesthouse, good self-catering deals available Nov-Mar. Also has a cellar bistro, **Bistro 76**, serving good food.
E Netherstove, Sandwick, T/F01856-841625, www.netherstove.com. 2 rooms. May-Oct. Neat B&B near Skara Brae, overlooking the Bay of Skaill, run by the delightfully named Mrs Poke. Also has 2 self-catering chalets and a cottage (available all year).
E Primrose Cottage, Marwick Head, T/F01856-721384. 3 en suite rooms. Comfortable B&B overlooking Marwick Bay. Evening meal and vegetarian options available.
E Thira, a few miles behind Stromness, at Innertown, T01856-851181. Comfortable, friendly and no-smoking modern bungalow with spectacular views of Hoy. Also serves an excellent cooked breakfast, and will provide a fantastic dinner made from the finest local ingredients on request.
F Brown's Hostel, 45 Victoria St, Stromness, T01856-850661, www.brownshostel.co.uk. 14 beds. This popular independent hostel has no curfew and is open all year round.
F Stromness Hostel, 6 Hellihole Rd, Stromness, T01856-850589, www.stromnesshostel. 3 en suite rooms and 2 8-person dorms. Open Mar-Oct. SYHA hostel a 10-min walk south from the ferry terminal.

Camping

F Eviedale Centre, beside the junction of the road to Dounby, T01856-751270, Apr-Oct, has a small bothy and campsite.
Ness Point T01856-873535. May to mid-Sep. There's a campsite a mile south of the ferry terminal. It's well equipped and has incomparable views, but is very exposed.

East Mainland and South Ronaldsay *p350*

There's a good selection of accommodation in St Margaret's Hope.
B Creel Restaurant & Rooms, Front Rd, St Margaret's Hope, T01856-831311, www.thecreel.co.uk. 3 en suite rooms. Offers comfortable rooms and superb, though expensive, food using deliciously fresh, locally grown ingredients. Dinner only. Good choice.
E Commodore Chalets, St Mary's, Holm, T01856- 781319, www.commodorechalets.co.uk. This place looks like an army barracks but offers good-value accommodation in 9 self-catering chalets and 6 overnight lodges. Good location, with views of Churchill Barriers and within walking distance of Italian Chapel.

For an explanation of sleeping and eating price codes used in this guide, see inside the front cover. Other relevant information is found in Essentials, see pages 40-47.

E Dundas House, South Ronaldsay, T01856-831315. 3 rooms. Refurbished and comfortable B&B 6 miles from St Margarte's Hope with good views. Also can provide evening meal.
E The Fisher's Gill, St Margaret's Hope, T01856-831711. Open all year. Good B&B, also offers seafood dishes.
E Vestlaybanks, Burray village, on the south coast, T01856-731305, vestlaybanks@btinternet.com. B&B also providing evening meals. Great views across Scapa Flow.
F Wheems Bothy, Wheems, Eastside, a few miles southeast of St Margaret's Hope, T01856-831537. Apr-Oct. Organic farm offering cheap and basic hostel accommodation.

Hoy *p353*
There's not much accommodation in the north of the island, except for the 2 SYHA hostels. There are a few very good B&Bs in the south of the island.
D Stromabank Hotel, Longhope, T01856-701494, www.stromabank.co.uk. 4 rooms. Great views across to Orkney and Scottish mainland. Also serves evening meal in summer months. Phone to book.
E Stoneyquoy, south of Lyness, T/F01856-791234, www.visithoy.com. Very comfy B&B on a 200-acre beef farm. Home-made bread and farm eggs for breakfast. The owner, Louise Budge, also runs guided tours of the island. Good value.
E-F Quoydale, 1 mile from ferry, T01856-791001, www.orkneyaccommodation.co.uk. 2 rooms. B&B on working farm, taxis and tours available, also evening meal.
F Hoy Centre, about a mile from Moaness Pier, hoy.centre@orkney.gov.uk. May-Sep. Refurbished hostel sleeping 32 in 8 rooms. Family room also available.
F Rackwick Outdoor Centre, in Rackwick Glen in the north of Hoy. Mid-Mar to mid-Sep. Book ahead for both hostels, contact Orkney Council, T01856-873535.

Rousay, Egilsay and Wyre *p354*
Accommodation is very limited on Rousay, and non-existent on Egilsay and Wyre.
D Taversoe Hotel, near Knowe of Yarso, about 2 miles west of the pier, T01857-821325. 3 rooms. Offers excellent-value meals. Seafood is particularly recommended (closed Mon to non-residents). Bar stocks local ales. Transport available to/from pier.
F Rousay Hostel, Trumland Organic Farm, T01857-821252, trumland@btopenworld.com. Open all year. Half a mile from the ferry, with laundry and camping and beds for 13.

Shapinsay *p355*
L Balfour Castle, T01857-711283, www.balfourcastle.com. 7 rooms. Live the life of a would-be aristo in this impressive baronial Victorian mansion, set in 70 acres of wooded grounds and still part-family home. The price includes dinner. The castle has a private chapel and a boat is available for birdwatching and fishing trips for residents.
D-E Hilton Farm House, T01857-711239, www.hiltonorkneyfarmhouse.co.uk. 3 rooms. This B&B is a little humbler but very comfortable, also offers evening meals as well as transport round the island and fishing tours.

Eday *p355*
C Sui Generis, Redbanks, 2 mins' walk from ferry, T01857-622219, www.suigenerisfurniture.co.uk. 2 rooms. Beautiful guesthouse/furniture maker, rooms are truly imaginative and unlike anything else you'll encounter in this part of the world. 3-course dinner is £15. Recommended.
D Skaill Farm, just south of the airport, T01857-622271. 2 rooms. Jun-Mar. Price includes dinner.
E Blett, Carrick Bay, opposite the Calf of Eday, T01857-622248. 2 rooms. Very friendly. Evening meal and packed lunch provided if you wish. Mrs Poppelwell also has a self-catering cottage for up to 3 nearby.
F Youth Hostel, T01857-622206. Apr-Sep, run by Eday Community Enterprises, just north of the airport. Basic lodging.

Sanday *p356*
D The Belsair, Kettletoft, T01857-600206. 3 rooms. Large house overlooking old harbour. Meals served in bar and dining room.
E Kettletoft Hotel, Kettletoft, T/F01857-600217. Serves meals and has a lively bar.
E Quivals, T01857-600467. One of a handful of B&Bs, this one is run by Tina and Bernie Flett. In addition to the B&B between them they operate a ferry service, run a car and bike hire service (T01857-600418), and Bernie also takes out tours, see Activities and tours, page 363.

F Ayre's Rock Hostel, Ayre, T01857-600410. Good facilities, only 7 beds though.

Stronsay *p356*

D-E Stronsay Hotel, T01857-616213, www.stronsayhotel.com. Has been refurbished and offers cheap bar food.

F Stronsay Bird Reserve, Mill Bay, south of Whitehall, T01857-616363. B&B or you can camp overlooking the wide sandy bay.

F Stronsay Fish Mart Hostel, T01857-616360. Open all year, is well-equipped and comfortable, see page 356. Their café does cheap meals.

F Torness Camping Barn, at the southern end of the island, on the shore of Holland Bay near Leashun Loch, T01857-616314. Very basic and very cheap. They also organize nature walks to the nearby seal-hide. Phone for pick-up from the ferry.

Westray *p357*

C Cleaton House Hotel, about 2 miles southeast of Pierowall, T01857-677442, www.cleatonhouse.co.uk. 7 rooms. This converted Victorian manse is the best place to stay. It serves excellent evening meals (ΨΨΨ) in the restaurant.

D Pierowall Hotel, in the village, T01857-677707, www.orknet.co.uk/pierwall. 6 rooms. Less stylish, but comfortable and friendly. It also serves good-value bar meals, try their fish and chips.

E 1 Broughton, T01857-677726, www.no1broughton.co.uk. 3 en suite rooms. Newly renovated house overlooking the bay in Pierowall, nicely furnished rooms. Packed lunch and light supper on request.

F The Barn, Chalmersquoy, T01857-677214, www.thebarnwestray.co.uk. Sleeps 13 in 5 rooms. High-quality hostel accommodation with great views.

F Bis Geos, T01857-677420, www.bis-geos.co.uk. Hostel housed in rebuilt crofthouse, sleeps 12 in 4 rooms, well-equipped throughout, a great place to stay. Also 2 self-catering cottages.

Papa Westray *p357*

D Beltane House Guest House, T01857-644267. A row of converted farm workers' cottages to the east of Holland House. It offers dinner (ΨΨ). Run by the island community co-operative.

E School Place, T01857-644268. Homely B&B with lunch and evening meals also available.

F Papa Westray Hostel, T01857-644267. Open all year, housed in the same complex at Beltane. A 16-bed hostel run by the island community co-operative which also runs a shop and restaurant serving lunch and evening meals. They have a minibus which takes ferry passengers from the pier to anywhere on the island.

North Ronaldsay *p358*

D-E Garso House, T01857-633244, christine.muir@virgin.net, about 3 miles from the ferry pier. Full-board. They also have a self-catering cottage (up to 5 people) and can arrange car hire, taxis or minibus tours.

E North Ronaldsay Bird Observatory, T01857-633200, www.nrbo.f2s.com. Offers wind-and solar-powered full-board accommodation in private rooms or dorms.

Camping

Phone T01857-633222, for information.

Eating

Eating options are very limited on the islands but most B&Bs and guesthouses will provide evening meals.

Kirkwall *p341, map p344*

ΨΨΨ-ΨΨ Foveran Hotel, see Sleeping, above. Probably the best place to eat in town. Friendly service but not the quickest.

ΨΨ-Ψ Albert Hotel, Mounthoolie La, T01856-876000. Serves decent bar meals made with home-grown produce.

Ψ The Mustard Seed Café, 65 Victoria St. The best place for a snack is this cafeteria-style café, serving substantial soups and main courses in a bustling and very friendly atmosphere.

Stromness and West Mainland *p345*

ΨΨ Hamnavoe Restaurant, 35 Graham Pl, Stromness, T01856-850606. The best place to eat in town. It specializes in local seafood but also offers good vegetarian dishes. Mar-Oct Tue-Sun from 1900.

ΨΨ Julia's café and bistro, opposite the ferry terminal, Stromness. Daily 0730-2200. Very good home-cooked food in pleasant surroundings.

ΨΨ **Stromness Hotel**, see Sleeping, above. Good bar meals.

Ψ **Ferry Inn**, near the ferry terminal, John St, T01856-850280, www.ferryinn.com. Serves decent bar food and has a lively bar.

East Mainland and South Ronaldsay *p350*

ΨΨΨ **Creel Restaurant & Rooms**, Front Rd, St Margaret's Hope, T01856-831311, www.thecreel.co.uk. See also Sleeping, above. Superb, though expensive, food using deliciously fresh, locally grown ingredients. Dinner only. Best on the islands by some way.

Ψ **Murray Arms Hotel**, Back Rd, St Margaret's Hope, T01856-831205. Not exactly haute cuisine but good-value bar meals.

Hoy *p353*

ΨΨ-Ψ **Hoy Inn**, near the pier and post office, T01856-791313. A bar and restaurant which serves good seafood (closed Mon). There's also an RSPB information centre here.

Ψ **Anchor Bar**, T01856-791356, in Lyness serves lunches.

Rousay, Egilsay and Wyre *p354*

ΨΨ-Ψ **Pier Restaurant**, beside the pier, serves food at lunchtime.

North Ronaldsay *p358*

ΨΨ-Ψ **Burrian Inn and Restaurant** is the island's pub, and also serves food.

Bars and clubs

Kirkwall *p341, map p344*

Nightlife in Kirkwall revolves around its lively pubs. Check in *The Orcadian* for folk nights, etc.

Ayre Hotel is quiet and relaxed but also stages folk music nights.

Bothy Bar, Albert Hotel, is a good place for a drink, and sometimes has live folk music.

Stromness and West Mainland *p345*

Stromness Hotel, the **Ferry Inn** and the bar of the **Royal Hotel** are the best places for a drink are in Stromness.

The Mistra, Evie, is the local village shop, post office and pub.

Entertainment

Orkney *p340*

For details of what's going on, buy *The Orcadian*, which comes out on Thu, or pick up a free copy of the Tourist Board's guide.

Kirkwall *p341, map p344*

The town's **New Phoenix** cinema is housed in the **Pickaquoy Leisure Centre**, Pickaquoy Rd, T01856-879900. It also has sports and fitness facilities, and a café and bar.

Festivals and events

Orkney *p340*

There are numerous events which take place throughout the year.

May Orkney Folk Festival, an excellent event, takes place for 3 days at the end of May at various locations throughout the islands. It is one of the most entertaining events of all.

Jun The acclaimed St Magnus Festival is the most prestigious and popular. Held in Kirkwall, it consists of 6 days of music, drama, literature and the visual arts, with many internationally renowned performers.

Jul During this month there are several regattas held on most of the islands.

Aug Festival of the Horse and Boys' Ploughing Match on South Ronaldsay. There are numerous agricultural shows in Aug which culminate in this festival, see page 351.

Sep Orkney Science Festival is during the 1st week in Sep, T01856-876214.

Dec The Ba' (ball), in Kirkwall, is amongst the best-known annual events. It takes place on Christmas Eve and New Year's Eve and is a bit like rugby, basketball and a full-scale riot all rolled into one, and is contested between 2 sides – the Uppies and the Doonies – representing different districts of the town. As many as 200 'players' may be involved, and a game can last up to 7 hrs as both sides attempt to jostle the ball along the streets until one reaches their 'goal' to win the prized ba'.

Shopping

Stromness and West Mainland *p345*

Stromness Books and Prints, 1 Graham Place, Stromness, T01856-850565. A wee

To dive for

Orkney offers some of the best scuba diving in the world, thanks to the part played by Scapa Flow in both world wars, see page 147. The wreckage on the sea bed, combined with the wildlife that teems around it – sea anemones, seals, whales and porpoises – make for great diving. Visibility is sharp and the water is not as cold as you expect, thanks to the Gulf Stream. Several companies offer diving courses for beginners and wreck diving for more experienced divers. This can be as a dive package, including accommodation, meals and boat charter, or simply as a boat charter. Most companies are based in Stromness. See page 363.

For a full list of dive operators, check out www.subaqua.co.uk.

gem. No 3 for 2 offers, no sofas, no internet, no skinny lattes with cinnamon, just books – ones that you might want to read – and an owner who knows what he's talking about. A real bookshop for real people.

Activities and tours

Kirkwall *p341, map p344*
Discover Orkney Tours, T/F01856- 872865, offers tours of Mainland as well as trips to Westray and Papa Westray.
Go-Orkney, South Cannigall, St Ola, T01856-871871, www.orknet.co.uk/orkney-tours, runs a series of tours of Mainland, and also to Hoy and Rousay.

Stromness and West Mainland *p345*
The Diving Cellar, 4 Victoria St, Stromness, T01856-850055, divescapaflow.co.uk, and **Scapa Flow Diving Holidays**, Stromness, T01856-851110, offer liveaboard packages or day trips on the *MV Invincible*, complete with its own bar.
Wildabout Orkney, 5 Clouston Corner, Stenness, T01856- 851011, www.wildabout.orknet.co.uk, offers highly rated wildlife, historical, folklore and environmental tours of Mainland for £16 per person for a full day.

East Mainland and South Ronaldsay *p350*
Orkney Divers, based at the Crowsnest bunk-house, St Margaret's Hope, South Ronaldsay, T01856-831205, www.orkney divers.com.
Scapa Scuba, T01856-851218, www.scapascuba.co.uk, take guided dives for £50, or -day dry-suit training course at Churchill Barriers for £130.

Rousay, Egilsay and Wyre *p354*
Rousay Traveller, T01856-821234, run very informative minibus tours from Jun-early Sep Tue-Fri, meeting the 1040 ferry from Tingwall, they last 6 hrs and cost £15, children £6.

Shapinsay
Orkney Island Holidays, Furrowend, T01856-711373, www.ornkneyislandholidays.com. Paul and Louise Hollinrake have 20 years' experience running week-long all-inclusive tours of the island from their home base.

Eday *p355*
Orkney Ferries, T01856-872044, also run the **Eday Heritage Tour** every Sun from mid-Jun to mid-Sep. It leaves Kirkwall at 0920, returns at 1955 and costs around £30 per person, which includes ferries, guided walks or minibus tour, entry to Carrick House and lunch. Book with **Orkney Ferries** or at the tourist office in Kirkwall.

Sanday *p356*
Quivals, see also Sleeping, above, T01856-600467. A B&B, the owners also run full-day tours of the island, on Wed and Fri, from mid-May to early Sep, departing from Kirkwall pier at 1010 and returning at 1940 (around £30 per person, minimum of 4 people).

Westray *p357*
Discover Orkney, T/F01856-872865, run day tours on a Sun to Westray from Kirkwall, leaving at 0940 and returning at 2015, and costing around £30 per person including ferry. They also run a day tour on a Mon to Papa Westray.

Island Explorer, T01856-677355. There are guided minibus tours of Westray with Alex Costie. They connect with the ferry at Rapness and cost £20 for a full day.
J & M Marcus, Pierowall, also runs bus tours and offers car hire.
Tom Rendall, T01856-677216, for boat trips to Papa Westray.

Transport

Kirkwall *p341, map p344*
Air An 8-seater aircraft flies from Kirkwall daily except Sun to **Stronsay**, **Sanday**, **North Ronaldsay**, **Westray** and **Papa Westray**, and on Wed to **Eday**. To Papa Westray and North Ronaldsay costs £15 one way (£12 with a one-night stay), and to the other islands listed costs £31 one way.

Bus There's a limited bus service around the Mainland. Peace Coaches, T01856-872866, runs regular buses Mon-Sat from Kirkwall bus station to **Stromness**, 30 mins. They also run 3-5 buses a day, Mon-Sat, to **Houton**, 30 mins, which connect with ferries to **Hoy**; and a daily bus, Mon-Sat, to **East Holm**, 25 mins, and **Stromness** via **Dounby**, 55 mins. Causeway Coaches, T01856-831444, runs 2-4 buses a day, Mon-Sat, to **St Margaret's Hope**, 30 mins. Rosie Coaches, T01856-751227, runs buses to **Tingwall** and **Evie**. The bus service between Kirkwall and **Burwick** is run by Shalders Coaches, T01856-850809. Note that there is no Sun bus service on Orkney.

Car Scarth Car Hire, Great Western Rd, T01856- 872125; WR Tullock, Castle St, T01856- 876262, and Kirkwall airport, T01856-875500.

Cycle hire Bobby's Cycle Centre, Tankerness La, T/F01856- 875777. Mountain bikes from £8 per day.

Ferry Northlink Ferries, T01856-885500, www.north linkferries.co.uk, sail from **Aberdeen** to **Kirkwall** (7½ hrs) on Tue, Thu, Sat and Sun at 1700, returning to Aberdeen on Mon, Wed and Fri at 2345. A single passenger fare costs from £15.60 up to £23.80 (peak season, Jul-Aug). A car costs from £61.50 up to £84.40.

Northlink Ferries also sail from **Lerwick** (Shetland) to **Kirkwall** (7 hrs) on Mon, Wed and Fri at 1730, returning on Tue, Thu, Sat and Sun at 2345. A passenger fare costs £13.30-18.80 single. A car costs £47.50-77.80. Return fares are double the cost of single fares and children under 16 travel for 50% discount. Cars should be booked in advance and all passengers must check in at least 30 mins before departure. 2-berth cabins are available on all journeys, costing from £76 up to £105 per trip.

John O'Groats Ferries, T01955-611353, www.jogferry.co.uk, operate a passenger-only (and bicycles) ferry service from **John O' Groats** to **Burwick** (twice a day, 4 times Jul-Aug, 40 mins) on South Ronaldsay, from May to Sep. There are bus connections between **Burwick** and **Kirkwall** (45 mins) for all ferry sailings. Return fare including bus is £26 (bicycles an extra £2). No bookings required. A free bus meets the afternoon train from Thurso at 1445 and connects with the 1600 or 1800 ferry to Orkney. They also operate the Orkney Bus, a daily direct bus/ferry/bus service between **Inverness** and **Kirkwall**, via **John o' Groats**. It leaves Inverness at 0730 and 1420 from Jun-Sep (at 1420 only in May). and costs £46 return. Journey time 5 hrs. Advance booking is essential. Check their website for details of their other tours of Orkney.

Stromness and West Mainland *p345*
Bus There are several buses daily (Mon-Sat) between **Stromness** and **Kirkwall**, 30 mins. On Mon there's a bus between Kirkwall and Birsay with Shalder Coaches, T01856-850809. To get to Skara Brae you'll need your own transport, or you can visit as part of a guided tour (see the TIC), or walk north along the coast from Stromness, via Yesnaby.

Car hire Brass's Car Hire, Blue Star Garage, North End Rd, Stromness, T01856-850850.

Cycle hire from Orkney Cycle Hire, 54 Dundas St, Stromness, T01856-850255.

Ferry Northlink Ferries sail from **Scrabster** to **Stromness** (1½ hrs) 3 times a day Mon-Fri and Sat mid-Jun to mid-Aug, and twice a day on Sat and Sun. Passenger fare is £12.70-14.80 single and a car costs £40.10-44.30. A bus links

Stromness with Kirkwall, via Hatston Ferry Terminal. **Rapstons Coaches** (T01847-893123) and **Citylink** (T08457-550033) operate bus services between Thurso and Scrabster. There are regular bus and train services to Thurso from Inverness.

East Mainland and South Ronaldsay *p350*
Ferry See Kirkwall Transport section for the ferry service from **John o' Groats** to **Burwick**. **Pentland Ferries**, T01856-831226, www.pentlandferries.co.uk, sail from Gill's Bay (between John o' Groats and Thurso) to St Margaret's Hope, 4 times daily 1 Jun- 31 Aug, 3 daily Oct-May, £12 single, £6 child aged 5-16, £28 for a car.

Hoy *p353*
Bus Transport on Hoy is very limited. **North Hoy Transport**, T01856-791315, runs a minibus service between **Moaness Pier** and **Rackwick**, which meets the 1000 ferry from Stromness. Call the same telephone number for a taxi around the island.

Car and bicycle Car and bike hire is available from **Halyel Car Hire**, Lyness, T01856-791240.

Ferry A passenger ferry sails between **Stromness** and **Moaness Pier** in the north (30 mins) 3 times a day Mon-Fri and twice on Fri evenings, twice daily Sat and Sun. There's a reduced winter service (mid-Sep to mid-May). There's also a car and passenger service between **Houton** and **Lyness** and **Longhope** (45 mins) up to 6 times daily (Mon-Sat). There's a limited Sun service from mid-May to mid-Sep.

Rousay, Egilsay and Wyre *p354*
Ferry A small car ferry sails from **Tingwall** (20 mins) to Rousay 6 times a day (Mon-Sat; 5 times on Sun). Most of the ferries call in at Egilsay and Wyre, but some are on demand only and should be booked in advance, T01856-751360. A bus connects **Tingwall** and **Kirkwall**.

Shapinsay *p355*
Ferry The small car ferry makes 6 sailings daily (including Sun in summer) from Kirkwall (25 mins).

Eday *p355*
Air There are flights from **Kirkwall** to Eday with **Loganair**, T01856-872494, on Wed only. There are ferries from **Kirkwall** (1¼ hr to 2 hrs) twice daily via **Sanday** or **Stronsay**.

Taxi and bicycle You can hire a taxi from **Mr A Stewart** by the pier, T01857-622206, or hire bikes from **Mr Burkett** at Hamarr, near the post office south of Mill Loch.

Sanday *p356*
Air There are **Loganair** flights to Sanday from **Kirkwall** twice daily Mon-Fri and once on Sat.

Ferry There's a ferry service twice daily from **Kirkwall** (1½ hrs). The ferry arrives at Loth, at the southern tip of the island, and is met by a minibus which will take you to most places.

Stronsay *p356*
Air There are **Loganair** flights to Stronsay from **Kirkwall**, twice daily Mon-Fri. A ferry service runs from **Kirkwall** (1½ hr) twice daily Mon-Sat (once on Sun), and once daily Mon-Sat from Eday (35 mins).

Car hire and taxi Taxis and island mini-bus tours are available from **M Williamson**, T01857-616255. Car hire and taxis are available from **DS Peace**, T01857-616335.

Westray *p357*
Air Flights to Westray with **Loganair** depart Kirkwall twice daily Mon-Fri and once on Sat.

Cycle hire Mrs Bain at **Twiness**, T01856-677319.

Ferry There's a car ferry service from **Kirkwall** to **Rapness**, on the south coast of the island (1½ hrs). It sails twice daily in summer (mid-May to mid-Sep) and once daily in winter. There's also a passenger ferry from **Pierowall** to **Papa Westray** (see below).

Papa Westray *p357*
Air The famous 2-min flight from Westray leaves twice daily Mon-Sat (£14 one-way). There is also a direct flight to Papay from **Kirkwall** daily Mon-Sat, except Fri (£15 one-way).
Ferry There's a passenger ferry from **Pierowall** on Westray 3-6 times daily (25 mins). The car ferry from **Kirkwall** to Westray continues to Papa Westray on Tue and Fri (2¼ hrs).

North Ronaldsay *p358*
Air There are **Loganair** flights from **Kirkwall** twice daily Mon-Sat, T01856-872494.

Ferry There's a car and passenger ferry which sails from **Kirkwall** (2 hrs 40 mins) once a week (usually Fri) and also on some Sun between May and Sep. Contact **Orkney Ferries** for details, T01856-872044.

Directory

Kirkwall *p341, map p344*
Banks Branches of the 3 main Scottish banks with cash machines are on Broad St and Albert St. Exchange also at the tourist office. **Laundry** The Launderama, Albert St, T01856-872982. Mon-Fri 0830-1730, Sat 0900-1700. **Medical services** Balfour Hospital, Health Centre and Dental Clinic, New Scapa Rd, T01856-885400. **Post** Junction Rd. Mon-Fri 0900-1700, Sat 0930-1230.

Stromness and West Mainland *p345*
Banks There are branches of **Bank of Scotland** and **Royal Bank of Scotland**, both with ATMs, on Victoria St, Stromness. **Laundry** Next to the Coffee Shop, Stromness, T01856-850904. Self-service or service washes.

Shetland

Shetland is so far removed from the rest of Scotland it can only be shown as an inset on maps. It is closer to the Arctic Circle than it is to London and it's easier and quicker to get there from Norway than it is from the UK's capital. This seems entirely appropriate, for Shetland is historically and culturally closer to Scandinavia than Britain. Many of its place names are of Norse origin, and people here still celebrate the vikings in the annual Up-Helly-Aa festival. Modern-day visitors tend to come by plane rather than longboat, and usually bring binoculars, for Shetland is a birdwatcher's paradise. It is home to countless species, many of them seeking refuge from the madding crowds. And, let's face it, there's no better place than here to get away from it all. ►► *For Sleeping, Eating and other listings, see pages 378-384.*

Ins and outs

Getting there

Shetland has good air connections with the rest of the UK. There are regular flights to and from several mainland airports which are operated by **British Airways/Loganair** (see page 340), plus a new twice-weekly service from London Stansted with **Atlantic Airways** (www.atlantic.fo). There are daily car ferry sailings from Aberdeen to Lerwick taking 12 hours and as well as ferries arriving from Kirkwall (Orkney).

Getting around

There is a regular scheduled inter-island service from Tingwall Airport near Lerwick with **Loganair** to Foula, Fair Isle, Papa Stour and Out Skerries. Frequent ferry services also link many of the islands with the Shetland Mainland. Booking is essential for all journeys. Shetland has around 500 miles of good roads, and an extensive public bus service links Lerwick with all towns, villages and tourist sights. There are several bus operators. A *Shetland Transport Timetable*, published by **Shetland Islands Council**,

Shetland

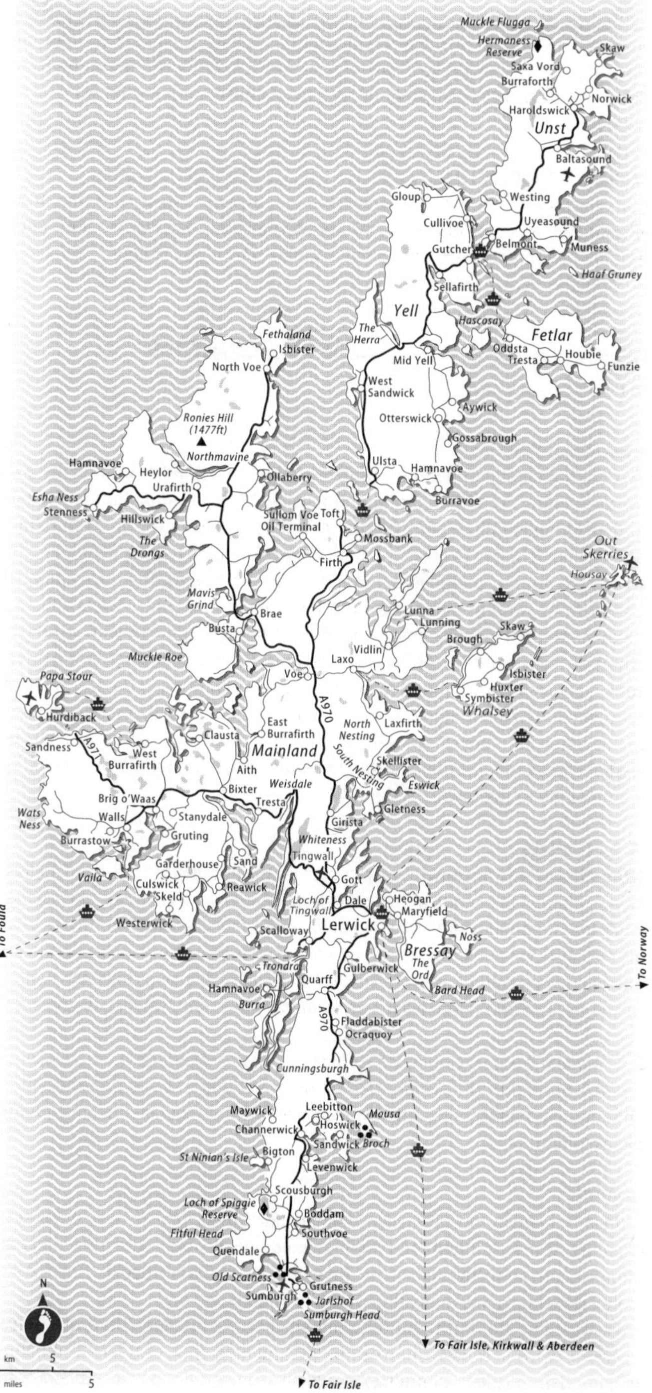

Muckle Flugga
Hermaness Reserve
Skaw
Saxa Vord
Burrafirth
Norwick
Haroldswick
Unst
Baltasound
Gloup
Westing
Cullivoe
Uyeasound
Gutcher
Belmont
Muness
Haaf Gruney
Sellafirth
Yell
Hascosay
The Herra
Fetlar
Oddsta
Tresta
Houbie
Funzie
Fethaland
Isbister
North Voe
Mid Yell
West Sandwick
Aywick
Otterswick
Ronies Hill (1477ft)
Gossabrough
Northmavine
Ulsta
Hamnavoe
Heylor
Ollaberry
Urafirth
Burravoe
Esha Ness
Stenness
Hillswick
Sullom Voe Oil Terminal
Toft
The Drongs
Mossbank
Firth
Out Skerries
Housay
Mavis Grind
Brae
Lunna
Busta
Lunning
Skaw
Brough
Muckle Roe
Vidlin
Laxo
Isbister
Voe
Huxter
Papa Stour
Symbister
Whalsey
Hurdiback
A970
East Burrafirth
North Nesting
Laxfirth
Clausta
Sandness
A971
West Burrafirth
Mainland
South Nesting
Skellister
Aith
Bixter
Weisdale
Eswick
Brig o' Waas
Tresta
Wats Ness
Walls
Stanydale
Gletness
Girista
Burrastow
Gruting
Whiteness
Sand
Tingwall
Garderhouse
Vaila
Culswick
Gott
Reawick
Skeld
Loch of Tingwall
Dale
Heogan
Maryfield
Westerwick
Lerwick
Scalloway
Noss
To Foula
Bressay
Trondra
The Ord
To Norway
Gulberwick
Quarff
Hamnavoe
Bard Head
Burra
A970
Fladdabister
Ocraquoy
Cunningsburgh
Leebitton
Maywick
Mousa
Hoswick
Channerwick
Sandwick
Broch
Bigton
St Ninian's Isle
Levenwick
Scousburgh
Loch of Spiggie Reserve
Boddam
Fitful Head
Southvoe
Quendale
Old Scatness
Grutness
Sumburgh
Jarlshof
Sumburgh Head
N
To Fair Isle, Kirkwall & Aberdeen
0 km 5
0 miles 5
To Fair Isle

 contains details of all air, sea and bus services throughout the islands. It is available from the tourist office in Lerwick. The best way to explore the islands is with your own private car. It is cheaper to hire a car in Lerwick rather than at the airport. Hitching is a feasible way to get around and is relatively safe. Cycling is a good way to experience the islands, though most places are very exposed and the winds can be relentless and punishing (Force 8 is considered pleasant is these parts). » *For further details, see Transport page 382.*

Tourist information

The main tourist office is in Lerwick (see below). Check out the excellent www.visitshetland.com, with links to events, transport, accommodation and local operators. Another recommended portal to all things Shetland is www.shetland-tourism.co.uk.

Lerwick and around

» *pp378-384. See map, page 367.*

→ *Phone code: 01595. Population: 7600.*

Lerwick is the capital and administrative centre of Shetland and the only sizeable town, containing more than a third of the islands' 22,000 population. Though the islands have been inhabited for many centuries, Lerwick only dates from the 17th century, when it began to grow as a trading port for Dutch herring fishermen, thanks to its superb natural sheltered harbour, the Bressay Sound. The town spread along the waterfront, where merchants built their lodberries, which were houses and warehouses with their own piers so that they could trade directly with visiting ships. By the late 19th century Lerwick had become the main herring port in northern Europe. Lerwick has continued to grow: the discovery of oil in the North Sea in the early 1970s led to the building of the Sullom Voe Oil Terminal, and the effect on the town has been dramatic. It is now the main transit point to the North Sea oil rigs and there have been major extensions to the harbour area, bringing increased shipping and prosperity to the town.

Ins and outs

Getting there and around Ferries from Aberdeen arrive at the main Holmsgarth terminal, about a mile north of the old harbour. There's a regular bus service between Lerwick and Sumburgh airport (50 minutes) run by John **Leask & Son**, T01595-693162. Taxis (around £25) and car hire are also available. All island bus services start and end at the Viking bus station, which is on Commercial Road, a short distance north of the town centre. The town is small and everything is within easy walking distance.

TIC ⓘ *Market Cross, Commercial St, T01595-693434, May-Sep Mon-Fri 0800-1800, Sat 0800-1600, Sun 1000-1300, Oct-Apr Mon-Fri 0900-1700*, is an excellent source of information, books, maps and leaflets. They will also change foreign currency and book accommodation.

Lerwick

The town's heart is the attractive **Commercial Street**, which runs parallel to the Esplanade. At the southern end are many old houses and lodberries, and you can continue south along the cliffs to the **Knab** or to lovely **Bain's beach**. *Lerwick Walks* is a leaflet detailing many interesting walks in and around town.

Overlooking the north end of Commercial Street is **Fort Charlotte** ⓘ *Jun-Sep daily 0900-2200, Oct-May 0900-1600, free*, built in 1665 and later rebuilt in 1780 and named after Queen Charlotte, George III's consort. It has since been used as a prison and Royal Naval Reserve base and, though there's little to see in the fort, there are fine views of the harbour from the battlements. One of Lerwick's most impressive buildings is the Victorian **town hall** ⓘ *Mon-Fri 1000-1200 and 1400-1530, free*, on Hillhead. The stained-glass windows of the main hall depict episodes from Shetland's history. Opposite the town hall, above the library, is the **Shetland Museum** ⓘ *T01595-695057, Mon, Wed and Fri 1000-1900, Tue, Thu and Sat till 1700, free*, which gives a useful introduction to the islands' history. Amongst the artefacts on display is a replica of the St Ninian's Isle treasure.

Also in town, in the Galley Shed off St Sunniva Street, is the **Up-Helly-Aa Exhibition** ⓘ *mid-May to mid-Sep Tue 1400-1600 and 1700-1900, Fri 1700-1900, Sat 1400-1600, £3, concession £1.50*. This gives a taste of the famous fire festival held annually in Lerwick on the last Tuesday in January, when there's a torch-lit procession through the town with hundreds of people dressed in Viking costumes (*guizers*). The procession is followed by a replica Viking longship built especially for the event. At the end of the procession the ship is set ablaze when the guizers throw their flaming torches on to it.

A mile west of town are the substantial remains of **Clickimin Broch**, a fortified site occupied from 700 BC to around the fifth or sixth century AD. A path leads to the site from opposite the supermarket on the A970. About a mile north of the ferry terminal is the **Böd of Gremista** ⓘ *Jun to mid-Sep Wed and Sun 1000-1300 and 1400-1700*, free, a restored 18th-century fishing *böd* (booth) which was the birthplace of Arthur Anderson (1791-1868), co-founder of the Peninsular and Oriental Steam Navigation Company, now P&O. One of the rooms features an exhibition on Anderson's life and involvement with P&O.

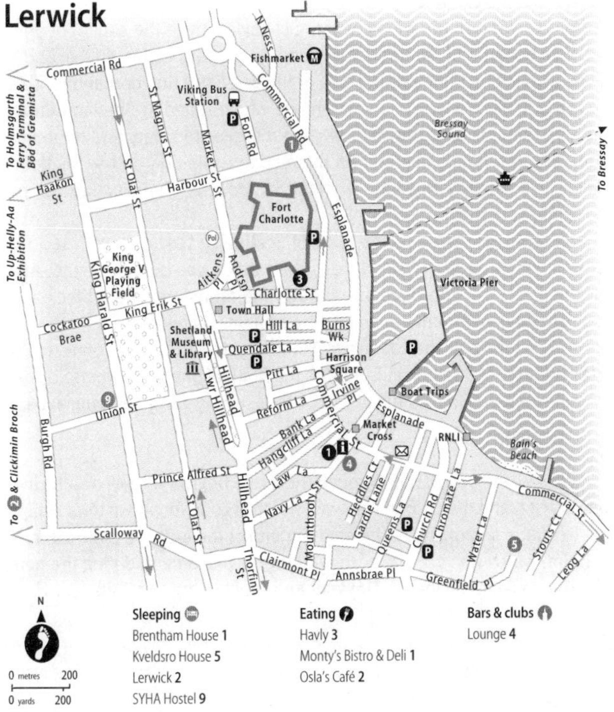

Bressay

Lying to the east of Lerwick across the Bressay Sound is the island of Bressay (pronounced 'bressah'), which creates a sheltered harbour for the capital and led to its establishment as a major trading port. Seven miles long by 3 miles wide, it makes an ideal day trip for cyclists. Another good way to get around is on foot, and there's a fine walk to the top of **Ward Hill** (742 ft), the highest point, from where you get great views of the island and as far afield as Foula and Out Skerries. There are also good coastal walks, particularly along the cliffs from Noss Sound south to **Bard Head, The Ord** and **Bressay Lighthouse**, where you can see large colonies of seabirds. For details of wildlife cruises to Bressay and Noss, see page 382.

Noss

Serious birdwatchers should head for Noss, a tiny, uninhabited island off the east coast of Bressay, which is a **National Nature Reserve** with over 100,000 pairs of breeding seabirds. A walk around the perimeter of the island takes at least three hours but is highly recommended. At the east side is the **Noup of Noss**, where the 600-ft cliffs are packed full of nesting gannets. The reserve is managed by Scottish Natural Heritage who have a small visitor centre at **Gungstie**.

Central Mainland

» *pp378-384. See map, page 367.*

→ *Phone code: 01595.*

The Central Mainland is Shetland's slim waist, and only a few miles of land separates the east and west coast. There's not a huge amount of tourist interest here but the area's history is fascinating and the Scalloway Museum is certainly worth a visit.

Scalloway and around

Six miles from Lerwick on the west coast is Scalloway, once the capital of Shetland and now a fishing port and fish-processing centre. In 1942, during the Second World War, Scalloway became the headquarters of the **Shetland Bus** operations. This was the name given to the Norwegian fishing boats which sailed to Shetland during the night from German-occupied Norway, bringing refugees to safety and returning with ammunition and resistance fighters. An interesting exhibition on the Shetland Bus can be seen at **Scalloway Museum** ⓘ *Main St, May-Sep Tue-Thu 1400-1630, Sat 1000-1230 and 1400-1630, free.*

The harbour is dominated by the ruins of **Scalloway Castle**, built in 1600 by the notorious Earl Patrick Stewart using local slave labour, see box, page 346. After his execution the castle fell into disrepair, though the four-storey main block and one wing remain. Inside, an interpretative display explains its history.

South of Scalloway lie the islands of **Trondra** and **Burra**, now connected to the Mainland by bridges. At Burland on Trondra is the **Spirit of Shetland**, where you can buy knitwear, while on West Burra is the attractive little fishing village of **Hamnavoe**.

Tingwall

North of Scalloway, the B9074 runs through the fertile Tingwall Valley, past a nine-hole **golf course** at Asta, and the **Loch of Tingwall**, which is good for brown trout fishing and also home to swans and otters. At the northern end of the loch is a promontory called **Law Ting Holm**, which was the site of the Althing, or parliament, during the period of Norse rule. Overlooking the loch is **Tingwall Kirk**, built in the late 18th century on the

Catpund Quarries, 10 miles south of Lerwick, to the south of Cunningsburgh, is where soft soapstone was quarried from Neolithic to medieval times, and was used for making a variety of stone implements and utensils.

site of the earlier church of St Magnus which dated back to the early period of Norse Christianity. In the graveyard is the old burial vault with several interesting old grave slabs. Nearby is **Tingwall Agricultural Museum** ⓘ *Jun-Aug Mon-Sat 1000-1300 and 1400-1700, £1.50*, which houses a collection of old crofting implements.

Weisdale

The A971 continues northwest towards Weisdale, a district with some worthwhile attractions. At the head of **Weisdale Voe** the B9075 branches north to **Weisdale Mill** ⓘ *T01595-830400, Wed-Sat 1030-1630, Sun 1200-1630, free*, which now houses the **Bonhoga Gallery**, a purpose-built art gallery featuring varied exhibitions of local, national and international works. There's also a nice café serving snacks. Weisdale Mill was part of the Kergord Estate, known until 1945 as Flemington, and was built from the stones of evacuated crofthouses. Over 300 crofters were forcibly evicted in the mid-19th century during the Clearances, when lairds expanded their more profitable sheep-farming activities. In 1940 the mill was requisitioned as the intelligence and administrative HQ for the **Shetland Bus** operations (see Scalloway, above). The Kergord estate today is the largest area of woodland in Shetland, and attracts a variety of migratory birds.

On the west shore of Weisdale Voe, south of the mill, are the ruins of the house where **John Clunies Ross** (1786-1854) was born. He settled in the Cocos Islands in the Indian Ocean in 1827 and the islands were owned by the Estate of the Clunies Ross family until purchased by the Australian government in 1978. In 1984 the islanders voted to become part of Australia.

The Westside

» *pp378-384. See map, page 367.*

→ *Phone code: 01595. OS Landranger Nos 3 & 4.*

The western Mainland of Shetland, stretching west from Weisdale to Sandness, is known as The Westside. This part of Shetland is notable for its varied landscape of spectacular sea cliffs, rolling green hills, bleak moorland, peaty freshwater lochs and numerous long sea lochs, or voes. This is excellent walking country, with many fine coastal routes, especially around **Culswick** and **Dale of Walls**. It is also great for birdwatching and trout fishing, and there are many opportunities for spotting whales, dolphins and otters.

Stanydale, Walls and Sandness

There are a few interesting archaeological sites here, too. At Stanydale, signposted from the road between the villages of **Bixter** and **Walls**, is the site of a Neolothic settlement with the remains of houses, field boundaries and clearance cairns. Near the **Brig o' Waas**, just north of Walls, is the **Scord of Brouster**, a prehistoric farm site which has been excavated.

The pretty little village of **Walls** (pronounced *waas*) is set around a sheltered natural harbour and is a popular spot with visiting yachts. It also attracts many visitors during its **Agricultural Show** in August, the biggest such event on Shetland. Walls is the departure point for ferries to the remote island of Foula, see below.

Northwest of Walls, the A971 crosses bleak moorland before descending to the crofting township of **Sandness** (pronounced *saa-ness*), surrounded by fertile land and facing little Papa Stour, about a mile offshore. There's a good beach here and also a **woollen spinning mill** ⓘ *Mon-Fri 0800-1700, free*, where you can watch how they spin the famously fine wool into yarn.

Close encounters of the bird kind

Shetland is famous for its birds. As well its huge seabird colonies, the islands attract Arctic species and are an important crossroads for migrating birds. Over 340 species have been recorded on Fair Isle, including rare and exotic birds from Asia and America. Twenty-one out of the 24 seabirds common to Britain breed in Shetland. These can be found around the coastline, but the largest colonies are at the Hermaness and Noss reserves.

Amongst the many species which can be seen are the puffin. About one fifth of Scotland's puffins breed in Shetland. Its cousins in the auk family, guillemots, and razorbills, are also here in abundance during the summer months, along with kittiwakes, shags and that most common of seabirds, the fulmar. Britain's largest seabird, the gannet, can be seen diving spectacularly for fish at Hermaness, Noss, Fair Isle and Foula, while its smallest seabird, the storm petrel, is best seen around dusk on the tiny island of Mousa.

Summer heralds the return of the Arctic tern which breeds along low coastlines, as do the eider, oystercatcher, ringed plover and black guillemot, or tystie, which stays here all year round. The best place to see waders and shelduck are the nutrient-rich tidal mudflats at the Pool of Virkie in the South Mainland.

Many birds breed on agricultural land, and these include the lapwing, skylark, meadow pipit and wheater. The hills and moorland provide breeding grounds for many summer visitors such as that pirate of the skies, the great skua, or bonxie, and the Arctic skua. Another Arctic species, the whimbrel, also nests here, mainly in Unst, Yell and Fetlar. Moorland habitats are also favoured by the curlew, golden plover and merlin, Shetland's only bird of prey, while the lochs are home to large numbers of red-throated divers. Fetlar is home to 90% of the population of one of Britain's rarest birds, the red-necked phalarope.

Many of Shetland's bird habitats are protected as RSPB Reserves and National Nature Reserves, and it is an offence to disturb the birds and their young at or near their nests. You also risk being dive-bombed by some of the more aggressively protective species. For a full list of all species recorded on the islands and more practical birdwatching information, be sure to get a copy of the *Shetland Bird Chart*,by Joyce Gammack, available from the tourist office in Lerwick.

Foula

Lying 15 miles west of the Shetland Mainland, tiny Foula – whose name derives from the Norse *fugl ey*, meaning 'bird island' – is the second most remote inhabited island after Fair Isle. It supports a population of around 40 people, who are greatly outnumbered by the many thousands of seabirds, including a small colony of gannets and the rare Leach's petrel. There are also about 2500 pairs of great skuas, the largest colony in the UK. The island is dominated by its sheer cliffs, which reach their peak at **The Kame** (1220 ft), the second-highest sea cliffs in Britain after St Kilda.

An interesting feature of the island's people is that they still observe the old **Julian calendar**, replaced in 1752 in Britain by the present Gregorian system which deleted 11 days from the year. Remote areas of the country kept to the old calendar, adding an extra day in 1800, which was a leap year, and some parts of Shetland continued to observe festivals 12 days after the dates in the new calendar. The most remote areas kept to the old calendar longest, and the people of Foula still celebrate Christmas on 6 January and New Year's Day on 13 January.

Papa Stour

A ferry sails from West Burrafirth on the Westside, near Sandness, to the little island of Papa Stour, only a mile offshore. The island, which has a population of around 30, is mostly made up of volcanic rock which has been eroded to form an amazing coastline of stacks, arches and caves, most spectacular of which is **Kirstan's Hole**. The island is home to large colonies of auks, terns and skuas, and also has a fascinating history of its own. Pick up the island trails leaflet from the tourist office in Lerwick.

South Mainland » *pp378-384. See map, page 367.*

→ *Phone code: 01950.*

From Lerwick a long, narrow finger of land points south. The main road runs down the east coast for 25 miles till it ends at **Sumburgh Head**, near Shetland's main airport. This southern part of the Shetland Mainland holds the islands' two most important archaeological sights and main tourist attractions.

Isle of Mousa

ⓘ *Mousa Boat Trips, T01950-431367, www.mousaboattrips.co.uk, sails to the island from Leebitton harbour in Sandwick: Apr, May and Sep daily at 1400 (Fri and Sun also at 1230), returning at 1700; Jun-Aug daily at 1230 and 1400, weather permitting. This allows 2½ hours to see the island. Trip takes 15 mins and costs £10, concession £9, children £5. Entry to the broch is free.*

Fifteen miles south of Lerwick, the scattered crofting communities of Sandwick look across to the Isle of Mousa, site of the best-preserved broch in Scotland. This fortified tower was built around 2000 years ago and still stands close to its original height of 45 ft. It's a very impressive structure when you see it from the inside and has chambers, galleries, an internal staircase and a parapet. The broch features in a Viking saga of the 12th century when the mother of Harald, Earl of Orkney, took refuge there with her lover. The Earl, who did not approve of the liaison, laid siege to the broch, but it proved impregnable and he gave up.

Mousa island is also home to many seabirds and waders, most notably the storm petrel, which is best seen at dusk as they return to their nests amongst the beach rocks (Mousa Boat Trips also run late evening trips to see storm petrels from late May to mid-July). You can also see seals on the white sand beach at West Voe. If you have time, it's a good idea to walk right around the coast, starting from the landing stage at West Ham and first heading south to the broch. Watch out for dive-bombing terns.

South of Sandwick

At Hoswick, between Sandwick and Levenwick, is **Da Warp and Weft Visitor Centre** ⓘ *May-Sep Mon-Sat 1000-1700, Sun 1200-1700, free*, which houses an exhibition on weaving, crofting, fishing and island life. Next door is the **Shetland Woollen Company**, where you can buy knitwear. Further south on the east coast, at Boddam, is the **Shetland Crofthouse Museum** ⓘ *May-Sep daily 1000-1300 and 1400-1700, £2*, a restored thatched crofthouse with 19th-century furniture and utensils.

St Ninian's Isle to Quendale

On the west coast, near Bigton village, a signposted track leads to the spectacular sandy causeway (known as a tombolo) which leads to St Ninian's Isle. The tombolo is the best example of its kind in Britain, and you can walk across to the island which is best known for the hoard of Pictish treasure which was discovered in 1958 in the ruins of the 12th-century church. The 28 silver objects included bowls, a spoon and brooches, probably dating from around AD 800, and are now on display in the Royal Scottish Museum in Edinburgh, though you can see replicas in the Shetland Museum in Lerwick.

The west coast south of Bigton is beautiful with long, sandy beaches interspersed with dramatic cliff scenery. On the other side of the road from the long, sheltered beach at **Scousburgh Sands** is the **Loch of Spiggie RSPB Reserve**. The loch is an important winter wildfowl refuge, particularly for Whooper Swans, and during the summer you can see various ducks, waders, gulls, terns and skuas. There's a hide on the northern shore with an information board. Nearby is the **Spiggie Hotel** which offers bar meals, afternoon tea or dinner.

A few miles south of the loch is the village of **Quendale**, overlooking a wide, sandy bay. Here you'll find the beautifully restored and fully working 19th-century **Quendale Mill** ⓘ *May-Sep daily 1000-1700, £2*, the last of Shetland's watermills. Not far from here, between Garth's Ness and Fitful Head, lies the wreck of the Braer oil tanker which ran on to the rocks in 1993. A disaster of epic proportions was averted by the hurricane-force gales which dispersed the huge oil spillage.

Sumburgh and Jarlshof

At the southern tip of Mainland is the village of Sumburgh, site of Shetland's main airport for external passenger flights and for helicopters and planes servicing the North Sea oil industry. South of the airport is Shetland's prime archaeological site, **Jarlshof** ⓘ *T01950-460112, Apr-Sep daily 0930-1830, £4, concession £3, children £1.60*, a hugely impressive place which spans 4000 years of occupation from Neolithic times through Norse settlement to the 16th century. The original Stone Age dwellings are topped by a broch, Pictish wheelhouses, Viking longhouses and, towering over the whole complex, the ruins of a 16th-century mansion. This remarkable site was only discovered at the end of the 19th century when a violent storm ripped off the top layer of turf. Jarlshof is, in fact, not a genuine name, but the exotic invention of Sir Walter Scott in his novel *The Pirate*. A useful guidebook available from the visitor centre helps to bring the place to life.

Another fascinating excavation has been going on nearby, at **Old Scatness**, and looks set to become just as impressive. Since 1995, a team from Bradford University have been working here and have revealed a mound over 5 m high and 80 m in diameter thought to have been inhabited for over 3000 years. In its centre is a an Iron Age tower, or broch. Visitors are welcome at the site (July and August only). For more details visit www.brad.ac.uk.

South of Jarlshof the Mainland ends abruptly at **Sumburgh Head**, an RSPB Reserve. The **lighthouse** on top of the cliff was built by Robert Stevenson in 1821, and the keepers' cottages are now rented out as self-catering accommodation. The lighthouse isn't open to the public, but from its grounds you can see many nesting seabirds such as puffins, kittiwakes, fulmars, guillemots and razorbills. Just to the east of the airport is **Pool of Virkie**, another good birdwatching area.

Fair Isle

» *pp378-384. See map, page 367.*

→ *Phone code: 01595.*

Fair Isle, 24 miles southwest of Sumburgh and 27 miles northeast of North Ronaldsay in Orkney, is the most isolated of Britain's inhabited islands. Only 3 miles long by 1½ miles wide, the island has a population of around 70 and is best known for its intricately patterned knitwear, which is still produced by a co-operative, **Fair Isle Crafts**. Co-operative could be said to sum up the friendly islanders, whose lifestyle is based on mutual help and community effort.

Ins and outs

Getting to Fair Isle requires patience, persistence and a strong stomach to survive the white-knuckle 4½-hour ferry sailing. There are also flights from Tingwall Airport. For more information on Fair Isle visit www.fairisle.org.uk, or call the **National Trust for Scotland** ⓘ *T0141-616 2266, www.nts.org.uk.* » *For further details, see Transport page 382.*

Sights

Fair Isle is a paradise for birdwatchers, and keen ornithologists form the majority of the island's visitors. Celebrity birdwatcher and former Goodie, Bill Oddie, has dubbed it the "the Hilton of the bird world". It stands in the flight path of many thousands of migrating birds, and over 340 species have been recorded here at the **Fair Isle Bird Observatory**, which also offers accommodation and where visitors are welcome to take part. As well as the almost obscenely rich birdlife there are around 240 species of flowering plants, making the island an especially beautiful haven for naturalists. Fair Isle's coastline, especially in the north and west, also boasts some outstanding cliff scenery.

The bird observatory was the brainchild of George Waterston, an ornithologist who first visited in 1935 and then bought the island in 1948 to begin his task of building the observatory. The island was given to the National Trust for Scotland in 1954 and declared a National Scenic Area. It was recently designated a place of outstanding natural beauty and cultural heritage by the Council of Europe. The **George Waterston Memorial Centre** ⓘ *May to mid-Sep Mon and Fri 1400-1600, Wed 1030-1200, donations welcome*, has exhibits and photographs detailing the island's natural history, as well as the history of crofting, fishing, archaeology and knitwear.

North Mainland

» *pp378-384. See map, page 367.*

→ *Phone code: 01806.*

The main road north from Lerwick branches at **Voe**, a peaceful and colourful little village nestling in a bay at the head of the Olna Firth. One branch leads to the Yell car and passenger ferry terminal at **Toft**, past the turn-off to the massive **Sullom Voe Oil Terminal**, the largest oil and liquefied gas terminal in Europe. The other road heads northwest to Brae (see below).

Brae

Brae is not a very pretty place and was built to accommodate workers at the nearby Sullom Voe oil terminal. It does boast a good selection of accommodation and decent facilities, though, and makes a good base from which to explore the wild and wonderful coastal scenery around the Northmavine peninsula to the north. There's also good walking and spectacularly good westerly views around the island of **Muckle Roe** to the southwest, and up the island's small hill, **South Ward** (554 ft). But be careful of the overly protective bonxies, or great skuas, which will attack if you get too close. The island is attached to the mainland by a bridge.

Northmavine

The charmingly named **Mavis Grind**, the narrow isthmus where it's claimed you can throw a stone from the Atlantic to the North Sea, leads into Northmavine, the northwest peninsula of North Mainland. It is one of Shetland's most dramatic and beautiful areas, with rugged scenery, spectacular coastline and wide empty spaces. This is wonderful walking country, and it's a good idea to abandon the car and explore it on foot. **Hillswick Ness**, to the south of **Hillswick** village, is a nice walk, but further west, around the coastline of **Eshaness**, is the most spectacular cliff scenery and amazing natural features, all with unusual and evocative names.

North of the lighthouse are the **Holes of Scraada**, **Grind o' da Navir** and the **Villians of Hamnavoe**, which are not the local gangs but eroded lava cliffs with blowholes, arches and caves. East of Eshaness are the **Heads of Grocken** and **The**

Drongs, a series of exposed sea stacks, which offer superb diving. Further north, overlooking the deep sea inlet of **Ronies Voe**, is the dramatic red-granite bulk of **Ronies Hill** (1477 ft), with a well-preserved burial cairn at the summit. The coastal scenery to the north and west of here is even more breathtaking, but very remote and exposed. You should be well equipped before setting out.

Between Eshaness and Hillswick, a side road leads south to the **Tangwick Haa Museum** ⓘ *May-Sep Mon-Fri 1300-1700, Sat and Sun 1100-1900, free*, which features displays and photographs on the history of fishing and whaling and the hardships of life in these parts.

Whalsay and Out Skerries » *pp378-384. See map, page 367.*

→ *Phone code: 01806.*

South of Voe, the B9071 branches east to Laxo, the ferry terminal for the island of **Whalsay**, one of Shetland's most prosperous small islands owing to its thriving fishing industry, which helps support a population of around 1000. The fleet is based at **Symbister**, the island's main settlement. Beside the harbour at Symbister is the **Pier House** ⓘ *Mon-Sat 0900-1300 and 1400-1700, Sun 1400-1700, free*, a restored böd which was used by the Hanseatic League, a commercial association of German merchants who traded in Shetland from the Middle Ages to the early 18th century. Inside is an exhibition explaining the history of the Hanseatic trade, and general information on the island. One of Scotland's great poets, **Hugh McDiarmid** (Christopher Grieve), spent most of the 1930s in Whalsay, where he wrote much of his finest poetry, until he was called for war work in 1942, never to return. His former home, at Sodom near Symbister, is now a camping böd, see Sleeping, page 378.

The Out Skerries is a small group of rocky islands about 5 miles from Whalsay and 10 miles east of Shetland Mainland. It's made up of three main islands: the larger islands of **Housay** and **Bruray**, which are connected by a road bridge; and the uninhabited island of **Grunay**. The Skerries boast some spectacular and rugged sea cliffs which are home to many rare migrant seabirds in spring and autumn.

Yell, Fetlar and Unst » *pp378-384. See map, page 367.*

Yell

→ *Phone code: 01957.*

Yell, the second largest of the Shetland Islands, was described rather damningly by Shetland-born writer Eric Linklater as 'dull and dark'. And it's true that the interior is consistently desolate peat moorland. But the coastline is greener and more pleasant and provides an ideal habitat for the island's large **otter** population. Yell is also home to a rich variety of birds, and offers some good coastal and hill walks, especially around the rugged coastline of **The Herra**, a peninsula about halfway up the west coast.

At **Burravoe**, about 5 miles east of the ferry terminal at **Ulsta**, is the **Old Haa Museum** ⓘ *T01957-722339, late Apr-Sep Tue-Thu and Sat 1000-1600, Sun 1400-1700, free*, housed in Yell's oldest building which dates from 1672. It contains an interesting display on local flora and fauna and history.

The island's largest village, **Mid Yell**, has a couple of shops, a pub and a leisure centre with a good swimming pool. About a mile northwest, on the hillside above the main road, are the reputedly haunted ruins of **Windhouse**, dating from 1707. To the north is the **RSPB Lumbister Reserve**, where red-throated divers, merlins, great and Arctic skuas and many other bird species come to breed. The reserve is also home to a

In the seas around Whalsay you can see porpoises, dolphins, minke whales and orcas, hence its Viking name which means 'island of whales'.

With nothing between you and the North Pole but water, this is the place to sit and contemplate what it feels like to be at the end of the world...

large population of otters. A pleasant walk leads along the nearby steep and narrow gorge, known as the **Daal of Lumbister**, filled with many colourful flowers. The area to the north of the reserve provides good walking over remote moorland and coastline.

The road continues north past the reserve and around **Basta Voe**, where you can see otters. North of **Gutcher**, the ferry port for Unst, is the village of **Cullivoe**, with some good walks along the attractive coastline.

Fetlar → *Phone code: 01957.*

Fetlar is the smallest of the North Isles but the most fertile, and is known as 'the garden of Shetland'. Indeed, the name derives from Norse meaning 'fat land', as there is good grazing and croftland and a wide variety of plant and bird life. The whole island is good for birdwatching, but the prime place is the 1700 acres of **North Fetlar RSPB Reserve** around Vord Hill (522 ft) in the north of the island. This area has restricted access during the summer months, and visitors should contact the warden at Bealance (T01957-733246). The warden will also let you know if and when you can see the one or two female snowy owls which sometime visit.

The north cliffs of the reserve are home to large colonies of breeding seabirds, including auks, gulls and shags, and you can also see common and grey seals on the beaches in late autumn. Fetlar is home to one of Britain's rarest birds, the **red-necked phalarope**, which breeds in the loch near **Funzie** (pronounced 'finnie') in the east of the island. You can watch them from the RSPB hide in the nearby marshes. Red-throated divers and whimbrel also breed here. The island is also good for walking, and a leaflet describing some of the walks is available from the tourist office in Lerwick.

The main settlement on the island is **Houbie**; on the south coast. Here you'll see a house called Leagarth, which was built by the island's most famous son, Sir William Watson Cheyne, who, with Lord Lister, pioneered antiseptic surgery. Nearby is the excellent **Fetlar Interpretive Centre** ⓘ *May-Sep Tue-Sun 1200-1700, free,* which presents the island's history and gives information on its bounteous birdlife.

Unst → *Phone code: 01957.*

Unst is the most northerly inhabited island in Britain, but there is more to the island than its many 'most northerly' credentials. It is scenically one of the most varied of the Shetland Islands, with spectacular cliffs, sea stacks, sheltered inlets, sandy beaches, heather-clad hills, fertile farmland, freshwater lochs and even a sub-arctic desert. Such a variety of habitats supports over 400 plant species and a rich variety of wildlife. Unst is a major breeding site for gannets, puffins, guillemots, razorbills, kittiwakes, shags, Arctic and great skuas and whimbrels, amongst others, and in the surrounding waters you can see seals, porpoises, otters and even killer whales.

In the east of the island, north of **Baltasound**, is the **Keen of Hamar National Nature Reserve**, 74 acres of serpentine rock which breaks into tiny fragments known as 'debris', giving the landscape a strange, lunar-like appearance. This bleak 'desert' is actually home to some of the rarest plants in Britain. Baltasound is the island's main settlement, with an airport, hotel, pub, post office, leisure centre with pool and Britain's most northerly brewery, the **Valhalla Brewery** which can be visited by appointment, T01975-711348.

To the north of here is the village of **Haroldswick**, home of Britain's most northerly post office, where your postcards are sent with a special stamp to inform everyone of this fact. Here also is **Unst Boat Haven** ⓘ *May-Sep daily 1400-1700, free*, where you can see a beautifully presented collection of traditional boats and fishing artefacts. A little way further north is the **Unst Heritage Centre** ⓘ *same opening hours as Boat Haven and also free*, which has a museum of local history and island life. Nearby is an RAF radar-tracking station at Saxa Vord. The road ends at Skaw, where there's a lovely beach and Britain's most northerly house. The road northwest from Haroldswick leads to the head of **Burra Firth**, a sea inlet flanked by high cliffs, and site of Britain's most northerly golf course.

To the west of Burra Firth is the remote **Hermaness National Nature Reserve**, 2422 acres of dramatic coastal scenery and wild moorland which is home to over 100,000 nesting seabirds including gannets, and the largest number of puffins and great skuas (or 'bonxies') in Shetland. There's an excellent **visitor centre** ⓘ *T01975-711278, daily late Apr to mid-Sep 0830-1800*, in the former lighthouse keeper's shore station, where you can pick up a leaflet which shows the marked route into the reserve, and see the artistic efforts of many of Unst's children. Whilst in the reserve, make sure you keep to the marked paths to avoid being attacked by bonxies; they are highly protective and they will attack if they think that their territory is being threatened.

The views from Hermaness are wonderful, out to the offshore stacks and skerries including **Muckle Flugga**, and then to the wide open North Atlantic Ocean. Muckle Flugga is the site of the most northerly lighthouse in Britain, built in 1857-1858 by Thomas Stevenson, father of Robert Louis Stevenson. The writer visited the island in 1869, and the illustrated map in his novel *Treasure Island* bears a striking similarity to the outline of Unst. Beyond the lighthouse is **Out Stack**, which marks the most northerly point on the British Isles. With nothing between you and the North Pole but water, this is the place to sit and contemplate what it feels like to be at the end of the world.

Sleeping

Lerwick and around *p368, map p369*

Shetland's best accommodation is outside Lerwick, whose hotels are mostly geared towards the oil industry. During the peak months of Jul and Aug and the Folk Festival in Apr, it's a good idea to book in advance. There are several decent guesthouses and B&Bs in town, which are all much of a muchness. The tourist office can supply details.

B **Kveldsro House Hotel**, Greenfield Pl, T01595-692195, www.shetlandhotels.co.uk. The most luxurious hotel in town. Pronounced 'kel-ro', it overlooks the harbour and has an upmarket (and 🍴🍴🍴) restaurant as well as cheaper bar food.

B **Lerwick Hotel**, 15 South Rd, T01595-692166, reception@lerwickhotel.co.uk. 10 mins from the centre, has a reputation for fine cuisine.

C-D **Brentham House**, 7 Harbour St, T01950-460201; www.brenthamhouse.co.uk. 3 en suite rooms and 1 suite. Without a doubt the best guesthouse in town. Luxurious rooms featuring Victorian bathtubs and continental breakfast waiting in the fridge. This is serious pampering at this price. Recommended.

F **SYHA hostel**, Islesburgh House, King Harald St, T01595-692114. Apr-Sep. Clean and well-run.

Camping

Clickimin Caravan & Camp Site, T01595-741000, near Clickimin Leisure Centre and loch on the western edge of the town.

Central Mainland *p370*

C **Herrislea House Hotel**, Tingwall, near the airport, by the crossroads, T01595-840208, www.herrisleahouse.co.uk. 13 en suite rooms. Open all year. Country house in lovely setting with well-furnished rooms. Their **Phoenix** restaurant (🍴🍴🍴) specializes in local meat (Mon-Sat 1830-2045), while the **Starboard café-bar** offers good home cooking daily till 2300, and the **Starboard Tack** bar has live music.

A böd for the night

There is only one youth hostel in Shetland, but budget travellers shouldn't panic. **Shetland Camping Böd** project has developed a network of camping *böds* (pronounced 'burd') which provide basic and cheap digs throughout the islands.

A *böd* was a building used to house fishermen and their gear during the fishing season and the name has been used to describe these types of accommodation which are similar to English 'camping barns'. They are all located in scenically attractive places and each has its own fascinating history. They are very basic and the more remote ones have no electricity or lighting. You'll need to bring a stove, cooking and eating utensils, sleeping bag and torch (flashlight). All *böds* must be booked in advance through the tourist office in Lerwick. They cost £5 per person per night, though they can also be booked for exclusive use by large groups. They are open from the beginning of April till the end of September. There are at present six camping *böds* on Shetland and these are listed in the relevant places.

C-D Inn on the Hill at Westings, Wormadale, near Tingwall, T01595-840242, www.originart.com/westings. 6 rooms. Modern hotel with fairly functional rooms, but great location overlooking Whiteness Voe, decent bar food and real ales, also campsite.
E Hildasay Guest House, Scalloway, in the upper part of the village, T01595-880822. Has disabled facilities and arranges fishing trips.

The Westside *p371*

A Burrastow House, 2 miles southwest of Walls, T01595-809307, www.users.zetnet.co.uk/burrastow-house-hhotel. 5 rooms. Open Apr-Nov. A restored 18th-century house in a stunning location overlooking Vaila Sound, it's full of character and the new Belgain owner cooks magnificent seafood (non-residents welcome but only at weekends). This is the best place to eat on the islands, so you'll need to book ahead. Price includes dinner. Recommended.
The best of the rest is is in Walls, and includes the friendly and comfortable.
E Skeoverick, a mile or so north of Walls, T01595-803349; and **E Pomona**, Gruting, east of Brig o' Waas, T01595-810438.

Camping

Voe House, Walls, is a camping böd – a restored 18th-century house overlooking the village. Open Apr-Sep. Book through Lerwick tourist office.

Foula *p372*

E Leraback, Foula, T01595-753226. Dinner included in the price.

Self catering

There is self-catering accommodation available on Foula, £90-150 per week for a cottage sleeping 4-6 people. Contact Mr R Holbourn, T01595-753232.

Papa Stour *p373*

D North House, on Papa Stour, T01595-873238. Full board (there's no shop on the island).

South Mainland *p373*

There's accommodation in Sandwick, around Sumburgh however it is limited.
C Sumburgh Hotel, next to Jarlshof, T01950-460201, www.sumburgh-hotel.shetland.co.uk. 32 en suite rooms. 19th-century former home of Laird of Sumburgh, great views across to Fair Isle, has 2 bars and restaurant (🍴).
E Barclay Arms Hotel, Sandwick, T01950-431226. A more modest affair but offers evening meals.

Camping

Betty Mouat's Cottage, next to the excavations at Old Scatness and the airport, is this camping böd. It sleeps up to 8 and is open Apr-Sep. Book through Lerwick tourist office.

Fair Isle *p374*
There are a few places to stay on the island, but accommodation must be booked in advance and includes meals. There are no hotels, pubs or restaurants.
C Fair Isle Lodge and Bird Observatory, T01595-760258, www.fairislebirdobs.co.uk. Full-board accommodation in private rooms or in a dormitory (**E**).
D Schoolton, T01595-760250. Full board.
D Upper Leogh, T01595-760248, kathleen.coull@lineone.net. Full board.

Self-catering

Self-catering cottage, T01595-760248, for 4 from £210 weekly.

North Mainland *p375*

B Busta House Hotel, Brae, T01806-522506, www.bustahouse.com. 20 rooms. Open all year. The best place to stay around Brae, and probably the next best on Shetland, is this luxurious and wonderfully atmospheric 16th-century country house overlooking Busta Voe about 1½ miles from Brae village. The superb restaurant (ŢŢŢ) is one of the finest on Shetland, with a selection of malts to match, and there are also meals in the bar.
E Almara, T01806-503261, Upper Urafirth. This friendly and comfortable B&B is the pick of the bunch.
E Westayre, T01806-522368. A working croft on Muckle Roe.

Camping

Johnny Notion's Camping Böd, in Hamnavoe, Northmavine, is reached by a side road which branches north from the road between Hillswick and Eshaness. This is birthplace of John Williamson, known as 'Johnny Notion', an 18th-century craftsman who developed an effective innoculation against smallpox. It's open Apr-Sep and has no electricity. Book through Lerwick TIC.
Sail Loft, in Voe by the pier. This former fishing store is now Shetland's largest camping böd. Open Apr-Sep.

Whalsay and Out Skerries *p376*

Hugh Mc Diarmid's Camping Böd, near Symbister, open Apr-Sep, with no electricity. The former home of this great poet, see page 376.

Yell *p376*

E Hillhead, in Burravoe, T01975-722274.
E Pinewood Guest House, in South Aywick, between Burravoe and Mid Yell,Yell, T01975-702427.
E Prestegaard, Unst, T01975-755234, a Victorian house at Uyeasound on the south coast near the ferry
E-F Post Office, in Gutcher, T01975-744201, which is friendly and welcoming.

Camping

Windhouse Lodge, Yell, a camping böd below the ruins of haunted Windhouse. It's well equipped and open Apr-Sep.

Fetlar *p377*

C-D The Gord, in Houbie, Fetlar, T01975-733227, for dinner, B&B.
E The Glebe, T01975-733242, a lovely old house overlooking Papil Water.

Camping

Gerth's Campsite, Fetlar, T01975-733227, overlooks the beach at Tresta and has good facilities.

Unst *p377*

There's a decent selection of accommodation on Unst.
C Buness House, Unst, T01975-711315,Unst, buness@zetnet.co.uk. Top choice has to be this lovely old 17th-century Haa in Baltasound. Staying here is a bizarre and rather surreal experience, given that you are on the most northerly island in Britain. The house is crammed full of Indian Raj relics, and the stuffed eagle, tiger and leopard skins hanging in the hallway are a wildlife close up almost as impressive, though considerably more unsettling and un-'PC', as the Hermaness Nature Reserve in the north of the island that the family own. The food is excellent (ŢŢŢ) and accommodation comfortable.

For an explanation of sleeping and eating price codes used in this guide, see inside the front cover. Other relevant information is found in Essentials, see pages 40-47.

E Cligera Guest House, Baltasound, T01975-711579.
F Gardiesfauld Hostel, Baltasound, T01975-755259, open Apr-Sep, an independent hostel which also hires bikes.
E Gerratoun, Haroldswick, T01975-711323.

Eating

Lerwick and around *p368, map p369*

Despite a ready supply of fresh local produce, Shetland is a gastronomic desert. The hotels and guesthouses listed above under Sleeping are far and away the best options, especially **Burrastow House** and **Busta House Hotel**.
TTT Monty's Bistro & Deli, 5 Mounthooly St, T01595-696655. The best place to eat in Lerwick. It offers good modern Scottish cooking in a cosy, informal setting. Tue-Sat.
TT Kveldsro Hotel and **Lerwick Hotel** (see Sleeping, above) are the next best choices after **Monty's** for dinner or bar lunch.
T Havly, 9 Charlotte St, 01595-741000. Mon-Fri 1000-1500, Sat 1000-1700. Scandinavian-themed café with nice vibe and good home-cooking.
T Osla's Café, 88 Commercial St, T01595-696005. Cosy café serving a wide range of coffees, pancakes and other snacks and boasting the islands' only beer garden. Mon-Sat until at least 1900, Sun 1200-1600.

Central Mainland *p370*

T Castle Café, New Rd, Scalloway, near the castle. Damn fine chippie serving takeway or sit-in fish and chips to grateful customers.
T Da Haaf Restaurant, T01595-880328. A canteen-style restaurant in the North Atlantic Fisheries college specializing in (yes, you guessed it) seafood. Does a good fish supper, as well as having a more up-market menu for the evenings. Open Mon-Fri 0900-2000.

North Mainland *p375*

TTT Busta House Hotel, Brae, see Sleeping, above. The best option hereabouts.
TT The Booth, Hillswick. Shetland's oldest pub serving food daily in summer.
TT-T Mid Brae Inn, Brae. A good place to eat and serves food daily till 2100.
TT-T Pierhead Restaurant and Bar, Voe, T01806-588332. Serves decent meals.

Yell, Fetlar and Unst *p376*

Eating options are very limited, though most B&Bs will serve evening meals on request.
Baltasound Hotel, Unst, T01975-711334, serves meals and drinks to non-residents.
Hilltop Restaurant and Bar, **Old Haa Museum Café**, and **Seaview Café**, are all on Yell.

Bars and clubs

Lerwick and around *p368, map p369*

Lounge, Mounthooly St near the tourist office. The upstairs bar here is best place for a drink. Local musicians usually play on Sat lunchtimes and some evenings.

Festivals and events

Lerwick and around *p368, map p369*

Jan Up-Helly-Aa. Annual fire festival celebrated on the last Tue in Jan with torch-lit processions, Viking costumes and the burning of a Viking longboat. See also Sights, page 369.
May Shetland Folk Festival Folk music has a strong following in Shetland and this is one of Scotland's top folk events. Over 3 days in early May the islands are alive with the sound of music as musicians from around the globe come to play. See also www.shetlandfolkfestival.com.
Mid-Oct Shetland Accordion and Fiddle Festival. For details of both events, contact the Folk Festival office, 5 Burns La, Lerwick, T01595- 694757.

The *Shetland Times*, www.shetland-times.co.uk, also details what is going on. Also check the tourist board's Events phoneline, T01595-694200.

Shopping

Lerwick *p368, map p369*

Ninian, 110 Commercial St, Lerwick, T01595-696655. Stocks a wide range of Shetland-made products and 'alternative' gifts.

Central Mainland *p370*

Shetland Woollen Company, next to Scalloway Castle, T01595-880243, where you can buy the famous Shetland wool and Fair Isle sweaters.

Activities and tours

Lerwick and around *p368, map p369*

Boat trips

A boat trip to the seabird colonies on Noss and Bressay is unmissable, so don't even think about coming here and not doing it. **Seabirds-and-seals**, T07831-217042, www.seabirds-and-seals.com. Award-winning wildlife cruises run by Jonathan Wills. If you go at the right time of year, you are almost guaranteed to see seals, porpoises and the astounding gannetry on the spectacular cliffs of Noss' east coast. Trips leave at 0930 and 1400 mid-Apr to mid-Sep, weather permitting, £35, £25 under 16, under 5 free.

Shetland Wildlife Holidays, Longhill, Maywick, T01950-422483, www.shetland wildlife.co.uk. Offer a number of guided tours to see the islands' outstandingly rich selection of wildlife; including boat trips to Noss and Bressay, a full-day Hermaness and Muckle Flugga Cruise, and the more upmarket week-long 'Ultimate Shetland' tour, at around £700.

Bus tours

John Leask & Son, The Esplanade, Lerwick, T01595-693162, offers a variety of bus tours costing from around £10 up to £20 depending on the destination.

Sea kayaking

Tom Smith, T01595-859647, www.eakayakingshetland.co.uk. Half-day trips £35, full days £60.

Travel agent

John Leask & Son, Esplanade, T01595-693162.

Transport

Lerwick and around *p368, map p369*

Air Getting to Shetland by air can be expensive. From Aberdeen fares range from around £100 one way, depending on the day and time of year. A return flight from Orkney is around £186. For details of the excellent value Highland Rover Pass, see page 36. Flights from several mainland airports in Scotland and England can be booked through British Airways, T08708-509850, or by calling **Loganair** in Lerwick, T01595- 840246. Shetland's main airport is at Sumburgh, 25 miles south of Lerwick, T01950-460654. Bus services operate linking Sumburgh with Lerwick. There are direct daily flights from **Aberdeen** (4 Mon-Fri; 2 on Sat and Sun), which has frequent services to all other major British airports. There are also direct flights from **Glasgow** (daily), **Edinburgh** (daily except Sun), **London Heathrow** (daily), **Inverness** (Mon-Fri), **Orkney** (daily except Sun), **Wick** (Mon-Sat) and **Belfast** (daily except Sat). There are also international flights to and from **Bergen** and **Oslo** (Norway) on Thu and Sun.

Bus For detailed information on all bus services, call T01595-694100 (Mon-Sat 0900-1715). There are regular daily buses (Nos 3 and 4) to and from **Sumburgh airport** which connect with flights. These buses also stop at several main sights, including **Jarlshof**, **Sandwick** (for Mousa Broch) and **St Ninian's Isle**. Bus No 2 runs to **Scalloway** (Mon-Sat). There are also buses (Mon-Sat) to **Walls**, **Sandness**, **Aith**, **Skeld**, **North Roe**, **Hillswick**, **Vidlin**, **Toft** and **Mossbank**. Buses depart from the Viking bus station.

Car hire Bolts Car Hire, Toll Clock Shopping Centre, 26 North Rd, T01595-693636; **John Leask & Son**, Esplanade, T01595-693162; and **Star Rent-a-Car**, 22 Commercial Rd, T01595-692075, which also has an office at Sumburgh Airport.

Cycle hire Grantfield Garage, North Rd, T692709, Mon-Sat 0800-1300 and 1400-1700.

Ferry Ferry links with the UK are provided mostly by **Northlink Ferries**, T0845-6000449, www.northlinkferries.co.uk. They operate car ferries to Lerwick from **Aberdeen** (and to Kirkwall, Orkney). There are daily sailings from Aberdeen (Mon, Wed and Fri at 1900, Tue, Thu, Sat and Sun at 1700), the journey takes 12 hrs. A single fare for a passenger seat with no accommodation costs from £21.40-31.20 (return fare is double), depending on the time of year. A car costs £82.80-111.30 single. A 2-berth cabin costs from £54.90 in low season up to £105.50 for a 'Premium' berth in high season. Children aged 4-16 travel for half price and under 4s go free.

There are also ferries from **Norway**, **Iceland** and the **Faroe Isles**, see page 32.

There are regular daily car ferries between Lerwick and **Bressay** (£3.10 per passenger, £7.40 per car, 5 mins), **East Mainland** and **Whalsay** (same prices as above, 30 mins), **North Mainland** and **Yell** (same prices as above, 20 mins), **Yell** and **Unst** (free, 10 mins), and **Yell** and **Fetlar** (free, 25 mins). **Noss** can only be visited from late May-late Aug Tue, Wed and Fri-Sun, from 1000-1700. From the 'Wait here' sign overlooking Noss sound on the east side of Bressay an inflatable dinghy shuttles back and forth to Noss during the island's opening hours. In bad weather, call the tourist office, T01595-693434, to check if it's sailing. A postcar service runs once a day (except Sun) from Maryfield ferry terminal to Noss Sound, T01595-820200. There's a less frequent car ferry service between **East Mainland** and **Skerries** (£2.70 per passenger, £3.70 per car, Mon, Fri, Sat and Sun; 1½ hrs), and **Lerwick** and **Skerries** (same prices, Tue and Thu; 2½ hrs). There's also a passenger/cargo ferry service between **West Mainland** and **Papa Stour** (same prices, Mon, Wed, Fri, Sat and Sun; 40 mins), **West Mainland** and **Foula** (£2.70 per passenger, £13 per car, Tue, Sat and alternate Thu; 2 hrs), **Scalloway** and **Foula** (same prices, alternate Thu; 3 hrs), **South Mainland** and **Fair Isle** (same prices, Tue, Sat and alternate Thu; 2½ hrs), and **Lerwick** and **Fair Isle** (same prices, alternate Thu; 4 ½ hrs).

These services are operated by Shetland Council, T01595- 744866, www.shetland.gov.uk. Fares vary according the route. Bookings are also essential. Times and fares are also available from the TIC in Lerwick (see below). Note that fares quoted here are for return trips.

Taxi There are several taxi companies in Lerwick: **6050 Cabs**, T01595-696050; **Sheilds Taxis**, T01595-695276; and **Abbys Taxis**, T01595-696666.

Central Mainland *p370*

Air Tingwall Airport, T01595-840246, has flights to most of the smaller islands, see the Lerwick transport. Getting to and from the airport is straightforward, as regular buses between Lerwick and Westside (see below) stop in Tingwall.

Bus There are several buses Mon-Sat between **Lerwick** and **Scalloway**, operated by **Shalder Coaches**, T01595-880217.

The Westside *p371*

See Lerwick Transport section, above, for details of flights and ferries to the area.

Air Loganair, T01595-840246, operates a regular service from Sumburgh to **Fair Isle**.

Bus There are daily buses to **Walls** from Lerwick, Mon-Sat, with **Shalder Coaches**, T01595-880217. A minibus runs to **Sandness** from **Walls** once a day (except Sun). Contact **Mr P Isbister**, T01595-809268.

Ferry Ferries should be booked with W Clark, T01595-810460.

South Mainland *p373*

See Lerwick Transport section, above, for details of flights and ferries to the area.

Bus There are several daily buses (Mon-Sat; 2-3 on Sun) between **Lerwick**, **Sandwick** and **Sumburgh Airport**. 2 buses daily (Mon-Sat) run to **Quendale** from **Lerwick**, with a change at **Channerwick junction**. There are regular daily buses from **Lerwick**, which stop at the **Sumburgh Hotel**, **Scatness** and **Grutness Pier** (for Fair Isle) en route to the airport.

Fair Isle *p374*

See Lerwick Transport section, above, for details of flights and ferries to the area.

Air A day-return flight allows about 6 hrs on the island. You can also fly from **Kirkwall** on Orkney, which allows 2½ hrs on the island, T01856-872420.

Ferry Ferries should be booked with J W Stout, T01595-760222.

North Mainland *p375*
Bus Regular buses from **Lerwick** to **Brae** and **Hillswick** to the northwest, and **Toft** and **Mossbank** to the north, pass through **Voe** Mon-Sat. Buses from **Lerwick** to **Hillswick** (see below) and to Toft/Mossbank (see under Yell, below) stop in **Brae**. There is a daily bus service from **Lerwick** to **Hillswick** (Mon-Sat), departing at 1710 and arriving at 1825. From there, a feeder service continues to **Eshaness** (20 mins). Contact Whites Coaches, T01806-809443.

Whalsay and Out Skerries *p376*
Ferry There are regular daily car and passenger ferries between **Laxo** and **Symbister**. To book, call T01806-566259. There are daily buses to **Laxo** and and **Vidlin** (see below) from Lerwick, run by Whites Coaches, T01595-809443.

There are ferries to the Skerries from Lerwick and also from Vidlin, about 3 miles northeast of Laxo. For bookings, call G W Henderson, T01806-515226. There are also flights from Tingwall Airport. See the Lerwick Transport section, above, for further details.

Yell, Fetlar and Unst *p376*
Bus 3 buses daily Mon-Fri; 2 on Sat, 1 on Sun run between Lerwick and Toft (1 hr). There's a bus service on Yell which runs between Ulsta and Cullivoe and stops at villages in between, T01975-744214.

Also on Unst, there's an island bus service which runs a few times daily (except Sun) between **Baltasound**, **Belmont** and **Haroldswick**, T01975-711666.

Ferry There are frequent car and passenger ferries from **Toft** on North Mainland to **Ulsta** on the south coast of **Yell**. It's not essential, but a good idea to book in advance, T01975-722259.

There are regular car and passenger ferries between **Oddsta** in the northwest of **Fetlar** and **Gutcher** on **Yell** and **Belmont** on **Unst**. There's a post car service which runs around the Fetlar from the ferry once a day on Mon, Wed and Fri, T01975-733227.

There are regular car and passenger ferries to **Belmont** on **Unst** from Gutcher on Yell. Booking is advised, T01975-722259.

For further details of ferries and flights see the Lerwick transport section above.

Directory

Lerwick and around *p368, map p369*
Banks Bank of Scotland, Clydesdale and Royal are on Commercial St. Lloyds TSB is on the Esplanade. **Embassies and consulates** Denmark, Iceland, Netherlands and Sweden at Hay & Company, 66 Commercial Rd, T01595- 692533; Finland, France, Germany and Norway at Shearer Shipping Services, Garthspool, T01595-692556. **Laundry** Lerwick Laundry, 36 Market St, T01595-693043, closed Sun. Service washes only. **Medical Services** Gilbert Bain Hospital, Scalloway Rd, T01595-743000. Opposite is the Lerwick Health Centre, T01595-693201. **Post** Commercial St (Mon-Fri 0900-1700, Sat 0900-1200), also in Toll Clock Shopping Centre, 26 North Rd.

Background

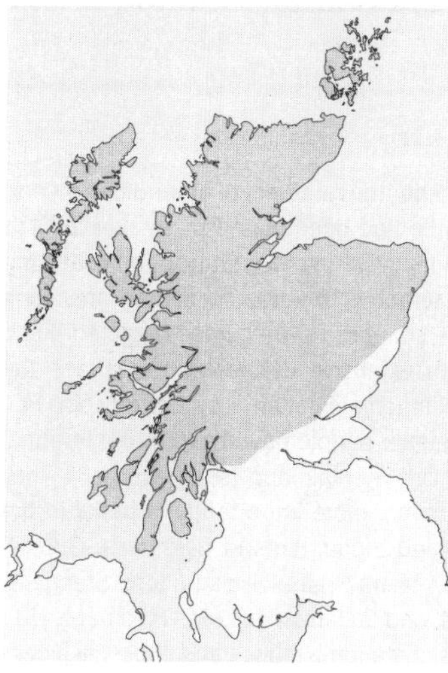

Footprint features

History

Prehistory

Scotland's earliest known inhabitants are the hunter-gatherers of around 6000-5000 BC. By 2000-1500 BC these Mesolithic people had been joined by Beaker folk, so named from their distinctive pottery, and grain-cultivating Megalithic people, arriving by sea via Spain and Portugal, who were tempted to settle by a then prevailing near-Mediterranean climate. Several climate changes for the worse triggered much population movement and also, along with extensive deforestation, caused the formation of peaty soil, now characteristic of much of Scotland, by around 1000 BC.

The pottery and other artefacts of the Beaker people have been found in burial mounds or cairns, such as Maes Howe on Orkney Mainland (see page 348). They suggest a complex social structure and perhaps, more importantly, a belief in the afterlife, as do the prehistoric settlements and monuments in Caithness, Orkney, Shetland and the Outer Hebrides, notably at Skara Brae (see page 347), Stenness, and the Ring of Brodgar on Orkney Mainland, and Callanish on Lewis (see page 310). But throughout Scotland there are hundreds of standing stones and circles, a legacy of the megalithic peoples. In Aberdeenshire surveys reveal precise orientations indicating their use as observatories charting lunar cycles and eclipses. The layout of Clava Cairns, near Inverness (see page 183), bears similarities to the great temple at Newgrange in Ireland. And at Kilmartin in Argyll (see page 183), cup and ring marks, stone alignments and burial cairns, formed in a complete 'landscape temple', suggest a geomantic sophistication that has now been forgotten.

At the beginning of the first millennium BC, Bronze Age traders from far afield were busy around the coasts. Celts arrived from Germany, bringing with them new agricultural technology and weaponry such as swords and shields, which in turn necessitated impressive earthwork defences in the form of hillforts and crannogs (see page 400) as competition for land increased. In about 200-100 BC more Celts arrived with superior iron-working skills, and consequently, more fortifications were also built. The brochs, or towers, the remains of many of which can still be seen dotted along the west coast and in the islands, date from this time (see also page 400).

The Picts and the Romans

Indigenous Iron Age tribes inhabited most of the country and were identified by the Romans as 'Picts' – possibly meaning 'painted, or tattooed, people'. They thwarted Roman imperial ambition in Alba, the land north of the Forth and Clyde, in around AD 80, and a string of Roman military outposts along the Highland line remain from this abandoned campaign. At Fortingall near Aberfeldy, the ancient yew tree is said to mark the birthplace of Pontius Pilate, possibly the son of a Roman soldier who later found preferment in Rome. To add credence to this theory, a gravestone marked 'PP' was found.

Defensive walls built by Emperors Hadrian (circa AD 123 from the Solway Firth to the Tyne) and Antoninus (from the Clyde to the Forth circa AD 143) against the Picts inadvertently set a precedent for the eventual polarization of Scotland and England, beginning around the ninth century, out of the mass of tribal kingdoms. An endlessly disputed border led to centuries of retaliatory raids and devastation on either side.

Picts south of the Antonine wall became semi-Romanized and were known as Britons, kin to the Welsh. Their kingdom of Strathclyde, with a stronghold on Dumbarton Rock near Glasgow, once extended into Lancashire and retained a separate identity into the 11th century. The Lothians, territory of the British Gododdin, was overrun by Anglians from Northumbria. In the seventh century the Anglians challenged the Picts in Alba and were finally defeated at Dunnichen.

Meanwhile an Irish tribe, the Scots, who claimed descent from an Egyptian Pharaoh's daughter, had been settling in Pictish territory in Argyll from around the fourth century. Once in Argyll, the sons of the Scots' leader, Erc, established a kingdom called Dalriada, sharing it between themselves under a high king at Dunadd (see page 128). When their fellow countryman, Columba, arrived in the sixth century on Iona, they were aided in their cause by his diplomatic skills at the hostile Pictish court of King Brude, in Inverness. In the ninth century the Scots under Kenneth MacAlpin took over the Picts. Although their written records were destroyed, or falsified by the conquering Scots, they left a rich legacy of unique sculptured stones denoting a civilized and artistic culture. When Kenneth set up at Scone, and Alba became Scotland, the seven kingdoms of Pictland in the north and east survived as great earldoms.

The early church

Some claim Joseph of Arimathea brought Christianity to Whithorn in Galloway, which had been a religious centre since the first century. Around AD 397 Ninian founded a Christian Mission in Whithorn, along eastern Mediterranean monastic lines vastly different from the Roman model. From here he and countless missionaries such as Kentigern, Moluag and Comgan went north to convert the Picts, as far as St Ninian's Isle in Shetland. Their communities, oak churches and cells are remembered in innumerable place names, wells and simple cross-marked stones, often established on pre-Christian sacred sites.

In AD 563 Columba arrived on Iona (see page 153), where he went on to found the Celtic Church, or the Church of the Culdees, with centres throughout Scotland, which differed in many ways from the Church of Rome. Iona became known as the 'Cradle of Christianity in Scotland', but the arrival of the Vikings inhibited sea travel and the monks were driven from Iona. About this time, the Scots took over the Pictish nation and the Columban church moved to Dunkeld, with Columba's relics transported in the breacbannoch, or Monymusk reliquary. This was carried at Bannockburn and is now in the Museum of Scotland in Edinburgh.

St Andrews later became the principal seat of the church, although Iona retained special status. Communities of Culdees (one of which was at St Andrews) survived into the 13th century, outwith the Columban and later Roman church. These were thought to be adherents of Ninian's church, preserving elements of pre-Christian druid religion.

A common origin for the cross symbol found on both the Pictish cross slabs and the free standing crosses of Iona and Islay is the *chi-ro*, or wheeled cross, as found at Whithorn. However, the enigmatic symbols, vivid hunting scenes and mythical beasts of the Pictish stones found throughout Pictland are unique, and their function remains a mystery. Another mystery is the brief flourishing in the early 13th century of an accomplished school of sculptors around Loch Awe, in Argyll. In ancient burial grounds throughout Knapdale are found grave slabs depicting swords, warriors and foreign ships, thought to mark the graves of the Knights Templar who fled here from France.

The Vikings

Pagan Norsemen in dragonships are first heard of in Argyll in AD 795, the first of many such coastal raids of unimaginable savagery, which included ritual killings. Colonies of monks were not spared; 68 suffered the 'red martyrdom' on Iona in 807, and its library, 'a shop window crammed with the loot of centuries' was a magnet for raiders. By the late ninth century Norsemen had colonized Orkney (see page 346), and from Birsay Palace Earl Sigurd wielded power as far south as Moray. A renegade bunch of mixed Norse and Gaelic ancestry, the Gall-Gaels, appeared in the Hebrides and Galloway. Some of these, like chieftain Ketil Flatnose's family, became early settlers of Iceland.

Once surrounded by aggressive Norse colonies, now also in Dublin and York, the newly formed 'Scotland' survived through a combination of fighting spirit and a network of shifting alliances with the various Norse powers. Some of these alliances were enduring. In the ninth century 'Torf' Einar, credited with introducing peat cutting, founded a dynasty from which sprang the Earls of Angus.

After the Dublin colony collapsed in 1014, a Viking kingdom of 'Man and the Sudreys' (Hebrides) filled the vacuum, and the isles continued to be ravaged by warring Norsemen. By around 1100 Norwegian king Magnus Barelegs' empire included the entire northern and western seaboard. Against this backdrop, pursuing his own interests, appears Somerled, Hebridean hero of Norse-Gaelic blood, progenitor of Clan Donald and the powerful Lordship of the Isles. In 1153 he supported a rebellion against the Scottish crown. Later, in the early 13th century, he built a series of castles around the coast, such as Sween, Tioram, Mingary and Dunstaffnage, which foiled the intermittent attempts made by the Scottish crown to assert control.

The last of the great Norse kings, Hakon, was defeated by the Scots in 1263 at Largs, with the aid of bad winter weather. Orkney and Shetland were only returned to Scotland in the 15th century. A Norse dialect was spoken there into the 18th century, and vestiges of Norwegian law still survive, as does the Viking St Magnus Cathedral in Kirkwall.

Macbeth and the battle for kingship

Macbeth, the earl-king of the vast land of Moray, rose to high kingship with popular support, reigning for a relatively long (1040-1057) and peaceful time with his queen Gruoch, grand-daughter of Kenneth III of Scots. The popular image of Macbeth as portrayed by Shakespeare is, in fact, a false one. The great bard vilified Macbeth in order to please his James VI, who claimed descent from Duncan, Macbeth's rival. But it was Duncan who was the nasty piece of work, and he was slain not at Glamis, as in the play, but on the battlefield, while invading Macbeth's territory. Duncan features in the *Orkneyinga saga*, a Viking history, as Karl Hundason, 'low-born son of the hound'.

Competition for the throne was a part of Pictish custom. A suitable 'tanist' or candidate was elected from anyone whose great-grandfather had been king, and the candidates would then fight it out: in practice, survival of the fittest. This competition for the right to be king was complicated by the ancient dynastic rivalry among the Dalriadic Scots and perpetuated when they merged with the Picts under Kenneth MacAlpin. This later precipitated the Wars of Independence.

One part of Shakespeare's Macbeth which is historical fact is the Birnam Wood incident, when Malcolm, Duncan's son, and his Northumbrian allies used tree branches as camouflage to advance on Macbeth in his Dunsinnan stronghold near Perth. He was later hunted down and slain at Lumphanan by Malcolm's ally, MacDuff, Earl of Fife, and is buried on Iona.

Macbeth, the last truly Celtic king, was also one of the most able early kings. He was the first to establish and implement a fair legal system and, a firm supporter of the Celtic church, he went on pilgrimage to Rome where an Irish monk observed him liberally scattering money to the poor; further evidence of the great disservice done to his memory by Shakespeare.

The Canmores and the Norman conquest

Macbeth's usurper, the uncouth Malcolm III, Canmore (meaning 'big head'), was an illegitimate son of Duncan and a miller's daughter. In 1067 Malcolm married Margaret, a Saxon princess born in Hungary and sister of Edgar Atheling, the English heir to the throne, who had fled north with his family to escape William the Conqueror and the Norman conquest. Margaret was a devout Catholic and was largely responsible for introducing the religious ideas of the Roman Catholic Church into Scotland, for which she was canonized in 1251. In 1072 she founded Dunfermline Abbey and introduced southern manners to the Scottish court.

Malcolm's belligerent instincts were not curbed by the influence of the saintly Margaret, however, and one of his many raids into Northumberland provoked a visit from William the Conqueror. The result was that Malcolm was forced to swear allegiance to William, an oath he didn't take too seriously, as he continued to raid England at whim, but one which would lead to a greater degree of southern interference in Scottish constitutional matters.

The Normans began to exert their influence over Scotland in many other ways. They were granted land as far as the Highland fringes, establishing a feudal system based on loyalty to the crown. The traditional patriarchal tribal culture was eroded, causing constant rebellions in the North and Galloway. The Norman successor to the Scottish throne, David I, like many of his Norman friends, had English estates, acquired through his wife. This wealth built the great Border abbeys and established the Roman church more fully. New parishes and dioceses revolutionized administration, and burghs were founded to develop international trade, attracting Flemish settlers. Society in medieval Scotland became more typically European than England or even France.

One of the depressingly familiar themes running through Scottish history has been the unwillingness of the Scots nobility to resist English ambitions towards Scotland. This has always been their Achilles heel and, in 1290, it provoked a crisis of succession, when the new child queen, Margaret, Maid of Norway, died en route from Norway. Margaret had been recognized as heiress of Scotland, the Hebrides and the Isle of Man, and the planned child marriage to the prince who would become Edward II, son of Edward I, was not to be. Following her death, no fewer than 13 rival contestants materialized. Two main factions emerged: the Balliols and Comyns against the Bruces. But instead of reverting to the traditional method of tanistry, or 'natural selection', the pusillanimous Scots nobles appealed to Edward I of England to adjudicate.

Wallace and Bruce: the Wars of Succession

Edward eventually chose John Balliol, and he was crowned king at Scone in June 1292. Balliol was anxious to prove to his fellow Scots that he was not as weak as they claimed him to be. He negotiated a defensive agreement with the French, the beginning of the Auld Alliance. He then invaded Cumberland in 1296, but in retaliation Edward attacked Berwick and slaughtered its inhabitants. The Scottish army was then defeated at Dunbar, and thereafter the castles of Edinburgh, Roxburgh, Perth and Stirling were captured.

In the same year, Balliol abdicated at Stracathro and went into exile. Edward then destroyed the great Seal of Scotland and, worse still, moved the Stone of Destiny, the traditional crowning throne for all Scottish kings, to Westminster Abbey, where it lay under the Coronation Chair for 700 years. Scotland, as a result, was left in disarray.

However, resistance found a leader in William Wallace, son of a Renfrew laird. He began a revolt against the English in 1297 and built up a substantial army. By September of that year he he had secured a small but strategic victory against English forces at Stirling Bridge. This galvanized support, and he was quickly declared 'Guardian of the Realm'. Following his defeat at Falkirk he was betrayed to Edward by one of the Scots noblemen, captured and taken south to be executed (disembowelled, then hung, drawn and quartered) in Smithfield, London, in 1305.

This stirred Robert the Bruce to take up the cause of independence. Encountering his treacherous rival, 'Red' Comyn, in a Dumfries church, he seized the initiative, stabbing him at the altar. With Comyn dead, and the support of patriotic church leaders, as well as Sir James, 'The Black Douglas', Bruce was able to consolidate his gains, and he was crowned king with full ceremony at Scone before the inevitable blow of Papal excommunication fell. But it was not only that Rome refused to recognize Bruce as king. Edward I, the self-proclaimed 'Hammer of the Scots', was not best pleased, and for the next seven years Bruce was a virtual outlaw fighting a guerrilla campaign against Edward from hiding in the west.

During this time the indomitable Edward died, and Bruce felt bold and confident enough to raid the northern counties of England as far south as Appleby and Richmond. Of his castles captured by the English, only Stirling remained to be wrested from Edward's successor, Edward II. So the scene was set for the most significant battle in Scottish history: in 1314 at Bannockburn, near Stirling, Bruce confronted Edward II's vastly superior army. His incredible victory, aided by Angus Og of the Isles, and a number of Knights Templar recently arrived seeking sanctuary from persecution in France, has ensured him a place in the heart of every patriotic Scot.

Bannockburn brought the Scots a rare victory over their southern enemy, and led to the 'signing' of the Declaration of Arbroath, manifesto of Scotland's independence, in 1320. There followed a temporary peace with England, and Bruce was finally recognized as king by the Pope, before he died in 1329. His friend Douglas, as requested, took Bruce's heart on pilgrimage to the Holy Land, but when Douglas died en route it was returned to Melrose Abbey.

The Stewart dynasty

From Robert the Bruce's title of 'High Steward' sprang the dynasty of Stewart kings. The early Jameses (of whom there were seven in all) all followed a tragic pattern: succeeding as infant kings, imprisoned throughout childhood, and suffering untimely deaths. James I and III were both murdered, and James II blew himself up accidentally with a cannon. Unscrupulous regents frequently took charge, and hugely powerful nobles like the house of Douglas competed both amongst themselves and against the king. James II hot-bloodedly murdered the Earl of Douglas over dinner at Stirling Castle by throwing him out of the window. The Lords of the Isles were put down by the Earl of Mar and his followers in one of the bloodiest battles of all, 'Red Harlaw' near Inverurie. Like the Douglases, they too were finally forfeited, in 1543.

However, the early Stewarts made progress towards rescuing the country from anarchy by laying the foundations for a modern state through a series of constitutional reforms. Mostly cultured and progressive, they found time to write poetry (James I wrote the *King's Quair*), to build Renaissance palaces, and to father sufficient illegitimate 'James Stewarts' to fill numerous ecclesiastical sinecures (James IV and V). James IV was a true Renaissance prince with a glittering court, but a self-destructive streak led to his early death – along with most of the nobility – at Flodden, in 1513, sacrificed for the long-standing 'Auld Alliance' with France.

Mary, Queen of Scots

There is no more tragic and romantic figure in Scottish history than Mary, Queen of Scots. Raised in France for safekeeping as a Catholic, her brief reign was dogged by bad luck, bad judgement and bad timing. She arrived back in Scotland in 1561, a young widow, at the height of Reformation turmoil in which both France and Catholicism were inimical. Something of a loose cannon, she was embroiled in a power struggle not helped by her disastrous choice of husbands. Implicated in the celebrated murder of the first one, her cousin, Henry Lord Darnley, she then swiftly married one of the chief suspects, the Earl of Bothwell, incurring the fury of everyone else. Imprisoned after the Battle of Carberry on the island fortress of Loch Leven, she escaped only to throw herself on the mercy of her cousin Queen Elizabeth I, who, mindful that in Catholic eyes Mary had the better claim to the English throne, locked her up at Fotheringhay for 19 years before deciding to do away with her altogether.

Reformation and the roots of Scottish education

The Reformation, converting the Catholic church to Protestant, came relatively late to Scotland and the motives were as much political as religious, though, of course, in 16th-century terms the two were inextricably linked. A pro-English Protestant faction had grown over decades, opposing the French Catholic Regent, Mary of Guise, and in

1560 a rebel parliament banned Catholic Mass, thus shattering for good the Auld Alliance with France, first formalized in 1295.

The casualties of the Reformation were countless, and included religious buildings, works of art and even whole libraries. It amounted to a complete obliteration of the past over which even today amnesia prevails, though, unlike in England, there were very few martyrs. So began 100 years of bitter struggle to establish the reformed church. Cue the Protestant exile, John Knox, a Calvinist rabble-rouser of dubious character and little diplomacy who was prone to blasting his trumpet off against the 'monstrous regiment of women,' namely Mary, Queen of Scots. Knox's skills as a colourful orator, and his self-appointed role as official historian of the Reformation, have allowed him to eclipse the real hero, Andrew Melville, who sacrificed his career of reforming university education to devote himself to the nuts and bolts of church reform.

Schooling for all as a passport to intellectual freedom and moral probity was a dream of the reformers. While grammar and song schools already existed, by the end of the 17th century most parishes had schools using the bible as textbook. The 'Dominie' (schoolmaster) was, until recently, a hugely influential community figure. Prior to the Reformation the Universities of St Andrews (1412), Glasgow (1451) and Aberdeen (1495) had been established, and Edinburgh University was added to the list in the 1580s.

James VI and the Union of Crowns

After Elizabeth's death, Mary's son became James VI of Scotland. Jacobean Scotland was vibrant and vigorously European. Religious extremists were checked by James VI, the 'Wisest fool in Christendom,' and unprecedented peace allowed Renaissance culture to blossom. But trouble was brewing. In 1603 James VI ascended to the English throne as James I, with the Union of Crowns. At this time the Scottish Parliament had so little power that James VI/I was able to write from his palace in London: "Here I sit and govern Scotland with my pen. I write and it is done." In contrast, the English parliament had begun to assume some genuine power.

Charles I and the Covenanters

James believed in the Divine Right of Kings – the God-given right of monarchs to rule their subjects. It was a belief that he passed on to his son Charles I, who succeeded in 1625 and quickly proved that he had little desire to consult parliament in either Scotland or England. Although he was born in Dunfermline, he showed little interest in Scotland and was essentially an absentee monarch. He did not even bother to come to Scotland to be crowned until 1633, calling a parliament at the same time – and then overseeing proceedings, making sure that the voting went his way.

Charles also showed little tact and diplomacy in matters ecclesiastical, and by reasserting the powers of the bishops he rode roughshod over the authority of the General Assembly of the Church of Scotland. Not surprisingly, the rumblings of revolution could soon be heard.

The struggle of the kirk (church) against the king erupted into full-scale civil war, with hostility towards bishops the recurrent theme. A riot in St Giles in Edinburgh expressed public feeling and resulted in The National Covenant, signed in Edinburgh in 1638, pledging faith to 'the true religion' and affirming the authority of the powerful General Assembly of the Church of Scotland in all matters spiritual. Covenanters and king came to blows, followed by an extremist group of Presbyterians allying with the English parliament against the king, in the Solemn League and Covenant. Battle-hardened Scots flooded back from European campaigns to take up arms.

A supporter of the original Covenant, Montrose, led a spirited but doomed campaign for the king against the extremists. At Ardvreck in Assynt he was betrayed to his arch-enemy 'King Campbell', Duke of Argyll, who gave him a traitor's death in Edinburgh. After the Restoration Argyll found himself on the wrong side and met the same end on the same spot.

What's in a name?

Before Culloden and the Clearances, Highland tradition decreed that a person's loyalty lay first and foremost with their own particular clan, or family group. There were two classes of clan: clansmen of the clan who were related by blood and shared the same family name, and individuals and groups who sought and obtained the protection of the clan. This resulted in a clan having septs, or sub-groups, of different surnames. The first Scots to be organized into clans or kindreds were known in early Scots Gaelic as *cenela*, and there is documentation of three such clans in the 7th-century kingdom of Dalriada, present-day Argyll. Certain features persisted from those early days until the demise of the clan system in the 18th century, in that chiefs could be elected or deposed, but there was no need for kilts or tartans. What held the clan together was a shared knowledge of history and genealogy, reinforced through the oral tradition of the bards and story-tellers. The great majority of 'clan' tartans are, in fact, a 19th-century invention, inspired by the creative genious of Sir Walter Scott.

Civil War

Throughout the 17th century the dark side of religious idealism – fanaticism and paranoia – were epitomized by the 'kirk sessions': courts in which the church conducted an orgy of scapegoating and witch-hunts. Fundamental differences of ideology, constitution and culture between two countries only recently 'twinned', opened cracks in the alliance with the Parliamentarians. The following year Civil War broke out in England, with parliamentarians led by Oliver Cromwell fighting to wrest power from the king. In 1649 Charles was executed and England became a republic. The Scots, however, wanted to keep the monarchy and proclaimed his son, Charles II as their king, despite falling under Cromwell's military 'Protectorate'. Cromwell acted swiftly to bring the country under his control. In 1651 he forbade the Scots from holding their own parliament – forcing them to send representatives to Westminster instead.

Charles II and Restoration

The Commonwealth under Cromwell lasted until 1660, when Charles II was restored to the English throne. The Scottish Parliament was revived and met again in 1661. This time the Presbyterian Covenanters, who had gained such control of Parliament prior to the Commonwealth, were tamed. The Scottish Parliament was again largely run by nobles loyal to the king.

Although Charles II was greeted with wild rejoicing, the reinstatement of the bishops once again proved problematic. Some unconsenting ministers of the church were outlawed and, finding a loyal following, especially in the southwest, they held illegal services, 'Conventicles', in the open air. Crippling fines and brutal persecution from officers of the crown, including Graham of Claverhouse, merely increased their resistance, and many died in the 'Killing Times' as martyrs to high principle.

Religion and the monarchy

Scotland and England continued to disagree, both about the succession and about religion. Charles II's brother and successor, James VII/II, was a Roman Catholic, and in 1687 he tried to introduce more tolerant policies towards Catholics. His actions were seen as a threat to the privileged position held by the Church of England, which since the time of Henry VIII had been the official church in England, and also displeased Presbyterians in Scotland. At first the feeling was that this state of affairs wouldn't last:

James was ageing, and as both his daughters were Protestants, the Protestant succession seemed safe. However, when his heir James Francis Edward was born and brought up as a Catholic, a crisis was precipitated, James was ousted from the throne, and fled ignominiously in 1689. His Protestant daughter, Mary, and her husband William of Orange, were invited to take the throne of England, and were later reluctantly accepted by the Scots under the terms of the Revolution Settlement.

The Darién Scheme

Although both countries shared a monarch, England was growing significantly wealthier than Scotland. Like other European countries, it was thriving economically through trade generated by its colonies. Scotland, however, had no colonies of its own. To remedy this, a monopoly company was founded with the approval of the king, modelled on the English East India Company. Wealthy Scots helped to fund it, but much of the capital was raised in England. However, the English East India Company exercised its considerable power to protect its monopoly. Strings were pulled and the House of Commons soon threatened to prosecute the Scottish company's English directors. The king, who had agreed to its establishment, now came under pressure to oppose it. Not surprisingly, most of the English backers withdrew and Scotland saw it as a matter of national pride to raise the starting capital itself – a sum of £400,000, roughly half the nation's capital.

The intention of the scheme was to establish a permanent colony at Darién, on the Panama Isthmus in Central America. Darién was a strategically important site, and the plan was that goods sent to and from Europe would sail to Panama, be carried overland across the isthmus, then reshipped – the new Scottish company carrying out this lucrative work.

However, the project had not been thoroughly researched. For one thing, the land was owned by Spain, a major world power who King William could not afford to offend. Consequently, he ordered English colonists in the area not to help the Scottish settlers defend their new home against the Spanish. In addition the terrain was hostile (which was why the Spanish had not set up a similar scheme already), and diseases like malaria and yellow fever were rife. Within months large numbers of colonists had died. Another attempt was made and was also unsuccessful, and by 1700 the colony had been abandoned.

The consequences were far reaching. Scotland lost a vast proportion of her wealth; national pride and confidence were dented; and the country lost faith in the dual monarchy. The king had sided with his wealthiest subjects – and Scotland felt betrayed.

Union of Parliaments

While Darién produced much anti-English feeling, a number of Scots began to feel that greater co-operation with England could be economically advantageous. At around the same time a further constitutional crisis was brewing. William of Orange had no children and was to be succeeded by James VII/II's daughter, Anne, who was Protestant. However, Anne had no surviving children and English politicians began to search for an heir – who had to be both Protestant and have Stuart blood. They decided on the Hanoverians, who were descended from the daughter of James VI/I. In 1701 the English parliament passed the Act of Settlement, ruling that on Anne's death the throne should pass to the House of Hanover. In 1702 William died and the throne passed to Anne.

The assumption was that the Scots would follow England's lead and accept the Hanoverian succession. But the nation was still smarting over Darién and, as Anne turned out to have little interest in Scotland, relations were strained. The difficulties over having two separate governments under one monarch would not go away. In 1703 the Scottish parliament passed the Act of Security which declared that on Anne's death Scotland would take a different successor to England, unless some settlement could be agreed upon that restored "the honour and sovereignty of this Crown and Kingdom". They wanted to guarantee the power of the Scottish parliament; the freedom of Scottish religion; and freedom of trade. In addition Parliament ordered people to arm themselves and prepare to fight. It was sabre rattling that the English could hardly ignore.

Although Anne signed the Act of Security, Scotland's triumph was shortlived. England passed the Alien Act, which declared that all Scots except those resident in England should be treated as aliens, and Scottish trade with England was to be blocked. The act was to remain in force until Scotland agreed to make moves towards parliamentary union, or accepted Hanoverian succession.

There were obvious economic advantages to closer ties with England, and Scotland was in a vulnerable position. Not only had the Darién venture weakened the economy, the country was also suffering from several years of harvest failure which had led to famine. Although public opinion was against Union with England, it counted for little. It certainly appealed to many in parliament. Financial inducements were offered – and accepted – causing Robert Burns to comment later that Scotland had been "bought and sold for English gold". The Church of Scotland, initially suspicious of Union, withdrew its objections when it was assured that Presbyterianism would be safeguarded. A propaganda campaign was carried out on both sides of the border, many of the pamphlets being written by the author Daniel Defoe. The English were assured that Union would end the threat of invasion from Scotland; the Scots assured of great economic benefits.

The people were not swayed. There were violent demonstrations in the streets, and riots in Glasgow, Dumfries and Edinburgh. Opponents even went as far as claiming that Union would be sinful. The riots in Edinburgh were particularly violent, causing Defoe, who was acting as a spy for the English government, to say: "A Scots rabble is the worst of its kind. "The Scots – he said – were a hardened and terrible people". Pro-Union MPs were attacked, and plans were made in Lanarkshire to raise an army to march on Edinburgh. But public opinion was not of consequence. The Duke of Argyll, for instance, stated that anti-Union petitions were only fit to make paper kites out of. Although some members, notably Andrew Fletcher of Saltoun, were opposed to Union, the treaty was comfortably passed by the Scottish Parliament on 16 January 1707. It had to be signed in secret in Edinburgh to protect politicians from the mob.

In April the act was passed in the English Parliament, and on 1 May 1707 the Union came into effect. The Kingdoms of Scotland and England were united into Great Britain, though Scotland preserved its separate legal system, educational system and church. Despite the vigorous opposition, threats and bribery assured that a bankrupt and exhausted Scotland was, in popular mythology, sold to England for £398,085 – part compensation for Darién, part wages for the Commissioners who closed the deal.

Jacobite rebellion

Rebellion against the imposition of William of Orange began in 1689, when William's government redcoats clashed with supporters of James II (the Jacobites) at Killiecrankie (see page 72). They were led by Graham of Claverhouse, 'Bonnie Dundee', who was killed in the battle. In 1692 an expedition to weed out the Jacobites in the Highlands resulted in the Glencoe massacre, which provoked unprecedented public outcry (see page 211).

The Act of Settlement was not forgotten, and dwindling trade and increased taxation fuelled dissatisfaction with the Union. A lively underground resistance, aided by long-standing French connections, revolved around the Jacobite court in exile at St Germain. Sympathy also came from English quarters.

Four attempts ensued to reinstate a Stewart monarchy, supported erratically by France, and culminating at Culloden in 1746 (see page 184). Much support came from

Death of the clans

Though events such as Culloden played a part in the demise of traditional clan society as central government sought to 'civilize' the lawless fringes of society, the repression of clanship had already been effected largely by the changing role of the clan elites.

By the time of Bonnie Prince Charlie's defeat at Culloden in 1746, the clan chief had virtually become a commercial landlord, no longer trustee of his people's territory but sole owner of the land, thanks to the new, legalistic definition of clanship agreed between the clan chiefs and central government.

Tensions between the state and the leading clans over authority and control of the Highlands and Islands of Scotland had grown in the wake of the Union of Crowns in 1603 and the government introduced a series of measures, known as the Statutes of Iona, in 1609 (revised 1615-1516) to curb the most disruptive aspects of clanship and to educate the clan chiefs about their responsibilites as members of the Scottish landed classes.

These new laws defined the clan elite's superior position at the expense of their clansmen. Traditionally, all clansfolk considered themselves noble, due to their relationship with previous chiefs, but the Statutes limited the wearing and use of arms, lowered expectations of hospitality, restricted the deployment of military retinues and made the clan elite accountable to the Scottish legal establishment. This had particular impact in the Hebrides where further measures such as the promotion of English schooling and establishment of a Protestant Church ministry were designed to force the pace of change and assimilation.

During the course of the 17th century central government control was further extended. The notion of heritable trusteeship exercised by the clan chiefs over their clan territories gave way to the more legalistic alternative of heritable title, ending the notion of collective land rights and replacing it with sole ownership of the land by the clan elite.

The spread of agrarian capitalism further changed the nature of the clan system, as the clan elites took a more propietorial role in their dealings with their kinsfolk. Civil War, occupation by Oliver Cromwell's forces and the massive ideological and financial pressures generated by the Covenanting movement all had a devastating effect on the Scottish Gaeldom, leading to social dislocation and a polarization of the clans.

The policies of the restored regime of Charles II only made things worse. The increased burden of high taxation and accountability for his clansmen consolidated the tendency of the clan chiefs to act in their own interests rather than as patrons and protectors. So clansmen became alienated from their elite and the role of the chief changed as head of the kindred was subordinated to his role as head of the elite.

The Jacobite Rebellions of 1715 and 1745 not only gave the British government the excuse to wipe out all traces of the clan system, and, in the process, the Gaelic language, in favour of commerce and 'civility', but also provided clan leaders with an excuse to end their traditional responsibilities.

north of the Tay, which was Catholic and Episcopalian country. The term 'Jacobite' popularly denoted anti-establishment and Episcopalian. There was also a linguistic, social and cultural divide between Lowlander and Highlander which had grown since the 15th century.

Highland culture and independence was not diminished after the demise of the Lords of the Isles, hence the rise of the Campbells to enormous power as government agents, dealing for instance with the troublesome MacGregors. Claiming descent from Kenneth MacAlpin, the MacGregors were almost annihilated in 1603, and outlawed until 1774. They played a significant part in the Jacobite rebellions.

Although traditionally indifferent to the monarchy, many clans came out in support of Prince Charles (of 'Bonnie Prince Charlie' fame) in 1745. After defeat at Culloden, savage reprisals were led by the 'Butcher' Cumberland. Rebels were beheaded or hanged, estates confiscated, and the pipes and Highland dress proscribed until 1782. Clansmen were enlisted into Highland regiments and 1150 were exiled, swelling the ranks of emigrants to the colonies. Gaelic culture was effectively expunged and Scotland as a whole suffered disgrace. See also box, page 395.

Rise and fall of Bonnie Prince Charlie

Charles Edward Stuart, the 'Young Pretender', grandson of James II, was born in Italy. First setting foot on Scottish soil aged 23 with seven companions (the Seven Men of Moidart), his forceful personality persuaded reluctant clan chiefs to join him in raising the Standard for his father at Glenfinnan in 1745. Inadequately prepared government troops under 'Johnny Cope' (of ballad fame) enabled his swift progress to Edinburgh, where he held court at Holyrood, dazzling the populace with a grand ball. Edinburgh was charmed but embarrassed.

With sights set on the English throne, he reached Derby. Encouraging reports about panic in London were offset by news of advancing government troops which prompted retreat. The pursuing redcoats were outwitted as far as Inverness, and the ensuing bloodbath at Culloden, though Charles' only defeat, was decisive. Fleeing to the Hebrides, he was given shelter by Flora MacDonald (see page 279) and then spent a summer as a lone fugitive. Despite a £30,000 reward for his capture, he managed to escape on a French frigate in 1746. Too late by just a fortnight, 40,000 louis d'ors then arrived from France, enough to have revived the whole campaign.

This failure has been ascribed to a fatal weakness of character and a collapse of resolve at Derby. He ended his days a degenerate and broken man, ensuring the complete collapse of the Jacobite cause. But Bonnie Prince Charlie is remembered in numerous nostalgic songs, a toast to 'the King over the Water', and a host of memorabilia.

The Enlightenment

Intellectual life flourished in late 18th-century Scotland. Embracing all the arts, its roots lay in the philosophical nature, shaped by European thought, underlying Scots law, education and the church. The sceptic David Hume (1711-1776) was the foremost of a school of philosophers, best known for his *Treatise on Human Nature and Essays, Moral and Political*. Kirkcaldy-born Adam Smith pioneered political economy in his *Wealth of Nations* (1776), a powerful impetus to later political reform.

An emphasis on research and practicality in the sciences fostered inventiveness in applied science, contributing much to industry and agriculture. James Watt (1736-1819) developed the steam engine which powered the machinery of the Industrial Revolution, medicine flourished at Edinburgh University, and further generations spawned engineers and inventors like Alexander Graham Bell and John Logie Baird, inventors of the telephone and television respectively.

Classicism was espoused in architecture and by painters like Allan Ramsay, Raeburn and Naysmth, and gave way in literature to the Romanticism of Robert Burns whose work profoundly influenced popular culture and notions of democracy.

Sir Walter Scott's best selling historical novels worked miracles for Scotland's public image. It was he who stage-managed the visit of George IV, who sportingly donned a kilt and, for modesty's sake, pink tights for the occasion. Later on, Queen Victoria was inspired to adopt a Highland home and, with the craze for 'Balmorality', the Highlands assumed a romantic glamour, becoming a fashionable resort for southern sportsmen.

Industrial revolution and the Clearances

Until around 1750 a large percentage of Scotland's population lived north of the Clyde and Tay. Emigration to the Lowlands or North America was already a problem, as a money economy threatened traditional ways of life. The decision of landlords to resettle their tenants on the coasts, replacing black cattle with sheep, was a disastrous economic and social experiment, with brutal evictions in some areas – although popular myth forgets that famine, disease and overpopulation were rife and many went willingly. Eventually, in 1886, crofters' rights were to some extent recognized (see also page 307).

The gap between Highland and Lowland life continued to widen as overgrazing, deforestation for industry, and deer 'forests', led to desolation in the Highlands, while improvements and drainage transformed Lowland agriculture.

At the same time industrialization was soon to bring a massive population shift. Wool, cloth and linen, long established as cottage industries, were undergoing mechanization. By 1820 mills were established in the coalfields of Lanark, Renfrew and Ayr. Linen declined in favour of cotton, spun and woven in Paisley and New Lanark, while tweed was first woven in Galashiels in 1830. Dundee substituted jute for linen and Kirkcaldy developed linoleum. Thriving on trade with America, Glasgow's population mushroomed, absorbing many from the Highlands, as well as thousands of Irish refugees from the potato famine of the 1840s. Poor housing, overcrowding and disease became chronic.

20th-century Scotland

By 1900 iron and later steel, mainly in the west, had become manufacturing mainstays, serviced by new canals, railways and roads. As well as emigrants, Scotland supplied goods to North America: locomotives, girders, bridges, textile machinery and tools. Shipyards flourished on the Clyde. The first iron steam ships were launched around 1800, although fast wooden clippers like the *Cutty Sark* were still competitive in the mid-19th century, when major shipping companies such as Cunard came to the fore. From 1880 skilled labour built steel ships for world markets as well as for the Royal Navy. Business boomed during the First World War, when political activity among skilled workers, inspired by the Bolshevik revolution and led by Marxist and Scottish Nationalist John Maclean, gave rise to the myth of 'Red Clydeside'.

Post-war slump hit all industries in the 1920s, from which they never really recovered. A dangerous dependency on mining, metalworking and heavy engineering was a crucial factor in industrial decline, and the innovative spirit of the 19th century is only now re-emerging among pioneering computer software development companies in the central belt.

In a long Liberal tradition dedicated to political reform, the issue of Home Rule reared its head repeatedly after the 1880s. The first stirrings of nationalism were heard after the First World War and voiced by writers in the 1920s, such as Lewis Spence, Hugh MacDiarmid and Neil Gunn. These sentiments took political shape as the Scottish National Party (SNP) in 1934. Support grew through the 1950s and 1960s, and in 1967 the SNP was revealed as a potent political force when Winifred Ewing won the Hamilton by-election.

Nationalist fervour reached its height in the 1970s, roused by expectations that revenue from the oil and gas recently discovered in the North Sea would reverse economic decline. These hopes were dashed by oil revenues disappearing into the British Treasury at Westminster. In 1974, 11 SNP MPs were elected to Westminster –

Sunny side up for Eigg

The 12th of June 1997 was not just a momentous day in the history of the Isle of Eigg, but a cornerstone in the long, hard struggle by successive generations of Highlanders to end 250 years of oppression and feudal law. This was the day that the Eigg Heritage Trust successfully bought their own island (for the knock-down price of £1.6 million), thus bringing it back into community ownership.

It brought to an end a decade-long battle with their rather idiosyncratic landowner, Keith Schellenberg, who had a penchant for flying in his rich buddies for a spot of good-natured war gaming (shooting the local peasants having already been declared illegal), and would tour the island in his Rolls Royce, issuing proclamations (until said Rolls mysteriously 'caught fire' one day in 1994, provoking the humorous *Sun* headline of "Burnt Eigg Rolls").

With the 60 or so residents behaving like "ungrateful children", "IRA terrorists" and even "Islamic fundamentalists", the "misunderstood" Schellenberg finally got the message and, in 1995, sold to a singularly bizarre German artist by the name of Professor Maruma. Even by the standards of Highland landlordism, Maruma cut an eccentric figure, and was discovered by the German press to be neither an academic nor an artist.

It couldn't last, and so the people of Eigg won a famous victory that would cause a seismic shift in Scottish landownership, paving the way for the landmark ruling of 2003, ending centuries of colonial abuse and injustice, and ensuring a viable future for the islanders.

and, although many felt that this was a protest vote, Labour was concerned. In 1979 it held a referendum on the establishment of a Scottish Assembly. Turnout was low and support was luke warm, so no assembly was established.

Labour were soon ousted from office and the Thatcher government swept to power in 1979, bringing with it a disdain for Scotland that was to have far-reaching consequences. The new Conservative government also introduced policies that did not sit easily with most Scots. When the unpopular Poll Tax, which notoriously taxed 'dukes the same as dustmen', was introduced in Scotland a year earlier than in the rest of Britain, the country felt that it was increasingly being governed by politicians who cared little for its people. Years of Tory rule served only to widen the gap between Scotland and Westminster, and it was almost inevitable that some form of devolution would follow.

The new parliament

Twenty years on, the Scots voted emphatically in favour of devolution, and the Scottish Parliament reconvened after 292 years on 12 May, 1999. The new Parliament has 129 MSPs (Members of the Scottish Parliament) who were elected by proportional representation. It has the power to pass legislation and to alter the rate of taxation. However, defence and foreign affairs are still handled by Westminster. The early years of the parliament have not been without controversy, and its relationship with Westminster has at times proved frosty. The most pressing issue is the so-called 'West Lothian Question', the anomaly that allows Scottish MPs at Westminster to vote on issues solely affecting England, while English MPs cannot vote on solely Scottish issues. MSPs, for example, recently voted to fund personal care for the elderly in Scotland. Yet this went against the policy of the Labour government, leading to the possible scenario of Scottish Labour MPs at Westminster voting against such funding for the elderly in England. As one commentator said: "The

The winds of change

The wild Atlantic storms that batter the Hebridean island of Lewis may seem but a minor squall compared to the storm of protest that has grown over the proposal to build three massive wind farms on the island with the potential to generate more than 1000 megawatts of electricity. The largest of these schemes, to be situated on the north Lewis moor, comprises 190 turbines, making it the largest onshore wind farm in Europe. Each turbine will be 140 m tall – twice the height of the Scott monument in Edinburgh – and the path the turbine blades will cut through the air will be greater than the wingspan of a jumbo jet.

The Western Isles Council, not surprisingly, are in favour of the plans, believing that the wind farms could turn around the island's fortunes, transforming Lewis into the renewable energy capital of Europe. Lewis Wind Power, which is made up of British Energy and energy group, Amec, claims that some 333 jobs would be created during the four-year construction period and a further 346 over its 25-year lifetime. In addition, it is offering £2-3.5 million in annual rental income to crofters.

But local opposition is strong and the depth and the strength of that opposition was keenly felt by the island's Labour MP of nearly 20 years, Calum MacDonald, who lost his seat in the 2005 general election. Lewis is home to one of the largest remaining peatland habitats in Europe. This blanket bog, which is only found in a few widely scattered areas such as Tierra del Fuego, Kamchatka in Russia and New Zealand, supports dozens of rare birds and insect species and is acknowledged to be equivalent to the Amazonian rainforest in South America.

Local residents on Lewis say that construction of the wind turbines will destroy this precious environment. But that's not all. The Royal Society for the Protection of Birds (RSPB) has serious concerns for the rare bird populations living on the moor. They estimate that 50 golden eagles and up to 250 red-throated divers could be killed by collisions with rotor blades.

The proposals for the Lewis wind farms have been submitted to the Scottish Executive, though some believe the matter could yet go to a public enquiry. If that happens then Lewis Wind Power could have quite a battle on their hands.

English have been the silent and uninvited guests at the devolutionary feast". In addition, Scotland still benefits from higher spending per head than any other part of Britain – a situation which is almost certain to change in the near future.

The bold, stunning new parliamentary building, which finally opened in October, 2004, has more than its fair share of critics and was even subject to a public inquiry into why its costs increased tenfold (from an estimated £40 million to over £400 million), and why it opened three years later than planned. Blame was eventually apportioned to beaurocrats and politicians (so what's new?). But now, at least, it's there, fittingly overshadowing the queen's residence. Whether devolution is a step on the road to full independence, however, remains to be seen.

Culture

Architecture

Early structures: from brochs to towers

A thousand years before Stonehenge, a Neolithic architect was supervising the construction of Maes Howe (see page 348) in Orkney. Dramatically accompanied by two stone circles, its massive precision-cut stonework houses a tomb. Religious architecture evolved into the Bronze Age, and over 22 centuries of chambered tombs survive, notably at Camster and Kilmartin. Henges and stone circles, as at Cairnpapple, also abound. At Skara Brae (see page 347) is a 5000-year-old village, a Neolithic Pompeii where stone furniture and utensils survive in rooms straight out of the *Flintstones*.

Brochs, fortresses not dissimilar to diminutive industrial cooling towers such as at Mousa on Shetland (see page 374), appeared around 75 BC. A staircase ascended within double walls and a well often provided water for the besieged within. On duns and hilltops, timber-laced forts, built from 700 BC into the Middle Ages, are sometimes found to have been fired to such an extent that stonework fused solid or vitrified. Whether this was intentional, or the result of attack, remains a mystery.

Ninth-century wheelhouses, with stone piers radiating from a central hearth, are visible at Jarlshof on Shetland, and appeared later in the Hebrides. Timber began to be used for Pictish hall houses, crannogs – lake dwellings on wooden rafts – and early churches (such as at Whithorn).

In the 11th century round towers, such as those at Brechin and Abernethy, were used for defence and as belfries by Culdee communities. Around this time the first cathedrals were built. The one at Birsay on Orkney, founded in 1050 by Earl Thorfinn, was soon replaced by another in Kirkwall commemorating the Norse St Magnus (see page 343). This was built by masons from Durham Cathedral after working at Dunfermline Abbey, also Romanesque, built for St Margaret. She also commissioned St Rule's in St Andrews, whose tall square tower suggests Northumbrian influence, echoed in those at Muthill, Dunning (in Strathearn) and Dunblane.

Abbeys and cathedrals

David I (1124-1153) granted land to Roman monastic orders and two centuries of abbey and cathedral building ensued, though mostly in the Lowlands. Years of neglect and depredations by English troops and iconoclastic reformers left many as picturesque ruins, stripped of magnificent wood and stone carving, stained glass and wallpainting. The wallpaintings at Fowlis Easter, 15th-century collegiate churches, are a rare survivor. The ruins of Oronsay Priory and the Valerian-clad cloisters of Iona's nunnery (see page 153) are the legacy of the Augustinians.

Medieval castles

Symbols of feudalism built by Norman settlers appear in the form of timber motte and bailey fortresses – timber towers with defensive earthworks – though they are found mostly south of the Forth and Clyde.

Square or oblong tower houses, with a defensive entry at first floor level, barrel vaulting and great hall, were to be an enduring form of dwelling, evolving from the 14th century into the 17th. More elaborate are L-plan and Z-plan versions, with one or two towers added at the corners to defend the entry.

Renaissance palaces

While ordinary folk lived in thatched turf and stone hovels (some into the 20th century), the cosmopolitan and cultured Stewart kings set about building new palaces and improving existing residences. The old castle at Linlithgow had emerged by 1540, a wholly residential Renaissance palace ranged around a quadrangle, which even impressed the French Mary of Guise. While the Great Hall at Stirling is a triumph of late Gothic, the later Palace block (1540-1542) reveals many Renaissance features, such as the recessed bays along the exterior with sculpted figures, and the famous carved wooden ceiling medallions, the 'Stirling Heads'.

The tower house

A minor building boom in the late 16th century was a result of church land being transferred over a long period into private hands. The old tower house formula found favour, preferred over earlier royal examples of Renaissance innovation. Everyone from nobility to minor gentry was afforded both defence against troublesome neighbours as well as gracious living. Claypotts in Dundee is a good example of 'the castle with a country house built on top', while at Craigievar (see page 98), finished as late as 1626, idiosyncratic inventiveness reaches its apogee where the roofline explodes in a flurry of fairytale turrets. Families of masons developed individual styles detectable in Aberdeenshire where many tower houses, great and small, are still inhabited or have been recently revived. Defensive features like gun loops (apertures for guns) survived less out of necessity than as status symbols, and interiors, especially timber ceilings, were vividly painted, with exuberant imagery, as at Crathes (see page 90).

16th- to 18th-century townhouses

'New towns' to promote trade were established by David I and settled with English and Flemish merchants, with a strict hierarchy of trading rights and privileges. Stone houses first replaced wood in the east coast burghs in the 16th century, setting a precedent for future urban design. Every burgh had its symbols of commerce and government at its centre: the Mercat (market) cross and the Tolbooth (town hall).

Two centuries later, the spirit of vernacular architecture had not changed dramatically. Nor had urban layout, many houses still being built gable end on to the street. The multi-storey tenement became a distinctive feature of urban living, pioneered in Edinburgh's Canongate, where buildings such as Gladstone's Land are still intact. Culross Palace and Argyll's Ludgings in Stirling are outstanding examples of grand town houses.

William Bruce and the 17th-century mansion

The country mansion was a concept pioneered by Alexander Seton, paragon of a new kind of architectural patron, at Pinkie House in Musselburgh, a daring essay in elegance and erudition. Post Restoration, William Bruce exemplifies a new concept: the architect. Introducing classical symmetry to existing buildings such as Holyrood and Thirlestane, he also designed Hopetoun in 1699-1703. The innovative oblong shape and hipped roof of Kinross are characteristic of his many other country house designs with their Anglo-Dutch interiors and plasterwork. He also revolutionized garden and landscape design. Bruce's protégé, James Smith, was a pioneer of British Palladianism. Rising from master mason to King's Master of Works and private architect, his own house, Newhailes (circa 1690), was the inspiration for countless lairds' houses, both grand and humble, built throughout Scotland in the 18th century.

Victorian Baronial

Not content with Classicism, architects raided the Gothic, Tudor, Jacobean and Scottish past, even Asia and Europe, for ideas. Late 18th-century country houses by Gillespie Graham were asymmetrical and castellated. Inspired by the picturesque movement, they are the harbingers of the High Victorian revival of Scottish baronial which reached its peak in the 1860s. New and unprecedented wealth found industrial tycoons and landowners beating a path to the doors of fashionable architects like Burn and Bryce, to build colossal and fantastic country seats with room for entertaining on a huge scale, and the latest in comforts – like plumbing. Some followed Queen Victoria's example at Balmoral, building extravagant Highland shooting lodges. Most eclectic of all is Mount Stuart on Bute (1870s) a neo-Gothic/Renaissance palace whose sumptuous interior even includes details from Charlemagne's tomb (see page 134). Flamboyant design extended to monumental industrial buildings like textile mills and foundries, also railway stations, viaducts and bridges.

Literature

Any overview, no matter how brief, of Scotland's literary tradition must begin with a poet who has become inextricably linked with the image of Scotland and all things Scottish across the globe. **Robert Burns** was born on 25 January 1759 in Alloway, Ayrshire, in very humble surroundings, later referring to himself as "a very poor man's son". Burns wrote in the dialect of plain country people and about the lives they led, but the emotions he described were so genuine that they appealed to all classes.

His poetry mainly concerned itself with life as he was living it. He was also keen to point out what he saw as a kinship between all living things, such as in his famous *To A Mouse*. The most frequently quoted lines of this poem; "The best laid schemes o' mice an' men – Gang aft a-gley," has entered the language, as have many sayings originated by Burns, and is a perfect summing up of his point of view. His most celebrated work, *Auld Lang Syne* expresses the joys of human companionship and is practically an anthem when friends gather to celebrate New Year around the world. His love of the companionship of friends is also a focus of *Tam O'Shanter*, which also serves as a cautionary warning against overindulgence and is a ghost story in the tradition of the mythic, while his irritation against the assumed superiority of some was put into words in *A Man's A Man For A' That*, which also returns to his theme of kinship.

The 'heav'n-taught' Ayrshire ploughman died on 21 July 1796, and was buried in St Michael's Churchyard, Dumfries. Such is his standing that his memory is celebrated every year on 25 January, his date of birth, now referred to as Burns Night.

Another writer forever associated with the Borders is **Sir Walter Scott**, who not only ruled the roost of his native Scotland but the world of literature in general. Born in 1771, the son of a wealthy Edinburgh lawyer, Scott spent much of his childhood in the Borders during which time he immersed himself in tales and ballads of Jacobites and Border heroes, giving him a passion for history which would infuse his later work. It was this material which would eventually become poems in his three volumes of *Minstrelsy of the Scottish Border* which established his name as a literary figure. Other romantic poetic works followed, such as *The Lady of the Lake*.

In 1811 Scott purchased Abbotsford, a farmhouse near Melrose, and during the following years developed the style which would remain his best-remembered contribution to literature, the historical novel. Collectively known as the Waverley novels, these included *Old Mortality*, *Rob Roy* and *The Heart Of Midlothian*. The original Waverley was a romantic tale of the Jacobite Rebellion of 1745 and the Highland society of the time. By 1819 Scott had moved beyond purely Scottish history and wrote *Ivanhoe*, set in 12th-century England. It remains his most enduring work, and he followed it with *Kenilworth*, *Redgauntlet* and *The Talisman*.

Scott died on 21 September 1832. His huge popularity was believed to have kept the spirit of Scotland alive and he is commemorated by the Scott Monument in Princes Street, Edinburgh.

Gaelic writers

Not surprisingly, given the relatively low numbers of people who can speak the language (around 80,000), Gaelic writers have never enjoyed anything like the same success of their English-language counterparts. Two writers who have managed to transcend the linguistic barrier are Sorley Maclean (1911-1996) and Iain Crichton Smith (1928-1998).

Sorley Maclean in particular is something of a cult figure, and it has been argued that he did for the Gaelic language what Hugh MacDiarmid did for Scots. The fact that Maclean translated much of his work into English made him accessible to a much wider audience and this sparked a Renaissance in Gaelic literature. He was also influencial in the preservation and promotion of the teaching of Gaelic in schools.

It was the publication of Gordon Wright's *Four Points of a Saltire* – poems from Goerge Campbell Hay, Stuart MacGregor, William Neill and Sorley Maclean – that brought his work to the outside world in the 1970s, and the bilingual *Selected Poems* of 1977 brought him a whole new generation of readers. He won the Queen's Gold Medal for Poetry in 1990 and died in 1996, at the age of 85.

Another important Gaelic writer of the 20th century was Lewis-raised Iain Crichton Smith. Like Sorley Maclean, Crichton Smith was bilingual, allowing him to reach a wider audience, as well as translate other Gaelic works – including the 'Gaelic Homer', Duncan Ban McIntyre. Smith was awarded an OBE in 1980 and won numerous literary prizes, travelling frequently to read his work around the world. His heart, though, remained in the Highlands of Scotland, and he lived in the village of Taynuilt, near Oban, until his death in 1998.

A contemporary of Scott's, though far less well known, was **James Hogg**, the Ettrick Shepherd, born at Ettrickhall Farm in Selkirkshire in 1770. Like Burns before him, Hogg was of humble origins and did not receive a proper education he but inherited a vast store of balladry from his mother, Margaret, some of which Scott published in his *Minstrelsy Of The Scottish Border*. Like Burns, Hogg was lionized by the Edinburgh elite as another heaven-taught rustic with a flair for poetry, but that is to severely undermine his importance to the world of philosophy and psychology as well as literature. His writings dealt with the notion of a divided nature within a single individual, reflecting Hogg's own double life as rough Border shepherd and sophisticated urban intellectual. Hogg's thinking and writing reached their apotheosis is his extraordinary *The Private Memoirs and Confessions of a Justified Sinner*, published in 1824 and one of the true masterpieces of Scottish literature. There is nothing else like it and, prior to the Freudian era, nothing to match its insight into fractures of human nature.

This exploration of the dual nature of man received its quintessential expression in **Robert Louis Stevenson's** *The Strange Case of Doctor Jekyll and Mister Hyde*, published some 50 years after Hogg's death and one of the classics of horror literature. The tale was inspired by Edinburgh's notorious Deacon Brodie, a seemingly respectable pillar of the community by day and a criminal, gambler and womanizer by night.

Stevenson's fondness of the macabre is also apparent in stories like *The Bottle Imp* and *The Bodysnatcher*, but it is for his romantic historical adventures that he is best known. Born at 8 Howard Place, Edinburgh, on 13 November 1850, Stevenson was fond of travel which led to his employment as a writer of travel articles and essays. While staying in Braemar in 1881, Stevenson drew pirate maps of an island,

 and these became the basis of his tale, *Treasure Island*, published two years later. For Stevenson it was just the first of the many adventure tales, including *Kidnapped*, its sequel, *Catriona* and *The Master of Ballantrae*, he wrote before his death in Samoa on 3 December 1894. The tradition of the adventure story has continued throughout the 20th century in the works of Perth-born **John Buchan**, author of *The Thirty-Nine Steps*.

One of Stevenson's contemporaries at Edinburgh University was **Sir Arthur Conan Doyle**. Born at Picardy Place, Edinburgh, on 22 May 1859, Conan Doyle was schooled in Lancashire before returning to study medicine at Edinburgh University in 1876. It was while serving as an out-patient clerk at Edinburgh Royal Infirmary that Doyle met Doctor Joseph Bell, the man who was to influence most the creation of his famous character. "His strong point", Doyle later noted, "was diagnosis, not only of disease, but of occupation and character".

Doyle was living in London and had published several short stories and essays when memories of his former mentor, combined with a love of the detective fiction of Edgar Allan Poe, inspired him to write *A Study In Scarlet*, which first appeared in the 1887 edition of *Beeton's Christmas Annual*. Doctor Watson recounted Sherlock Holmes' unique detective skills in this, followed by a further three novels and 56 short stories, with all but *The Sign Of Four* making their initial appearance in *The Strand Magazine*.

Holmes became a phenomenon that not even Doyle could control. In fact, by 1893 he was so annoyed that his more serious literary endeavours were being neglected that he achieved what many criminals had failed to do. He killed Holmes. Following publication of *The Final Problem*, in which Holmes and his mortal foe, Professor Moriarty plunged over the Reichenbach Falls, there were public displays of grief and mourning. It was clear that the public were not going to let Holmes rest in peace, and eventually Doyle was forced to find an ingenious way of reviving the character. He penned his last Holmes story in 1927, a mere three years before his own death. Doyle's other famous character was Professor Challenger, who famously discovered the Lost World, which later inspired Steven Spielberg's *Jurassic Park*.

Another classic of literature was written by Doyle's older literary friend, **JM Barrie**. Born in Kirriemuir in 1860, James Matthew Barrie was the son of a weaver. Educated at Glasgow Academy and Edinburgh University, Barrie spent some years in Nottingham as a journalist before returning to Kirriemuir to write. He moved to London in 1885, and it was there that he wrote his first novel, *Better Dead*. More novels and plays followed, best known of which is *Peter Pan* and *The Lost Boys*. First published in 1904, it was written for the children of a friend, Llewelyn Davis. Before his death in 1937, he bequeathed the copyright for Peter Pan to Great Ormond Street Hospital in London.

20th century

A common criticism of 19th- and early 20th-century Scottish literature was the relative absence of novels dealing with the whole issue of industrialization, growing social division and immigration. Rather than explore the vexed issues of poverty, class division and the growing Celtic influence, most writers belonged to the 'Kailyard School', which presented a romantic, sentimental and completely unrealistic image of Scotland, perhaps reflecting the overwhelmingly middle-class background of novelists at that time.

The Kailyard came to be detested by a growing band of writers in the 20th century, and a new phase of realistic literature – known as the Scottish Renaissance – began in the 1920s, inspired by one of the greatest novels to emerge from Scotland, **George Douglas Brown**'s ground-breaking *House of the Green Shutters*. Published in 1901, the novel brings Greek tragedy to 19th-century rural Ayrshire and, more than any other, destroyed the bucolic escapism of the Kailyard School.

In the same year **James Leslie Mitchell** was born in rural Aberdeenshire. Better known by his pseudonym **Lewis Grassic Gibbon**, his novel, *Sunset song*, published in 1932 (only three years before his untimely death), has become one of the mainstays of modern Scottish literature, and taught as part of the national curriculum. It was written as the first book in the trilogy, *A Scots Quair*, which charts the life of Chris Guthrie, from late 19th century through to the 1920s. Written from the girl's perspective, it is remarkable not only for its strong evocation of this part of Scotland, but also for its uncanny emotional resonance.

Another renowned northeast writer is **Neil Gunn**, born in Dunbeath, Caithness, in 1891. His writings, which deal with the disintegration of the old Highland way of life in the wake of the Clearances and the struggle to adapt to new conditions, also convey a strong sense of place and are as important to Scottish literature and identity as Faulkner and Dostoevsky are to the USA and Russia. Amongst his best-known works is *Silver Darlings* (1939), the title of which refers to the booming herring industry. Gunn died in 1973.

For its size, Orkney has produced a disproportionate number of well-loved and much-read authors. The poet, novelist and playwright, **George Mackay Brown**, gained even more popularity after the posthumous publication of his autobiography, following his death in 1996. Like Gunn and Grassic Gibbon before him, Brown is inextricably linked to his homeland and evokes the spirit and landscapes of his beloved Orkney with a deft sensitivity, bringing a strong poetic impulse to bear on the social realism of his novels. Amongst his best is *Greenvoe*, published in 1972. **Eric Linklater** (1899-1974) is another Orcadian whose copious output of books and poems gained him international recognition. *The Dark of Summer* best represents his compelling style.

One of the most important 20th-century Scottish writers, perhaps *the* most important, is **Hugh MacDiarmid** (1892-1978). Born Christopher Murray Grieve, in the Scottish border town of Langholm, MacDiarmid, as with many Scottish writers of the 20th century, was fiercely political, becoming a founding member of the Scottish National Party (SNP) in 1928. During the 1930s, MacDiarmid moved to the remote Shetland island of Whalsay. He continued writing ground-breaking poetry, becoming increasingly convinced that the essential Scottish human condition could not be fully expressed through the English language alone but rather through a plurality of voices, including Lowland Scots dialect and the Gaelic language. Though recognized as the major force behind the Sottish Literary Renaissance, MacDiarmid's life was a frugal one and he died a man of modest means, near Biggar, in 1978. His best-known work, *A Drunk Man Looks at the Thistle*, was published in 1926.

Another 20th-century giant is **Robin Jenkins**, referred to as 'the Scottish Thomas Hardy'. It was Jenkins who put his native city of Glasgow firmly on the literary map. His most Glaswegian of novels, *A Very Scotch Affair* (Gollancz, 1968), is still regarded as a high point in pre-1970s Glasgow fiction. Jenkins is also recognized as the founder of new Scottish fiction and a precursor to Kelman and Welsh as portraying an unsentimental view of Scottish life. Among his other novels are *The Cone Gatherers* (MacDonald 1955), *Fergus Lamont* (Edinburgh Canongate 1979) and *Childish Things* (Canongate 2001).

Another Glasgow literary talent of this time is **William McIlvanney**. Though he had already published two Glasgow novels in the 1960s, it was the following decade which saw him emerge as one of the city's greats. In *Laidlaw* (Hodder and Stoughton, 1977), McIlvanney explored Glasgow's seedy, criminal underbelly through the eyes of the eponymous police Detective-Inspector, who became as much a part of the city as Ian Rankin's *Rebus* has become a part of Edinburgh. Two subsequent crime thrillers featuring Laidlaw, *The Papers of Tony Veitch* (Hodder and Stoughton, 1983) and *Strange Loyalties* (Hodder and Stoughton, 1991) helped McIlvanney transcend the crime novel genre, in the same way that Ian Rankin has done today.

Writers, of course, are interested in people and as Ian Rankin says: "Edinburgh's dualism makes it perfect for tales of people who are not what they seem. It's a very secretive place, its residents reticent". It was this characteristic that **Muriel Spark** captured in her classic novel *The Prime of Miss Jean Brodie* (1965). In 1981 **Alasdair Gray**'s totally original debut novel, *Lanark: A Life in Four Books* (Canongate, 1981), changed everything. It single-handedly raised the profile of Scottish fiction. Suddenly, the outside world stood up and took notice. Since then,

Scottish writers have gone from strength to strength, most notably with **James Kelman**, a giant on the literary scene, whose brilliant fourth novel, *How Late It Was, How Late* (Secker and Warburg, 1994), won the Booker Prize. A one-time bus conductor, Kelman is a committed and uncompromising writer whose use of dialect has attracted as much criticism from the literary establishment as it has praise from fellow writers at home. When some reviewers accused him of insulting literature, he retorted that "a fine line can exist between elitism and racism. On matters concerning language and culture the distinction can sometimes cease altogether."

Kelman has revolutionized Scottish fiction by writing not just dialogue but his entire novels in his own accent, and the debt owed to him by young contemporaries is immense. Writers such as **Duncan Mclean**, **Alan Warner** and **Irvine Welsh** all cite Kelman as a major influence on their writing. Cairns Craig, who has written widely on the modern Scottish novel, states that Kelman's real importance lies in his original use of the English language. "He can be seen as a post-colonial writer who has displaced and reformed English in a regional mode". Among Kelman's finest is his first novel, *The Busconductor Hines* (Polygon Books, 1984) and *A Disaffection* (Secker and Warburg, 1989). Kelman's *Translated Accounts* (Secker and Warburg, 2001) is believed to be his most 'difficult' to date. One literary critic claimed that, while it took Kelman three years to write, it might take the reader three years to understand it.

There are many other notable Glasgow novelists who began to make their name from the 1980s onwards. **Jeff Torrington**, the Linwood car-plant shop steward who was discovered by Kelman, won the Whitbread Prize for his debut novel *Swing Hammer Swing* (Secker and Warburg, 1992), which is set in the Gorbals of the late 1960s. **Janice Galloway** received much praise for her first novel, *The Trick is to Keep Breathing* (Vintage, 1990), which was on the short-list for Whitbread First Novel, and followed it up with an excellent collection of short stories, *Blood* (Secker and Warburg, 1991). Another brilliant collection of mostly Glasgow short stories is **AL Kennedy**'s *Night Geometry and the Garscadden Trains* (Edinburgh: Polygon, 1991), while *So I am Glad* (Jonathan Cape, 1995) is a Glaswegian take on Magic Realism.

Scottish literature has long been known for its dark hue. Crime, poverty and social dysfunction have provided rich copy for writers in a world where detectives are never less than hardened and profanity is as prevalent as punctuation. **Irvine Welsh** whose 1994 cult novel, *Trainspotting*, shone a spotlight on the city's drug-ridden underbelly, spawned an entire generation of gritty, realist writing. After a succession of hit and miss follow-ups, Welsh is back to rude health with his latest, *Porno* (2002), a sequel to *Trainspotting*, which sees the return of Renton, Sick Boy, Spud and Begbie.

From the same stable is **Alan Warner**, whose bleakly humorous *Morvern Callar* not only put Oban on the literary map but also signalled the arrival of a major and serious new talent, and **Laura Hird**, whose debut novel, *Born Free* (Rebel Inc 1999), tells the tale of a dysfunctional family trying to cope with life in one of West Edinburgh's most notorious housing schemes.

One of the most successful and best-known Scottish authors is **Iain Banks**, whose shocking debut, *The Wasp Factory* (1984), heralded a new Scottish writer of considerable imagination and wit. Banks has gone on to become one of the most prolific writers around, penning his best-seller, *The Crow Road*, and many others, as well as science fiction novels written under the name **Iain M Banks**.

Perhaps the most successful current Scottish writer is Fife-born **Ian Rankin**, currently the finest exponent of so-called 'Tartan Noir'. Rankin's Inspector Rebus novels give a striking depiction of contemporary Edinburgh. Rankin lives in Edinburgh and walks around the city a lot while researching new titles. He uses real locations and gruesome historical events in his books. Rebus drinks in a real city pub, the Oxford Bar, and in one book *Set in Darkness*, Rankin uses the story of an act of cannibalism which took place in the 18th century Scottish Parliament. Like the rest of Rankin's Inspector Rebus novels, this paints a stark, honest picture of contemporary

Great Scots

For such a small country, Scotland has produced a remarkable number of intellectual geniuses who have been peculiarly influential. Many of them were great scientists, like James Clerk Maxwell, described by Einstein as the most important physicist after Newton, and who paved the way for Einstein's theory of relativity. There was also John Napier, the inventor of logarithms, Lord Kelvin, who devised the second law of thermodynamics, and James Hutton, Roderick Murchison and Charles Lyell, who together created modern geology.

In medicine, Scotland led the world. Robert Liston and James Young Simpson discovered the benefits of chloroform, and Alexander Fleming discovered penicillin, the most effective antibiotic ever devised. The number of technologists is incredible, and includes James Watt, who developed the steam engine, R W Thomson, who invented the fountain pen and pneumatic tyre, John Macadam, who gave us the metalled road, Charles Mackintosh, who invented waterproof fabric, Alexander Graham Bell, who invented the telephone, and not forgetting John Logie Baird, the father of television.

Scotland has also given the world the Bank of England, the decimal point, colour photographs, the fax machine, the photocopier, the bicycle, the bus, the thermos flask, the thermometer, the gas mask, the gravitating compass, the fridge, the grand piano, fingerprinting, Bovril, interferon, insulin, the gel-filled bra and Dolly, the cloned sheep.

Edinburgh through the eyes of a cynical detective straight out of the Philip Marlowe school of hard cops. His other Rebus novels include *The Falls* (2001), *Black and Blue* (1998), *A Question of Blood* (2003), and *The Naming of the Dead* (2006), his most recent. Rumour has it that, like Conan Doyle with Sherlock Holmes, Rankin is planning to get rid of Rebus.

Music

It could easily be argued that, in its music, Scotland produces the finest and clearest expression of its culture. All tastes are currently catered for within its music scene, reflecting the cosmopolitan nature of a country standing at the threshold of a new era with its own parliament and a deep sense of love of its history and traditions, while keeping a weather eye on the future. Although the words 'Scottish music' often conjure up images of a tartan-clad piper on a mist-covered moor, that same piper is just as likely to be found supplying stirring melodies to the decidedly 90s edge of 'drums and bass' styles heard in clubs around the country. And that's not all – the sheer number of options available to those seeking any style of music, ranging from folk to funk, from 'Tattoo' to 'T In The Park', is truly remarkable.

Yet, despite the fact a new millennium has come and gone, bringing with it so many changes in music and technology, Scotland as a nation still responds, virtually as one, to the skirl of a full set of **Highland bagpipes**. Little wonder the pipes have been a dominant instrument for centuries – in celebration, in battle, in mourning – and are never far from the traveller's notion of all things Scottish. The pipes' unique sound is enjoyed the world over, not just in Scotland – witness the large numbers of pipe bands in the USA, Canada, across Europe, Australia and New Zealand. However, perhaps the best way to enjoy the pipes is to visit the country in summer when, accompanied by a full complement of drummers, many pipe bands can be seen taking part in competitions or playing at Highland Games in the open air. It would also be totally remiss not to mention the **Edinburgh Military Tattoo**, which takes place annually during August at the world-renowned Edinburgh Festival on the esplanade of Edinburgh Castle.

Traditional Scottish music can be passionate or jocular, mournful or joyous. In the hands of a good player, few instruments compare to the violin, or **'fiddle'**. For confirmation, simply seek out the work of **Ally Bain**. With The Boys Of The Lough, Phil Cunningham or solo, his handling of all traditional Scottish styles is superb. The folk circuit is alive and well and, crucially, features many contemporary songwriters as well as tradionalists. Apart from those already listed above, the players worth checking out include Dougie Maclean, Eric Bogle, Hamish Imlach, the Battlefield Band, Dick Gaughan and the Tannahill Weavers, all of whom have a worldwide following.

Delving a little deeper into traditional Scotland's music, you may come across Strathspey and Reel societies. These are groups of fiddlers, large or small, which are well attended across the length and breadth of Scotland. Most welcome visitors to their meetings to enjoy the music and, as most of these take place in pubs and hotels, to enjoy the local brew. On a more informal level, there are ceilidhs which often employ the help of a 'caller' to call out the moves to beginners and experienced dancers alike. The emphasis here is on enjoyment rather than precision and it is well worth seeking out some of the finest ceilidh dance bands, such as Tayside's Benachally Ceilidh Band, featuring former members of Silly Wizard and Capercaillie, The Craigenroan Ceilidh Band, The Occasionals and Alisdair MacCuish and the Black Rose Ceilidh Band.

There are also numerous Scottish music festivals, which range from the massive **Celtic Connections** (see page 49) and the well-respected **Shetland Folk Festival**, to smaller events which feature ceilidhs and more informal jam sessions.

Folk fusion

Scottish folk music struggled hard to shake off its couthy image, no doubt fuelled by too many dreadful hogmanay TV shows and shameless shysters in kilts. Things then took a turn for the better in the 1970s with the emergence of bands such as North Uist's **Runrig**, who married Gaelic lyrics to rock stylings and even reached the UK Top 10, and **Capercaillie**, whose reworkings of traditional West Highland songs with Karen Mattheson's haunting vocals have brought them significant commercial success. These two in particular have managed to promote Gaelic language and culture as well as promoting the image of traditional music as an exciting, innovative and relevant medium. Another innovative folk fusion band are **Afrocelts**, formerly the Afro Celt Sound System, who have been at the cutting edge of Celtic/World Music for several years and strongly identified with the new age/rave scene.

Others worth checking out include **Silly Wizard** (featuring Phil Cunnigham), **Salsa Celtica, The Easy Club, Mouth Music, Deaf Shepherd** and **Shooglenifty**, whose radical mixing of folk music with trance – 'acid croft' as they call it – has made a huge impact internationally. Also worth listening to are **The Peatbog Faeries**, from Skye, with their high-octane fusion of Celtic folk with reggae, dub and soca, and newcomers **Pipedown**, from Edinburgh, who successfully marry the pipes with guitar, mandolin and percussion. Their debut album, *The First Measure*, has won many plaudits.

Scottish rock, pop and dance

The Scots may be stereotyped as a bunch of kilt-wearing, haggis-munching bagpipe players, but there's so much more to the country's musical heritage. This is the country that gave the world **Lonnie Donegan, Lulu, Donovan** and **The Incredible String Band**. Ex-Faces lead singer and sun-tanned bad-hair boy, **Rod Stewart**, though born in England, still remembers his roots and wraps himself in tartan every time Scotland (used to) qualify for a World Cup. And speaking of tartan, there's the **Bay City Rollers**, who blazed a trail in the 1970s as the forefathers of the teeny-bop market. The 1970s were also notable for the peerless white funk of **Average White Band**, whose singles *Pick up the Pieces* and *Let's Go round Again*, dented the charts. Glasgow-born **Sheena Easton** made it big stateside in the 1980s, while that decade was dominated by the **Eurythmics**, led by Aberdeen-born singer, **Annie Lennox** and **Dave Stewart**. Also big in the 1980s were **Simple Minds**, whose early post-punk sound and look gave no hint of their later stadium rock credentials.

One of the most influential bands of the 1980s were the **Jesus and Mary Chain**, whose distinctive feedback-drenched sound and notoriously shambolic live gigs brought them a huge cult following. Their drummer, **Bobby Gillespie** went on to form the equally influential **Primal Scream**, whose prodigious alcohol and drug consumption was only matched by the size of their egos.

The 1980s also saw the emergence of the innovative Postcard label, which launched the careers of **Orange Juice**, whose frontman **Edwyn Collins** went on to huge international solo success with A Girl Like You, Josef K, the Bluebells (featuring Lonnie Donegan's son) and the 16-year old **Roddy Frame** and his band, **Aztec Camera**. Also big in the 1980s was the Celtic-influenced guitar sound of **Big Country**, fronted by former Skids man, **Stuart Adamson, Wet Wet Wet**, who still hold the record for the number of weeks at number one (15) with *Love is all around*, and who could forget **The Proclaimers** who released the unashamedly sentimental *Letter from America*. Other notable Scots names from that decade include **The Cocteau Twins, Love & Money, Altered Images, Texas, Del Amitri, Blue Nile, Billy Mackenzie** and **The Associates, Waterboys, Danny Wilson, Goodbye Mr Mackenzie** (who featured Shirley Manson on vocals, later of Garbage). As dance began to take hold in the latter half of the decade, another Scottish band provided one of the key albums of the period, namely **Primal Scream**'s epic *Screamadelica*.

The 1990s were no less productive with **Bronski Beat**, **The Shamen**, **Soup Dragons**, the hugely important **Teenage Fanclub**, and the bizarre and enigmatic **KLF**, who produced one of the soundtracks of the time with their 1990 ambient classic, 'Chill Out'. The 90s also saw the arrival of **Travis**, whose 1999, *The Man Who*, brought them massive commercial success.

Behind the scenes, too, Scots have been influential, and none more so than **Alan McGee**, whose Creation label signed up the cream of talent north of the border in The Jesus and Mary Chain, Primal Scream and Teenage Fanclub (as well as a bunch of Mancunian upstarts by the name of Oasis). And Glasgow's fecund indie scene continues to produce a stream of contenders. There are established favourites like **Belle and Sebastian**, **Idlewild**, **Mogwai**, **Arab Strap**, **Idlewild**, **The Delgados**, **The Cosmic Roughrider** and **Uresei Yatsura**, and the fabulous avant garde funk of **Franz Ferdinand**. Not to be outdone, Edinburgh, too, has produced some fine pop bands, including the very melodic **Aberfeldy**, named after the Perthshire town. One of the most interesting performers of recent years is **Kenny Anderson**, whose Anstruther-based Fence Collective spawned the massively successful **KT Tunstall**. His own band, **King Creosote**, feature regularly in Highland music festivals with their own folk-inspired music.

Language

Though the vast majority of Scots speak English, one ancient Scottish language which survives is Scottish Gaelic (*Gaidhlig*, pronounced 'Gallic'). Preceded by the speech of the Celts, it is now Scotland's oldest surviving language. Often referred to as the national language, it has been spoken the longest. Introduced to the country by Irish immigrants in the third and fourth centuries, its use soon spread and became well established. The language is spoken by about 60,000 people in Scotland (just over 1% of the population). This is in the **Gaidhealtachd**, the Gaelic-speaking areas of the Outer

Hebrides, parts of Skye and a few of the smaller Hebridean islands. Gaelic is one of the Celtic languages, which has included Irish Gaelic, Manx, Welsh, Cornish and Breton. Today only Scottish and Irish Gaelic, Welsh and Breton survive.

Argyll (which means 'coastland of the Gael') was the prime Gaelic-speaking area from the time Columba landed there in 563. Scottish Gaelic expanded greatly from the fifth century to around the 12th century and became the national language, spoken throughout most of the country with the exception of the Norse-speaking Orkney and Shetland isles. Galloway had a Gaelic community which was separated from the Highlands, but the language died out there about the 17th century.

From that point, Gaelic began a steady decline over the following centuries and, even before Union with England, was being usurped by English as more and more wealth and power passed into non-Gaelic hands. This transfer of power was given a major boost by the Reformation in the mid-16th century, as strong anti-Gaelic feeling was to the fore in the Church of Scotland.

Gaelic culture still flourished in the Highlands, but the failure of two successive Jacobite rebellions in the 18th century helped to seal its fate. In the wake of Culloden, all features of traditional Gaelic culture were proscribed and the clean sweep by government and landlords culminated in the Highland Clearances of the 19th century. The final nail in the coffin came in 1872, with the Education Act that gave no official recognition to Gaelic.

After two centuries of decline, Gaelic is now staging a comeback, thanks to financial help from government agencies and the EU which has enabled the introduction of bilingual primary and nursery schools and a massive increase in broadcasting time given to Gaelic-language programmes. This renaissance can also be seen, and heard, in the fields of music and literature, and the recent return of the Scottish Parliament can surely only help to strengthen the position of Gaelic in Scottish society.

Arts and crafts

Many of the handicrafts you'll see during your visit to the Highlands and Islands, such as pottery and jewellery, though undeniably beautiful, are produced by non-indigenous residents. Two traditional craft skills which have survived are weaving and knitting. Two areas where these skills reach their apotheosis are Harris and Orkney and Shetland and Fair Isle.

Knitting

Scottish sheep, particularly Orkney and Shetland, are characterized by their fine wool. The sheep of the original breed of Orkney and Shetlands, small bodied with low carcass weights, were probably a cross with Scandinavian animals. These Moorit sheep still thrive on North Ronaldsay, protected by the Rare Breeds Survival Trust. For most of the year they feed on seaweed but are moved on to grass in the lambing season. All the males and 20% of the females are horned.

Gossamer fine shawls made from Shetland wool are soft but hardwearing. Shetland wool is very loosely spun, which adds to the lightness of the finished garment. Knitted on fine needles the famed characteristic of the shawls is that they can be pulled effortlessly through a wedding ring.

Intricate patterns in bright colours characterize Fair Isle knitting. When not being worked into the design, the wool in the spare colour is taken across the back of the work, caught at regular intervals in the stitches so that there are no long loops. It is important for the tension to be correct as too tight carrying of the spare wool would distort the finished garment. This double use of wool also means that Fair Isle garments as well as being extremely colourful, are very warm, consisting as they do of two or more layers of wool.

Before the advent of mass-produced fleece clothing and other warm store-bought wear, a Scottish fisherman wore a sea jersey, sometimes known as a Guernsey or a Gansey. Tradition says that each village had its own peculiar design. Thus, if a man were lost at sea, his jersey pattern might be the only means of identification if he were not found very quickly. But in reality, every family and knitter in that family would have their own pattern. Cable stitch represented rope; hearts, anchors and waves could also be part of a design. The jerseys were made from five-ply Yorkshire 'wheeling', still available from Richard Poppleton of Wakefield, Yorkshire. This is a pure wool worsted yarn, tightly spun which makes it warm and hardwearing. When unwashed, the wool would contain lanoline, the natural oil, which would make garments practically waterproof too. Wool with the natural oils would be widely used for the knitting of seaboot stockings.

The jerseys are knitted in the round on four or five needles. There is no sewing together of the garment, all is done by knitting. Some jerseys have three little pearl buttons to close the neck. The sleeves are knitted from the armholes downwards and are never too long as they get wet as the seamen work with the nets. Also, when the wrist edges eventually become frayed, the knitter unravels the cuff and knits it up afresh.

The needles are long as more than 500 stitches are cast on. In order to make the work easier to handle, the right-hand needle would be anchored at the waist by a 'shield', a pouch of straw or a bunch of feathers. Quite an intricate design might be woven into the shields and they fetch a good price in auctions today. Alternatively, a knitting stick or knitting goose would anchor a needle under the right arm.

It is said that Kaffe Fasset, who is now one the world's leading knitwear designers, began his career thanks to Scottish wools. He was in the north and saw for sale wools of every delicious colour. Knowing little about knitting at that point, he nevertheless bought wool of every shade and also two needles. Boarding the train from Inverness back to London, he was in a carriage with several women. Soon after they began the journey he said 'I'm sure that some of you ladies can knit?' Indeed they could. By the time that they reached London, they had shown Kaffe Fasset how to cast on and off and how to increase and decrease. This was all that was needed to start his amazingly successful career. To this day, his designs use no complicated stitches, their unique beauty derived from inspired use of vibrant or subtle colours.

Religion

The Highlands and Islands of Scotland are largely Protestant, and religion, as in the rest of the country, plays a relatively small part in the lives of most people. This does not apply, however, in the Outer Hebrides, where religion plays a vitally important role in the islanders' lives, and priests and ministers still wield considerable power in the community. This particularly applies in the Calvinist Protestant islands of North Uist, Harris and Lewis, which still strictly adhere to the creed of Sabbatariansim. Here, Sunday is the Lord's Day and the whole community stops work. But despite the fact that the Outer Hebrides are sharply divided between the Protestant northern islands and the Roman Catholic southern islands of Benbecula, Barra and South Uist, there has been little confrontation.

The only conflict has arisen within the Presbyterian Church of Scotland (or Kirk) itself, which has split into various factions over the years. The main split had its roots in the 1712 Patronage Act, which allowed a landlord the right to choose the parish minister, thus breaking the fundamental rule of the church ministers and elders. In 1843, in protest at the state's refusal to change the Patronage act, a third of Scottish ministers walked out of the established Church of Scotland to form the Free Church of Scotland – the so-called 1843 Disruption. In 1893 a second disruption occurred, this time within the Free Church of Scotland itself when a minority seceded and formed the

 Free Presbyterian Church. Now it becomes really confusing. In 1900 most congregations in the Free Church of Scotland and the United Presbyterian Church joined together to form the United Free Church of Scotland. However, a large proportion of people in Lewis were opposed to this union and the largest congregations decided to continue as the Free Church of Scotland, or 'Wee Frees' as they are popularly known. Later, in 1929, the United Free Church joined with the Established Church of Scotland. And it doesn't end there. As recently as 1988, the Wee Frees split over the threatened expulsion of a minister who attended a requiem mass during the Catholic funeral of a friend. He and his supporters have since formed the breakaway Associated Presbyterian Churches.

Now all this may seem pedantic in the extreme to many outsiders, but to the people of Lewis, Harris and North Uist (and also much of Skye and Raasay), the Free Church is of enormous social and cultural, as well as spiritual, importance. Not only did it organize resistance to the infamous Highland Clearances but it has also done the most to preserve the Gaelic language.

Land and environment

Geographically, Scotland can be divided into three areas: Southern Uplands, Central Lowlands and Highlands. The Southern Uplands is the area south from Edinburgh and Glasgow to the English border, and consists of a series of hill ranges sandwiched between fertile coastal plains. The Central Lowlands, the triangle formed by Edinburgh, Glasgow and Dundee to the north, contains most of the population, and is the country's industrial heartland. The Highland Boundary Fault is the geographical division running northeast from Helensburgh (west of Glasgow) to Stonehaven (south of Aberdeen). To the north of this line lie the Highlands and Islands, which comprise roughly two-thirds of the country. This is an area of high mountain ranges punctuated by steep-sided valleys, or glens, and deep lochs. The northwest coastline is indented by numerous steep, fjord-like sea lochs, and offshore are some 790 islands, 130 of which are inhabited. These are grouped into the Outer Hebrides, or Western Isles, the Inner Hebrides, and, to the north, the Orkney and Shetland Islands.

Much of Scotland was long ago covered by the Caledonian forest, which consisted mainly of the Scots pine, along with oak, birch and other hardwoods. Over the centuries, the trees were felled for timber and to accommodate livestock, and now only around 1% of this ancient forest still remains. Small pockets of native Scots pine can be found scattered around the Highlands, at Rothiemurchus, near Aviemore, at Glen Tanar, near Ballater in Deeside, around Braemar, at Strathytre near Callander and Achray Forest near Aberfoyle, at Rowardennan on Loch Lomond, in Glen Affric and on the shores of Loch Maree.

Several decades ago the Forestry Commission, a government body, set about fencing off large areas of moorland for reforestation. Now much of the landscape is dominated by regimented rows of fast-growing sitka spruce, which are not particularly attractive. There are also serious concerns over the damage coniferization causes to the unique habitats in many areas, in particular to large areas of bogland in the 'Flow Country' of Caithness and Sutherland, a unique natural environment as precious as any tropical rainforest. This and other endangered habitats are registered as an SSSI – a Site of Special Scientific Interest – but this has proved less than adequate. The only real guarantee of protection is for such areas to be owned or managed by environmental organizations such as Scottish Natural Heritage, the Scottish Wildlife Trust, the Royal Society for the Protection of Birds, the Woodland Trust and John Muir Trust (see page 59).

In recognition of this, the new Scottish Parliament produced a draft bill to establish a series of national parks, based on advice from Scottish National Heritage. This is aimed to reduce the conflict between social and economic development and long-term protection of the natural and cultural environment. The first new park to open, in April 2002, was Loch Lomond and Trossachs National Park, and the other was Cairngorms National Park, which opened in early 2003.

Wildlife

The Scottish countryside plays host to some of Europe's rarest and most celebrated wildlife, though much of it has disappeared over the centuries. The ancient Caledonian forests were once home to wildlife that we now identify with other far-flung countries: including the brown bear, lynx, wolf, reindeer and beaver to name but a few. Small numbers of beaver and reindeer have been reintroduced in recent years and there is the ongoing controversial debate regarding the reintroduction of the wolf.

Coastal wildlife

Scotland boasts over 13,000 km of the British coastline. As a result seabirds and some sea mammals abound and both the resident and visitor list is impressive. Some of the more notable avian 'stars' include the eider duck, most famous for its feather down which the birds use to keep their eggs warm and we use in quilts to keep us cosy. Both sexes are about the size of a small goose yet are quite different in appearance. The male, for courting purposes, looks very regal, being predominantly black and white with lime green cheeks and a pastel pink breast, while the female, for the purposes of camouflage, is a dull brown colour. During the breeding season on the coast fringes and off-shore islands it is not unusual to encounter the females at very close quarters while sitting on the nest. They are very confident about their camouflage and will stay perfectly still even when you are within a few feet.

During the winter the firths (large coastal inlets) and estuaries play host to large numbers of predominantly arctic seaduck including the beautiful jet black common and velvet scoter, the scaup (very similar to the common tufted duck) and the spectacular and rare king eider. Waders too are present in large numbers around the coast and again, especially in winter. Knot, dunlin and turnstones are also common along the beaches and mudflats. During the summer perhaps the most commonly seen coastal wader is the oystercatcher which is black and white with a conspicuous orange beak. While around estuaries keep your ears open for the high-pitched call of the curlew.

These estuaries, along with many of the offshore islands also play host to Scotland's two resident seal species, the common seal and the grey seal. Although the two are at long range quite hard to distinguish, the common is generally lighter in colour and smaller with more delicate dog-like facial features. The common seal breeds in summer and generally tend to be independent of one another, while the grey breeds in mid-winter in rookeries predominantly on offshore islands. Both species can be seen throughout the year with the common most common on the west coast and the grey on the east.

Dolphins, porpoises, basking sharks and some species of whale can also been seen regularly around the Scottish coastline. The resident pod of bottlenose dolphins in the Moray Firth is best viewed between May and September, while minke whales, basking sharks and even orca (killer whales) are not entirely unusual off the west coast and Western Isles.

Island wildlife

The many offshore islands scattered around the Scottish coast provide sanctuary to a wide variety of seabirds, often in huge numbers. These islands are important both nationally and internationally for many breeding species and as such are designated National Nature Reserves (NNRs) and Sites of Special Scientific Interest (SSSIs). The most noted are the islands around Orkney and Shetland and on the west coast Handa Island near Cape Wrath

To visit these islands and the massive seabird colonies that inhabit their towering cliffs in the breeding season (April to September) is an unforgettable experience. Classic residents include members of the auk family, including the guillemot, razorbill and the puffin, without doubt the most colourful and charming seabird in Britain. Unlike the hardy guillemots and razorbills that nest precariously on the cliff ledges, the puffin nests in burrows, which they excavate with razor-sharp claws. After the eggs are incubated and the eggs hatch the chicks are raised in the burrow and this is the best time to view the birds.

The best places to see puffin and the seabird colonies are in Orkney and Shetland, or Handa Island in the far north west of the country, near Cape Wrath. Several other species inhabit other neighbourhoods within these seabird cities including the Manx shearwater and fulmar, which are both specialist pelagic petrels. The fulmar is worth special mention because it has the admirable habit of vomiting all over you should you stray too close. One of the most famous seabirds around Scotland is the large and very stern looking gannet which is black and white in colour with a 6-ft wing span and an ochre-coloured head. Its most famous international breeding site is the Bass Rock in the Firth of Forth (see *Footprint Scotland* for more details) where over 50,000 pairs breed annually. So famous is the Bass that it lends its name to the Northern or Atlantic gannet's official scientific name, Morus bassanus.

Other more unusual rare and resident species you might be very lucky to see on the coast is the white-tailed sea eagle around the Western Isles or the beautiful snowy owl on Fetlar in Shetland. The sea eagle used to be fairly common but was wiped out in Scotland by early last century. Now, after a successful reintroduction on the Isle of Rùm on the west coast, several pairs breed. The specific nesting locations are understandably keep secret but you may still see one on a fishing foray over its huge territorial range. Like the golden eagle its sheer size is an instant give away while the tail of course distinguishes it from its more common relative. The snowy owl is rarely seen outside Shetland and of course is instantly recognizable.

Some islands around the coast of Scotland are also well known internationally as migratory stopovers for vagrant species. Fair Isle between Shetland and Orkney is particularly important and well known often providing life-saving shelter in spring and autumn storms for such exotically named species as the jack snipe or black redstart.

Rivers, lochs and wetlands

Otters are more commonly found along riverbanks in Europe but in Scotland are best observed on the tidal fringes searching for seafood. The Isle of Skye and Shetland are the best venues. The otter was for decades almost hunted to extinction in Britain but is now fully protected. It is often confused with the feral mink or ferret, which is far more commonly seen in the countryside throughout Britain.

Loch Garten in Speyside near Aviemore is the home to the **osprey** and the venue of one of Scotland's most successful avian conservation stories. After being absent for many years the Loch Garten breeding site became a catalyst for what is now the successful national comeback of the species. You can view the birds nesting in summer at Loch Garten but if you are really lucky you will see one catching fish in a spectacular display of aerial acrobatics on the lochs and rivers of the region. The rivers Tay and Spey are world famous for their salmon. Some of the hydroelectric dams in Scotland have fish ladders where you can observe this archetype of inherent motivation as the fish struggle relentlessly upstream to breed. Pitlochry is one such venue.

Although not endemic to Scotland one of the most beautiful bird species you may encounter on the more remote lochs are **divers** (or loons as they are called in North

America) – most commonly the red-throated diver, the rarer black-throated diver and occasionally the largest, the great northern diver. All three can be seen on the coast in winter. The best time to see these birds is in their superb summer breeding attire but it is perhaps their call that is most memorable. The haunting cry of the great northern or black throat that carries for miles across the moors and wide-open spaces is quite simply unforgettable. Red-throated divers breed on lochs throughout the highlands while black-throated divers can be found in the far north, especially round Lochinver and in Caithness. Also both rare and beautiful is the delicate black-neck grebe which supports a headpiece in the breeding season to beat any human fashion label at the annual Royal Ascot horse races. Loch Ruthven near Inverness is an excellent place to observe this particular avian fashion parade.

For any Scot who is in tune with the countryside the first calls of greylag and pink-footed **geese** are a sure sign that summer has ended. Huge numbers winter in Scotland especially in the central lowlands and parts of the west coast. Similarly, barnacle geese invade the Solway Firth in the south in their thousands. The V-shaped flying formations and constant honking of course make the type of bird if not the actual species instantly identifiable. Of course no mention of Scotland's waterways and wildlife would be complete without mention of Scotland's most famous aquatic creature – the **Loch Ness Monster**. Nessie does of course exist but like the wild haggis is very very shy and elusive.

Forests and lowlands

As opposed to its introduced North American cousin the native red **squirrel** is a delicate and shy creature. Their beautiful rustic colours can often herald their occasional public appearance in the forests of the Central Highlands, especially Speyside. If it were not for the grey squirrel pushing them out of former habitats and man destroying the habitat itself they could once again be classed as common. Even rarer is the elusive and rarely seen **wildcat** and **pine marten**. The wildcat is larger than the domestic 'moggy' and has a much courser, thicker fur coat, piercing, wild eyes and untamed attitude. Over the years the feral cat and wild variety have interbred and now it is very unusual to see the species in its rawest form. The pine marten is about the size of a mink and is occasionally seen in forested areas of more remote and unpopulated areas of the country.

The forests and lowlands are also home to some familiar bird species. The quite bizarre and wonderfully named **capercaille** (pronounced 'capper-kay-lee') is a member of the grouse family and the largest of the three species found in Scotland. It is the handsome black male that is most often seen deep in the forests, most commonly crossing forest paths and fire breaks while guarding his extensive territory. This is necessary not so much as protection from predators, but invasion by other highly sexed males intent on one thing and one thing only. An encounter and subsequent dispute results in audible threats and much puffing up of the plumage. Even more spectacular are the fights between the capercaillie's smaller relative the **black grouse**. Their version of a 'boxing ring' is called a 'lek' and can be the sight of spectacular displays of male hormonal overload.

Other unusual birds of the forest includes the **crossbill**, which is about the size of a overweight canary and has a beak that intersects, which it uses to expertly extract pine seeds from the cone. Crossbills can regularly be seen in the central highlands with National Nature Reserves like Loch Garten being a good bet. While in the Loch Garten area you may also see the delicate little crested tit, which although not endemic, only breeds in this part of Scotland. In much of western Scotland the **hooded crow**, or 'hoodie' replaces the common crow found throughout Britain. The hooded crow can be distinguished by the diagnostic grey patches on its plumage.

Britain's only venomous snake, the **adder**, is relatively common throughout Scotland and is mainly found on open ground covered in bracken or heather. It is rarely seen and generally keeps well out of your way, though you may be lucky enough to encounter one sunning itself on rocks early in the day.

Highlands

The **red deer** are as much an environmental problem as a feature of the Scottish landscape. They now number over 300,000 and in the absence of natural predators are essentially out of control in the Central Highlands. Extensive management through hunting and culling has so far failed to keep numbers in check. In summer they remain in herds on high ground and, despite their size, they are actually very hard to spot. In winter however you can often see them in large numbers on lower ground in the glens and beside the main roads. During the 'rut' in autumn the males (stags) become highly aggressive and use their impressive antlers in fierce combat to win the females (hinds). This fighting is often accompanied by a loud roar that carries for miles. Other deer species seen commonly in Scotland in the Highlands, Central Lowlands and Borders are the **roe, sitka** and **fallow deer**.

Another famous Highlands inhabitant is the **golden eagle**. After periods of decline they are now present in relatively healthy numbers especially in the Central and Western Highlands but are not exactly widespread or commonly seen. To the uninitiated the eagle is very often confused with the common buzzard, though the latter is actually much smaller. The golden eagle also dwarfs the large and menacing **raven** that is also a regular sight in central and western Scotland – usually accompanied by a raucous, 'throaty' call. Another regal and masterful lord of the highland skies is the **peregrine falcon.** In both flight and appearance they are the epitome of power. To watch a peregrine hunting other birds in flight is to witness one of the most spectacular acts in nature.

Two quite common masters of camouflage on the mountain slopes are the **mountain hare** and the **ptarmigan**, a bird similar in size and appearance to a red grouse. Both go through an incredible phase of moult from dark browns in summer to pure white in winter. They do this of course in order to blend in with their surroundings and avoid predators like the peregrine. Any time spent around the ski-fields in summer or winter should reveal one or both species.

Other rarer birds found breeding on the inhospitable high tops, especially in the Cairngorms, are the **dotterel**, a small attractive wading bird and the sparrow sized **snow bunting**. The snow bunting, like the mountain hare and ptarmigan, assumes a predominantly white plumage in summer. Few breed in Scotland as it is predominantly a winter visitor to the coast. On the lower slopes the **red grouse** is a common sight. Vast tracks of land are maintained to provide the ideal breeding habitat for this 'game bird' which are then hunted for sport.

Books

→ *See also page 402.*

History, politics and culture

Daiches, D, *The New Companion to Scottish Culture* (Polygon, 1993). A comprehensive guide to Scottish culture.

Kennedy, L, *In Bed with an Elephant* (Corgi, 1996). An entertaining account of Scotland's often turbulent relationship with England.

Lynch, M, *Scotland A New History* (Pimlico, 1999). A worthy contender.

Macdonald, M, *Scottish Art* (Thames & Hudson, 2000). Good overview.

Magnusson, M, *Scotland the Story of a Nation* (Harper Collins, 2000). A mighty tome, and after reading it you're unlikely to pass on any questions on Scottish history.

McIntosh, A, *Soil and Soul: People Versus Coporate Power* (Aurum Press, 2004). Inspirational and poetic in equal measure, this remarkable book weaves ecology, spirituality and politics into a spellbinding tale of the power of the community.

Nairn, T, *The Break-up of Britain* (Common Ground pub, 2003). Gives a radical perspective of Scottish independence. *Scotland's Story* (Fontana) is also insightful.

Prebble, J, *1000 years of Scotland's History, The Lion in the North, Glen Coe, Culloden* and *The Highland Clearances* (Penguin). For a more emotive and subjective view of highland history.

Smout, T C, *A History of the Scottish People* (1560-1830) (Fontana, 1998) and *A Century of the Scottish People* (1830-1950) (Fontana, 1997). The best general overview of Scottish social history.

Tranter, N, *The Story of Scotland* (Neil Wilson publishing, 1992).

Biographies, travelogues and memoirs

Banks, I, *Raw Spirit: In Search of the Perfect Dram* (Arrow, 2004). Slightly uneven but generally enjoyable romp around Scotland's distilleries.

Bathurst, B, *The Lighthouse Stevensons* (HarperCollins, 1999). A well-documented account of the fascinating story of Robert Louis Stevenson's family, who built many of the lighthouses around Scotland's coast.

Boswell and Johnson, S, *A Journey to the Western Islands of Scotland* (UK Penguin). If you only read one travelogue, make it this.

Crumley, J, *A High and Lonely Place and Gulfs of Blue Air – A Highland Journey* (Mainstream). Decent travelogue.

Duff, D (ed), *Queen Victoria's Highland Journal* (UK Hamlyn). Another interesting read.

Fraser, A, *Mary, Queen of Scots* (UK Mandarin). Excellent biography.

Grant of Rothiemurchus, Elizabeth, *Memoirs of a Highland Lady* (Canongate).

Maclean, F *Bonnie Prince Charlie* (Canongate). Excellent biography.

Maxwell, G, *The Ring of Bright Water* (Penguin). One of the best known Highland memoirs, a tale of otters and other wildlife set in Glenelg.

Miller, K, *Electric Shepherd: A Likeness of James Hogg* (Faber & Faber, 2003). For a fascinating study of the life and works of one of Scotland's most enigmatic literary figures look no further.

Morton, H V, *In Search of Scotland* (Methuen). Another notable travelogue.

Nicolson, A, *Sea Room* (HarperCollins, 2002). Beautiful and lyrical 'love letter' to the obscure and tiny Shiant Islands, written by the man who owns them.

Skinner Sawyers, J (ed), *The Road North – 300 years of Classic Scottish Travel Writing*, (The Inn Pinn, 2000). A selection of the best, including **Daniel Defoe**, **Edwin Muir** and **Jan Morris**.

Tomkies, M, *A Last Wild Place*, by naturalist Mike Tomkies is a fascinating account of life in a remote West Highland croft.

Outdoor activities

Walking

There are numerous walking guides available and this is only the briefest of selections. Two of the best are *Great Walks Scotland* by **Hamish Brown**, and *100 Best Routes on Scottish Mountains* by **Ralph Storer**.

Two helpful hillwalking guides published by the **Scottish Mountaineering Trust** are *The Munros* by **Donald Bennett** and *The Corbetts* by **Scott Johnstone et al**. The SMT also publishes a range of district guides listing mainly high level walks. Also useful are *The Munro Almanac* and *The Corbett Almanac* by **Cameron McNeish**.

Those wishing to attempt one of the long-distance walks should read *The West Highland Way* or *The Southern Upland Way*, both highly informative guides by **Roger Smith** (HM Stationery Office).

An excellent guide for both walkers and mountain bikers is **Ralph Storer**'s *Exploring Scottish Hill Tracks*.

Cycling

Other recommended cycling guides include: *The Scottish Cycling Guide* by **Brendan Walsh**; *101 Bike Routes in Scotland* by **Henry Henniker** (Mainstream); *Cycling in Scotland* by **John Hancox** (Collins Pocket Reference, Harper Collins); and *Cycling in Great Britain: Bicycle Touring Adventures in England, Scotland and Wales* by **Tim Hughes & Jo Cleary** (Bicycle Books, US).

Birdwatching

A good birdwatching guide is *Where to Watch Birds in Scotland* by **Michael Madders and Julia Welstead** (UK Christopher Helm).

Miscellaneous

Black, G, *The Surnames of Scotland: their origin, meaning and history* (New York, 1940). Available in most public libraries.

HM Stationery Office, *Exploring Scotland's Heritage*. A beautifully illustrated series of books on historic buildings and archaeological sites in different regions of Scotland.

Jackson, M, *The Malt Whisky Companion* (UK Dorling Kindersley). Those wishing to bone up on their malt whiskies should refer to this.

MacDonald, Lady C, *The Claire MacDonald Cookbook* (UK Bantam). An excellent Scottish recipe book by Lady Claire, who runs a hotel on Skye.

Sinclair, C, *Tracing your Ancestors* (HM Stationery Office). For more detailed genealogical study.

Stuart, M and Balfour Paul, J, *Scottish Family History* (Edinburgh, 1930). For a comprehensive history of Scottish clans and families. In most public libraries.

Poetry

Crawford, R and Imlah, M (eds) *The New Penguin Book of Scottish Verse*, (2000). An excellent overview.

Crichton-Smith, I, *Collected Poems*. Bilingual (English and Gaelic) poet writing passionately about life in the Outer Hebrides.

McCaig, N *Selected Poems*. Challenging poet whose work is deeply rooted in the landscapes of the Highlands.

McDiarmid, H, *Selected Poems*. A huge figure on the Scottish literary landscape. His nationalist views and use of Scots have been as influential as they have been provocative.

Morgan, E, *New Selected Poems*. Scotland's new poet laureate is one of the country's foremost living writers and both entertaining and experimental.

Muir, E, *Collected Poems*. Recognized as one of the most distinguished poets of the last century, received an MBE in 1953 for his significant contribution to Scottish poetry.

Paterson, D, *Landing Light*. This is the latest work of a genuinely innovative new voice in Scottish poetry.

Footnotes

Glossary

Scottish terms

ben hill or mountain
bothy farm cottage/mountain hut
brae hill or slope
brig bridge
burn brook
clan tribe bearing same surname
crannog Celtic lake or bog dwelling
croft small plot of farmland and house
dram small measure of whisky
elder office bearer in Presbyterian church
factor manager of estate/landlord
firth estuary
ghillie personal hunting or fishing guide
howff traditional pub/haunt
kirk church
lade mill stream
laird landowner/squire
Mac/Mc prefix in Scottish surnames denoting 'son of'
machair sandy, grassy coastal land used for grazing
manse vicarage
merse saltmarsh
Munro mountain over 3000 ft
provost mayor
Sassenach literally 'Saxon', ie English
sept branch of clan
Wee Frees Followers of the Free Church of Scotland
wynd lane
yett gate or door

Useful Gaelic

abhainn river
aonach ridge
aros dwelling
ault, allt stream
bagh bay
bal, baile town or village
ban, beinn mountain
bealach mountain pass
beg, beag small
cairn heap of stones marking a spot
camas bay or harbour
ceilidh social gathering involving singing, dancing and drinking
cnoc, knock hill
coll or coille wood or forest
corran point jutting into the sea
corrie, coire hollow in mountainside or whirlpool
craig, from **creag** rock, crag
drum ridge
dubh black
dun fort
eas waterfall
eilean island
fin or fionn white
gare, gear short
garv, garbh rough
geodha cove
glen, glean valley
inch, innis meadow or island
inver, inbhir river mouth
kyle, caolas narrow strait
liath grey
loch lake
more, mór great, large
rannoch bracken
ross, rubha promontory
sgeir sea rock
sgurr sharp point
sheiling shepherd's hut
strath wide valley
tarbet, tairbeart isthmus
tigh house
tir, tyre land
torr hill, castle
tràigh shore
uig shelter
uige water

Index

C

D

J

K

L

M

T

U

V

W

Y

Map index

Map symbols

Administration

- Capital city
- Other city/town
- International border
- Regional border
- Disputed border

Roads and travel

- Motorway
- Main road
- Minor road
- 4WD track
- Footpath
- Railway with station
- Airport
- Bus station
- Metro station
- Cable car
- Funicular
- Ferry

Water features

- River, canal
- Lake, ocean
- Seasonal marshland
- Beach, sand bank
- Waterfall

Topographical features

- Contours (approx)
- Mountain
- Volcano
- Mountain pass
- Escarpment
- Gorge
- Glacier
- Salt flat
- Rocks

Cities and towns

- Main through route
- Main street
- Minor street
- Pedestrianized street
- Tunnel
- One way street
- Steps
- Bridge
- Fortified wall
- Park, garden, stadium
- Sleeping
- Eating
- Bars & clubs
- Entertainment
- Building
- Sight
- Cathedral, church
- Chinese temple
- Hindu temple
- Meru
- Mosque
- Stupa
- Synagogue
- Tourist office
- Museum
- Post office
- Police
- Bank
- Internet
- Telephone
- Market
- Hospital
- Parking
- Petrol
- Golf
- Detail map
- Related map

Other symbols

- Archaeological site
- National park, wildlife reserve
- Viewing point
- Campsite
- Refuge, lodge
- Castle
- Diving
- Deciduous/coniferous/palm trees
- Hide
- Vineyard
- Distillery
- Shipwreck
- Historic battlefield

Acknowledgements

Alan would like to thank all those helped in the research, writing and preparation of this guidebook. Suzy Kennard for writing the History and Architecture sections, Duncan Lindsay for Music, Darroch Donald for Wildlife and Frank Nicholas for Literature.

Thanks also to all the staff at the various tourist information centres who were so willing and helpful, to the National Trust for Scotland for their assistance and for supplying many of the images used in the Foot in the Door section, and to Historic Scotland. A big shout to all at Footprint for their help and support, especially Flick for her due diligence and for showing grace under pressure.

This book, as always, is dedicated to Philippa for her love, support and encouragement, and for single-handedly looking after our kids for such a long time, to the point where they screamed and ran off when I finally finished writing and emerged from my office, unshaven and bleary-eyed.

Colin Hutchison, an Edinburgh-based travel and adventure sports journalist, researched and updated the Argyll and Inner Hebrides and Central Highlands chapters and part of the North and Northwest Highlands chapter, as well as updating the Sports and activities section.

The chance to enjoy terrific scenery, food and local banter whilst cycling and driving around Scotland made contributing to this guidebook all the more enjoyable for Colin. He would like to thank the staff at Historic Scotland and Visitscotland for their respective assistance, and Gill, for her unstinting love and support.

Complete title listing

Footprint publishes travel guides to over 150 destinations worldwide. Each guide is packed with practical, concise and colourful information for everybody from first-time travellers to travel aficionados. The list is growing fast and current titles are noted below. Available from all good bookshops and online Www.footprintbooks.com

(P) denotes pocket guide

Latin America & Caribbean

Antigua & Leeward Islands (P)
Argentina
Barbados (P)
Bolivia
Brazil
Caribbean Islands
Chile
Colombia
Costa Rica
Cuba
Cuzco & the Inca heartland
Discover Belize, Guatemala & Southern Mexico
Discover Patagonia
Discover Peru, Bolivia & Ecuador
Dominican Republic (P)
Ecuador & Galápagos
Havana (P)
Jamaica (P)
Mexico & Central America
Nicaragua
Peru
St Lucia (P)

North America

Discover Western Canada
Vancouver (P)

Africa

Cape Town (P)
Kenya
Morocco
Namibia
South Africa
Tanzania

Middle East

Dubai (P)
Egypt
Jordan

Australasia

Australia
Discover East Coast Australia
New Zealand
Sydney (P)

Asia

Borneo
Cambodia
Discover Vietnam, Cambodia & Laos
India
Laos
Malaysia & Singapore
Rajasthan
South India
Sri Lanka
Thailand
Vietnam

Europe

Andalucía
Antwerp & Ghent (P)
Barcelona (P)
Bilbao and the Basque country (P)
Bologna (P)
Cardiff (P)
Copenhagen (P)
Costa de la Luz (P)
Croatia
Dublin (P)
Lisbon (P)
London
London (P)
Madrid (P)
Naples & the Amalfi Coast (P)
Northern Spain
Paris (P)
Reykjavík (P)
Scotland Highlands & Islands
Seville (P)
Siena & the heart of Tuscany (P)
Tallinn (P)
Turin (P)
Valencia (P)
Verona (P)

Lifestyle guides

Body & Soul Guide to the World
Diving the World
European City Breaks
Snowboarding the World
Surfing Britain
Surfing Europe
Surfing the World
Wine Travel Guide to the World

Also available
Traveller's Handbook (WEXAS)
Traveller's Healthbook (WEXAS)
Traveller's Internet Guide (WEXAS)

Credits

Footprint credits
Editor: Felicity Laughton
Map editor: Sarah Sorensen
Picture editor: Kevin Feeney

Publisher: Patrick Dawson
Editorial: Sophie Blacksell, Nicola Jones, Sarah Sorensen
Cartography: Robert Lunn, Kevin Feeney
Design: Mytton Williams
Sales and marketing: Andy Riddle
Advertising: Debbie Wylde
Finance and administration: Elizabeth Taylor, Vassia Efstathiou

Photography credits
Front and back cover: eye35/Alamy (Loch Assynt), Scottish Viewpoint/Alamy (Tobermory)
Inside colour section: The National Trust for Scotland Photo Library, age fotostock/ Superstock, Brian Lawrence/Superstock, SuperStock Inc./SuperStock, DC Lowe/ SuperStock, Hugh Webster/Alamy, Seb Rogers/Alamy, Scottish Viewpoint/Alamy, Leslie Garland Picture Library/Alamy, Arch White/Alamy Doug Houghton/Alamy, Chris Joint/Alamy

Print
Manufactured in India by Nutech Photolithographers, Delhi
Pulp from sustainable forests

Footprint feedback
We try as hard as we can to make each Footprint guide as up to date as possible but, of course, things always change. If you want to let us know about your experiences – good, bad or ugly – then don't delay, go to **www.footprintbooks.com** and send in your comments.

Ordnance Survey

Publishing information
Footprint Scotland Highlands and Islands
3rd edition

February 2007

ISBN 978 1 904777 809
CIP DATA: A catalogue record for this book is available from the British Library

Published by Footprint
6 Riverside Court
Lower Bristol Road
Bath BA2 3DZ, UK
T +44 (0)1225 469141
F +44 (0)1225 469461
discover@footprintbooks.com
www.footprintbooks.com

Distributed in the USA by
Publishers Group West

Neither the black and white nor coloured maps are intended to have any political significance.

Every effort has been made to ensure that the facts in this guidebook are accurate. However, travellers should still obtain advice from consulates, airlines etc about travel and visa requirements before travelling. The authors and publishers cannot accept responsibility for any loss, injury or inconvenience however caused.

Scotland

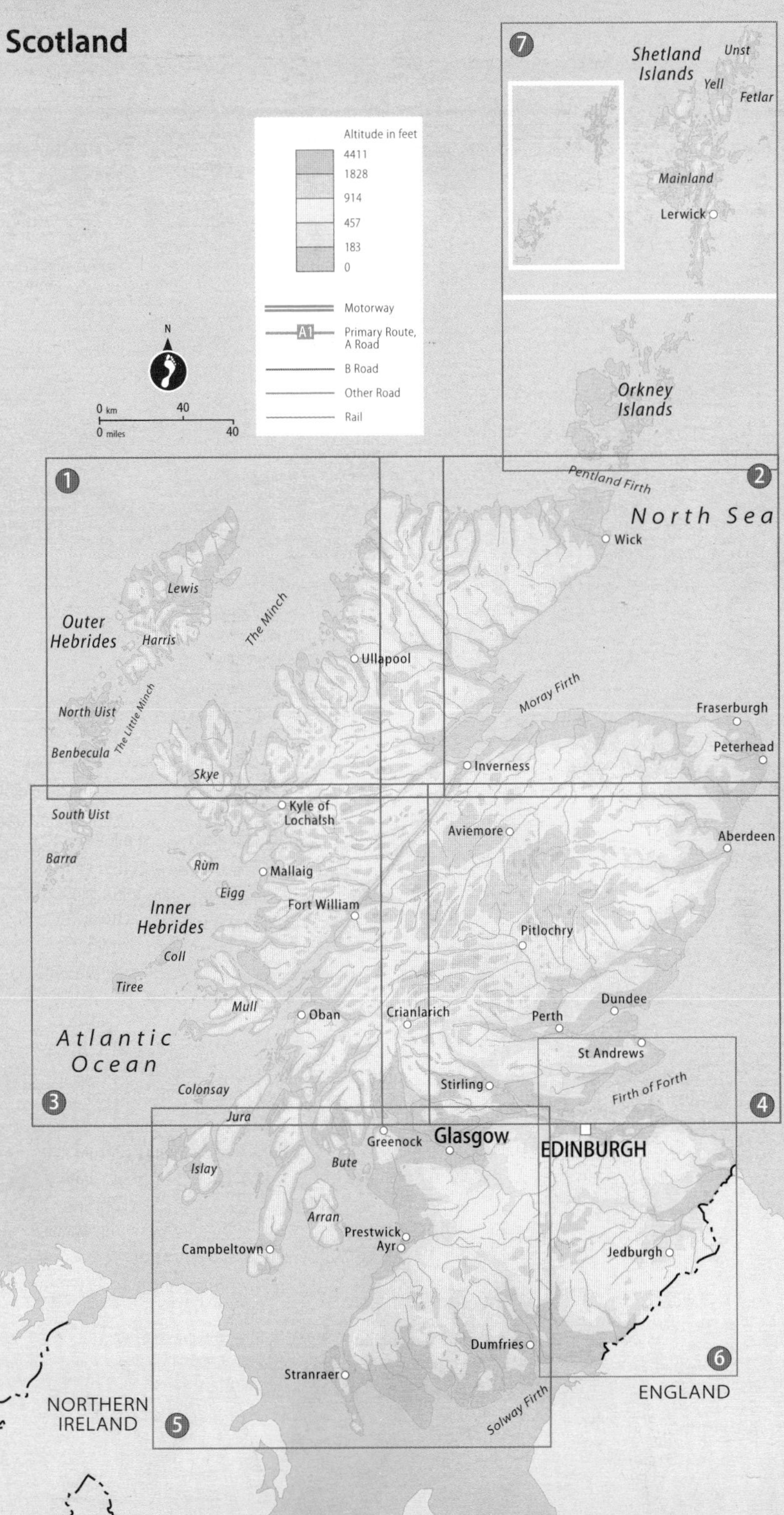

Altitude in feet
4411
1828
914
457
183
0
Motorway
A1
Primary Route, A Road
B Road
Other Road
Rail
N
0 km
40
0 miles
40
7
Shetland Islands
Unst
Yell
Fetlar
Mainland
Lerwick
Orkney Islands
1
2
Pentland Firth
North Sea
Wick
Lewis
Outer Hebrides
Harris
The Minch
Ullapool
North Uist
The Little Minch
Benbecula
Moray Firth
Fraserburgh
Peterhead
Inverness
Skye
South Uist
Kyle of Lochalsh
Aviemore
Aberdeen
Barra
Rùm
Mallaig
Eigg
Inner Hebrides
Fort William
Pitlochry
Coll
Tiree
Mull
Oban
Crianlarich
Dundee
Perth
Atlantic Ocean
St Andrews
Stirling
Firth of Forth
Colonsay
3
4
Jura
Greenock
Glasgow
EDINBURGH
Islay
Bute
Arran
Prestwick
Ayr
Campbeltown
Jedburgh
Dumfries
Stranraer
6
ENGLAND
NORTHERN IRELAND
5
Solway Firth

Map 1

N
A
B
C
1
2
3
0 km 10
0 miles 10
Flannan Islands or Seven Hunters
57° 50'
Boreray
Hirta
Soay
Dun
8° 30'
St Kilda
Outer Hebrides
Rubh Robhanais
Port Nis
Eoropaidh
Tabost
Dail Bho Dheas
Sgiogarstaigh
Gabhsann Bho Dheas
Siadar
A857
Baile an Truiseil
Muirneag (814ft)
Arnol
Barabhas
Tolastadh Úr
Tolsta Head
Siabost
Bragar
Leodhais (Lewis)
Gearrannan
A858
Carlabhagh
Griais
Loch a'Tuath
Bearnaraigh Beag
East Loch Roag
West Loch Roag
Tolastadh a'Chaolais
Beinn Mholach (958ft)
A857
Tunga
Rubha an t-Siumpain
Newmarket
Port nan Giúran
Miabhig
Bearnaraigh
Breascleit
Steornabhagh (Stornoway)
Siulaisiadar
Timsgearraidh
Calanais
A866
An Rubha
Cruiabhig
Gearraidh na h-Aibhne
A858
Mealisval (1884ft)
Loch Suainaval
Einacleit
Achadh Mór
Crosbost
Breanais
Uig
Mealasta Island
Baile Ailein
Loch Erisort
Loch Langavat
Ceann a Tuath na Hearadh (North Harris)
Cearsiadar
Grabhair
Scarp
Loch Reasort
Airidh a'Bhruaich
Leumrabhagh
Huisinis
Tirga Mor (2228ft)
Airidh a'Mhulaidh
Beinn Mhór (1877ft)
Loch Shell
Gasker
Clishham (2622ft)
Abhainnsuidhe
A859
Loch Seaforth
Loch Claidh
Bun Abhainn Eadarra
Aird Asaig
Loch Bhrollum
Tarasaigh
Tarbert (An Tairbeart)
Urgha
Reinigeadal
A859
Caolas Scalpaigh
Toe Head
Ceann a Deas na Hearadh (South Harris)
East Loch Tarbert
Scalpay (Eilean Scalpaigh)
Shiant Islands
Shillay
Taobh Tuath
Pabbay
A859
Sound of Pabbay
An t-Ob
Sound of Harris
Roghadal
Bearnaraigh
Boreray
Renish Point
Grimnis Point
Vallay
Otternish
Baile Mhartainn
Solas
Rubha Hunish
Duntulm Castle
Kilmaluag
A865
Hogha Gearraidh
Uibhist a'Tuath (North Uist)
Lochamaddy (Loch na Madadh)
Kilmuir
Quiraing
Staffin Bay
Cean a'Bháigh
A855
Sound of Monach
A865
A867
Vaternish Point
Linicro
Staffin
Claghan na Luib
Loch Euphoirt
Trotternish
Little Minch
Ben Geary (932ft)
Culnaknock
Heisker or Monach Islands
Saighdinis
Uig
Baile Seal
Trumpan
Waternish
Loch Snizort
Cairinis
A87
Baile a'Mhanaich
Uachdar
Dunvegan Head
Lusta
A855
A865
Loch Dunvegan
The Storr (2360ft)
Beinn na Faoghla (Benbecula)
Boreraig
Edinbane
Kensaleyre
Dunvegan Castle
A850
Bernisdale
Milovaig
Creag Ghoraidh
Duirinish
Dunvegan
Borve
Sound of Raasay
Neist Point
Carbost
Ardivachar Point
Wiay
Loch Bee
Roskhill
Skye
Bagh nam Faoilean
Portree
Healabhal Bheag (1602ft)
Bracadale
Stadhlaigearraidh
Loch Sgioport
A87
Oskaig
Uibhist a'Deas (South Uist)
Clachan
A863
Peinchorran
Portnalong
Sconser
Rubha Ardvuie
Talisker
Carbost
Sligachan
A87

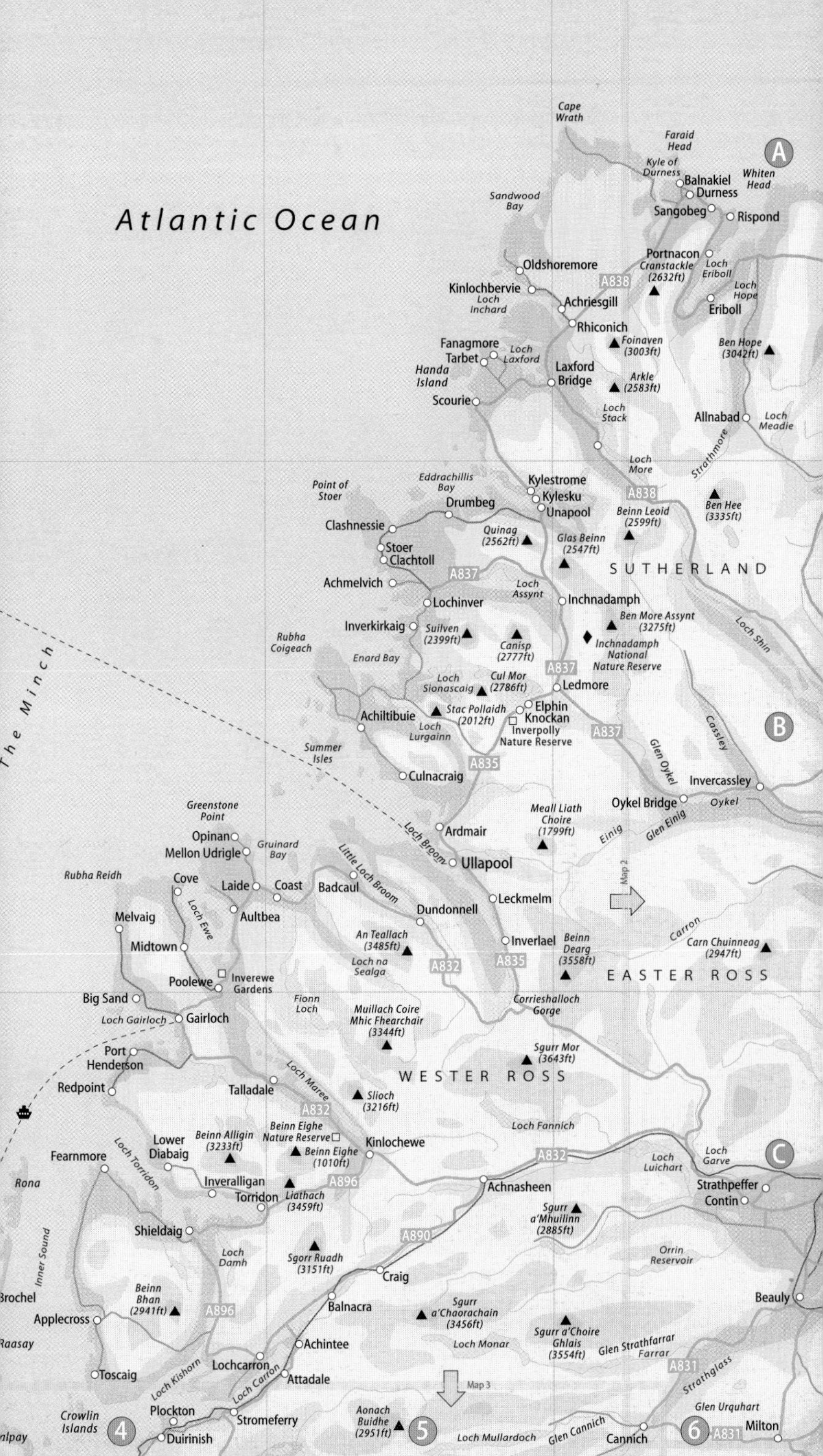
Atlantic Ocean
The Minch
Cape Wrath
Faraid Head
Kyle of Durness
Balnakiel
Durness
Whiten Head
Sandwood Bay
Sangobeg
Rispond
Portnacon
Cranstackle (2632ft)
Loch Eriboll
Loch Hope
Oldshoremore
Kinlochbervie
Loch Inchard
A838
Achriesgill
Eriboll
Rhiconich
Foinaven (3003ft)
Ben Hope (3042ft)
Fanagmore
Tarbet
Loch Laxford
Handa Island
Laxford Bridge
Arkle (2583ft)
Scourie
Loch Stack
Allnabad
Loch Meadie
Loch More
Strathmore
Point of Stoer
Eddrachillis Bay
Kylestrome
Kylesku
Unapool
Drumbeg
Ben Hee (3335ft)
Beinn Leoid (2599ft)
Clashnessie
Quinag (2562ft)
Glas Beinn (2547ft)
Stoer
Clachtoll
A837
SUTHERLAND
Achmelvich
Loch Assynt
Lochinver
Inchnadamph
Ben More Assynt (3275ft)
Inverkirkaig
Suilven (2399ft)
Canisp (2777ft)
Inchnadamph National Nature Reserve
Loch Shin
Rubha Coigeach
Enard Bay
Loch Sionascaig
Cul Mor (2786ft)
Ledmore
Stac Pollaidh (2012ft)
Elphin
Knockan
Achiltibuie
Loch Lurgainn
Inverpolly Nature Reserve
Cassley
Summer Isles
A835
Glen Oykel
Culnacraig
Invercassley
Oykel Bridge
Oykel
Greenstone Point
Meall Liath Choire (1799ft)
Opinan
Ardmair
Einig
Glen Einig
Mellon Udrigle
Gruinard Bay
Loch Broom
Little Loch Broom
Ullapool
Rubha Reidh
Cove
Laide
Coast
Badcaul
Map 2
Loch Ewe
Aultbea
Leckmelm
Melvaig
Dundonnell
Carron
An Teallach (3485ft)
Inverlael
Beinn Dearg (3558ft)
Carn Chuinneag (2947ft)
Midtown
Loch na Sealga
A832
Poolewe
Inverewe Gardens
EASTER ROSS
Big Sand
Fionn Loch
Corrieshalloch Gorge
Loch Gairloch
Gairloch
Muillach Coire Mhic Fhearchair (3344ft)
Port Henderson
Sgurr Mor (3643ft)
Loch Maree
WESTER ROSS
Redpoint
Talladale
Slioch (3216ft)
Loch Fannich
Beinn Eighe Nature Reserve
Lower Diabaig
Beinn Alligin (3233ft)
Beinn Eighe (1010ft)
Kinlochewe
Loch Luichart
Loch Garve
Fearnmore
Loch Torridon
Inveralligan
A896
Achnasheen
Strathpeffer
Rona
Torridon
Liathach (3459ft)
Contin
Sgurr a'Mhuilinn (2885ft)
Shieldaig
A890
Inner Sound
Loch Damh
Sgorr Ruadh (3151ft)
Orrin Reservoir
Craig
Brochel
Beinn Bhan (2941ft)
Balnacra
Beauly
Applecross
Sgurr a'Chaorachain (3456ft)
Sgurr a'Choire Ghlais (3554ft)
Raasay
Achintee
Loch Monar
Glen Strathfarrar
Farrar
Lochcarron
A831
Toscaig
Loch Kishorn
Attadale
Strathglass
Loch Carron
Map 3
Glen Urquhart
Crowlin Islands
Plockton
Stromeferry
Aonach Buidhe (2951ft)
Milton
Glen Cannich
Cannich
Duirinish
Loch Mullardoch
A
B
C
4
5
6

Map 2

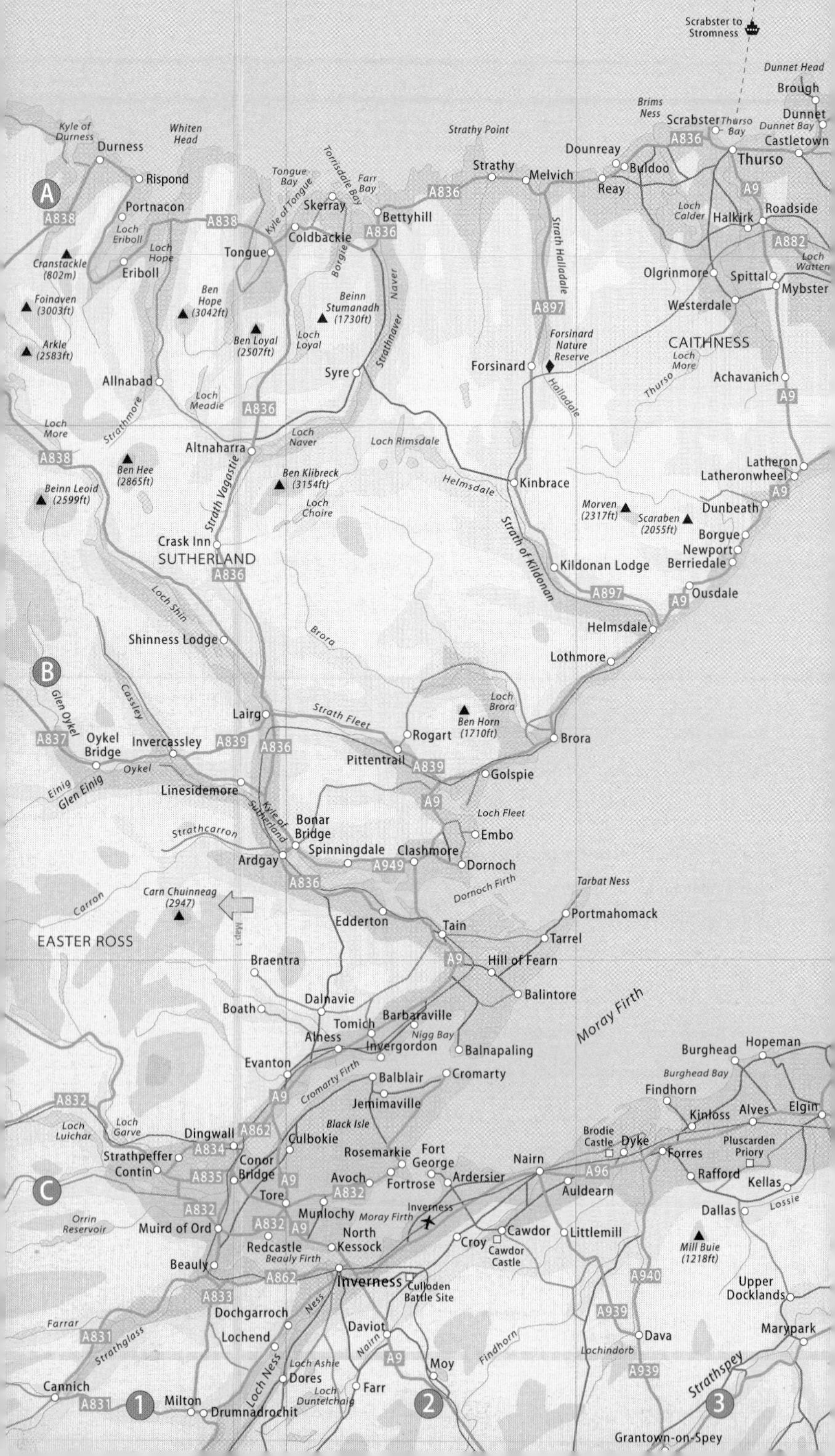

Scrabster to Stromness
Dunnet Head
Brough
Brims Ness
Dunnet
Scrabster
Thurso Bay
Dunnet Bay
Castletown
Kyle of Durness
Whiten Head
Strathy Point
Durness
Dounreay
A836
Thurso
Buldoo
Rispond
Tongue Bay
Torrisdale Bay
Strathy
Melvich
Reay
Farr Bay
A836
A9
A
Kyle of Tongue
Skerray
Loch Calder
Roadside
Portnacon
A838
Bettyhill
Halkirk
A838
Loch Eriboll
Coldbackie
A836
A882
Loch Hope
Strath Halladale
Loch Watten
Tongue
Borgie
Cranstackle (802m)
Eriboll
Olgrinmore
Spittal
Naver
Mybster
Beinn Stumanadh (1730ft)
Westerdale
Foinaven (3003ft)
Ben Hope (3042ft)
A897
Forsinard Nature Reserve
CAITHNESS
Ben Loyal (2507ft)
Loch Loyal
Arkle (2583ft)
Strathnaver
Loch More
Syre
Forsinard
Achavanich
Allnabad
Halladale
Thurso
A9
Loch Meadie
A836
Loch More
Strathmore
Loch Naver
Loch Rimsdale
A838
Altnaharra
Latheron
Ben Hee (2865ft)
Latheronwheel
Helmsdale
Kinbrace
Beinn Leoid (2599ft)
Ben Klibreck (3154ft)
A9
Strath Vagastie
Loch Choire
Morven (2317ft)
Dunbeath
Scaraben (2055ft)
Strath of Kildonan
Borgue
Crask Inn
Newport
SUTHERLAND
Kildonan Lodge
Berriedale
A836
Ousdale
A897
A9
Loch Shin
Helmsdale
Brora
Shinness Lodge
Lothmore
B
Glen Oykel
Cassley
Loch Brora
Ben Horn (1710ft)
Lairg
Strath Fleet
A837
Oykel Bridge
Invercassley
A839
A836
Rogart
Brora
Pittentrail
A839
Oykel
Golspie
Einig
Glen Einig
Linesidemore
A9
Kyle of Sutherland
Loch Fleet
Bonar Bridge
Embo
Strathcarron
Spinningdale
Clashmore
Ardgay
A949
Dornoch
A836
Dornoch Firth
Tarbat Ness
Carn Chuinneag (2947)
Carron
Map 1
Portmahomack
Edderton
Tain
EASTER ROSS
Tarrel
A9
Hill of Fearn
Braentra
Balintore
Moray Firth
Boath
Dalnavie
Tomich
Barbaraville
Nigg Bay
Alness
Invergordon
Balnapaling
Hopeman
Burghead
Evanton
Cromarty Firth
Burghead Bay
Balblair
Cromarty
A9
A832
Findhorn
Jemimaville
Elgin
Alves
Kinloss
Loch Luichar
Loch Garve
Black Isle
Dingwall
A862
Brodie Castle
Dyke
Pluscarden Priory
Culbokie
Fort George
A834
Rosemarkie
Nairn
Forres
Strathpeffer
Conor Bridge
A96
Contin
Rafford
A835
Avoch
Fortrose
Ardersier
Auldearn
Kellas
C
A9
A832
Tore
A832
Inverness
Lossie
Munlochy
Moray Firth
Dallas
Orrin Reservoir
Muird of Ord
A832
A9
North Kessock
Cawdor
Littlemill
Croy
Cawdor Castle
Mill Buie (1218ft)
Redcastle
Beauly Firth
Beauly
A862
Inverness
Culloden Battle Site
A940
Upper Docklands
A833
Ness
Dochgarroch
A939
Farrar
Daviot
Marypark
A831
Lochend
Nairn
Dava
Strathglass
Findhorn
Lochindorb
A9
Loch Ashie
Moy
A939
Strathspey
Dores
Cannich
Loch Ness
Loch Duntelchaig
Farr
A831
1
Milton
2
3
Drumnadrochit
Grantown-on-Spey

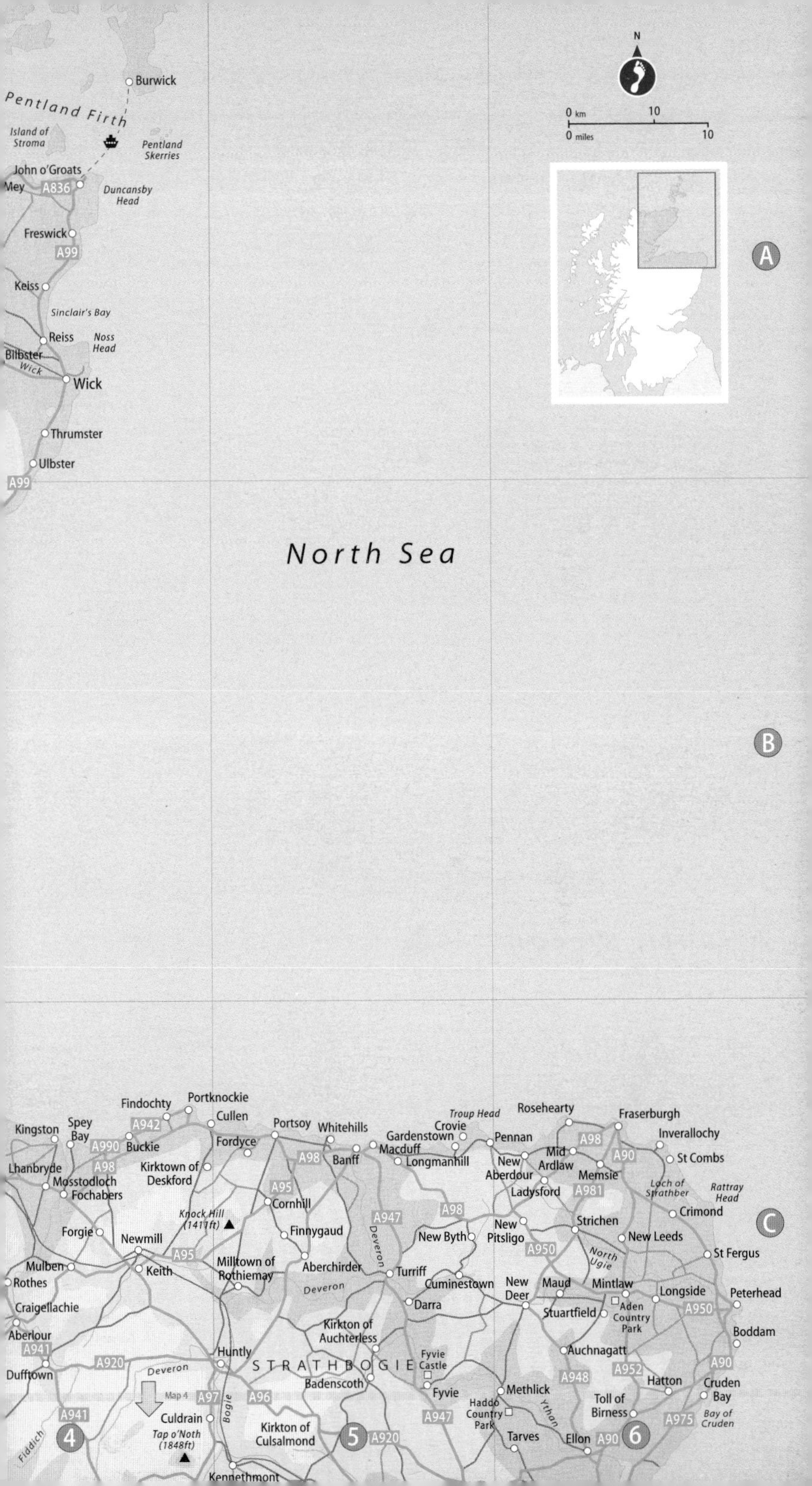

N
0 km
10
0 miles
10
A
B
C
Burwick
Pentland Firth
Island of Stroma
Pentland Skerries
John o'Groats
Mey
A836
Duncansby Head
Freswick
A99
Keiss
Sinclair's Bay
Reiss
Noss Head
Bilbster
Wick
Wick
Thrumster
Ulbster
A99
North Sea
Findochty
Portknockie
Cullen
Portsoy
Whitehills
Troup Head
Rosehearty
Fraserburgh
Kingston
Spey Bay
A942
A990
Buckie
Fordyce
Gardenstown
Crovie
Pennan
A98
Inverallochy
A98
Banff
Macduff
Longmanhill
New Aberdour
Mid Ardlaw
A90
St Combs
Lhanbryde
Mosstodloch
Fochabers
Kirktown of Deskford
A95
Cornhill
Memsie
A981
Loch of Strathber
Rattray Head
Ladysford
Knock Hill (1411ft)
A947
A98
Crimond
Forgie
Newmill
Finnygaud
New Byth
New Pitsligo
Strichen
New Leeds
A95
Deveron
A950
Mulben
Keith
Milltown of Rothiemay
Aberchirder
Turriff
North Ugie
St Fergus
Rothes
Deveron
Cuminestown
New Deer
Maud
Mintlaw
Longside
Peterhead
Craigellachie
Darra
Aden Country Park
A950
Stuartfield
Aberlour
Kirkton of Auchterless
Boddam
A941
Auchnagatt
A920
Huntly
STRATHBOGIE
Fyvie Castle
A952
A90
Dufftown
Deveron
A948
Hatton
Cruden Bay
Badenscoth
Methlick
Map 4
A97
A96
Fyvie
Toll of Birness
Haddo Country Park
Ythan
A941
Bogie
A947
A975
Bay of Cruden
Culdrain
Tap o'Noth (1848ft)
Kirkton of Culsalmond
Tarves
Ellon
A90
Fiddich
4
5
A920
6
Kennethmont

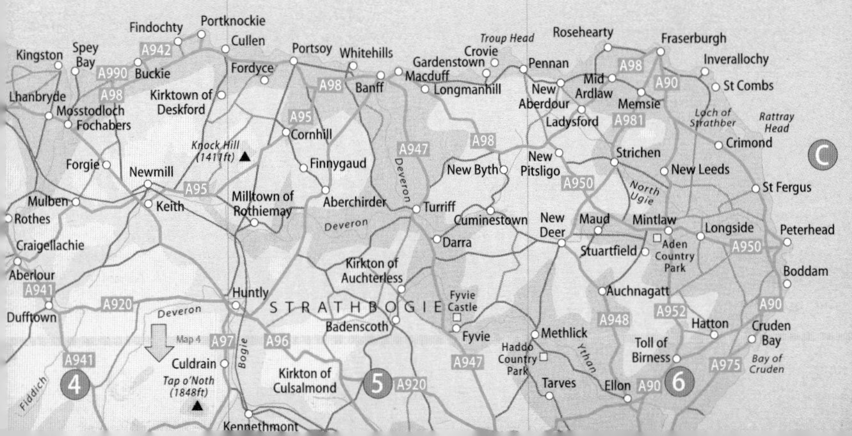

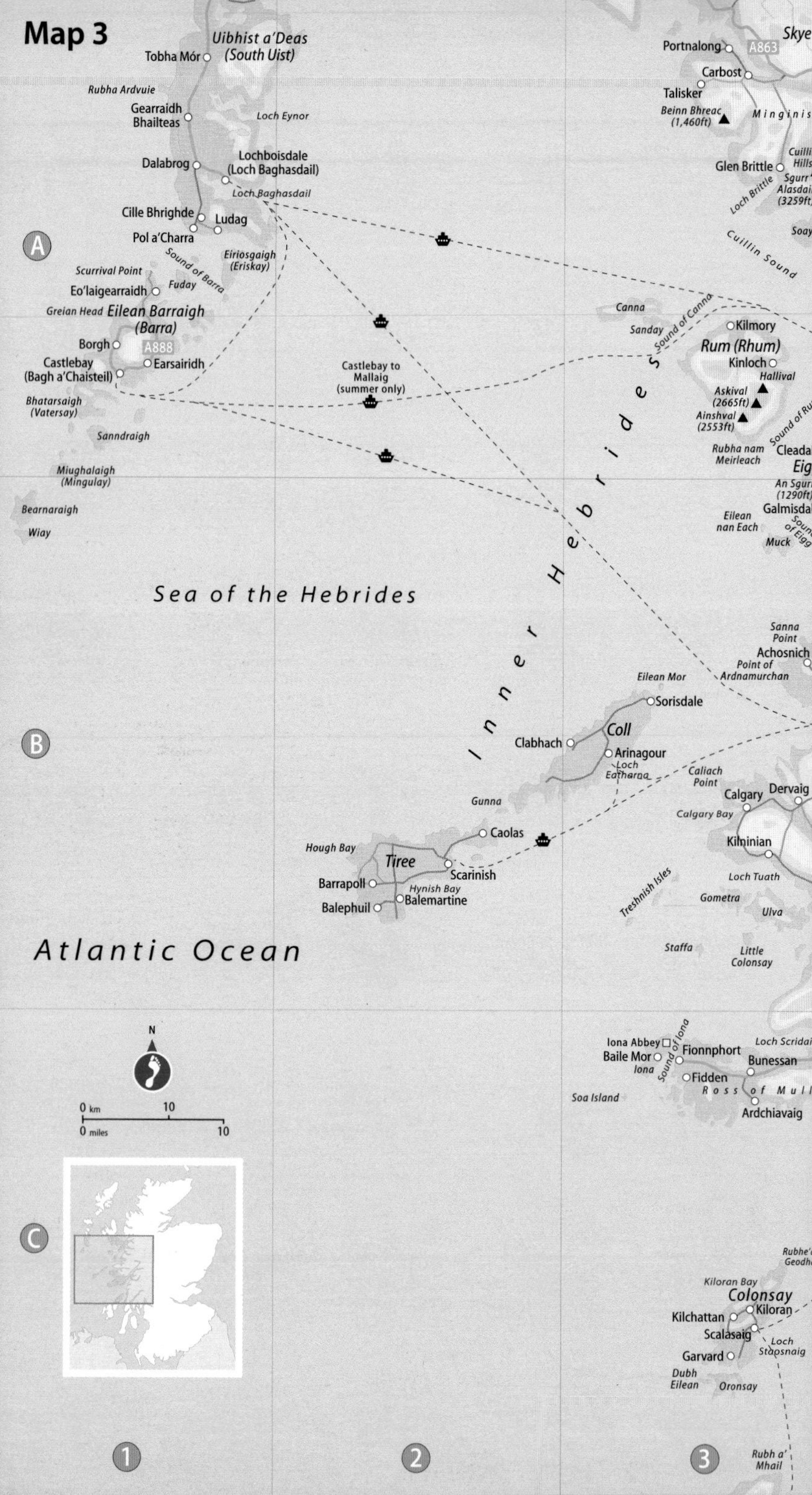

Map 3
Uibhist a'Deas (South Uist)
Tobha Mór
Rubha Ardvuie
Gearraidh Bhailteas
Loch Eynor
Dalabrog
Lochboisdale (Loch Baghasdail)
Loch Baghasdail
Cille Bhrighde
Ludag
Pol a'Charra
Sound of Barra
Eiriosgaigh (Eriskay)
Scurrival Point
Fuday
Eo'laigearraidh
Greian Head
Eilean Barraigh (Barra)
Borgh
A888
Earsairidh
Castlebay (Bagh a'Chaisteil)
Bhatarsaigh (Vatersay)
Sanndraigh
Miughalaigh (Mingulay)
Bearnaraigh
Wiay
Castlebay to Mallaig (summer only)
Sea of the Hebrides
Inner Hebrides
Atlantic Ocean
Skye
Portnalong
A863
Carbost
Talisker
Beinn Bhreac (1,460ft)
Glen Brittle
Loch Brittle
Cuillin Sound
Soay
Canna
Sanday
Sound of Canna
Kilmory
Rum (Rhum)
Kinloch
Hallival
Askival (2665ft)
Ainshval (2553ft)
Rubha nam Meirleach
An Sgurr (1290ft)
Eilean nan Each
Muck
Sanna Point
Achosnich
Point of Ardnamurchan
Eilean Mor
Sorisdale
Coll
Clabhach
Arinagour
Loch Eatharna
Caliach Point
Calgary
Dervaig
Calgary Bay
Gunna
Caolas
Hough Bay
Tiree
Scarinish
Barrapoll
Hynish Bay
Balephuil
Balemartine
Kilninian
Loch Tuath
Treshnish Isles
Gometra
Ulva
Staffa
Little Colonsay
Iona Abbey
Baile Mor
Iona
Sound of Iona
Fionnphort
Bunessan
Loch Scridain
Fidden
Ross of Mull
Soa Island
Ardchiavaig
N
0 km 10
0 miles 10
Kiloran Bay
Colonsay
Kiloran
Kilchattan
Scalasaig
Loch Staosnaig
Garvard
Dubh Eilean
Oronsay
Rubh a' Mhail
A
B
C
1
2
3

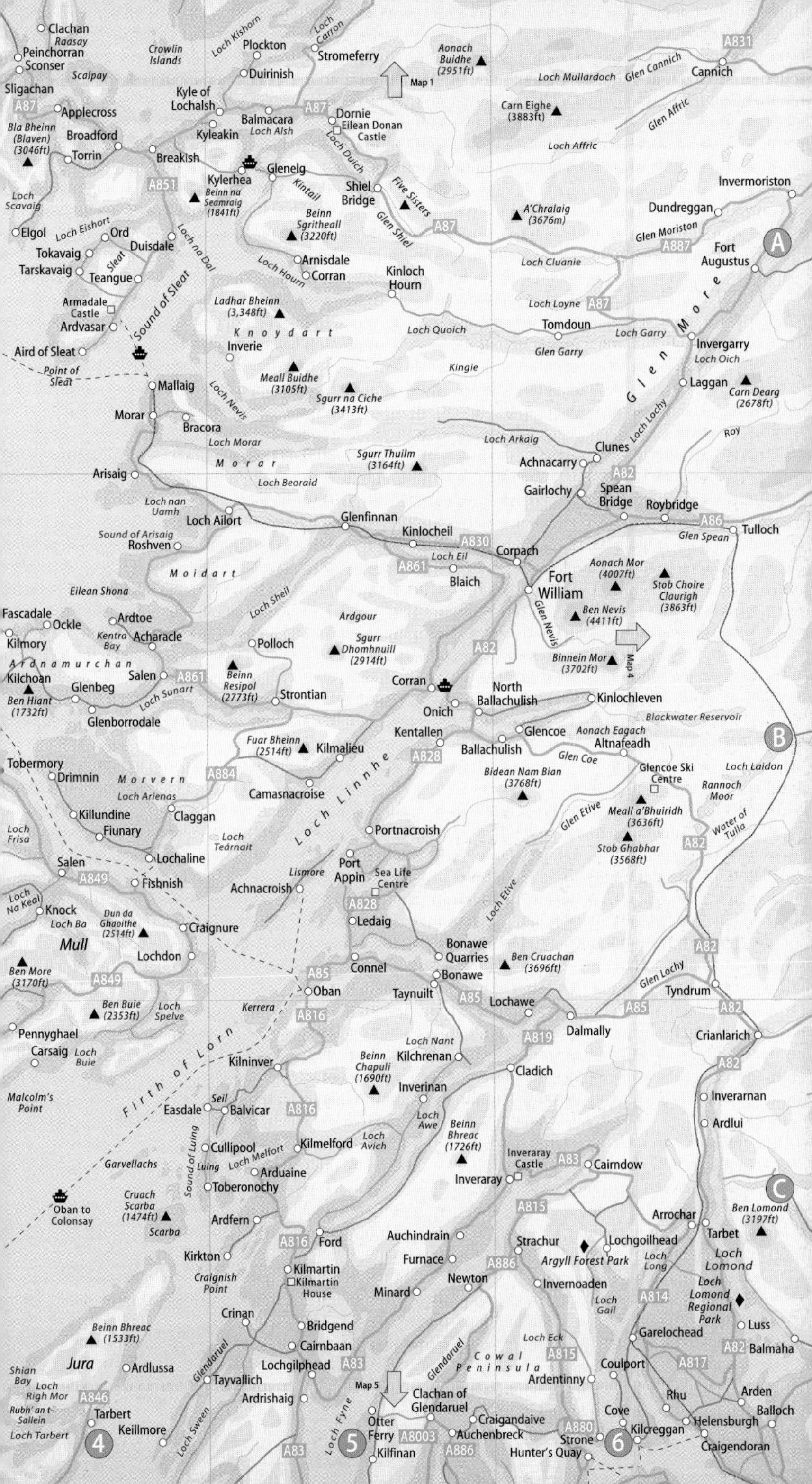

Clachan
Raasay
Peinchorran
Sconser
Scalpay
Sligachan
A87
Applecross
Bla Bheinn (Blaven) (3046ft)
Broadford
Torrin
Crowlin Islands
Loch Kishorn
Plockton
Duirinish
Kyle of Lochalsh
Kyleakin
Balmacara
Loch Alsh
Loch Carron
Stromeferry
Map 1
Dornie
Eilean Donan Castle
Loch Duich
Aonach Buidhe (2951ft)
Loch Mullardoch
Glen Cannich
Cannich
A831
Carn Eighe (3883ft)
Glen Affric
Loch Affric
Breakish
Glenelg
Kylerhea
A851
Beinn na Seamraig (1841ft)
Kintail
Shiel Bridge
Five Sisters
Glen Shiel
A87
A'Chralaig (3676m)
Invermoriston
Dundreggan
Glen Moriston
A887
Fort Augustus
A
Loch Scavaig
Elgol
Loch Eishort
Ord
Tokavaig
Duisdale
Sleat
Tarskavaig
Teangue
Loch na Dal
Beinn Sgritheall (3220ft)
Arnisdale
Corran
Loch Hourn
Kinloch Hourn
Loch Cluanie
Armadale Castle
Ardvasar
Sound of Sleat
Ladhar Bheinn (3,348ft)
Knoydart
Inverie
Loch Loyne
A87
Tomdoun
Loch Quoich
Loch Garry
Glen Garry
Invergarry
Loch Oich
Glen More
Aird of Sleat
Point of Sleat
Mallaig
Meall Buidhe (3105ft)
Kingie
Laggan
Carn Dearg (2678ft)
Sgurr na Ciche (3413ft)
Loch Nevis
Morar
Bracora
Loch Morar
Morar
Loch Arkaig
Loch Lochy
Roy
Clunes
Achnacarry
Sgurr Thuilm (3164ft)
Arisaig
Loch Beoraid
A82
Gairlochy
Spean Bridge
Roybridge
Loch nan Uamh
Loch Ailort
Glenfinnan
Kinlocheil
A86
Tulloch
Glen Spean
Sound of Arisaig
Roshven
A830
Loch Eil
Corpach
A861
Blaich
Aonach Mor (4007ft)
Fort William
Stob Choire Claurigh (3863ft)
Moidart
Eilean Shona
Loch Sheil
Ardgour
Glen Nevis
Ben Nevis (4411ft)
Fascadale
Ockle
Ardtoe
Kilmory
Kentra Bay
Acharacle
Polloch
Sgurr Dhomhnuill (2914ft)
A82
Binnein Mor (3702ft)
Map 4
Ardnamurchan
Kilchoan
Salen
A861
Beinn Resipol (2773ft)
Corran
North Ballachulish
Kinlochleven
Glenbeg
Ben Hiant (1732ft)
Loch Sunart
Strontian
Onich
Glenborrodale
Blackwater Reservoir
Kentallen
Glencoe
Aonach Eagach
Altnafeadh
B
Fuar Bheinn (2514ft)
Kilmalieu
Ballachulish
A828
Glen Coe
Tobermory
Drimnin
Morvern
A884
Loch Linnhe
Glencoe Ski Centre
Loch Laidon
Bidean Nam Bian (3768ft)
Rannoch Moor
Loch Arienas
Camasnacroise
Killundine
Claggan
Meall a'Bhuiridh (3636ft)
Glen Etive
Loch Frisa
Fiunary
Loch Teàrnait
Portnacroish
Water of Tulla
Stob Ghabhar (3568ft)
A82
Lochaline
Salen
Port Appin
Sea Life Centre
Lismore
A849
Fishnish
Achnacroish
Loch Na Keal
Knock
Loch Ba
Dun da Ghaoithe (2514ft)
A828
Ledaig
Loch Etive
Craignure
Mull
Lochdon
Bonawe Quarries
Ben Cruachan (3696ft)
A82
Ben More (3170ft)
A849
Connel
Bonawe
Glen Lochy
A85
Oban
Taynuilt
Tyndrum
Ben Buie (2353ft)
Loch Spelve
Kerrera
A816
A85
Lochawe
A85
A82
Pennyghael
Dalmally
Loch Nant
A819
Crianlarich
Carsaig
Loch Buie
Firth of Lorn
Kilninver
Beinn Chapuli (1690ft)
Kilchrenan
Cladich
A82
Malcolm's Point
Seil
Easdale
Balvicar
A816
Inverinan
Inverarnan
Loch Awe
Beinn Bhreac (1726ft)
Ardlui
Sound of Luing
Cullipool
Kilmelford
Loch Avich
Garvellachs
Luing
Loch Melfort
Arduaine
Inveraray Castle
A83
Cairndow
Toberonochy
Inveraray
Oban to Colonsay
Cruach Scarba (1474ft)
Scarba
A815
C
Ardfern
Arrochar
Ben Lomond (3197ft)
Tarbet
Ford
A816
Auchindrain
Strachur
Lochgoilhead
Loch Lomond
Kirkton
Kilmartin
Furnace
A886
Argyll Forest Park
Loch Long
Craignish Point
Kilmartin House
Newton
Loch Lomond Regional Park
Minard
Invernoaden
Loch Gail
A814
Crinan
Bridgend
Luss
Beinn Bhreac (1533ft)
Cairnbaan
Loch Eck
Garelochead
Glendaruel
Cowal Peninsula
A815
A82
Balmaha
Jura
Ardlussa
Lochgilphead
A83
A817
Coulport
Shian Bay
Loch Righ Mor
Tayvallich
Glendaruel
Ardentinny
A846
Map 5
Clachan of Glendaruel
Rhu
Arden
Rubh' an t-Sailein
Tarbert
Ardrishaig
Loch Fyne
Cove
Balloch
Loch Tarbert
Keillmore
Loch Sween
Otter Ferry
Craigandaive
A880
Kilcreggan
Helensburgh
4
A83
5
A8003
Auchenbreck
Strone
6
Craigendoran
Kilfinan
A886
Hunter's Quay

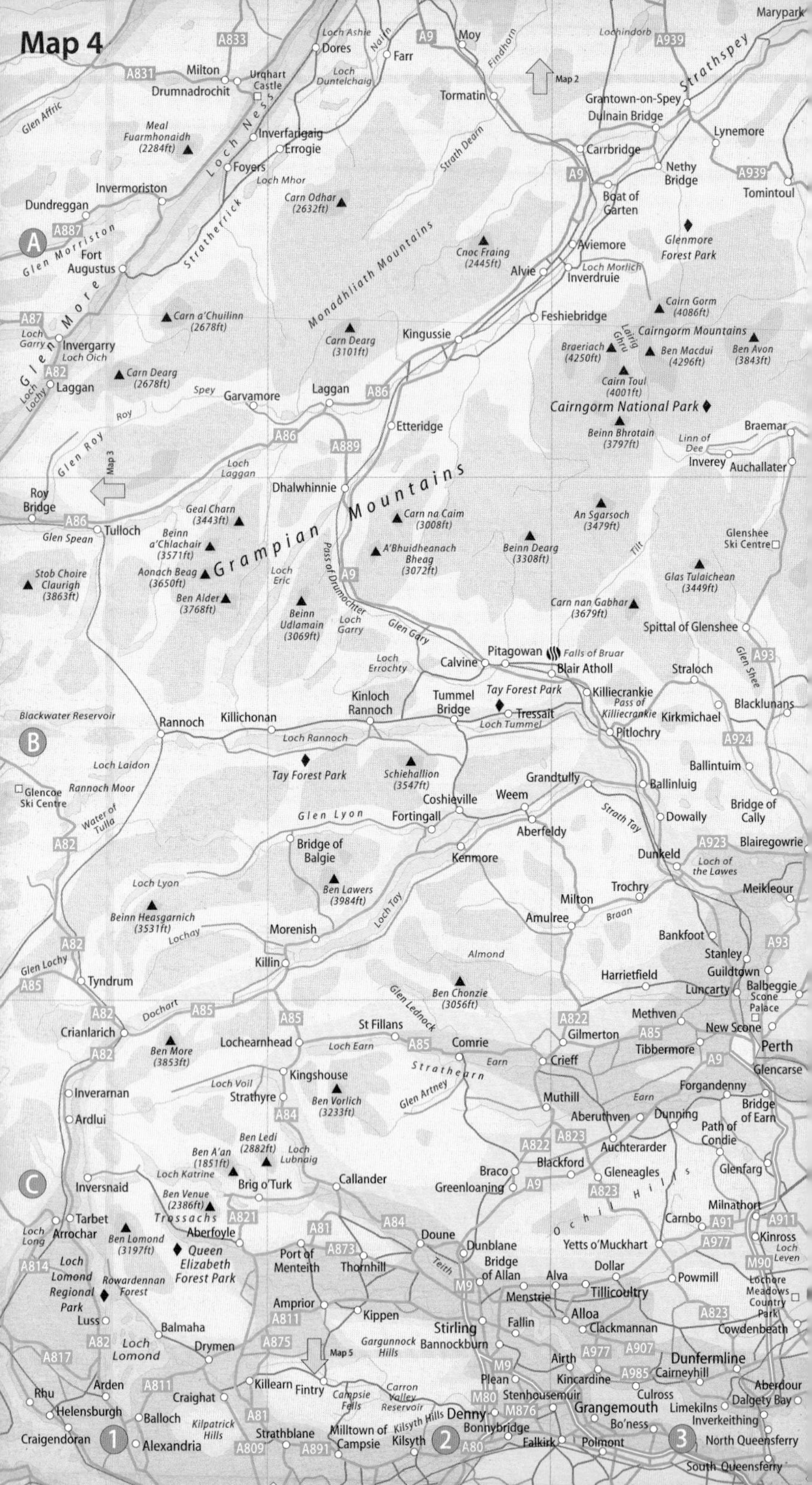

Map 4
A833
Loch Ashie
Dores
Nairn
A9
Moy
Farr
Findhorn
Lochindorb
A939
Strathspey
Marypark
A831
Milton
Drumnadrochit
Urqhart Castle
Loch Duntelchaig
Map 2
Tormatin
Grantown-on-Spey
Dulnain Bridge
Glen Affric
Meal Fuarmhonaidh (2284ft)
Loch Ness
Inverfarigaig
Errogie
Strath Dearn
Lynemore
Carrbridge
Foyers
Loch Mhor
A9
Nethy Bridge
A939
Tomintoul
Invermoriston
Carn Odhar (2632ft)
Boat of Garten
Dundreggan
Stratherrick
A887
Glen Morriston
Glenmore Forest Park
A
Monadhliath Mountains
Cnoc Fraing (2445ft)
Aviemore
Fort Augustus
Alvie
Loch Morlich
Inverdruie
Glen More
Cairn Gorm (4086ft)
A87
Carn a'Chuilinn (2678ft)
Feshiebridge
Loch Garry
Invergarry
Carn Dearg (3101ft)
Kingussie
Lairig Ghru
Cairngorm Mountains
Loch Oich
Braeriach (4250ft)
Ben Macdui (4296ft)
Ben Avon (3843ft)
A82
Carn Dearg (2678ft)
Cairn Toul (4001ft)
Loch Lochy
Laggan
Spey
Garvamore
Laggan
A86
Cairngorm National Park
Roy
Etteridge
Beinn Bhrotain (3797ft)
Braemar
A86
A889
Linn of Dee
Glen Roy
Map 3
Inverey
Auchallater
Loch Laggan
Grampian Mountains
Roy Bridge
Dhalwhinnie
Carn na Caim (3008ft)
An Sgarsoch (3479ft)
Geal Charn (3443ft)
A86
Tulloch
Beinn a'Chlachair (3571ft)
A'Bhuidheanach Bheag (3072ft)
Beinn Dearg (3308ft)
Glenshee Ski Centre
Glen Spean
Pass of Drumochter
Tilt
Stob Choire Claurigh (3863ft)
Aonach Beag (3650ft)
Loch Eric
A9
Glas Tulaichean (3449ft)
Ben Alder (3768ft)
Beinn Udlamain (3069ft)
Loch Garry
Carn nan Gabhar (3679ft)
Glen Gary
Spittal of Glenshee
Loch Errochty
Calvine
Pitagowan
Falls of Bruar
Blair Atholl
A93
Glen Shee
Straloch
Kinloch Rannoch
Tummel Bridge
Tay Forest Park
Killiecrankie
Pass of Killiecrankie
Tressait
Blacklunans
Blackwater Reservoir
Rannoch
Killichonan
Loch Tummel
Kirkmichael
B
Loch Rannoch
Pitlochry
A924
Loch Laidon
Tay Forest Park
Schiehallion (3547ft)
Ballintuim
Grandtully
Glencoe Ski Centre
Rannoch Moor
Ballinluig
Coshieville
Weem
Water of Tulla
Glen Lyon
Fortingall
Strath Tay
Bridge of Cally
Dowally
Aberfeldy
A82
Bridge of Balgie
A923
Blairegowrie
Dunkeld
Kenmore
Loch of the Lawes
Loch Lyon
Ben Lawers (3984ft)
Meikleour
Trochry
Milton
Beinn Heasgarnich (3531ft)
Loch Tay
Amulree
Braan
Lochay
Morenish
Bankfoot
A82
Almond
Stanley
A93
Killin
Glen Lochy
Guildtown
Harrietfield
A85
Tyndrum
Ben Chonzie (3056ft)
Luncarty
Balbeggie
Glen Lednock
Scone Palace
A82
Dochart
A85
A85
A822
Methven
Crianlarich
St Fillans
Gilmerton
A85
New Scone
Ben More (3853ft)
Lochearnhead
Loch Earn
A85
Comrie
Tibbermore
Perth
A82
Earn
Crieff
A9
Glencarse
Strathearn
Kingshouse
Loch Voil
Inverarnan
Forgandenny
Muthill
Earn
Strathyre
Ben Vorlich (3233ft)
Bridge of Earn
Glen Artney
Aberuthven
Dunning
Ardlui
A84
Path of Condie
A823
Ben Ledi (2882ft)
Loch Lubnaig
A822
Auchterarder
Ben A'an (1851ft)
Blackford
Glenfarg
Loch Katrine
Braco
Gleneagles
Hills
C
Inversnaid
Brig o'Turk
Callander
Greenloaning
A9
Ben Venue (2386ft)
A823
Milnathort
Trossachs
Ochil
Tarbet
A821
Carnbo
A91
A911
Loch Long
Arrochar
Ben Lomond (3197ft)
Aberfoyle
A81
A84
Doune
Kinross
Queen Elizabeth Forest Park
A873
Dunblane
Yetts o'Muckhart
A977
Loch Leven
A814
Loch Lomond
Port of Menteith
Thornhill
Bridge of Allan
Dollar
M90
Rowardennan Forest
Teith
Alva
Powmill
Lochore Meadows Country Park
Regional Park
M9
Menstrie
Tillicoultry
Ampriot
Kippen
Luss
A811
Alloa
A823
Stirling
Fallin
Clackmannan
Cowdenbeath
Balmaha
A82
Loch Lomond
Drymen
A875
Gargunnock Hills
Bannockburn
Map 5
A817
M9
Airth
A977
A907
Dunfermline
Plean
Kincardine
A985
Cairneyhill
Rhu
Arden
A811
Killearn
Fintry
Carron Valley Reservoir
Aberdour
Craighat
Campsie Fells
M80
Stenhousemuir
Culross
Dalgety Bay
Helensburgh
M876
Grangemouth
Limekilns
A81
Kilsyth Hills
Denny
Balloch
Kilpatrick Hills
Bo'ness
Inverkeithing
Bonnybridge
Strathblane
Milltown of Campsie
Craigendoran
1
Alexandria
A809
A891
Kilsyth
2
A80
Falkirk
Polmont
3
North Queensferry
South Queensferry

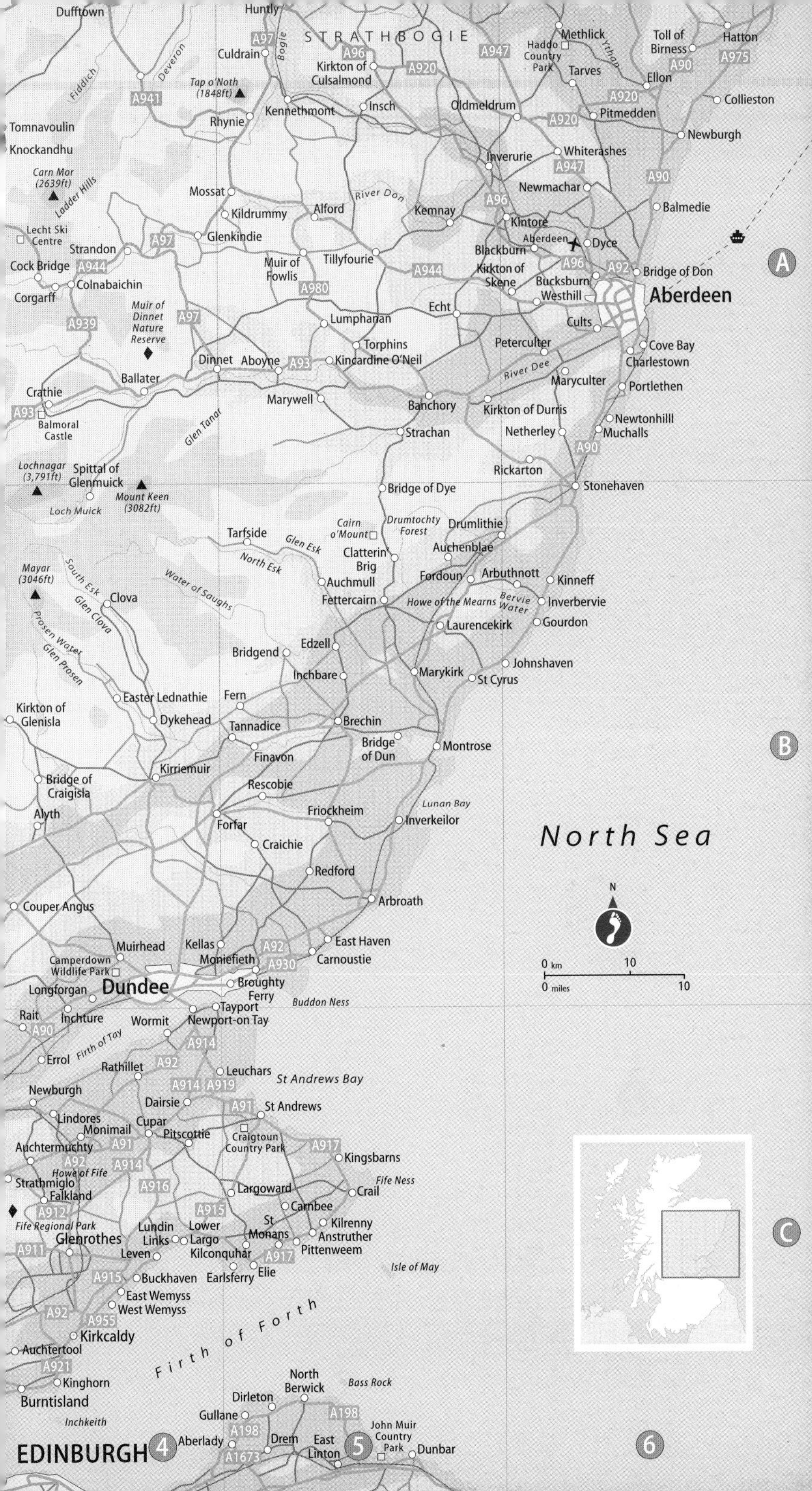

Dufftown
Huntly
STRATHBOGIE
A97
Bogie
A96
A947
Methlick
Haddo Country Park
Ythan
Toll of Birness
Hatton
A975
A90
Culdrain
Kirkton of Culsalmond
A920
Tarves
Ellon
Deveron
Fiddich
A941
Tap o'Noth (1848ft)
Kennethmont
Insch
Oldmeldrum
A920
Pitmedden
Collieston
Rhynie
A920
Tomnavoulin
Knockandhu
Newburgh
Inverurie
Whiterashes
A947
Carn Mor (2639ft)
Ladder Hills
A90
Mossat
River Don
Newmachar
A96
Balmedie
Kildrummy
Alford
Kemnay
Kintore
Lecht Ski Centre
A97
Glenkindie
Aberdeen
Dyce
Strandon
Muir of Fowlis
Tillyfourie
Blackburn
A
Cock Bridge
A944
A944
Kirkton of Skene
A96
A92
Bridge of Don
Colnabaichin
A980
Bucksburn
Corgarff
Westhill
Aberdeen
Muir of Dinnet Nature Reserve
Echt
A939
A97
Lumphanan
Cults
Torphins
Peterculter
Cove Bay
Dinnet
Aboyne
A93
Kincardine O'Neil
Charlestown
River Dee
Maryculter
Ballater
Portlethen
Crathie
Marywell
Banchory
Kirkton of Durris
A93
Balmoral Castle
Newtonhill
Glen Tanar
Strachan
Netherley
Muchalls
A90
Rickarton
Lochnagar (3,791ft)
Spittal of Glenmuick
Stonehaven
Mount Keen (3082ft)
Bridge of Dye
Loch Muick
Cairn o'Mount
Drumtochty Forest
Drumlithie
Tarfside
Glen Esk
Auchenblae
Clatterin' Brig
North Esk
Arbuthnott
Kinneff
Mayar (3046ft)
South Esk
Water of Saughs
Fordoun
Auchmull
Bervie Water
Inverbervie
Clova
Fettercairn
Howe of the Mearns
Glen Clova
Gourdon
Laurencekirk
Prosen Water
Glen Prosen
Edzell
Bridgend
Johnshaven
Inchbare
Marykirk
St Cyrus
Easter Lednathie
Fern
Kirkton of Glenisla
Dykehead
Brechin
Tannadice
Bridge of Dun
B
Montrose
Finavon
Kirriemuir
Bridge of Craigisla
Rescobie
Lunan Bay
Alyth
Friockheim
Inverkeilor
Forfar
Craichie
North Sea
Redford
Arbroath
N
Couper Angus
East Haven
Muirhead
Kellas
A92
Carnoustie
Monifieth
Camperdown Wildlife Park
A930
Dundee
0 km 10
0 miles 10
Broughty Ferry
Longforgan
Tayport
Buddon Ness
Rait
Inchture
Wormit
Newport-on Tay
A90
A914
Errol
Firth of Tay
Rathillet
A92
Leuchars
St Andrews Bay
A914
A919
Newburgh
Dairsie
A91
St Andrews
Lindores
Cupar
Monimail
Pitscottie
Craigtoun Country Park
A91
A917
Auchtermuchty
Kingsbarns
A92
A914
Howe of Fife
Fife Ness
A916
Strathmiglo
Largoward
Falkland
Crail
Cambee
A915
A912
St Monans
Kilrenny
Fife Regional Park
Lundin Links
Lower Largo
Anstruther
C
Glenrothes
A911
Pittenweem
Leven
Kilconquhar
A917
Isle of May
Elie
A915
Buckhaven
Earlsferry
East Wemyss
West Wemyss
A92
A955
Firth of Forth
Kirkcaldy
Auchtertool
A921
Kinghorn
North Berwick
Bass Rock
Burntisland
Dirleton
A198
Gullane
Inchkeith
A198
John Muir Country Park
EDINBURGH
4
Aberlady
Drem
East Linton
5
A1673
Dunbar
6

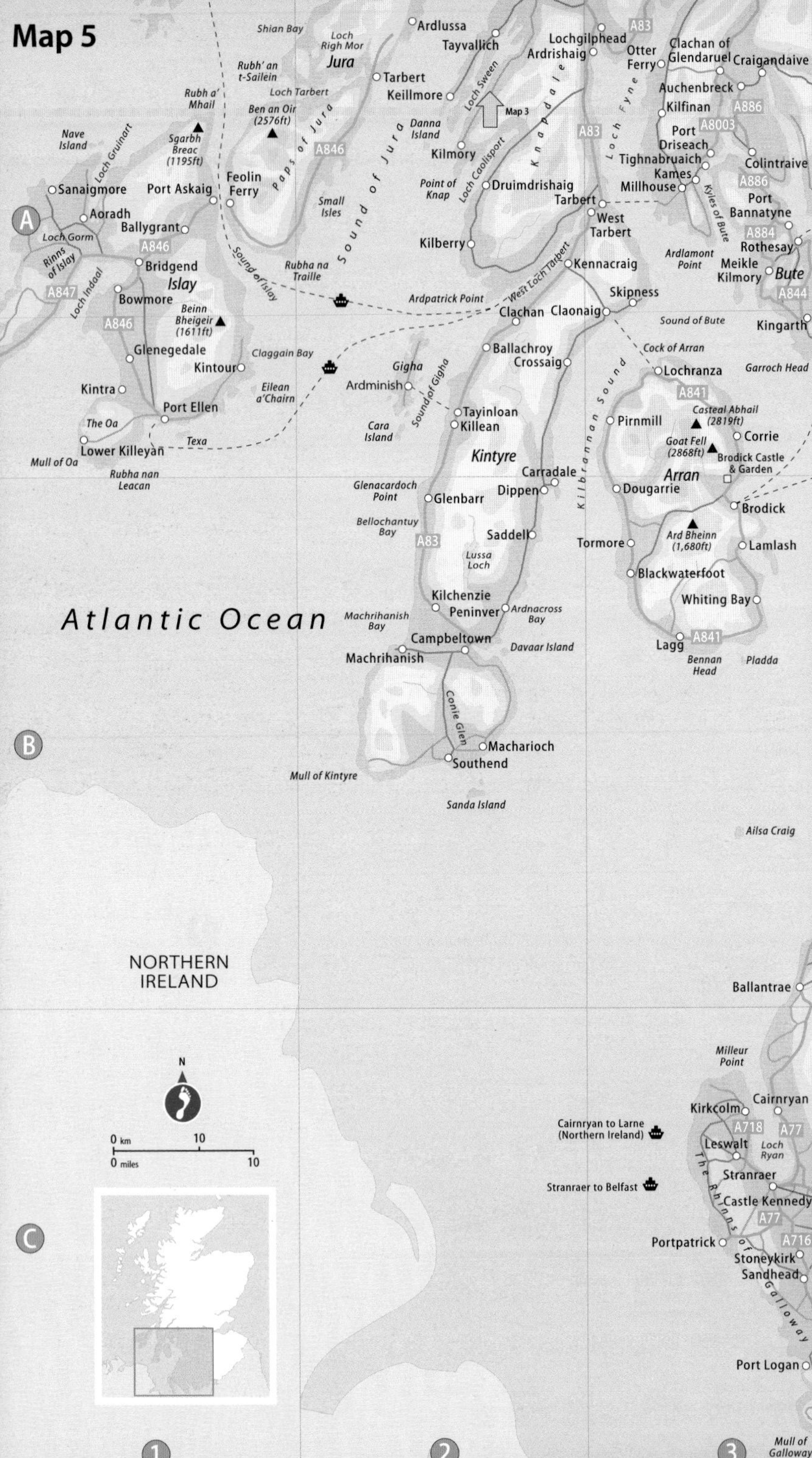
Map 5
Shian Bay
Ardlussa
Loch Righ Mor
Jura
Tayvallich
Lochgilphead
A83
Ardrishaig
Otter Ferry
Clachan of Glendaruel
Craigandaive
Rubh' an t-Sailein
Tarbert
Loch Tarbert
Keillmore
Loch Sween
Auchenbreck
Rubh a' Mhail
Ben an Oir (2576ft)
Map 3
Kilfinan
A886
Nave Island
Sgarbh Breac (1195ft)
Paps of Jura
Danna Island
Knapdale
A83
Loch Fyne
Port Driseach
A8003
Loch Gruinart
A846
Kilmory
Tighnabruaich
Colintraive
Sanaigmore
Port Askaig
Feolin Ferry
Sound of Jura
Point of Knap
Loch Caolisport
Druimdrishaig
Kames
Millhouse
A886
Aoradh
Small Isles
Tarbert
Kyles of Bute
Port Bannatyne
Ballygrant
Loch Gorm
West Tarbert
A884
A846
Kilberry
Rothesay
Rinns of Islay
Bridgend
Sound of Islay
Rubha na Traille
Ardlamont Point
Meikle Kilmory
Islay
Kennacraig
Bute
A847
Loch Indaal
Bowmore
West Loch Tarbert
Skipness
A844
Ardpatrick Point
Beinn Bheigeir (1611ft)
Clachan
Claonaig
Sound of Bute
Kingarth
A846
Glenegedale
Claggain Bay
Ballachroy
Cock of Arran
Crossaig
Kintour
Gigha
Lochranza
Garroch Head
Kintra
Ardminish
Eilean a'Chairn
A841
Port Ellen
Sound of Gigha
Tayinloan
Kilbrannan Sound
Casteal Abhail (2819ft)
The Oa
Pirnmill
Killean
Corrie
Cara Island
Goat Fell (2868ft)
Texa
Lower Killeyan
Brodick Castle & Garden
Kintyre
Mull of Oa
Carradale
Arran
Rubha nan Leacan
Glenacardoch Point
Dippen
Dougarrie
Glenbarr
Brodick
Bellochantuy Bay
Saddell
Ard Bheinn (1,680ft)
Tormore
A83
Lamlash
Lussa Loch
Blackwaterfoot
Kilchenzie
Whiting Bay
Ardnacross Bay
Atlantic Ocean
Machrihanish Bay
Peninver
Campbeltown
A841
Davaar Island
Lagg
Machrihanish
Bennan Head
Pladda
Conie Glen
Machariogh
Southend
Mull of Kintyre
Sanda Island
Ailsa Craig
NORTHERN IRELAND
Ballantrae
Milleur Point
N
Cairnryan
Kirkcolm
Cairnryan to Larne (Northern Ireland)
A718
A77
0 km
10
0 miles
10
Leswalt
Loch Ryan
Stranraer to Belfast
Stranraer
The Rhinns of Galloway
Castle Kennedy
A77
Portpatrick
A716
Stoneykirk
Sandhead
Port Logan
Mull of Galloway
A
B
C
1
2
3

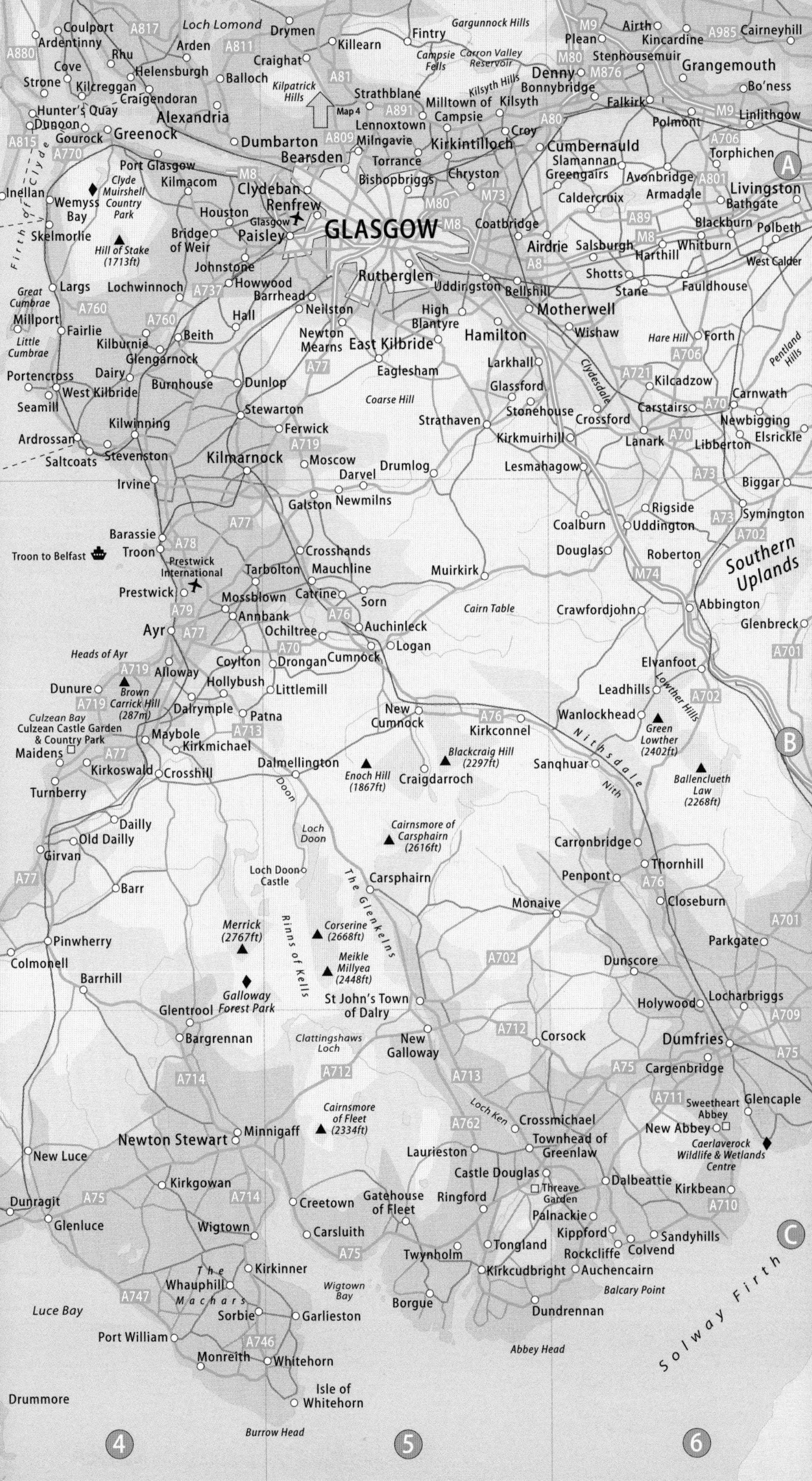

Coulport
A817
Loch Lomond
Drymen
Killearn
Fintry
Gargunnock Hills
M9
Airth
A985
Cairneyhill
Ardentinny
Arden
A811
Plean
Kincardine
A880
Rhu
Craighat
Campsie Fells
Carron Valley Reservoir
M80
Stenhousemuir
Grangemouth
Cove
Helensburgh
A81
Denny
M876
Strone
Balloch
Kilsyth Hills
Bonnybridge
Bo'ness
Kilcreggan
Kilpatrick Hills
Strathblane
Craigendoran
Map 4
A891
Milltown of Campsie
Kilsyth
Falkirk
Hunter's Quay
Alexandria
Lennoxtown
A80
Polmont
M9
Linlithgow
Dunoon
Gourock
Greenock
Croy
A706
A815
Dumbarton
A809
Milngavie
Kirkintilloch
Cumbernauld
Torphichen
A770
Firth of Clyde
Bearsden
Torrance
Slamannan
A
Port Glasgow
M8
Bishopbriggs
Chryston
Greengairs
Avonbridge
A801
Clyde Muirshell Country Park
Kilmacolm
Clydebank
M73
Livingston
Inellan
Wemyss Bay
Renfrew
M80
Caldercruix
Armadale
Bathgate
Houston
Glasgow
GLASGOW
M8
Coatbridge
A89
Blackburn
Polbeth
Skelmorlie
Hill of Stake (1713ft)
Bridge of Weir
Paisley
Airdrie
Salsburgh
M8
Whitburn
Harthill
West Calder
A8
Johnstone
Rutherglen
Shotts
Great Cumbrae
Largs
Lochwinnoch
A737
Howwood
Uddingston
Bellshill
Stane
Fauldhouse
Barrhead
A760
Neilston
Motherwell
Millport
A760
Hall
High Blantyre
Wishaw
Fairlie
Beith
Newton Mearns
East Kilbride
Hamilton
Hare Hill
Forth
Little Cumbrae
Kilburnie
Glengarnock
Pentland Hills
A706
A77
Eaglesham
Larkhall
Portencross
Dairy
Clydesdale
A721
Kilcadzow
Burnhouse
Dunlop
Glassford
Carnwath
West Kilbride
Coarse Hill
Carstairs
A70
Seamill
Stewarton
Stonehouse
Newbigging
Strathaven
Crossford
Kilwinning
Ferwick
Kirkmuirhill
Lanark
A70
Elsrickle
Ardrossan
Libberton
A719
Saltcoats
Stevenston
Kilmarnock
Moscow
Drumlog
Lesmahagow
Darvel
A73
Irvine
Biggar
Newmilns
Galston
Rigside
A77
Coalburn
Uddington
A73
Symington
Barassie
A78
A702
Troon to Belfast
Troon
Crosshands
Douglas
Roberton
Southern Uplands
Prestwick International
Tarbolton
Mauchline
Muirkirk
M74
Prestwick
Mossblown
Catrine
Sorn
Cairn Table
Crawfordjohn
Abbington
A79
Annbank
A76
Ayr
A77
Ochiltree
Auchinleck
Glenbreck
A70
Logan
Heads of Ayr
Coylton
Drongan
Cumnock
A701
Elvanfoot
A719
Alloway
Dunure
Brown Carrick Hill (287m)
Hollybush
Littlemill
Leadhills
Lowther Hills
A702
A719
New Cumnock
Dalrymple
Wanlockhead
Green Lowther (2402ft)
Culzean Bay
Patna
A76
Culzean Castle Garden & Country Park
A713
Kirkconnel
Nithsdale
B
Maybole
Maidens
A77
Kirkmichael
Blackcraig Hill (2297ft)
Dalmellington
Sanqhuar
Kirkoswald
Crosshill
Enoch Hill (1867ft)
Craigdarroch
Ballenclueth Law (2268ft)
Doon
Nith
Turnberry
Dailly
Cairnsmore of Carsphairn (2616ft)
Loch Doon
Old Dailly
Carronbridge
Girvan
Thornhill
Loch Doon Castle
The Glenkens
Carsphairn
A77
Penpont
A76
Barr
Monaive
Closeburn
A701
Merrick (2767ft)
Rinns of Kells
Corserine (2668ft)
Pinwherry
Parkgate
Colmonell
Meikle Millyea (2448ft)
A702
Dunscore
Barrhill
Galloway Forest Park
St John's Town of Dalry
Holywood
Locharbriggs
Glentrool
A709
A712
Corsock
Clattingshaws Loch
New Galloway
Dumfries
Bargrennan
A75
A75
Cargenbridge
A714
A712
A713
A711
Glencaple
Sweetheart Abbey
Loch Ken
Cairnsmore of Fleet (2334ft)
Crossmichael
A762
New Abbey
Minnigaff
Townhead of Greenlaw
Caerlaverock Wildlife & Wetlands Centre
Newton Stewart
New Luce
Laurieston
Castle Douglas
Kirkgowan
Threave Garden
Dalbeattie
Kirkbean
Dunragit
A75
A714
Creetown
Gatehouse of Fleet
Ringford
A710
Glenluce
Palnackie
Wigtown
Carsluith
Kippford
Sandyhills
C
Tongland
A75
Twynholm
Rockcliffe
Colvend
The Machars
Kirkinner
Kirkcudbright
Auchencairn
Whauphill
Wigtown Bay
Balcary Point
A747
Borgue
Solway Firth
Luce Bay
Sorbie
Garlieston
Dundrennan
Port William
A746
Abbey Head
Monreith
Whitehorn
Isle of Whitehorn
Drummore
Burrow Head
4
5
6

Map 6
Newburgh
Lindores
Monimail
Abernethy
Auchtermuchty
Path of Condie
Strathmiglo
Glenfarg
Falkland Palace
Fife Regional Park
Milnathort
Carnbo
Kinross
Loch Leven
Glenrothes
Lochore Meadows Country Park
Lochgelly
Cowdenbeath
Kirkcaldy
Auchtertool
Dunfermline
Aberdour
Kinghorn
Cairneyhill
Burntisland
Dalgety
Limekilns
Inverkeithin
Inchkeith
South Queensferry
North Queensferry
Dairsie
Cupar
Pitscottie
St Andrews Bay
St Andrews
Craigtoun Country Park
Kingsbarns
Fife Ness
Crail
Largoward
Carnbee
St Monans
Kilrenny
Anstruther
Pittenweem
Kilconquhar
Leven
Elie
Buckhaven
East Wemyss
Isle of May
Firth of Forth
North
Bass Rock
Dirleton
Auldhame
Gullane
Aberlady
Drem
John Muir Country Park
Dunbar
Map 4
Cockenzie & Port Stenton
EDINBURGH
Lauriston Castle
Cramond
Leith
Kirkliston
Broxburn
Edinburgh
Livingston
Water of Leith
Musselburgh
Prestonpan
Longniddry
East Linton
Haddington
Stenton
Tranent
Macmerry
Bolton
Garvald
Whitecraig
Ormiston
Pencaitland
Gifford
Cockburnspath
St Abb's Head
St Abbs
Ecclaw
Loanhead
Dalkeith
Bilston
Bonnyrigg
Scald Law (1900ft)
Pentland Hills Regional
Roslin
Rosewell
Penicuik
Gorebridge
North Middleton
Humbie
Lammer Law (1733ft)
Lammermuir Hills
Meikle Says Law (1756ft)
Whiteadder Water
Grantshouse
Coldingham
Eyemouth
Auchencrow
Reston
Burnmouth
(1844ft)
Carlops
Leadburn
South Esk
Gilston
Chirnside
Foulden
Berwick-upon-Tweed
Pentland Hills
West Linton
Moorfoot Hills
Heriot
Oxton
Dirrington Great Law
Duns
Blackadder Water
Romannobridge
Gala Water
Westruther
Dolphinton
Blackhope Scar (2137ft)
Lauder
Ladykirk
Swinton
Elsrickle
Blyth Bridge
Eddleston
Stow
Houndslow
Greenlaw
Windlestraw (2613ft)
Leader Water
Gordon
Peebles
Colquhar
Eccles
Coldstream
Stobo
Broughton
Tweeddale
Innerleithen
Galashiels
Greenlaw
Stichill
Southern Uplands
Traquair House
Abbotsford House
Melrose
Floors Castle
Kelso
Dun Rig (2439ft)
Minch Maw (1861ft)
Melrose Abbey
Newtown St Boswells
Kelso Abbey
Town Yetholm
Selkirk
Tweedsmuir
Mountbenger
Yarrow
Midlem
Nisbet
Eckford
Kirk
Broad Law (2758ft)
Black Knowe Head
Lilliesleaf
Morebattle
Bowmont Water
Glenbreck
Cappercluech
Ettrick Water
Hassendean
Bonjedward
Jedburgh
Jedburgh Abbey
Oxnam
Map 5
White Coomb
Hawick
Teviotdale
Hart Fell (2652ft)
Ettrick
Roberton
Capplegill
Bonchester Bridge
Chesters
Camptown
Cheviot Hills
Southdean
Carter Bar
Loch Fell (2258ft)
Teviothead
Moffat
Beattock
Annandale
Eskdalemuir
Hermitage Castle
Roan Fell (1861ft)
Liddlesdale
Johnstown Bridge
Boreland
Eskdale
Newcastleton
Langholm
ENGLAND
Lochmaben
Locherbie
Waterbeck
Canonbie
Ecclefechan
Eaglesfield
Kirkpatrick-Fleming
Blacksmith's Shop
Annan
Gretna
Eastriggs
N
0 km
10
0 miles
10
A
B
C
1
2
3
A912
A914
A919
A91
A917
A92
A914
A916
A915
A912
A911
A977
A915
A955
M90
A92
A823
A921
A198
A198
A1673
A1
A8
M8
A71
A702
A7
A1
A6093
A720
A6094
A702
A701
A68
A7
A68
A7
A6105
A6112
A6105
A697
A72
A72
A703
A6105
A6089
A7
A699
A698
A701
A698
A708
A6088
A701
A7
M74
A75

Map 7

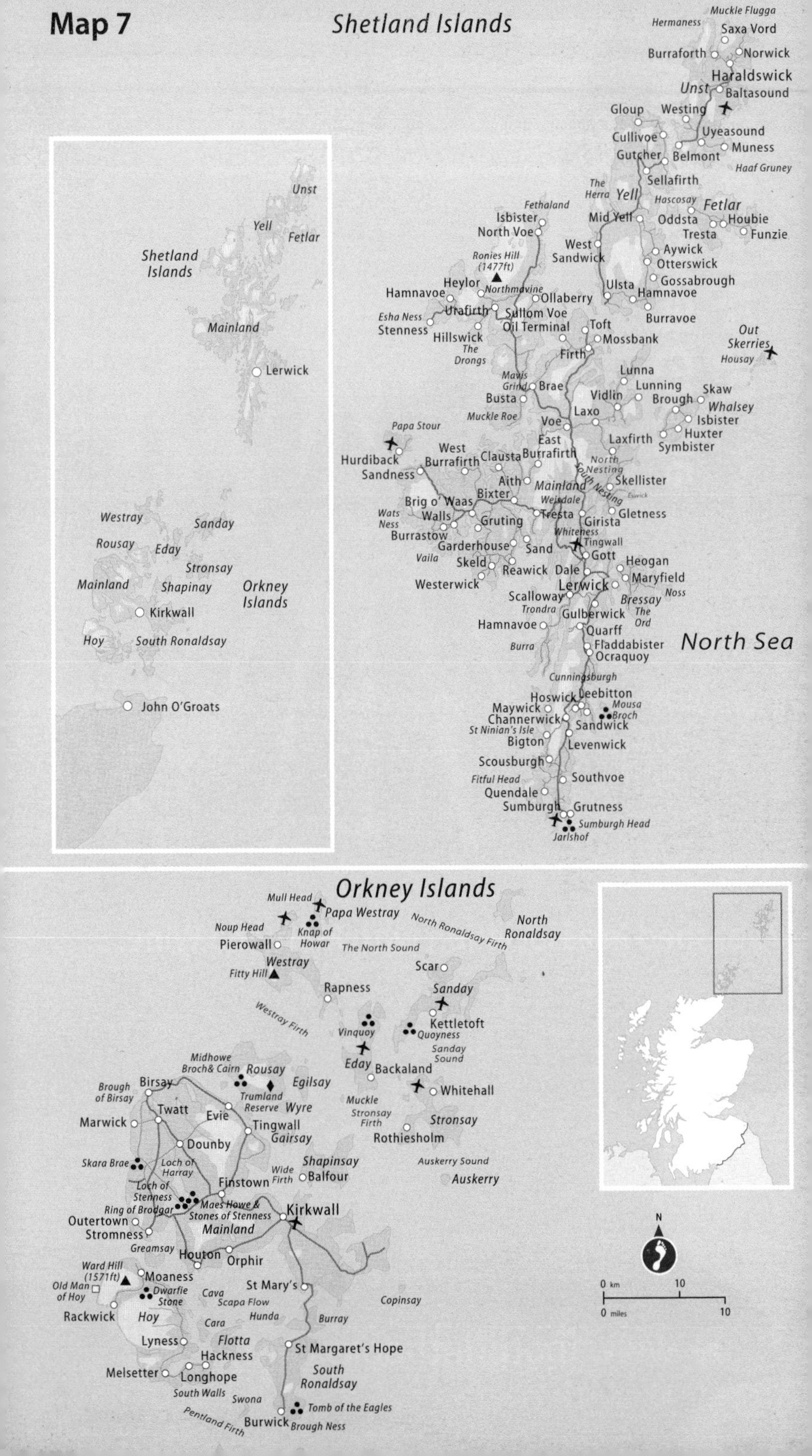

Shetland Islands

Muckle Flugga
Hermaness
Saxa Vord
Burraforth
Norwick
Haraldswick
Unst
Baltasound
Gloup
Westing
Cullivoe
Uyeasound
Muness
Gutcher
Belmont
Haaf Gruney
Sellafirth
The Herra
Yell
Hascosay
Fetlar
Fethaland
Isbister
Mid Yell
Oddsta
Houbie
Tresta
Funzie
North Voe
West Sandwick
Aywick
Otterswick
Ronies Hill (1477ft)
Gossabrough
Heylor
Ulsta
Hamnavoe
Hamnavoe
Northmavine
Ollaberry
Burravoe
Esha Ness
Urafirth
Sullom Voe Oil Terminal
Stenness
Hillswick
Toft
Mossbank
Out Skerries
The Drongs
Firth
Housay
Lunna
Mavis Grind
Brae
Lunning
Busta
Vidlin
Skaw
Brough
Whalsey
Muckle Roe
Laxo
Isbister
Papa Stour
Voe
Huxter
Laxfirth
East Burrafirth
Symbister
West Burrafirth
Hurdiback
Clausta
North Nesting
Sandness
South Nesting
Aith
Mainland
Skellister
Eswick
Bixter
Brig o' Waas
Weisdale
Wats Ness
Walls
Tresta
Gletness
Burrastow
Gruting
Girista
Whiteness
Garderhouse
Sand
Tingwall
Vaila
Gott
Skeld
Reawick
Dale
Heogan
Westerwick
Lerwick
Maryfield
Scalloway
Bressay
Noss
Trondra
Gulberwick
The Ord
Hamnavoe
Quarff
Burra
Fladdabister
North Sea
Ocraquoy
Cunningsburgh
Hoswick
Leebitton
Maywick
Mousa Broch
Channerwick
Sandwick
St Ninian's Isle
Bigton
Levenwick
Scousburgh
Fitful Head
Southvoe
Quendale
Sumburgh
Grutness
Sumburgh Head
Jarlshof

Unst
Yell
Fetlar
Shetland Islands
Mainland
Lerwick
Westray
Sanday
Rousay
Eday
Stronsay
Mainland
Shapinay
Orkney Islands
Kirkwall
Hoy
South Ronaldsay
John O'Groats

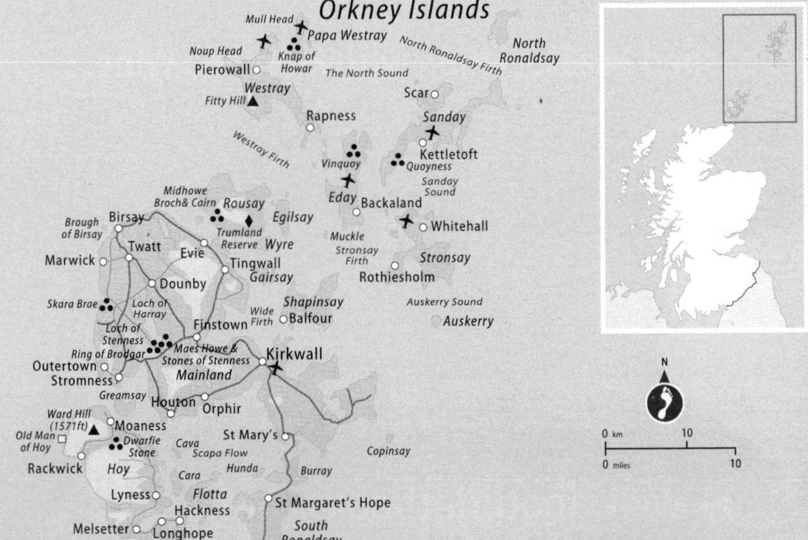

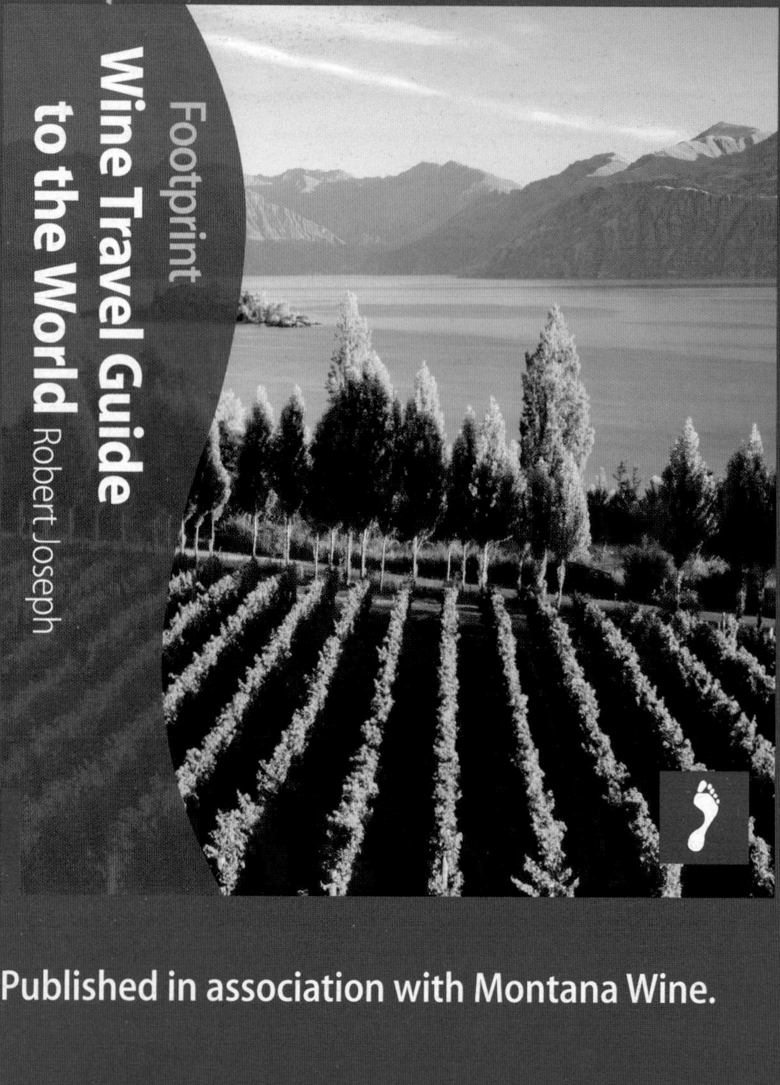
Footprint
Wine Travel Guide
to the World
Robert Joseph

A guide specifically conceived and written for anyone who travels and enjoys wine.

In Margaux, I want to tread the warm, well-drained gravel outcrops... I want to see the Andes water gushing down off the mountains into the fertile vineyards of Chile's Maipo Valley. I want to feel the howling mists chill me to the bone in California's Carneros, and then feel the warm winds of New Zealand's Marlborough tugging at my hair. I want it all to make sense. *Oz Clarke*

ISBN 1 904777 85 6

Footprint
Travel guides